D1095952

Pass of the North

Four Centuries on the Rio Grande

BOOKS *by* C. L. SONNICHSEN

BILLY KING'S TOMBSTONE

ROY BEAN: LAW WEST OF THE PECOS

COWBOYS AND CATTLE KINGS

I'LL DIE BEFORE I'LL RUN

ALIAS BILLY THE KID

THE MESCALERO APACHES

TEN TEXAS FEUDS

TULAROSA: LAST OF THE FRONTIER WEST

THE SOUTHWEST IN LIFE AND LITERATURE *(Anthology)*

THE EL PASO SALT WAR

OUTLAW

PASS OF THE NORTH

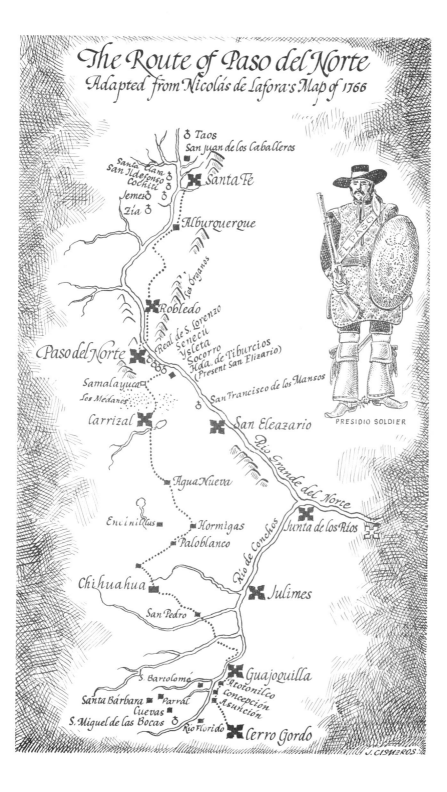

The Route of Paso del Norte
Adapted from Nicolás de Lafora's Map of 1766

Taos
San Juan de los Caballeros
Santa Clara
San Ildefonso
Cochiti
Jemez
Zia
Santa Fé
Alburquerque
Los Organos
Robledo
Real de S. Lorenzo
Senecú
Ysleta
Socorro
Hda. de Tiburcios
(Present San Elizario)
Paso del Norte
Samalayuca
Los Médanos
San Francisco de los Mansos
Carrizal
San Eleazario
Rio Grande del Norte
Agua Nueva
Encinillas
Hormigas
Paloblanco
Rio de Conchos
Junta de los Rios
Chihuahua
Julimes
San Pedro
S. Bartolomé
Guajoquilla
Atotonilco
Concepción
Santa Bárbara
Parral
Asunción
Cuevas
S. Miguel de las Bocas
Rio Florido
Cerro Gordo

PRESIDIO SOLDIER

J. CISNEROS

El Paso Street, looking south from Pioneer Plaza in 1880

The same view one year later

El Paso Street in the early 1900's

Pass of the North

Four Centuries on the Rio Grande

by

C. L. SONNICHSEN

TEXAS WESTERN PRESS

THE UNIVERSITY OF TEXAS AT EL PASO

1968

COPYRIGHT 1968

BY C. L. SONNICHSEN

Library of Congress Catalog Card No. 68-30889

S. D. MYRES, *Editor*

Map and Chapter Initials by

JOSE CISNEROS

Third Printing 1975

Foreword

FOUR CENTURIES and more have gone by since Alvar Núñez Cabeza de Vaca crossed the Rio Grande somewhere within sight of Mount Franklin. The year was 1536. In 1981 it will be four hundred years since Brother Agustín Rodríguez, the first European to visit the unknown lands beyond the Pass of the North, looked speculatively at the pools and swamps near where we live now and decided that the place would be good for farming. Incredible things have happened during those centuries. The early ones were terribly dangerous and difficult for the generations of Spaniards and Indians who maintained a precarious foothold on the banks of the Great River. Many times they prayed and petitioned to be allowed to go away and live somewhere else. Poor old Governor Otermín, ailing and harassed, spoke for practically everybody in his suffering colony when in 1682 he wrote to Father Ayeta in Mexico City, "For the love of God and Saint Anthony, do everything you possibly can to get me out of here!"

In 1968 we sometimes meet a man who feels the same way — someone who hasn't been here very long or who can't stand the desert — and we understand his feelings, for the land around us has never been easy to tame or to love. We live among green fields and orchards in a narrow garden created by the waters of the river, but close by are mountain slopes which would be hard climbing for a goat, endless miles of stony soil inhabited by horned toads, jackrabbits, and an occasional rattlesnake. Wild creatures are still our neighbors. On the outskirts of town on summer nights people can hear the coyotes talking, and the paisano (road runner, chaparral cock) teeters across our university campus now and then, balancing his outthrust head with his outthrust tail. One of our new grade schools out on the Alamogordo road has a "rattlesnake patrol" which searches the grounds every morning for overnight arrivals. Nature is not just close; it can be dangerous. West of the river along the international boundary the country is so rough and wild that men of the Border Patrol, following the tracks of a Mexican who has crossed under cover of night, always move fast lest the illegal entrant be dead before they can catch up with him. Names like Jornada del Muerto (Day's Journey of the Dead Man — a waterless segment of the Royal Road of Spain beginning just above Las Cruces) remind us of the perils of life in former times; and the screaming winds and billowing dust of a March sandstorm remind us further that things have not changed much in spite of automobiles and air conditioning.

Yet almost three-quarters of a million people (counting everybody on both sides of the river) live in this valley now and most of them prefer it to any other spot in the world, including California. They are always explaining to newcomers what fine things it has to offer. A few dust storms in the spring and a little dry heat in the summer are trifling hardships compared to the blizzards and tornadoes and floods which happen to other people in other places. And we do have wonderful moments — when the sunset colors work magic with those barren mountain slopes; when we see the snowy top of Sierra Blanca a hundred miles away in New Mexico shining in the clear air; when the far mesas in the Indian summer days of early fall are clothed in blue shadow. We live and play out of doors all year long.

Climate, however, is only part of what we have to enjoy and be proud of. Our location next door to Mexico makes us unique. El Paso and Juárez are the largest border cities in either country. They are to a great extent bi-racial and bi-lingual. Everywhere we go we hear the Spanish language, eroded and changed by time and distance, but still the language of Cervantes and Alarcon; and with the language come many of the gracious ways of Spain. The politeness and decorum of our Latin neighbors, their strong sense of family, their love of joy — these things make life richer for us as well as for them. Sooner or later we all become part Mexican, speaking at least a few words of Spanish, enjoying the spicy food, the fiestas and parades (maybe even the bullfights), the *matachines* doing their sacred dances at Tortugas and Ysleta, the families in the cemeteries on All Souls' Day taking picnic lunches and visiting their dead.

And then we have those four centuries. A sense of history develops easily in a place where so much has happened — where so many unusual human beings have played such wonderful parts on such a tremendous stage. The Pass has always been a meeting place, a crossroads, where Indian and Spaniard and Anglo have met and mingled. Conquerors and colonists, wild Indians and devoted friars, trappers and traders and Forty-niners have played their parts in their time. Gunmen and gamblers and fancy women had their hour seventy-five years ago. Manufacturers and missile men are taking the lead now.

It adds up to a remarkable story — a story that should be told — a reminder in a rootless age of the deep roots of one community. It must be a tale of two cities, for El Paso is part Mexican, and Juárez is more American than it sometimes likes to admit. The river brought them both to life. They could not do without each other. This is the story of how they came to be, how they grew, and how they changed from the old days to the new.

Table of Contents

Illustrations

Pass of the North

Four Centuries on the Rio Grande

DeVargas the Reconqueror

CHAPTER I

Men with Beards and Armor

 AFTER CORTEZ laid his rough hand on the Indian civilizations of Mexico, the Spaniards spread out rapidly over the beautiful new country. It took many years and much blood to bring the Indians under more or less firm control, start big ranches, and get the mines into operation, but the line of settlement crept farther and farther north until it reached Southern Chihuahua.[1] There it stopped for a while, held back by the need to consolidate what had been gained and by the vast and forbidding *terra incognita* stretching to the Rio Grande and into the unknown distance beyond.

With visions of the wealth of Peru and Mexico haunting the dreams of the Spaniards, their imaginations were left free to do their wonderful best. Far to the north, they believed, the Straits of Anian[2] would undoubtedly be found, opening a new passage by sea to the treasures of the Orient. Closer at hand there was a vast lake somewhere in the West where natives paddled canoes ornamented with pure gold.[3] The Blue Mountains, veined with precious metals, lifted their heads beyond the horizon somewhere,[4] and there were great golden cities where the land was rich and the women were fair. Considering what the Spaniards had already found in Peru and Mexico, they can hardly be blamed for expecting even greater wonders. Every traveler who could provide a scrap of information or conjecture was listened to eagerly, especially if his tale was unbelievable.

The earliest first-hand report was made by a gaunt and weather-beaten Spaniard, naked and bearded with ribs showing like the bars of a cage, who walked all the way across the continent between 1528 and 1536. Survivor of an unfortunate expedition which had set out to occupy Florida, Alvar Núñez Cabeza de Vaca, with two Spanish companions and a colored serving man, came at last to the vicinity of El Paso on his way to the Pacific coast. Just where he crossed the Rio Grande is a much debated question,[5] but whether or not he was the first white man to walk up North Oregon Street, as one El Paso historian humorously suggests,[6] he must have come close. A few weeks later he was back among "civilized" men in a land devastated and depopulated by a band of his fellow Christians out hunting slaves, "carrying away many people in chains."[7]

Núñez reported his adventures to the King of Spain and to the world, and his story was eagerly discussed by many a Spaniard who wondered about the riches on the other side of the last frontier. One of them had curiosity enough and resources enough to go and see for himself what was beyond the horizon. This was Francisco Vázquez de Coronado, who in 1541 and 1542 pushed through New Mexico to the plains of Kansas. He went far and observed much, but brought back none of the riches he had hoped to find. His route to the unknown lay to the west of the Rio Grande. His route back was down the Pecos. He missed El Paso going and coming.

Coronado's unimpressive effort discouraged the Spaniards in Mexico, and it was forty years before anyone plucked up courage to try it again. Meanwhile the whole matter of colonial policy was being reexamined as a result of frontier troubles.[8] The King issued an edict in 1573 declaring that future expeditions would have to be authorized, and that they would be authorized only if their purpose was conversion of the Indians. From that time on a good, healthy interest in gold and jewels had to be played down while a passion for making worried Christians out of satisfied savages had to be played up.[9]

As the frontier crept northward into southern Chihuahua, adventurous men undoubtedly struck out ahead of it. There were wildcat expeditions of one sort or another — by soldiers pursuing marauding Indians, by slave hunters, by curious men who wanted to look at the country.[10] Naturally no reports exist for the unauthorized excursions, but we know something about the ones with official blessing — the Rodríguez-Chamuscado affair, for instance, which brought the first Europeans into the El Paso valley.

There was a little mining camp, known as San Bartolomé, northeast of the larger camp of Santa Bárbara in Chihuahua, where a group of enthusiasts gathered. One was a soldier named Pedro de

Bustamente who had heard from a captured native, in the course of a punitive expedition to the north of the settlements, that somewhere back of the beyond were Indians who raised cotton and made clothes from it. He yearned to go and find those cotton-raising Indians.[11]

His yearnings were shared by another soldier, a fiery-bearded old man named Francisco Sánchez and nicknamed Chamuscado — the singed or scorched one. Sánchez was nearly seventy and in poor health, but he hoped and believed that he could make one more exploring expedition which would be the crowning achievement of his life.[12]

The two fighting men were joined in their councils by a pioneer as dedicated as themselves — a Franciscan named Fray Agustín Rodríguez who was mightily moved to undertake the conversion of the heathen. Father Francisco López, an older religious, was interested likewise, though his enthusiasm was probably not as violent as that of Rodríguez.

Far out on the mining frontier these men, all exiles from Spain, dreamed, read the words of Cabeza de Vaca, and came to a decision. They would go if they could. Brother Rodríguez journeyed to Mexico City and spoke with the Viceroy, Don Lorenzo Suárez de Mendoza y Figueroa. He must have been a good talker, for Don Lorenzo approved his scheme on account of his "great zeal," and told him he could take other priests under the convoy of as many as twenty soldiers. He even promised Rodríguez that he might name the leader of the soldiers.[13]

This was exactly the arrangement that Rodríguez wanted. He flew back to San Bartolomé, appointed Sánchez Chamuscado the captain of eight soldiers who were interested in making the trip, and named Fathers Francisco López and Juan de Santa María as his priestly companions. Father Juan was skilled in astronomy and astrology, a fact which may have cost him dear later on.[14]

They left Santa Bárbara on June 5, 1581, together with nineteen Indian servants, six hundred head of livestock (including ninety horses), and a supply of goods for barter. Nothing was said about making money out of the expedition, but the men were undoubtedly thinking about it.[15] Hernán Gallegos, who kept a record, says they were "fortified with the hope of attaining temporal and eternal reward."[16]

Rodríguez the priest and Sánchez the soldier started out as firm allies, but their opposite aims put them at odds as time went on. One might say that they set the pattern for the succeeding chapters in the history of Spanish conquest north of the Rio Grande. It was friction between church leaders and government officials which helped to bring about the breakdown of the whole system and the expulsion from New Mexico of all the Spaniards except dead ones. But that comes later.

They followed the Conchos down to its junction with the Rio Grande, turned northwest as the river ran, and after many adventures came to the swamps below El Paso which later travelers always particularly noticed. They had seen no human being for three days and encountered none above El Paso for another fifteen. They noted, however, that the El Paso valley, even the eight leagues of marshy land on the west bank just below the present site of the town, was "suitable for ranches and for the cultivation of anything that might be desired."[17] Our first visitors were our first boosters.

It is almost certain that Rodríguez and Chamuscado were the first Europeans to pass over the river at the Frontera crossing — the old Spanish Ford. In those days the Rio Grande ran deep and strong all year long, flooding the whole valley from time to time in the spring and returning to its banks the rest of the year. The gorge, where the water had cut through the rocky hills forming the Pass of the Great River of the North, offered no passageway for men and animals. The terrain east of the river was rugged and impassable. It was necessary then, and for the next two centuries, for travelers to leave the channel north of the settlement, swing westward around the base of Mule Drivers' Mountain (now Cerro de Cristo Rey), and come back to the river somewhere near the present site of Sunland Park. There it was possible in ordinary weather to get carts and pack horses across. Nobody crosses there now, of course. In fact, nobody even knows just where the river ran so long ago. Naturally the people who watch the thoroughbreds run at the race track never think of the jaded Spanish ponies and pack mules which passed that way four centuries ago, perhaps right where they are sitting. They might enjoy the races more if they did.

The story of the Rodríguez-Chamuscado expedition after they

passed the old Spanish Ford is one of the great adventure tales of the Western world. The tiny band of Spaniards acted as if it numbered a thousand men, went where it pleased, took careful notes of the location and size of the pueblos, and made a beginning of preaching the gospel to the heathen natives. The men went west as far as Zuñi and east to the buffalo plains beyond the Pecos. Hernán Gallegos kept the official record, but two other soldiers made mental notes and later added their testimony to the record.[18] They knew they were doing an incredible thing.

Their greatest danger was a split in their own ranks. The soldiers prospected industriously for precious metals. The friars prospected just as zealously for souls to save and felt tremendous excitement as they surveyed these broad fields, ripe for God's harvest — and themselves ready to bring in the first ears. They did not seem to realize the precariousness of their position. If they did think of it, they probably welcomed the possibility of a martyr's crown, not considering how much such a distinction might cost the other members of the expedition. The soldiers were by no means lacking in religious conviction, but the euphoria of the friars worried them.

Their fears were justified. At the pueblo of Malpartida in the Galisteo Valley, a little way south of the future site of Santa Fe, Father Juan de Santa María made an announcement. The rest could go on to the buffalo plains, he said. He was starting for Mexico to report what he had seen. He was going now, and alone. With the help of astrology he had figured out a short cut down the east side of the Manzano Mountains and the other ranges screening the east bank of the Rio Grande.[19]

"Wait till we have seen everything the natives have told us about," the soldiers remonstrated. "Don't go alone into country none of us has ever seen."

He would not listen.

"Think what this will do to the Indians. You will put us all in danger."

"I am going back," the priest insisted. "I must make a report of what I have seen to my superiors."

And go he did on September 8, 1581. Captain Sánchez well knew that if anything happened to Santa María, the soldiers would be blamed and he took what precautions he could. He called his men together and reminded them that he was their leader, duly com-

missioned. They agreed that he was and told him they were ready
to do as he said. Thus reassured, he had Gallegos draw up a paper
stating that Father Juan had left them against the advice of the
captain and his men and would not be persuaded or stopped. They
all signed it. The paper is still to be seen in the Archives of the
Indies in Spain. It did not help, for the Church historians who
reported the matter later made it appear that the soldiers had
deserted the priests and that Father Santa María had volunteered
to go back for help.[20]

Already the Indians were losing their first awe of the bearded
white men with their horses and armor and firearms. They counciled and debated, concluded that the departing father might
bring back enemies to plague them, and set out to cut him off.
The pursuers caught up with him on the third day, waited till he
went to sleep under a tree, and killed him. They told the remaining Spaniards about it later on.[21] With their help Father Juan became the first Spanish martyr in New Mexico.[22]

Now began the real explorations of the Chamuscado party. They
visited Acoma and Zuñi. They went north to Taos and east to the
buffalo plains. They saw much that even Coronado had missed.
And they found themselves closer and closer to Indian trouble. At
the pueblo of Piedrahita in the Galisteo Valley the Indians refused
to give them supplies and yielded only when the soldiers walked
into the central plaza and discharged their guns. Since the death
of Father Juan, however, they had been aware that these men in
beards and armor were mortal and could bleed and die. The Spaniards knew very well what the Indians were thinking and resolved,
after several of their horses had been killed, to try a stratagem.
Those nine soldiers attacked the pueblo of Malagon, captured three
of the inhabitants, and made a great show of preparing to cut off
their heads. It was arranged that the two friars would rush in at
the last minute, plead for their lives, and save them from death.
The Indians were deeply impressed by this little drama — deeply
grateful.[23]

In spite of the success of their scheme the Spaniards all realized
that it was time to turn back. They were so few and so vulnerable
that they could be swept away in a few minutes by the increasingly restless and rebellious Indians. Besides, they had accomplished
what they came for. It was time now to go back and reap the re-

wards of what they had done. Gradually, not wishing their departure to look like a retreat, they moved southward.

The final blow fell when they reached the Tigua pueblo of Puaray (Sandía) near Albuquerque. Fathers López and Rodríguez announced that they would go no farther. Here they would remain and minister to the Indians.

Chamuscado and his fighting men were horrified and must have wondered if all Franciscans were out of their minds. They argued and remonstrated to no avail. "You have no interpreter," they said. "You can accomplish nothing. You will be killed like Father Juan."

"Oh no," the friars replied. "God will protect us. We will stay and preach the gospel."

"What you are doing is tempting God," Chamuscado said bitterly, "and causing a scandal and a disorder. Leave with us now, and we will come back to preach and colonize."[24]

"No one," the friars said, "can make us give up our purpose of preaching the holy gospel to these Indians. We will have you excommunicated if you try to make us go by force."[25]

There was only one thing to do — go back to Mexico and bring reinforcements. Chamuscado went to work on the Indians. He told them he was going, but that he was coming back soon with many more Spaniards and their wives. They replied that this would be a fine thing, and when he returned they would have the fathers "fat and well kept."

Chamuscado left everything he possibly could with the friars — tools, medicines, supplies, Indian servants. On January 31, 1582, the soldiers started for home. Down the Rio Grande they slogged, weakened by sickness and exhaustion. The captain moved with great effort and finally broke down completely, conquered by his "old disease," whatever it was. The men found means to bleed him, but it did no good. His hands and feet became paralyzed. They killed a horse for its hide and made him a litter. They prayed that he would live to see San Bartolomé again, and he almost made it; but thirty leagues short of the goal he died and was buried beside the road by his grieving comrades in arms.[26] Hernán Gallegos took command and brought the company back to an astonished community which had long ago given them up for lost. They had been gone for eleven months.

There was much excitement in Mexico City over the reports of these men. They had prospected assiduously along the way and had found signs of mineral wealth.[27] The Indians were there by the thousands waiting to be baptized. New Mexico had attractions for everybody.

The Franciscans, of course, were concerned about their brothers preaching and teaching so industriously back there in the wilds, far away and in peril. The Viceroy was concerned too, but not enough to order immediate action. While he was taking advice about how many men would be needed for a rescue operation, two servants, Francisco and Gerónimo, who had remained with the friars when Chamuscado left, reappeared at San Bartolomé with the news that López and Rodríguez were dead — murdered by the Indians they had hoped to convert. The word was passed on to the Viceroy. The Viceroy drew up a report to send to the King in Spain, and there the matter rested. It would take a year or more for instructions to arrive. The New World could never get things done very fast.

The Franciscans could not wait. Somehow, on some sort of authorization, an expedition was assembled. Fray Pedro de Heredia, an energetic Franciscan, was the moving spirit. Without waiting for permission to start, Brother Pedro took his men out of San Bartolomé on November 10, 1582. There were two priests and fifteen soldiers. Of the latter the most important was a gentleman and landowner named Don Antonio de Espejo. When Heredia was called back by his ecclesiastical superiors for presuming to start off without clearance, Espejo got himself elected leader of the expedition.

Don Antonio was a very rich and very high-spirited[28] man whose recklessness had got him in trouble. He had been charged with murdering one of his ranch workers (his brother actually did the killing but Don Antonio was present) and he wanted (1) to stay away from the settlements for a while and (2) to make an impressive record as an explorer to counteract public disapproval of his misdeeds.[29] The expedition was a lifesaver for him.

Now the Indian grapevine brought word that the abandoned brothers had not been killed after all. The friars felt great eagerness to push forward and rescue them. Up the river they went over a trail which was soon to become familiar — on to the marsh lands below El Paso dotted with pools of water from the overflow of the

Rio Grande. Here they found Indians whom they called Tampa-
choas. Without pausing, Espejo and his men pushed on up the river
and confirmed the story that the fathers had actually met their
deaths at the hands of the Indians of Puaray. Espejo himself swung
over to the Pecos Valley on his way home, and the site of El Paso
saw him no more. Father Beltrán and a few soldiers came back by
the route through the Pass of the North and arrived safely at Santa
Bárbara.

After this it was just a matter of time until somebody would head
a major colonizing expedition into the new-found lands. The King
approved the idea, and half a dozen ambitious Spaniards began
jockeying and angling for the job. Seventeen years after Chamuscado laid his bones beside the road to San Bartolomé, Juan de
Oñate, the colonizer, came to the Pass.

CHAPTER II

The Tread of a Conqueror

 THE GREAT COLONIZING expedition reached the banks of the Rio Grande fifteen miles below the Pass on the twentieth of April, 1598. There were 400 men, 138 families. Their baggage was carried in eighty-three wagons and carts, and they drove a herd of over 3,000 sheep, goats, cattle, mules, and horses.[1] Nothing like this had been seen in these parts before, and nothing like it would be seen again for many a year. The natives could hardly have missed the long procession of people and animals, but not an Indian was seen for four days.

All sorts and conditions of men were among the colonists. Lists had been opened in the Viceroy's palace in Mexico for the gentlemen. Many had pledged money and supplies; some had even committed everything they had to the expedition. In some cases a whole family enlisted — a father and his sons, with their women in the background. The common citizens had been notified of the enterprise by criers accompanied by drum and trumpet who went about the streets of Puebla, Zacatecas, and other frontier towns. Similar efforts were being made to recruit men for California and the Philippines,[2] but there were special advantages attached to the New Mexico enterprise. For one thing, every colonist was assured that he and his descendants would be considered noblemen — *hidalgos* — thenceforward, with rights and privileges equal to those of the best blood of Spain.[3]

Untouched by such wordly considerations were the six friars who were charged with the conversion of the Indians in the new land. They had their own problems, however. They were chagrined to find that Father Diego Márquez of the Spanish Inquisition had been commissioned to accompany them. Anxious to avoid being dominated by the Holy Office, the Franciscans petitioned to have

Father Márquez recalled. They succeeded in having him sent back to Mexico City, and it took the Inquisition another twenty-five years to gain a foothold in the new province, but the six friars lost so much time and enthusiasm that they too gave up their plans and went back to the capital.[4]

The colonists ranged from boys in their teens (the youngest was fifteen) to gray-headed men in their sixties. Most were in their twenties and thirties. Some had little or nothing in the way of arms. Others had horses and weapons and body armor.

At the top were a handful of brave and competent gentlemen including Captain Marcos Farfán de los Godos, a sturdy, chestnut-bearded native of Seville, forty years old. The Governor trusted him and made him stay behind the main body to escort a second group of friars with Fray Alonso Martínez at their head — "a man of singular virtue and noble qualities."[5] Captain Marcos had a taste in literature and could write plays.

Notable also were the Governor's two nephews, Juan and Vicente Zaldívar. Juan was the *maestro de campo;* Vicente was the *sargento mayor.* They were young men of great courage and tenacity who distinguished themselves in feats of arms after the settlement, though they were accused of cruelty and harshness by disgruntled settlers later on.[6]

The most interesting and unusual of all was Don Gaspar Pérez de Villagrá, a Spaniard of distinguished family who had been in the New World since 1580. He was not an impressive figure, being short, stocky and plain in features with deep furrows in his forehead, thinning hair and a full red beard streaked with gray. His carriage, however, was that of a man who had been at home in the court of Philip II before the call of unknown lands had reached him. Later he proved to be a tough and ruthless fighter — an officer to whom difficult and dangerous enterprises were trusted. But military distinction was not his object. What he wanted to do was to write a heroic poem about the conquest.

This was nothing new for a Spaniard in the great days of expansion. One of Don Gaspar's relatives had assisted in the conquest of Chile, about which the great and noble poem, the *Araucana*, had been written. Why shouldn't the conquest of New Mexico open the doors to immortality for one who saw it all with his own eyes and recorded it all for a grateful posterity? Gaspar was an educated man — a graduate of the University of Salamanca — who loved and reverenced the classics. He got himself appointed historiographer of the expedition — a position of great importance in a time and place devoted to the most meticulous record keeping — and missed no opportunity to see and hear everything.

The sense of destiny which lay heavily on the mind of Gaspar Pérez de Villegrá was likewise the motivating force in his leader, Governor Juan de Oñate, who had wanted the governorship with all the passion of his nature and had paid, prayed, cajoled and waited to get it. He was a great man and the son and grandson of great men.[7] His father, a leader of many responsibilities and much enterprise, had discovered and exploited the mines at Zacatecas. This won him tremendous credit with the King, who loved the royal fifth of what the mines produced. Juan in his turn hunted successfully for mineral riches, discovering and developing the rich veins at San Luis Potosí. By the time he was fifty he was fabuously wealthy in his own right. He was married to a granddaughter of Cortés, a great - granddaughter of Montezuma, and took off his hat to no man but the Viceroy. Still he was unsatisfied. He wanted to lead some great enterprise; carve his name deep in the hard rock of history; rule the destinies of wide lands and mighty peoples. We should not be far wrong in saying that Oñate wanted to be a king.

His eye turned naturally to the vast and mysterious realm to the north. Ever since the survivors of the Rodríguez-Chamuscado expedition had come back to spread their eyewitness reports of the cities and nations they had seen, a colonizing expedition had been inevitable and more than one unauthorized dreamer had tried his luck,[8] but Oñate, a friend of Viceroy Velasco, was given the place on September 21, 1595.

For four years his appointment brought him nothing but trouble and frustration. His friend Velasco moved on to Peru. The new ruler, the Count of Monterrey, was unwilling to approve the expedition without looking into everything for himself. He was uneasy over many of the petitions Oñate had presented. In the first place the man had asked to operate directly under the Crown and the Council of the Indies, bypassing the Viceroy entirely. He had asked for permission to raise his own military forces. He wanted the right to found ports on both the Atlantic and the Pacific when his exploring parties reached them (the Spaniards of this era visualized the continent as much narrower than it proved to be). He asked for the title of marquis.[9] The count suspected, and not without reason, that Oñate was trying to snatch a kingdom from his hand, and he moved slowly, waiting for word from Spain on Oñate's requests, most of which were turned down.

Meanwhile recruiting went on. During the autumn of 1595 and the spring and summer of 1596 men continued to arrive at the encampment on the Río de las Nazas in southern Chihuahua. Once the King almost appointed another man to lead the expedition, but when this interloper asked for money, the King's approval of Don Juan suddenly revived. Don Juan was asking for very little support from the Crown.[10]

Still the word to move did not come. It did not finally come until the summer of 1597.[11] Then came a final inspection, without which movement was impossible, and the expedition prepared to venture into the great unknown.

The only trail which had been followed up to this time was the safe and circuitous route down the Conchos River to its junction with the Rio Grande where Presidio, Texas, stands today. There previous explorers had turned to the left and ascended the Big River. Oñate decided to march directly north across the base of the triangle. He sent out an advance party under Vicente Zaldívar to find a wagon route with adequate water supplies. Zaldívar set out, guided by three men who said they knew the country, but no European really knew what lay beyond the hills. They had a gruesome time. Once they were three days without water, but when it seemed there was no hope, they captured four Indians who showed them a spring. They sent a messenger back to Oñate with instructions to report favorably on the route and to say nothing of the hardships.[12]

The messenger arrived on March 10 at the camp on the San Pedro, and Oñate gave the command to advance. As the great caravan crept along over the barren landscape, it fell into the route which ever since has been the main highway north to the modern city of Chihuahua and to El Paso on the Rio Grande. Then as now the water holes were none too frequent, especially for a party which could go only as fast as the sheep and cows it was driving. The colonists were soon in bad shape. Food was growing short and water was hard to find. A second party was sent out to see what was ahead. Among the volunteers was Gaspar Pérez de Villagrá, who didn't want to miss anything. With characteristic modesty he remarked that he went along "more to fill the required number than to add strength to this noble band."[13]

Not a member of the patrol knew what he was doing or where he was going. "We were sadly lacking in all knowledge of the stars, the winds, and other knowledge by which to guide our steps. I doubt if there was a single one of us who, once the sun had set, could with certainty say, 'There is east, there is west.' "[14]

They had a terrible Indian scare when a roving band captured them and held them prisoner for a while. Finally the red men turned them loose with the smiling explanation that it was all in fun. The indignant Europeans decided that they could play the same game, crept up on the Indian encampment that night, and gave their playful friends a fright of their own.[15]

Their shoes wore out. Their horses wore out. Once they were rained on for seven days. Then there was no water at all. They ate weeds and roots. After a final four waterless days they reached the Great River at last, where it flowed deep and majestic among the cottonwoods and salt cedars and tornillo brush. Horses and men went mad. Two of the animals drank till they burst; two others drowned in the swift current. The men were almost as bad. They wallowed and drank, and drank again, finally laying their water-logged bodies beside the stream "like foul wretches stretched upon some tavern floor."

When they recovered from their aqueous debauch, they found themselves ravenous for food, and they set to work hunting and fishing. The river was full of fish in those days and there were ducks and geese in the marshes.

About this time they saw the front of the great column creeping into view and soon all the Spaniards were reunited in the shade of the cottonwoods beside the swift-flowing river. Everybody had a story to tell. The main body had been saved by divine intervention. After seven days without water they lost all hope. Only God could help them, so they prayed fervently. Suddenly clouds spread over one half of the sky while the sun continued shining in the other half. A great deluge came down and saved them all from inevitable destruction.[16]

To the miserable travelers the tree-shaded river bank was a heavenly place. "It seemed," said Villagrá, "that these were, indeed, the Elysian fields of happiness, where, forgetting all our past misfortunes, we could lie beneath the shady bowers and rest our tired aching bodies, enjoying those comforts so long denied us. It was with happiness that we saw our gaunt horses browsing in the grassy meadows, enjoying a well deserved rest. . . .

"The mighty river flowing swiftly by was such a pleasing sight that its turbulent waters seemed to us a calm and placid lake with scarcely a ripple to disturb its peaceful surface. Its bountiful waters teemed with many fish, and we easily caught a great number. The hunters then shot a large number of ducks and geese. . . . We built a great bonfire and roasted the meat and fish, and then all sat down to a repast the like of which we had never enjoyed before."[17]

With full stomachs and thankful hearts the entire company assembled and compared experiences. The *sargento mayor*, Vicente Zaldívar, told what the scouts had gone through. The Governor himself addressed the crowd and described the experience of the main body of travelers. He praised them for their endurance and promised them a day of rest for everybody.

It seemed time for a celebration. The Governor ordered a chapel built under a grove of trees and the religious ceremonies began. "Here the priests celebrated a solemn high Mass, after which the learned Commissary preached an excellent sermon. Then some of the soldiers enacted a drama written by Captain Farfán. This drama pictured the advent of the friars to New Mexico. We saw the priests coming to this land, kindly received by the simple natives, who reverently approached on bended knees and asked to be received into the faith, being baptized in great numbers.

"After this was over the entire army began celebrating with great joy and mirth."[18]

By order of the Governor everybody put on his best clothes. The horsemen, armor and weapons glittering, assembled and the footmen were drawn up in orderly ranks. Flanked by his civil and religious aides, the Governor stepped forward with a scroll in his hand and went through the solemn ceremony of taking possession:

"In the name of the most Holy Trinity, and of the eternal Unity, Deity and Majesty, God the Father, the Son, and the Holy Ghost, three persons in the one and only true God, who by his eternal will, almighty power and infinite wisdom, rules, directs, and governs from sea to sea, from one end to another, as the beginning and the end of all things . . . and in honor of His most holy and venerable Mother, the holy Virgin Mary, our lady . . . and in the name of the most blessed Saint Francis, image of Christ, God in body and soul, His royal ensign and patriarch of the poor whom I adopt as my patrons, advocates, and intercessors that they may intercede with God himself, that all my thoughts, deeds, and actions may be directed to the service of His infinite majesty to increase the number of the faithful and the extension of the holy Mother church, and to the service of the most Christian of kings, Don Philip, our lord, pillar of the Catholic faith. May God guard him many years for the crown of Castile, and the prosperity of his kingdoms and provinces.

"Be it known that I, Don Juan de Oñate, governor, captain general, and adelantado of New Mexico, and of its kingdoms and provinces, as well as those in its vicinity and contiguous thereto, as the settler and conqueror thereof, by virtue of the authority of the king, our lord, hereby declare that:

"Whereas, by virtue of my appointment . . . and, whereas I desire to take possession of this land this 30th day of April, the feast of the Ascension of our Lord, in the year fifteen hundred and ninety-eight, through the person of Don Juan Pérez de Donís, clerk to his majesty, secretary of this expedition, and to the government of said kingdoms and provinces.

"Therefore in the name of the most Christian king, Don Philip, the second of that name, and for his successors (may they be many) . . . I take possession, once, twice, and thrice, and all the times I can and must, of the actual jurisdiction, civil as well as criminal, of the lands of the said Rio del Norte, without exception whatsoever, with all its meadows and pasture grounds and passes."[19]

So saying, Don Juan solemnly took the royal standard and with his own hands raised it in the place prepared, setting on one side of it the coat of arms of King Philip, and on the other the imperial arms.

At the conclusion of the standard raising the trumpeters blew a great blast, the arquebusiers fired a volley from their weapons, and every man woman, and child in camp shouted at the top of his voice.

One day for ceremony and celebration was all that could be allowed. Early the following morning the caravan was on the move. Five of the best swimmers were sent up river to look for a ford. Villagrá, always anxious to see everything, went along. They ducked in and out of the water looking for shallow places and having a good time all round. Suddenly they came on a camp of Indians, and the red men were upon them before the naked Europeans could run. They had no weapons, of course, and were prepared for the worst, but the Indians proved to be friendly and they were soon hard at work trying to understand each other. The swimmers persuaded four of the natives to come back to the main party with them. Fearfully the red men came. The governor was delighted to see them, put some clothes on their naked bodies, and "loaded them with gifts." Dazed with happiness, the Indians left and soon came back with "great quantities of fish." It was joy upon joy for everybody.[20]

The red men led them to the ancient ford, which they had been using from time immemorial, the crossing above the narrows or gorge of the Rio Grande. Soldiers and citizens plunged into the water, leading horses, shoving carts, pushing and carrying whatever needed to be pushed or carried. Forty Indians armed with bows and arrows appeared and joined in getting the sheep across. Exhausted but happy, the colonists trailed out on the long road which led to New Mexico and a new life.[21] It was May 4, 1598.

No prophet told them that at the foot of their rainbow there would be nothing but years of toil and hardship and disappointment — long frustration and lonely death — but it turned out that way. The mines they had hoped to find did not materialize. Agricultural resources in the new land were limited. The only real harvest was the ingathering of heathen souls. And from the beginning something else was wrong: the soldiers and governors pulled in one direction and the priests in another. Each side exploited the natives and each blamed the other for what its own people were doing. It never occurred to anybody that the Indians had any rights. To the colonists of those early days, it seemed proper to insist that the Indians were there to have their souls saved whether they liked it or not. At the same time it seemed reasonable that if this service were performed for them, the Spaniards should at least get their expenses back. Hence the emphasis on mines, buffalo hides, salt, cotton, wool, and anything else that could be squeezed out of a new country. They had not come, they said, to *regoldar cabrito y beber agua clara* (belch from eating goat meat and drink clear water). Everybody wanted to get rich as soon as possible.

The intention of the King and the Council of Indies was benevolent towards the Indian. The laws were humane and were intended to protect the weak and ignorant from the intelligent and powerful. The trouble was that two groups claimed dictatorial power. The Church with its allied organizations the Crusade and the Holy Office attempted, sometimes intemperately, always persistently, to maintain its authority. The civil officials likewise considered themselves paramount because they were the representatives of the King.[23] Everyone professed himself ready to serve "the two majesties." The question was: How to serve two masters who couldn't get along together.

CHAPTER III

Laying the Foundation

FROM THE VERY BEGINNING the Pass was a meeting place of races. First it was Spaniard and Indian who had to learn to live together. The soldiers and priests who came here were sent to restrain the bodies and sustain the souls of the Indian population. If there had been no Indians, there would have been no Spaniards — and no racial problems.

Two tribes were at hand to be dealt with. Downriver were the Sumas, a wandering group without a systematic economy and with few scruples about causing trouble for the Europeans. They may have been poor relations of the great Jumano group which Cabeza found living in mud villages in the Rio Grande Valley and which extended its branches far out onto the plains of Texas.[1] The Sumas or Zumas or Zumanos, a wilder and more primitive group than the ones Cabeza saw, lived on the western fringes of Jumano territory. They ate mescal, mesquite beans, the fruit of the prickly pear and anything else they could find, wandering over the country south and west of El Paso from Casas Grandes eastward to the Rio Grande as the spirit and the food supply moved them.

Above the Pass, dominating the country northward for perhaps a hundred miles, lived a fiercer group called the Mansos, who probably came from the same linguistic and racial stock.[2] Now *manso* in Spanish means gentle or tame, and that was just what the Mansos were not.[3] They acquired their name when they presented themselves to Oñate himself with cries of "Manxo, manxo!" — meaning that they meant him no harm.[4]

From 1598 on there was constant traffic through the Pass, and the Mansos were often on hand to greet and be greeted. Father Benavides, who came to New Mexico in 1625, described them five years later in his famous *Memorial:*

They too are savage Indians, like the preceding ones, and also naked, except for the women, who wear two deer skins, one in front and one behind. They sustain themselves on fishes from that river, which are plentiful and good, devouring them raw, just as they do the meat of all the animals they hunt, not leaving even the blood. As for the entrails, they do not even take much trouble to clean them; they devour it all like animals. They are a robust people, tall and with good features, although they take pride in bedaubing themselves with powder of different colors which makes them look very ferocious. As this is a unique ford, the friars have crossed over so many times that these Indians already desire to become Christians.[5]

The Spaniards noted that the Mansos, although they could hardly go in for fads in clothing, managed to make their appearance distinctive by bobbing their hair and plastering it to their skulls with mud, making it appear as if they were wearing skullcaps or *gorretas*.

Between 1630 and 1650 the group seems to have moved up the river to the vicinity of Las Cruces — perhaps to camps in the Organ Mountains, which were called for many decades *La Sierra de los Mansos*.[6] At the time of the founding of the mission at El Paso they were brought back to their former home and continued to live there until they were swallowed up by the mounting tide of immigration. Bandelier thought he had found some of their descendants living in Juárez three hundred years later.[7]

Records are scanty about the growth of a spirit of friendship and understanding between the fathers and the Indians at the ford, but there was pretty constant contact. From the beginning of settlement supply trains came from Mexico City at irregular intervals,[8] and when the river was high, travelers sometimes had to wait for weeks until the waters subsided. The site of El Paso and Juárez was a well-known camping place long before it was a town, and both races used it.

Five years after his arrival, Father Benavides recommended that a mission be established at the Pass. It was a strategic location and a good place to operate from in converting the Indians. It seemed to Father Alonso that the Mansos were begging to be saved, and he told about one episode which helped to convince him:

I cannot refrain from telling at this time what happened to me the first time I passed through this nation. Some Indians took me to the rancheria and, having regaled them with bells, feathers and beads of different colors . . . I made a cross the length of a lance and set it up in the center of the rancheria. Then, as best I could, I explained to them that if they worshiped this holy symbol with all their hearts they would find therein the aid for all their needs. Falling on my knees I kissed it. They all did the same. With this my soul was comforted greatly, for it was the first cross they adored in this place. . . . The devil speaks in person to this nation in diverse disguises, but the blessed fathers came out of it unharmed, although amid great dangers.[9]

Father Benavides' thought bore little fruit for the next twenty-five years,[10] but by 1656 Fray Francisco Pérez and Fray Juan Cabal had settled at the Pass as missionaries. They had built a church — no doubt a primitive structure — and had assembled some of the Mansos for instruction.[11] The fathers hoped to teach them farming as well as religion and convert them to a settled and civilized way of life. Over and over the Indians gave up and went back to the wilds; over and over the priests led them back. This went on year after year for many decades.

In 1656 prospects looked good enough at the Ford to induce the fathers to ask for more help, and help was actually granted. The caravan of 1658 escorted a party of Franciscans including four additional religious assigned to El Paso. On the road, however, ten of these friars deserted — appalled, no doubt, by the leagues of wasteland piling up between themselves and all they held dear. The collapse of these ten broken reeds was a setback for the hopeful little community at the Pass but it did nothing to dampen the energy and devotion of the real founder of El Paso, a Franciscan named Fray García de San Francisco y Zúñiga.

We know a little about this good and devoted man of three hundred years ago. He was twenty-six years old when he came to New Mexico with the caravan of 1628-29 — a modest young Franciscan lay brother whose quiet gifts probably did not make him conspicuous among the twenty-nine other recruits who arrived at the same time.[12] He was so humble that he did not consider himself worthy to take orders and did so only at the insistence of his superiors.[13] Fray Estevan de Perea, the *custos*, must have been aware of his capabilities, however, for he encouraged him and entrusted him with great responsibilities.

He plunged into the field at the southernmost point of Spanish occupation in New Mexico — the pueblo of Senecú in the Rio Grande Valley near the future site of San Marcial. In the year 1620 the Reverend Father Antonio Arteaga had converted the natives and set up a church and convent dedicated to St. Anthony of Padua.[14] From this base of operations the new priest sallied forth and soon had a conversion of his own set up at Socorro, twenty miles up the river. The place got its name from the willingness of the natives to succor travelers with bread or beans or whatever they had. Seven hundred persons awaited Father García, and he must have converted them all, for his biographer says that before he died he brought ten thousand converts into the fold of the church.[15]

What love and care he lavished on his mission field! He "adorned" the church and sacristy, added "rich ornaments, an organ and music." He was of a warm and generous heart and loved to provide for his friends. One of his joys was a lush garden, complete with grape vines (imported from vineyards far away), which gave pleasure to the eye and to the palate. He supplied wine for religious services in conversions many leagues from his own.[16]

In his middle years he became vice-custodian of the New Mexico missions, which meant that many cares must be laid on his shoulders and much time must be spent away from his Piro Indians and his garden at Socorro.[17] Among his responsibilities was the little mission at El Paso. Fathers Pérez and Cabal were having trouble with the Mansos and Sumas, who were showing the "repugnance of their natures" toward the Christian life. They even plotted to kill their teachers, who retired in haste to their home convent at Socorro.

"Never mind," Father García advised them. "Don't wear yourselves out, for the time has not yet come."[18] On his own initiative, however, he began to prepare for an establishment at the Pass, and in the fall of 1659[19] he was ready. Armed with a license from Governor Manso and instructions from his superiors, he sallied forth from his convent at Socorro accompanied by Father Blas de Herrera and six Christian Indians from Senecú. In the *auto de fundación* he himself described what followed.

. . . having gone down as I was ordered, with no little labor, to the ford of the Rio del Norte on the frontier of New Spain and the custodia and province of New Mexico; and having assembled the greater part of the rancherias of the pagan Mansos at the said site, and having offered them the word of the gospel, and they having accepted it for their guide and having permitted me to construct a small church of branches and mud and a monastery roofed with grass, the said pagans received me as their preacher and minister.[20]

The date traditionally accepted for the founding of the mission at El Paso is December 8, 1659. It took García almost ten years more to build his church and convent. Construction problems were many — for one thing there were no timbers in this land of little rain. Where were the roof beams to come from? Father Vetancurt, writing forty years later, had heard how that difficulty was overcome: "Before the building was started, there were no timbers for it; but one day while he was kneeling in prayer, some Indians came and took him a league and a half away where they showed him a grove of pines, very beautiful, which they cut down and transported easily to the pueblo of the Mansos."[21]

That there was ever a grove of pines within five miles of Juárez, Mexico, is a matter for serious doubt. With God, all things are possible, of course, but some say that the pillars supporting the ceiling beams are trunks of palm trees brought from Spain to Vera Cruz and carried to El Paso on the shoulders of faithful Indians.[22]

With the coming of a new custodian to New Mexico in 1661, Father García was relieved of his duties as vice-custodian and had more time for his conversion. He laid the cornerstone of his church on April 2, 1662. Six years later the building was finished along with a convent big enough to house thirty friars. When asked why he had provided for so many, Father García merely observed that the space might be needed later on. And of course it was!

The whole establishment was dedicated to Our Lady of Guadalupe on January 15, 1668. The custodian himself, the Reverend Juan Talaban, sang the mass. Four hundred Mansos attended and a hundred of them were baptized, the men coming in at one door and the women at another. Fresh from the baptism, they found themselves in the middle of the new church undergoing the marriage ceremony.[23]

To celebrate this spiritual housecleaning, the citizens kept bonfires going and shot off rockets.[24] It was a great time for all.

You can step inside the door of the old cathedral in Juárez, parts of which belong to the original structure, and view the whole scene in your imagination — the priests in their vestments, soldiers in armor, a sprinkling of Spanish ladies, and the long-haired Indians kneeling on the floor. Since then three sun-soaked centuries have drifted over the roof of Father García's cathedral, "the most beautiful temple of those provinces and that custodia." Some of the years have been bloody and terrible and some have been happy and triumphant, but none has been more exciting and significant than that year of dedication, 1668, when civilization in visible and tangible form was revealed to those poor Indians.

By 1668, says Vetancurt, the total number of parishioners at the Pass had reached a thousand,[25] mostly permanent settlers who had their land under cultivation and had accumulated 9,000 head of cattle plus 13,000 sheep and goats.[26] Most of them were Indians or mixed bloods, but there was a leavening of Spanish families. The missionaries usually saw to it that their wants and needs were taken care of by a few of their own people who felt that it was a privilege to serve a holy man. The mention of vineyards and orchards in documents of the late sixties points to the presence of many Spaniards at this important way station on the road to Santa Fe.[27]

The Indian population would have been predominantly Manso and Suma, but Apache pressure was beginning to tell on the outlying missions in Eastern New Mexico, and natives from Abó, Chililí, Isleta, Humanas, Senecú and Quarai were commencing to filter southward as their pueblos declined.[28] The presence of all these converts taxed the resources of the mother church and expansion became necessary. Actually two branches had been established before the cathedral was dedicated. One was San Francisco de los Sumas (1665), located a league and a half from old San Lorenzo, which seems to have occupied a site twelve leagues below El Paso near present-day San Elizario.[28] The second was called La Soledad de los Janos. Nobody knows exactly where it was, but it must have been off to the southwest in the direction of Casas Grandes seventy leagues away in Chihuahua.[29]

Not all the Mansos were converted. In fact there was one band of die-hard heathens who refused to come in at all and lived somewhere north of the Pass (they were heard of in the Organs and in the Floridas near Deming) under a tough chieftain called Capitán Chiquito, The Little Captain. With such holdouts serving as a bad example, the Christianized Mansos more than once grew restless and had to be punished and restrained. One such episode happened in 1667. Captain Andrés de Gracia, the *alcalde mayor,* asked for help from Santa Fe, but before help could be sent a second dispatch informed the Governor that de Gracia had solved his own problem by hanging two of the rebels. These hangings convinced some of the Mansos that there was no future for them under the Spaniards and led to a larger Manso uprising in 1684.[30]

The Sumas too had their moments of dissatisfaction which resulted in later uprisings, but all this takes nothing away from the magnitude of Father García's achievement. Before the 1660's were over, El Paso was a thriving community with the mission at its heart. The fathers had fields and flocks, gardens and orchards, grapes and flowers.[31] Hundreds of Indians were learning the ways of peace and religion. El Paso was a promising and flourishing unit in the vast web of colonization and conversion which Spain had flung over the New World.

The wisdom and benevolence of the Indian policy of the Franciscan missionaries is being questioned by skeptical historians now. One of them calls it a "militarily enforced tyranny."[32] Sometimes perhaps it was. But a devoted and humble teacher like Father García shows us what the noblest of the Spaniards dreamed of accomplishing.

In his later years the good *padre* rose to eminence in the church. As vice-custodian and *procurador* he was called on to take action during the troubled administration of Governor Bernardo López de Mendizábal (1660-1661) when Church and State were at bitter odds, and it was he who drew up the list of complaints against that greedy and garrulous man.[33] López replied to these charges when his time came to be heard in Mexico City, and countered with awful blasts against the manners and morals of the clergy. No breath of scandal blew on Father García, however. And if his life had not been spotless, the world would have heard about it.

With these struggles and achievements behind him, he went to his eternal reward on January 22, 1673, in the convent of Senecú, of which he was the head. *Fue de caridad ardiente en socorrer así a los religiosos como á los naturales liberal,* says his biographer. He was warmly charitable not only toward his fellow churchmen but also toward the natives. "He was a mirror for others in prayer and other virtues; he was zealous in the conversion of souls."

He was more than that. He was a noble human being who enjoyed the good things of life when he could have them and loved to share them with others. And in a time of scandal and recrimination, no one spoke evil of him. What better could be said of any human being, priest or layman?

CHAPTER IV

The Loss of Everything

 THE NEWS CAME at daylight on the morning of August 25, 1680. It came in the form of two sweat-stained letters in the hands of two weary Indian runners who had been traveling by night for fear of the Apaches. They presented themselves at the portal of the convent of Our Lady of Guadalupe at El Paso del Norte and asked to see Father Francisco Ayeta as quickly as possible. Their business was of the utmost urgency.

The brown-robed Franciscan brother turned after hearing the first words of explanation and hastened with all possible speed to the modest cell where the Reverend Father had done his sleeping and praying since the first of April, waiting for the flooded river to subside so he could take his supply wagons across and get on with his journey to Santa Fe.

In a matter of minutes the news had gone to the farthest limits of the little mission community: the Indians of the New Mexico pueblos, aided and encouraged by the wild Apaches, had risen and wiped out the Spanish settlements. Many, perhaps most, of the Christians had been killed. The families who lived along the river below the capital — some 1,500 Spaniards plus some friendly Indians — were making their way south in pain and peril. There was no word from Governor Otermín and he and the settlers from Santa Fe northward were presumably dead. The whole province had gone in a welter of smoke and blood. Everything — the fruits of nearly a hundred years of occupation — was lost.[1]

Ayeta, a man of much refinement and great modesty, was overwhelmed by the news of disaster but he was not greatly surprised. He had been living in the shadow of the danger for six years and had been spending all his time and energy trying to avert it. Sick as he was at heart, he rose to this as to every other occasion. He sent for the military and civil authorities.

By eight o'clock he had them assembled in his convent cell. There was first of all the *maestro de campo,* sixty-year-old Pedro de Leiva — personification of the tough and hardy Spanish soldier. With him came his two *sargentos mayores* Diego Lucero de Godoy and Lorenzo de Madrid. The civil power was represented by the *alguacíl mayor,* Gregorio de Valdés, and the *regidor,* Alonso del Río. These leaders, with twenty-seven men, had come down from Santa Fe several weeks before to meet the great supply train from Mexico City, to welcome their beloved Father Ayeta, and to see that he made the last stage of his six-months journey in peace and safety. Now they summed up in their own persons the power of the Spanish Crown in this most isolated outpost in the New World. If, as they feared, the Governor and all his staff had perished, they were the government — all that was left of the Cabildo which ruled from the Royal Houses at Santa Fe. It was a solemn moment for those men, frantic as they were about the fate of their own families far to the north and mourning in their hearts for the ruin of their personal fortunes.

Father Ayeta looked at them and thought of all that they represented. For over eighty years they and their fathers and grandfathers had lived in the wilderness in turmoil and discontent. They had exploited and antagonized the Indians whom the fathers (not always above reproach themselves, though some were saints and martyrs) were trying to civilize and christianize. They had feuded and fought each other, harried the governors (had killed one of them), and kept the country in turmoil.[2] A few families, all intermarried, had become prosperous. The rest were poor and eager to leave a hostile land where the laws compelled them to stay.[3] There was little opportunity for education, and few of them outside the official family could read or write.[4] They wenched and gambled. They were superstitious[5] and contentious. They were inbred and at the same time had produced many crossbreeds. Convicts and fugitives had found refuge among them.[6] Mexico and Spain, with their civilizing influences, were far removed, part of another world of which they could only dream. They can hardly be blamed for being products of their time and environment, but they were a problem for any governor, too much of a problem for poor old Antonio Otermín, who called them, quoting a distracted predecessor, "a people abandoned by God."[7] From the moment their forbears had arrived in New Mexico, they had been preparing for this day of wrath. Now it was here.

Part of the trouble was the possession by a good many Spaniards of *encomiendas* or grants of permission to levy tribute on this or that Indian community.[8] Part of it was the unwillingness of the natives to give up their ancient religious traditions. The worst punishments they underwent were for apostasy and they learned to carry on their primitive worship in secret.[9] Even the ones who came to Mass could not be relied on. Ayeta strongly suspected that some of the governors had encouraged them in their errors.[10]

The leaders in the pueblos had been getting ready for something like twelve years[11] to throw the Spaniards out and several times had actually laid far-reaching plans which were detected in the nick of time.[12]

Governor Treviño made the fatal error in 1675 of trying to go too far and too fast in putting down the spirit of revolt. He arrested forty-seven of the Indian shamans and hanged three of them. He would have hanged more, but the Indians made such strong protests, pointing out the consequences of this cruelty, that he had to back down.[13] The forty-four shamans who escaped with their lives got back to their homes, but they went nursing bitterness. Among them was a Tewa of Taos named Popé. For five years he built up the organization which engineered the great revolt.[14]

Ayeta himself — Procurator of his order for the provinces of New Mexico, Custodian and Visitor in them, Commissary General of the Holy Office and *juez ordinario* of the Custodia[15] — was the man who saw most clearly what was coming and tried hardest to circumvent it. In 1676, the year after the hanging of the Indian leaders, he traveled to Mexico City with a letter from the Governor and a memorial of his own urging the Viceroy to send reinforcements and supplies lest all be lost. In 1677 he arrived in Santa Fe after nine months on the road with the fruits of his efforts. These included forty-three fully equipped soldiers (all convicts) and a thousand horses — plus armor, leather jackets, saddles, shields, and other military supplies.[16] He had convinced the Viceroy and his officials that if New Mexico went, the provinces to the south would probably go too, and they had given him this handful of men and equipment.

As soon as he was back in Santa Fe, Ayeta realized that it would not be enough. The contempt of the Indians for the Spaniards was now complicated by desperation induced by several years of drouth and famine.[17] The danger was mounting steadily. In 1679 Ayeta was back in the Capital asking for fifty more soldiers. The Viceroy was quite willing to present the matter to the King; the letters went off; and in due course of time the King rendered a favorable decision.[18] But by then it was too late.

Meanwhile Ayeta had assembled twenty-eight wagons and loaded them with supplies for the missionary priests in New Mexico. When the caravan of 1680 set out, he joined it, as he felt he must, without waiting for the word from Spain. The spring floods were making swamps along the bottom lands when he arrived at the Pass and it was necessary for him to wait, with what patience he could muster, till the river could be crossed.

His welcome, as always, was a warm one, for Father Ayeta was one of the great men of his time and place — a man whom his associates instinctively loved and reverenced. We know only a little about his personal life and background. A Spaniard — a *gachupín* — born in 1640 in Pamplona, he came to the New World early in his life. When he was only nineteen he put on the brown robe of a Franciscan and a year later took his vows.[19] We can be sure that he cherished memories of long years in the great monastery and school of San Francisco de Mexico. In later times his qualities of "gentlemanliness, faithfulness, and nobility" were recalled by his successors, and he was valued and respected even in the Royal Court in Spain. He had wealthy and powerful friends in whose great houses he was sometimes able to snatch a few hours of relaxation among people of education and refinement.[21]

As a gentleman he was careful of his appearance and elegant in his manners — fit for responsibilities of the highest importance, yet truly devout and humble. The two sides of his character appeared in his writing. On the one hand he was a skillful stylist with a fine, flexible flow of language and great power in argument. On the other, the courtly self-abasement affected even by the proudest grandees of his time sounds honest and natural in his mouth: "Your most humble chaplain kisses the feet of your Excellency."

Physically he was not robust and sometimes remarked regretfully, "I find myself in very poor health, to such a point that I know neither what I am saying nor what I am doing" — yet there was a core of iron in him which held him steady and enabled him to make decisions in spite of weakness and debility. Patient in most things, he was impatient in one. He disliked long debates and acrimonious discussion. On one occasion, when a *junta* threatened to become heated, Ayeta stayed away, pleading sickness, and sent by letter his views on the matters in question.[23] This was the man who called together at the convent the responsible officials of the settlement.

When all was quiet in his cell, Ayeta addressed his guests and told them the sad news. The letters left no doubt of the magnitude of the tragedy. One was from Juan Severino Rodríguez to Father Diego de Mendoza. The other was from Mendoza to Ayeta. They had been sent forward from the column of refugees moving down the river. "There is such a multitude of small children that all are traveling on foot, and the poor women as well,"[24] Mendoza wrote.

The question was, what could be done?

Leiva went out to call his men together for a *junta de guerra,* and Ayeta and his priests retired for a session of prayer in the convent.

The council of war convened about nine o'clock and agreed that the first thing to do was to get help to the refugees. Ayeta offered to unload his wagons and send them on with the food and clothing needed. He would send two hundred head of cattle. He would go himself, and so would any of his clergy who were needed.[25]

The next step was to set up some machinery of government. That meant another meeting — this time a meeting of all the Spaniards in the settlement. Drum and trumpet went forth to summon them. In all such cases the Spaniards were thoroughgoing democrats who believed in free debate and majority rule. When all were assembled — probably a hundred or so — the situation was explained and candidates were proposed. The vote was for Pedro de Leiva, probably because Ayeta was for him. In the next parcel of dispatches the father commended him to the Viceroy: "He has much experience and courage in warfare, for which he is held in high esteem. I assure you, most excellent sir, that if he does not save the present situation, I have no hope that anyone, after God, can do so."

The hours that followed were full of furious activity. It took two days to unload the wagons of the supply train and store the contents. On the third day the wagons were reloaded with supplies for the refugees. Two more days passed as the military company was organized. The rescue force numbered seventy-eight arquebusiers, and Ayeta noted with acid humor that "not even one affected to be crippled in order to be rejected."[26] Fifty-six citizens, armed with whatever weapons came to hand, completed the force. Four priests were detailed to go along to serve in any way they could.[27]

On the thirtieth of August they left, most of them in great sorrow and uncertainty for the families and friends whose fate they dreaded to learn. Ayeta remarked that they were "absolutely raging; I believe under God that each one must be reckoned as ten men."[28]

The rescue party proceeded by forced marches up the river, not knowing what they might encounter. At San Cristóbal, the campground at the north end of what we now call Elephant Butte Lake, they found some of the refugees encamped. The contingent from Santa Fe had not caught up yet, having pushed southward only as far as Socorro.

Governor Otermín was not dead, as had been feared. He and the fugitives from Santa Fe had escaped with not much more than their skins and had moved south along the river in destitution and discouragement. When he caught up with the families who had been living in the valley below present-day Albuquerque, he found to his intense anger and disgust, that they had been able to salvage much of what they owned, loaded it into wagons and brought it along, with their livestock.

The Governor was outraged. He was a fussy, self-important man, full of worries and resentments, one who worked furiously at enterprises that never quite succeeded and laid careful plans which never quite came off. After each misfortune he accumulated voluminous records with the object of blaming somebody else. Like so many good but ineffectual people, he was apt to fret himself into ill health, and his affairs got themselves into worse tangles as he tried to recover. Ayeta called him "a very Christian gentleman and zealous for the honor of God and our lord, the King, excellent in his measures for peace and war" — one who shared his own "scanty possessions" to aid the poor settlers.[29] When all was going well in the kingdom, Otermín spoke of the priest as his "most beloved Fray Francisco Ayeta."[30] Their friendship cooled considerably when the bad times came.

The unauthorized and selfish departure of the southern colonists while he was fighting for his life in the Royal Houses at Santa Fe galled Otermín for the rest of his career in New Mexico. He was prepared at first to hang somebody for it, but actually he got no farther than some furious grumbling and the accumulation of an extensive collection of notes. He never forgot the insult, however, and later on found ways of expressing his resentment where it would do the most damage.

Meanwhile something had to be done to get the colonists out of danger. El Paso was the obvious destination, but there was not enough food to support two thousand persons on the long journey. The Governor sent Leiva back to the Pass for more supplies.

Ayeta was anxious to do all he could when he heard Leiva's story. He loaded twenty-five wagons with clothing and provisions, rounded up guards and teamsters, and headed for the crossing. By the time he skirted Mule Driver's Mountain and arrived at the Ford, the river was impassable. Rain had fallen and the stream was up again. The caravan struggled up the west bank for four leagues, hoping to find a crossing. On the morning of September 18, it arrived at a point across from present-day Canutillo. The campground called La Salineta (little salt lake) was in sight on the east bank. In desperation Ayeta had six spans of mules hitched to one wagon and plunged into the swift water. The wagon stuck in the middle of the stream, with Ayeta in it. Hoping to save the animals at least, he cut the traces and the horses got across. Himself, however, he could not save.

At this moment Governor Otermín, with an advance party of refugees, arrived at the bank and came to the rescue of the valiant padre. Indian swimmers carried him out on their shoulders and spent the rest of the day getting the wagon ashore. The horses were then loaded with flour, chocolate, corn and bread and urged across to the east bank.[31]

The pack train met the main body of New Mexicans and made it possible for them to move wearily on to La Salineta. There they went into camp and stayed for many dreary weeks. Several good reasons existed for keeping them there. In the first place, there was no room in El Paso for this horde. In the second, the government had to keep them together if possible and curb free souls among them from scattering out along the dim trails to far-away towns in Mexico. Even so, a small but steady stream of colonists trickled away—first to El Paso; then to Casas Grandes, Namaquipa, Torreon, or any other place which was far away from New Mexico.[32] Otermín tried to stop the outflow by appealing to Governor Estrada of Nueva Vizcaya to turn the fugitives back, but he tried in vain.

Ayeta noted that though they looked "like dead people," they were as "discontented and arrogant" as ever, demanding that they be allowed to move on and leave their desolate campground. They could not understand, or did not care if they did understand, that if New Mexico was to be reclaimed some day, there must be people to reclaim it — and that they were the people who would have it to do.

Ayeta did the best he could for them, sending off to Casas Grandes and Taraumares, far to the southwest, for corn and beef. "In the year '80 I have been obliged to learn something about trade," he wrote to the Commissary General. "May God in his holy compassion bring me safely through it."[33]

In October, with cold weather coming on, Otermín was forced to make a decision. Following a universal muster intended to account for all the refugees and a great council to discuss what was to be done, he received a petition from all the people in camp asking that they be allowed to move across the river to the vicinity of the convent "because of the many dangers and inconveniences which beset them at La Salineta." The next day the Governor granted this request.[34] It was the beginning of the real settlement of the El Paso Valley.

The influx of those two thousand hungry, disorderly refugees was, of course, a terrible thing. The mission had existed for some twenty years and the Franciscans had things well in hand with gardens, orchards, and herds of cattle for themselves and a reasonable number of dependents and visitors, but there was not enough of anything for two thousand additional people. Something had to be done, however, and something was done.

Before long they had been sorted out and settled in three new towns below the mother church. Farthest to the south the Governor established his headquarters at a place he called the Real de San Lorenzo (after the saint on whose day the revolt broke out). It was six leagues from the original settlement. Five priests were stationed there and Father Ayeta let them take his portable altar on its cart "as being more decent."[35] The site of San Lorenzo was already a historic spot, for it was "at the place where the wagons arrive on the outward trip" — the spot where the river turned east and where the caravans left the Valley to strike out across the sand dunes on their way south.[36] It was near, perhaps on, the spot where Oñate had taken possession of New Mexico for his God and King. The other two communities — San Pedro de Alcántara and El Santísimo Sacramento—were spaced two leagues apart toward El Paso.

Each family constructed its own house of "sticks and branches," a type of building still observable in the El Paso neighborhood and still called a *jacal*. The houses in San Lorenzo were said to be "built in an orderly manner,"[37] but to the colonists, some of them accustomed to a considerable degree of comfort, they must have seemed grim enough.

While the settlers were establishing themselves as best they could, Ayeta was on the road again under the October sky, headed for Mexico City with letters from the Cabildo and the Governor. His object was to report and plead for more help. The great ones were ready to listen to him this time. They promised him a presidio garrisoned by fifty men at a salary of 350 pesos annually. They arranged for aid to the settlers — tools and arms and supplies plus "twelve pairs of fetters and six chains of two arrobas with their collars and padlocks, two hinges and padlocks for the stocks."[38]

When the Junta General in Mexico asked Ayeta to take charge of the caravan, he told them that he had just received notice of his appointment as Procurator General for all the provinces of New Spain and a summons to Spain on official business. He vindicated his reputation for diplomacy in the way he handled this delicate situation. He asked the Viceroy to decide for him what he should do. After appropriate consultations the Viceroy requested him to postpone his acceptance of his new position since nobody else could be trusted to do what needed to be done in New Mexico. Ayeta accepted the decision "with entire willingness"[39] and went off to assemble his caravan.

Meanwhile things were going from bad to worse at the Pass. Supplies were almost used up. No word had come from Mexico City. The colonists became more disgruntled and disrespectful than ever as poor old Otermín developed symptoms of illness and dreamed of going away on sick leave.

They all wanted to leave, and of course he could not let them go. At a *junta de guerra* on April 5, 1681, he tried to tell them why. "You tell me," he said, "that you are all perishing of hunger. I know this to be true for I am experiencing the same need. Nevertheless, if all the men should go, the women and children left behind would certainly perish, and to grant permission to everyone to leave this camp would manifestly expose this body of Christian Indians to being destroyed."[40]

There was also the Reconquest. Not to go back eventually and wrest their old country from the rebellious Indians was unthinkable. Naturally most of the colonists must consider themselves under orders to try to regain the ground that had been lost. Otermín tried to impress this view upon them at the *junta* but he was unable to work up much enthusiasm for the enterprise. In fact, only two members of the assembly were willing to advise the governor to attack at once. These, however, were of a quality to command attention. Old Pedro Duran y Chávez and his nephew Juan Domínguez de Mendoza were top men in the group from the Rio Abajo settlements. The Chávez and Domínguez families had done well for themselves in New Mexico. Tough and ruthless, they were also strong and efficient and loyal to each other.

Of Pedro Duran y Chávez we know little except that he was "turbulent," and that he was accused of planning the murder of Governor Rosas in 1642."[41] Domínguez, however, was already the leading military figure in New Mexico and was on his way to becoming a legend. He had attained his eminence because he was better at his job than any other military leader in the province. True, his own career was his chief concern and he cared for nobody outside his own family, but he could be a very practical man, as he showed on this occasion. His argument for an immediate reentry was that there should be plenty of corn at the pueblo of Isleta, and it would be well to go and get it.

His uncle Pedro de Chávez sided with him. The rest voted against organizing an expedition, even for food. They wanted to wait till Ayeta returned from Mexico City with supplies.[42]

Otermín shook his head, thought a while, and made his decision. He would send Pedro de Leiva off to Casas Grandes to buy as much livestock as possible "at my expense."

The sequel showed what those refugees were really like. Of the ten men detailed to assist Leiva, only one went along, and he did nothing. In trying to get 150 head of cattle home without assistance, Leiva and his servants lost forty. Otermín heard of this sorry business and took down Leiva's sworn statement on June 15, 1681, but apparently did nothing about it. After all, what could he do?[43]

At the end of the first week in September Ayeta arrived, twenty leagues ahead of his wagon train, and for a little while Otermín felt better. There were arms and supplies for a military expedition and fifty soldiers for the new presidio. Now the Reconquest could be organized. He issued orders for a general muster and placed Juan Domínguez de Mendoza in charge of the proceedings.

The results were appalling. Usable equipment was almost nonexistent. Practically every arquebus was out of order. Pascual Naranjo was only one of many who reported "with his person and a lance, on foot, and without any other equipment."[44] Horses were in fairly good supply but leather jackets for the men and horse armor for their mounts were scarce. Food was hard to find. Apparently the refugees had not bothered to plant what they needed to feed themselves and bad weather had ruined what there was. Again Father Ayeta had to step in and provide maize and beef.[45] Otermín, already shaken, had a worse shock coming. He was authorized to issue equipment and make a cash payment to the enlistees, but to his astonishment and chagrin, he found that almost nobody wanted his money. Only a fraction of the authorized force of 150 men was willing to sign up. Anxious to find out why, he conducted an investigation and kept careful *autos* of what everybody said.

The most important people, he found, were causing the trouble. Tomé Domínguez de Mendoza complained of "gout and stomach disorder, besides being sixty-one years old." He would be pleased, he said with sublime effrontery, "to accept an alms of his Majesty (whom God keep), because of his great poverty, but can't accept any responsibilities as a soldier or settler."[46]

Pedro Duran y Chávez pleaded similarly, asking for remuneration "for the services I have rendered, so that my family may not perish, I being extremely poor and destitute."[47]

Even the sturdy Juan Domínguez de Mendoza pleaded enfeebled health. "Only a few days ago he had a fainting fit, after which they carried him to his house, and if the people of his household had not found him, he would have died."[48]

Since Juan was one of two who had advised an immediate re-entry, his attitude needs explanation. Actually he was just looking out for Juan Domínguez. He and his clan realized that if they accepted the King's pay, they would be subject to his discipline, and they wished to remain as free as possible. Some agreed to go without pay but they refused to obligate themselves by accepting money. These people were doing very well where they were. Ayeta noted "how little desire many, who had managed to attain some small degree of comfort, had to return for this reduction."[49]

When Otermín probed deeper, he found that the equipment issued to the men already signed up was disappearing at a great rate. This called for another proclamation in October, 1681, ordering that nobody "shall dare to gamble with any of the arms, horses, or clothing which are strictly necessary to them," and that "whatever any of them shall have won from another shall be returned immediately. . . ."[50]

Otermín knew well enough that the Chávez and Domínguez families were living off the bounty of the King while they profiteered at the expense of the poor. He prepared a series of interrogatories to throw light on their habits and situation and found that they had more cattle now than when they arrived — had even driven some off to be sold in other communities. Father Ayeta had bought some of this livestock back to feed the hungry. They had taken the wool distributed to the wretched settlers for clothes-making, added it to their own supply, and used it for commercial purposes. Don Pedro de Chávez himself had set up a loom and was weaving sackcloth and blankets for sale outside the community and was baking bread for those who could pay for it.[51]

That they were sick is as doubtful as that they were starving. Otermín remarked with grim irony that there seemed to be "more sick people in El Paso than in a hospital."[52]

These interrogatories were made in early October of 1681. It was late to start the Reconquest, but the Governor was determined to go, and to go now. On November 5, 1681, he marched out of the *plaza de armas* with 146 Spaniards under arms, many of them mere boys. Beside them trotted 112 Indians.[53]

Ayeta and his little church on wheels went along, but with many misgivings.[54]

CHAPTER V

The First Reentry

 THE ISLETA INDIANS were assembled in their ancient plaza when the Spaniards appeared after a month of cautious movement. The natives seemed overjoyed, all 500 of them, at the reunion, and they participated heartily the next day in religious exercises when Father Ayeta brought up his portable altar and said Mass. It was the day of the Immaculate Conception, a day for giving and rejoicing, which the natives celebrated by making a "free gift" of supplies.[1]

That same day Otermín took a final step in organizing the Reconquest. With considerable ceremony, he appointed the indispensable Domínguez a Lieutenant-General of Cavalry and put him at the head of a flying squadron which was to investigate the Indian pueblos to the north: San Felipe, Cochití, and Santo Domingo. He instructed him to take away all the Spanish arms which the Indians had captured, burn all the kivas, and sack the houses of those who refused to surrender. This was to be done "always with deliberation, resolution, and Christianity."[2] He gave him the best horses and equipment and bade him a hopeful farewell on December 8, 1681.[3]

The appointment was no surprise to anyone, least of all Domínguez, but the fact that it was made by a man who did not like or trust him is some measure of what Domínguez meant to the people and government of New Mexico. Since he begins to be the central figure in the story, some knowledge of his background and career will be useful:

His family came into the country some time between 1640 and 1650 when old Bartolomé (Tomé) Domínguez moved his family up from Mexico City and occupied lands in the vicinity of present-day Albuquerque. His descendants allied themselves with the first families of New Mexico, including the Mendozas, whose name they added to their own. They considered themselves to be members of the Spanish aristocracy and never for a moment forgot that they were important people.[4]

Old Tomé died at the age of 96 in 1656. His son, Tomé the second, settled south of the Indian village of Isleta at the place still called Tomé after him. Our subject, the second son Juan, lived in the same general vicinity.

It is hard to tell how old the man was. In 1680, he gave his age as forty-six and the year following he said he was fifty-two,[5] a characteristic piece of inconsistency. In another account he declared that he came to New Mexico as "a child of twelve,"[6] and in 1686 mentioned that he "had served his Majesty in the provinces of New Mexico for forty-two years."[7] These figures in combination indicate that he was forty-eight years old in 1680, which is probably about right.

After he became able to bear arms, he rose from private soldier through all the ranks: *alférez,* captain, *sargento mayor, maestre de campo,* lieutenant governor. Through sheer efficiency, he became the top military man in the kingdom,[8] for though most of the colonists, both lay and clergy, feared and even hated him, they had to call on him in difficult times, and they knew they had to.

The mere recital of his commissions and certificates, drawn up at his request by the Cabildo or Council of State at El Paso in 1684, is most impressive, showing as it does that Domínguez had been employed and promoted by thirteen governors up to and including Otermín. He had been lieutenant-governor four times. He even had "a writing of favor and privilege from his Majesty in five pages, having been copied and made at the time when General Francisco Martínez de Baeza was Governor, being signed with his name, sealed with the seal of his arms, and countersigned by his secretary of government and war."[9]

This statement came from his friends. His enemies had their turn later.

A record which purports to give a complete account of Domínguez' services to King and country was prepared at his instigation for the King of Spain and supported by documents prepared at his request by others. Historians strongly suspect that he falsified parts of this record of his *servicios* and forged some of the accompanying papers.[10] The chances are, however, that his actual experiences and accomplishments would turn out to be as hair-raising and horrifying as anything he invented.

The testimony showed that his career began as early as 1644 when he put down a revolt of the Zuñis and Picuríes.[11] He would have been in his teens when he did this — if he did it.[12]

In 1654, he went with Sargento Mayor Diego de Guadalajara's expedition to the Río Colorado far out in Texas, in the course of which the Spaniards supported the Jumanos in one of their private wars and emerged with victory and much plunder. Later, Domínguez claimed to have been the leader of this foray and supplied details of various fights he led against the Apaches and a combination of the Excanjaques and Aidos. In a three-day battle against the latter, he captured 1,600 of the enemy and liberated 127 Christian captives. One is not surprised to learn that present-day scholars consider the story to be "a product of the forger's imagination."[13]

His next exploit, as he tells it, was a campaign against the Mescaleros, who had raided the Humanas pueblo on the site now known as Gran Quivira. Twenty-seven captives were recovered. Next he took on the Navajos, recapturing 211 Indian prisoners, forty Christian natives, and a Spanish girl.[14]

Next he claims to have pacified the Mansos of the El Paso area, hanging two of their leaders. The time was the early 1650's.[15]

Later in the decade, he went out against the Apaches again, supposedly in a time of peace, and "butchered" some of his captives. For this crime Governor Medrano is said to have condemned him to death, but the sentence was commuted — no doubt because Juan was more useful alive than dead.[16]

During these years, Domínguez seems to have stood well with the governors sent out from Mexico, though this is little credit to him since they were mostly a poor lot. In the summer of 1659, the most incompetent of all of them appeared in New Mexico, the unfortunate Bernardo López de Mendizábal. The friars accused him of encouraging the Indians to practice their "heathen rites," and he fought a hard battle against the churchmen which eventually cost him his position and his life.[17] Domínguez was under fire along with his governor. When poor, half-demented López was tried by the Inquisition in Mexico City, Fray Salvador de Guerra's testimony included an accusation against Domínguez:

I also swear that Juan Domínguez de Mendoza, who was lieutenant general in the time of the government of Mendizabal — whom I know and knew as a man conspicuously inimical to the ecclesiastics, who persecuted them by his writings, prevented them from administering the holy sacraments, took away the cantors, sacristans, and others who attended divine worship, and who beat the Indians in the churches and churchyards to prevent them from serving their spiritual pastors — this man after the four above-mentioned persons were arrested by the Holy Office, took his pistols, arquebuse, and leather jacket, and wandered about the fields, telling people everywhere that he does this, not staying in his house even at night, but has his weapons ready, in case they should come to arrest him for the Inquisition. He says he will kill every one who comes, or be killed himself, before he will allow himself to be taken, and that the four men who were arrested allowed themselves to be taken through pure cowardice.[18]

Obviously the Inquisition could have finished Domínguez as well as López, but it didn't, perhaps because he was next to indispensable in the harried province.

Those were years of famine and great hardship. The Christian Indians starved and died. The Apaches and Navajos raided with increasing boldness, robbing and burning, carrying off many captives, and desecrating the sanctuaries. All roads were dangerous. The country was actually in a state of siege.

Now was the time for Domínguez and his fellow *encomenderos* to take action. In return for their privileges in exploiting their Indian charges, they were expected to defend them and the Kingdom.[19] In practice, this meant that they drove the Indians to defend themselves, for the Spaniards were few, and the military squadrons were made up mostly of red men who had to fight either the enemy or their Spanish masters. Such a system lent itself to graft and corruption, and apparently Domínguez got his share.[20]

Some of his activities in the Indian campaigns of this period are known to us through his own statements, and more from the records of official investigations provoked by his questionable conduct. In 1666, for instance, he led a detachment against the Apaches west of the Rio Grande in the neighborhood of the Rock of Acoma. On March 26, he and his soldiers, returning from their punitive expedition, camped for the night at the foot of the great mesa with the Indian town on top. A number of the natives came down to visit Domínguez in his camp in order to complain of Father Nicolás de Freitas, their priest, who had beaten them for small offenses.

Domínguez ordered one of his men to write down what they said.

News of this act was carried back to the top of the rock, where it reached the ears of Father Diego de Santander, a priest so old and worn-out in missionary work that he could not climb up and down the Indian trail. He was not too old or too feeble to fly into a rage, however. He ordered several able-bodied Indians to carry him to Domínguez' camp, where he expressed himself freely on the subject of a priest's immunity from investigation by lay authorities. Domínguez was serving as Lieutenant Governor and Captain General at this time, and Father Diego could not have gone any higher without attacking the Governor himself.

The next step after an episode of this kind was to send off a barrage of letters to the Viceroy, accusing or defending according to one's sympathies. In spite of the fact that Domínguez' soldiers stood up for him, a series of complaints went off to Mexico City from both Santander and Freitas.

They denounced Domínguez for being chronically hostile to the clergy and said that Don Bernardo López de Mendizábal, a priest-hater himself, had felt it necessary to reprove him for a "shameful" letter attributing terrible wickedness to a Sandía friar. They were sure he had encouraged the Sandía and Isleta tribesmen to relapse into heathenism, and they suspected that Domínguez was a heathen himself. They wondered how he had managed for so long to keep out of the clutches of the Inquisition.[21]

Many of their fellow colonists wondered likewise, but somehow Domínguez managed to stay in the clear. Through the sixties he played a leading role in holding the frontier against the Apache.

The most exposed of the Christianized settlements were the pueblos east of the site of Albuquerque, beyond the Manzano Mountains, in the Salt Lakes region; the most vulnerable of these villages was Humanas. The Siete Ríos Apaches raided here repeatedly and it became necessary to campaign against them. Domínguez led the pursuit more than once. In May, 1669, he was made *encomendero* of Humanas. He got a cotton blanket and a *fanega* of corn from each house in the village every year, and it was understood that he was to get out and earn his income. He earned it. By June of 1670, he is reported to have killed thirteen Apaches and freed six Indian captives.[22]

This spurred the Seven Rivers band to organize the greatest raid of all. They struck Humanas in September of 1670, leaving behind them eleven dead and escaping with thirty-one captives. The Spaniards sent out a counter expedition, and it is safe to suppose that Juan Domínguez was one of the leaders. What success he had we do not know.

Juan was no ordinary man. He must have had great capacities for both good and evil — great gifts and even greater faults. We have only to add that he was also a man of great ambitions, wilful and selfish ambitions which were to develop into dangerous obsessions. His acquaintances could say under oath: "His reputation is so bad that he is generally said to be worse than the devil."[23] But for many years he was New Mexico's indispensable man.

We know what he looked like. The Cabildo of Santa Fe, in exile at Paso del Norte, on October 8, 1684, set down at Juan's own request a description of himself and his two sons:

> The said Maestre de Campo is a tall man, not excessively so, of good stature, dark-skinned, of good countenance, already gray headed and apparently some sixty years of age, more or less, with a good mustache, and has three scars, all on the left side. The first in a shoulderblade which he broke at the Rock of Acoma which has left him with a shrunken shoulder, and the second in the left hand, the entire first joint of the thumb being removed from the said hand, and the third he has above the knee of the said left side, crossing the thigh muscle, and another scar on the head on the left side, all of which he received in combat.[42]

Otermín had to use this scarred and broken warrior, though he simmered with indignation over what he considered Domínguez' desertion in 1680 and his lack of enthusiasm for the reconquest. In spite of all, the Governor made him his lieutenant, giving him "jurisdiction of El Paso in civil and military affairs."[25] Now at the crucial moment of reconquest, Domínguez was singled out again for the position of maximum responsibility. The probe of Indian towns upriver was a mission of utmost importance. Information which the flying company might provide would determine Otermín's course of action, and he knew he must put his best man in charge. Consequently Domínguez rode out at the head of the column.

They were gone eleven days. Otermín passed the time, with Father Ayeta's help, in burning the pueblos of Alameda, Puaray and Sandía and in examining all the Indians he could find who might throw some light on conditions in the revolted province.[26]

Domínguez sent back several messengers with reports, and on December 19 he himself appeared. He brought some loot and a story, and not much else. The story threw Otermín into a renewal of his old frenzy at all the colonists, but especially at Juan Domínguez de Mendoza.

The company had passed through six pueblos. They had burned none but had sacked several. Otermín thought they were more interested in "prying into the trap doors of the pueblos than in reclaiming the apostate tribesmen."[27] Domínguez explained that he thought the rebels would come in for conference more readily if he did not burn their houses, and he actually blamed the Governor's incendiary habits for spoiling his own negotiations. He told the Viceroy later on that as his men and the natives were weeping together with joy over their happy reunion, "an Indian came from the pueblos below with the report that the governor was burning those of Alameda, Puaray, and Sandía, angering the whole community that had now become pacified. When the petitioner saw this, he returned to call the said governor to account for committing the blunder of burning all those pueblos and provisions. . . ."[28]

Domínguez may have had a point here, but the Governor was not convinced. He assembled testimony which fixed responsibility for the failure of the *entrada* on his lieutenant, showing that he had fraternized and traded with the enemy and had made no attempt to seize any of the Indian leaders, some of whom were actually in his power.[29] One suspects that Juan had in fact enjoyed a sort of old-home-week celebration with his Indian acquaintances and did as little as possible to disturb them beyond dipping into their abandoned storehouses — a procedure to which they were well accustomed after almost a hundred years of experience.

In time, Otermín's accusations reached the *fiscal* in Mexico City. This official condemned Domínguez for what he had done or failed to do and condemned Otermín for appointing him to do it. Domínguez' conduct, he said, smacked of "malice or treason, for which . . . the *oidor fiscal* makes criminal complaint against the above-said."[30]

This, of course, came later. At the moment of Juan's return from his scouting expedition, the Spaniards were worrying mostly about their next move. It was cold, and a chill December wind reached their bones. The ground was covered with snow. After moving camp downriver to a place where they could get wood for fires, Otermín called his inevitable *junta de guerra* to discuss the situation. Father Ayeta, bored to tears by these interminable fruitless conferences, asked to be excused because of sickness. His opinions, submitted in writing, indicated that he disapproved of almost everything that had been done, felt that the entire camp was disaffected, and guessed that the Governor would not be able to get ten votes for going back to finish what Domínguez had left undone. In his view there was "an epidemic of hatred in these parts toward any person who governs and commands. . . ."[31]

All agreed at the *junta* that it would be impossible to winter in the north "for we should all perish."[32] They agreed also that they must take the 400 Isleta Indians back with them. Otermín went along with this recommendation, moved the 385 Indians then present into his camp, and proceeded to destroy their pueblo and all its stores: 1,000 *fanegas* of maize "besides beans, of which there was a quantity." Don Martín Solís de Miranda, the *fiscal*, felt that this amount of food would have carried the men through the winter.[33]

The retreat began on January 1, 1682, and continued through bad weather which developed into a raging storm. The Governor was ill, and one of his legs swelled. The horses and mules exhausted themselves and had to be abandoned a few at a time. They got through to Doña Ana at the south end of the snow-covered Jornada del Muerto on February 4th and straggled on downriver toward home, miserable, discouraged, and resentful.

And now a new difficulty arose. With almost 400 more Indians added to the already overcrowded colony at the Pass, something had to be done about providing permanent homes for the refugees. Otermín surveyed the land up and down the river and found that there was no place as good as the El Paso Valley.

The trouble was, it was already occupied. The original settlers had scattered for a considerable distance downstream on both banks, grouping themselves in nine small settlements — three Spanish communities and six Indian mission villages — six more than the original and official three.[34] Otermín was convinced that the colony would be better off if everybody was reshuffled and settled in not more than three villages. The government subsequently agreed to this, but Ayeta and his Franciscans were infinitely shocked at the idea. It was part of their theory that Indians and Europeans must be separated. The native was potentially good as long as he could be kept from the oppressions, the diseases, and the vices of the invaders.[35] He became a bad Indian when he got too close to the settlers. And now Otermín was talking about bringing Indians and Spaniards together for mutual defense. Ayeta sent off two letters to the Viceroy describing the situation. The settlement, he said, was torn by "a terrible, formidable tempest of complaints, discords, enmities, hatreds, and ill will."[36] The settlers were on a diet of seeds and herbs. Twelve had died since the first of January, and the Indians had made off with 400 animals. Conditions were about as bad as they could possibly be.

On March 1 the settlers in an open meeting resolved that the colony could not continue without royal aid. Otermín agreed that something had to be done. He said the old and the ill could leave, and others could go in search of food if they asked his permission. The penalty for unauthorized departure was death.[37]

Already a number had gone from San Lorenzo without permission. The Cabildo had decided to make a secret appeal to the Viceroy to ask that Otermín be removed. It was an extra irritation to the Governor, when he found out about it, to learn that the Cabildo's messengers had left on horses belonging to him.[38]

Otermín, of course, did not know what they were saying about him, but he knew he must defend himself. He wrote two letters — one to Father Ayeta, who left for Mexico City on March 30, four days after the messengers. He closed his plea to Ayeta with these words: "For the love of God and Saint Anthony as soon as you arrive in Mexico, do everything you possibly can to get me out of here."[39]

Father Ayeta was not able to do much to help him. He himself was so crippled and ill when he left that he was forced to accept the loan of the Governor's coach because he was unable to mount a horse.[40] Fifty leagues from Parral he wrote to the Viceroy apologizing for his infirmities and protesting once more against the proposed plan of settling Indians and Spaniards together.[41]

It was his last effort in behalf of the miserable group at the Pass. He never returned to the frontier, and the next we hear of him, he is in Spain. He came to Madrid in 1683 and plunged at once into a furious pen-and-ink warfare defending the "regulars" — the missionary priests — against the encroachments of the bishops and the secular clergy. He turned out at least four stout tomes, armored in pigskin and bristling with citations from church law and papal bulls, which can still be found in collections of religious documents.[42] "He played no undistinguished role," says one commentator, "in the battles which near the end of the seventeenth century took place between the Episcopal power and the Regulars."[43] Another adds: "We must confess that our Ayeta wielded a terrible pen; and he appeared to have no respect for the bishops."[44]

It was said by the Franciscan chroniclers that Ayeta might have been a bishop himself, but he preferred to spend his life "in defense of these provinces."[45] He never realized it, probably, but this was a sad and wasteful thing. Other learned and conscientious men could have fought these library battles, but who else could have matched Brother Francisco in patience, courage and resourcefulness in meeting the problems of the wild Spanish frontier? When he died in Spain some time in the 1690's, New Mexico lost one of her greatest men.

With Ayeta out of the way and Otermín stranded in El Paso, the messengers sent by the Cabildo should have had a clear field, but their luck turned out to be bad. They were thrown in jail on arrival because they "came back here desperate and raving mad without following the head they were legally obligated to."[46] They were out in less than a year, however, and apparently nothing was done to them. They probably came back to the Pass in the caravan of Don Domingo Jironza Petris de Cruzate, the new Governor who gave Otermín the release he had so long and so vainly craved.[47]

Meanwhile the Viceroy's council had met and made some decisions affecting El Paso. The presidio was to be retained. The Spanish settlement was to be given the status of a villa. Indians and Spaniards were to be kept absolutely separated. Nobody was to leave without license.[48]

Finally the *junta* considered the case of Juan Domínguez de Mendoza. They blamed him for the failure of Otermín's reentry but refrained from condemning him officially. They recommended that the new Governor look into the matter and send whoever was guilty to Parral for punishment.[49]

Far from the capital and ignorant of what was going forward, Otermín spent his final months, as he had spent all the rest, in finding problems which could have no solution and applying remedies which could never cure the disease. In September and October of 1682 he took another census and found that the settlement had almost disappeared. Only forty names were recorded at El Paso; only eighty at San Lorenzo, the seat of government. Nineteen soldiers manned the presidio. One had died. Seven had deserted. Three were absent without leave. The rest were unaccounted for.[50] Everybody was hungry, and not a single sheep or cow was left in the colony.[51] Weapons, armor, tools were missing, often "sold for food," and as a result the colony was practically defenseless. Only seventy-two men in the settlement were capable of bearing arms, and they had nothing to fight with.

Otermín's reports to Mexico City reveal the slackness, irresponsibility, laziness, and dishonesty of many of the refugees.[52] Something must be subtracted from these reports for Otermín's grudges and sickness of soul, but the Pass community had obviously reached the lowest point in its fortunes.

One constructive measure taken by the retiring Governor was the exiling of Tomé Domínguez de Mendoza, Juan's older brother, and their uncle Pedro Duran y Chávez. The two were forced out on the grounds that they had impeded the *entrada* and obstructed the wellbeing of the colony. Probably these men took their families elsewhere with entire goodwill, since everybody who happened to be there had long wished himself away.

The indestructible Juan, of course, was still around, though he was under indictment in Mexico. The indispensable man was still indispensable. Furthermore, he had been bitten by a new ambition. It had occurred to him that the only man who could ever make something out of the struggling colony was none other than Juan Domínguez de Mendoza.

CHAPTER VI

Ambitions and Disappointments

 AUGUST OF 1683 saw the arrival at the Pass of a man who should have been a great and successful governor. Don Domingo Jironza Petris de Cruzate (his family name was Jironza) had every quality which should distinguish a chief executive. In another capital he would have made a brilliant record, but the odds against any governor of New Mexico were very great indeed — too great for even an extraordinary administrator.

Jironza was a Spanish captain who came to the New World in 1680 after distinguished military service under Don John of Austria. Recommended to the Viceroy by Don Payo Enríquez de Rivera, great priest and greater statesman, Don Domingo spent two years as *alcalde mayor* of Mextitlán before his appointment to the governorship. Once appointed, he went vigorously to work and proved to be the best man at getting what he wanted that the colony had ever known. Before he left Mexico City, he had petitioned and demanded and required until the government officials were weary of him. But every time they refused him, he immediately charged in again, asking for more than his previous requests, always emerging with something.[1]

He got money for housing at the presidio, money for powder and lead, money for subsistence for the soldiers, and so on — much less than he wanted but something substantial. He had reason to hope that better times were ahead for the exiled settlers when he arrived among them with his wagonloads of supplies, his soldiers, and his retinue of servants.

His skill as a diplomat appeared as soon as he set foot in his new dominions. His first duty was to hold the *residencia,* the official investigation of his predecessor. Shrewdly, he listened only to Otermín's friends and sent the old Governor out of the colony with a clean bill of health. Next he suspended proceedings against Juan Domínguez de Mendoza and Pedro de Chávez, though these proceedings had been instituted at the command of the Viceroy, in order to avoid "greater unrest and damage."[2]

At the same time he was building himself comfortable adobe quarters at San Lorenzo, seven leagues downriver from the Pass community. With the outbreak of Indian troubles in the spring of 1684, however, he shifted the whole settlement to within two leagues of Paso del Norte to a new San Lorenzo, the little community that you see on your left when the Mexico City road turns right and heads south for Chihuahua. The eastward expansion of Juárez has almost engulfed the old town, but some traces of the village of almost three centuries ago can still be made out.[3]

Before the move, Jironza had set up his military post on the same spot where Otermín had maintained his own — at old San Lorenzo.[4] This community extended up and down the river for a distance of four leagues,[5] and the exact location of the government houses and presidio is hard to determine. Most historians have placed them at or near the present site of San Elizario, though the location has been questioned.[6] When in 1684 the colony had to be concentrated for purposes of defense, the fort was moved to, or close to, Paso del Norte where it could offer better protection against the Indian raiders.

The settlement badly needed protection. Only a few horses were left in the hands of the settlers, thanks to the Apaches, and those the Spaniards still possessed were tied to the doors of their houses at night for safekeeping.[7] There was work for every soldier Jironza could muster, and he found soldiers to do the work. The fifty men he had enlisted in Zacatecas had dwindled, through desertion, to twenty-seven by the time he reached Paso del Norte. He had been expressly forbidden to swear into his force any of the settlers, but since there was no other way, he enlisted twenty-three of them. This little band went valiantly to work, wiping out Apache camps wherever they could be found. In the following July Jironza reported that his men had not had "one hour of rest."[8]

As busy as the soldiers was the new priest, Fray Nicolás López, an ambitious, bustling person who arrived with Jironza to become vice-custodian of the district. In the absence of the *custos*, who was in Mexico City, he was the religious head of the colony and able to make what changes and innovations he pleased. López seems to have looked on the situation at the Pass as his great opportunity. Things were bad; he would make them better. The work had been contracted; he would expand it again. Almost as soon as he arrived, he rushed off and established a mission at a lonely desert outpost called Ojito (later Ojo de Samalayuca) eight leagues south of Paso del Norte. When that was accomplished, he began casting about for other ways of increasing his influence. For a while things played into Father López's hands, and it looked as if he might realize his dream of organizing the biggest missionary effort the northern frontier had ever seen.

Far out on the buffalo plains to the east, leagues beyond the Pecos river, was the main body of the people called Jumanos. A number of them lived the year round on the Rio Grande, at and above the site of today's town of Presidio, Texas. Some of the wandering bands came back to the river valley every winter, fanning out into the country north and east when warm weather came again to hunt buffalo, gather the fruits and nuts of the fertile areas, and trade with other tribes. These Jumanos were wonderful at getting around the country, seeing the sights, exchanging goods, and retailing gossip.[9]

Their leader at this time was an extraordinary chieftain named Juan Sabeata, a Christian who had been educated and baptized in Parral, far down in Mexico.[10] He was an extremely busy Indian, a schemer and arranger, a purveyor of news across hundreds and even thousands of miles. Undoubtedly he was clever and intelligent, but one gets the impression that his was a volatile and somewhat devious character. At the end of Otermín's day as Governor, Sabeata and twelve of his tribesmen came up from their camp at La Junta to ask for trade, friendship, teachers, and help in fighting the Apaches, who were pressing them hard.

According to his story, his people were eager for missionaries and instruction. Once when they were going into battle they had had a vision of a cross — had won a victory as a result. Would Otermín please send priests at once? It is possible that Sabeata was being cut off from his annual expedition to the buffalo plains by his feud with the Apaches and was merely trying to get the Spaniards to provide him with an escort.[11] On the other hand, he may really have wanted his people to be Christians.

Otermín took the envoys seriously but had to put them off. What could he have done for them at this moment, even if he had wished to be bothered? He turned them over to Father López, who asked them if they had a church ready for the fathers. No, they had none. Well, no Mass could be said without a church to say it in. On August 11, 1683, they went away; but before they went, they took the measurements of the altar in the church at Paso del Norte.[12]

On October 15, while Jironza was getting ready to hold the *residencia* for his predecessor, six of the Jumanos came back with Juan Sabeata again at their head. He was more insistent and eager than before. Ten thousand of his people, he said, were thirsty for the water of salvation.[13] The Apaches were troubling them and they needed help. He added craftily that "Spaniards" from the east had come in ships to trade. He knew very well that his listeners would be alarmed at the thought of an invasion by the French.

As a clinching argument, he revealed the happy fact that churches with altars were ready for the use of the friars. Now there was no reason for waiting.

Governor Jironza was interested in Sabeata's proposals and reported favorably on them to the Viceroy.[14] Father López was interested likewise, eager as he was to organize a great and successful missionary enterprise. And Juan Domínguez, for reasons of his own, was the most enthusiastic of all.

For some time, against all likelihood and against all custom, Juan had yearned to be Governor of New Mexico. Why he wanted to take charge of those contentious, ungrateful, violent people is hard to imagine, but he was sure he could handle the assignment and wanted it above all things. He had occupied the Governor's chair four times on a temporary basis and no doubt reasoned that his familiarity with the job would weigh in his favor. If he could prove himself to be extraordinarily capable and enterprising, he might have a chance. The Jumanos expedition looked like the opportunity he had been waiting for. So López the priest and Domínguez the soldier began to work together.

López moved first. As soon as he had set up his new mission of Santa Gertrudis at El Ojito, he turned to Juan Sabeata's business. Apparently he had the Governor's encouragement.[15] With two friars as eager as himself, he made preparations to set off for La Junta. Jironza cooperated by authorizing a volunteer force which would explore the Texas plains after escorting the priests to their new conversion. Juan Domínguez, naturally, was named to lead it.[16] The Governor directed him to bring back pearls from the Nueces River and samples of all products of the country, cautioning him to pay particular respect to the fathers for the sake of example to the Indians.[17]

López could not wait for the escort. On December 1, 1683, with Fathers Acevedo and Zavaleta, he set off in a cloud of dust and zeal, barefooted and protected only by a squad of Juan Sabeata's Indians.[18] A full two weeks later, on December 15, Domínguez was ready to follow and took the road with some twenty men, including his sons Baltasar and Juan the younger and his son-in-law Diego Lucero de Godoy. When he reached La Junta on December 29, the three friars were already hard at work converting and baptising.

Pausing for only two days, Domínguez left the mission on December 31, 1683, to begin his work of exploration. Only Father Acevedo remained to remind the natives that the Spaniards were there to stay.

Lost as he was in the trackless wastes of West Texas, Domínguez carefully recorded each day's march in his itinerary, described and named his camping places, and usually made mention of the fact that he erected a cross on some eminence near camp. It was his way of establishing his loyalty to the church in case somebody should be skeptical later on. His long record as a priest hater had to be compensated for; there was also the fact that he was under indictment for treason.

On they went — five leagues, six leagues, seven leagues a day, stopping where they could find fuel and water. They passed the spot where Alpine, Texas, stands now; paused a few leagues beyond for the accompanying Jumanos to organize a "surround" of deer and other animals to relieve their food shortage; slogged on to the springs where Fort Stockton later took root. On January 13 they reached the Pecos River and followed it for nine leagues downstream. Now they began to find buffalo.

On January 17, still beside the Pecos, they met Juan Sabeata coming to meet them with a band of his people. Both parties fired salutes and the Indians offered to provide shelter for the soldiers in their reed huts, but old campaigner Domínguez made excuses and set up his tentless camp on a hill "according to the usage of war."[19] Two days later a great council was held in the course of which Domínguez asked the tribesmen what they wanted of him. They begged "for the love of God I should make war on the hostile Apaches." The Spaniard agreed that his men would do what they could against the common enemy.[20]

The two parties went on together to the Middle Concho with its wild hens and songbirds, its live oaks and grapevines, its fish and clams. Always the Apaches hovered near, stealing when they could. Already Domínguez was losing faith in Sabeata and recorded that "in nothing has he told the truth."[21]

As they approached the site of San Angelo, the wild Indians attacked repeatedly, wounding one Spaniard and killing several of the Jumano allies. They pushed on, however, until they stood on the spot which two hundred years later was to be called Ballinger, Texas.[22] Here they stayed from March 16 to May 1, built a combination fort and chapel, and counciled with the native bands who came to see them. Christian Indians appeared and eagerly helped with the Masses which were celebrated every day, reminding the Spaniards that trading expeditions from New Mexico had been meeting these tribesmen on the plains every year for some time. According to his own account Father López preached to these savages in their own language, he "having a very large vocabulary in the said tongue."[23]

Domínguez had expected to meet and consult with forty-eight nations or tribes, but many did not come in. On the second of May, unable to wait longer for the groups which had not appeared, the Europeans left their camp. Juan Sabeata was long gone. Domínguez thought "he had plotted with some nations to kill us, and then found out that we had learned it already from the same nations. . . . His conduct having been so bad, he was perhaps afraid they would kill him, for he remained in bad repute with all those nations."[24]

So passed Juan Sabeata from the picture with Domínguez' condemnation fastened upon him forever. He would have told another story, and from what we know of Domínguez, the Indian's version might have been nearer the truth. From here it looks as if two shrewd and selfish men came together with the intention of using each other, and when each found out what the other had in mind, they parted with mutual recrimination.

Sabeata continued for another eight years or so to make his incredible journeys across the measureless plains. In 1692 he was in Parral carrying two-year-old letters from the fathers in East Texas reporting the incursions of the French. After that we hear no more of him.[25]

The Spanish force marched homeward by easy stages. The leader records no disagreement and no mishap beyond the misfortune of young Francisco de Archuleta, who went hunting and got lost — so he said. Three days after his disappearance, as they approached the Pecos River, they came upon his tracks, and his rescue soon followed. On the twenty-fifth day the party cut the trail it had made on the way out and shortly afterward it was back at La Junta.

Domínguez, probably with very good reason, hurries over this part of his journey. Not daring to go home by the river route because of the Manso and Suma uprisings which had broken out during his absence, he led his men westward to the Sacramento River where Chihuahua now stands, spent two weeks with his brother Tomé and his uncle Pedro Chávez (in exile there),[26] and returned to El Paso by the Mexico City road.

What he did not want to talk about was the discord which had broken out during his long journey. When the whole sad business was aired some months after his return, sworn testimony accused him of behaving savagely toward the volunteers, beating them, cursing them (they "never heard a good word from his mouth"),[27] threatening to shoot them,[28] and treating the Indians so badly that it "was only through providence that they were not all killed."[29] The expedition had to return prematurely because the natives became resentful,[30] and on the way back, nine of the Spaniards had deserted and come home by themselves "lest worse things happen."[31]

Of all this Domínguez said not one word in his itinerary. Some of it was certainly true.

It was true also that he had led a handful of Spaniards through hundreds of miles of unknown land and thousands of potentially hostile natives and had not lost a man; that he had claimed rich regions for the King and protected the fathers while they baptized hundreds of savages. In the strange pattern of Domínguez' life the good and the evil were twisted together so tightly that, as usual, no man could separate them.

He returned to a colony rent by rebellion, broken and discouraged. His old friends and neighbors were trying again to find a way to leave the country. The Mansos and Sumas were in revolt. Lives had been lost, and the missionary enterprise which had brought Paso del Norte into existence was cancelled out for the time being. The triumph which Domínguez had hoped for was cancelled out likewise.

The supposedly "reduced" Indians had never forgotten how Captain Andrés López de Gracia had executed two of their number some years before. Their burdens seemed heavy, and they looked with envy on their apostate cousins to the north, unpunished and living as they pleased. Add to this the fact that they were hungry, like everybody else in the colony, and it is no wonder they began to talk about freedom. Their plan was to catch the Spaniards at Mass on Easter Sunday and wipe them out.[32] Francisco Tilagua, the Tigua chief, got wind of the plot, however, and reported it to Jironza. The Governor extracted confessions from eight of the leaders and sentenced them to be garrotted at seven o'clock that very night.[33]

This scared the settlers and marked the beginning of bad feeling between them and Jironza. Led by Fathers Farfán and Espinola, they came in a body to his house, told him that the execution of these eight men would mean the end of every Spaniard in the Valley, and persuaded him to suspend the sentence. They could not convince him that he should revoke it. The Mansos did not wait to see what would happen. They fled at once to the camp of Capitán Chiquito, the renegade leader who was living a hundred miles away in the Florida Mountains, and went back to the wild ways of their ancestors.[34]

Their departure brought the colonists to the Plaza at Paso del Norte in fear and trembling, and again the Cabildo begged the Viceroy to do away with the entire settlement and let them depart.[35] The only result of their frantic plea was the resettlement already mentioned when San Lorenzo was moved to its present site just east of present-day Juárez. In their new homes their woes were, if anything, multiplied. They had to sell "even their wives' clothing" to keep life in their bodies. Worst of all, other tribes had caught the germ of rebellion from the Mansos. The Sumas at La Soledad, at or near Janos, rose on May 6, killed their priest Father Beltrán, burned the convent, and plundered the mission. It was the same at Father López' new conversion at Ojito, where the Archuleta family was destroyed. At La Junta, the two resident fathers barely escaped with their lives.[36] When Jironza led an expedition to bring the *revoltosos* back from Capitán Chiquito's camp, there was fierce fighting and it became obvious to the Spaniards that the Indians were determined to remain free.

On his return from this expedition, Jironza ordered the execution of the Manso plotters who had been under suspended sentence. At three in the afternoon of August 5, 1684, *maestre de campo* Alonso García, with the assistance of the mulatto Captain Roque de Madrid, twisted the cords around their necks one by one, and when all were dead he hung their bodies in the Plaza according to his original instructions.[37] The Spaniards were greatly surprised to find that this drastic act did not put an end to the revolt. Instead there was heavier fighting, and a real peace was not achieved until 1686.

By this time, Jironza was going the way of all governors. Ragged and hungry,[38] the colonists blamed him for their troubles and tried again to get away. On August 18 the Cabildo asked formally for leave to go south and settle on one of the rivers in Chihuahua. He would not — could not — listen, but on September 20 they sent a second plea more urgent than the first.[39] Only López and Domínguez opposed abandonment of the colony, and their reasons, as we have seen, were far from disinterested.

Jironza stood up to the Cabildo, as in all conscience he had to, pointing out that the petitioners had neglected to sow crops the preceding spring and that they would have to be helped even to leave the place. They were beyond this sort of reasoning. They were not affected even by the Governor's generosity in sharing all he had, even his clothes, with them, or by the fact that he was as poor as the poorest of them in spite of his office.[40] They only knew that they had to get out of this intolerable situation and that Jironza could not be replaced soon enough to suit them.

Father López departed for Mexico City in September and immediately on his arrival began to pull wires and make arrangements. Word came back that a successor for Jironza was being considered and that López was working hard to get the appointment for Domínguez.[41] By this time the whole colony knew that Juan intended to be the next governor and was shocked by the knowledge. The Governor was more shocked than anybody because he expected to be reappointed at the end of his term, which had one year to run. He sent off a letter to the Viceroy which listed Domínguez' shortcomings and revealed how "greatly agitated" the citizens had become.[42]

To make things worse for Jironza, the fall elections in 1685 placed the Domínguez and Chávez families in control of the machinery of government. Their men dominated the Cabildo, and the Cabildo became openly hostile to the Governor. On the Mexico City front, Father López was working underground trying to move the colony upriver to the abandoned pueblo of Isleta, plotting against Jironza, laboring to get himself appointed custodian.[43] Stalemated in one of these enterprises, he launched another. It was probably at his instigation that the Cabildo on September 27, 1685, addressed a secret letter to the Viceroy accusing the Governor of misconduct and had it smuggled out of the colony by Lazaro de Mizquia, who had gone on such missions before. His escort included Juan Domínguez de Mendoza, Juan's son Baltasar, and his son-in-law Diego Lucero de Godoy. Domínguez was about to ask for a showdown in Mexico City.

The Governor had forbidden such unauthorized departures, and when news of the expedition reached him, he hurried to San Lorenzo to investigate. The same day he took legal action against the deserters.[44] Witnesses were called in to give answers to a prepared list of questions intended to expose Domínguez, most flagrant sins over the past twenty years. His conduct during the re-entry of 1682 was blasted again;[45] the death sentence imposed by Governor Medrano (recalled because of the troubled times) was canvassed. He was described as "a man of bad conscience" — in fact, "worse than the devil."[46]

His greatest offense was aspiring to be Governor. The testimony indicated that he thought himself sure of the office, intended to get even with his foes once he was in it, and thought he could pass it on to his sons "for three lives."[47] As his first official act he meant to hang the nine men who had deserted from his expedition to the Jumanos.

Felipe Serna, a veteran of this expedition, described Juan's behavior:

... the said Juan Domínguez had gone about in many places saying that he was going to be governor ... and then he would have much maize and would hang all those who came back from Jumanas. .... Father Nicolas López had told him to come to Parral to receive the office of Governor and Captain General ... the witness likewise heard it said that ... the said Juan Domínguez was very bad and that it would be better for all of them to go to Julimes to live. ....

While Jironza was taking this testimony, the accused was hurrying down the long road to the capital, resolved to make a great and final effort. He expected to succeed. His enemies were far from the seat of government and were having troubles of their own. Before their accusations could reach the *audiencia,* Father López would have had time to present his recommendations in Domínguez behalf, and López was backed by Father Posadas, head of the Franciscans in Mexico.[48] How could he lose?

From June through November of 1685, the Council considered these matters and called in New Mexicans living in the capital who might have knowledge of the situation.[49] It was against all custom, of course, for an insider to become the chief executive of the colony — and there were the disturbing aspects of Domínguez' record and personality. On the other hand, his distinction as a soldier could not be denied, and New Mexico needed a strong hand. The members of the *audiencia* hesitated.

Domínguez himself played his high card in a memorial dated November 18, 1685, addressed to the Viceroy. It told Domínguez' story as Domínguez saw it, recounting his long and distinguished military service, justifying his mistakes, and pointing with pride to his successes. Without mentioning the governorship, he intimated that it was no more than his due and that it would be a simple thing for a man of his attainments and experience to restore order and prosperity to the beleaguered province.

It is necessary for me to bring this to the exalted attention of your Excellency, so that you may see and know the reward with which I now find myself after having served his Majesty for forty-two years, and having lost my fortune, which was not small, as is well known, and having lost more than sixty-six persons of my blood alone. As a loyal vassal of his Majesty I must report and present to your Excellency this truth, for I perceive that the preservation of this New Spain depends upon the settlement of that kingdom [New Mexico] and I see how easy it is to accomplish it. If it should be necessary, I will make agreements, with my life as forfeit, for settling it. . . .

I pray your Excellency that with your accustomed Christianity you will be pleased to reward my services. . . . I hope to receive justice from the zeal and greatness of your Excellency in all respects.[50]

It was all useless, all wasted. In the end Domínguez' great hope collapsed, leaving him bitter and disappointed. Pedro Reneros de Posada received the appointment as Jironza's successor for reasons which no one now can understand. Thirty-year-old Reneros had been a common soldier in the garrison at Paso del Norte in 1681[51] and had risen through the ranks to the post of Captain of the Presidio. In 1684, the Governor had sent him on a mission to Mexico City,[52] and somehow he came out of it with the Governor's job.

Father López, shaken and fearing the worst, wrote to Antonio Ortis de Otalora, the Royal Secretary, that the post had been given to "a person entirely incompetent for the business, from whom there may be expected many losses."[53]

López and Domínguez made one final and futile effort. López wrote to the Viceroy in the early months of 1686, pointing out that the Spaniards were morally obligated to return to the country of the Jumanos, where 500 souls had been saved and where "many other nations" were waiting for salvation. He followed with another letter on April 24 suggesting that Domínguez was the man to lead such an expedition. "He is the only one for this affair, in the present state of things, for he is fully experienced in matters of war and, moreover, is known to be a man of singular good fortune in it."[54]

The father was not hopeful of a favorable reply and added a final request from his disappointed friend: "The said general has desired to take ship and place himself at the feet of his Majesty to inform him concerning all these kingdoms and provinces . . . but, finding himself in fallen fortunes (for in the loss of New Mexico he lost more than 40,000 pesos . . .), the small means that he now has have not permitted him to carry out his wish."[55]

The *fiscal* finally and definitely said no to the missionary enterprise on May 26, 1685. There would be no such adventure until the New Mexico business was settled. And that was the end of Juan Domínguez' hope of promotion.[56]

The criminal charges against him were not finally settled until April 30, 1687, when Viceroy Monclova pronounced sentence. Domínguez was acquitted on three of the four charges against him. He was cleared of mismanagement of the expedition to the Jumanos. He was exonerated in the matter of the first reentry under Otermín. He was declared innocent of presumption in boasting that he would be Governor of New Mexico. One count stood up: Domínguez had left the El Paso colony without permission and therefore had to pay the costs of litigation.[57]

Meanwhile Governor Reneros was having his day. With two bosom cronies who had assisted him formerly in carrying out his nefarious enterprises, he arrived on the Rio Grande in September, 1686, and started at once to build a reputation for ruthlessness and dishonesty. He could have made a fine record, for the first good growing years since 1682 occurred during his term,[58] and at least the people had something to eat. The welfare of the colonists, however, meant little to him. He ruled harshly, cheated his troops, profiteered, and kept the colony stirred up and unhappy during his entire term of office.[59]

His one constructive effort was the organization of an expedition which penetrated as far as the pueblo of Santa Ana north of Albuquerque. He brought back fourteen Indian leaders — four to be executed and ten to be sold into slavery. This was success of a sort, but not the kind to bring order and tranquillity to the province. Instead, under his rule the Sumas tried once more to rise against their masters.

The situation improved when Reneros' term was up and Jironza was appointed to succeed him. The Governor plunged into vigorous campaigning against the rebel Indians. His nephew Captain Juan Mateo Manje, who told his story many years later, says that he conducted three expeditions into hostile territory, penetrating as far north as present-day Albuquerque.

He made overtures of peace, but the rebel Indians replied with blasphemies against God; whereupon he destroyed the capital of Sia. The battle went on from dawn until 10 o'clock of the following night. Although 50 of 80 soldiers were wounded, he killed 600 heathen Indians, burning many more who would not surrender.[60]

To Mateo, and presumably to the rest of the Spaniards in the colony, this was an admirable achievement. With no sense of incongruity Manje declares that Jironza "was acclaimed by the people not so much as governor, but as an example of charity, being more of a father to them."[61]

Given a little more time Jironza might have been the one to accomplish the Reconquest; but to his bitter disappointment, he was superseded. De Vargas, his successor, arrived at Paso del Norte on February 22, 1691, with the news that Jironza's career in New Mexico was ended. After Vargas' departure from Mexico City a dispatch from Spain arrived recommending that Jironza be retained in office. It came too late to do him any good.[62]

During Jironza's second term Juan Domínguez de Mendoza made his final moves in the New World. He had been living in Mexico City, probably in reduced circumstances, but his family was still in El Paso. He could hardly go back himself but he had influence enough to bring his wife and children to the capital. A petition on his behalf was presented by his son Baltasar at Paso del Norte on March 1, 1691, nearly four years after Juan's unauthorized departure. The document stated that Doña Isabel Duran y Chávez, his wife, and other members of his household needed medical treatment, something which was not available in El Paso. Through somebody's influence the request for leave was granted and the Domínguez clan left New Mexico for good.[63]

Their reunion was brief. Juan was still determined to lay his case before the King. He must have known that there could be no future for him in the New World, but his obsession was stronger than his reason. He took ship for Spain, carrying with him, in addition to the testimony which he had collected from his friends, or which he had invented, a report from Father López on the provinces traversed by the expedition to the Jumanos and a proposal drawn up by himself for conquering and exploiting these provinces. A contemporary reporter summarized his proposition: "Among other things he gave assurance that it was easy to penetrate into those lands in order to settle them. He offered, if given two hundred soldiers, supplied and clothed, to go as far as the Río de los Nueces, which is four hundred leagues from Mexico, that he would obligate himself to conquer a great empire, and . . . to maintain with the natural products of the land, not only two hundred men, but, if it should be necessary, 200,000. . . ."[64]

Still hopeful, he took ship with his son Baltasar, probably in 1693. As they neared their destination, Juan's evil fate struck again. The vessel was wrecked and he lost all the goods he had brought with him. Nevertheless he presented himself with his statement of his *servicios* and his proposals at the court of King Charles II. There is no record of how he was received or what progress he made. We know only that he died in a Madrid hospital before he could accomplish anything of importance.[65]

Baltasar continued the campaign and actually emerged with a recommendation from the King that he be appointed to one of several positions of trust in New Spain, the governorship of New Mexico being one of them. When he returned to Mexico, however (probably in 1695), all the posts were taken. De Vargas was already in New Mexico preparing for the reconquest. So Baltasar, like his father, faded into the limbo of lost ambitions.

CHAPTER VII

The End of Rebellion

DON DIEGO JOSE DE VARGAS ZAPATA Y LUJAN PONCE DE LEON Y CONTRERAS, who took over the government at Paso del Norte on February 22, 1691, came of the bluest blood in Spain, on both sides. His ancestors had included some of the most distinguished figures in the kingdom, and the Vargas line went back to the eleventh century. Soldiers, governors, ambassadors, friends of kings, they had done signal service for the crown in both the Old World and the New, had risen to high rank and won much honor, and were rich with the accumulated wealth of centuries — proud as only Spanish *hidalgos* can be.[1]

Don Diego was the last legitimate male heir of his line, and all this ancestral pomp and power converged upon him. Whether he thought of his career in such terms or not, he spent his life trying to live up to his ancestry; and when the accounts were all in, he had reason to feel that he had done well. He paid a high price for his fame, but he deserved it.

Unlike most of his contemporaries, Don Diego has left us a good likeness. In his late twenties or early thirties he sat — or rather stood — for his portrait, a reproduction of which forms the frontispiece of Dr. Espinosa's unique work on his exploits.[2] He appears in elaborate dress — a brocaded coat with wide, half-length sleeves designed to show off the tremendous puffed sleeves of his silk shirt, knee breeches with white lace garters, elegant white silk stockings, a plumed hat in one hand, an eight-foot lance in the other. His straight black hair is parted neatly in the middle and hangs below his shoulders. His face is long and oval with commanding black eyes, a long, slightly curved nose, and a small, precise mouth dominated by a full, self-important upper lip. He wears two hair-line mustaches and a thin perpendicular line of chin whisker. He appears to be tall but not particularly robust, with narrow shoulders and slender legs. He seems more elegant than enduring, but he has the air of command, which includes command of himself. And the rapier by his side and the spear in his hand are indicators of his mettle.

Born in 1643 in Madrid,[3] the family seat, he shaped his life in accordance with the tradition of his line. At twenty-one he married, and his wife was as rich and as blue-blooded as himself. Her name was Doña Beatriz Pimentel de Prado of Torrelaguna, and that is all we know of her or are likely to know.

The young husband was much abroad on official business for his King. He fought in Italy and dreamed of fighting in the New World. In 1673 opportunity came his way and he sailed for New Spain as the King's *capitán del pliego del aviso* or official messenger. We know nothing of his sentiments on leaving Doña Beatriz and their eight-year-old daughter, Doña María Isabel, or of their feelings on seeing him go. Some deductions may be made, however, from the fact that he never returned to Spain, that he arranged informally for a new family in Mexico City not long after his arrival, and that he revealed on his death bed in 1704 that he was the father of three illegitimate children,[4] ages twenty-four, twenty-three, and nineteen.

For a few years after his advent in 1673, Don Diego disappears behind the scenes as he goes about building his career. By 1679 he begins to emerge into public business with the good word of the King himself to back him. In that year he appears as *alcalde mayor* of Teutila and he went on to occupy other positions of trust in the mining towns of Michoacán. The Viceroy found occasion to speak of him as a person of complete integrity, experience, and intelligence.[5] Little by little his employments grew in importance until finally, on June 18, 1688, the King gave him the appointment he wanted — the governorship of New Mexico for a term of five years.

Merit had something to do with Don Diego's advancement, but money probably had more. The court was always in need of more funds for the colonies, was always hesitant about spending any more than the absolute minimum on colonial enterprises. A man who could and would pay for an important and expensive project like the Reconquest was a real godsend to the Viceroy and the *real hacienda,* and Vargas was willing to spend his large fortune on the enterprise. He got the appointment. It took time to go through the formalities, but he received his first salary installment on October 12, 1690, and reached the Pass on the following February 22.[6]

Jironza was taken completely by surprise. His appointment had a full year to run; he was planning another attempt at reconquest; and he had no notion that his services were to be thus cut off. The papers were in order, however, and he had no recourse.

The new Governor was appalled by what he saw at the Pass of the North. The colony was decimated by desertions and deaths. Famine conditions prevailed and life had been reduced very close to an animal existence. Nobody had clothes enough to appear decently in public. The Indians were doing as they pleased.

Vargas put first things first. He flung himself into a punitive expedition against the hostiles and quieted them considerably. All the while he was reporting to his superiors on the chances of finding valuable minerals in northern New Mexico in order to insure their continued interest in what he hoped to do.[7]

By March of 1692 he was ready to organize his reentry and asked only for fifty more soldiers. The actual expenses of the expedition he would bear himself. The finance committee met in Mexico City on May 28, 1692, and approved his proposals with relief and thanksgiving,[8] ordering that the reinforcements should be assembled in the neighborhood of Parral. Vargas, always independent, fixed a day for departure and announced that he would leave whether the detachment from Parral arrived or not. This was his proclamation, read in the Plaza of Paso del Norte in front of the old cathedral, and in other public places where people could be assembled at the sound of drum and bugle:

Since it is getting late in the season, and in order to profit by present conditions . . . I designate Saturday, the sixteenth of this month of August, as the day of departure from this parade ground of the presidio of El Paso; that on this day the three squads of the company of this presidio and captain and maestre de campo, Roque de Madrid, shall leave with the pack animals, wagons, livestock, and the one hundred selected friendly Indian warriors, and travel as far as the place called Robledo, twenty-nine leagues from here, which I designate as their parade ground and where the said captain will camp. Then, upon the arrival of the soldiers from Parral, I, the said governor and captain general, will sally forth with them . . . to join forces at the said parade ground and place of Robledo.[9]

The orders said that assembly would be at eight o'clock on the designated day. The day came, however, and at eight o'clock the Plaza was practically empty. Such punctuality as Vargas demanded could not be expected in Mexico in that time, or in this. By ten o'clock, however, everything and everybody were present and accounted for. By two the wagons had moved out to the ford of the river and the crossing began. There was much equipment to move — horses and men, provisions including a herd of cattle, a small cannon, and a stone mortar. It was dusk when all was safely over, and the weary men camped where they were. The next day they trailed off to the Robledo campground close to today's Radium Springs. Vargas went back to the village to wait a little longer for the men from Parral.

On the twenty-first, no word having come from the reinforcements, Vargas gave up and at five in the afternoon started north himself with his escort, leaving behind a functioning government, set up with his usual care and diligence, and a letter of instructions for the recruits when and if they showed up, as they later did.[10] He arranged for supplies to see them through their march to the north — "bread, pinole, sugar, chocolate, meat, tobacco, and soap" — and wrote a final letter to the Viceroy. Then the wilderness swallowed him up and Paso del Norte saw him no more for four months.

He returned, as he noted, "at about eleven o'clock in the morning" on December 20, 1692, with a wonderful story. He had traversed all of New Mexico — north to Taos, west to Zúni and Hopi. He had shed not one drop of blood and everywhere he had gone he had won the Indians back to acceptance of the Spanish King and the Spanish religion, mostly by sheer persistence and the force of rhetoric.

The natives were prepared for the traditional soft approach and tough follow-up. In fact, their Apache friends told them that if they so much as listened to the Spaniards, they might as well hang themselves. They were invincibly suspicious and terribly frightened, fleeing to the mountains ahead of the conquerors and coming back to be forgiven only after superhuman efforts and superhuman patience on the part of Vargas.

He knew exactly what he had to do — what risks he had to run. He and his small band went to pueblo after pueblo, persuaded the few tribesmen who were present or who would listen that the

Spaniards came only to forgive, not to punish. Vargas himself embraced and caressed the Indian leaders and showed great perspicacity in picking out the intelligent ones whom he could reason with and trust. He gave them food and friendly words, treated them with affection, showed them the picture of the Virgin on his banner in token of his good faith, and assured them that he "esteemed and loved them from the bottom of my heart."[11]

More than once when they made hostile demonstrations against him and threw dirt in his face, he went into their villages unarmed and even alone, and faced them down by sheer courage and persistence. He pinned them down and talked them into submission.

His words were backed up with reassuring deeds. He would not sleep in the pueblos, camping outside on the ground with his men. He destroyed nothing and demanded nothing, and he paid for what he used.[12] When he had hypnotized an entire pueblo into assembling before him, he would command his two priests to absolve them of the "sin" of rebelling against the Spaniards and the Church. Then he would have the babies baptized, he himself and his soldiers standing as godfathers for them. Afterward he would take a kindly farewell, promising to return soon and admonishing the reconverted Indians to say their prayers.

Now this was something those Indians had never seen or heard of and their astonishment and incredulity are quite understandable. After the punishments they had undergone in the past, after the indignities they had suffered, they could hardly believe their own eyes and ears. Vargas had to go back a second time to Pecos Pueblo before they would believe him. The Indians at Acoma insisted on taking a night for council before they yielded, and even then Vargas practically forced his way through hostile groups into the Plaza before they gave in.

They expected the Spaniards to be gracious when all was going according to their desires and to be ruthless when their wills were crossed. They knew that punishment was regarded as a duty and a necessity in the Spanish military philosophy. Why should it be different now?

As a matter of fact, it was not different. Vargas was determined to win bloodlessly, if he could. He knew it was the best way. But he was prepared to slay and burn if the Indians refused to submit. Later on, he proved himself as ruthless as the rest, but from beginning to end of the preliminary invasion of 1692 he showed iron restraint and an imperturbable bravery in the most deadly peril. It is a temptation to speculate on the wonders this treatment might have worked in the century preceding and in the centuries that followed — on what could have happened if the Spaniards had always acted toward the Indians like true Christians and brothers.

Vargas did not mean to slip up in any detail. He kept a campaign journal which he required his officers to sign at the end of each day's proceedings, and in it he reveals his own nature on every page — all his intelligence, skill and determination; all his ambition, vainglory, and egotism.

In his innermost thoughts the Indians were "rebellious, traitorous apostates," and he spoke of the spirit that moved him to invade their territory as "the daring that burns within me."[13] When he acted with kindness and forbearance, it was not for humanity's sake but because it was "a judicious and prudent resolution."[14] He refers approvingly to his own "sagacity" and speaks of his "justifiable vanity" over his accomplishments.[15] When he reported to the Viceroy, he was capable of writing this paragraph:

> As for me, I will be satisfied and proud in knowing that no one has been audacious enough to undertake that which, by the divine will, I have achieved to date. And so I will have the satisfaction of knowing that no one will censure my actions, since the triumphs, by divine mercy, have been exactly as recorded in my reports; and once they are obtained, the news will spread and envy will be the slave of prowess, and I will be able to say that even in the face of the most impossible obstacles no one should lose hope if valor accompanies his evident disinterestedness.[16]

We have to admit that Vargas could back up his good opinion of himself with real achievements. His success in getting himself and his men back from the wild country in the dead of winter was worthy of the highest praise. He and his men went days without water,[17] camped out in ice and snow, endured wind and sleet, and lost some of their livestock to Apache bands which kept them under constant surveillance. The Spanish aristocrat held his own with the tough and experienced soldiers and with the Indian guides and auxiliaries.

He noted that he had subdued and reclaimed twenty-three pueblos, freed seventy-four captives, and baptized 2,214 children and adults.[18] He failed only in omitting to visit the site of a deposit of quicksilver of which he had been writing to the Spanish officials.

He did get samples of vermilion earth and continued to speak of this as one possible justification for the great labor and expense involved in his invasion until the assayers finally got hold of his sample and judged it to be worthless.

There was great rejoicing over his safe return, not merely in Paso del Norte, but in Mexico and Spain. The Viceroy and his council could not speak too highly of his achievements, approved all his actions, and prepared to send off a special report to the King "so that he may honor him and grant him the favors conformable to such distinguished and singular services."[19] Vargas himself took pains to let the King know that he expected some special recognition and mentioned some of the acknowledgments that would be welcome. First he asked for the title of Marqués de Los Caramancheles (an estate which had once belonged to his family). Next, "in order that I may continue to serve your majesty," he asked for a governorship in Guatemala, the Philippines, or South America.[20]

This was building for the future. Meanwhile there was work at hand. Vargas wanted a presidio of a hundred soldiers at Santa Fe and five hundred Spanish families in New Mexico to prevent another revolt.[21] The Viceroy agreed — he was prepared to agree with anything Vargas suggested — and made available to him 40,000 pesos for buying seeds, livestock, carts, and all else that might be needed for the final effort.

The effort began with a survey of conditions at Paso del Norte, and they were bad. The total population was now approximately a thousand souls — less than half the number which had come out of New Mexico twelve years before.[22] The colonists were existing in the direst poverty. Only one man in four had a horse. They were in no condition to go back to their old homes.

Vargas the indomitable was not dismayed by any of this. He swept through northern Mexico enlisting new recruits, urging fugitives from New Mexico to come back to the fold, buying wagons and flour and horses and cattle, enlisting soldiers for the presidio. The miracle he dreamed of was finally accomplished when, on October 4, 1693, the real reconquest began. Two squads of ten soldiers each led off as the long procession left the Pass. Behind them came colonists on horseback and in ten twelve-mule wagons. Six supply wagons and three field pieces followed. Drum and trumpet beat and blared as the expedition moved out toward the

Ford and passed out of the life of the Valley.[24] There was land enough for everybody now, and the community settled back into its old tempo, geared to the moods of the river and the sky.

Word came back of the success of the recolonizing project, and the news was not all good. Conditions were much as they had been before Vargas had shown what could be done by kindness and patience. Only four of the reclaimed pueblos had remained faithful. The rest were ready to die rather than submit to the Spaniards again. Santa Fe was fortified and defiant. After camping for two weeks outside the walls in bitter weather and losing twenty-one of the colonists, the soldiers stormed the place and executed seventy of the Indian leaders afterward. This was what the natives had expected all along and they fought harder when they heard the news.

In June of 1694, sixty-six more families arrived from Mexico and the food shortage with which the colonists were contending became worse. It was necessary to raid the pueblos to find grain supplies, and as a result more battles and sieges took place. Finally the last remaining islands of resistance were wiped out and New Mexico became Spanish again.[25]

For Vargas life had exhausted nearly all its rewards. He survived an Indian uprising in 1696 which cost the lives of five missionary priests and twenty-one Spaniards, but he was not reappointed as Governor. Don Pedro Rodríguez Cubero succeeded him. The report was that he had "bought the governorship for a term of five years."[26] The *residencia*, during which all new governors evaluated the record of the preceding administration, lasted for thirty days, and when it was over, Vargas was sent to prison. He remained there for almost three years. Apparently the colonists had turned against him and were glad to see him go.

Ironically, back in Spain high honors were being paid him by a King and Court entirely ignorant of his evil plight. He was reappointed to succeed Governor Cubero, was granted the title of Marqués de la Nava de Bracinas, acquired a large *encomienda* in New Mexico, became the subject of a two-volume history, and was honored with the title of "Pacificator." And all the while he was sitting in a cold prison cell in the province he had brought back under Spanish dominion.

The Spanish court had no news of his real situation until the spring of the year 1700, and he was not released until later in the same year. In the winter of 1703 he resumed his post as Governor, fell sick the next spring while out on campaign against the Apaches in the Sandía Mountains, and died at Bernalillo on April 8, 1704.

The great September Fiesta in Santa Fe still celebrates his recovery of New Mexico for the Crown and the Cross, and his name is still honored in his old haunts.[27] These were the rewards Vargas worked and suffered and died for, and from what we know of the man, he probably would not consider the price he paid too high.

CHAPTER VIII

A Century of Trouble

 As THE YEAR 1700 brought the New Mexico settlements to the beginning of a new century, the Spanish colonials were still struggling to retain control of the northern frontier. Apparently they had learned very little from the Revolt and the Reconquest. For a century and more, life went on in the old pattern of feuds within the settlements and Indian attacks from without. Paso del Norte was a focal point in this turbulent epoch when the Spanish-Mexicans were not so much living in the country as holding desperately onto their slippery footing.

The great enemy was the chain of Apache bands running all the way from the San Antonio region to the mountains west of the Rio Grande in New Mexico. The names of these bands changed and their habitats shifted through the years; but the ones we hear the most about are the Mescaleros in the mountains of southeastern New Mexico, the Natagés from the lower Pecos who raided as far west as Paso del Norte, and the Gilas in the wilderness west of the Rio Grande.[1]

These tribal units visited each other, sometimes intermarried, and took great pleasure in combining forces for raids on exposed communities. Raiding was their business, and they labored in their vocation diligently as long as the price they paid for booty and glory was not too high. When they found themselves in danger from the soldiers or an aroused citizenry, they would sue for peace and settle down for a while.

It is hard to convey in words the dreadful isolation of the place — a pinpoint of resistance against an enemy scattered all over the almost illimitable wastelands of Chihuahua and New Mexico. The convent made it a center of missionary activity. Its cattle and wheat and fruit and vineyards made it a minor commercial center.

But it was still a little, lonely, exposed outpost on the farthest frontier of New Spain.

The first recorded description of Paso del Norte after the Reconquest was set down in 1706 by Father Juan Alvarez, who came to put the sacked and ruined churches of the custodia back into operating order. When he asked the Governor for help, he was told to write an account of all the missions with a commentary on their lacks and losses. Father Juan obliged. He noted that fifty soldiers were quartered in Paso del Norte, that Fray Francisco de Gonzáles was the father preacher and the commissary of the Inquisition, and that "the mission is supplied with the necessities, because it is one of the old ones." San Lorenzo, Senecú, Isleta, and Socorro were still functioning, and there was a new mission called Santa María Magdalena "composed of Sumas Indians, who are beginning to be reduced."[2]

The Sumas were not as close to reduction as Father Juan thought. In 1712 and again in 1720 they rose in revolt. What their grievances were we do not know, but in the light of their previous experiences, we could make a good guess. Both times the soldiers went after them and brought them back to San Lorenzo or Santa María Magdalena, but other uprisings were still to come.

In the early years of the century there were not many intervals of peace. The settlements were under constant Apache surveillance and sometimes under siege. When Don Francisco Cuervo y Valdés came north in 1705 to become Governor *ad interim*, he had to stop at Paso del Norte and fight Indians.[3] Captain Antonio Valverde y Cosío, Lieutenant General and Commandant in charge of the presidio, was having more trouble than he could conveniently handle and the Governor's men were needed on the firing line.

Until recent times, there was never any question about who was in the wrong. The Spaniards, who were offering the blessings of religion and civilization to the barbarous heathen, were met with ingratitude, treachery, and violence. Now we are beginning to hear a different story. The Indians, we are told, were only trying to follow their old ways and hold to their own culture. They were really freedom fighters. As Jack D. Forbes puts it, "the enemy of native civilization in New Mexico was primarily the Spaniard and not the Apache."[4]

Such a view of the situation is distressing to good and loyal Catholics in the Southwest and is probably no more than partly true. It is certainly a fact, however, that the Spaniards were their own worst enemies. The tide of civil strife rose higher during these years, priest against soldier and priest against priest.

Since the earliest times — since the 1630's — the bishops of Durango had claimed Paso del Norte, and even all of New Mexico, as part of their jurisdiction. The Franciscan missionary priests, with headquarters at Santa Fe, resisted vigorously every proposal of the bishops to send secular priests to take charge of the parishes. Between 1725 and 1760, a few of the hardier bishops conducted visitations of the northern outposts,[5] picking up stories of the indolence, inefficiency, and worldliness of the fathers and relaying these tales to Mexico City as evidence of the need for secular clergy. Then the missionaries would write furious replies which fill many a thick file in the archives of Spain and Mexico.[6] This went on for several decades, neither side able to win a clear-cut victory, though by 1750 the Bishop of Durango had managed to place *jueces ecclesiasticos* (judges of the ecclesiastical courts) at Paso del Norte and Santa Fe and was able to collect tithes in both places.[7]

When the fathers were at peace with each other, they attacked the civil authorities. They accused the soldiers of horrible excesses, and the soldiers in turn accused the priests of parasitism, luxury, laziness, and ignorance. The governors were mostly bitter against the clergy and the clergy were violent against the governors.

The Indians were in the middle, pulled in one direction by the civil authorities and pushed in the other by the priests. They protested whenever they had a chance, which was not often, against the cruelties and exactions of the *alcaldes* and governors. The fathers supported them as much as they could. There were some bad priests; the Franciscans admitted that.[8] But it is impossible to avoid the conclusion that the brown-robed brothers were almost the only Europeans who were really concerned for the misfortunes and sufferings of the Christianized Indians. In the first decade of the century, for instance, the soldiers were murdering the Hopis and Zuñis while the priests were trying to move the military out so that love and leadership might take the place of naked force. In 1709 the *custos*, Father Juan de la Pena, was struggling in vain to stamp out heathen rites among his Indian charges and at the same time complaining of abuses by the *alcaldes* who were making the Indians work without pay.

With the Spaniards thus divided, the Apaches probed for weak spots and struck hard when they found one. Sometimes for a few years conditions got better, but the raiders always returned and the Christian Indians were always wondering if it might not be better to go back to their old free life and their old half-forgotten religion. The "abominable hostilities and tyrannies of the governors and alcaldes mayores" were sometimes enough to drive them back to savagery. Father Carlos Delgado of Santa Bárbara in Chihuahua told his superior in Chihuahua City of one such case that happened in Paso del Norte in 1750:

These punishments are so cruel and inhuman that sometimes for a slight offense, sometimes because the Indian resists the outrages that they inflict upon him, or sometimes because they are put in jail for many days, are confined in the stocks, or — and I cannot say it without tears — the officials flog them so pitilessly that, their wrath not being appeased by seeing them shed their blood, they inflict such deep scars upon them that they remain for many years. It is a proof of this second point that when I went among the heathen to reduce the apostates there were among them some who, with an aggrieved air, showed me their scars, thus giving me to understand that the reason why they fled and did not return to the pale of the church was their fear of these cruel punishments.

A further distressing proof of this practice is what was done in the past year at El Paso by a captain to a Catholic Indian of the Zuma nation, sacristan of the mission of El Real. A servant of the captain of El Paso had hidden three ears of corn which he had stolen from his master. The sacristan took them from him, and, without any more proof or reason than having found him with them in his hands, and because the said servant, to escape punishment, said that the innocent Indian often stole corn from the granaries, the said captain became so angered that, in violation of all natural and divine laws, he ordered six soldiers to take the Indian out and kill him in the fields.

They carried out the order, and when the unfortunate Zuma cried aloud for confession they did not yield to his entreaties, but gave him a violent death, perhaps being fearful that the missionary religious, whose duty it was to administer the holy sacrament to him, would prevent the execution of that unjust order, even though it might be at the cost of his life.

The outrage did not stop here, for when the Zuma Indians of the mission of El Real learned of the death of their countryman, they began to rise up, all crying out: "Why, since we are Christians, do they not permit us to confess at the hour of death? Let us flee to the mountains!" They did not flee, our father, either because the soldiers restrained them or because the fathers appealed to them. A still greater injury, however, arose from the remedy, for the governor having ordered a large troop of Zumas of both sexes to come to this city, simply because an Indian woman and two men were not able to travel as fast as the others, having crippled feet, the corporal who was leading them ordered them to be beheaded at a place called El Gallego, where he left the bodies unburied, to the intense grief of their companions and relatives, whose sorrow was not lessened on seeing that the said corporal and the rest of the escort robbed them of their little children in order to sell them as slaves in various places along the road.[9]

The "civilized" Indians had long memories and brooded over such abuses for years — until they were ready to fight or go back to the wilderness.

There was less trouble in the 1730's than New Mexico had known for a long time, possibly because the Spaniards were trying new methods. It is recorded that one Spanish Governor, Enrique de Olavide y Michelena, spent part of the year 1738 visiting all the New Mexican pueblos, inviting Indians who had grievances against any Spaniard in or out of office to come forward and make his complaint.[10] Apparently no complaint was made — possibly because no native believed he would get anywhere by making it.

In the 1740's the raiding started up again and blood flowed once more along the El Paso road. Traders had difficulty in getting to the annual fair held at Paso del Norte, the route being "infested with savages."[11] In fact, all of New Mexico during this period was in great trouble. The French were building up trade with the Plains Indians — Comanches, Utes, and other hostile tribes — and were trading guns for horses. As a result, the outlying settlements were unable to continue in existence and settlers retreated to the larger centers. The eastern frontier north from Albuquerque was depopulated.[12]

The eastern Apaches, under heavy pressure from the newly arrived Comanches, retreated farther and farther south, endangering the Spanish communities wherever they found themselves.[13] Some of the Mescalero bands drifted far into Mexico and lived there for many decades. Others moved westward. By the seventies the Comanches had actually pushed these Apaches to the Rio Grande and were occupying their hunting grounds in the Sierra Blanca. One or two of the Apache bands took up quarters at Hueco Tanks, thirty miles east of the Pass.

During all this time, in spite of trouble and danger, crops were planted and babies were born, the yearly caravans passed through and the annual fiesta brightened the existence of the *Paseños*. The community was expanding a little and ambitious young men were venturing farther from the mother church and the presidio. We get a glimpse of what was going on from a report written in 1744 by Fray Miguel Menchero, "apostolic preacher-general, *calificador* of the Holy Office of the Inquisition, apostolic notary, ex-custodian of this holy province of El Santo Evangelio, ex-visitador of the *custodia* of the province of San Pablo of New Mexico," who was making a visitation of all the New Mexico missions.

Only a few Spaniards were living in the Valley towns,[14] but two new communities, La Ranchería and El Capitán, were in existence over twenty miles downriver from Paso del Norte. At El Capitán a chapel was erected in honor of Santa María de las Caldas where a "black priest," or lay priest, was in charge. The presence of Father Joseph de Ochoa, sent to Santa María by Bishop Crespo after his visit in 1730, was a scandal to the missionary fathers, who declared that the chapel (a made-over stable) was a disgrace and the worship conducted there was "indecent."

Father Andrés Varo, the angry man of that time and place, tells about it in his reports to his superiors and adds that the Indians at El Capitán were so unhappy that they rose in the year 1745, threatening to destroy everything, and in the year 1749 they finally did so.[15]

In complete contrast to the views of Father Andrés was the report of Father Manuel de San Juan Nepomuceno y Trigo, who visited the missions in 1758 under orders from the Procurator General of the Franciscans. His description of the mother mission is worth quoting:

This mission is the flower of them all, both on account of its fruits and garden products and of its climate. Although the region is cold, it is not so cold as that of the interior missions, for, while some snow falls, the average weather is like that of summer. At a distance of half a league to the east, the residents have their vineyards and fruit-trees — peaches, apples, plums, and several kinds of pears. In the same neighborhood they have their garden, in the midst of the settlement, and a vineyard which is cultivated and pruned by a horticulturist furnished each week by the Indians, whose wines defray the necessary expenses of the celebration of the sacrament in the mission.[16]

Senecú, Isleta, and Socorro were flourishing and, as Father Trigo saw the situation, the Indians were cooperative and contented. He was thinking, of course, of the Indians who were left. Many had gone back to the old wild life. At San Lorenzo only "six or eight" families remained, "for the Zumas, who formerly composed the mission, revolted, and returned to their heathenism and the mountains." [17]

The last visitation by a Bishop of Durango happened in 1750 when Dr. Pedro Tamaron y Romeral, a *gachupín* from Toledo who had spent the previous forty years in Caracas, set out on a two-year tour of his vast domain. In spite of his sixty-three years he was an "inveterate tourist" [18] who could not rest till he had seen everything. The Franciscan clergy at Paso del Norte in their hearts denied his right to supervise them, but had to make the best of the situation. They ushered him into the little city on April 23, 1760, and gave him a "solemn welcome."

The Bishop's notes tell us something about how life was carried on in those days. The main irrigation ditch, he says, took half the water of the river, but in flood times the crops and sometimes the dam might be destroyed.

The method of restoring the conduit every year is to make some large round baskets of rather thick rods. When the freshets are over, they put them in the current, filling them with stones, and they act as dams and force the water to seek the mouth of the ditch. This is not necessary when the river is in flood. Indeed, so much water flows that if the river is somewhat higher than usual, they are alarmed, fearing that they may be flooded and inundated with great damage.

In 1760 the Valley boasted a "large number" of vineyards which produced excellent full-bodied wines and some brandy. Tamaron noted that "it is delightful country in summer." [19]

He found that there were two lay priests in the community, one serving as vicar and ecclesiastical judge. To keep the peace, Tamaron gave the office of Vicar to the Custodian who was, of course, a Franciscan. Then he went on his way.

From a military man we get a different picture of life at the Pass during this period. In 1765, Don Pedro José de la Fuente of the presidio garrison kept a diary which has been preserved. It is mostly devoted to Indian troubles, present and expected. He had three squads of soldiers, one at Carrizal thirty leagues south on the Chihuahua road and two at Paso del Norte. A militia company stood ready to go into action when the need arose, and many friendly Indians scouted constantly for signs of enemy concentration.

Hostile tribesmen were never far away. They were always leaving their traces across the river from the settlement; the citizens were always running about in alarm at the sight of smoke signals on Mount Franklin and answering signals going up from the Organs far to the north. At such times de la Fuente would call for "the greatest vigilance by our garrison."[20]

Sometimes, as on January 31, 1765, the chiefs would send messengers to the commander to talk about peace. De la Fuente knew very well that there was only slight possibility of seriousness on their part, but he always felt he had to give them a chance. Meanwhile, small raids were occurring at fairly frequent intervals. On January 11 Apaches stole two horses from the settlement and outdistanced pursuers. On February 27 they got eight oxen and again disappeared in the rugged fastnesses of the Organ Mountains before the friendly Indians sent after them could catch up.[21]

The same pattern was followed throughout the six months covered by de la Fuente's diary. Apaches came in to spy, to trade, to ask for peace, to steal. The Spaniards gave them soft words, admonished them, and pursued them when they fled with their loot — all to very little purpose.[22]

It was not an all-out war. People came and went in small parties — messengers, soldiers, the annual caravan from Santa Fe to Chihuahua. And in this situation, somewhere between war and peace, the first half of the century passed into history. The second half was a much more strenuous time. The new developments began to appear in the year 1766 when the Marqués de Rubí came to New Mexico to inspect the frontier posts and improve the efficiency of the Spanish forces. His grand tour of all the presidios was a belated effort to do something about the impossible situation on the northern frontier. Hard pressed on all sides by the French, the British, and the Russians, the declining Spanish Empire had to strengthen its hold on its colonial possessions from Mexico northward or watch them slip away. A complete reorganization of frontier defenses was indicated.[23]

Rubí was on the road from 1760 to 1768, arriving at the Pass on July 19, 1776. Nicolás de Lafora, his captain of engineers, described for posterity everything he saw and drew a priceless map of the Valley and its settlements. He estimated that 5,000 souls were living in a "continuous settlement seven leagues long below El Paso."[24]

When the survey was complete, Rubí made recommendations which shook the Pass community to its foundations. He wanted a chain of presidios forty leagues apart located at strategic points all the way across the continent from California to eastern Texas. Local militia would defend Paso del Norte. The presidial soldiers would operate from Carrizal, thirty leagues to the south.[25]

In 1772, four years after they were made, Rubí's recommendations became the law of the land and a man with the unlikely name of Don Hugo O'Conor was selected to put them into operation. He became *inspector comandante* at Chihuahua on February 17, 1772.

He stepped into a bad situation. Since the outbreak of major hostilities in 1748, 4,000 human beings had died at the hands of the barbarians on the northern frontier — twelve million pesos worth of property had been destroyed.[26] The troops were in need of food, clothing, and pay. The citizens were without necessities.

O'Conor at least tried to do something about it, though the word "incompetent" has been applied to him.[27] He struck the southern Mescalero bands far to the east in the Bolsón de Mapimí — the Lipans in the Guadalupes a hundred miles east of Paso del Norte — the western Apaches near Janos. The tribesmen were impressed, and on February 7, 1775, a group of Gileños came to him to ask for peace. Skeptical of their good intentions, Don Hugo stated his terms and sent them back to their tribes. He was not surprised when they stole thirty head of horses and mules, and escaped to the Organs. He knew they would have to be soundly beaten before there could be any real peace. While the settlements to the west in Arizona and Sonora reeled under blow after blow, he went about strengthening his defenses and mounting his attack. By the spring of 1775, he was ready to move all along the line from Sonora to Texas.[28]

Captain Bellido of the presidio (located since 1774 in the Valle de San Elizario fifty-four miles southeast of present-day Juárez on the banks of the Rio Grande)[29] was to provide 140 men, and the other communities were to contribute what forces they could. The leader of each segment of the little army of 2,228 men followed detailed instructions. Bellido's group was to sweep through the Apache haunts north and east — the Cornudas, the Guadalupes, the Sacramentos. The Lieutenant Governor, in charge at Paso del Norte, was to lead another squad north to the Organs and eastward to the Sierra Blanca. Wherever the Apaches turned, they would run into a Spanish force.

If we can trust O'Conor's reports, the plan worked pretty well. He inflicted upon the savages "fifteen defeats of devastating proportions. In all the Spaniards killed one hundred and thirty-eight warriors, captured one hundred and four of all ages and sexes, and recovered one thousand nine hundred and sixty-six animals."[30]

On into 1776 O'Conor continued his campaigning. He was given a timely assist by the Comanches, who caught a large group of Apaches off guard in the Sacramentos and Guadalupes east of the Pass and slaughtered several hundred of them.[31] Before the year was done, however, Don Hugo had worn himself out and had to be transferred to more tranquil surroundings. His place was taken by a greater man, Don Teodoro de Croix.

Nephew of a former viceroy, a knight of the Teutonic Order, a brigadier and a veteran of long and distinguished service, the Caballero de Croix (as he called himself) had the background and the energy to do what could be done.[32] His opportunities likewise were very great. By this time the Council of the Indies had decided to divorce the northern provinces from the jurisdiction of the Viceroy of New Spain and set them up as a political entity under a commander responsible in most things directly to the King. Don Teodoro was actually to rank as another viceroy.

Naturally Viceroy Bucareli in Mexico City resented de Croix's independent status and the frank reports which he sent describing the confusion and terror in those remote outposts.[33] This lack of harmony handicapped the new commander in the monumental labors which he was about to undertake.

In spite of O'Conor's efforts, the most appalling conditions existed on the frontier. Between 1771 and 1776 in Nueva Vizcaya alone 7,764 persons had been murdered, 154 captured. The number of abandoned ranches and settlements was 116. Cattle and horses stolen, 68,256. The statistics did not include soldiers killed in battle, livestock stolen from the presidios, or travelers waylaid on the highway.

Captain Antonio de Bonilla, de Croix's official secretary, wrote a gloomy report on the various frontier communities. This was his picture of the situation at Paso del Norte:

> The pueblo of El Paso is surrounded on all sides by hills in which the Apaches live and from which they come down to commit hostilities without risk of suffering retaliation because of the scattered situation of the dwelling places, each one a little ranch.

There were plenty of men in the settlements, he added, but lack of arms and horses (the Apaches had most of them) paralyzed the community.[34]

Helpless as they were, the *Paseños* seemed overly anxious to conciliate the Indians. Bonilla heard that Captain Pedro del Barrio (who succeeded de la Fuente) actually admitted them to the village on friendly terms. He said his force was so weak he had no choice, but this excuse did not save him from a reprimand, and from arrest and imprisonment in Chihuahua when Don Antonio Daroca came in 1773 to move the presidio to Carrizal. Daroca had orders to arrest the Apaches who were camped peacefully in the vicinity of Paso del Norte, and he attempted to do so, but he got only a few of them — mostly women who "ended their days miserably in the wool mills of Ensenilla."[35]

De Croix threw his full energies into the war effort, making a personal inspection of the northern regions and holding three councils with his top soldiers to establish policies and lay plans. The council held at Chihuahua on June 19, 1778, brought together the governors of Coahuila, Nueva Vizcaya, and New Mexico, along with lesser officials, and some new developments resulted.[36] Alliances with the Comanches and the Mescalero Apaches were to be sought, and the frontier garrisons were to be reorganized and improved. De Croix had it in mind to get rid of useless presidios, take better care of the horse herds, and organize a sort of light cavalry which could move faster than the old-style mounted troops with their unwieldy equipment and cumbersome supply trains.[37]

Almost at once, conditions began to improve. Governor Anza of New Mexico gave the Comanches a severe beating in 1779 and brought them in to ask for peace and alliance.[38] Early in 1780, de

Croix made peace with the Mescaleros. The Lipans, under attack from the Comanches, were forced to ask for peace likewise.[39] In 1781, de Croix was able to report that all but the Gila Apaches had been pacified.[40]

Meanwhile Don Teodoro proceeded with his reorganization of the frontier line of defense, modifying the long line of presidios, setting up new communities of settlers behind the line, and organizing flying corps of local militiamen to back up the presidial soldiers. Two companies were assembled for the defense of the Valley towns, each composed of forty-odd Spaniards and thirty Indians.[41]

If de Croix's description of the presidial officers is anywhere near the truth, the citizen soldiers were far superior to the military. These officers, he said, "openly embrace all the abominable excesses of drunkenness, luxury, gambling and greed, but under cover and away from the forts, vices have free rein. This sets a bad example for the troops." Very few of them, he thought, "give any hope of improving their behavior and conduct."[42]

In spite of everything, de Croix made progress. He had judgment and experience and unshakable determination. When men or circumstances upset his plans, he wasted no time in hand wringing. He drew up new plans and started over. A man like that could not be entirely defeated and some successes came his way.

In September of 1779, for instance, some of the Mescaleros actually gave serious thought to settling down and taking up farming. With de Croix's permission, they were allowed to occupy the pueblo of San Francisco de los Sumas, long since abandoned, in the valley below town, and a second group settled at the pueblo of Nuestra Señora de la Buena Esperanza still farther down the river.[43] In his report of 1781 de Croix described the result. Most of the Apaches, he said, "prefer the vagrant life. They have not seemed able to build an adobe, or to apply themselves to work in the field, which has been done for them by our field workers, or to incline them or their sons to these labors. Besides there are well-founded suspicions of their having committed various murders and robberies in different parts of the province. . . . Notwithstanding the little captain, Domingo Alegre, and other Mescaleros of his band, are proceeding, as it appears, in good faith."[44]

By 1782 bigger fish had begun to come into de Croix's net. In the summer four principal chiefs and one hundred thirty-four warriors gave themselves up at Paso del Norte and were sent into the interior under guard.[45] The Spaniards had some success, too, against the Gila Apaches as their flying squadrons penetrated the mountain fastnesses and attacked the red men in their *rancherías*. But forces which were out of his control now began to work against the great general. In 1779 the King of Spain began his downfall by ordering him to use "suave and gentle" methods of dealing with the natives. The declaration of war against England finished him.[46] He was never able to set up the sweeping campaign he had dreamed of — a campaign reaching all the way from the Gulf of California to the Gulf of Mexico. Discouraged but never defeated, he went off in 1783, after six and a half years of command, to become Governor of Peru.[47]

His successors, Phelipe de Neve and Joseph Antonio Rengel, were willing and able men, but troops and funds were in short supply, as always, and when the supreme command was returned to the Viceroy in 1784, the days of the great campaigns were over.

This should have meant a return to full-scale raiding by the tribesmen, but the New Deal which came to *Apachería* after 1786 changed the Indian situation almost completely.[48]

Viceroy Bernardo de Gálvez was the man with the idea. A noble Spaniard who had shown great courage and resourcefulness in managing Spaniards and fighting Indians during his early youth, he held the Viceroy's post for only a year, dying of a fever in the epidemic of 1786. During his brief tenure, however, he worked out a set of rules which were used effectively by his successors.

First, the Apaches must be subdued by force. Then they were to be corrupted. Liquor, he thought, was a better weapon than guns. "With a little effort and in a short time they will acquire a taste for these drinks, in which case it will become with them the most valuable trade. . . . After all, the supplying of drink to the Indians will be a means of gaining their good will, discovering their secrets, calming them so that they will think less often of conceiving and executing their hostilities, and creating for them a necessity which will oblige them to recognize their dependence upon us more directly."[49]

Second, he determined that the Indians should be given firearms and ammunition. However, the guns were to be of inferior quality. The red men would not "be able to preserve their firearms," giving the Spaniards an advantage they had not enjoyed before.[50] Any band which asked for peace should be encouraged to settle down, though no Spaniard was to trust an Indian any farther than he could see him. "Peace being established, if the Indians give indications of quietude and good faith, and reveal actual needs, they may be aided with regular rations of food."[51]

Paso del Norte was to be a center for negotiations with the hostile tribes. "The aforesaid town is a very suitable place for establishing peace and maintaining commerce with the Apaches."

Just how, and how far, these instructions were followed, we do not know. We do know, however, that for something like twenty-five years after Gálvez laid down this crafty policy, the frontier was comparatively peaceful. Apparently the Apaches were handled with gloves, fed with some regularity, tolerated in the vicinity of the towns and presidios, cajoled, bribed, and intoxicated into the status of harmless nuisances. "We hear of no serious depredation in these years," says Bancroft, "or in the beginning of the next century. Neither does it appear, however, that the Apaches were making very rapid progress in the great work of being exterminated, of becoming drunkards, or in forming an ineradicable taste for Spanish luxuries. They were rather biding their time and awaiting the accumulation of plunder. Meanwhile the expense of the royal treasury was . . . about one million dollars per year . . . besides the amount expended in gifts and rations to the savages."[52]

There may have been no "serious depredations," as Bancroft says, but there were plenty of minor ones. News was always coming in of attacks and raids somewhere in the region. There was always coming and going of soldiers and militia on escort duty, punitive expeditions, reconnaissance. The reports of robberies and murders never ceased — a sheepherder ambushed here, a herd of horses stolen there, pursuers turned back by a snowstorm in the Caballo Mountains.[53] In 1799, large parties of soldiers and citizens were reconnoitering the mountains and escorting herds of cattle to the settlement at the Pass.[54] On August 24, 1806, during a special time of peace, five Apaches stole ten horses and five oxen from the citizens of Ysleta and three horses at Socorro.[55] And so it went. The Apache was by nature and training a raider, and sometimes he was going to raid.

Most of the reports from this time, however, are hopeful. As early as September 7, 1790, Comandante Jacobo Ugarte y Loyola wrote that "all the nations" were staying within their prescribed bounds and keeping good faith. In 1798, by permission of the Governor, a band of Apaches established a semi-permanent camp close to the presidio at San Elizario. From a letter of Pedro de Nava, the officer in command, it appears that in return for rations, the Indians were expected to stay in such camping spots and not move without giving notice.[56]

Lieutenant Zebulon Pike saw what was happening when he passed through under guard on his way to Chihuahua in March of 1807. He was entertained at Paso del Norte by Don Francisco García, a merchant and rancher who possessed 20,000 sheep and a thousand head of cattle. These animals must have been pastured near the settlement and could not have been accumulated in such large numbers had the Indians not been quiet.

It was not fear of the Spanish soldiers which kept the Apaches in line. At San Elizario Pike observed the manners of the garrison, an idle, careless crew who gambled and drank and let tomorrow take care of itself. "Around this fort," he remarked, "were a great number of Apaches, who were on a treaty with the Spaniards. These people appeared to be perfectly independent in their manners and were the only savages I saw in the Spanish dominions whose spirit was not humbled, whose necks were not bowed to the yoke of the invaders."[57]

At the end of the century, then, conditions were not all good or all bad, but they had certainly improved, and for the first time in two hundred years there was a little security, a little prosperity. Old Father Andrés Varo, laboring in his vineyard at Senecú, could raise his hands to heaven and exclaim with justification: "Oh Land and Kingdom of New Mexico: So long oppressed, humiliated, and persecuted, so often not governed but tyrannized over by these unworthy chiefs. . . ." But on the other hand we must not forget Don Francisco García's 20,000 sheep. In all her history Paso del Norte had not seen such wealth.

CHAPTER IX

Prosperity and Peril

 FROM 1790 to 1830 was Spanish New Mexico's golden age. Ranchers and farmers prospered as never before. Caravans from the Pass showed up annually at Santa Fe to trade at the great fiesta in September and the reputation of Pass wine and Pass brandy spread farther than ever. Since the arts of war were practiced less, the arts of peace — including dissension and disaffection — flourished more. The people feuded with the Lieutenant Governor and civil authorities feuded with the religious.[1] Since there were few major dislocations, minor ones took on a new importance, for instance the epidemic of whooping cough, measles, and dysentery which played havoc with the children of New Mexico from Paso del Norte to Santa Fe in 1805.[2]

Times were not exactly booming, but business was better. There was talk about having another annual fair in September to compete with the one at Santa Fe.[3] Yearly caravans convoyed by soldiers came through carrying the wool, hides, feathers, salt, piñon nuts, brandy, fur, and cotton of the north to settlements in the interior and bringing back tools, arms, tobacco, sugar, paper, books, boots, and other supplies needed in the New Mexico communities. Paso del Norte profited by and participated in this traffic.[4] The mail was supposed to go through from Chihuahua to Santa Fe twice a month,[5] and sometimes it did, though the service became irregular and uncertain in the twenties and thirties.

Education took a shaky step forward. By 1800, schools which progressed through five or six grades[6] existed in several New Mexican towns. A report on the number of children in classes in the El Paso Valley was sent off to Santa Fe on June 7, 1807. In five towns (Paso del Norte, San Elizario, Senecú, Ysleta, and Socorro) and in eight country districts, a total of 460 students were enrolled.

Paso del Norte accounted for 316 of them. The names of teachers are given for all schools except those in Paso del Norte.[7] One wonders what problems were encountered by José Rosas in Pueblo del Real (San Elizario) and José Alderete at Ysleta; probably the same difficulties faced by their successors in the same towns today. A note at the bottom of the report reminds one of conditions in Kansas or Illinois or Alabama not many years ago: "Some children have left school because they have learned to write passably well, and others because they are old enough to help their parents in their work, because they are very poor."

Antonio Barreiro in his *Ojeada sobre Nuevo Mexico* in 1832 mentions schools in six New Mexico towns but does not include El Paso in his "glance." He does remark that teachers are well paid but that education is in "distressing condition" because of public apathy and the "neglect, laziness, and ignorance of the schoolmasters."[8] The truth is that special training for children was, and continued to be for many years, available mostly to the well-to-do. Upper-class people could read and write, and some had gone to centers of learning for instruction; but the common sort had small chance to become literate. Their day, however, was coming closer.

One special evidence of progress arrived, at least in idea, in 1797. The town was to have a bridge. Commerce and mail service would benefit immeasurably. There would be no more month-long delays while the angry waters subsided. This was real progress. On June 1, 1797, fifty-four men went forth from Paso del Norte and headed northward to meet a party of New Mexicans at the town of Sabinal some forty miles below Albuquerque. They were to cut timber, probably in the Manzano Mountains, and bring it to the river where it could be floated to the Pass.

They had a most unhappy time. Having left without provisions, they had to sell their clothes to buy food, and on the way back their log raft turned over and left them unprovided again. On June 20, Acting Lieutenant Governor Francisco Xavier Bernal wrote to Comandante Pedro de Nava, complaining of the misfortunes suffered by his men.[9]

It is certain that the bridge was built, but not very well built, and that it gave way within the next two or three years when there was an unusually destructive flood. During the early months of the year 1800, Governor Chacón decided to rebuild it; and on

July 4 we hear that more timbers were on their way to the Pass.[10] The bridge builder wrote that he arrived on August 24 and was going to work without delay.

He notes that the structure is only half a league from the center of population, which should place it just above the "falls" which supplied power for Ponce de León's flour mill and for Hart's mill later, and close to the spot where the soldiers from Old Fort Bliss paraded later still.

This poses a problem for the historian, since the old Spanish trail did not, and could not, follow the river. Where the Rio Grande broke through the mountain wall, the steep and rocky slopes came down to the water's edge and prevented all passage except when the river was dry and its bed could be used as a road. The old Spanish trail swung westward around Mule Driver's Mountain and came back into the Valley at Frontera crossing. It is certainly a fact, however, that the Spaniards did build a bridge, and they must have reached the eastern end by making a trail through the rugged hills somewhere near the future site of the A.S. & R. smelter. Doniphan's men followed it in 1846 and crossed the river "about at the foot of the rapids below the dam at Hart's Mill."[11] Major Emory of the Boundary Commission blasted a passage through the rugged slopes above the watercourse in the 1850's, and he may have followed the trace laid out years before by his Spanish predecessors, but we have no way of knowing exactly where that trace was.

We do know that Governor Chacón came down from Santa Fe to be present at the opening of the reconstructed bridge in 1802, and that he had a fall from his horse which damaged him seriously. At the ceremonies of dedication, however, he was able to appear and take part.

The bridge was something to be proud of. It was five varas (seventeen feet) wide and 157 varas (over 500 feet) long, and was supported on eight caissons. Since it was only half a league from the town, and since there was no park or recreation area available to the citizens, the builder laid out the approaches on both sides in terraces, with a *glorieta* or summer house at each end.[12] The grand opening must have been a proud and happy moment for all the townspeople.

Anything as elaborate and expensive as that bridge should have lasted for generations, but it turned out to be a continual trouble and expense to all concerned. It had to be rebuilt in 1802 [13] and repaired in 1805. [14] It was seen two years later by the only American ever to mention it. This was Lieutenant Zebulon M. Pike, who came to the Pass under guard on March 21, 1807. He crossed the bridge and noted that it spanned the river at the place where the dam diverted water and the irrigation ditch began. [15]

Nine years later it was still there, and again in need of repairs. [16] In 1819, it was rebuilt for the last time, to the great indignation of *paisanos* as far away as Taos, who were called on for help of one kind or another. [17] We do not know what flood in what year finally brought the bridge crashing down into the swirling waters, but when the Americans arrived in 1846, they had to ford the river as the *conquistadores* had done before them.

The Apaches may have had something to do with the destruction of that bridge, for evil days were at hand. Their ambushes and incursions made life a burden in the northern provinces and the repair of bridges impossible.

At the time Mexico won its independence in 1821, the tribesmen had been quiet for so long that the defenses of Chihuahua and Sonora had fallen into decay. Along with the *Reglamento de Presidios* which reorganized the frontier garrisons in 1772, a policy of conciliation was initiated, as we have already seen. Presents and rations continued to be passed out for almost forty years. The Indians depended on them and expected them and to a large extent laid aside their old raiding habits as long as these benefits were provided. [18] Even after the fight for independence had begun, the Apaches remained quiet. A recent authority thinks they were waiting to see what could be expected from the new regime. [19]

So confident were the Mexicans that peace could be maintained for the foreseeable future that the first Constituent Congress of Chihuahua in 1824 passed a Colonization Law opening certain selected localities to settlement. As a result the little town of Canutillo sprang up some twenty miles above the Pass alongside the river. It lasted until 1832. [20]

Another byproduct of those relatively placid days was the establishment of the first public school in Paso del Norte in 1826, by order of the state legislature of Chihuahua. It was in this year also that Paso del Norte became a villa[21] — significant evidence of the growth of the town in size and importance.

In 1831 the good days came to an end. Quite certain now that rations and presents would no longer be forthcoming, the Apaches attacked everywhere. Toward the end of January they overran the community of Carrizal and the ranch of El Carmen south of Paso del Norte;[22] and that was only the beginning. The governments of Chihuahua and Sonora tried to cope with the situation. A "general contribution" was levied—the first of many—to finance the campaign, and in the fall of 1831, at Santa Rita del Cobre (today's Santa Rita Copper Mines), a treaty was imposed upon the tribesmen.[23]

It was a bad treaty, penning the Apaches up in three zones, demanding that they work for a living, and not even mentioning the word "rations." The warriors went back to raiding as fast as they could.

In July, 1834, a peace was signed at Paso del Norte with a group of Comanches and Kiowas who were living at the bottom of the Big Bend of the Rio Grande.[24] But hostilities were interrupted for only a few months so far as these Indians were concerned; and attacks by the Apaches were never interrupted at all.

Sonora was crucified. Chihuahua suffered almost as much. The mail service between the capital and Santa Fe could not maintain a schedule, "the riders being almost totally at the mercy of hostile Indians while on the road."[25] Don Francisco García lost his sheep and cattle. Men and women in the outlying settlements were massacred and their children carried off into captivity. All over the frontier states it was the same. Don Ignacio Zúñiga, commander of the northern presidios in the thirties, estimated that between 1820 and 1835, 5,000 Christians were killed, 100 settlements destroyed and 4,000 settlers driven out of the country. Tucson and Tubac alone were left in northern Sonora. The rest were *despoblados* — abandoned.[26] The archives of the north-Mexican towns are stained with blood and tears — heartbreaking chronicles of torture, death and destruction, renewed year after year.[27]

Hardly anything could be done to stem the tide. The Mexicans were forbidden by their government to own serviceable arms, while the Indians had no difficulty in exchanging livestock, captives, and other plunder for good guns and ammunition. The warriors swarmed over northern Mexico, depredating almost at will. They boasted that they could wipe out the entire Mexican population any time they chose, but preferred to let the *paisanos* raise livestock and children for them to steal.[28]

In 1835, in desperation and despair, the State of Sonora revived the old Spanish custom of paying for scalps — one hundred pesos for the scalp of a male fourteen years old or older. In Chihuahua, militia companies were organized and sent to reinforce the garrisons of the frontier forts.[29]

Scalp hunting proved the more profitable and practicable measure of the two. It attracted a good deal of outside talent as time went on. Chihuahua became the "scalp capital of the world,"[30] and a goodly number of adventurers — American, Mexican, and even Indian (from the United States) — made a business of killing Apaches, and anybody else with black hair who fell in their way, for cash and half the loot of the Indian villages. The industry was sometimes called "scalp mining" or "barbering."

James Kirker was the most expert and ruthless operator.[31] This native of Ireland got started when his friend and former employer Robert McKnight (the same McKnight who spent nine years in prison in Mexico with the first Santa Fe traders between 1812 and 1821) was put out of the mining business at the Santa Rita copper mines by a group of Apaches who had legitimate grievances. Out of loyalty to his old friend, Kirker assembled a band of twenty-three Delawares, Shawnees, and white men and attacked an Apache village. He emerged from the battle with fifty-five scalps, nine prisoners, and four hundred head of captured livestock. As a result, his fame spread far and wide through the Spanish borderlands, eventually reaching the Governor of Chihuahua and bringing Kirker an invitation to come south and go into the hair-and-ears business.

He continued to contract with the government until Don Francisco García Condé took charge of affairs in Chihuahua. Don Francisco considered scalp hunting to be a vile and dishonorable thing; besides, the efficiency of the Americans threw many good Mexicans out of work. He sent Kirker away, and at once the wild men returned to the attack, laying everything waste in their traditional manner. Unwillingly the Governor put Kirker to work again, offering him a liberal contract which included rewards for restoring stolen livestock. Aided by 100 hard-case bounty hunters, Kirker brought in a plentiful supply of scalps and collected $37,500 for recapturing 15,000 mules from the Apaches.[32]

The treasury could stand only so much of this sort of thing and the Governor tried to remedy the situation by putting the hunters on what amounted to a salary, a step which Kirker refused to put up with. He withdrew to the mountains and for three years lived with his erstwhile enemies. According to one source, he became their chief.[33] When Don Angel Trias became Governor in 1845, he determined to revive the bounty system, offering a special bonus — $9,000 — for anyone who would bring in the locks of the Apache leader Santiago Kirker. Kirker, however, was equal to the occasion. He opened negotiations with Trias and was soon slaughtering his Apache friends and followers for what their hair would bring.[34]

There is no doubt that he was a master workman. He had many good days, but probably his best was July 7, 1846, when he killed and barbered Chief Reyes and 148 tribesmen near the town of Galeana. The scalps and other trophies were brought to Chihuahua and displayed according to law on the Cathedral Square. The English traveler George Frederick Ruxton saw those scalps (he counted 170) — trophies, he remarked ironically, "of Mexican valor and humanity."[35] He obviously did not understand the situation.

Kirker's day was soon over. He fell out with the authorities, possibly because he was turning in too many Mexican scalps along with those of *bona fide* Apaches,[36] and he joined Doniphan's Missourians on the Rio Grande just before the Battle of Brazito on Christmas Day, 1846.

After the Treaty of Guadalupe Hidalgo, scalp hunting became an even bigger business with a new cast of characters. Half a dozen Americans took the field — especially Major Michael Chevalier and Captain John Joel Glanton — and as many as fifteen Mexican leaders, each with his trusty band of killers.[37] "By the end of 1849," says Ralph Smith, a long-time student of this gruesome business, "the state of Chihuahua alone had paid out $17,896 for scalps and was still advancing money to empresarios."[38]

In these wild and whirling times Paso del Norte bore her part. The hundred dragoons quartered at San Elizario could not control the situation in the Valley — never had been able to. Militia companies were organized by Governor General Calvo and in the early 1840's were expanded to include 700 men. This group gained one of the few victories recorded during this unhappy period. "About fourteen years ago," wrote Captain John Pope in 1854, "these Arabs of New Mexico, the Apaches, having made a desperate foray upon the Mexicans, retreated with their plunder to these mountains, the Huecos, thirty miles east of El Paso. The Mexicans surprised and surrounded them, hemming them up in the rocky ravine forming the eastern tank. Here an engagement took place, in which the Indians were totally defeated and nearly exterminated, only two or three escaping. It is said that upwards of one hundred of them were killed."[39]

Josiah Gregg picked up a story of another episode that may have been connected with the Hueco Tanks massacre. In the summer of 1839, he says, a number of Apache prisoners were being held in the jail at Paso del Norte. One was the wife of a chief — a man who did not take his loss lightly. With some sixty warriors he rode into the center of the community and demanded the captives. The *Comandante*, hoping to work out a stratagem which would defeat them, told them they could have the captives next morning. That night the available troops were concentrated around the jail but kept out of sight. In the morning the chief and twenty of his men were lured inside and done to death.

They took a few Mexicans with them. When the *Comandante* shouted, "*Maten a los carajos!*" the chief replied, "*Entonces moriras tu primero, carajo!*" (Then you will die first, you rascal) and the *Comandante* perished with a knife in his heart.[40]

It is hard to believe that the crafty and resourceful Apaches would have been caught in such a trap, but they were able to make mistakes, like other human beings. They lost their hair occasionally in the wild desert country beyond the Valley, and Paso del Norte was a minor center for the redemption of their scalps.[41] They continued to pilfer and plunder about the river towns, however, for another twenty years. In 1965 Anastacia Cooper of Ysleta, over a hundred years old, could still remember those Indians "yelling at night as they were driving livestock belonging to the settlers."[42] She was the last living human being who could recall that dreadful sound, once all too familiar to every person in the region.[43]

In spite of the Indians, life grew richer. Economically, the citizens did well enough during the first half of the nineteenth century. Mostly they were farmers who raised quantities of wheat which they ground into flour at grist mills in Ysleta, San Elizario, and Paso del Norte. Their other great crop was the mission grape — direct offspring of vines planted by Father García de San Francisco so long before — from which they made raisins, wine and their famous *aguardiente* or brandy. Almost all the potables obtainable in Chihuahua and New Mexico were imported from this Valley.[44] When Americans came into the region, they were uniformly and emphatically impressed by the local wines.[45]

Practically everything would grow here. Fruit trees — apples, pears, peaches — ornamented the patios and orchards. There were melons, onions, squash, beans, sweet potatoes, sugar cane and maize. Usually there was plenty for everybody, thanks to the canals and laterals which had been delivering the river water to the fields with more or less efficiency since 1659, Father García himself having engineered the first ditch.[46] Livestock belonged mostly to the rich. The poor ate chile and tortillas and beans as they do now unless they organized hunting parties which brought back deer from the mountains and antelope from the plains. The meat was cut into strips and dried in the sun for winter consumption and sometimes for export.[47] Much of the home-grown mutton was sent out of town, on the hoof, as a cash crop. In good years a great herd of sheep was driven south annually.[48]

The dangers and hardships of life were balanced by much that was good and beautiful. The fruits and vines, the whispering corn fields and the fragrant roses growing along the *acequias,* made an oasis in the wasteland. The life these people led had some of the pastoral charm of the landscape. For almost two centuries these *paisanos,* cut off from the rest of the world, passed on their customs unchanged to their descendants, and relics of the old ways and attitudes survive to this day, enriching the lives of even the Anglos who hardly know they exist.

Everybody in the Valley was, of course, related to everybody else, at least to those on his own social level, and family affairs were the center of everybody's interest. On Sundays the normal Mexican attended church and visited relatives. Family ties extended even into economic matters. It was expected that one should share what he had with his *primos* (cousins) and if anybody in a poor family had beans, everybody had beans. This material courtesy and generosity was accompanied by a verbal decency and formality which still distinguish the Mexican people, even the humblest of them.

The Church with its festivals was the center of all activity. The great feasts — especially Holy Week and Christmas — were times of solemn devotional observance. The Nativity and the death and burial of Christ were acted out in plays and pictured in tableaus. The Nativity plays — *Los Pastores* and *Las Posadas* — are still occasionally seen in the El Paso neighborhood but since the 1930's they have ceased to be a natural and accepted part of Mexican life. Feasts of the patron saints of the various parishes were commemorated with processions, music, fireworks, and musket volleys. There was always something going on or something to prepare for.

Weddings were times of special celebration when whole villages came together to feast on beef and wine, watch the *matachines* dance, and cheer on the contestants in races and roping contests. Well-to-do citizens gave dances when the spirit moved, and in good weather it moved rather often. Girls were carefully chaperoned and kept pretty much at home, but they managed, as girls always have, to know the boys in their neighborhoods and marry the ones they liked. The impression passed on by American travelers in later years that Mexican young ladies were easily interviewed and eager for acquaintance with young Americans was based on wishful thinking and contact with the lower orders of society. These travelers would have had difficulty in even getting an introduction to girls of good family, though it did happen if they were properly sponsored.

Because of the difficulties of travel, every community was thrown pretty much on its own resources. There were carpenters and shoemakers, blacksmiths and tanners. Since it was a two-day trip by ox team from San Elizario to *La Plaza* (Paso del Norte) twenty miles away, the people didn't go very often.

There were no newspapers and very few books, particularly of the kind that "contribute so largely in disseminating ideas,"[49] but by 1846 when Americans arrived in large numbers and reported on what they saw, Paso del Norte was by no means a slough of complete and abysmal ignorance. Susan Shelby Magoffin, who came in that year and was in close contact with the best people, visited one family whose children were studying English and French. Their father, she noted, not merely looked like George Washington but was a student of the great American's career and principles. He did not think, incidentally, that the great leader's countrymen were living up to his precepts. The Mexican ladies were more interested in *modas americanas* and personal gossip than in books.[50] They spent much time in visiting and playing cards and were probably about on the same intellectual level as average American and Mexican ladies today who have been to school but don't remember much about it.

Even the men were less agitated by the changing currents of ideas than their countrymen in other districts. The tremendous and far-reaching changes which shook Mexico during the first two decades of the nineteenth century were felt on the northern frontier, but not as something close at hand. The geographical remoteness of the *Paseños* was part of it, but only part. They were outside the arena also because the roots of the trouble scarcely reached them. The snobbishness of the *gachupines* (Spaniards from Spain) and the parasitism of the *criollos* (Spaniards born in the New World) were not part of the social structure of the northern states.[51] The *mestizos* (people of mixed blood), whose energy and ambition were repressed elsewhere, had things pretty much their own way in Paso del Norte. There was an aristocracy, but it was an aristocracy of agriculture and commerce. Its top men were traders and owners of fields and flocks.[52] Although the gap between the rich and poor was wide, it was probably not so wide as in other parts of Mexico, and the greed of high officials which "germinated the seeds of general rebellion"[53] could not be as conspicuous in this remote region as in the centers of population farther south.

Nevertheless Paso del Norte shared in the general dismay over the impotence of the Spanish government as the eighteenth century ended and it welcomed the liberal philosophies which began to be adopted by the Mexican intellectuals. The names of Jefferson and Franklin meant something to these people, and were flung in the faces of the invaders when American soldiers entered Mexico in 1846.

When independence was achieved in 1821 and Mexico embarked on a new era of self-government, legislators from Paso del Norte took their seats in legislative assemblies in Chihuahua and in the Capital. A look into the Juárez Archives will remind us that orders and *avisos* did arrive and that the population was affected by the battles far away.

The historian of Juárez remarks that at this period the *Paseños* had enough on their minds to make their interests "state rather than national,"[54] particularly after Chihuahua was organized and the first meeting of its legislature was held in 1824.

So matters stood on the eve of the American invasion — an event which would eventually remove the Indian menace and bring the mixed blessings of American-style culture to the north bank of the river, but which would interfere seriously with traditional ways on the south bank and subject the population to pressures it had never known or even suspected before.

CHAPTER X

The Americans Arrive

THE HALF-CENTURY from 1800 to 1850 changed the whole pattern of life at the Pass. From a tiny community, isolated beyond belief, the settlement was transformed into a well known stopping place for Santa Fe traders, Forty-niners, and the United States Army. Its orientation changed from the north-south direction of the Santa Fe - Mexico City axis to the east-west routes of American traffic. Its inhabitants, cut off from the rest of mankind for two hundred years, were conquered by foreign troops, inundated by gold seekers, tempted by the wares of Missouri traders, and infiltrated by marrying Americans. It was a revolutionary fifty years.

During the first two decades of the century nobody in his right mind would have predicted even a small part of what was to happen. Things were as they had always been, for the most part, as far back as grandfathers and great-grandfathers could remember. There was nothing much between Albuquerque, 200 miles to the north, and Chihuahua, 200 miles to the south, but dust and thirst and Indians. Anyone obliged to traverse the primitive road in either direction took a solemn farewell of his family and attached himself to as large a party as possible. The outside world began at Mexico City, almost 2,000 miles to the south — so far away that not one man in a thousand saw it in the course of a lifetime. The United States, almost as far removed as the Capital, was infinitely farther away in other ways, a foreign country inhabited, it was said, by a race without manners or morals or religion. The vast, untraversed plains between Santa Fe and St. Louis were probably put there by God to protect the *gente de razon* — civilized people — from that strange and unpredictable nation.

Actually the *Paseños* were well acquainted by 1830 with a small group of Americans who had come to live among them, but these familiar faces had come to be part of the home scene and their owners were thought of as more Mexican than gringo. Their presence did not change the general estimate of the trappers and traders who occasionally visited the country — violent bearded creatures so different from the Spanish ideal of true manhood. They chewed tobacco and tried to make friends with the Mexican women. They knew nothing of the forms of polite intercourse. Their presence created many problems.

The American newcomers, for their own part, were apt to underestimate the Mexicans. They did not understand the caste system or the rules which kept women in the background and, ideally, out of sight. They underestimated the courage of the Mexican men, many of them great Indian fighters but not accustomed to or sympathetic with the eye-gouging and fisticuffs of their northern neighbors. The two groups had much to learn before they could appreciate and understand each other.

The first American to appear on the banks of the Rio Grande seems to have been one James Purcell of Illinois who came to Paso del Norte late in 1806, accompanied by a Frenchman named Lorenzo Durocher. He had permission "to work at his trade of carpenter for Don Juan Antonio García in this settlement." What he was doing there is a matter for conjecture,[1] but *Comandante* Isidro Rey of the garrison was so unaccustomed to seeing people from the outside world that he asked for instructions on how to behave.[2]

Lieutenant Zebulon Pike is the first American to tell what he saw in the El Paso Valley. A prisoner, he arrived at Paso del Norte on March 21, 1807. Although he was not able to make notes, he was curious and observant and retained his impressions. "The settlement," he says, "is by far the most flourishing town we have been in," and adds that the natives had "as finely cultivated fields of wheat and other small grain as I ever saw, and also numerous vineyards from which were produced the finest wine ever drank."[3]

After Pike's brief visit, *norteamericanos* appeared from time to time, welcome or not. Robert McKnight, James Baird, John Stephenson, and several others, the first to attempt to bring goods to the Southwest from the Missouri settlements, were taken to Durango in 1812, undoubtedly by way of El Paso, and confined until 1821. Their confinement was probably not rigorous, and they may not have wished to leave. Several of them are heard of in the region later on.

Tougher and more elusive than the traders were the trappers. Some of them are said to have worked the Rio Grande and its tributaries in very early times, but their status was at best ambiguous and they did not show themselves often in the centers of population. It was illegal for any except *bona fide* New Mexicans to take beaver, and even they had to have licenses when they wished to trap. "The North Americans," says José Agustín de Escudero, "began to corrupt the New Mexicans by purchasing their licenses from them, and, with this authorization, undertaking immense hunting expeditions; not only did they use ordinary traps, but they even loaded certain types of traps on rafts and floated noiselessly down the rivers and thus surprised their prey. . . . Thus they traveled hundreds of leagues, from the remotest source of the Rio Bravo to El Paso. . . ."[4]

One who complained of these interlopers was James Baird, a member of the original party of unfortunate Santa Fe traders who came in 1812. He returned to Missouri after his release in 1821 but was back in Spanish territory in 1822. Apparently he became a Mexican citizen as soon as he conveniently could and in 1825 was operating a distillery near Taos.[5] A year later he had settled in Paso del Norte, from whence he sallied forth to hunt beaver.[6]

He was heard from, in a high state of indignation, in the fall of 1826 when Vicente St. Vrain and perhaps as many as a hundred associates traversed New Mexico and northern Sonora on what was supposed to be a trading expedition but was really a fur-hunting foray. Baird, the Mexican citizen, was indignant that these foreigners were invading his homeland. "I have learned," he wrote to the President of the El Paso District, "that with scandal and contempt for the Mexican nation a hundred-odd Anglo-Americans have introduced themselves . . . and with such arrogance and haughtiness that they have openly said that in spite of the Mexicans, they will hunt beaver wherever they please."

Baird reported that in the last year and a half the invaders had taken pelts worth $100,000. Now he wanted to go hunting himself and the game was gone.[7]

It would seem that a good many adventurous Americans were entering the Spanish Southwest by the back door, and it is certainly a fact that by 1825 the total isolation of the region, including the El Paso Valley, was becoming a thing of the past. Two who took pains to enter New Mexico legitimately were Sylvester and James Ohio Pattie who worked the copper mines at Santa Rita and who, according to the latter's *Personal Narrative*, were at home almost anywhere in the Southwest. James visited the Pass in 1826 and described a little of what he saw. The town, he says, "has a length of eight miles and a breadth of nearly three. I was struck with the magnificent vineyards of this place, from which are made great quantities of delicious wine. The wheat fields were equally beautiful, and the wheat of a kind I never saw before, the stalks generally yielding two heads each. The land is exceedingly rich, and its fertility increased by irrigation."[8]

During the thirties, Americans came in increasing and even alarming numbers. By this time the Santa Fe trade had been in existence for some time, though it was not until after Mexico became independent in 1821 that traders were encouraged to do business in New Mexico. Once their great wagons began to roll, the trade expanded and the traders pushed southward to Paso del Norte, to Chihuahua, to Durango, and beyond. By 1830 the tobacco-stained beards and Missouri twang of the gringo merchants had become familiar to the Valley Mexicans. From these traders we get a fairly detailed picture of Paso del Norte and its tiny, just-born sister community on the north bank in the decade before the American take-over.

Josiah Gregg — trader, scholar, confirmed traveler and life-long student of the West and its people — came to the Pass with his wagons on September 12, 1839. The river was up and he had to ferry his goods over in a dugout. A "stern, surly officer" (ancestor of some later customs men) went through the merchant's papers and let him pass to Chihuahua. Gregg put down in his everpresent notebook his impressions of the settlement, already familiar to him from previous trips.

The valley of El Paso is supposed to contain a population of about four thousand inhabitants, scattered over the western bottom of the Rio del Norte to the length of ten or twelve miles. These settlements are so thickly interspersed with vineyards, orchards and cornfields, as to present more the appearance of a series of plantations than of a town: in fact, only a small portion at the head of the valley, where the *plaza publica* and parochial church are located, would seem to merit this title. Two or three miles above the *plaza* there is a dam of stone and brush across the river, the purpose of which is to turn the current into a dike or canal, which conveys nearly half the water of the stream, during a low stage, through this well cultivated valley, for the irrigation of the soil. Here we were regaled with the finest fruits of the season: the grapes especially were of exquisite flavor.[9]

Gregg liked the place and spoke highly of the people of "that delightful town of vineyards and orchards, who, take them altogether, are more sober and industrious than those of any other part of Mexico I have visited; and are happily less infested by the extremes of wealth and poverty."[10]

Another traveler who had his say about the community was James Josiah Webb, a big Yankee from Connecticut with a rattrap mouth and considerable experience as a merchant and trader, who came to the Pass in 1846, traveling in haste to outrun the wagons which had crossed the plains and entered Santa Fe under the protection of Kearny and his United States troops. The fact that Webb and his partners could travel through a country with which their own was actually at war shows that the traders were in a way a race apart, tolerated and even encouraged because of the services they could perform to brighten the lives of these isolated people.

They crossed the river a little above the dam at the Pass, went into camp, and prepared to repel visitors. A good many people, Webb says, "came to our camp to sell provisions, fruit, etc., to gratify curiosity, and others to show their hatred of the Texans and heretics, and still others to do a little legal work in mules."[11] It seems that mules stolen in Chihuahua, mostly by Apaches, were sold in New Mexico. Sometimes these animals would pass into the hands of the traders, who would drive them south to Paso del Norte, where the authority of the State of Chihuahua commenced.

Before Webb and his men had finished pitching camp, a silent Mexican appeared driving a cart loaded with what the traders took to be old iron. Actually he had a load of branding irons. He inspected every team as it arrived on the south bank, and when all were over he had matched his irons to the brands on four mules, which he formally claimed. In the days that followed other claimants appeared and took so much of the work stock that orders were given to move out and "stop the game."

Traders like Gregg were transients, here today and gone (*gracias á Dios*) tomorrow. But a second type of gringo adventurer began to move in during the twenties. This was the marrying American, often a man of superior manners and some means, who married a local girl of good family, embraced Catholicism, changed his citizenship, and became a substantial member of the community. The aristocrats of Paso del Norte, even in those far-off times, were not entirely provincial, and neither were the Americans who were taken into their families. They lived graciously, accepted the responsibilities imposed upon them by a patriarchal society, and considered themselves inferior to nobody.[12]

The men of El Paso were brave Indian fighters, far travelers, possessors of flocks and herds. The women were firmly religious, busy with good works, keenly conscious of their far-reaching family ties, proud of their positions. An outsider who married into one of those families needed to be an exceptional person, and as time went on so many special cases arrived that the whole pattern of existence in the community was affected.

An early arrival of this type was a Kentuckian, lately from Missouri, named Hugh Stephenson, a big, brave, responsible, busy person who did much to develop the resources of the area and who passed his talents on to descendants who occupy positions of trust on both sides of the border. He "followed the rivers" and the beaver south in 1824, [13] liked what he saw in the El Paso vicinity, and went into business as a Santa Fe trader with headquarters near Mesilla on the future site of Las Cruces. In August, 1828, he married Juana Ascarate, only daughter of Juan and Eugenia Ascarate and heir to a considerable fortune in land, cattle, and mines.[14] Between 1830 and 1840 Hugh and Juana built their great house called *La Casa Grande el Alto* in their own little community of Concordia at the eastern end of the settlement on the north bank.[15] Concordia Cemetery and the few adobes that remain of the old Concordia military post are all that is left to tell us where Concordia was.

The Stephensons lived like the aristocrats they were, and they took their obligations to society seriously. Hugh's great-grandson observes that Don Hugo's "greatest zeal was in personally helping, counselling, and befriending the poor, sick and needy. These came to him from far and near, surely knowing that his house was always open to them and that they would not be disappointed."[16]

His portrait, made when he was sixty years old or better, shows an erect and vigorous man with long white hair combed across a high, bald forehead, a pair of keen, indomitable eyes, a tight, determined mouth and a firm chin. His face is clean shaven. His clothes are well cut and well kept. He remains a Kentucky gentleman after thirty years or more in an environment which is supposed, at least by fiction writers, to convert brisk Americans into debilitated and degenerate expatriates.

Don Hugo stayed out of trouble most of his life, though his Southern loyalties cost him much of his property after the Civil War.[17] He was respected and beloved even by such hard-nosed Yankees as W. W. Mills, and he continued to be esteemed by his fellow townsmen until he died in October of 1870.

Of similar calibre was James Wiley Magoffin, likewise a Kentuckian and a Santa Fe trader. The Mexicans called him Don Santiago and made a place for him in the most exalted circles of provincial society. His services in preparing the way for Kearny's bloodless conquest of New Mexico are well known and were recognized and rewarded by the United States government.[18] His service to the Southern cause during the Civil War was almost as important. His great adobe mansion, built when he settled in the Valley in 1849, was a center of culture and hospitality, especially after Fort Bliss was established, practically in his back yard, in 1853.[19] Don Santiago himself was a lively, witty, companionable person, like Hugh Stephenson a Southern gentleman. His first and second wives, sisters, belonged to the important Valdéz family of San Antonio.[20]

These marrying Americans, and others like them, appeared in the Valley in the 1820's. In due time they set up their own private communities on the north bank, but they were not the first to take up land on what is now the American side. In 1827 development was begun by one of the most important citizens of Paso del Norte — Juan Ponce de Leon, a rich and important person with a practical monopoly of the hauling and freighting done to and from the town, a flour mill at the south end of the dam where the "falls" of the Rio Grande provided water power, and many fertile acres on the south bank of the stream.

In February, 1827, Ponce petitioned the *ayuntamiento* for title to a piece of land half a league from the plaza and across the river. He apparently had been cultivating these acres for some time but now wished to make it legal.[21] Appraisers valued the grant at 80 pesos, which Ponce considered too much, but he went ahead with the steps necessary to acquiring title. The surveyors moved in, and eventually the *alcalde* from Paso del Norte went through the time-honored formalities of giving possession. He took Ponce by the right hand and led him over his two *caballerías* of land. Ponce did his part by picking up a few clods, breaking them in his hands, and scattering them to the four directions.[22] He received a second grant on May 4, 1830. The two tracts together were known for many years as *El Rancho de Ponce* and their fields of corn and wheat waved where downtown El Paso now presents its acres of brick and asphalt.

The river at that time ran approximately down Second Street, on the edge of our downtown section. Ponce's irrigation ditch followed San Francisco Street, watering the fields en route, and nourishing the vineyard which flourished where the United States Courthouse and the City County Building now stand.[23]

Probably nobody lived at the ranch for some time. Ponce built a shack on the river bank on what is today the corner of Second and El Paso streets and is said to have had a tannery near this location.[24] These buildings washed away in 1830. Where the White House Department Store and the Mills Building stand now, Ponce later put up a two-room shelter. Sometimes a herdsman or a farmer spent a night there, but Ponce never lived there at all according to the most recent authorities.[25]

In the years that followed, Ponce's grant passed into other hands,[26] but his *rancho* was the first attempt at occupation of the north bank of the river and was the beginning of El Paso, Texas.

While Ponce was cultivating his acres and growing richer, news came from Mexico that the gringos in Texas had revolted against the Mexican government. This fact did not affect the local citizens much. Texas was so far from their sphere of interest that they felt little personal concern, and the fact that the Congress of the newly created republic claimed all the land east of the Rio Grande from the mouth to the source — including Ponce's ranch — was not a thing to take seriously.[27]

The Pass community, however, was obliged to participate in these issues sooner than anybody in the town expected or desired. The first sharp reminder of the new developments was the arrival of a forlorn and dejected group of Anglo prisoners, the survivors of what has come to be called the Texan Santa Fe expedition. Leaving Austin, Texas, in the late summer of 1841, this group marched across the Staked Plains to offer the New Mexicans the blessings of citizenship in the Republic of Texas. The lost and demoralized members broke up into small parties which were arrested one by one by the waiting Mexican soldiery as they came into the Pecos Valley. They were herded down the *camino real*, afoot and miserable, to prison in Chihuahua, shepherded by a sadist named Damasio Salazar. Following instructions (he said), he removed the ears from those who died, or were shot, strung them on a wire, and delivered them to Don José Manuel Elias González, the commanding officer at Paso del Norte.[28]

General Elias was indignant and promptly put Salazar in his place. His fellow townsmen shared his indignation and did their best to feed, clothe and comfort the prisoners. Foremost among them was the young *cura* of Paso del Norte, Father Ramon Ortíz. He could not take care of all 180 prisoners personally, but he did everything he could, and his household was busy for days making shirts and underwear, cooking uncounted meals and heating water for uncounted baths.

An unusual friendship sprang up between the priest and a prisoner named George Wilkins Kendall, co-founder of the New Orleans *Picayune,* who had joined the group in order to report its activities. Kendall was a lively and talented young man who responded to the real nobility of the young priest's character, and Ortíz was just as much drawn to the young journalist. "Seldom," said Kendall, in the book which carried the story of these events all over the world, "have I parted from a friend with more real regret than with Ortíz, and as I shook him by the hand for the last time, and bade him, perhaps, an eternal adieu, I thought if ever a noble heart beat in man it was in the breast of this young, generous and liberal priest."[29]

Until his death in 1896, Ortíz commanded the love and respect of everybody on both sides of the International Boundary,[30] but his contacts with Americans in the years which followed brought him more grief than joy. His next involvement came in 1846. In May of that year the forces of Mexico and the United States came to blows on the lower Rio Grande and the two countries prepared for war. President Polk, with one eye on the profitable Santa Fe trade, lost no time in directing the Governor of Missouri to raise a volunteer force to cooperate with the regulars under Colonel (later General) Kearny. The First Regiment of Mounted Missouri Volunteers was quickly organized and chose as its commander a tall, red-headed Kentucky lawyer named Alexander Doniphan, whose exploits thereafter made some important Southwestern history.

After his bloodless occupation of Santa Fe, Kearny detached Doniphan's regiment for special duty. First came a campaign against the Navajos, and when this was successfully concluded, the unit struck southward along the Rio Grande, leaving its artillery with Colonel Price, who feared a native uprising. The plan was to join forces with General Wool, who was to come from the lower Rio Grande to Chihuahua.

Those Missourians were a strange and wonderful lot. Doniphan's men were mostly farm boys. They didn't believe much in uniforms and they thought even less of military drill and discipline. Doniphan, who combined a rugged firmness with considerable kindness of heart, loved his boys, and they loved him. As a result they did what he told them to do, but they expressed themselves freely about what they were doing and about the officers for whom they were doing it.[31]

The English traveler George F. Ruxton came upon them in camp at Valverde in the park-like bottom lands of the Rio Grande twenty miles below Socorro. A concentration of traders shepherding over 300 wagons and a million dollars worth of goods had stopped there weeks before the troops arrived, unwilling to go on into hostile territory and happy to follow military orders to wait for Doniphan to catch up.[32] Their wagons were arranged on the east bank to make a formidable fortification in case of need. Across the stream was the campground and Ruxton, once an officer in the British army, was amazed at what he saw in their camp: "From appearances no one would have imagined this to be a military encampment. The tents were in line, but there all uniformity ceased. There were no regulations in force with regard to cleanliness. The camp was strewn with the bones and offal of the cattle slaughtered for its supply, and not the slightest attention was paid to keeping it clear from other accumulations of filth. The men, unwashed and unshaven, were ragged and dirty, without uniforms, and dressed as, and how, they pleased. They wandered about, listless and sickly looking, or were sitting in groups playing at cards, and swearing and cursing, even at the officers if they interfered to stop it (as I witnessed). . . . The greatest irregularities constantly took place. These very men, however, were as full of fight as game cocks and shortly after defeated four times their number of Mexicans at Sacramento, near Chihuahua."[33]

While all this was going on, there was much alarm at the Pass and in Chihuahua, the capital city. The news of the outbreak of hostilities reached Chihuahua in June and provoked great indignation against the "unjustified and iniquitous aggression" which threatened the land. In the Legislature Roque J. Morón rose to protest. Addressing the Americans in general, he asked, "What has this unfortunate country done to you? . . . Oh! Is a benign and hospitable state, afflicted and desolated for fifty years by savages and inundated by the blood of its men and by the tears of its widows and orphans — is this a fitting theatre for displaying the power of the United States, drowning out in the clamor of an unjustifiable war the indignant voices raised from the tombs of Franklin and Washington?"[34]

In this spirit of righteous wrath the citizens of Paso del Norte and its environs prepared for battle. On June 22 Don Sebastian Bermúdez, the Prefect, wrote to the Secretary of Government in Chihuahua declaring that all the inhabitants of his district "with the greatest enthusiasm have offered their persons and every variety of sacrifice to repel the unjust aggression of the North Americans." Colonel José Ignacio Ronquillo was named head of the auxiliary forces to be raised in the district, and the enlistment of volunteers began in the Valley towns.[35] Father Ortíz was foremost among the organizers.

General Angel Trias, in charge of all defense efforts, ordered a scouting party out while all this was going on. At the end of the second week in August Colonel Mauricio Ugarte brought 380 soldiers into Paso del Norte on his way to investigate the state of affairs in the north. Within a few days he was back, having marched as far as Socorro, a hundred miles from Santa Fe. There he met the fleeing Governor Armijo and learned of Kearny's take-over. Armijo advised him sensibly to go back to Chihuahua. What could his three hundred do against Kearny's six thousand? Ugarte wasted no time in following this advice.[36]

What were the people of Paso del Norte thinking and feeling during this time? They have been charged with indifference to the occupation of their town and even indifference to the fate of their country. Senator Benton, who knew them only by report, describes them as "comfortable"[37] burghers who valued their prosperity above all. Dr. Wislizenus, who was in El Paso when Ugarte passed through, reported that "the people of El Paso seemed very indifferent to who should be the conqueror."[38] Some American historians like to think that the citizens secretly wished for American rule.[39] Anyone who knows the Mexicans could never believe this. A fiercely patriotic people with a strong sense of national honor, they have died by the thousands during the last century for their country's welfare. They could not have been indifferent to this invasion.

Actually it was a confusing time for these people, so far from the political heart of their nation. The country was going through a difficult period and to even the most devoted Mexican it was not always clear where his loyalties lay. Armando B. Chávez in his history of Juárez notes that "from 1846, the date of the invasion, to 1848, the date of the treaty, seven different men governed Chihuahua at eleven different periods."[40]

The orders which came from headquarters were not consistent. At the moment when the defense organization was beginning to shape up, a letter was received from the Secretary of Government in Chihuahua: "Since it is impossible for the forces of the state to risk a complete and decisive battle on account of the chances of its complete ruin with small probability of favorable outcome on account of the lack of arms, horses and munitions; and since a war of extermination must be waged against the Americans until they or the state succumb . . . at the moment that the enemy is known to have begun to march toward this capital, your Excellency will take measures to disperse through the interior all livestock and all supplies of all classes; and all the troops, State Guard and local volunteers will march to the Villa of Aldama, retreating in such a manner as to give constant annoyance to the enemy."[41]

The government at this moment apparently intended to pursue a scorched-earth policy and let the Americans starve themselves into defeat. Something changed the plans, however, and by the end of September Don Sebastian Bermúdez, the Prefect, was admonishing his followers: "The hour has come when with much ardor and firmness we must as good Mexicans give to the world, and particularly to the North Americans, a testimony that while we exist we will not permit ourselves to be oppressed. . . ."[42]

Stories circulated about the brutality of the invaders — the same sort of inventions that had made the Santa Feans shudder: the Americans were coming to take everything, and "besides abusing the women, these ruffians would brand them on the cheek as mules were branded."[43] Indignation at the fate the Americans were preparing for them, or simple patriotism, or both, induced a band of local militia to march northward on October 12. But there was dissension and dissatisfaction in the ranks, and by the time they reached Doña Ana, fifty miles away, the men were close to mutiny. They turned around and came back.

In Chihuahua the news of this second retreat aroused Governor Trias to make a supreme effort. He gathered all the troops and supplies he could and sent them off to Paso del Norte with his last exhortation ringing in their ears:". . . chastise the enemy if he should have the audacity to set foot upon the soil of this state."[44]

By the middle of December a sizable force had assembled at the Pass — close to 1,200 men with four pieces of artillery. About 400 of them were regulars, including some of the useless presidial troops, for whom nobody had any respect. Several hundred more were members of the National Guard and the rest were local boys who, according to a Mexican authority, were used to fighting Indians and very effective in ambushes and personal combats but unskilled in managing pitched battles.[45] This mixed and undisciplined group went into camp at the dam, where the old Spanish bridge had once spanned the river and where Juan Ponce de León had his dilapidated flour mill, and waited for orders to march. In their ears still rang the passionate rhetoric of Sebastian Bermúdez, the Prefect of the community: "In a cause as just as that in which we fight, we must not doubt for one moment that the God who protects the innocent is on our side and will defend us against the perfidy and bad faith of our neighbors who, with arms in their hands, invade today the territory of our district."[46]

Meanwhile Doniphan had mustered his men in the campground at Valverde and prepared for the difficult march across the Jornada del Muerto. On December 12 the first detachment of his troops moved out. Two more detachments followed. By December 23 the three groups had united at Doña Ana, cold and tired but still full of Missouri spirit. They moved downriver, and on Christmas Day, 1846, halted just below the old campground called *Bracito* (from an arm of the river) near a group of round-topped sand hills known as *Los Temescalitos.*[47] They were about thirty miles from El Paso. Behind them the force was strung out for miles in typical careless fashion, some guarding the slow-starting traders' caravan, some herding loose horses, some just taking their time.

Word of their approach was brought to Colonel Gabino Cuilty in camp at the Pass. The Colonel was contending with a serious illness which had been diagnosed as "brain fever." Shortly after the news arrived, he left for Chihuahua with the regimental physician, and the command devolved upon Lieutenant Colonel Luis Vidal.

Vidal decided not to stake everything on one pitched battle. He kept perhaps half his force at the narrows and put them to extending and improving the fortifications which were already in existence. He ordered Lieutenant Colonel Antonio Ponce de León (no relation of the El Paso capitalist, so far as we know) to take command of the dragoons and some of the El Paso militia[48] and make contact with the enemy.

He did not believe that the coming operation would amount to much. The American force, he told his troops, consisted of some three hundred ragged volunteers who could be "lanced like rabbits."[49] His orders indicate that he considered the expedition in the light of a scouting foray, and that he may have meant to make his real stand at the Pass:

The enemy shall be engaged until put to flight . . . provided its numbers do not exceed, according to assurances, from three hundred to four hundred men. In case the enemy should have received reinforcements to such extent that it may be superior in numbers, you will take precautions, according to your military knowledge, to fall back, with object of holding the line of defense established at this camp. . . .[50]

Nobody in Doniphan's camp had any suspicion that there would be a battle. No sentries were out. The men were scattered through the bottoms foraging for wood to cook supper with and looking for grass which might be worthy of their horses. Not all of the force had come up, and some units were miles to the rear. Colonel Doniphan and several of his officers and men were playing cards to determine the ownership of a horse belonging to a couple of Mexican scouts who had been detected and shot the day before, and the Colonel was piling up points in a game known as Three-trick Loo.[51]

It was about three o'clock when a man came to the Colonel in haste and called his attention to a dust cloud rising in the hills in the direction of El Paso. At first Doniphan was skeptical that the moment of truth had really arrived and was inclined to continue with the business in hand. But when he actually saw the banners and uniforms of the Mexican cavalry, he jumped to his feet, remarking that the game would have to be finished later. "But remember that I am ahead," he cautioned the players.[52]

The bugle sang assembly. Men came running in from every direction, lining up wherever a troop was forming, hunting frantically for rifles, working against time. In a matter of a few minutes they were in line of battle, or what had to serve as a line of battle — all cheerful and excited. They were quite ready for whatever was going to happen, but their ragged appearance and raggeder formation must have persuaded the Mexican regulars that Lieutenant Colonel Vidal was right.

Colonel Ponce had arranged his own troops in a long line which overlapped the smaller American force on either end. The cannon was in the middle, guarded by the local volunteers. On either wing he placed his cavalry — on the right the five hundred dragoons from Vera Cruz and Zacatecas, smartly uniformed men in blue trousers, green coats with red trimmings, and tall caps trimmed with brass and surmounted by horsehair plumes. This imposing body halted three-quarters of a mile from the Americans while a well mounted officer spurred forward, holding erect a slim lance with a small black flag flying at the tip. The little black flag was a threat. It meant "No Quarter."

Colonel Doniphan advanced a few steps in front of his men with his interpreter, a Missouri youth named Colbert Coldwell[53] who had learned some Spanish in the Santa Fe trade. He told Coldwell to see what the Mexicans had in mind. Whether the Colonel instructed him what to say in the ensuing conversation is not clear from the record.

"Our general orders your commander to come before him."

"Tell him our commander will meet him half way."

"No, he must come into our camp."

"If your general wants peace, tell him to come here."

"Then we will charge and take him. We will not ask or give quarter."

"Charge and be damned."[54]

The trumpet sounded in the Mexican lines and the whole body began to move forward. The ground was rough and broken, dotted with sandy hillocks and underbrush, and their progress was not rapid but the dragoons looked very military and the infantry worried the Americans with four or five rounds of rifle fire, mostly ineffective because they aimed too high. Twice the brass howitzer paused to discharge two pounds of scrap metal which whistled over the invaders' heads.

The Missourians stood firm and did not return the fire until only about sixty yards separated the two lines, although the officers had a hard time to hold them back. Doniphan even ordered some of the men to lie down until he gave the word to fire.

The Mexicans were much encouraged and thought everything was going their way. There were only about 500 men in the American ranks and they seemed to be falling down. Nobody was shooting. Could it be possible that they intended to give up without a fight? The Mexicans had their answer when the word was passed, "Let them have it," and the riflemen began to fire. They made almost every bullet count.

Meanwhile the dragoons brought their force to bear against the left side of the American line, coming in at a diagonal. The tip of the line pulled back on the left so as to present a solid front to the charge. Convinced that the enemy was retreating, the dragoons rode in at a gallop, only to be blasted by more bullets from the Missouri rifles. Those who were still in the saddle veered off toward the wagons, which were parked on the American left, but the wagoners were sharpshooters too, and poured in a heavy fire which sent the dragoons into precipitate retreat.

Meanwhile the detachments of Doniphan's force which were coming up from the rear when the firing started made haste to get into the battle. The dust raised by their approach rose into the sky and the Mexicans thought a huge number of reinforcements were approaching.[55] Caught off balance and unable to regroup,[56] the Mexican force was soon in full flight, pursued by sixty mounted soldiers who followed the retreat for miles but never caught up with the fleeing dragoons.

Only one of the four Mexican cannons was brought into action. After it had fired a couple of rounds a Missourian, unidentified, asked "What the hell you reckon that is?"

"A cannon, I believe," one of his friends replied.

"Then let's go and get it." And they did.[57]

Everything fell into their hands — ammunition, weapons, supplies. Among the supplies was a quantity of the El Paso specialty, Pass wine. This provided a stimulus for the celebration that followed the fight and the victors did not quiet down until well into the night.

They had reason to be triumphant. Not one American was killed and only seven were wounded. The Mexicans lost perhaps a hundred killed and wounded. An exact count was, of course, not possible.

It was not much of a fight. Historians have spoken scornfully of this "farcical brush, lasting thirty or forty minutes in all," and expressed doubt that it ever should have been called a "battle."[58] It happens, however, that it is the only battle that was ever fought in the El Paso vicinity and since it is ours, we shall continue to be impressed by it.

It was a sad day for the Mexicans, in particular for Colonel Antonio Ponce de Leon. In his official report he described the action, as he saw it. As the battle began, he said, "I shouted victory to the glorious General Santa Anna and to my country; and finding that all my troops responded with enthusiasm and decision to the desire for combat, I was led to predict a certain victory; therefore I ordered my line of attack to move forward in regular time; and perceiving the entire column of cavalry on my left had ceased to move, I repeated my orders. . . . I saw that the Vera Cruz dragoons were running at full speed towards the right, where the firing did not reach, and that the whole of the left wing of the cavalry and

National Guard also took no part in the combat, but, on the contrary, some of them were already running away. Under such conditions, I wished to force the charge myself and to lead it in person, as in fact was undertaken; but some close volleys of the enemy and the endless number of hand grenades which they threw at us exactly at the most critical moment of the attack, completely disorganized the cavalry which turned tail with incredible haste. . . . I with my aides and Captain Juan Ruiz, who was my adjutant, remained at the enemy's front until wounded by a shot which I received in my left side; and without hope of any rally, I proceeded in search of the rest of the force. I . . . make the request that you, as Commander of the Department, will order an investigation with respect to me and my conduct in the unfortunate action of the 22nd, as it touches my honor, and the pure and simple truth as to the part I took."[59]

The investigation that Ponce asked for took place with unaccustomed speed. He was arrested, charged with cowardice, and taken to Chihuahua for trial. There we lose track of him.

His men went through Paso del Norte in small groups like a series of small whirlwinds, pausing only to commandeer supplies and horses and leaving the natives more disgusted than ever with their defenders.[60]

When on the twenty-seventh the advance guard of Doniphan's troops appeared in the Pass where Vidal had meant to make his stand, there was nobody to oppose them. Instead a delegation of townspeople met them to explain that they had been forced to take up arms against their will and to restore a number of horses that had been stolen from the Americans. They all rode into town together taking the rougher but less sandy route on the left bank which passed by Ponce's ranch — "a very pretty bottom with rows of cottonwoods and vineyards on each side"— on their way to the ford.

It was surprising and gratifying to the soldiers as they came into the settlement to note the cordiality of the townspeople. By the time they reached their campground in a field or vineyard some distance beyond the Plaza, all the men were carrying grapes, apples, pears, peaches, gourds of wine — all presents from the friendly townspeople.[61]

The men were favorably impressed by everything but the weather. A standard-model local dust storm was in progress as they went into camp. There were few tents and most of them were exposed to the full force of the December wind. They found it almost impossible to prepare food and complained that what they cooked was about equal parts nourishment and dirt. They endured the flying sand for four days, after which they moved to more comfortable quarters on the Plaza.[62]

The important men of the town came to Doniphan on the morning of December 28 and mutually satisfactory arrangements were worked out. Three American prisoners in the jail, Arkansas citizens on their way to California, were liberated. The Colonel proclaimed a peaceful policy toward those who "remained peaceable and neutral." He promised to pay for all supplies needed by his men and to punish all who abused the citizenry. He forbade the sale of spiritous liquors to his men (though they seemed to get all they wanted in the days that followed). Actually the only oppressive measure he took officially was to order a search of all houses for arms.

When his intentions became known, the fearful citizens who had fled in fear of the American barbarians came back, and during the time (forty-two days) that the troops occupied the town, they reached a rather good understanding with the people. There were abuses and exactions and misunderstandings, of course, but on the whole this first large-scale contact between Latin and Anglo did not turn out badly.

Juan Ponce de León, the richest man in town, and Guadalupe Miranda, formerly a state official and now an *alcalde* of Paso del Norte, were most attentive to Doniphan and helped to make the occupation not merely bearable but sometimes pleasurable for all.[63]

The only man among the top citizens who was less than patient was Ramon Ortiz, the *cura*. Father Ortiz was a notable patriot who could not bring himself to regard the invasion of his country with patience though he was able and willing to love his enemies, as he had shown on the occasion of the visit of the Santa Fe Expedition prisoners in 1841. He refused to give lip service to Doniphan, and the Colonel had him confined lest he organize the opposition to American control. In fact, Doniphan took him along as a hostage when he eventually took the road to Chihuahua, letting it be known that any hostile movement would result in the death of the beloved priest.[64]

The other civic leaders entertained the officers, wined them and dined them, and created an era of good feeling which none of the invaders could have hoped for a few days previously.

The traders who had moved southward under Doniphan's protection arrived in the wake of the invaders and set up shop in hired rooms and stores. They supplied the soldiers as well as the townspeople and trading was lively and profitable.

In spite of almost daily alarms and rumors of the approach of Mexican forces from Chihuahua,[65] the men enjoyed themselves. One group spent ten days upriver on a hunting expedition and had "much sport." The soldiers made friends with the citizens, called on the girls, learned a few words of Spanish, and had their mouths burned by the chile-flavored food. The ones who wanted to carouse managed to do so — particularly in a saloon kept by a Frenchman at the southeast corner of the Plaza. A couple of brawls occurred there, and one stabbing in which an officer named Wells had a knife driven entirely through his neck. Miraculously he recovered.[66] There were dances and much strolling in the Plaza. And there was gambling. The Missourians found the Mexicans as keen gamblers as themselves, which was saying a good deal, and before long games were running full blast in the open street around the Plaza — monte, faro, chuck-a-luck, black jack. "When the weather was pleasant the streets about the plaza were crowded with Mexicans and American soldiers engaged in betting," John Hughes wrote in his diary. "This vice was carried to such an excess at one time," he adds, "that Col. Doniphan was compelled to forbid gambling on the streets, in order to clear them of obstruction."[67]

Gambling was not all that went on. Hughes notes on Wednesday, January 13, that three men were court-martialed for rape. There were "novel occurrences" at the fandangoes or dances, as Hughes noted. On one occasion "negroes took the shine & danced with the belle of El Paso."[68] Unfortunately we do not know who the belle of El Paso was, but apparently the dances went from bad to worse. On the seventeenth Col. Doniphan by order put a stop to "horse & mule racing & fandangoes."[69]

The men who were there took widely different views of what went on. George Rutledge Gibson, who did the quartermaster's chores for Doniphan's little force, remarked that "The army was composed of men of a restless and roving disposition, and the little discipline which prevailed was totally insufficient to prevent rioting and dissipation."[70] Marcellus Ball Edwards, commenting on the death of a comrade, remarked: "Our hospital affairs are conducted scandalously. There is not a surgeon or steward who can much more than determine calomel from quinine, and not one who would leave the card table to attend the deathbed of his patient."[71]

One modern commentator is probably quite right when he declares that "Mexico was hard-used by Johnny Gringos who, as Susan Magoffin remarked, were 'not careful at all how much they soil the property of a friend much less an enemy.'"[72]

Whatever the Mexicans thought of the gringos (and it certainly was not all bad), the boys from Missouri were mostly charmed with the Mexicans and their town. They agreed on the kindness and hospitality of the *Paseños,* whom they regarded as having "more intelligence than exists in Santa Fe, and both men and women present a neater appearance and have more refinement."[73] They praised the wine, the fruit, the climate. They found the architecture interesting, especially the patios — cheerful green oases with flowers and birds, privacy and peace, hidden behind the "dismal doors" of the adobe houses.[74] They made curious visits to the ancient church with its five bells "pretty much used up, only one of them making tones superior to a brass kettle."[75]

One of them, John T. Hughes, talked himself into believing that the place was a potential paradise and sent off an account to the War Department which he hoped would result in an American take-over. The scenery, he said, was "grand and picturesque beyond description." All the country needed was "an energetic American population" to bring in the millenium.[76]

They were young men, and the most interesting thing in the world, even for the intellectuals and the diary writers, was girls. The shapely young women were good for a thrill, as they have been for thousands of soldiers and travelers and staid local citizens ever since. It was something to see one of them on her way to church, sitting sideways in the saddle, her escort holding the reins with his arms around her. "I could not see the face of the lady, but judging from the brilliancy and sweet expression of her dark, melting eye, peeping like a star through the folds of her rebozo, it must have been beautiful."[77]

George Rutledge Gibson was fortunate enough to be on good terms with the women of the Espinosa family. Juan Espinosa, he confided to his diary, "has taken such a fancy to me that he brought all his women to see me. . . . His sister is a pretty girl with dark eyes, black hair, and a brunette complexion, and, like all women in the country, has a fine form and pretty hands and feet. Generally the women have small hands and tapering fingers, and altogether are superior in form to the American, probably because lacing and such things are unknown. I, of course, embraced her when she left, according to the fashion of the country, and had no objection to repeat the ceremony at another visit which she subsequently paid me."[78]

Colonel Doniphan's reason for lingering at Paso del Norte was not his fascination with the town. On his arrival, he found to his consternation that General Wool, to whom he was expecting to report at Chihuahua, had not come near the place. Now the boys from Missouri were cast adrift in the sea of sand and had to decide whether to retreat or go on. Rumors came constantly to their ears that ten thousand Mexicans were gathering at Chihuahua or were actually marching north to wipe them out. They would be slaughtered if they went on, and they would be disgraced if they retreated. As volunteer troops organized on the American frontier plan, they had some right to a voice in the decision, and one observer says the question was actually put to a vote.[79] The majority decided it would be better to press on. Doniphan, however, was unwilling to face heavy odds without his artillery, so he waited at Paso del Norte for forty-two days, until his guns caught up with him. Colonel Price would send him only six pieces, for the Taos revolt was simmering, and Price knew he was going to need firepower. He spent the interval accumulating supplies, gathering what arms and ammunition he could find, and enjoying the people and the climate. One of his special orders sent a crew of men to repair Ponce's mill at the dam above the town so that enough wheat could be ground to provide for the journey.[80]

The guns arrived on February 1, six of them,[81] and fired a salute which brought the people out of their houses and sent them up on their flat roofs in droves to see what was going on. The Missourians acknowledged the salute as best they could with a feeble blast from the two-pounder taken at Brazito, and the artillerymen marched in to the tune of *Yankee Doodle*.

A week later, February 8, the column moved out, leaving half a dozen of their number in the local cemetery and two privates who had become attached to local girls and preferred desertion and connubial bliss to any further chances at military glory. The battle of Sacramento was fought and won just outside Chihuahua on February 28 and the Missourians went home by way of Monterrey and New Orleans to more wining, dining, and hero worship than any group of Missourians had enjoyed up to that time — probably more than any have enjoyed since.

General Sterling Price arrived with another contingent of Missourians on November 8, 1847, moved on to Chihuahua, and had the dubious distinction of winning the battle of Santa Cruz de Rosales after the war was over.[82]

It is worth noting that the Mexican historians regard the engagement at Santa Cruz as atoning for the "national disgrace" of Brazito and Sacramento. Governor Trias "fought with 200 patriots against 1,500 North Americans of the three branches of service, under command of Colonel Price, who violated the treaty of Guadalupe Hidalgo. When General Trias had to surrender after eight hours of combat, he had not one cartridge left to fire."[83]

Price's men, who seem to have been rowdier and wilder than Doniphan's, remained in Chihuahua until July, 1848, when they were ordered back across the Rio Grande.[84]

One of El Paso's future first citizens arrived with Price's men. Simeon Hart was a New York Stater who grew up in St. Louis,[85] a man of complicated personality, proud, intense, gentlemanly, ambitious. He was thirty-two years old when he became Colonel John Ralls' adjutant and struck out for Santa Fe, Paso del Norte, and Chihuahua. He fought with distinction at the final battle of Santa Cruz de Rosales[86] and was wounded during the action. With some prisoners and some wounded Missourians he stopped to rest at the *hacienda* of a hospitable miller, Don Leonardo Siqueiros. The *molino* at Santa Cruz was famous throughout the region.

Don Leonardo had five daughters, all pretty, vivacious, gracious and refined. Simeon fell in love with Jesusita, the oldest, and informed her parents that he wanted to marry her. They replied that since their countries had been so recently at war, they could not approve of such a thing. Undaunted, Simeon said he would be back in a year; and he was. When they became man and wife, he was thirty-four and Jesusita was seventeen.

In 1849 Hart was building his mill across from Ponce de León's establishment on the Mexican side of the dam, and by 1854 he and Jesusita and their growing family were living in their own house — a house which still stands. It formed one side of a great courtyard with stables and storerooms forming the others, and a sundial in the middle.

Though Simeon became rich and influential he was always hospitable, especially to travelers. He served the South well during the Civil War and passed his drive and energy on to his son Juan, an engineer and a long-time editor of the El Paso *Times*.

After this there were two El Pasos, one Mexican and one American, but in spite of irritations and misunderstandings, the relations of the two peoples after 1846 were on the whole good, and sometimes warm and close.

CHAPTER XI

The Pivotal Fifties

THE YEARS BETWEEN 1848 and 1861 revolutionized life in the Valley. With the signing of the Treaty of Guadalupe Hidalgo on February 2, 1848, the Rio Grande became an international boundary, not a private, domestic sort of river flowing between two Mexican towns. Within a short time our remote little outpost was a halfway station for transcontinental travelers; more-or-less regular mails began arriving; and stage passengers could take scheduled accommodations to somewhere else.

For various reasons people far away began to be interested in us. Texas tried unsuccessfully to grab New Mexico in 1848[1] and actually organized El Paso County in 1850;[2] the capitalists who had been talking since the 1830's about a route for an ocean-to-ocean railroad now included El Paso in their speculations; and the once-sleepy community was invaded by hundreds of soldiers, gold-seekers, Boundary Commission employees, and vagabonds of all descriptions. They brought with them boom times of a sort, but so many evils came with them that the Valley merchants and farmers often yearned for the good old days when Indians were all they had to dread.

Two things triggered the change: first, the discovery of gold on January 24, 1848, on the south fork of the American River in California; second, General Orders No. 58, issued by the Adjutant General in Washington on November 7, 1848, ordering six companies of the Third Infantry from eastern Texas to El Paso "as soon as the necessary reconnoissance can be made."[3] Gold fever and military necessity worked together to transform the life of the Valley.

The gold craze hit Texas late in that year of 1848 as a considerable segment of the population of the United States began moving west. A surprising number of emigrants decided to go overland from the Gulf Coast of Texas — a route which was fine in theory because "the distance looked shorter, the climate milder, and spring came much sooner."[4] The fact that there were no roads across the wilds of West Texas made little difference to the eager travelers. They would find a way.

General Orders No. 58 was intended partly for their benefit, partly as a first step toward the establishment of frontier defense in the newly acquired territory. General William J. Worth, commander of the Eighth Military District, worked with the emigrant organizations which gathered in several Texas towns during the winter and spring of 1849,[5] and Major Jefferson Van Horne, waiting in San Antonio for the "reconnoissance" which would establish his route, announced that he would provide protection for any emigrant group which chose to follow him.

Meanwhile a crash program of exploration began, aiming to establish routes across the cruel and inhospitable *terra incognita* west of the Texas settlements. It was so little known that when exploration began, the guides who were supposed to have some acquaintance with the terrain promptly got themselves lost.[6] A route had to be found, however. Manifest Destiny demanded it, and so did the merchants of San Antonio and Austin, who wanted a cut of the Santa Fe trade and who were rivals for the business of the assembling caravans of Forty-niners.[7]

The trail from San Antonio to Presidio, through the Big Bend, had been blazed in 1846 by Captain George W. Hughes of General Wool's invading army on his way to Saltillo.[8] John Coffee Hays and Captain Samuel Highsmith, subsidized by the merchants of San Antonio, wandered about over West Texas in the fall of 1848, followed the Hughes trail to Presidio, and turned back exhausted and defeated.[9]

The merchants of Austin tried their luck next. Colonel Robert S. Neighbors had been encouraged by General Worth to find a way west,[10] and the Austin merchants commissioned their first citizen, Doctor and Editor John S. (Rip) Ford to go along. These two tough old Texas Rangers established a route through what is now San Angelo, across the Pecos at Horsehead Crossing, and through the pass at the southern end of the Guadalupe Mountains — approximately the route of the Butterfield stages later on. It was called the Upper Road.

They noted that Americans were already gravitating toward the Pass, among them El Paso's first female resident. This was a six-foot amazon known since the Mexican War (in which she participated to the consternation of both sides) as the Great Western.[11] She was built like a battleship and was capable of knocking a man down if she thought he needed it, but was willing to get up in the night to cook him a meal if that was what he needed.[12] She was as generous with her affections as with everything else and seems to have made several men happy during her career as a camp follower with Taylor's army in Mexico. She liked them big and strong, and her current love was apt to be replaced by one bigger and stronger. When Ford and Neighbors arrived at the Pass, she was keeping a hotel or rooming house. Ford remarks humorously in his memoirs: "She has the reputation of being something of the roughest fighter on the Rio Grande; and was approached in a polite, if not humble manner by all of us — the writer in particular."[13]

A few weeks later Lewis B. Harris saw and described her, concluding his remarks with the statement, "She treated us with great kindness."[14]

This unusual woman, about whom we really know very little, has provoked a good deal of discussion and speculation.[15] We cannot tell now just how good or bad she was, but we can safely say that there has never been another El Paso resident like her.

While Ford and Neighbors were establishing the Upper Road, an official Army reconnaissance was under way, conducted by Lieutenants W. H. C. Whiting and W. F. Smith of the Corps of Topographical Engineers. They left San Antonio in February, 1849, under orders to try the trail through the Big Bend to the Rio Grande and to locate a better one if necessary. It proved to be necessary. They followed John Coffee Hays' traces to Presidio and moved from there along the Rio Grande to El Paso. It was very hard going — wagons could hardly have got through — and on the way back they pioneered a more northerly passage, following the river downstream for about a hundred miles and then striking eastward. The route they located, called the Lower Road, was the one used thereafter by the Army and by a good proportion of those traveling between East and West Texas. The frontier army posts were served by this road later. Much of it follows roughly the El Paso - Del

Rio - San Antonio highway we drive today — at seventy miles an hour instead of two or three.

The troops marched early in June, six companies and the headquarters unit plus surveyors, road builders, 275 loaded wagons, 2,500 animals (horses, mules, and beef cattle), and a number of emigrants en route to the West Coast. Colonel Joseph E. Johnston and a construction crew were in the lead.

This mighty caravan moved slowly but steadily forward, clearing and building as it went. When the terrain called for improvement, working parties from Major Van Horne's troops were assigned to the task while men, wagons, and animals waited for the road to be made.[16] Under these circumstances the hundred days consumed in covering 673 miles was not really an excessive amount of time. One by one the landmarks dropped astern — sites of future towns and forts: Uvalde, Fort Clark, Fort Stockton, Fort Davis, Fort Quitman. Then San Elizario, Ysleta, and at last the Pass community. The date of their arrival was September 8, 1849.[17]

Van Horne did not find a military post waiting for him. He did find young Benjamin Franklin Coons, a St. Louis trader operating out of Santa Fe, busily rebuilding and improving the old Ponce de León ranch. He had a store and several dwellings in operation and was enlarging corrals and storerooms to accommodate his freighting business. The Major took advantage of these preparations, leased land and buildings from Coons, and erected other structures to suit his needs and tastes. Once established, he settled down to the business of protecting tenderfeet on their way west and fighting the Apaches who were busily picking up what they could from the defenseless or the unwary. We know what the place looked like, for H. C. Pratt of the Boundary Commission painted a picture of it which has survived[18] — the first graphic representation of the town.

This was the beginning of an association between El Paso and the military which has continued with few interruptions to the present and which has had a tremendous impact on the American community at the Pass. The first post, which lasted only two years (when the troops were moved forty miles north to Fort Fillmore), was known simply as The Post Opposite El Paso, Mexico. In 1854, a new post was established at Magoffinsville, and in that same year the name was changed to Fort Bliss to honor a Mexican War hero.[19] The location has been shifted several times since and the character of the Fort has changed likewise — from an infantry post to a cavalry post to an artillery post to the largest guided-missile school in the world — the center today of a complex of integrated ranges which occupy the Hueco and Tularosa Basins for 200 miles north of the town.[20] The economy of El Paso has benefited greatly from the army payrolls, and the social life of the place has acquired a tone which it would otherwise have lacked. During the days when the Cavalry occupied the barracks and stables on Lanoria Mesa and played polo every Sunday in the arroyo below, so many second lieutenants found wives in El Paso that the town came to be known as the Mother-in-Law of the Army. Many of those second lieutenants rose to high military rank in the years that followed, and the El Paso girls who married them rated, and still rate, as generals' ladies all over the world.

Meanwhile the Forty-niners loaded their wagons and crossed the wilds in such numbers that at times the Pass community looked like one vast campground. There was no holding them back. One group actually got through on the Upper Road ahead of Ford and Neighbors, the pathfinders. This party traveled up the Pecos and across the mountains in such fashion as to strike the Rio Grande twenty-five miles above the settlement,[21] arriving with no adventures to report. The companies which followed were not so lucky. Several small parties waited at Fredericksburg for the soldiers, who were preparing to pioneer the Southern route. Disappointed in their hopes of an escort, they trailed westward anyway, some without sufficient provisions, some poorly armed, all completely unprepared for what was ahead. "Most of them," says their historian, "were lost, some were on the road to El Paso sixty days, many were without water for days at a time, and some almost died of starvation."[22] Ford and Neighbors, on their way back from El Paso in May, began meeting these parties at the Pecos and continued to meet them for some time.

The worst stretch was between the Pecos and the Rio Grande. C. C. Cox traveled this stretch in June and saw evidence of great distress and misfortune. An eyewitness reported to him that there were "no less than sixty wagons abandoned on the road between the River and this place [the Guadalupes] and that it was really distressing to witness the dead and dying animals strewn along the way." Cox himself was saved only by a series of timely rains.[23]

Lost, thirsty, sometimes under attack by Indians, they never stopped or turned back, and most of them reached the Valley settlements. D. C. Sullivan arrived in Austin early in August and reported that the emigrants camped above and below the Pass numbered "upwards of four thousand. There are 1,200 or 1,500 wagons at the same point. Provisions are scarce — not to be had."[24]

It was a bad time for the *Paseños,* who were completely unprepared for this invasion. Threatened with starvation if they parted with their stores of beans and onions and corn, they hid their supplies and sold them only when tempted by soaring prices. The less scrupulous emigrants, faced with famine in their turn, got supplies any way they could, bullying the natives and stealing from them and from the Army.[25] It was small wonder that the citizens of Paso del Norte received their visitors, when they came across the river, with something less than cordiality.

It would have been easier if the companies had kept moving, but most of them stayed several weeks to rest and reorganize and prepare for the second half of the long journey. Many of them had second thoughts about continuing. Some even decided to stay and make a start in business.

A surprising number of them recorded their impressions in letters, diaries and newspaper stories. Let us look at one of our visitors, who can stand for several thousand more. His name was C. C. Cox — an Ohio boy who came to Texas to live with his sister near Houston and joined the Thomas Smith group which reached El Paso in June. On July 4, 1849, he was in camp ten miles above the settlement, where there was grass and wood. Being a young man of conscience and sentiment, he regretted the fact that "several hundred Americans are assembled together upon this great anniversary without manifesting some special interest in the day." Since his friends were indifferent, he took up his journal. His party had arrived on June 27 without seeing a buffalo or an Indian and without loss or sickness. He liked what he saw. "The sight of this little place is truly refreshing to the weary traveller of the plains — indeed, the cool shady avenues, fragrant breezes, delicious fruits, and luxuriant appearance of everything around, makes one almost feel that he is transported to the bowers of Eden."[26]

A few days later he noted further: "During our stay here, I have devoted myself to learning the language and character of the Mexicans both of which being easily acquired, I may say that I made some progress — the former I found an agreeable pastime, particularly when instructed by the *Ladies*. . . . I must agree with the established opinion, and pronounce ignorance, indolence, and cowardice to be the predominant characteristics of these people. But in justice to the women . . . I have found them warm-hearted and generous, even to a *fault*. The Mexican man has great antipathy for the Texicans — and our men have already had several difficulties with them at this place."[27]

The beauty and warm-heartedness of the Mexican women seems to have become legendary and some of the Forty-niners reached the Valley with preconceptions which the ladies of the region could hardly have lived up to. Thomas Eastland, who came in September, 1849, wrote to his wife about it in terms which might have been different if he had been writing to somebody else. "The Señoritas of El Paso are a poor looking set," he said. I have looked in vain for those 'dark liquid eyes,' 'long silken eye lashes,' and 'fawn like figures' *some travelers* talk of — no such things in these diggings — all poetry —."[28]

The number-one topic of conversation was always Indians. In every emigrant camp, and in every home and gathering place the talk always came around to the latest depredations and what had been or could be done to stop them. Since the early 1830's the Apaches and Comanches had harried the north-Mexican states and depopulated the outlying settlements. Now the American caravans offered them new and richer pickings. As the Forty-niners swarmed across the vast vacancies of west Texas, there were hardly enough warriors to go around, but the Indians did the best they could. They ran off mules and horses and oxen, sometimes killed a tenderfoot, and kept everybody in a state of alarm.

Scalp hunting was responsible for some of their savagery. As we have seen, the governments of the Mexican states had been paying good money for scalps, off and on, for twenty years. Since 1846 the business of bounty hunting had increased prodigiously and the red men were furiously resentful. Chief Gómez, a particularly tough and hardy leader of the Mescaleros in the Davis Mountains, let it be known that he was in the business himself and would pay $1,000 for the scalp of any American or Mexican. He arrived at this figure because Governor Trias had set this price as the value of Gómez' own hair.[29] His offer did not stop such experts as Major Michael H. Chevalier and Captain John Joel Glanton from beating the Apaches at their own game. Glanton in the winter of 1849-50 is said to have surprised a band of Mescaleros in Santa Elena Canyon and "harvested" 250 scalps.[30]

The emigrants passed the reports and rumors around and C. C. Cox in July of 1849 put down what he heard: "Considerable excitement prevailed yesterday in consequence of a drove of mules having been stampeded by Apaches. These Indians make frequent descents upon El Paso and the settlements near, and inhabitants are in constant dread of their approach. Apache scalps are worth two hundred dollars, prisoners two hundred and fifty — The Authorities here offer great inducement to those who are fond of fighting — A company is being made up among the Americans for that purpose and no doubt at least a hundred will join it — I understand Major Chavalle with a small company is engaged in the business."[31]

Armando B. Chávez, the Juárez historian, confirms Cox's figures (in pesos, which were equivalent to dollars in those days) and adds that an Indian of less than fourteen years was worth fifty pesos.[32] Some of the Forty-niners may have joined one or another of the companies of Indian hunters in hopes of earning a few badly needed dollars.

The year 1849 saw the business at its peak. By 1850, according to historian Ralph Smith, the rowdy American partisans were scalping more Mexicans than Indians and had to be driven out of the country by the military.[33]

Stimulated perhaps by the bounty hunters, the Apaches worked very hard at their trade during these years. Ben Coons the freighter had a hard fight with them in November of 1849 near Guadalupe Peak and had to send to Major Van Horne at El Paso for help.[34] They ran off forty of James Magoffin's mules from the mesa no more than three miles from his house in January of 1851 and got thirty more from his corral a week later.[35] Word was constantly coming in of theft and murder somewhere in the territory where they ranged. The November 13 issue of the Los Angeles *Star* in 1852 reported that nine men had been killed within fifteen miles of El Paso during the two months preceding.[36]

The Mexicans suffered as much as the Americans, or more, and conditions became so unbearable that in 1852 Don Mariano Varela, the mayor, took personal charge of a company of determined volunteers who chased the red men as far as the Lago de Guzmán in western Chihuahua, "cleansing our villa," says Armando B. Chávez, "from this chronic calamity of our time."[37] A few months later, of course, the Indians were back in business.

All through the fifties the raids continued. "When I arrived in El Paso," Anson Mills remembered (he came in 1857), "it was dangerous to go far from the village. Mesquite root gatherers were attacked, the men killed and the animals driven off within a half-mile from the village."[38] The end was not in sight until after the Civil War.

Worse than Indians for our Latin neighbors were the fruits of war. The cession of territory was a terrible humiliation to patriotic Mexicans whose love of country, then as now, was real and passionate. The loss of Texas and the territories taken away by the treaty of Guadalupe Hidalgo reduced the national area by almost half, and during the interval between the signing of the treaty and the establishment of the boundary four years later, Nature herself added another blow to those already so deeply felt. On January 12, 1849, the river flooded and changed its course, cutting a new channel which left the three Valley towns, Ysleta, Socorro, and San Elizario, on the east bank. The land enclosed between the old channel and the new was known as "The Island." The Americans claimed it, and it is American territory today.[39]

The boundary was discussed during a series of conferences in El Paso and Paso del Norte in 1850 — conferences which were conducted in an atmosphere of complete cordiality and courtesy but which, nevertheless, were painful in the extreme to the Mexican gentlemen who had to assist at the partition of their country.

Commissioner John Russell Bartlett, who arrived in November, 1850, was a scholar whose business was publishing and selling books. His real object — which he actually attained — was to write an immortal travel book based on his experiences as Boundary Commissioner.

Establishing the dividing line was no problem to him, nor was it a problem to his opposite number, General Pedro García Condé. Each had a large staff of experts of one kind or another who proceeded to work with the utmost good will. The official map named in the Treaty of Guadalupe Hidalgo proved to be greatly in error in both latitude and longitude, but the commissioners worked out a compromise and agreed to establish the starting point of their westward progress forty-two miles north of El Paso.[40]

Then the trouble began. The "expansionists" in Washington and even important members of the Commission felt that Bartlett had bargained away the route of the transcontinental railway which was some day going to be built to the West Coast. There was much confusion, delay and anger. The Commission ran out of money. Bartlett went off on a tour of the North Mexican states. The area between the misplaced line on the official map (just north of Paso del Norte) and the Bartlett-Condé line became an area of international dispute and the two nations bristled at each other again. The Mexicans moved troops into the Mesilla Valley and the Americans almost did the same.

The solution which was found in 1853 was a final humiliation to Mexico. Santa Anna was again in power, but his regime was shaky in the extreme, in desperate need of money, and faced with general insurrection unless funds were forthcoming. James Gadsden, the United States Minister to Mexico, undoubtedly told Santa Anna that unless he would part with the disputed land for a cash consideration, the United States would take it anyway. For ten million dollars down, the United States got a boundary on the 32nd parallel, which was far enough south to provide space for the railroad. The original idea was to pay up to fifty million dollars for Lower California and the whole northern part of Mexico.[41]

A bit of drama happened at Paso del Norte as a result. Governor Angel Trias was still in town with his eight hundred soldiers at the time the treaty was signed, determined not to part with another foot of Mexican soil without a fight. David Meriwether, the new Territorial Governor of New Mexico, had accepted his position with the understanding that his job was to expedite the boundary settlement, but he found the situation delicate in the extreme. William Carr Lane, his predecessor, had proclaimed United States jurisdiction over the disputed territory, and all that saved the situation was Colonel Edwin V. Sumner's refusal to back Lane up with troops.

Late in 1854, with tension unrelaxed, Meriwether learned that the Gadsden treaty had been signed. He secured a certified copy of Santa Anna's order that the newly purchased territory be surrendered to the United States forces, opened communications with Governor Trias, and asked if, "on the production of such a paper, he would feel at liberty to surrender possession of the territory in dispute. To this he responded in the affirmative, provided I appeared with a force sufficient to protect the citizens from Indian depredations." It seems hardly likely that Meriwether could have got Trias' orders before Trias himself received them, but that is the way Meriwether tells it.

In order to complete the transaction, Meriwether, escorted by several companies of United States troops, traveled south to El Paso. At Fort Bliss, then located at Magoffinsville, he met Trias and had a pleasant interview. It was agreed that a ceremony of transfer should take place the next day at noon. "Our forces," Meriwether remembered later, "should cross the river above the falls at 12 o'clock the next day, and, on seeing the American flag approaching, he would pull down the Mexican flag, march his troops out of the fort leaving the gates open for our entrance."

It happened exactly that way. In spite of the suspicion of some of the younger officers that they were being led into a trap, Meriwether insisted on going ahead with the transaction and nothing happened to mar the spirit of the occasion. The Americans hoisted their own flag on the vacated flagpole, fired off two cannon in salute, and listened to *Hail, Columbia* and *Yankee Doodle* played by the band. Meriwether made a speech to the crowd of Mexicans who had been attracted by the solemnities and harmonies, saying that he hoped they would be law-abiding citizens of the United States but they could be Mexicans if they chose to move to Mexican territory. "The Mexicans appeared to be satisfied with what I had said to them," says Meriwether, "and applauded lustily, many coming to be introduced to me, and to whom I gave a cordial shake of the hand."[42]

In view of the fact that Meriwether and his men crossed the river "above the falls" (where the old Spanish bridge used to be, and where first Ponce de León and then Hart had their flour-milling machinery), there can be little doubt that the fort which changed hands was the stronghold erected in 1846 to prevent Doniphan's march on Chihuahua. The spot is on Mexican soil now, and certainly was then, whatever Meriwether may have thought. But it was a fine spot for a ceremony.

With the establishment of the boundary line across New Mexico and Arizona, all debate on this subject should have been at an end. For the next century and more, however, there was to be dissatisfaction and argument. More than once between 1853 and 1863, the river shifted its bed in and below El Paso. In 1864, the worst flood ever known in the Valley shifted it still more. In 1867, the river rose again, destroying Magoffinsville and the low-lying sections of Paso del Norte[43] and moving the channel far to the south and west, somewhere near its present course. From then on an area between El Paso and Paso del Norte was claimed by both sides.[44] This was the Chamizal, meaning a place where the *chamizo* — English chamisso — shrub grows freely. The question came to a head in 1894. Eventually it was submitted to an arbitration board which in 1911 decided in favor of Mexico. The United States, however, refused to accept the decision on the grounds that it was impossible to determine the location of the river at the time the International Boundary was established and that the change in its course was the result of erosion and accretion (gradual change) and not of avulsion (sudden change). The Chamizal was a grievance and an irritation to Mexico for many years and a matter of conscience to Americans who stopped to think about it. Both nations were happy and relieved when the matter was finally adjusted in 1963 and the agreement was approved by the congresses of both nations.[45] Considerable drama was added to the accord when the Presidents of the two countries met on September 25, 1964, and, in an atmosphere surcharged with international good will, unveiled a marker commemorating the agreement. It is worth noting, since this book is partly a chronicle of international relations, that while the embracing and speechmaking were going on at the site of the marker, a large crowd of Mexican citizens almost stormed the international bridge. They said they had been informed by a Mexican radio station that everybody could cross as soon as Presidents Johnson and López Mateos had left the bridge after their initial meeting. American Immigration Service men were not about to allow such a thing to happen, but their will did not prevail until they sent for the El Paso Fire Department and made preparations to wash the crowd into the river.[46] The Mexicans felt that since the Chamizal now belonged to Mexico, there was no reason why they should not enter it.

It has always been hard for Americans of decency and good will to realize how hollow the talk about a Good Neighbor Policy sounds in Mexican ears even now — though episodes such as this one at the Stanton Street Bridge should make it understandable. It is no wonder that such phrases can be and have been used with heavy irony, especially by Latins who like to talk about Yankee Imperialism and *la plutocracía de Wall Street*.[47] It is greatly to the credit of the individual Mexican that he can accept a friendly American for what he is, politely disregarding his country's grievances and remembering, as his grandfather did in 1846, that friendship and generosity and forbearance can exist between human beings in spite of what their governments do to each other.

Bartlett's arrival brought to a climax one situation which had been steadily worsening since 1849. Vice and crime were getting out of hand. A great number of undesirables had crossed the West Texas desert with Major Van Horne, and many others had been left behind when various emigrant parties reorganized and moved on. Now came Bartlett with a crew of thugs who at least equaled those already on the ground in devotion to villainy. Shorthanded, the Commissioner had been obliged to take on a number of teamsters who could give no evidence of good character. He promptly discharged them on reaching the Valley, but this was no help to the community, for they simply joined the reprobates already in residence.

They made a headquarters of the little Mexican town of Socorro in the Valley below the Pass, a place where wagon trains of the Forty-niners often stopped, and their numbers and their confidence grew to such an extent that the natives went in fear of their lives. Some of these scoundrels forced themselves into the houses of the villagers, and several families, unable to help themselves, moved out and went away. "Houses were opened for the indulgence of every wicked passion," says Bartlett, "and each midnight hour heralded new violent and often bloody scenes for the fast filling record of crime."[48]

The American soldiers stationed in the old presidio at San Elizario hesitated to become involved. They said the civilian government was responsible. It was not until a Boundary Commission employee named Edward C. Clarke was stabbed to death at a dance that effective action was taken.

Eight or nine suspects were rounded up by a posse of Mexicans, Americans, and Boundary Commission employees but the prisoners refused to take their arrest seriously, "making vulgar and obscene remarks upon their position." Although a county government had been functioning since 1850,[49] no officer had had the hardihood to contend with the lawless element, and the rascals thought they were safe. This time, perhaps because a government employee was the victim, things were different. Attorneys were appointed for prosecution and defense and the trial opened in the home of Justice Alex Berthold[50] before judge and jury — the latter made up of six Socorro citizens and six members of the Boundary Commission staff. Bartlett's description of the proceedings has become famous:

It is doubtful whether in the whole history of trial by jury a more remarkable scene than the one here presented was ever exhibited. The trial took place in one of the adobe or mud-built houses peculiar to the country, which was dimly lighted from a single small window. Scarcely an individual was present who had not the appearance and garb of men who spend their lives on the frontier, far from civilization and its softening influences. . . . There sat the judge, with a pistol lying on the table before him; the clerks and attorneys wore revolvers at their sides; and the jurors were either armed with similar weapons, or carried with them the unerring rifle. . . . The fair but sunburnt complexion of the American portion of the jury, with their weapons resting against their shoulders, and pipes in their mouths, presented a striking contrast to the swarthy features of the Mexicans, muffled in checkered *serapes*, holding their broad-brimmed glazed hats in their hands, and delicate cigarritos in their lips. The reckless unconcerned appearance of the prisoners, whose unshaven faces and dishevelled hair gave them the appearance of Italian bandits rather than of Americans or Englishmen; the grave and determined bearing of the bench; the varied costume and expression of the spectators and members of the Commission, clad in serapes, blankets, or overcoats, with their different weapons, and generally with long beards, made altogether one of the most remarkable groups which ever graced a court room.[51]

For two days it went on, under the stern eyes of a detachment of troops sent by Major Van Horne. Three men — William Craig, Marcus Butler and John Wade — were declared guilty and condemned to death.

Immediately after sentence was passed, the three were taken to the plaza in front of the church for execution. Craig and Wade refused the good offices of a priest and continued their ghastly levity till the last. Butler, who was only twenty-one, cried bitterly until his companions told him to be quiet — he could die but once.[52] And so the three of them were hanged from the same cottonwood tree while groups of determined men stood about with guns in their hands in case some of the desperadoes should attempt a rescue. It was dark before the work was finished.

A fourth man, Alexander Young, who was considered the ringleader, had escaped, but a reward was posted for him and he too stretched a rope. After that, disturbers of the peace were hard to find in the Valley for some time.[53]

As the fifties progressed, emigrant wagons became less common, but traffic continued through the Pass. Herds of cattle destined for the camps and settlements in California became a familiar sight,[54] and sometimes a temptation. In 1853 one such herd created an international incident. James Magee was the owner of most of the animals — a man about whom we know nothing but about whom we could make some informed guesses in the light of what happened. He and his men were approaching El Paso on the northern road when a gang of thieves ran off several hundred head of cattle. Magee estimated their worth at $20,000. He made two trips across the river in pursuit of his stolen stock and the second time he went, he was arrested and thrown in jail. After a week of bitter and fruitless negotiations, members of the emigrant colony, led by District Attorney Esler Hendree, tried to storm the jail and get Magee out. Hendree was killed, another American died of wounds, and Magee was hustled off to Chihuahua, where his trail ends.[55] Both governments were concerned over this breach of international etiquette; but a few months later the United States consul was able to report that all was forgotten and "the best feeling appears to exist between the people on both sides of the river."[56]

Two years later there was another invasion. On Christmas Day, 1856, a number of American soldiers got into a fight in a Paso del Norte barroom and were jailed. When the prefect refused to turn them loose, some members of the Fort Bliss garrison undertook to liberate them. Two were killed and the rest fled across the river.[57]

The Mexicans seem to have invaded the United States about as often as the Americans invaded Mexico. "On many occasions," says Morgan Broaddus, "detachments of the Mexican army appeared on the north side of the river to seek Mexican citizens who were under investigation by the Prefecto in El Paso del Norte. In January, 1853, a detail of the Mexican army entered the settlements of San Elizario and Socorro, where they demanded that the justices of the peace at both locations aid them in capturing deserters.

"The justice at Socorro refused, and the Mexican officer in charge entered his home, drawing his sword to force compliance by the public official. The residents of Socorro threatened mob violence if the Mexican soldiers attempted to arrest the deserters. *Los soldados* returned to their post south of the Rio Grande, and the deserters remained on Texas soil."[58]

The fact that nobody stayed angry over such episodes tells us something about the way the two groups got along on the border in those early times; the fact that they worked together to prevent trouble tells even more.[59]

And all the while a better day was coming closer. For one thing, the outside world was no longer so far away. The mail began to go through, and people began to go through with it. Captain Henry Skillman is reported to have been the first to carry a regular monthly horseback mail from San Antonio to El Paso in 1849 and 1850.[60] By 1851, he was operating under a regular contract.[61] In 1852, Bigfoot Wallace was doing some of the driving[62] and he continued the contest with mules and Indians over the long route for a number of years.

Not a great deal is known of the activities of the mail carriers during the early stages, but there can be no doubt that theirs was a rugged, dangerous business. Old Bigfoot used to tell tales of his experiences to his adopted family, the Bramlettes, in the Frio country south of San Antonio — tales which the children never forgot. He would describe the way he felt when the Indians attacked him some eighty miles downriver from El Paso, ran off his mules, and forced him to walk all the way to town.[63]

Always full of tales, Bigfoot would go on to tell about the trip he made one time with a friend of his called Dutch Pete. The two of them went to sleep under the stage and were still dreaming when the Indians jumped them. In the excitement Pete ran his head through the spokes of one of the wheels and nearly turned the vehicle over trying to get loose.[64]

The mail was probably carried on horseback for the first few years, and the first stages were undoubtedly buckboards or "Celerity" wagons. Concord coaches came later. But the mail did go through and the volume was sufficient to persuade the United States government that a post office was needed at El Paso. In 1852 Jarvis Hubbell became our first postmaster. At various times El Paso has been known by various names — *El Rancho de Ponce,* Franklin (probably from Franklin Coons, whose place the Mexicans called *El Rancho de Franquilín*), Smithville, Coons' Ranch. The name of the post office, however, has always been El Paso.[65]

Mail service was extended through the Pass in 1853 when George H. Giddings received the contract to carry the mails from San Antonio to Santa Fe. Operations began in July, 1854.[66] The first stagecoach in the area was probably used on the El Paso-Santa Fe portion of the run. In 1857 James E. Birch contracted for the San Antonio-San Diego route. George Giddings was in charge of the El Paso-San Antonio portion and succeeded as general manager when Birch lost his life at sea.[67]

This was the famous Jackass Trail — the first mail stage and public carrier linking the East and West coasts — so called because mules were used on some portions of the road. It was at that time "the longest uninterrupted route in the United States if not in the world."[68] Legend says that a New York shipowner bet Giddings $100,000 that one of his vessels, leaving New York on the same day the first coach left San Antonio, would arrive in San Diego first. Giddings took the bet and won it, his coach rolling into San Diego a few hours ahead of the ship. The date was August 31, 1857. The trip had taken thirty-eight days.[69] Captain Henry Skillman was in charge of the coach and the mails, and Bigfoot did part of the driving.[70]

The Jackass Trail was a pioneering venture. Its operators had to set up stage stations, establish a road west of El Paso,[71] and survive a series of weird accidents and financial reverses in order to stay in business. Simeon Hart is said to have provided financial assistance when funds ran out early in the organizing period.[72] Actually the bi-monthly stage ran over the entire distance only about forty times, but on every one of those trips the through passengers had an initiation into hardship which they never forgot. Experience would no doubt have improved the service, but the advent of the Butterfield Overland Mail led to cancellation of the portion of the Jackass Trail linking El Paso and Yuma.[73] Between San Antonio and El Paso, however, coaches traveled every week until the Civil War made all normal travel impossible.

The Butterfield Mail has had a great deal more publicity than the Jackass Trail, but undoubtedly it owed a good deal to the pioneer work of George Giddings. In the fall of 1858 the first Butterfield coach ran from Tipton, Missouri, where the rails ended, through Fort Smith, Arkansas, to Fort Chadbourne (between San Angelo and Abilene, Texas), on to "Franklin City" at the Pass of the North, and finally to San Francisco, arriving at the San Francisco Plaza at 7:30 on the morning of Sunday, October 10, after a trip of "twenty-three days, twenty-three hours and a half."[74]

The Butterfield coaches continued in operation for less than three years. In the summer of 1861 the Civil War wrote finis to this enterprise as it did to many others. But relics of John Butterfield's work can still be found here and there along his rugged route. Traces of his stage stations east of El Paso can still be seen — Pinery, Ojo del Cuervo, Thorne's Well, Alamo Springs, Hueco Tanks[75] — by people who like to look for their history away from the beaten tracks. The station at Mesilla, where according to local sages the east-bound and west-bound coaches met, is now a popular Mexican restaurant appropriately called *La Posta*.

A permanent reminder of stagecoach days in El Paso is preserved in the titles of the downtown streets, some of which were named for the destinations of one or another of the stage lines. The west-bound coaches left town by way of San Francisco Street. By the same process San Antonio, Santa Fe, and St. Louis (now Mills) Streets were labeled.

The glory of the Overland line's mid-point, the El Paso terminal, is long gone, of course, replaced by brick commercial buildings a couple of blocks from downtown El Paso. It stood on the corner of South El Paso and Overland streets, occupying two acres of ground between El Paso and Oregon street, with corrals and storage space, thirty rooms in all.[76] In 1860 a second story was added for the Frontier Hotel, which advertised large, airy rooms, careful servants, good meals, and a fine bar.[77] The Overland Company kept a large stock of goods on the premises and carried on a mercantile business of no mean proportions along with the mail and passenger enterprise.

After 1854 stagecoaches became familiar features of the El Paso scene,[78] but the year 1857 brought the natives a real surprise in the field of transportation. On July 23 of that year a party of strangers reached San Elizario in company with a local citizen named Ford. The word spread that they were the advance guard of Lieutenant E. F. Beale's camel caravan which was finding out for Jefferson Davis if the American deserts could be conquered by these ungainly beasts as the Arabian deserts had been. The precursors were in town for two days before the camels actually arrived — time enough for excitement and curiosity to reach a high pitch among the townspeople. This was decades before a circus was seen in the Valley and natives were quite naturally open mouthed and goggle eyed, following the strange creatures through town and out of town and surrounding them when the camel drivers went into camp. Beale's charges had better luck in creating excitement in the Valley towns than they did in making progress across the rocks and cactus of their new home.[79]

Members of the advance group were entertained at Fort Bliss the next day and attended a party given by the hospitable Mr. Magoffin the following night.[80] A few hours later the caravan was over the horizon, leaving a few camel tracks in the dust and an assortment of memories for the citizens to pass on to their grandchildren in later years.

As transportation and commerce picked up, the tempo of life picked up likewise. In spite of the evolution which was going on, El Paso had been a pretty dismal spot in the middle 1850's. F. R. Diffenderfer, who became the U. S. Consul in Paso del Norte and an important citizen, says of his arrival in 1857, "there were perhaps 20 small adobe houses in the place, only a portion of which were occupied. The population certainly did not exceed 50, all told. It began to show signs of progress soon afterwards when the great Overland mail line between Memphis, Tenn., and San Diego, Cal., began to run its coaches through the place. In 1857 there was only one mail a month with the States, and that by the way of San Antonio, Tex. Mail day was an event in those days. The overland mail company built a large mail building and spent a good deal of money for corn, hay and other supplies for its animals."[81]

The stage company primed a pump which continued to flow. Money came to the town. People followed the money. It is true that many of the people were bad, and El Paso's reputation as a rough and violent town was fixed for the next forty years, but that did not make it any less interesting to curious citizens in gentler regions. Gambling was probably its favorite vice, though the others were not neglected. In 1859, according to one traveler, a hundred thousand dollars would change hands in a single night.[82] Of the small American population of the town, some twenty were professional gamblers.[83]

Before the fifties were over, the steady flow of immigrants, gamblers and non-gamblers, caused El Paso to begin to think of itself as a town. In 1858 it was surveyed and platted and became a town indeed. The map maker, however, had his difficulties — the result of the peculiar temperament of Uncle Billy (William T.) Smith, at that time owner of the Ponce Grant. Uncle Billy was a white-haired, boyish-faced, almost illiterate Kentuckian who made up for his ignorance of letters by an extra measure of the milk of human kindness. After purchasing the Ponce *rancho* in 1854, he settled down to a career of cultivating his acres and his friends. When one of the latter, for any reason, decided to own a plot of ground, he had only to mention the fact to Uncle Billy and for a small consideration, or none at all, the plot became his. Boundaries were highly tentative. The new owner sowed his seeds or built his adobe house according to his fancy, and the streets of downtown El Paso reflect to this day Uncle Billy's generous but unsystematic nature.

An example of the consequences of such procedures resulted from the marriage of Judge J. F. Crosby to Josephine Bremond of Philadelphia and Austin in 1856. Josephine was a lovely lady and Uncle Billy felt that he must express his admiration of her in concrete terms. Three acres of land in the downtown section conveyed his sentiments adequately, and on these three acres, fronting Texas Street, the Crosbys built a fine house. As a consequence Kansas Street between San Antonio and Texas was not opened until after 1900.[84]

The surveyor was a young man named Anson Mills who left his mark deeply impressed on the community. An Indiana boy who had failed in mathematics at West Point and was ashamed to go home, he came to Texas in the spring of 1857, taught school for a year, and finally, with his younger brother William, took the Butterfield stage for El Paso. He had heard that it was "a promising settlement" and might eventually be an important town.[85] It was May 8, 1858, when he arrived.

Several old acquaintances from his West Point days were stationed at Fort Bliss, and with their help and the recommendation of District Judge Josiah Crosby, he secured an appointment as surveyor for the El Paso and Presidio land district and immediately became the busiest man in the place. He traveled widely, laying out army posts and surveying public lands. He even contracted with the Butterfield people to build their imposing new station. Meanwhile he was thinking, like everybody else, that the Memphis, El Paso and Pacific Railroad was surely coming and streets and business blocks needed to be ready for the wave of immigration which was just ready to break.

By this time a townsite company had actually been organized by six men who thus became the fathers of the city we live in today. Their names were Josiah F. Crosby, J. S. and H. S. Gillett, W. J. Morton, Vicente St. Vrain, and Uncle Billy Smith. The land they controlled included the Ponce grant and a 640-acre tract north of Ponce's acreage acquired by Uncle Billy through the use of land scrip. In view of his original ownership of the entire tract, he was allowed a fourth interest in the company.[86]

Mills had no difficulty in persuading these six men that a survey should be made, and they employed him to make it — something he certainly had in mind all the time since he was the only man in West Texas at that moment who was capable of doing the job.

"I continued for several months during the winter to make different sketches," Mills wrote forty-seven years later, "ignoring as far as the proprietors would allow me the irregular parcels of land and adobe buildings then existing. All these were rejected until finally about May or June, 1859, I produced one that all the six proprietors adopted and were willing to sign and did sign."

He complained that on the approved map no street ran parallel, or at right angles, to any other street in what is now our downtown section.[87]

It must be remembered that land was worth very little in 1854, and Uncle Billy had no idea that the citizens of a town of a quarter of a million people would some day be confused by his inability to draw a straight line.

For his efforts Mills was paid $150 and given four of his newly surveyed lots. He put up a tent on one of them alongside the community irrigation ditch. There he did his own cooking and lived a Spartan life completely at variance with the dignity in which he spent his latter years at 2 Dupont Circle in Washington, D. C. His map shows two of his lots on the corner of San Francisco and Santa Fe streets, the present location of the Mart Building. Louis Cardis, the Ben Ficklin Stage manager and a victim of the Salt war of 1877, lived there later, and he was succeeded by James P. Hague, the brilliant twenty-one-year old Republican District Attorney who came in 1871 from East Texas.[88] It is a historic corner, and Anson Mills in his tent was the first of a line of distinguished citizens who have occupied the premises. Bankers and businessmen taking dinner at the International Club on the top floor of the Mart Building would do well to recall these things.

CHAPTER XII

Life on the Border

 THE TOWNS which loom largest in the legendry of the west — Dodge City, Tombstone, Cripple Creek, Deadwood, Cheyenne, and the rest — were frontier towns for only a few years. Civilization moved in and ended the wide-open days after a comparatively brief interlude of violence and lawlessness. El Paso was a tough town longer than most. In the fifties she won fame of a sort as a rendezvous of hard-drinking, quick-shooting specimens — a fame which faded during the Civil War as most of the male population departed for the duration. Again in the early eighties, as the railroads raced for the Pass accompanied by a wave of shady or desperate characters, new legends of blood and sin arose and traveled throughout the land. It was not until several years after the turn of the century that civilization really caught up with El Paso — a fact which may well give our town the doubtful distinction of staying wide open longer than any other American frontier community.

There were good people, of course, but in those early times they minded their own business and did not interfere as their fellow townsmen went about the pursuit of joy or profit. And in some ways the community of the late fifties was more interesting than the one which grew up in the early eighties. With all its violence and vice, it was a cleaner, simpler place than El Paso after the railroad — or at least it seems so from this point in time.

This was partly due to the fact that it still had a rather pastoral feeling. W. W. Mills, who later became for a time the political boss of the region and left the best account of what went on before and after the Civil War,[1] says that in the fifties "nearly all that portion of the village or 'ranch' south of San Antonio and San Francisco streets was then cultivated in vineyards, fruit trees, fields of wheat and corn and gardens, for at that time and for years later there was an abundance of water in the Rio Grande all the year round, and El Paso was checkered with acequias (irrigation ditches)."[2]

The center of town was what we call now the Pioneer Plaza or Little Plaza, where San Francisco Street strikes westward to the Union Station. The main ditch ran through that sun-soaked little square and there were ash and cottonwood trees which added to the comfort of the vendors of this and that for whom the bridge across the *acequia* was a focal point. An adobe *tienda* on the southwest corner of the plaza dispensed meat, fruit, vegetables and other edibles. On the northeast corner, where the Mills Building now stands, Mrs. Gillock and her Kentucky-born husband, Major Braxton Gillock, kept a hotel. The remaining business houses straggled for a short distance down El Paso Street, so called because it led to the ford and ferry by which the citizens passed to and from Paso del Norte.

The social center, at least for the males of the community, was Ben Dowell's place on the corner where the Paso del Norte Hotel stands today. It was another thick-walled adobe structure which housed a number of attractions — the post office (from 1857 to 1860), a store, a billiard table, a bar, and accomodations for poker and gambling devices. Most meetings in El Paso in those days, friendly or unfriendly, were held in Ben Dowell's place and a fair share of the killings which redden the annals of those years happened inside or outside of Dowell's establishment.

It was the center also of the sporting life of the town — a life in which horse racing was a major ingredient. The racetrack was a three-quarter-mile straightaway stretch of dirt road which is now a part of West Overland Street. Differences of opinion about the speed of various horses were settled here, and considerable amounts of real, personal, and pecuniary property changed hands as a result. The finish line was near the junction of Overland and El Paso streets, a block from the front door of Dowell's place.

Dowell himself was the owner of a fantastically swift mare named Kit who is said never to have lost a race, and she won her share of the money.[3]

Dowell (Don Benito, the Mexicans called him) was one of the colorful characters of those days. He was a Kentuckian, big, brave and busy — almost completely uneducated but shrewd and enterprising. He had prematurely white hair, a noble beard "like corn tassels" (as his daughter described it),⁴ and sharp blue eyes.

He arrived in 1850, thirty-two years old and still shuddering over his experiences in a Mexican prison during the late war. He had absolutely nothing when he came but got a job supervising Ponce de León's vineyards spread over the acres where the streets of El Paso now run. Before long he was able to marry Juana Márquez of Ysleta. But then came years of terrible drouth when many good men left the country, Dowell among them. He tried California, where his first child Mary was born in 1854. But that country and its dying mining boom did not suit him. He was back in the Valley in 1855 working for Uncle Billy Smith — later for the Butterfield stage people.⁵

It was now that he began to lay the foundations for the fortune which was to elude him till the end of his life. Although he is always mentioned as the owner of a saloon, he was by training and instinct a farmer. He was the first to send for and keep on file the bulletins of the Department of Agriculture, and he kept up a correspondence with the officials of the Bureau. He is said to have introduced sweet potatoes and alfalfa to the valley and to have taught the fruit growers of Paso del Norte how to make peach brandy. His skills included carpentry, surveying, and butchering, and he was a wheelwright and wagon maker. He was a Mason (one of the first in the Southwest), a justice of the peace, postmaster from 1857 to 1860,⁶ El Paso's first mayor (in 1873) and the town's father confessor for many years. It goes without saying that he was able to take care of himself in a fight and accounted for at least one desperado who needed killing. This happened on August 7, 1856, when a character named Blair, whom Dowell had accused of robbing the customhouse safe a year previously, appeared in El Paso breathing threats of vengeance. Somebody tipped Dowell off, and when Blair stepped through the door of the saloon, Dowell greeted him with a charge of buckshot. There were no repercussions.⁷

If Ben Dowell had an obsession it was the idea that the railroad was coming and would make them all rich. With this in mind he accumulated property — several lots in town and 3,000 acres of prime Valley acreage north of the village. It is worth noting here that when he died of pneumonia in 1880 (after getting soaked while repairing a break in an irrigation ditch), the railroad was only six months away from El Paso and Ben had already begun to reap his profits. It was said of him, "He lived poor but he died wealthy."[8]

El Paso before the Civil War was never much more than a village. The census of 1860 lists 428 residents — 144 Americans and 263 who bore Spanish names. Only seven Anglo women are reported,[9] obviously not enough to go around, and it was natural that many of the gringos should marry, or live with, Mexican women. It is only fair to add that W. W. Mills, no sentimentalist, describes the Mexican population as "a much better class than those who came in later with the advent of the railroad."[10]

The Anglos had their points too, and Mills remarks that although they did not usually come to the frontier to teach Sunday school, "there were good people here also, and for the few who were capable of doing business and willing to work, the opportunities were as good then and as profitable as they have ever been since that time."

Society was more diversified than one might think. The coming and going of troops at Fort Bliss brought to the border many a name which later became famous — many a charming army wife who looked back on her stay in El Paso as a specially pleasant interlude. The Harts, Magoffins, and Stephensons were rich and hospitable, had libraries, and maintained contact with the outside world. Mingling with this superior group to a greater or less degree, the remaining Anglos constituted a hierarchy beginning at the top with merchants and lawyers and proceeding downward through speculators and adventurers of various kinds to gamblers and confidence men.

It was a masculine society and it made its own rules. Public opinion was the controlling force,[11] since formal law and order had only one foot in the door, and, like Tombstone and Tonopah and Abilene and Poker Flat, El Paso depended more on custom than on constables in managing its affairs. W. W. Mills learned about this on his second night in town when a gambler named Tom Massie came into the post office with the intention of killing Samuel Schutz, a merchant with whom he had had a quarrel about a house. Schutz grappled with the would-be killer and eventually escaped with a knife wound. When the struggle started, Mills the greenhorn stepped forward and said, "Gentlemen, would you see this man murdered?" Not a man answered him, or moved from his tracks. The day after the battle Uncle Ben Dowell, among other things the keeper of the town's conscience, buttonholed Mills and gave him a piece of useful advice:

"My young friend, when you see anything of that kind going on in El Paso, don't interfere. It is not considered good manners here."[12]

Mills comments, with some nostalgia, that the men who watched the fight in Ben Dowell's saloon were men of character — by which he means men of courage and decision. "They were neither assassins nor thieves nor robbers. Vices? Plenty; but they were not of the concealed or most degrading kinds. Violence? Yes, but such acts were usually the result of sudden anger or of a feeling that under the conditions then existing each man must right his own wrongs or they would never be righted."[13]

David Diffenderfer, an observant citizen who kept a diary, points out that conditions in communities far from El Paso had their repercussions in our corner of the remote frontier. "It was about the time of the Vigilance Committee in San Francisco," he says, describing the situation at the time of his arrival in 1857, "and gamblers, murderers, and thieves from that and every other quarter began to make El Paso their headquarters. Here they were comparatively safe. Ten minutes would take them across the river into a foreign country where they could not be reached. Many a dark deed was done there at that time. I well remember one morning when I opened my store door and saw two men dangling from the limb of a cottonwood tree close by. No inquiry was ever made as to the perpetrators. On another occasion I heard seven shots near at hand soon after going to bed. Next morning the body of a man riddled with buckshot lay a few yards away. I was a member of the inquest held next day. I forget the merits of the case, but at all events we decided there was no one to blame and the defunct got what he deserved."[14]

W. W. Mills recollected in later years that business for these El Paso pioneers was sporadic. When a wagon train came in or court was in session or there was money to be made somehow, they could work as hard as any Connecticut Yankee. But there were long periods of inactivity, and that fact no doubt accounted for the prevalence and persistence of drinking in the village. The drinking, in turn, certainly brought on some of the killings recorded by Mills and others.

During the last years of the decade, when Northern and Southern sympathizers began drawing away from each other and blackening each other's character, life became precarious in a new way. Anson Mills' political enemies called him an abolitionist and Mills replied by attaching a notice to the community bulletin board which was nailed to one of the trees in the Little Plaza. J. S. Gillett, W. J. Morton and J. R. Sipes, he said, were "lying scoundrels."[15] The three posted Mills as "a damned black Republican scoundrel" and John Gillett (a wholesale merchant) challenged him to a duel — a challenge which Mills ignored. About the same time the passionate Southerners, who had formed a vigilance committee to deal with such men as Mills, summoned him to appear before them and answer for his opinions and convictions. This too he ignored and suffered no ill consequences,[16] but the old days of live and let live were obviously over, and life at the Pass had lost whatever of the idyllic it may once have possessed.

The divisions which were leading the country into war were as deep here as anywhere in the land. Hart, Magoffin, Ben Dowell, Major Gillock, District Judge Josiah Crosby, and almost everyone else in the community were deeply and passionately Southern. The Mills brothers were probably the only Northern sympathizers and they were despised accordingly. But here the contradictory character of life in this frontier hamlet appears again. Even under circumstances which called forth such passionate loyalties and rejections, friendship could be stronger than any other feeling. Both W. W. and Anson Mills, for instance, were on the best of terms with P. T. Herbert, a violent character who had killed a man in Washington when he was a member of Congress from California. As a result of the scandal, he left the state by invitation and came to El Paso.[17] He aligned himself firmly with the Southern faction, but when the time came in 1861 for El Paso County to vote for or against secession, he apparently accompanied the brothers to the polls in Dowell's place of business.

Anson's story says that Herbert came to his house and offered to go with him. "I know how you are going to vote," he said. "I am going to vote for secession, but I would like to go with you. If there is trouble, I will defend you."

Inside the saloon the usual crowd of billiard players, card players, and drinkers were assembled. Mills had brought a sheet of paper on which he had written in large letters: "NO SEPARATION." He displayed it to the company with the words, "This is my ballot." Major Gillock, in charge of the ballot box, refused to take the proferred sheet until Herbert forced him to. "This is a legal vote. Place it in the box,"[18] he said. And Gillock did so.

W. W. Mills tells an even better story. As he entered Dowell's place to cast his ballot, Simeon Hart spoke up: "Champagne for a vote for secession and a noose for all Unionists." Turning to Herbert, he called on him to dispose of that black Republican.

Herbert replied, "I am as strong a Southerner as any man alive, but I am no assassin." When Hart attempted to use his cowhide whip on Mills, Herbert took it away from him and used it on its owner.[19]

Herbert's hatred and contempt for Hart led him to publish a printed broadside in which he branded Simeon as an "ignominious poltroon,"[20] and may have provoked him to assault the man again. Mills was as angry as Herbert and he and Hart were deadly enemies for the rest of their lives. Mills' account of the scene in Dowell's place was written many years later when he was trying to prevent restoration of citizenship to Judge Hart. His memories were undoubtedly colored by his resentments. The point to remember here, however, is that the Mills brothers and several Southern men remained friends in spite of the war or forgot their differences after it was over.

Another bright spot in the picture was the good understanding which persisted between the best Americans and the best citizens of Paso del Norte. El Paso was still a corner of Mexico in many ways. In customs, currency, and language it had never changed, and the Americans who came to the border had adjusted to the tempo and mores of Mexican life.[21] They were partners of Mexican businessmen and husbands of Mexican wives. "Common trials and dangers united the two races as one family," W. W. Mills remarked nostalgically in 1896, "and the fact that one man was a Mexican and another an American was seldom mentioned, and I believe as seldom thought about. Each man was esteemed at his real worth, and I think our estimates of each other's characters were generally more correct than in more artificial societies."[22]

The feeling of mutual tolerance and respect between Mexican and American continued, with some interruptions, for a good many years after 1861, but shortly after the vote on secession, the American community began to break up. Anson Mills took the last Butterfield Overland Mail stage out, on his way to Washington to hunt a commission for himself. W. W. Mills stayed in the area and served the Union cause as best he could. A third brother, Emmett, an employee of the Overland Company, tried to get through to California but perished with his party at the hands of Mangus Colorado and his Apaches in one of the bitterest last-ditch fights in the history of Indian warfare.[23]

The Civil War was under way, and it was the end of an era at the Pass of the North.

CHAPTER XIII

War in the Desert

AN OUTSIDER would never have believed that El Paso could be a point of interest to either the Confederates or the Yankees. The mesquite and sand of West Texas were certainly no objects in themselves. But the Pass of the North was an object, and an important one. Jefferson Davis, when he was Secretary of War in Franklin Pierce's cabinet, was in charge of the surveys which aimed to locate the best route for a transcontinental railway, and he recommended the southern route through the Pass. The government which he headed after secession was fully conscious of the importance of this remote community as an avenue to the Pacific coast and as a barrier to invasion from California.[1]

The campaigns which were waged in West Texas and New Mexico were mere skirmishes compared with the vast involvements farther east, but they were not without excitement and drama, and they had their own importance.

El Paso was the focal point. And at first El Paso was as Southern as Savannah. According to Anson Mills only two votes were cast against secession in the referendum which followed the convention in Austin[2] — presumably those of himself and his brother. Colonel I. V. D. Reeve, in charge of Fort Bliss, was a Union man also, and possibly a few of his brother officers shared his views. His superiors, however, were Southerners, and early in 1861 they ordered him to turn over the money and supplies in his charge to duly designated local commissioners and to proceed with his fourteen officers and 426 men under parole to San Antonio.

The night before Anson Mills left for Washington, he had dinner with Reeve and they talked about the government stores which would fall into the hands of the rebels if the order were carried out. The colonel asked Mills to see the Secretary of War and ask him to authorize movement of men and supplies into New Mexico. Mills carried out the request, but Secretary Cameron did not issue the necessary orders.[3]

The Confederates were more ready to take action. Before Colonel Reeve was gone from Fort Bliss, a "Convention of the People of Arizona" was held at Mesilla (March 16, 1861) which declared for the Confederacy, organized a state government, and invited all who did not approve to leave the country. W. W. Mills, on his way north to join General E. R. S. Canby, saw the Confederate flag flying in the street and heard the leaders ordering Union men to get out.[4]

Mills was trying to get the Union forces in New Mexico to march to El Paso before the Texan column from San Antonio could arrive. His endeavors bore no fruit, however, and Major Edwin Waller, with five companies of Texas Mounted Rifles, arrived at Fort Bliss on July 14, 1861. Colonel John R. Baylor was only a few days behind them.

It was a time of triumph for Hart, Crosby, and the Magoffins. Hart in particular went all out for the cause, entertaining officers, putting all his resources to work rounding up supplies, acting as one of the commissioners in charge of confiscated United States property, and even organizing a band of horse thieves to steal the cavalry mounts at Fort Fillmore.[5] His best efforts, however, were devoted to the destruction of W. W. Mills. By July of 1861 Mills was lurking in Paso del Norte, where he could keep an eye on Baylor at Fort Bliss and report to General Canby on his activities. "Several attempts were made to decoy me off the streets of Juárez," Mills declares, "so as to kidnap me, but I saw through the design and avoided them."[6] At last, however, a German named Albrecht Kuhn (acting sheriff at the time), whom Mills did not suspect of rebel sympathies, caught him off guard and hurried him across the river. He was placed in the guardhouse at Fort Bliss by order of Major Waller, and none of his friends, including P. T. Herbert the California firebrand, could get him out. Only when General Canby picked up a prominent secessionist in Santa Fe and threatened him with whatever treatment was meted out to Mills, did Baylor "enlarge" the limits of his captivity. Eventually he simply walked back to Paso del Norte. In the meantime he saw Baylor march out on his way to take Mesilla, capture the Union commander, Major Isaac Lynde, with all his men, and organize the Territory of Arizona for the Confederacy.

Mills' two months of imprisonment, part of the time in irons, rankled for the rest of his life and led to a long post-war battle with Hart, whom he held responsible for his humiliation.

The stage was now being set for the arrival of General H. H. Sibley, an Army major who had "gone South,"[7] as they said in those days, journeyed to Richmond, and sold Jefferson Davis on the idea of invading New Mexico and Arizona, probably intending to go all the way to California after the proposed take-over on the Rio Grande.[8] On December 14, 1861, he arrived at Fort Bliss with a force of Texas volunteers and took active charge of the campaign.

Before he arrived, Hart and Crosby were in communication with him, promising supplies and support. Crosby wrote late in October: "I have made arrangements with a responsible party to proceed at once and buy up a quantity of corn, beans, etc., in Mexico for your use. . . . I shall engage all the arms and munitions possible to be had."[9] Hart sent over thirty wagons to Sonora for wheat to add to the 50,000 pounds of flour he had on hand. He wrote in a letter dated October 27, "I can command here now from $40,000 to $50,000, all or most of which must go into Sonora immediately to pay for flour, etc."[10]

When Sibley actually arrived, Crosby joined his staff as temporary replacement for his chief quartermaster. Magoffin signed on as a volunteer aide. Hart was too busy with what he called his "breadstuffs" to play soldier at the moment.[11]

For a while all went well. Sibley marched north, defeated the Union forces at Valverde on the Rio Grande between Socorro and Hot Springs, moved triumphantly on to Albuquerque and Santa Fe, and was heading for the important post of Fort Union when misfortune in the shape of a detachment of Colorado volunteers struck his troops at Glorieta Pass. Glorieta was the Gettysburg of the West. Sibley turned back, and his men retreated as fast as they could to Fort Bliss. About half of them arrived in a body, short of blankets, shoes, horses, everything. The rest were scattered in small groups between Mesilla and the Pass.

Now came the time of reckoning for all of them. Sibley was ailing, sometimes tipsy, a poor planner. From the beginning small-pox and pneumonia had plagued his troops, and supplies were so short that the Mexicans had been raided and robbed unmercifully. As a result, observers said, the native population was "much opposed" to the invaders.[12] They were even more opposed when Sibley's defeated and exhausted men returned to Fort Bliss. An unidentified observer, obviously no Southern sympathizer, wrote as the Texans moved down the Valley: "They have acted about El Paso in such a manner as to enrage the whole community against them. All Mexicans are down on them, and they will find very little sympathy when they return. The officers have no control over them, and they do just as they please, and you know what men off a long trip please to do; females neither in nor out of their houses are safe. Blankets, onions, wine, and everything they can lay their hands on they carry off."[13] Colonel Steele himself reported that he was obliged to seize the supplies he needed and "this occasioned so much ill-feeling on the part of the Mexicans that in many instances armed resistance was offered . . . one captain and several men of my regiment were killed. . . ."[14]

It did not help any that Colonel Baylor, pursuing a band of Indians who had stolen one hundred head of his horses and mules, had invaded Mexico as far as the village of Corralitos, 150 miles below the border of Arizona, surrounded the house of a prominent citizen, and shot some of the inmates who tried to escape to the mountains. It is true that he killed some Indians and got his horses back, but he made no friends in Mexico.[15] Baylor himself remarked early in the campaign, "The Mexican population are decidedly Northern in sentiment, and will avail themselves of the first opportunity to rob us or join the enemy."[16]

A member of Sibley's command, reminiscing in later years, recalled that the men pastured their horses in the Mexicans' wheat fields and abused their hosts in other ways. "When the weather turned cold, it was much more comfortable to sleep in a warm adobe house than in a tent (by the way, very few had tents). The owners rather objected to being crowded into one room or being driven out altogether. This with the appropriation of their donkeys and very often their wives and daughters (always, however, with the women's consent), worked up feelings of hostility that made it a sad state of affairs for many of us, when as fugitives we were leaving the country a few months later."[17]

The great retreat began less than nine months after Sibley's arrival at El Paso. News of the approach of the California Column from the west sent the Confederates hurrying toward San Antonio, leaving Fort Bliss a shambles except for the hospital, where Dr. Southworth and twenty-five disabled men awaited the coming of the enemy. It was a sad and humiliating experience for those Texas boys. Many of them had sold their weapons in order to buy food and clothing.[18] As they straggled downriver in small groups, they were pursued and harassed by as many as 1,500 of the native population who took away the captured artillery they were trying to save and put them in such fear of their lives that many never expected to see San Antonio again.[19]

Magoffin, Crosby, Dowell and Hart went with the retreating troops. Hart sent his furniture and books across the river to Paso del Norte but left the mill untouched, somewhat to the surprise of the Union forces when they arrived. A volunteer who was quartered on the premises wrote back to his hometown paper that Hart did not destroy the place because "he fully believed that another Secesh force would arrive in a few months to retake the country."[20]

A rare picture of what El Paso was like in 1862 comes from one of the harried Southern soldiers on his way back from the campaigns in the north. Sergeant A. B. Peticolas, a member of the Victoria Invincibles, arrived at Hart's Mill on May 5. He was about out of everything, having no hat and only one pair of socks, and he was in great need of a square meal. When he had time to collect himself and acquire a few creature comforts, he wandered down to the village and observed the scene which took place daily at the center of town — this being the bridge over the irrigation ditch at what we call now the Little Plaza, the corner of San Francisco and El Paso streets:

Franklin is an interesting place on some accounts. The scenes that are daily met with here and the peculiar habits of its present inhabitants form interesting subjects to an inquiring mind, and while there is nothing transpiring to arouse our painful or passionate activities there is plenty to interest and amuse. The bridge across the *acequia* is the market place of the town. Here the copper colored Mexicans, with their broad brimmed *sombreros,* bring their baskets with lettuce, onions, *peloncillos,* and little mince pies, and to this place the soldiers saunter during the morning to trade old clothes, meat or paper for the various articles exhibited for sale. Here too the sentinel with his gun is posted as a sort of a police guard to maintain inviolate the peace of the town, but, happily, this soldier has nothing to do. Then there are the gambling saloons: a decided feature in the *tout ensemble* of the town, and though I never gamble myself, I sometimes visit the rooms and look on and see money change hands and it induces in me a long string of semi-philo-sophic, semi-moralistic reflections on this singular passion.[21]

The California boys, who had been making their way across Arizona under the cold and careful eye of General Carleton, were not far behind the retreating Southerners. Colonel E. E. Eyre, in charge of the advance guard, entered Fort Bliss on August 20, 1862, and his commander arrived a few days later. He recovered twelve wagon loads of supplies which the Southern forces had sent across to Paso del Norte and busied himself in conciliating and reassuring the Valley people. "When they found we treated them kindly and paid them a fair price for all the supplies we required," he said, "they rejoiced to find, as they came under the old flag once more, that they could now have protection and will be treated justly. The abhorrence they expressed for the Confederate troops and of the rebellion convinced me that their loyalty to the United States is now beyond question."[22]

Carleton sent troops to occupy the country as far east as Fort Davis and to see that the Confederate wounded were escorted in the direction of San Antonio until they could be turned over to their own people.[23] Then he went off to Santa Fe to replace General Canby, leaving a detachment at El Paso to keep the peace and watch for a Confederate riposte.

The post was a sensitive one. The Southern sympathizers who had not gone east with the troops were living in exile in Paso del Norte, a few yards from their old homes. Safe in Mexico, they watched the Union forces and prophesied the return of the Texans.[24] Major William McMullen, still somewhat dazzled by his newly acquired rank, was in charge of the Union force. His most pressing problem was General Baylor, who was said to be raising a force of 6,000 men to reinvade New Mexico.[25]

McMullen, whose temperature rose easily, reacted at once to the prevailing tensions on his arrival. By December 5 he had set up headquarters at San Elizario and had begun worrying the *prefecto* of Paso del Norte about danger from the east. Courteous and co-operative, Don José Uranga offered to keep a party of scouts at San Ignacio, a downriver hamlet, to watch for a Confederate approach.

McMullen was not satisfied. He had heard that as many as 9,000 men were ready to march against him, and he was certain that messages were passing between these forces and the Confederate sympathizers in Paso del Norte. His solution to the problem was an invasion of Mexico. He did not advise or consult with anybody. It was his own idea. Very shortly he received an indignant letter from Uranga:

> This office has been informed by Mr. Oran Lowry that a picket of soldiers of your command has been camped at the place called Loma Colorada on the right bank of the Rio Grande, and eight more soldiers have been stationed at Loma Blanca, also on the right bank of the said river, each with the object of detaining and seizing strangers on the road which passes these two places. If this act, Major, has actually been committed, there is no doubt that, without your knowledge, international rights have been violated and treaties existing between the two nations have been broken. . . .
> This occasion enables me to offer you my earnest good wishes and regards.
> God and Reformation, December 24, 1862.[26]

McMullen flung back a belligerent reply: "I . . . will not permit Mexican soil to shield our enemies when protected by Mexican authority in violating international obligations." He explained that his men had been watching for eight Americans said to be leaving for Chihuahua under a pass signed by Uranga himself.[27]

Uranga was so shocked by this extraordinary declaration that he took four days to formulate an answer. Then he tried reasonably to convince the Major that in allowing Don Juan Gillett to leave for the interior, he had simply conformed to "the right of asylum which every citizen in the world is guaranteed," not only in Mexico but in the United States as well.[28]

By this time Major McMullen had begun to worry about the consequences of his rash act and explained to Colonel West, his superior officer, at some length his reasons for doing it.[29] He need not have worried. West wrote: "You did perfectly right and your straightforward letter to the prefect will be too much for Mexican diplomacy, I think."[30] And that ended what might have been a serious international episode.

Relations between the Mexicans and the Union forces actually seem to have been extraordinarily good. Carleton's orders to pay for everything requisitioned and to treat the citizens with consideration certainly had a good effect. By the end of 1863 Reuben

W. Creel could report to General Carleton from Chihuahua: "That things are now placed upon such a good footing so far as Chihuahua and Arizona are concerned, and that such good order and discipline prevail, should be a source of pride to the commanding officer."[31]

A fine demonstration of these good relations was the tremendous welcome extended to General Carleton and his staff when they arrived on January 30, 1864. The principal citizens of Paso del Norte, said a correspondent for the Santa Fe *New Mexican,* "came over in large numbers to pay him their respects and offer him their friendly hands. Don Juan Zubiran, Dr. Samaniego and other prominent residents of El Paso, wishing to extend the hospitality of their city to the General and the gentlemen with him, promptly arranged for a grand *baile* at the residence of the Doctor. Cards of invitation were soon distributed for the Ball, to be given on the 1st of February. The Ball came off and was one of the most brilliant and recherche displays of the kind, ever seen upon these frontiers. . . . Col. Bowie's brass band, from Franklin, reached the city in advance of the guests, and after serenading some of the principal families, repaired to the Doctor's and at 10 o'clock in the evening, the dancing began. . . . The supper was a grand banquet. The table was mounted with the purest wines, choice fruits and all varieties of sweet meats. In the center was a pyramid cake of enormous size, from the top floated the colors of the United States and Mexico beautifully commingling. At two o'clock in the morning, supper was announced. . . . The only look of sorrow visible, was when daylight forced all to say a hurried goodbye. The General and his party, and all who attended this dance, are unanimous in its praise and will remember it as one of the 'green spots' in their frontier lives."[32]

International relations on the border were improving, as Dr. Samaniego's party indicated, and the Indian situation was improving likewise. For a while in the early 1860's the tribesmen took advantage of the confusion caused by the war and mounted full-scale raids, especially in the neighborhood of Fort Stanton and in the Mimbres country west of the Rio Grande, where every day saw new and "appalling additions to our black list of Indian murders."[33] The larger towns, however, suffered very little, perhaps because of the presence of Union or Confederate troops.

When General Carleton arrived, it was the turn of the hunters to be hunted. Partly because he had a passion for order and partly because he had to keep his young men busy, Carleton campaigned intensively against the Mescalero Apaches and the Navajos. In 1863 he confined most of them in very unsatisfactory quarters on a reservation near Fort Sumner on the Pecos in New Mexico. The story of that unfortunate experiment need not be told here, but the fact that it was made helps to explain the lack of Indian trouble in the Valley until after the war. It was not until the first week in December of 1865 that a band of red raiders invaded the outskirts of El Paso and ran off 200 head of beef cattle belonging to Captain French and W. W. Mills.[34]

The Valley people were actually much more concerned about a Confederate reconquest than they were about Indians. Even after hostilities were over, the country was worried about a force of adventurers organized in San Antonio by Spruce Baird, an old-time Texas and New Mexico politician, for a last fling at the Union troops at Fort Bliss. Carleton felt enough concern about this menace to warn the citizens, through the columns of the Santa Fe *Gazette*, to forget their differences and prepare to meet the challenge.[35]

With Lee's surrender on April 9, 1865, four years of civil strife came to an end and the men on the left bank of the Rio Grande took up the task of rebuilding their part of the nation. As the tensions eased on the American side, however, they became more severe for the Mexicans. Since 1854 the country had been torn asunder by revolution, the birth-pangs of a new nation. There was constant fighting. The treasury was empty. England, France and Spain were threatening intervention. The Liberals won in 1861 and President Benito Juárez gathered up the reins in Mexico City. He had, however, almost nothing to work with in his destitute and divided country, and the Americans, who were nominally on his side, had pressing business of their own after the firing at Fort Sumter in July. On May 31, 1862, Juárez had to leave the Capital, and a week later the French army arrived. From then on for several weary years the possibility of the return of democratic government to Mexico rested on the shoulders of this one indomitable, unpretentious, utterly honest, dedicated man, a great patriot and a mighty leader in the world's long fight for human freedom.

He knew that history was with him, and that his enemies would defeat themselves if he could only hold out. The difficulty was to hold out. The aristocrats were against him. The bishops were against him. The selfish and ambitious leaders were never securely for him. The French were occupying his country and in May of 1866 they brought in Archduke Maximilian of Austria and set him up as Emperor of Mexico. Somehow Juárez kept armed forces in the field, maintained a government, and functioned with dignity as the chief executive of a great and sovereign state. But his life was the life of a fugitive. As his enemies pressed hard upon him, he moved from one Mexican city to another with his cabinet and top military officers, the national archives following in a wagon. He was in San Luis Potosí in 1864, in Chihuahua the same year, in Paso del Norte in 1865.

He controlled only the arid north-Mexican states, though his generals and his liberal supporters were doing what they could in the South. Here his back was to the wall. While he lived, he would stay on Mexican soil, but this was Mexico's farthest outpost. The land was mostly barren, the people were poor, the town was hundreds of miles from other centers of population. But Paso del Norte and the State of Chihuahua had one supreme virtue: they were liberal and loyal. As one Juárez friend and compatriot put it, the inhabitants were distinguished by "the most profound hatred of intervention, the most energetic resolve to maintain the autonomy of the country, the greatest loyalty and respect for the supreme government, and the most heartfelt sympathy for the person of the President of the Republic."[36]

The first notice of the President's impending arrival came on August 14, 1865, when two mounted men rode through the streets crying: "Juárez is coming! Juárez is coming!"[37] Henry Cuniffe, the United States consul in Paso del Norte, had advance notice of the visit, but the citizens of Paso del Norte were learning for the first time that the French were invading Chihuahua and the government was being moved again.

Later in the day the presidential party arrived. It included the cabinet, the military staff, and about 500 soldiers. Still later General Luis Terrazas, Governor of Chihuahua, joined Juárez with some 300 men. This force camped on high ground to the west of the town where their five pieces of artillery could command the

Chihuahua road. Eventually ten more cannon were obtained from the United States. Supposedly General Carleton condemned them, plus a quantity of small arms and ammunition, on orders from Washington, offered them for sale, and accepted the bid of Don Juan Zubirán, collector of customs and prominent citizen of Paso del Norte.[38] The United States supplied a good deal of war materiel to the Mexicans by such subterfuges.

Quarters had been arranged for the President in a large house on the Plaza directly across from the front of the cathedral, and there he welcomed visitors who came to pay their respects, including leading men from across the river.

By this time the post of Magoffinsville was being put back into livable condition, and two companies of the Fifth Infantry were preparing to leave their temporary quarters in El Paso and move in.[39] Major D. H. Brotherton of the California Volunteers was in command and Major S. R. Marston, United States paymaster, was the ranking officer. Marston and Deputy Collector of Customs (under W. W. Mills) I. S. Bartlett were introduced to Juárez by Don Juan Zubirán. Bartlett has left an account of the interview and of his impressions of the great Mexican:

I saw before me a descendant of the Aztec race, of pure lineage, a short, solidly built, thick-set man, probably a little over five feet in height with a face darkly bronzed, handsome dark eyes, high cheek bones, a strong, prominent nose, and black hair cut close. His expression of countenance was winning and serene. His manner was that of a cultivated gentleman and scholar, easy and dignified. His conversation lacked the fluency and vehemence characteristic of the Spanish. His voice was low and pleasant and he frequently paused as if weighing the import of his words.

His dress was that of a "citizen" president and from an American point of view, faultless. He wore coat and trousers of black broadcloth, a white vest, standing collar, black neck tie, kid gloves and highly polished boots. His hair was cut short and his face smoothly shaven. His dress fitted his sturdy, compact figure to a nicety and was worn with the grace of a finished cosmopolitan.

. . . .

Juárez spoke with serene confidence of the ultimate downfall of Maximilian's scheme of empire and the success of the republic. In alluding to American affairs he showed great intimacy with the history of the struggle for the Union and the purposes of President Lincoln and Secretary Seward. . . . .

As we rose to depart the President requested us to be seated a few moments longer and . . . ordered wine. When the wine was served Major

Marston proposed a parting toast: "Viva la Republica Mexicana," to which the President responded by giving "The brave men who established liberty and union in the United States."

The days that followed were anxious ones for Juárez, but he never slackened his pace. I. S. Bartlett's diary for the period notes that the first issue of the *periodico oficial* to be disseminated from the new headquarters appeared on September 2 and that important dispatches began to come to Juárez by way of El Paso. On November 14 the presidential party left for Chihuahua, hearing that the French had withdrawn, but on December 13 they were back again and rumors began to fly that the French were preparing to march on Paso del Norte. On January 31, 1866, the Cabinet met in emergency session and decided that a forced loan must be imposed on the merchants and ranchmen to pay for the steps that must be taken to put the town in a posture of defense. This was the third levy of the kind imposed by the government on the citizens. When the news came that the French had actually departed from the state capital, General Terrazas led his 300 men out of town after taking two wagon trains belonging to Rafael Velarde and Ynocente Ochoa and requisitioning the supplies he and his men would need. Obviously the presidential visit was not an unmixed blessing to the citizens.[40]

Such matters did not diminish by even one degree the gaiety and good will of the parties which were constantly taking place. Don Juan Zubirán gave an "elaborate ball" on October 31, 1865. The President attended but did not dance. Early in November the American officers at Fort Bliss began to make arrangements for a great reception but Juárez notified them that he could not cross the river. "I have resolved never to leave the soil of Mexico during its occupation by foreign invaders." To save the day and the party,[41] Don Rafael Velarde offered his fine house for the occasion, and on November 10 the ball took place. "The affair was a great success in every way," Bartlett confided to his diary, "and especially marked the high regard and honor in which Juárez was held by the Americans." Don Benito himself remarked that the Americans "were very kind to me and to all who accompanied me."[42]

Perhaps the most impressive evidence of American regard for the Mexican president came into his hands ten days after his arrival on the border. General Carleton wrote from Santa Fe to offer asylum if it should be needed and to assure the President of his good will.

You must believe that in your reverses you have our deepest sympathy; and I am one of those who believe that not many months will elapse before you will regain the Capital of the Republic and be among a people as faithful and free as their chief executive with neither foreign influence nor foreign bayonets to coerce or distract you from the free discharge of your duty.[43]

In a courtly and sincere reply Juárez thanked Carleton for "the interest which with so much generosity you take in the welfare of Mexico and of myself in particular. For these things I offer you my most profound thanks."[44]

Juárez accepted his American friends with great cordiality. W. W. Mills says he "visited the President very often." A photograph exists which shows Mills, Consul Henry J. Cuniffe, Juárez, and two other Americans playing cards, and when Mills set off for the East in 1866, the President entrusted him with letters to Doña Margarita, his wife, and the Mexican minister to the United States.[45]

Grateful as he was for the sympathy and friendship of these men and of all Americans, Juárez never forgot the danger of being patronized by a government which had taken advantage of the Mexican nation before. Any aid from that quarter, he wrote to his son-in-law in April, 1865, must come from "a friend, not a master, and with no loss of Mexican soil or dignity."[46]

It is quite probable that no American suspected the heartbreaking personal dislocations which the President was undergoing during these times. He had already lost several children in infancy. His second son José had died the previous January. Now he learned of the loss of fifteen-months-old Antonio in New Rochelle, New York, where his family was living. Juárez loved his children passionately and grieved for them deeply, at the same time worrying constantly about his poor unhappy wife, far away, among strangers, distracted by grief and loneliness.[47] "My brain is overwhelmed and I can hardly write these lines," he said in a letter to his son-in-law after the news of Antonio's death reached him.[48]

His private griefs, of course, had no influence at all on his attention to public business. "That man is not a man," said his friend Ignacio Altimirano in 1865. "He is duty incarnate."[49] And he was still doing his duty when the tide began to turn during those months in Paso del Norte.

The good news that the French had really left Chihuahua arrived on May 20, 1866, and by the first of June the President was getting ready to go south once more. Bartlett noted in his diary on June 17, "Juárez with all his forces, attaches and war material left El Paso today for the south. The whole population was stirred with excitement by the event and before the march began, gathered around the great chief to say farewell. While there was universal joy over the bright prospects of the republic, genuine affection of the people for Juárez gave to the leave taking a tinge of sorrow."

A year later he was back in Mexico City.[50] The end of the Civil War had freed the energies of the Americans and they had become increasingly impatient of the French intrusion, increasingly anxious to support democratic government in their sister republic. Troops assembled on the border. General Sheridan assisted the cause by "condemning" quantities of arms and ammunition and leaving them "conveniently beside the river, and then making sure that the Mexican republicans knew that he had done so."[51] Napoleon withdrew his support of the unfortunate Maximilian and eventually Juárez had him shot. The interlude was over and the next chapter had already begun.

In 1888 Paso del Norte changed its name to Juárez in commemoration of those months in 1865 and 1866 when Benito Juárez was its first citizen and the town was Mexico's capital. The heroic statue of the great President which stands in the central park of Mexico's northernmost city not merely commemorates events of a century ago but serves as a rallying point for all gatherings and demonstrations of civic importance. On that spot, so sacred to the Mexicans, the present unfolds in the presence of the past.

CHAPTER XIV

Peace at Last

FOR ALL PRACTICAL PURPOSES El Paso was wiped out by the Civil War. After 1862 there was no law except military law; no travel to speak of except military travel.[1] Everybody went away — to Chihuahua; to San Antonio and New Orleans and Richmond; to St. Louis and Washington. Only a handful of these departed citizens drifted back to join another handful of new-comers who for one reason or another had decided to call El Paso home. Prominent in this latter group were members of the California Column who had found a foothold in communities all the way from Las Cruces to San Elizario. Their presence helped to change the course of Valley history.

The Union men were firmly in charge for a decade after the war was finished. W. W. Mills, collector of customs since 1863 by appointment of President Lincoln, was for the moment the most powerful man in the region. The old Southerners, however, never stopped trying to regain the ground they had lost.

There was Ben Dowell, for example. Ben had sent his family to Paso del Norte when the Confederates left and had removed himself to East Texas, where he kept busy running cotton through the Yankee blockade.[2] Later he became a captain and served as a recruiting officer.[3] In the last sad years of the war, broke and home-sick, he found his way back to his family in Paso del Norte. His only hope of getting back on his feet was to return to El Paso, and the only way he could come back to El Paso was to get W. W. Mills on his side. On October 12, 1864, he sent Mills a letter explaining that he had left the Confederate service "because it did not suit me" and that he wished to abandon the "dog's life" he had been leading. "I hope you will pass over in forgetfulness any hard feelings you might have entertained for me," he said, "and report favorably to the commanding officer at your post."[4]

Ben's little daughter Mary — who was born in California in 1854 and survived until the 1940's — brought the letter to Mills' office. For old time's sake, or for some other reason, Mills reacted favorably and sent back word that he would do what he could.

Dowell came across the river the next day riding Kit, his famous racing mare, the pride of his life. The two old cronies were in the midst of a friendly reunion when a file of soldiers halted in front of Mills' door and informed Dowell that he was under arrest. Despite vigorous protests, they put the man in the guardhouse and the horse in the government corral.

Mills, much incensed, went directly to Colonel George W. Bowie, the commanding officer, and informed him that Dowell was ready to take the oath of allegiance. Bowie replied that that might well be, but he, Bowie, was not about to administer the oath. In view of Mills' position in the community, however, Dowell and his mare might return to Paso del Norte.

Although Mills made no further protest, his busy mind was at work. The next day he appeared with Dowell before Henry Cuniffe, an old friend of both of them who had come back from exile in Chihuahua after the Union take-over and in 1865 became United States Consul.[5] Cuniffe administered the oath. Colonel Bowie admitted that he had been outwitted — probably glad in his heart that Uncle Ben was back.

And now the reason for Mills' generosity appeared. He knew what the Kit horse could do, and he persuaded Dowell to form a sporting partnership. They took on all comers who were willing to risk their money on their horseflesh. Dowell furnished the horse. Mills furnished the capital. The track was the same three-quarter-mile straightaway on what is now West Overland Street used for horse racing before the war. Many a good horse was imported to test Kit's speed, and thousands of dollars changed hands on these occasions.

The greatest race El Paso ever saw or ever will see happened on January 6, 1872. Pete Maxwell of Las Cruces, New Mexico, had a horse named Fly in which he had complete confidence. He brought her to El Paso and the race was arranged. All along the course were people with money to bet, stacks of bills and heaps of coin laid out on *serapes* or blankets. Something like $25,000 was wagered.[6]

Dowell gave his jockey final instructions. "Hold her back," he said, "until you get to that little clump of trees half way to the finish line. Then give her a touch of the quirt."

For the first half of the race, Fly was in the lead. Then they passed the clump of cottonwoods and Kit assumed command. As she passed Fly in a cloud of dust, her rider turned around, thumbed his nose at his rival, and shouted out so all could hear him above the thunder of hooves: "Shoo Fly."[7]

It is sad to relate that Kit lasted only three years longer, her death, ironically, being the result of an excess of green alfalfa, the crop which her master had introduced to the Valley.[8]

Mills helped other repentant Southerners besides Dowell, but one Confederate he could not forgive. Simeon Hart had arranged to have him kidnapped off the streets of Paso del Norte and put in the Fort Bliss guardhouse. Now it was Mills' turn, and he made the most of it. Since 1862, the property of any man who fought for the South had been subject to forfeiture and sale. Almost as soon as the California Column reached New Mexico in 1862, the indictments for treason began.[9] Joab Houghton, district attorney at Santa Fe, and U. S. Marshal Abraham Cutler were eager to bring charges. Among those libeled in 1862 were Samuel Magoffin, Simeon Hart, Josiah F. Crosby, John S. and Henry Gillett, and James Wiley Magoffin — all of El Paso.[10] Hugh Stephenson's Brazito grant and his mining claims in the Organ Mountains were declared forfeit. Property involved in the proceedings was located all the way from Canutillo to Fort Quitman and included the valuable assets of Hart's Mill and Magoffinsville.

Actual confiscation began when the cases were called in the Third Judicial District Court of New Mexico against individuals in "armed rebellion" against the United States. United States District Attorney Theodore D. Wheaton brought the suit. Judge Joab Houghton ordered United States Marshal Abraham Cutler to attach the property and notify the owners that the court would hear them on November 6, 1865. Cutler advertised the confiscation proceedings for two weeks in El Paso, San Elizario, Las Cruces, and Mesilla. These formalities having been duly completed, he proceeded to the actual selling. On December 18, 19, and 20, 1865, he stood in the Plaza at El Paso and conducted a public auction.[11]

It was a cheap and disgraceful performance. Houses and lots and parcels of land went for a fraction of their value to the old Unionists who were present and the hungry newcomers who had come to join them. Collector of Customs W. W. Mills was there bidding. So was Henry Cuniffe, the consul. Among the newcomers were Louis Cardis (on his way to becoming the political boss of the region) and ex-California Columnists George Kohlhaus and Charles E. Ellis of San Elizario. One parcel of good Valley land — 320 acres — sold for thirty dollars. Half of the Magoffinsville land on which Fort Bliss stood went to Henry Cuniffe and Albert H. French (Hugh Stephenson's son-in-law) for $4,000. Hart's Mill brought $3,000.[12] Only two rebels were allowed, by W. W. Mills' intercession, to keep what they owned: Ben Dowell and Major Braxton Gillock.[13]

Marshal Cutler had somebody "staked out" to buy up some of the property for resale to him. His profiteering was so brazen and flagrant that he was later indicted for embezzlement. His bills for handling the cases amounted to more than the collections, and he got hold of a good deal of real estate himself. At his trial in 1887, however, he was acquitted.[14]

The owners of the libeled property could not defend themselves until and unless they could make their peace in Washington, and this they proceeded to do at once. Hart went directly to the Capital and applied for a Presidential pardon. Now his long years of hospitality and cordiality toward the wayfarers of the West began to pay off. He is said to have been on friendly terms with Secretary of War Edwin M. Stanton,[15] through what earlier contact it is impossible now to say, and he probably was acquainted with a hundred other government officials who could and would do him a good turn. On November 6, 1865, he got his amnesty papers from President Andrew Johnson.[16]

James Wiley Magoffin had a much harder time. He too made the pilgrimage to the Potomac, was apparently turned down, and had to go back a second time. With the help of Benjamin W. Brice, paymaster general of the Army, he finally was granted a pardon.[17] By now, his health was bad. Instead of returning to El Paso, he went to live with his son-in-law Joe Dwyer in San Antonio. There he died on September 27, 1868. His property was not restored to the family until 1873.[18]

The other old Confederates who were able to stand up and fight took their battle to the courts and asked to have the confiscations set aside on the grounds that the New Mexico courts had no jurisdiction. They went all the way to the Supreme Court, and decision in their favor was handed down on March 28, 1868.[19]

The most disappointed man in El Paso over this decision was W. W. Mills. For $1,800 he had acquired a share of the Hart's Mill property. Now the transaction was void. "Without a murmur," Mills says, "I reconveyed all the property to the original owners and lost the eighteen hundred I had paid the Marshal."[20]

He even lost the $50,000 awarded him after years of litigation as damages for the kidnapping and imprisonment he had suffered during the war — a judgment, he says, which "was twice affirmed by the Supreme Court of Texas."[21] This long and painful struggle was concluded on May 5, 1873, when W. W. Mills and his brother Anson Mills accepted a payment of ten dollars through their attorney Charles H. Howard and released the Mill property to Hart.[22] A year later, his battle won, Hart lay down and died quietly.

Mills, less and less impressed by the human race and its works and more and more driven to the oblivion of the bottle, grew old with his memories. For a while he lived on a piece of ranch property which he owned on the Mexican side.[23] In 1897 he became United States Consul in Chihuahua and functioned there until 1907. He died in Austin, old, sick and not in good mental health, on February 10, 1913, leaving for posterity a singularly bad and singularly useful book which he called *Forty Years at El Paso* — with all its faults the best single record we have of the curious and wonderful days in the Valley before and after the Civil War.

CHAPTER XV

Buildup to Trouble

EL PASO AFTER THE CIVIL WAR was small but tough. We were short on political organization, law and order, religion, morality, and good women. Since we have no newspaper files for this period,[1] and other records are sparse, the full story of what went on is not always easy to reconstruct, but some rather lurid episodes get into the record.

S. H. Newman, who first saw the place in 1876, says no more than fifty or a hundred people were living here in that year (he probably means Anglos).[2] Buildings enough were standing, he says, "houses enough for a population of several hundred souls, but more than half of them unoccupied." He was told that only twenty-seven people in the county could serve on a jury because only twenty-seven people could read and write.[3]

Communication with the outside world was difficult. W. W. Mills had his own "ambulance" which could be slept in, and with a driver, a friend or two, and a couple of armed *mozos* he defied the Indians and made the trip to Austin when need arose, but not everyone could do that. Wagon trains operated by Gabriel Valdéz (James Magoffin's brother-in-law) or Ynocente Ochoa or Isaac Lightner made slow journeys to and from San Antonio, Chihuahua, or Santa Fe. Army supply caravans crossed the wild country from time to time and stage travel began in 1866, but all transportation was irregular and dangerous. Even after the government contracted with the San Antonio and El Paso Mail Company in 1867 to run a tri-weekly stage to El Paso,[4] people were "practically without mail facilities" for years on account of graft and inefficiency in the management. W. W. Mills and other citizens had to take their case all the way to Washington before they got any relief.[5]

Paso del Norte, across the way, was a metropolis, busy and prosperous. American travelers commented on its muddy streets and the presence of "the worst element in Mexico" among its lower-class citizens,[6] but permanent residents of the Valley found some aspects of its life delightful.

Ernest Kohlberg was one who liked what he saw. Ernest was an eighteen-year-old German Jewish boy who came to the border in 1875 to work for his relative Solomon Schutz and lived to become one of El Paso's leading business men. He described for his far-away German family a typical *baile* in Paso del Norte:

> I attended a nice Mexican ball in Paso del Norte last week and had an enjoyable time. The Mexican men with their politeness and their ladies with their grace are really in their element at a function of this kind. . . . The dance which I attended was in honor of a Mexican official and was particularly brilliant. . . . It is customary for the gentlemen to take a lady to supper, not to eat with her, but to wait on her. He sees that she gets something of everything that is served, cuts her meat, changes her plate and gives her some of the different wines that are served. While the lady is enjoying her supper the gentleman attends her by standing behind her chair. . . . Before the ball starts, the young men sit at the entrance of the home and as the ladies arrive, they offer them their arms and escort them to the room in which they assist them to lay aside their wraps and then take them to a seat in the ball-room. The dance takes place in the patio which has been covered with carpets over which canvas has been spread. It was about eight A. M., the sun was shining brightly and we had breakfast, before the ball was over. . . .[7]

Ernest endured heat, family quarrels, bandits, and slow business in the store which he managed in Paso del Norte. He had times of homesickness and despair, but he grew a noble mustache, learned to carry a six-shooter ("It is necessary after nightfall to be prepared for any eventuality"), and began to think like an American. "I did receive the newspapers, which were full of 'Your Excellencies' and 'Your Highnesses,' etc. As this sort of address and cringing are not known here, the whole thing makes a funny and ludicrous impression." Like all the other early arrivals, he hoped for better days. "With patience and spit one can catch many a gnat," he said.

It did take patience and courage to hold out in this wild, new country. The revolutions in Mexico had their repercussions on the border. The Indians raided and robbed. And the bad men made trouble and had to be controlled. Daniel W. Jones, a Mormon missionary, saw how the citizens handled one such case when a party of ruffians came in and "started to run the town." A warrant was issued for their arrest, but they defied the officers. Melton A. Jones was mayor and Ben Dowell was acting as marshal (this must have been in 1875 or 1876) and somehow they managed to bring the rascals in.

The dockets show that these men were arrested, brought to trial and found guilty of murder in the first degree; that the court sentenced them to be shot; that Ben Dowell and others were ordered by the court to execute the orders.

Accordingly the orders were duly executed, and Dowell and his assistants, the judge being one of the party, proceeded to shoot four of these condemned men on the street in front of the main saloon of the town. They were buried, as the records show, and the costs of court and all proceedings duly recorded.

Judge Jones showed me the record and explained how it was done. I never heard any complaint about the proceedings but, on the other hand, Judge Jones and Ben Dowell were very much respected by the average citizens of the country.[8]

One would think that in this isolated village common problems and common dangers would have welded the citizenry into a tight little unit, but they were actually divided and torn by personal and political differences and by competition for the meagre resources of that barren countryside. Those were bad and bitter times, and the hatreds and resentments built up to a bloody climax in the Salt War of 1877.

To understand the situation we must take a look at the men who walked those dusty streets in the sixties. There were several groups. The first would include the few Anglos who had remained in the vicinity through the war years. The Schutzes, Joseph, Samuel and Solomon, were among them. Natives of Westphalia, they had come in the fifties and grown up with the country. Mrs. Sam Schutz owned a piano, one of the first to be imported, and her music making was a revelation to little girls like Lillian Hague, who lived just across San Francisco Street. Sam Schutz constructed and operated a second-story opera house over his place of business, the pride of the town for a number of years. Solomon Schutz served as mayor in 1881.[9]

A second group, made up of Southerners who drifted back after 1865, included Simeon Hart, Ben Dowell, Braxton Gillock and the Gillett brothers, Henry and John. The Gilletts were rich men before the war, members of the original townsite company. Henry, who married Gillock's daughter Ellen, moved to Silver City. John, according to Anson Mills, went downhill rapidly after his return and had no further influence.

A member of this group who became a power in civic affairs was Joseph Magoffin, James Magoffin's portly, serious, full-bearded son. He made his peace with the government and the ruling Republican faction and rose to modest civic heights. From 1869 to 1872 he was a justice of the peace. He served as collector of customs in the seventies, four terms as mayor, and continued to be influential till his death in 1923.

These and a few other ex-soldiers of the South had their problems during the sixties and seventies, especially if they did not enjoy the friendship of W. W. Mills, leader of the Union men who formed a third group. Mills was the Republican boss and the most important citizen in his bullet-scarred hamlet. His backers included a few Unionists from pre-war days: David Diffenderfer (former U. S. consul in Paso del Norte), Frank Diffenderfer his brother, and Henry Cuniffe, who became consul in 1866. More numerous than the old timers, however, were the Union men who came as soldiers with the California Column. Prominent among them was black-haired, straight-backed James A. Zabriskie, who married Hugh Stephenson's daughter Adelaida in 1864 and became district attorney in 1866. Although he moved to Tucson in 1878, he stayed with the ship during the stormiest weather. A fellow officer with Zabriskie was Albert French, a hard-drinking captain of engineers — capable and energetic until his weakness destroyed him. He married Benancia Stephenson and helped to save what could be salvaged of the Stephenson property. Zabriskie and French were close friends and business associates of W. W. Mills.[10]

In every village in the Valley one of these California men was likely to turn up, men like Charles E. Ellis who established a store and mill in San Elizario, married a Valley girl and involved himself in local politics. He served as tax assessor and collector in 1866, county treasurer in 1870, sheriff in 1871.[11]

The most unusual of the group was an incredible character named Albert Jennings Fountain, a storm center throughout the region until his untimely and mysterious death in 1896. He says that his name was really Albert Jennings.[12] Born in 1838 in New York City, he was the son of sea captain Solomon Jennings and

Catherine de la Fontaine, offspring of French Huguenots. He says he matriculated at Columbia College though his name does not appear on the records.[13] His school days came to an end in the middle fifties when his father disappeared with his ship in the Far East. Albert shortly thereafter traveled to Europe, ostensibly for his health but actually to begin a search for his father. Once abroad, he took his mother's name — which he kept for the rest of his life — and got aboard an East Indiaman bound for Calcutta.[14] Eventually he wound up in Hong Kong in jail for having been caught aboard a smuggling vessel. With the help of the United States consul he reached San Francisco, probably in 1859. He was just twenty years old.

As a reporter for the Sacramento *Union* he went to Nicaragua to report the Walker filibustering expedition but Walker sentenced him to be shot for indiscreet reporting and he barely made it out of camp, disguised as a woman.

Back in California he abandoned his newspaper career for the safer profession of law and had just been called to the bar when war was declared.[15] He enlisted, came to New Mexico as a corporal, was promoted to sergeant, and ranked as a second lieutenant when he was discharged in August, 1864.[16] He immediately re-enlisted as a captain in the regiment of volunteer cavalry which had been organized to fight Indians.[17]

Meanwhile he had settled into the mold of the country. With a member of his command named Pérez he spent some time in El Paso soon after his arrival, fell in love with his friend's fourteen-year-old sister Mariana, and married her on October 27, 1862.[18]

He had his share of hard fights and hairbreadth escapes, which he loved to talk about and write about in his later years. A swashbuckler, a speech maker, a man who loved to play a part, a great organizer of amateur theatricals, he seemed a windbag to his enemies but was actually a very brave and very useful man. In a great number of skirmishes with Indians and outlaws after he moved to New Mexico in 1874, he proved to be a good field general, a resourceful guerrilla fighter whose contribution to the peace and safety of his state has been too soon forgotten.

He had the wounds to prove his prowess when he came to El Paso to recuperate and make a new start in 1866. Apparently he had engaged in a business enterprise which failed, possibly because his appointment (by General Carleton) as a captain of volunteer cavalry kept him out in the wilds looking for hostile savages. The wounds which laid him low had been received during a campaign in Arizona, a long way from his private enterprises, whatever they were.[19]

Somehow he recommended himself to W. W. Mills and — for a time — became his friend and assistant. According to Mills, Fountain came to ask for work doing odd jobs of painting. He had left New Mexico "after squandering other men's money" and was most grateful for anything that was done for him. Mills quotes a letter which Fountain is supposed to have written on May 13, 1869 — a letter which must have made its writer writhe when it appeared in an Austin newspaper six months later. It said in part:

> The year previous to my coming to El Paso to live, I had been engaged in an enterprise, which promised, if successful, a fortune. I had partners, who advanced a small portion of the original capital invested, and who, when I was confined to my bed, suffering for months from wounds received while risking my life, to advance their interest as well as my own, not only robbed me of all I had, but slandered me to my friends to excuse their conduct . . . some of these parties have since acknowledged to me in humble tones that they villainously slandered me, because they had to do it to save themselves. They also acknowledged that they endeavored to poison *your* mind against me when I had a prospect of again rising, and that if you had not stood my friend, they would have succeeded in their threats of driving me from the country. It was then through your interposition that these parties failed. . . . I believe that you were my friend when I most needed one; *you shall never have cause to regret that act,* and I would consider myself as great a villain as the world contains, if *under any circumstances whatever,* I arrayed myself among the number of your enemies, personal or political. . . .[20]

Thanks to Mills, Fountain became assistant assessor and deputy collector of internal revenue in 1866, and in that same year he functioned as district surveyor.[21] He says that he took time out from these jobs to accept the rank of colonel in Benito Juárez' army and organize his artillery.[22] Within a few short months he had risen from the very bottom of the heap to the very top, ranking next to Mills in the ruling political faction and conscious of great opportunities waiting for him just around the corner.

He and his associates were known as Radical Republicans. Theirs was the dominant party in Texas during the early post-war years — the party which said the South should not rise again. The

Radicals held on longer in El Paso County than anywhere else in Texas, and it took a small war to get them out.

Hardly less powerful than Fountain and Mills was another extraordinary character named Luis Cardis, an Italian who did not become a citizen till 1869,[23] but who nevertheless was a man to reckon with in the Valley. He was a rather strange and lonely figure among those aggressive Americans. A captain in Garibaldi's army in 1848 and '49, he came to the United States in 1854, appearing in El Paso toward the end of the War, exactly why we do not know.[24] A. J. Fountain says he "was a member of the Italian Carbonari, had betrayed his associates, and fled to save his life from their vengeance."[25] He was Mills' friend and henchman for a while, "my lieutenant in political affairs during the sixties," Mills says.[26] In 1869 when the Ben Ficklin stage line went into operation, Cardis became a mail contractor, managing the service between El Paso and Fort Davis.[27] He never married and he always lived in bachelor's quarters, but he was a gentleman in appearance and manners — a short, rather stout man with black hair and goatee who dressed neatly in dark clothes and kept his white linen spotless.[28] No fighter, he became the leading politician in the Valley by learning to speak Spanish well and functioning as the great and good friend of the Mexicans.

Even more influential with the Mexicans was the parish priest of San Elizario, the Reverend Antonio Borajo, a strange and violent figure about whom opinion is still divided. He was certainly a dedicated religious leader and yearned with all his soul for the welfare of his people and the prevalence of the will of God. The difficulty was that he allowed nobody to speak for God but himself. A thin, pale, long-faced, stoop-shouldered old man with a mane of white hair and a volcanic temperament, he ruled his parish with an iron hand and defied the gringos — all the gringos but Mills and Fountain, and he had his doubts about them.

He hated the Americans for interfering with the schools, insisting that girls should go to classes long after they should have been doing women's business and demanding that boys and girls — big boys and girls — should study in the same room, a practice which civilized people naturally viewed with horror.[29] He hated them for trying to close his cemetery. In 1871 District Judge Simon B. Newcomb — for sanitary reasons, he said — ordered the priest not to bury any more people in the *campo santo* next to the church and in the middle of town. Sheriff Charley Ellis, Borajo's fellow townsman, served the papers in due form. The very next day Borajo appeared at the head of a funeral procession, buried a child in the holy earth, and left his enemies wondering what they could do about it.

He tolerated no opposition. When a man was brought in to cast a bell for his church and failed to produce the desired results, Borajo got rid of him and cast the bell himself — very badly. At the thought of the stupidities he had to endure he would toss his white mane and exclaim, "*Ba, ba, ba, que burrada!*" (What asininity!) [30]

Daniel W. Jones, the Mormon missionary, encountered this supercharged ecclesiastic when he came to the Valley in the middle seventies. Borajo knew the Mormons were there, and when several of them visited his church one Sunday morning, he mounted the pulpit to denounce them. Brother Jones went home and wrote down what Borajo said as nearly word for word as he was able.

"The world's history gives an account of great plagues that have visited the world from time to time," Borajo began, and listed all the calamities he could think of, ending with the plague of Mormonism. "And there," he declared, pointing to Jones and his companions, "stand the representatives of this plague. Look at them. Their faces show what they are." He denounced them as polygamous and immoral barbarians and ordered his people to bring him the Mormon books so he could burn them. [31]

The missionaries managed to get out without being lynched but "for some days," Jones remembered, "when women in the streets would see any of us coming, they would jump into the first door and close it and then look out through what all Mexican houses have in their doors — a peep hole. Some of the women who ran from us were of the class that do not often scare at a man, yet they acted as though they dreaded us."

Along with this powerful padre a good many prominent Mexican - Americans were associated with Mills and his organization. Among them was J. M. Lujan — Don Mauro — who lived in a big adobe house near the church in San Elizario, the county seat. His fellow townsman Telesforo Montes, a famous Ranger and Indian fighter, was another, as were Maximo Aranda, judge, legislator, collector of customs, business man, and Gregorio García, justice of the peace. Martín and Benigno Alderete of Ysleta, leaders of a prosperous and prominent clan, belonged to the group.[32] In fact, almost everybody who was anybody was on the side of the Mills-Fountain-Borajo faction.

Civil government returned to the Pass in full array in 1866. The Constitutional Convention, which met in Austin in that year, authorized general elections. The will of the people, as expressed at the polls in June, put the leading Republicans in office. Albert H. French was county judge and judge of the "Police Court." James A. Zabriskie was district attorney, William P. Bacon was district judge, and so on down the line.[33] All were friends, and some were business associates, of W. W. Mills.

The combination held together through 1867, but its unity was precarious at best. In 1868 cracks began to appear in the structure. Time was running out for Mills and an opposition was beginning to organize. The leader of the dissenters, of all people, was A. J. Fountain.

To this day their feud has not been satisfactorily explained. They were both strong-willed, ambitious characters, good haters and good fighters, and no doubt they got in each other's way. Each one accused the other of many kinds of wickedness and both, or neither, may have been right. Then there was the basic division in the Republican Party separating the Radicals from the Conservatives. Fountain was a strong supporter of Radical Republicanism and Mills was conservative. There may have been other and deeper causes of contention which we do not know about.

It is possible that the whole affair was a matter of economics. Both the men were interested in the great salt deposits near Guadalupe Peak a hundred miles east of El Paso.

These deposits were considered to belong to all the towns of the Valley in common and were a resource of no small importance in times of drouth and hardship. Salt was a precious and sometimes a rare commodity in that country and many a man made a business of hauling it to the Valley towns and into the interior of Mexico. When all other ways of making a living failed, one could haul salt. The Spanish government had never allowed a resource of such general importance to be appropriated by individuals, and it was hard for the Mexicans to realize that under gringo law a man with a handful of scrip could preempt any piece of government land, including the *salinas*.

The natives had known about the salt deposits under Guadalupe Peak from the earliest times and may have used them.[34] The gringos became aware of them in 1862. They were not exploited until after the war, however, since there were other beds easier to get at. These were the San Andres saline lakes on the east side of the mountains of that name a hundred miles due north of El Paso. The old salt road started at Stephenson's Concordia ranch and followed the foothills past two or three springs which made travel easier. Caravans from all the Valley towns assembled several times a year and traveled together in a group large enough to discourage even the most ambitious band of Apaches from attacking.

This arrangement was disturbed in 1854 by the "Magoffin War" — the result of an attempt by American entrepreneurs to charge the Doña Ana Mexicans for the salt they took.[35] Magoffin's men used rough tactics — even firing off a small cannon into the ranks of the *salineros*. This may have been a factor in the decision which was reached in the El Paso Valley after the war to give up the San Andres lakes and open up the Guadalupe deposits.

The year 1862 was a bad one for everybody — drouth, the war — everything. It was in times like these that the salt became a life saver and the natives thought about going into the salt business to make ends meet. Besides, the soldiers had increased the demand. This time they determined to use the Guadalupe deposits, and men from all the towns joined forces to break a road from Fort Quitman in the Valley below El Paso across the sandhills. They had to carry their water, and they could expect Indian attacks, but there seemed to be no other way out of their troubles. Surely no one would envy them anything as difficult and dangerous to acquire as the salt.

They did not know the gringo politicians, who were willing to make money from almost anything. The El Paso rulers were well aware of the economic possibilities of the salt traffic. The trouble was that they depended on the Mexican vote for everything, and the Mexicans took it for granted that the salt could not be owned by any man or group of men. It would be fatal to make an open grab for it. The deal would have to look good. So they hesitated and shuffled their feet, and thereby nearly lost out entirely. For Samuel Maverick — the same Samuel Maverick for whom little lost calves are named — stepped in in 1865 and took up two sections of the best acreage in the salt lakes.[36] He had the land scrip and the knowhow to complete the transaction.

At first the Mexicans were dejected by this turn of events, and the El Paso politicians were chagrined. Both groups cheered up, however, when it was found that there was plenty of salt-producing territory outside of the Maverick survey.[37] The Mexicans resumed their hauling and the gringos began to think seriously how they could get hold of the unclaimed parts of the deposits. As a result of their special interest, they are said to have formed in 1868 an organization which outsiders called the Salt Ring.

The names of the ring members are familiar: W. W. Mills, A. J. Fountain, Frank Williams, Charles Conley, Albert French, Ben Dowell, Gaylord Clarke, J. M. Lujan[38] — plus Luis Cardis and Father Borajo. A few more names were added later, but these were the nucleus. They actually attempted to preempt the unclaimed part of the salt deposits on the basis of a certificate belonging to Ben Dowell, but the papers proved to be defective and the popular outcry was so violent that they dropped the enterprise promptly and completely.[39] When Fountain fell out with Mills in 1869, he became the leader of the opposition called by later historians the Anti-Salt Ring.

The rift began in an undercover conspiracy to get Mills removed from the collectorship. In May of 1869, when Fountain wrote his famous letter to Mills declaring his undying loyalty, he was, in the latter's words, "secretly conspiring with my most unscrupulous and most relentless enemies."[40] The conspirators saw to it that word got back to Washington that Mills was running a "Customhouse Ring" for the benefit of himself and his friends, that he was alienating the Mexicans, and playing fast and loose with government money. "There is no man now living of the same calibre, who has done the Republican Party and the Government so much injury," said one of them later. "His plan was to attack any person or corporation simply for the purpose of blackmail."[41]

The man selected to spearhead the attack was one D. K. Wardwell, formerly a clerk in the customhouse under Mills' supervision. The San Antonio *Express* in September, 1869, published the charges. Wardwell made fourteen specific accusations involving smuggling, falsification of records, failure to keep accounts, and the use of money from the customhouse safe for gambling, betting on horse races, and other private and illegitimate uses. "I can swear conscientiously," said Wardwell, "that I believe that Mills has robbed the Government of fifty thousand dollars a year ever since he has been in office. I was Inspector, and in a position to ascertain facts in relations to his frauds."

Mills had the charges printed in the Austin *Republican* with his answers and comments. All he had to say to the final preposterous accusation was: "As I have been in office eight years, this would amount to $400,000: *I wish I had the money!*"[42]

The newspaper war was carried on into December when Mills printed Fountain's letter of the previous May 13 declaring his eternal gratitude to his preserver and benefactor W. W. Mills. The same issue of the *Republican* which reproduced this extraordinary document carried an answer by Fountain which did not deny the authenticity of the letter but declared that Fountain was "astonished at the unblushing effrontery of this man" and revealed that he had in his possession "documentary evidence of his own writing, and signed by him, sufficient to convict him of charges of a more serious nature than any which have yet been made against him." With a specious show of humanity Fountain continued: "Sympathy for his family, and unwillingness to trample upon a sinking man had prevented me from publishing these documents. If he desires their publication, let him deny their existence."

On the same page Mills did deny their existence, though he indicated his belief that during Fountain's employment in the customhouse he had purloined some of his superior's private papers and forged Mills' signature to others. He did not question Fountain's assertion that 390 registered voters, and 150 who were not registered, had signed a document in which Mills was declared to be "undeserving the support or confidence of the people."[43]

By the time these matters were aired in the *Republican,* Mills was already out of office and was fighting a rearguard action. He was removed from his collectorship in the summer of 1869[44] by the Secretary of the Treasury and replaced by Dr. D. C. Marsh, a man described by the Republican press as a "sleek and sanctimonious" carpetbagger.[45] All Mills could salvage from the wreckage was an appointment as delegate to the Constitutional Convention held in that same year, and the affection of Mary Hamilton, the Governor's daughter, a lovely and gentle lady whom he married on February 8, 1869.[46]

Those who knew Mary Hamilton would never believe that he was a loser as long as he had her, but they sometimes wondered why she picked a man as obstreperous and cantankerous as W. W. Mills.

The summer of 1869 passed uneventfully, except for Mills' demotion, but the election of November, 1869, brought the Fountain-Mills feud into the open. Mills was running for the Legislature as a conservative Republican in the camp of his father-in-law, A. J. Hamilton. The old guard in El Paso backed him, and so did two newcomers — Gaylord Judd Clarke and B. F. Williams. Mills describes Clarke, a fellow New York Stater, as "my college chum and the most intimate friend of my early manhood." According to him, Clarke "had failed at everything and was destitute" and had reached the end of the line somewhere in Nebraska. Mills says he sent him the money to come to El Paso, found him a job in the customhouse, and arranged for his wife and children to join him.[47] Clarke's descendants reply indignantly that he succeeded as a lawyer in Albany, New York, but sacrificed a bright future and moved west for the sake of his wife's health.[48] Whatever the reason for their coming, the Clarkes brought a tremendous lift to the cultural life of their new home. Clarke himself wrote poems which show considerable verbal skill and sensitivity of spirit.[49] He had done newspaper work, was well read, and was gifted as a speaker and conversationalist. In addition he was deeply religious and an earnest Episcopalian. His wife was a charming, refined, and hospitable person ("ardent" is the adjective used to describe the couple by their historian)[50] who belongs with Mrs. Hague and Mrs. Mills and Mrs. Solomon Schutz as the first civilizers of their untamed little community. She was one of the first El Paso teachers.[51]

Williams was a less gracious character — a lawyer and an ex-Confederate soldier who seems to have changed his original Democratic loyalties in hopes of a political job. He came about the same time as the Clarkes, in 1867, and in 1869 was backing Albert Fountain while Clarke was supporting Mills. At the same time, strangely enough, Fountain and Clarke were the best of friends — were, in fact, living under the same roof in the old Overland stage station on south El Paso Street and finding many mutual interests and attitudes.

They continued to be friends during and after the election of 1869, though that election was apparently a fearful and wonderful thing. It took place at San Elizario, the county seat, with the military in charge to prevent violence, and lasted four days. When it was over, Fountain was in and Mills was out, but Mills protested loudly and vigorously that he had been deprived of his right. In his reminiscences he quotes a letter from his friend Albert French, the county judge: "We won the election, but the first night, we having one hundred and forty-three to their forty-eight votes, they opened the box and scratched our one hundred and forty-three votes for themselves. Fountain's name represents yours on the scratched tickets. I have sworn two hundred and seventy-seven men who voted for you. You got only one hundred and thirty-four as counted."[52]

Fountain's story, of course, was entirely different. He said later that the only plank in his platform during the campaign was the acquisition of the Guadalupe salt lakes for all the people of the El Paso area.

Shortly after the election, according to Fountain, he was honored by a call from Father Borajo. The conversation was short and to the point:

"Senator, what will you do about the salt lakes when you get to Austin?"

"I mean to get title to them for the people of the El Paso district."

"Well, such is not my desire. And remember what I did for you during the election."

"I do remember it."

"What I want you to do, then, is to acquire title to the salt lakes for yourself. You can charge a reasonable price for the salt. I will advise my people to pay it, and they will. You will get rich, and so will I, for we will divide equally."

"No," said Fountain. "I won't do it."

This is Fountain's story. The other side never got into print. Fountain concludes by saying that Borajo flew into a rage, told Fountain he was through as a public servant, threatened his life, and stormed out.[53]

In complete defiance of the militant priest, Fountain moved to carry out his campaign promises. From Austin he sent word back to El Paso that if the people would pay for the surveying, he would provide the land scrip needed to acquire unlocated portions of the salt lakes. Cardis and Borajo, says Fountain, would have none of it. They persuaded the people that he was trying to get the salt for himself. While Fountain was preparing a bill allotting the unclaimed salt to the County of El Paso "for the use of her citizens forever," they were circulating a petition which would put a stop to his efforts. Before he could bring his bill to the floor of the Senate, the petition, signed by "some six hundred" of his constituents, arrived in Austin. It asked him to drop the matter. He dropped it.[54]

This was one of the few setbacks Fountain suffered during his four years in the Senate. He served for a time as its president and introduced some important legislation including the bill which established the much-hated State Police. He was chairman of the Indian Affairs Committee, served on several others, and was instrumental in setting up a system of frontier defense.[55] When he left Austin for good, his colleagues presented him with a fine gold watch in recognition of his energy and effectiveness as a legislator.[56]

Outside the legislative halls, however, his course was anything but smooth. His enemy W. W. Mills, implacable and resourceful, had nursed his grievances for four years and in July of 1870 he found a way to pierce Fountain's armor. The Senator was arrested on Mills' complaint and taken before the United States Commissioner, where he was charged with a number of high crimes of which the chief was the impersonation of a deputy collector of customs and the attempt to collect money in that capacity. Fountain made bond and went off to El Paso.

He found the factions still in violent opposition — so violent, in fact, that the leaders were becoming afraid of the consequences and were making attempts to patch matters up. Going between the two parties was Albert French, once Mills' friend but now on Fountain's side since through Fountain's efforts he had been made captain of the local unit of the State Police. He brought Luis Cardis around for a conference. Borajo did not come, but he sent a letter stating that Cardis was speaking for him.

Cardis talked and talked. He wanted a reconciliation of the factions with all former resentments forgotten and an equal distribution of jobs and patronage to both sides. And what, Fountain wished to know, did Borajo want out of this? Well, he didn't want much — just complete control of the schools, a free hand in appointing teachers, and a definite understanding about the salt lakes.

Cardis paused here to explain. "Borajo has salt lakes on the brain," he said. "He seems to think he can make a fortune out of them."

"Why don't you and Borajo locate the lakes yourselves?"

"Because we can't afford to make money that way. It would destroy our influence with the people."

"Supposing I do what Borajo wants, how do you know I won't keep all the profits?"

"Because," Cardis told him, "it would cost you your life if you did, and you know it."

Again Fountain refused to have any part of these schemes, as he tells the story, and Cardis and French went away.[57]

Now it became public knowledge that Fountain the unpredictable had done the unexpected again. During his stay in Austin he had used his influence to get the appointment as district judge for Mills' friend Gaylord Judd Clarke. No one could say why he did it. Perhaps we need look no farther for an explanation than Fountain's high regard for his friend and neighbor. It is more likely, however, that Fountain the politician liked to seduce men from the opposition by offering them good jobs, as he had done in the case of Albert French. Mills says Fountain did it "to placate at least one gentleman and at the same time win away from me my friend."[58] Mills and Clarke continued on good terms after the appointment, however, which may or may not have been a disappointment to Fountain.

Actually the explosive element in the situation was not Mills. It was lawyer Benjamin F. Williams, who had supported Fountain with complete confidence that the Senator would make him the next district judge. Apparently he had gone to some lengths to deserve the appointment. His enemies said that "he acted with Fountain in perpetrating the fraud by which the people of El Paso were cheated out of the candidates of their choice a year ago." They said further that "he stood by Fountain, pistol in hand, while he (Fountain) committed a murderous assault upon Mr. Cardis a Hamilton man." Such loyalty should be rewarded, and Williams and his friends felt that he was entitled to the appointment. In May of 1870 over forty of them petitioned Fountain to get it for him.[59] There is some evidence that he had broken with Fountain before the election, denouncing him to the governor as "a forger and a thief."[60] The important thing is that in 1870 Fountain and Williams were enemies.

Their difficulties came to a climax on December 7, 1870. Williams had been brooding on Fountain's ingratitude and duplicity and drinking to reinforce his resentment. It was a fine, crisp winter day, but he took no note of the wonderful weather. Leaving his house on El Paso Street, he made a morning visit to Ben Dowell's saloon, where he took on more stimulants and began to denounce Fountain and Clarke to all within earshot. At the height of his tirade, Fountain himself stepped through the door. In an instant Williams had opened fire with a derringer. He emptied the weapon while Fountain, hit in two places and severely wounded, defended himself as best he could with his cane.

His ammunition spent, Williams backed out of the door in the rear and headed for his quarters, a few doors away. Once inside he barricaded the entrance and waited for the enemy to attack.

Fountain reached the front door of the saloon about the time Williams disappeared through the back entrance. Bleeding and angry, he hurried to his home two blocks away to get his rifle, stopping only to explain to Judge Clarke what had happened. Clarke took charge at once. He found Captain French of the State Police and ordered him to arrest Williams.

Together they went to the front door of the man's house and when they were refused admittance, they began trying to break in. This further exasperated the already frantic Williams, who now took away his own barricade, opened the door, and stepped out with a shotgun in his hand. Clarke dodged behind one of the adobe pillars of the *portal* or covered walk which extended the length of the block. Williams turned in the opposite direction and met him face to face. Leveling his weapon, Williams fired a double charge of buckshot into Clarke's heart. They were so close together that the blast set the victim's clothes on fire. He died instantly.

French immediately brought his pistol into action, placing bullets in Williams' right side and right eye. Fountain was close enough by now to get in a long shot with his rifle which finished the fight.[61]

A year after this terrible and tragic affair, Fountain found himself in difficulties of another sort. Mills was now ready to make his second move in his campaign to destroy the Senator. Early in December a capias was sent from Austin to El Paso requiring Fountain to appear and answer the charges against him in the United States District Court. The Austin *Statesman*, always bitter against the Radicals, reported the fact with sadistic satisfaction:

> The Honorable (?) Senator Fountain's personal appearance is so greatly desired in Austin that a capias has been sent to El Paso to bring the said gentleman in, dead or alive, to answer eighteen indictments — to such little charges as swindling, embezzlement, fraud and forgery; personating Collectors and Assessors, signing their names and swearing to documents, and disposing of pay-rolls at half price to Dutch saloon-keepers, are said to be only a portion of the indictments against him.
>
> Several pressing legal notices have been heretofore issued to him to appear, but having failed to do so, capias has been issued to bring him.[62]

All through these years Mills had harassed Fountain with every means at his disposal, repeatedly attacking him in the Austin papers and speaking ill of him on all occasions. Some time during that year of 1871 he collected his diatribes in a pamphlet, published at Austin at his own expense, called *El Paso. A Glance at Its Men and Contests for the last few Years: The Election Fraud, the Marshes, Williams, Pearson, Verney, and Fountain the Infamous.*

It was a real triumph of invective, the high-water mark of Mills' career as a gadfly. He told the story of his military career and his campaign against graft in the El Paso mail contracts as a warm-up. Then he recounted how he had befriended Fountain at the beginning of their association and how Fountain had turned against him. He produced affidavits showing that Fountain had won the election of 1869 by fraud; then let loose with charges that Fountain had stolen private papers and money when he was deputy collector and had falsified his accounts while Mills was away in Washington fighting the mail cases. He concluded by showing that Fountain's closest associates were in danger of prosecution for attempted assassination, tampering with the mails, theft, and defamation of character. "*These* were my accusers," he concluded. "Radicals in Texas sometimes complain of 'social ostracism.' I do not believe our people here desire to persecute any man for opinion's sake; but if the charge is that respectable people refuse to invite such men as Fountain into their parlors, we should plead guilty."

Having delayed his appearance long enough to make this case a celebrated one, Fountain finally showed up in Austin early in 1872 and stood his trial while the entire state watched with interest. W. M. Walton and ex-Governor A. J. Hamilton (Mills' father-in-law) were the prosecutors. It was to be an all-out attempt to finish Fountain off once and for all.

He was acquitted on every count. A correspondent for *Flake's Daily Bulletin,* originally convinced of Fountain's guilt, wrote to the editor from Austin on March 9, 1872: "The entire amount of money claimed to have been lost was less than five hundred dollars. The trial of these cases shows that every cent was paid over by Fountain — not one mill was lost by the Government — and that Senator Fountain did not forge anyone's name, did not personate any other person, did not illegally collect a dime, and did not neglect his business either criminally or carelessly. I believe the court and jury to be fair, conscientious and impartial — at least no man will accuse them of bias in favor of Fountain. . . . Senator Fountain has been the best abused man in Texas for the past six months, while evidence shows that he has been lying dangerously sick at home. He never fled, never sought to evade arrest, and never had committed a crime against the department."[63]

In view of the ruthlessness and unscrupulousness of political factions during these years, one would be rash to say that either Mills or Fountain was absolutely right.[64] But the fact remains that Fountain was acquitted.

His career in Texas was about over, the acquittal notwithstanding. He came home after the trial convinced that his enemies would resort to violence to get rid of him since they had failed of their purpose in the courts. He says that he learned later from Charles Howard that "Cardis and Borajo had determined to have me assassinated."[65] He may have had cause for alarm. Firearms were always handy in El Paso in those days and practically everybody was handy with them. A man who was angry or outraged enough would go after his enemy with a gun. Fountain was capable of doing exactly that himself, and he knew what he was up against. When his term of office was completed in 1874, he decided for the sake of his young wife and growing family (his final score was twelve children) to take no further risks. In January, 1875, he removed himself from the scene of his perils and triumphs and settled in Mesilla, New Mexico, where he continued his career as lawyer, editor, Indian fighter, and political wheelhorse. Trouble followed him like a shadow, but he was valiant and tenacious and held out until 1896, when he was finally done away with under circumstances which are still, and probably always will be, mysterious.[66]

Before he finished his career in the Texas Legislature, he helped to bring to El Paso two Radical Republicans who became locally famous. One was Simon B. Newcomb, a Nova Scotian who moved to Texas after a career in Canada and another in Ohio. Thanks to connections in Austin, he succeeded Gaylord Judd Clarke as district judge. Very shortly after his arrival he was embroiled with Mills and the moderate Republicans. When the grand jury addressed him in September of 1871 complaining of excessive taxation, election frauds, and government by "strangers appointed against our wishes" (meaning Simon B. Newcomb), the new judge responded with considerable heat.[67] So much bad feeling was generated that the military was called on to guard the courthouse and the governor was informed that bloodshed was imminent in El Paso County.[68] The trouble did not end until Newcomb was removed by the Legislature in 1874 and went off to Las Cruces to make his mark in New Mexico.[69]

The other Radical immigrant who arrived during these years was James P. Hague, a brilliant twenty-three-year-old lawyer, born in Missouri but reared and educated in East Texas. At twenty-one he was admitted to the bar in Austin, where he had been serving as clerk of the State Senate. Governor Davis gave him the appointment as district attorney which brought him to El Paso in May, 1871. He continued to be a significant figure in the life of the town until his premature death in 1893.[70]

One notable figure who came to town without Fountain's blessing, or the knowledge and consent of any other Radical Republican was Charles H. Howard. In retrospect his is a rather strange and terrible figure, for without him the troubles of 1877 would never have happened. At the time of his arrival, however, he was exceptional mostly because he was a Democrat — a dedicated Democrat who came to do battle with the entrenched Republicans and to conquer if possible. It took a brave man to undertake such a mission, and whatever else may be said of Charley Howard, nobody questions his bravery. The Radicals had held out in El Paso longer than anywhere else in the state and he meant to attack them in their citadel.

He was a Missouri lawyer, lately a lieutenant in the Confederate forces, a man with a reputation for "the daring and coolness with which he carried out the most dangerous enterprises."[71] He was a good speaker, though he mostly kept his mouth shut, a hard fighter, and a famous pistol shot — perhaps the best in the state.[72]

Physically he was burly and powerful, a bulldog of a man, dour and dangerous to his enemies, kind and benevolent to his friends. His new associates felt at once that he was to be respected — even feared. "From the first moment I saw him," one of them said later, "I feared him."[73]

One other immigrant who arrived during this period, a complete contrast to the contentious and self-seeking politicians we have been dealing with, was the Reverend Joseph Wilkin Tays — "Parson Tays" — who arrived in the fall of 1870 and founded the first Protestant church in our town. He came because Gaylord Judd Clarke and Albert Jennings Fountain had gone all the way to Austin to ask Bishop Gregg to send them a missionary. Tays was the man.

Born in Nova Scotia, he studied at King's College, taught at West Point, and was ordained in Texas. He lost his wife and baby son during a yellow-fever epidemic at Indianola, spent a year as chaplain of the Senate in Austin, and arrived with his broken heart and unbroken spirit in the village on the Rio Grande on October 2, 1870, bringing his two motherless boys with him. Clarke and Fountain found him a place to live and work just north of the Plaza west of where the Angelus Hotel later stood. He conducted a school, held services on Sundays, and made a living by dealing in real estate and holding down the job of county surveyor. He helped with his own hands to build the first St. Clement's Episcopal Church, a block south of his first location on Mesa Avenue. The bell, cast in Mexico, which hung first from a cross-bar outside his adobe sanctuary, now occupies the place of honor in the great stone church which rose on Montana Avenue in 1907 to carry on the work of this good and humble man.[74]

His energy and dedication appeared in a story which came back to Austin a month after his ministry began. He sent word that the situation was bad in El Paso but that he was doing his best. He was studying Spanish; and already one saloonkeeper had closed his doors and taken up another calling.[75]

CHAPTER XVI

The Storm Breaks

 WHEN CHARLES HOWARD AND WESLEY OWENS, his Negro servant and confidant, climbed down from the stagecoach early in 1872 and beat the dust of travel from their garments, their arrival in El Paso could not have been better timed. The Republican organization was in ruins, shattered by the Fountain-Mills feud and blown up in the shotgun blasts which killed Clarke and Williams. More than that, the rule of the Republicans in Texas had run its course. Conservative Republicans had combined with the Democrats to get rid of E. J. Davis and carpetbag rule.[1] It was time for a realignment.

Not long after Howard hung out his lawyer's shingle (he settled first in San Elizario),[2] he and Luis Cardis made contact with each other. Cardis still controlled the Mexican vote, but he was a wirepuller, a worker behind the scenes. Howard could make a speech and, if necessary, a fight. Cardis was a good inside man; Howard was a good outside man. They combined their forces, and their mutual affection was for a time a wonderful thing to behold. Cardis discovered that at heart he had been a Democrat all the time and prepared to give Howard all the help he could in ejecting the Republican rascals from their places of power and influence.

The combination met its first test of strength in 1872 when Howard ran against James P. Hague for district attorney. Howard got 477 votes to Hague's 120.[3] Cardis's influence, of course, made the difference.

Howard's joy and gratitude knew no bounds, and he fired off a letter to the San Antonio *Herald* ascribing all honor and glory to Cardis for bringing about this "great political revolution."

"For months and months preceding the election," he said, "unassisted and alone, with an energy and perseverance absolutely astonishing, Mr. Cardis worked day and night to rouse up the people. . . . I think no county in the State deserves more credit than El Paso, and no man more than L. Cardis."[4]

Cardis made no such revelation of his own feelings, but he could not have remained unmoved by such a eulogy! For two years these ambitious and wilful men prolonged their honeymoon. In 1874 they pooled their forces again to put Cardis into the State Legislature. Father Borajo was in the thick of the campaign using every bit of influence he possessed for his friend Don Luis. An unsympathetic observer reported that "The priest Borajo went from house to house threatening that those who did not vote for Cardis should not be buried in consecrated ground, but on dung hills like dogs. Yes, a sworn statement even says that he 'gathered his flock like a herd of sheep, and marched them to the polls, sprinkling holy water over the Cardis tickets and distributing them.' "[5] Howard told a friend in Austin that but eleven radical votes were cast in the entire county.[6]

Cardis would probably have won without any such drastic gestures, for things were going from bad to worse for his people, and they needed his help desperately. The panic of 1873 had made life more difficult than it had been for some years and many of the Americans gave up and moved away. The railroad, so long expected, made such slow progress that others gave up and moved on that account. In 1874 unusually high water sent the Rio Grande out of its channel and caused great damage in El Paso, Paso del Norte, and the smaller communities northward.[7] And along with the other plagues of nature, the Indians were becoming steadily more troublesome. They were haunting the outskirts of the Valley towns and driving off horses and cattle under the noses of the inhabitants, while stagecoaches on the San Antonio road were being regularly attacked.[8]

The Adjutant General finally authorized the organization of a local Ranger company which was mustered into service on May 27, 1874, with Telesforo Montes of San Elizario in charge. Lieutenant Montes and his men chased Apaches all that summer and all through the next year, sending reports to the Adjutant General which indicate that the Indians were more than holding their own. On August 18, 1875, they captured four horses in the outskirts of

San Elizario. The next day they attacked a salt train seventy miles out from the Valley and ran off six mules.⁹ And so it went.

The Valley people were having a hard time even keeping their bodies and souls together in those desperate years. Cardis tried to help them by introducing a bill in March of 1874 which set aside eight sections of irrigable land for each mile of new ditch which the people of any town in his home district might construct. "They ask it," said a reporter who had probably been indoctrinated by Don Luis himself, "as an act of justice, having suffered intolerable burdens and persecutions at the hands of political vampires until the people are almost in a starving condition, with no resources left."¹⁰

The passage of this bill did little to relieve the Valley Mexicans, whose problems were less political than meteorological that year, but at least they felt that their representative was doing something. Meanwhile District Judge Simon B. Newcomb, E. J. Davis' appointee, had been removed by his political opponents in Austin, and the day after the Legislature disposed of him, Charles Howard was given the appointment. It was only two years since he first set foot on the streets of El Paso, and now he was the biggest man in the Valley. It would be hard to match such a success story anywhere, and the speed of his rise may have given him some delusions about himself. He celebrated by getting married, his bride being Miss Louisa Zimpelman of Manor, Texas, daughter of Major George B. Zimpelman, banker, soldier, and financier of Austin. On New Year's Day, 1876, the newlyweds with two Negro servants for escort set off in a buggy on the eight-hundred-mile trip to El Paso.¹¹

Lou Zimpelman, a quiet, delicate girl, was not prepared for life on the frontier, apparently, for she died in the summer of 1877.¹²

Meanwhile Cardis and Howard had come to the end of their friendship. Howard was inclined to be arrogant. His new eminence may have made him more so. In addition there was trouble about the salt deposits. Cardis and Borajo tried to get Howard to commit himself somehow, and Howard refused. Cardis told Fountain some months later that the Judge had "violated his pledges"; Howard, when his turn came, assured Fountain that he had broken with his former friends "on account of their trying to force him into some monstrous schemes" which involved turning over to them two-thirds of the salt-lakes property.[13]

Hatred was a weak word for their feelings toward each other. Howard called Cardis, in print, "a liar, a coward, a mischief maker, a meddler; such a thing as could only spring from the decaying carcass of an effete people."[14] Cardis said nothing, but he expressed himself in other ways. A ditch project had been started in San Elizario as a result of Cardis' legislative effort of the year before. The state had not provided the help Cardis thought he had a right to expect, and he told his people that Howard was to blame, with the result that Howard lost what credit he had with the Valley Mexicans.[15] And every few weeks Ben Dowell would warn the judge that some of Cardis' friends and supporters were out to kill him.[16]

The Constitutional Convention of 1875 brought the feud into the open. Cardis and Howard opposed each other for the post of delegate. Howard won at both the precinct and district conventions while Cardis wrote letters to the Texas papers declaring that the elections were frauds. In August Cardis entered the final go-round as an independent and drew 370 votes to Howard's 104. He went off in triumph to represent his district at the convention in September.[17]

Howard suffered further humiliation in the regular elections of 1876 when he lost his judgeship and Cardis was returned to the Legislature.[18] His cup of bitterness overflowed and naturally he yearned for a chance to hurt and disgrace his enemy. At home Cardis kept out of his way, but once in San Antonio and once in Austin the little Italian was in the wrong place at the right time and Howard gave him a physical beating.[19]

He came near ending Cardis once and for all in the summer of 1877. Lou Zimpelman Howard was ill — was, in fact, dying — and her father, Major Zimpelman, came out from Austin to visit her. It was during this time that he first became interested in the salt lakes. He and Howard conferred and planned, and at last set out for the lakes with a surveyor to locate unclaimed acreage. In June, on his way back to the salt deposits to complete the survey, Howard cornered Cardis again in the stage station at Fort Quitman and intended to kill him but couldn't bring himself to pull the trigger. "He ran under a table and acted so cowardly I didn't have the heart to shoot him," he said. Cardis, badly frightened, went back to El Paso and had Howard indicted at the September term of court.[20]

Meanwhile Howard, acting for his father-in-law, perfected title to the unlocated portions of the lakes[21] and acquired the Maverick survey of ten years before. Thus legally in possession, he posted notices warning all and sundry not to take salt without clearance from him or his agents. When he heard that José María Juárez and Macedonio Gándara of San Elizario had said they would go after salt any time they felt like it, he had them arrested.[22]

Howard was on his way to Fort Davis to hold court when the arrests were made, and the action nearly cost him his life. A mob assembled, locked up the county judge and the justice of the peace when they refused to issue warrants for Howard's arrest, and sent a detachment off down the road to ambush him "and say it was Indians."[23] His agent, John McBride, heard about the proposed ambush and got to Howard in time to turn him back. He retreated to Ysleta, where he spent the night with Sheriff Charles Kerber, burning with anger at that "coward, thief, sneak, and liar" Cardis. On the road he said to his man Wesley Owens, "Wesley, when I get back from Fort Davis, if Cardis don't let me alone I'm going to kill him. I'm going to kill him anyway. He has been bothering me long enough."[24]

In the morning he woke to find Kerber's house surrounded by the San Elizario mob. When he and McBride went out to face them, they seized him, took him back to San Elizario, and confined him in Mauro Lujan's big house near the old church.

A week later he described his experience to Colonel Fountain: "I was kept for three days and nights; at all times surrounded by three or four hundred armed pelados, raving and raging like hungry coyotes. I was not allowed to see my friends or write to anyone. I was told that unless I would agree to certain conditions that the mob would impose, I would be killed. For two days I refused to subscribe to the conditions required or in any way treat with the mob. On the third day, finding that there was no assistance, that could be had in time to save my life, and that the mob was growing more ferocious every moment, and that not only my safety was involved but also that of every American in the country, I agreed to sign any papers required of me, and late in the evening of the third day of my confinement did sign a document. . . ."[25]

The idea of making Howard sign a bond may have originated in the mind of Luis Cardis, who seems to have been asked for advice by the leaders of the mob.[26]

The man who handled the negotiations was the new priest at San Elizario, the Rev. Pierre Bourgade (later a bishop). Borajo had moved across the river, most unwillingly, to the parish of Guadalupe when the east or American bank was taken from the jurisdiction of the Bishop of Durango in 1877 and placed in the Diocese of Tucson.[27] Bourgade secured Howard's promise that he would not prosecute the members of the mob if they allowed him to go free, and after the agreement was signed, the priest put his hand on Howard's shoulder, steered him through the menacing assembly to a waiting carriage and did not leave him until he was past Ysleta on his way home.

The paper Howard had signed said he would "forget all that has passed," let the courts determine ownership of the salt lakes, leave the country for good within twenty-four hours, and give bond for adherence to the terms of the agreement. The bond — for $12,000 — was signed by four of his San Elizario friends: John G. Atkinson, Charles E. Ellis, Jesús Cobos, and Tomás García — all men of property and standing in the community.[28]

Convinced at last that he had unleashed a tiger, Howard took refuge in Mesilla with A. J. Fountain, an "honorable enemy,"[29] and began sending telegrams (the line had reached Las Cruces by now) warning the Governor of Texas that there was danger of an invasion from Mexico. District Judge Allen Blacker rushed a dispatch to the governor from Fort Stockton, where the telegraph wires from eastern Texas ended: "Civil authorities powerless. . . . Life and property still in danger."[30]

Cardis, on the other hand, sent off a much more cheerful wire: "The late disturbance in this Co. is over and everything seems to be quiet. It is mainly through my efforts that peace has been established, though reports may come to you to the contrary. Full particulars by mail."[31]

He never lived to write the letter. Howard was brooding and raging against him, calling him an "infamous monster who has brought these poor, ignorant, deluded, and credulous people, into this trouble for his own cowardly and selfish ends. I can think of nothing in Earth or Hell, bad enough for him."[32]

In this frame of mind, he drove from Mesilla to El Paso on October 7 with a detachment of soldiers ordered by Colonel Hatch from Fort Bayard to make sure San Elizario was not taken over by aliens from Mexico. Fort Bliss had been abandoned as a useless outpost in January, 1877, and there were no soldiers nearer than this. The troops camped at El Paso and Howard stayed in town also. On October 10, after eating his noon meal at the hotel where the Mills Building now stands, he said to his colored man, "Wesley, I feel very restless and must have my revenge."[33] So saying, he picked up a double-barrelled shotgun and left the dining room.

At this moment, Cardis was sitting in a rocking chair in Schutz Brothers' store, a long block west on San Francisco Street. Howard must have known exactly where he was, for he walked directly to the Schutz place of business, entered, and shot Cardis as he got up from his chair and tried to take refuge behind a tall bookkeeper's desk. Howard later said that Cardis was pointing a pistol at him when he fired. This may be true. Cardis had been carrying two pistols, and only one was found on his body. But the technicality does not alter the fact that Howard went to the store to kill him and did so.[34]

Every American in the Valley had heard the news within a very short time, and every one of them knew that his life was in danger. "We are expecting a terrible catastrophe," said a telegram that went off to Colonel Hatch. "Can you send immediate help for God's sake?"[35]

Help was on the way, but not from Colonel Hatch. Major John B. Jones, chief of the Frontier Battalion of Texas Rangers, was sent from Austin to look into the situation. He had to go to Topeka, Kansas, and take the Santa Fe down into New Mexico, finishing the trip by stagecoach, in order to get to El Paso in the shortest possible time. He spent Saturday and Sunday, November 5 and 6, with Howard and Fountain in Mesilla.[36] On Monday he came to El Paso and found that the lawless element was in control in the Valley. The mob at San Elizario was looking for some way to kill Charles Howard and had notified the four bondsmen who had guaranteed his good conduct that the bond was forfeit. On Tuesday, the day after the Major arrived, a letter was smuggled out and delivered in El Paso: "Some eight or ten of us have got together and will fight till we die. We are in Atkinson's house — send us help for the honor of the Gringos." A postcript addressed to Sheriff Charles Kerber read: "Help us Charlie for Christ's sake, and we will do our damndest in the meantime."[37]

Jones decided to face the mob himself and went down to San Elizario for that purpose, first sending word to the leaders that he wanted to see them. They met him at Mauro Lujan's house, which was their headquarters, all the leading agitators except the two top men, Chico Barela and Sixto Salcido. They were probably waiting nearby. Father Bourgade translated.

They talked in the morning and they talked that afternoon. At first the Major was encouraged since they received him courteously. But when he announced that he was going to form a company of Texas Rangers and refused to let the leaders organize their own group, they turned sullen and angry, and he went back to El Paso with nothing accomplished.[38]

Three days later, on November 12, he sent a telegram to the Adjutant General requesting a commission for John B. Tays as a second lieutenant in the Rangers. He was to head a new detachment — Company C of the Frontier Battalion.

John was a brother of the Reverend Joseph W. Tays, the Episcopal missionary. Unlike Joseph, John was not well educated and had developed no particular skills. He dug wells and made furniture and did odd jobs. His fellow townsmen testified later that he was "a man of unblemished integrity, cool, courageous, and discreet."[39] These things he may have been, but he was no fighting man and had no background whatsoever for what he had to do. The reason he got the appointment was that among the handful of Americans in the village of El Paso he was the best that could be found. The men who were induced to enlist in his company were poor risks also. Not one of them would have been a Ranger under ordinary circumstances. Nevertheless, since the job had to be done and they were there to do it, they waited only until arms, ammunition and supplies could be assembled and then followed their lieutenant down to San Elizario where they took over an adobe house beside the highway at the north edge of town and went into quarters.

Meanwhile Howard had been busy on his own. With the help of Joseph Magoffin, collector of customs, and the Rangers, he persuaded the local justice of the peace, Guadalupe Carbajal, to admit him to bail. On the morning of November 17 he appeared on the streets of El Paso a free man and nobody seemed inclined to object. Major Jones was sure everything was under control and went back to Austin. On the 29th Tays wrote him about the local situation:

> Things are about the same as when you left the Mexicans gave Howerd a scare the other nite on his way down to Franklin at the ranch 15 miles above Franklin his man shot a dog belongen to the ranch as they past and fifteen armed men rushed out on Howard with the entention of killen him but for some nice talks and $100 he got off but badly scared he is now in Franklin.
>
> Yours respectfully
> Lt. J. B. Tays.[40]

The players were now in position and the game was ready to begin under conditions which boded ill for everybody concerned. There was serious unrest on both sides of the Rio Grande. The river was dry above El Paso by the middle of September and crops were going to be short.[41] Indians were troublesome, attacking trains and stages, killing the people and stealing the horses and mules.[42] Cardis had queried the Adjutant General on October 3, "Are El Paso and Presidio Counties to have protection and if so when?"[43]

On the Mexican side the turmoil was even worse. Benito Juárez was dead. His party was divided by ambitious men into several contentious groups. Sebastian Lerdo de Tejada, Juárez' close associate and confidant, became President, but Porfirio Díaz, often defeated but never crushed, finally forced him into exile — though not before several Mexican states, including Chihuahua, were overrun with soldiers and subjected to the rigors of war. Ernest Kohlberg, watching from his store building in Paso del Norte, noted the skirmishing and the executions near Chihuahua and prophesied in June, 1876, that troops would soon be in Paso del Norte "in order to get control of the customhouse and its revenues."[44]

Actually *lerdistas*, who hoped for the restoration of Lerdo de Tejada, were in and out of Paso del Norte for some time. Kohlberg noted in November that an officer of this "revolution" named Ferrales escaped being shot by fleeing to the American side,[45] but there were bands of revolutionists on the loose elsewhere in the state,

and the merchants and officials of the border town were uneasy
for many months. Toward the end of March, one of these bands
entered the city. "Two weeks ago," Ernest wrote on April 8, "there
were 100 Mexican cavalrymen here. I have never seen so many
cut-throats together at one time." They stayed only two days, but
they forced the merchants to pay their taxes a year in advance.
Ernest had to disgorge $160.00. "This money will not be lost if no
other party gets control," he remarked. "However, if another crowd
gets the upper hand, they will declare the levying of the tax as
illegal and will make us pay them again."

A month later a larger force of insurrectionists under Colonel
Machorro rode in and made more trouble. Machorro proclaimed
himself military governor of Chihuahua and tried to mulct the
merchants again. Fortunately for them, however, his violent tactics aroused such resentment in Paso del Norte that the entire
population rose against him and forced him to cross the river to
the American side, nearly drowning himself in his haste.[46]

It seemed that the whole country was restless and ready for
trouble. At San Elizario the local Mexican population gathered
here and there and discussed the difficult times they were going
through. They agreed that if it had not been for Howard, they
could have made a little money hauling salt and decided that his
interference was a thing not to be endured. Some of them resolved
that they would not pay more taxes to a government which deprived them of their ancient rights in this fashion.[47] They quoted
Father Ortiz, the priest of Paso del Norte, who thought they had
a moral if not a legal right to the salt.[48]

The guerrillas and government troops marching in and out of
Paso del Norte gave some of the Valley people ideas they would
have been better off without. A lerdista officer actually crossed
the dry bed of the Rio Grande to San Elizario and conducted drill
sessions.[49] There was talk all along the Border of another war between the United States and Mexico. "We have been expecting a
declaration of war between the United States and Mexico all summer," Ernest Kohlberg wrote to his people in Germany. "If this
came about it would be the best thing that could happen." Ernest
was sure that the United States would take over the North Mexican
states in case of hostilities, and from his point of view everybody
would be better off.[50]

This sort of gossip made the Mexicans on the north bank more conscious of their heritage than usual. At San Elizario during one of the frequent *juntas* somebody remarked, "You must remember, Gentlemen, that you are American citizens." This brought the whole assembly to its feet shouting, "No, no. We are not Americans. We are Mexicans to the death. *Hasta la muerte! Hasta la muerte!*"[51]

Somehow the salt question always came back into every discussion. Howard had no right to do what he was doing. It was necessary to make him see that he could not defy the people in this matter. Finally they decided to act. They organized a *conducta* of sixteen wagons and sixty yoke of oxen and set out for the lakes, intending to bring back salt in spite of Howard and his preemptions. The word came to Joseph Magoffin, the customs collector, and he set out in a buggy with an escort of soldiers to see if there was any truth in the story — especially to determine if any Mexicans nationals were involved.

Halfway from Fort Quitman to the lakes there was a campground where Magoffin met three loaded wagons coming back. The two parties went into camp near each other. During the night the drivers dumped their salt on the ground and fled. Magoffin learned later that they had considered cutting his throat but had decided not to risk it. All the men were from Chihuahua. Not one was an American citizen.[52]

It was time now for Howard to make a decision. He could fight or he could run. He chose to fight. His friends and even such "honorable enemies" as Colonel Fountain advised him as earnestly as they could to stay away from the Valley towns. He refused to listen, considering himself honor bound to do whatever he could to protect the interests of his father-in-law, Major Zimpelman, even at the risk of his life. He said he "would feel as if he were recreant to his trust were he to allow himself to be driven from his post of duty by the menaces of a mob."

Although Fountain tried to convince him that Zimpelman would not expect him to take such risks "in the performance of a professional obligation,"[53] Howard was determined to go in person to prosecute the salt runners, and go he did on the afternoon of December 12, escorted by a detachment of Rangers who had come up to El Paso at his request.

A considerable concentration of friends and enemies was waiting for him at San Elizario. One was lawyer James P. Hague, who went down that same day, broke a leg when his horses ran away and smashed his buggy, and was lying in Mauro Lujan's house, unable to stir. Judge Hague had come close to taking Cardis' place as a friend of the poor, and there were those who thought that he and Mauro Lujan were the real leaders of the mob,[54] though Hague had written to his wife in October, "I have no connection with the affair and I don't want or intend to have."[55]

Much concerned about what was going on was Father Pierre Bourgade, the local priest, who had written to Major Jones: "Three fourths of these fellows are already starving in consequence of their bad crops and are determined to get something from the salt or fight to the death."[56]

Most concerned of all was Lieutenant Tays of the Rangers. He watched the men in the streets and realized what they were capable of doing. Some hours after the detachment went off to El Paso to act as Howard's escort, he decided that more protection might be needed and set off himself at the head of another group to meet and reinforce his men. At the edge of town he encountered Chico Barela, the strong man of the mob, with about eighteen men, most of them from Mexico.[57]

Chico has carved a small but solid foothold in Valley history and deserves a few words to himself. A native of Ysleta, he was illiterate but a leader of great force and talent. He was a quiet man, fair for a Mexican, with brown hair and blue eyes. His daughter Pancha is said to have been engaged to Luis Cardis at the time of the latter's death,[58] but the story cannot now be verified. He was certainly loyal to Cardis' memory, as were his chief lieutenant Sixto Salcido of San Elizario and most of the *insurrectos* in the mob.

The sight of Chico's picket line on the outskirts of town alarmed Tays still further and he instructed one of his troopers to ride on to El Paso and alert Captain Blair, in charge of the soldiers from Fort Bayard. Blair answered the call, we might add, and arrived with fourteen men at the outskirts of San Elizario about nine o'clock that night, but when Barela told him there were no aliens in the mob — all good Americans — he turned around and went back to camp. His credulity destroyed the last hope for Howard.

Meanwhile the reinforced Ranger detachment had brought

Howard safely to their adobe headquarters in the village late in the afternoon. The night, however, was marked by violence. Before morning Charles Ellis, the storekeeper and miller, Howard's friend, had been dragged and stabbed to death by the mob when he tried to reason with them. In the morning Howard and his hosts found themselves surrounded and under siege. Sergeant C. E. Mortimer was killed in the street outside as he was doing sentry duty and bullets crashed from time to time through doors and windows. John Atkinson, one of Howard's bondsmen, somehow got through the Mexican lines with a trunk containing $11,000 and asked the Rangers for protection, but nobody else went in or out. The fighting continued all that day and through the next night. Young Miguel García, one of a group who had been holding out in Ellis' store, was killed when the mob broke through a wall and overran the place.

The siege, which had begun on Wednesday, continued through Friday and Saturday. The mob made assault after assault and the Rangers, worn out and sleepless, fought them off.[59] There was a parley Sunday night which led to a cease-fire until Monday morning. With daylight the talks were resumed. "If Howard gives himself up," the Mexicans said, "and gives up all claim to the salt lakes, no harm will come to him."

The judge had already made up his mind what he would do. "I will go," he said. "It is the only chance to save your lives. But they will kill me."

"Then don't go," Tays told him. "We are here to protect you, and we will do so to the very last."

"No, I'll go. McBride, take care of my money and papers. Goodbye, boys." Smiling cheerfully, he shook hands all round and left the building."[60]

Whatever may be said of Tays, he was no coward. When Sergent C. E. Mortimer had been shot down in the street, it was Tays who walked out under fire, picked him up, and brought him inside the Ranger quarters. He was unwilling now that Howard should face the music alone, and he walked beside him as he stepped into the street and proceeded toward the Mexican headquarters at Guillermo Gándara's house. Chico Barela was so glad to see Howard that he is said to have "hugged and kissed him."

Neither Howard nor Tays had much Spanish so a messenger

was sent back for John Atkinson to come and translate. Leaving his eleven thousand dollars, he came to Gándara's house and immediately went into a huddle with the leaders. The upshot was that he agreed to turn over his money if the mob would cancel Howard's bond. Chico, who engineered the deal, seems to have promised that all could go free if the money was turned over and Howard left the country forever. There can be little doubt that if Chico had remained in control, bloodshed would have been avoided. But he had unleashed forces that were more powerful than he.

Atkinson played the game out to the last card. He was back at the Ranger's house within half an hour bearing assurances that all was peaceful at last. He told the men that their horses would be taken care of, and that Tays was expecting them to come at once. They fell into the trap and straggled out, two or three at a time. As each group reached the rebel stronghold, their arms were taken away and they were shoved into "a dirty room" and placed under heavy guard. They were too close to exhaustion to feel anything but relief that the fight was over at last. Most of them lay down on the dirt floor and went to sleep.[61] They had earned the doubtful distinction of being the only body of Texas Rangers who ever surrendered.

Tays and his men could have gone free at this point. The leaders of the mob told the lieutenant repeatedly that he could depart now that they had Howard. He refused to go. "I will not leave till Howard goes free," he said. Finally they lost patience, picked him up bodily, and locked him up in a room they were using as a guardhouse.

Meanwhile Chico Barela had sent word to Father Borajo that he had reached an agreement with the Americans and had Howard in custody. Borajo is said to have sent back a reply: "Shoot all the gringos and I will absolve you."[62] It is hard to believe that any priest would have made such a statement.

His advice, if he gave it, was probably not needed. Howard was doomed the moment he left the protection of the Rangers, and his final great moment was not slow in coming. As soon as it was known that he was in custody, the great crowd in the plaza set up a chant: "Kill him! Kill him!" Almost everybody from the villages on both sides of the river was there that day, and they made a mighty noise.

Somewhere there must have been a *junta* which pronounced the death sentence, for shortly after Howard gave up, a committee of twelve or fifteen men entered Gándara's house where he was under guard and reappeared, shoving him ahead of them. They marched him into a vacant space between two houses. He turned to face the mob, silent now, as a firing squad of five men filed up led by Desiderio Apodaca. Every one of them was a citizen of Mexico.

Howard tried, in his broken Spanish, to tell them that his death might cost the lives of three hundred men, but he could not find the words he wanted and gave up. Seeing the squad was ready to do its work, he braced himself, gave the command to fire, and fell to the ground in his last agony. Jesús Telles, a horse thief who swung back and forth between Ysleta and Mexico, ran up with a *machete* raised to strike and aimed a blow at Howard's face. The dying man twisted away as the blow fell, and Telles cut off two of his own toes. Others with better aim hacked and chopped at the body.[63]

Atkinson and McBride were brought out next. Chico Barela objected furiously. He had promised that all could go free, Howard included. He had not objected too much when Howard was shot because he thought the man deserved it. These two could not, in honor, be killed. His objections were brushed aside and the men were shot down. But when the mob called for more blood, Chico got control at last. He stood up and said his men would fight if there was any more killing. The mutilated bodies were dragged off and pitched into an old well half a mile away, where they were later found.

While the mob fell to looting the stores and homes of the Americans, the Rangers, disarmed and disgraced, went back to their quarters. Next morning Chico overrode the voices of those who wanted to "shoot all the gringos," gave them back their horses, and sent them out of town.[64]

Now that the horse had been stolen, everybody flocked in to lock the barn. Colonel Hatch came to El Paso and took charge of the troops which marched in from Fort Davis and Fort Bayard. Sheriff Kerber assembled a posse of hard characters, mostly from

Silver City, New Mexico, under instructions from Governor Hubbard. This group marched to San Elizario, committing rape and murder en route, and camped there till Christmas, quarrelling among themselves and shooting each other when no better prospects for homicide were available.[65]

The Salt War was scandalous enough to call for a congressional investigation, and a four-man board assembled in El Paso on January 22, 1878. On March 16 a final report was filed,[66] but Major Jones, dissatisfied with the majority opinion, continued taking testimony, and filed his own minority report on March 22. Jones was convinced that the international aspects of the affair were more important than his colleagues were willing to admit. He thought the damage done to property amounted to $31,000 (as against the majority estimate of $12,000), and he recommended that the Mexican government be asked to punish the Mexican citizens involved and to pay for the damages. He agreed with the others that it would be advisable to reestablish Fort Bliss in case of future trouble.

Washington paid attention to this last recommendation, and in 1879 steps were taken to set up a new Army post on property purchased from Simeon Hart's estate close to the old mill.[67]

The grand jury of El Paso County indicted six men, the leaders of the mob, and the Governor of Texas later offered rewards for Chico Barela, Sixto Salcido, and four others. Nobody turned a finger to collect the money and the indicted men lived out their lives in peace and safety on the Mexican side of the river.[68]

The question of payment for salt ceased to be a matter of controversy. A new agent was appointed by the Zimpelman interests. The Mexicans applied to him politely for permission to haul salt and paid for what they took.

CHAPTER XVII

The Boom Begins

 ABOUT THE MIDDLE OF JULY, 1877, before the Salt War broke out, a man whom we know only as Juan paid a visit to El Paso. Juan was from the Valley town of Socorro, fifteen miles below the Pass, and was a correspondent for the Mesilla *Independent,* a weekly paper issued by Colonel Fountain and two associates. With humorous condescension, like an Englishman describing the quaint customs of the Hottentots, Juan noted his sensations and impressions in our primitive little community. It must be remembered that San Elizario (the county seat), Ysleta — perhaps even Socorro — were larger than El Paso. Juan intimated that the place was little and stagnant and dull, as it undoubtedly was. He described the great event of that summer, the completion of Joseph Magoffin's new house (the one we call the Old Magoffin House now), a "magnificent country seat, which is pleasantly situated one mile south of this renowned metropolis."

"It is not given us (wicked sinners) to see into the future," Juan continued, straining his imagination, "but judging from the past progress, who knows but that in a few years hence the Judge's palatial rural domicile will be the center of the city." Smiling inwardly at this fantastic thought, he closed his piece with a poetical sneer:

> Not a drum was heard,
> Nor the voice of a goat;
> Nor a doleful or joyful ditty.
> But a dog struck his teeth
> Through the tail of my coat
> As I left that famous city.[1]

The year before S. H. Newman had estimated the population as somewhere between fifty and a hundred[2] and had remarked that half the houses were unoccupied. What impressed Newman particularly was the strength of purpose which fired those fifty-odd pioneers. Every one of them had dreamed a dream — a vision of a Great Day coming when the railroad would arrive and untold riches would reward the faithful, all of whom were hanging grimly to the lots and plots they had acquired. Ben Dowell and Colonel Zabriskie and W. W. Mills and Joseph Magoffin and James P. Hague had important holdings. Even Parson Tays had considerable acreage, much of it given in payment for his services as surveyor.

"The few people living here never wavered in their faith that this was to be a great city," Newman recalled. "I remember how the same Col. Zabriskie pointed out the exact spot where the railroad would cross the Rio Grande, and I smiled and accused him of drawing upon his imagination. Years afterward when the Southern Pacific railroad company built its bridge above the city, I smiled again and in imagination took off my hat to Col. Zabriskie. It was on the exact spot he had pointed out."[3]

The Great Day was slow in coming. The Texas and Pacific reached Fort Worth in 1876 and never moved an inch farther for four years. The Galveston, Harrisburg and San Antonio (one day to be part of the Southern Pacific system) arrived in San Antonio in 1877 and sat on its hands for three years. True, the Southern Pacific began to build eastward from Yuma in December of 1878, but Yuma was a long way from El Paso.[4]

Meanwhile life at the Pass was alternately dull and dangerous. The Apaches provided what excitement there was. On February 6, 1877, Gregorio García, an important citizen of San Elizario, wrote to Adjutant General William Steele at Austin: The Indians "have left me and my two sons destitute, having carried off all our stock." He asked for more protection from the Rangers.[5]

Lieutenant Tays, who continued to command the Ranger company after his humiliation at San Elizario, had one brush with Apaches in the salt lake region, losing one man and three horses. A complaint went in to Austin that he was using his force to protect a herd of his own sheep.[6]

A year after the outbreak of the Salt War Tays resigned in order to take a job in the customs service at Presidio.[7] His successor was a famous fighter, a real professional, George W. Baylor — a brother of General Baylor of the Confederate forces in the campaign of 1861-62.

With his family and an escort of six Rangers, Baylor arrived at his quarters in Ysleta in September, 1879.[8] Within a month he was chasing Indians. Victorio, the great and ruthless Apache leader, had broken out of the Mescalero Reservation during the summer and begun his two-year carnival of death and destruction. Circling through New Mexico and Arizona, he dropped below the border into Old Mexico and went to earth in the Candelaria Mountains fifty miles below El Paso. Here he succeeded in ambushing — twice — parties sent against him from the town of San José, said to have been the property of Dr. Mariano Samaniego of Paso del Norte.[9] Twenty-nine Mexicans from San José and Carrizal were dead. The word came to Paso del Norte. Men from the little towns on the Mexican side, with ten Rangers under Baylor, rendezvoused at the Ojo de Samalayuca. Chico Barela, lately in command of the San Elizario mob, was one of the party. Victorio slipped away from his mountain hideout before they arrived, and it was not till a year later, on October 14, 1880, that the great Apache was finally cornered in northern Chihuahua and killed. In the meantime he had circled El Paso again, moving through New Mexico and Arizona like a devouring flame and defying pursuit. Baylor's Rangers and United States troops were cooperating with the Mexican forces just before the end, but General Joaquín Terrazas requested them to leave when he saw that he had the situation firmly in hand.[10]

The last Indian fight in Texas took place a little later when a remnant of Victorio's band attacked the San Antonio stage in Quitman Canyon, killing the driver and his lone passenger. With some Mexican helpers who had personal grievances against the Apaches, Baylor took up the pursuit and after a long chase surprised the Indian encampment at daybreak on January 29, 1881, in the Diablo Mountains southwest of Guadalupe Peak. Four warriors, two women and two children were killed as the band scattered and fled.[11]

While these troubles were creating difficulties on the perimeter of the El Paso region, matters were going from bad to worse in the town itself. El Paso had never been a prudish place. The frontier code required every man to mind his own business and as Owen White, our first historian, puts it, a citizen was judged by his shooting ability and his liquid capacity.[12] But the honest old ways were passing, and people were now arriving who made the original settlers look like a parcel of Puritans. Behind this situation was the fact that the railroads had at last begun to move. The Southern Pacific reached Tucson on March 20, 1880 — Benson in June — Lordsburg in mid-October — Deming on December 15.[13] The Texas and Pacific at the same time was racing (if one uses the term loosely) across northern Texas, reaching Baird on December 4, 1880, Sweetwater on March 12, 1881, Big Spring on April 28.[14] And that was not all. The Santa Fe, without much chance of being in first, was making good progress south of Albuquerque, and the Mexican Central had started the long haul from the border to Chihuahua and Mexico City. It was obvious that the Great Day was at hand, and as the railroads came closer, the population of the town began to grow and multiply wildly. A stage line linked each end-of-track to the booming village, and every day another batch of strangers crowded in. By May of 1881, according to one estimate, the fifty citizens of 1876 had grown to 1,500.[15] Accommodations were at a premium. Prices skyrocketed. The streets were crowded day and night. El Paso was dull and lonely no longer.

Some of the newcomers were men of substance and character who came to build a city, and many of the names you see on schools and streets and subdivisions were first heard in the community in 1880 and 1881 when the boom began. Zach White, who had a part in practically every progressive venture during the next forty years, appeared in February, 1881, with ten thousand dollars sewed into the back of his vest. He sold groceries at first and went on to hardware, brick manufacturing, and real estate.[16]

In February, 1880, O. T. Bassett and his special friend Charles R. Morehead arrived. Morehead in his forty years of life had proved himself in times of danger and difficulty as a wagon boss for the great firm of Waddell and Majors. He had been mayor of Leavenworth just before he came to the Southwest. Small in stature, he was big of brain, tremendously shrewd and courageous — a quiet little man who got things done. Bassett was an Indiana businessman looking for new opportunities.

The two men came by train and stage from Fort Worth, dodging Victorio on the way, put up at Mrs. Rohman's hotel, where the Mills Building now stands, had dinner with Joseph Magoffin and

Judge Allan Blacker, and bought 400 acres of land from the former.[17] A year later they were back in town and in business. Bassett started a lumber yard which was a landmark in the early days.[18] Morehead picked up a contract for building a section of the Texas and Pacific Railroad, brought the first big money to El Paso as a result, and with Bassett, W. H. Austin, and others, chartered the State National Bank — a major force in El Paso business ever since.[19]

Other men who were to build our city were not far behind. Dr. Hugh White, Judge Llewellyn Davis, Major W. J. Fewel, William Rheinheimer, Dr. Walter Vilas, James H. White — these and many more arrived just before or just after the railroad.[20] Every day brought more pilgrims looking for a chance to put their money or their talents to work — so many that housing was nonexistent and rooms were hard to find. Building materials were in short supply in spite of O. T. Bassett's new lumber yard. Until the railroads actually arrived, there was no way of importing nails and locks and doors enough to satisfy the demand. The hopeful ones came crowding in, however, regardless of shortages. They all felt like Llew Davis, who rode the stage in from the west on the first day of May, 1881. "Down through old Fort Bliss we came," he said, "and I thought it was the most beautiful sight I had ever seen in my life when I looked out over this lovely country . . . I wanted to be in the coming metropolis; I was anxious to grow up with the frontier town."[21]

Many of the immigrants, unfortunately, were not of Llew Davis' calibre. The railhead communities which were moving closer from north, west and east were lively and wicked places — tent towns which kept ahead of the law and attracted the worst kind of human parasites. Inevitably some of them joined the rush to our booming community and inaugurated twenty-five years of virtual dominance of the town's affairs by the "sporting element." In 1878 Ranger Lieutenant John B. Tays had remarked in a letter to his commanding officer, "The temtation is great in this town for men to go astray."[22] In 1880 the "temtation" was greater.

Responsible citizens saw it coming and did what they could to stem the tide. For one thing they tried to set up a city government. The abortive attempt of 1873-75 had made them a bit wary, but now self preservation demanded that they get organized. A petition went to the county court. An election was held. And on July 23, 1880, Mayor Solomon Schutz and his aldermen — Ben Dowell, Adolf Krakauer, J. D. Ochoa, Antonio Hart, S. C. Slade, and Joseph Magoffin — met for their first session. Their chief concern was to establish machinery for assessing and collecting taxes ("every drinking saloon shall pay a yearly occupation tax of ten dollars"[23]). Their next most pressing worry was keeping the village *acequia* (irrigation ditch) clean. Under severe penalties it was forbidden "to bathe in any acequia in this city or to cast offal, filth, or impurities of any kind therein . . . or to drive any herds of sheep, goats, cattle, hogs, or other animals into any acequia within the city. . . ." The measure seems a bit oversolicitous until one remembers that everybody's drinking water came out of the ditches.

The real problem, however — the one that made everything else look unimportant — was what to do about the influx of sports, tinhorns, barflies, confidence men, dance-hall girls, and gunmen. They were taking over the town, and the council had to find a way to control them.

Actually El Paso was not anxious for a complete cleanup. From where we sit now, it appears that law and order was about the last thing we wanted, for there was money in all this vice and sin. It was not just that vice paid fines and taxes. It did that. But the men and women who ran the sin business — at one time more than half the population — ate three meals a day, wore clothes, and lived in houses. As long as they provided a major source of income for the town's businessmen, no successful effort was made to run them out.

Before long there was a saloon for every two hundred people. Every other building in the downtown section seemed to be a grog shop, and conscientious little girls, whose mothers had told them never to walk past a saloon, were apt to zigzag from one side of the street to the other and arrive at home quite late.[24]

The big saloons had gambling rooms in the back and several of them added variety shows to their other attractions. Jack Doyle's place on the corner of El Paso and San Antonio streets was famous in 1881 (the First National Bank acquired the site after a brief interval). Then there was the Gem just south of Dowell's old saloon on El Paso Street and directly across the way from Doyle's establishment. Farther south, below Overland Street, the Coliseum offered girls and gaiety to the sporting crowd in 1881 and 1882. By

1883 it had been replaced by the National Theatre, which offered first-class vaudeville acts and vied with the Gem for the town's business. According to W. W. Bridgers, whose adolescent imagination soaked up all such details, each had a fine brass band which was sent out to parade the streets and work up interest just before show time each evening. The bands arranged their routes so that they had to pass each other at the climax of their maneuvers, and the resulting "battle of the bands" was considered one of the major cultural attractions of the city.[25]

It was these theatres which stepped up the "temtations" which John Tays had deplored in 1878. The female entertainers who flocked in were not there to teach Sunday School. Between performances, they circulated among the patrons, inducing them to buy drinks, sitting on their laps, making assignations. A free spender, a "live one," might squander several hundred dollars in the course of an evening, mainly on five-dollar bottles of champagne.[26]

There was some show of elegance, if not refinement, in such places, but over on Utah Street (now South Mesa — the name had to be changed when the town attained respectability) was located a row of bordellos where anything went. S. H. Newman, editor of the *Lone Star*, reported in 1883 that the *filles publicques* were arousing the indignation of respectable people in the neighborhood by sitting on their porches every afternoon in little or no clothing, often on the laps of their male guests, and after dark they bandied obscenities and fired off pistols to the scandal of the community.[27] This had undoubtedly been going on for some time.

Meanwhile on El Paso Street, the town's only business thoroughfare, the crowd milled and jostled twenty-four hours a day. "At night," says James B. Gillett, who saw it all, "there was not enough room for people to walk on the sidewalks and they filled the streets. . . . Each drinking place had a gambling house attached. . . . If one wished a seat at the gaming tables he had to come early or he could not get within thirty feet of them."[28]

Something had to be done to curb the sin and violence. But what? It seemed nearly impossible to find effective police officers, mostly because there was no money in the city treasury and would not be until the spring of 1881. Could Law and Order be purchased on time? Possibly, if the marshal could live on fees. The council appointed John B. Tays, the ex-Ranger. He lasted three months, from August through October. The next to wear the badge was George Campbell, a Kentuckian "of fair education and respectable family"[29] who had been a deputy sheriff in Young County, near Fort Worth. Captain Baylor of the Rangers vouched for him. He inherited as his assistant an alcoholic named Bill Johnson and was sworn in on December 1, 1880.

For a short time these two officers labored, not very hard, at keeping the peace in a disorderly town. Campbell allowed the saloon keepers and gamblers to be friendly with him, and the result was what might have been expected. City Attorney W. M. Coldwell, who liked him, thinks that he was too young and unsophisticated to use crooked tactics himself, but "his connection with the disturbers of the public order was too intimate to make it a pleasant duty for him to be energetic in their arrest, conviction and suppression."[30] In short, he let the tenderloin do as it pleased, and he was popular as a result.

His troubles started when he began to believe that he ought to have a salary, whether there was any money to pay him or not, and so indicated to his employers. Disturbed by the whole situation, Mayor Schutz, speaking for the city government, asked the Governor to send the Ranger company stationed at Ysleta since the city and county officers could no longer protect life and property.

"The Southern Pacific and the Rio Grande and El Paso Railways," he wrote, "are on the eve of completion to this point: and as the forerunners and followers of such enterprises, we now have turned loose upon us hordes of vagabonds, gamblers, burglars, thieves, and particularly murderers.

"Like classes have also poured into El Paso, Mexico — one mile distant from this place, and thus, one place is a refuge for the criminals and fugitives of the other. We have no doubt that in each of the El Pasos, confederacies for crime are now formed, with aids and confederates in the other."[31]

If any response was made to this plea, it has not been recorded. Since there was no recourse, the council agreed to pay Campbell a stipend, probably postponing payment until money became available. But Campbell was unwilling to take the will for the deed, brought suit, and won his case.[32] Still he remained unpaid, because there was no money to pay him. He decided to resort to sterner measures.

The scheme, evolved either by himself or by his friends in the sporting crowd, was to shoot up the town in order to convince the citizens that police protection was absolutely necessary. Campbell would be called in and ordered to go to work. He would reply that they must pay him first. They would see the point and find the money.

Apparently the first part of the campaign went off according to plan. All hell broke loose on El Paso Street one night, the focus of the attack being the house of Alderman Krakauer, who lived on the corner of San Francisco Street. The next night an attack was planned on Alderman Hague's house, a block west. Several of Hague's friends armed themselves to repel the assault, however, and as a result the assault never came.[33] Meanwhile, in desperation, the mayor and council had appealed to Captain Baylor for aid. The Rangers were not actually moved to the vicinity of El Paso until the next year, but they helped get the situation in hand in that fall of 1880 when James B. Gillett and five men were ordered to report to the mayor and carry out his orders.[34] Campbell, of course, was out. In fact, a warrant was issued for his arrest, though it was never actually served and he was eventually allowed to resign. Bill Johnson sobered up enough to take on the duties of acting marshal after some futile attempts on the part of the city government to find a peace officer who was big enough for the town.

It took four months more to find him, but around the first of April, 1881, he appeared. He was a tremendous and formidable person, six feet two, 180 pounds, with auburn hair and hazel eyes, a broad, pale face, a record as a gunman, and a complete absence of fear or compunction. No more dangerous, ruthless, relentless character ever walked our streets, and you had only to look at him to know it. His name was Dallas Stoudenmire.

A native of Alabama born in December, 1845, he served in the Confederate army, picked up four severe wounds and some minor ones, and surrendered with Joe Johnston at Greensboro when the war was over. In 1874 he moved to Texas and became a farmer near Columbus in Colorado County, where his name is still remembered. In the same year he enlisted in Captain J. R. Waller's A Company of the Frontier Battalion of Texas Rangers and served for several months. Discharged, he became a wheelwright in the little town of Alleyton near Columbus, leaving when he got in trouble with his German neighbors and wounded several of them in a fight. His next stop was the Texas Panhandle, where he engaged in sheep raising with his brother-in-law Doc Cummings, and from there he moved south to Llano County, running a store there until further trouble sent him to San Antonio. There is evidence that he spent some time in New Mexico. His last move was to El Paso,[35] where Doc Cummings was already established as owner and manager of the Globe Restaurant, first on San Antonio Street and later on El Paso Street, which from all accounts was one of El Paso's better eating places. Stoudenmire presented himself before the city council on April 11[36] and reminded them that they needed a marshal. Major Noyes Rand knew him or knew of him and gave him a "warm recommendation."[37] W. M. Coldwell, the city attorney, prepared the necessary papers and had him sworn in before Justice James Tays.

The exchange that followed was characteristic. "Do you know what you are expected to do?" asked the lawyer.

"Yes, and I will do it."

He stepped out of Coldwell's office, crossed the footbridge over the *acequia* which still flowed occasionally through the Little Plaza,[38] and headed down El Paso Street. The reign of Dallas Stoudenmire had begun.

From his first appearance on that street, he was the man in charge. As a result he was anything but popular with a large segment of the population, but it was a long time before the malcontents mustered up courage to do anything about it.

One of the most disgruntled was Acting Marshal Bill Johnson, whose name appears in the city council minutes with the word "resigned" the day Stoudenmire was appointed.[39] Apparently his resignation was not his idea. According to legend, one of Stoudenmire's first acts after his appointment was to call on Johnson at the city jail and demand the keys. Johnson was in no mood to give up anything and said so. Stoudenmire seized him by the collar, shook him dizzy, and took the keys out of his pocket.[40] From that day forward Bill Johnson lived to get even.

The first big difficulty which the new marshal had to face came on April 14, only three days after his appointment, and involved an affair of jailbreaking, rustling, and murder. George Look, new in town at the time, saw it all and in 1909 wrote down an eyewitness account.

Several of the "real, truly hard ones," members of "the gang" which had come close to running El Paso for a while, were in jail in Mexico for robbery. Their Mexican girl friends smuggled arms to them and they broke out of the *juzgado*. A Mexican cowboy who happened to have a Winchester on his saddle left his breakfast across the plaza from the jail, pursued the fugitives, and killed three of them. It developed that these men were friends and associates of one Johnny Hale, manager of a ranch near Canutillo belonging to the four Manning brothers who operated saloons and places of entertainment in El Paso. Hale was said to be close to a gang of rustlers who were at home in the *bosque* twenty miles north of the Pass. All of them were friends of George Campbell, the deposed city marshal.

The Mexican cowboy — whose name Look does not give — paid for his sharpshooting some days later when he and two companions crossed to the American side to search for missing livestock above town. "Hale, Campbell, and others heard they were here," says Look, "and went up after them."[41] Two of the Mexicans were ambushed as they were eating lunch and shot to pieces.

The word got back to the friends of the dead men. About seventy-five of them came across the river in a group and asked for someone to go with them to recover the bodies. Constable Gus Krempkau, formerly a well regarded member of Baylor's Ranger company, volunteered to go along.[42]

By eleven o'clock they were back with a wagon containing their murdered friends and stopped for inquest proceedings at Judge Buckler's office near the corner of El Paso and San Antonio streets. Johnny Hale and George Campbell were in the street looking on. The fact that they were close to the men who did the killing, might even have had a hand in it, was well known and the Mexicans were close to the boiling point. They were more anxious to get the bodies back across the river than to punish the slayers, however, and showed signs of impatience with the law's delay.

Ben Schuster, in his store across the street from Buckler's office, noted that everybody's hand was close to his firearms and the situation was growing more precarious by the minute. He joined the group as a peacemaker, asked them to be quiet and put up their guns, and told Judge Buckler he had better call off the proceedings and send the Mexicans on their way. The inquest was actually discontinued and the wagon moved out.

At this point the voice of George Campbell was heard. "Where is our new marshal?" he wanted to know. "Where is Stoudenmire? These Mexicans are carrying guns and ought to be arrested."[43]

At this moment Krempkau came out of Paul Keating's Chief Saloon, Winchester in hand, stepped across to his riding mule, and started to place the weapon in the saddle scabbard.

"Any American who takes the part of those Mexicans ought to be hanged," Campbell shouted.

Krempkau, who was obviously unhappy about the whole business, stopped what he was doing, turned about to face Campbell, and said, "George, I hope you don't mean me."

Campbell reached up to untie his own mount, which was anchored to the branch of a tree, and as he did so he snapped his fingers and spat out, "If the shoe fits, put it on!"

Just at that instant Johnny Hale thrust a six-shooter under Campbell's upraised arm and shot Krempkau through both lungs, at the same time shouting, "Turn loose, Campbell, I have got him covered!"

Krempkau did all a man could. His strength ebbing, he began to slide down beside the door casing of Judge Buckler's office, but he got his pistol out and put a bullet through Campbell's right wrist, causing him to drop the gun he had just drawn. As he reached to pick it up with his left hand, Krempkau got him again in the foot.

Stoudenmire was not far away, a block or so down the street, and he came up on the run, his pistols out and firing. His first shot missed its mark and caught one Ochoa, an innocent and inoffensive Mexican, square in the belly — Look says the man was buying peanuts from Charley Lawrence. His second got Campbell in the same place and brought him to earth. His third hit Johnny Hale in the forehead as he peered around an adobe pillar.[44]

By now Doc Cummings, Stoudenmire's brother-in-law and buddy, came charging out of his restaurant on El Paso Street, still wearing his cook's apron, with a shotgun in his hands. He took his stand by the marshal and began shouting for the Rangers. Stoudenmire joined him in the chorus: "Where are the Rangers? Close in, Rangers!"

The Rangers did not appear, but Zach White did. Zach had opened up a small grocery store right next to what had been Ben Dowell's place and was now Frank Manning's billiard room and bar. The shooting erupted just outside and startled him as he was going about his mercantile chores. The thought went through his mind that some of his men might be involved and he dashed for the door to see about it. Powder smoke was still drifting above his head as he reached the open. Three men were lying in the street and he looked them over quickly to make sure none of them belonged to him. Satisfied, he was starting back to the store when he noticed Stoudenmire "standing within ten feet, waving his six-shooters, one in each hand, saying, 'You —— — —— stand back!' "

Moving as fast as he could out of the danger zone, White saw one of his men "behind one of the big adobe posts, about four and one-half feet thick, in front of the store. He had stood there during the fight as the other boys had locked him out. He was selling candy to Ochoa when he was hit. He said, 'The damn post is too small to hide a man in such a battle!' "45

The only other bit of action occurred when Stoudenmire, Look and Cummings walked over to Campbell. He lay on his back with his arms folded, quite conscious, looking up at Stoudenmire. "You big son-of-a-bitch," he said distinctly. "You murdered me." They carried him to the Overland Building, where he died the next day.

This happened on Thursday, April 14, 1881. Very little business was done in the town that weekend. The vigilantes (we do not know who they were or anything about them except that they made their headquarters in Ben Schuster's store) patrolled the streets and the place was quiet enough. Even the saloons were empty. But more trouble was brewing. Bill Johnson, ex-assistant marshal, had been brooding and drinking and working himself up to revenge. Undoubtedly he had had encouragement from others. On Sunday evening he figured out a plan of action and took his stand behind a pile of bricks left over from the construction of the new State National Bank on the north side of San Antonio Street near the intersection with El Paso Street. He was only a few steps from the bloodstains left by the killings of two days before. The marshal was a methodical man and his movements could be predicted. On schedule Stoudenmire appeared at the intersection and crossed to the north side of San Antonio Street. Doc Cummings was with him. Johnson waited, as he thought, just long enough — then rose up and turned loose both charges of his double-barrelled shotgun. He probably hoped to get both the men. He missed completely, however, though he nearly rubbed out George Look, who happened to be passing in front of the brick pile. In an instant eight bullets from the pistols of Stoudenmire and Cummings perforated Johnson's body and it was all over with him.[46]

There may have been more shooting. Zach White and others are sure that Johnson's friends began firing at Stoudenmire from all directions, though only one shot nicked him. The episode passed into the folklore of the Frontier West and expanded as such stories will. When Edgar Beecher Bronson picked it up and passed it on in 1910, it came out this way:

At least a hundred men fired at him . . . and it was a miracle he did not go down at the first volley. But he was not even scathed. Drawing his pistols, Stoudenmire marched upon the enemy, slowly but steadily, advancing straight, it seemed, into the jaws of death, but firing with such wonderful rapidity and accuracy that seven of his foes were killed and two wounded in almost as many seconds, although all kept close as possible behind the shelter of the *portal* columns. And every second he was so engaged, at least a hundred guns, aimed by cruel trained eyes, that scarce ever before had missed whatever they sought to draw a bead on, were pouring out upon him a hell of lead that must have sounded to him like a flight of bees.

But stand his iron nerve and fatal snap-shooting the thugs could not. Before he was half way across the street, the hostile fire had ceased, and his would-be assassins were flying for the nearest and best cover they could find. Out of town they slipped that night, singly and in squads, boarding freight trains north and east, stages west and south, stealing teams and saddle stock, some even hitting the trails afoot, in stark terror of the man. The next morning El Paso found herself evacuated of more than two hundred men, who, while they had been for a time her most conspicuous citizens, were such as she was glad enough to spare.[47]

It is too bad that in cases like this fiction should be so much stranger than truth.

To say that El Paso became a quiet and peaceful town after that lethal weekend would be an exaggeration, but it was certainly quieter, and Marshal Stoudenmire's stock stood high. As time went on, he showed himself to be highhanded and irritable, but these things were charged up to his genius and excused. Nobody opposed him openly, and the town calmed down to such an extent that the police force was threatened with boredom. "Some of our peace officers say it is getting painfully peaceable here," the *Herald* commented humorously on October 12, "and if there is not a change, they will have to move to Tombstone or some other lawless locality."

Perhaps because there was little to challenge him, Stoudenmire began to drink heavily. It was the flaw which was to end his career — but he still had plenty of time.

Meanwhile the town continued to boom. All sorts of new businesses sprang up. Most of them were saloons or places of entertainment but legitimate enterprise was on the move too. The old Central Hotel added a second story and was the best in El Paso until the Pierson was opened in 1883, long after the railroad came.[48] Marcellus Washington Carrico arrived in April of 1880 and, with the backing of James L. Marr and a number of others, began to prepare for publication of the El Paso *Times*. Simultaneously Barron F. Deal and Charles Baker were hurrying down from Colorado, carrying another printing plant in a wagon and hoping that the El Paso *Herald* would be on the street first. Actually both papers seem to have made it on the same day — April 2, 1881.[49]

Long before this the council had granted a franchise to a street railway company (the action was dated January 14, 1881),[50] and though nobody rode a mule car until September of 1882, the mere mention of the possibility of public transportation raised the spirits of the citizens.

In the spring of 1881 likewise the El Paso Water Company was organized, an enterprise which would make obsolete a number of traditional procedures: settling the Rio Grande mud out of the drinking water, bringing home whatever liquid happened to be running through the *acequia*, filling the water bucket from the cart of a street vendor. True, Mr. Sylvester Watts of St. Louis, who took over the franchise of the original company, did not complete his project until the fall of 1883, and even then his water was muddy and intermittent.[51] But again, the thought of a bona fide water works in dusty El Paso was exciting.

Even a gas company was organized that same spring — hopefully, and with the consciousness that modern living could not be achieved overnight.[52]

The names of the promoters who now began to implement their dreams are interesting to read. The men who came early and hung on are there, side by side with the energetic new capitalists who had sniffed the scent of opportunity and beaten the railroad in: Zach White, Joseph Magoffin, J. P. Hague, Solomon Schutz, James A. Tays, Charles R. Morehead, O. T. Bassett. Ynocente Ochoa. Mariano Samaniego and Benjamin Degetau from Paso del Norte were eager investors also. The field was ready for the harvest.

FATHER RAMON ORTIZ
Beloved Priest of Paso del Norte
[María Luisa Flores]

The Old Mission Church at Paso del Norte, 1850
[J. R. Bartlett's *Personal Narrative*]

Smith's Ranch, 1853 — site of downtown El Paso
[Texas Memorial Museum]

HUGH STEPHENSON
*Mountain Man and Santa Fe
Trader*
[Hugh Dwyer]

JUANA ASCARATE STEPHENSON
Mistress of Concordia
[María Luisa Flores]

SIMEON HART
Missourian and Miller
[María Luisa Flores]

Don Santiago
JAMES WILEY MAGOFFIN
[Aultman Collection]

Hart's Mill and the Hart Home.
An early landmark and an oasis in the desert.

[María Luisa Flores]

YNOCENTE OCHOA
Merchant Prince of
Paso del Norte
[María Luisa Flores]

JOSE MARIA FLORES
Merchant and Mayor of
Paso del Norte
[María Luisa Flores]

Fort Bliss at Magoffinsville in 1854
[F. A. Percy]

ALEJANDRO DAGUERRE
and REFUGIO SAMANIEGO, *his wife*
Early-Day Aristocrats

DOCTOR MARIANO SAMANIEGO
First Citizen of Paso del Norte
[María Luisa Flores]

CARMEN SIQUEIROS DE SAMANIEGO
Wife of the Doctor
[María Luisa Flores]

BENJAMIN DOWELL
Agriculturist, Saloon Keeper,
First Mayor
[Pioneer Association of El Paso]

GAYLORD JUDD CLARKE
A Civilized Immigrant
Assassinated in 1872
[Pioneer Association of El Paso]

ALBERT JENNINGS FOUNTAIN
Storm Center of the Salt War
[Pioneer Association of El Paso]

JAMES P. HAGUE
A Power in the Eighties
[Pioneer Association of El Paso]

LUIS CARDIS
Politician Extraordinary
[Pioneer Association of El Paso]

CHARLES H. HOWARD
Victim of the Salt War
[Pioneer Association of El Paso]

JOSEPH MAGOFFIN
Pioneer Businessman, Mayor,
Collector of Customs
[Aultman Collection]

President BENITO JUAREZ *relaxing with American friends,*
W. W. Mills and Henry Cuniffe on his right
[Mrs. Evelyn Rosen]

The Butterfield Stage Station, El Paso, built in 1858
[Aultman Collection]

The Ferry at the foot of El Paso Street, 1880
[Aultman Collection]

Santa Fe train in the El Paso station, 1881
[Aultman Collection]

CENTRAL HOTEL
Second story added, after arrival of the railroads.
[Aultman Collection]

Scene of the Street Battle, April 17, 1881
Bill Johnson died on the brick pile beside State National Bank.
[Aultman Collection]

DALLAS STOUDENMIRE
The Mighty Marshal
[Aultman Collection]

JAMES B. GILLETT
Ranger and Peace Officer
[El Paso Public Library]

ZACH T. WHITE
Pioneer Capitalist
[Stout-Feldman]

The McGinty Club gets its name, 1889
[Aultman Collection]

THE McGINTY LIGHT GUARDS
Standing: Peg Grandover, Frank Gaskey, Henry Ong, Billy Schumann, Jim Longwell (Captain), Henry Moore, Tom Booth, Jimmy Watts. Kneeling: Frank Hughes, Billy O'Brien, Herbert Stevenson, Kinney Leathers, Harry Moss, Joe Schneider
[Aultman Collection]

The McGinty Club String Orchestra

Top Row: Charles Taylor, Ray Pollard, Max Hester, John C. Bushong, William Hester, Otto Heckelmann.   Bottom Row: E. H. Offley, Dr. G. W. Dengler, Carl Pitzer, William Bridgers, Dan Reckhart, Frank Bell   [Aultman Collection]

The Myar Opera House, El Paso's Pride
[Aultman Collection]

Chopin Hall, April 2, 1902.
Mexican voters being paid off the morning before an election.
[Aultman Collection]

Grand Central Hotel and San Jacinto Plaza, just before the fire
[Aultman Collection]

Mandy and the Mule Car, First Baptist Church in background
[Aultman Collection]

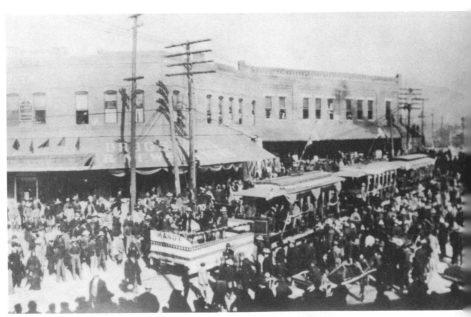

First electric streetcar takes Mandy for a ride
[Pioneer Association of El Paso]

The Great Day

 THERE WAS JOY and thanksgiving in the air as the steel rails, the bringers of all good things, came within miles—came within view — came inside the city limits. The crowd on the streets increased and the pace of night life grew faster as the end of track drew near. Pigtailed Chinese railroad workers began to show up on the streets as the grading crews penetrated the heart of the village. The bridge men hurried to get their part of the work done before the tracks reached the river, and in a hurricane of orderly confusion, the railroad arrived.

The historians argue about when it happened. The date usually given is May 13, 1881, but actually nobody is sure when the first work train rolled down the trackage or when it was possible for passengers to get off within the borders of the town. All we really know is the date of the ceremonies which officially welcomed the railroad and its builders, opened the floodgates of El Paso oratory, and launched the Valley community on its fourth and most impressive century. The day was Thursday, May 26, 1881.

The ceremonies and festivities were described by the *Herald* on the following Wednesday in its tenth issue, using its finest adjectives and all its capital letters. The editors well knew that not since Father Rodríguez passed the ford in 1581 had the Valley seen such a day as this. For on May 26, 1881, El Paso, with its sister town beside the Great River, began to be a metropolis.

Everything was done to make the day memorable. A "pavillion" was erected near the future site of the railroad station for the reception of distinguished guests. The business houses were decorated with bunting and greenery. Atop Mundy's Market on the Little Plaza a huge Texas star split the sky. Fort Bliss agreed to provide cannon for salutes to greet the special train bearing the

Southern Pacific officials. Speeches had been prepared and rehearsed. Prince Albert coats and top hats were out of the mothballs. Refreshment and entertainment had been provided. It was to be the perfect celebration; and no doubt it would have been but for one small detail: The time of celebration was set for ten o'clock in the morning. The train from the west arrived too soon — a little after nine.

The crowd arrived early — from the Valley, from Paso del Norte, from New Mexico. Even some Chinamen were present. But where were the cannon? It was time for the salutes, and there was nothing to salute with. A frantic messenger went off to hurry the gunners along, and some time later, still ahead of scheduled time, the guns arrived and went into booming action.

Events proceeded as announced from then on. The reception committee, consisting of Judge T. A. Falvey, Judge Joseph Magoffin, M. W. Carrico, James P. Hague, Joseph Schutz, J. D. Ochoa, J. R. Currie, C. R. Morehead, H. C. Cook, William S. Hills, Benjamin Degetau, and several others, boarded the train to welcome the officials. They emerged accompanied by C. F. Crocker, president of the railroad, Colonel Bean, superintendent of the Tucson Division, and W. E. Brown, president of the Southern Development Company. The officials were led to their places on the east side of the pavilion and the batteries of El Paso oratory were trained upon them. Judge Falvey introduced Judge Blacker, who welcomed the guests in polished prose as he peered into the glorious future of El Paso and its surrounding territory. "From a ranche we have sprung into a city," he intoned. "We are not fit to be American citizens if we do not avail ourselves of the great advantage we have as residents. His Excellency, the Governor of Texas, said to me only last winter, that if he was a young man, he would settle in the Valley of El Paso, with the firm belief that it would be within his power to become a millionaire — that El Paso is the best place in the United States to make a fortune in a single lifetime."

Don Espiridión Provencio, for his own country, assured the guests in ornate Spanish phrases that "Mexico, my country, salutes and congratulates you today." Next came a round of refreshments in the tent, after which a procession formed and the entire assembly marched down San Francisco Street to the hall over Schutz's store, where the second part of the program got under way. Here the fine ladies of the town made their appearance, and here James P. Hague, no mean maker of speeches, achieved the pinnacle of his oratorical career. One passage will serve to illustrate: "We now here, by our presence in these surroundings, are met to celebrate the advent, into our midst, of the Southern Pacific Railroad itself. It has been decreed: The Lone Star, in the splendor of her course, shall now enter the portals of the Golden Gate; the Nereid of the Pacific shall now add to the wealth of her dominion, the chief jewel that once adorned the diadem of the Montezumas."[1]

James Hague had every right to make the principal speech that day. He had deeded thirty acres in the heart of the future city to the railroad for right of way and had thereby contributed as much as any man, if not more, to the future of the community.[2]

The celebration was not over until late that night. The banquet at the Central Hotel was a brilliant affair, with toasts and responses and an overflowing of good feeling. This was followed by a grand ball (not a *baile* this time) in Schutz's Hall, which was newly floored and handsomely decorated. At ten minutes past nine the best Mexican band in Paso del Norte began the Grand March, with waltzes, quadrilles, schottisches and polkas following until the supper hour.

The list of guests was a roll-call of early El Paso: Joseph Magoffin, J. P. Hague, Ben Schuster, Jacob Calisher, O. T. Bassett, W. H. Austin, W. M. Coldwell, A. Krakauer, W. S. Hills, Maurice Ullman, George Edgerton, T. A. Falvey, C. Q. Stanton, Zach T. White, James L. Marr, James Gillett, H. S. Scotten, Dr. Alexander, J. A. Buckler, N. S. Newland, G. F. Neill, Albert Schwartz, J. R. Currie, and C. R. Morehead.

Something like a supreme effort had been made by the ladies to achieve costumes worthy of the occasion. Mrs. Austin wore black silk with coral jewelry; Mrs. Zork, "very handsome dress of white tulle, gold and diamond ornaments." Mrs. James Gillett of Ysleta, a bride, "wore her wedding dress of white tulle, trimmed with blue satin, wreath of orange blossoms, and was voted by the ladies even the most graceful dancer in the room."

Dallas Stoudenmire was there, and very much the man of the evening. The reporter noted his presence and remarked that "Marshal Stoudenmire wants a railroad celebration and ball every day in the year." Dr. S. M. Cummings, Stoudenmire's brother-in-law, brought his wife, who was handsome in black cashmere and coral jewelry. The Mannings were not mentioned and all four of the brothers may have stayed away because of the feud which was developing between themselves and the Stoudenmire faction.

The railroad officials left the ball about eleven o'clock and an hour later were steaming back to San Francisco. It was no doubt just another party to them, and possibly not as impressive as some they had attended. At Tucson, for instance, the cannonading far outdid El Paso's belated salute. But as Judge Blacker said to the Southern Pacific officials: "We have come with full hearts and willing hands to do the best we possibly could to make your brief stay among us pleasant, enjoyable, and instructive." Whatever the officials thought about it, it was El Paso's finest hour.

CHAPTER XIX

The Boom Continues

THE GREAT DAY was the beginning of a revolution. Everything seemed to be happening at once in 1881 and 1882. The railroads, for instance, kept on coming. When the Southern Pacific arrived, the Santa Fe was only twenty-five miles away.[1] The Texas and Pacific was working west of Big Spring.[2] The Mexican Central, which was starting from Paso del Norte for Chihuahua, commenced heavy construction in early November and actually reached Chihuahua a year later in the fall of 1882.[3]

The Santa Fe came in for a good deal of abuse from the El Paso newspapers on account of its arrogant attitude and high rates.[4] But when its passenger depot was built — a two-story wooden structure with a brick platform — the wicker furniture, wall-papered interior, and iron stoves attracted so many visitors that the place threatened to become a sort of municipal club.[5]

Other building went forward at full speed. John Dougher, employed by Anson Mills and Josiah Crosby, began work on the Grand Central Hotel (where the Mills Building is today), a structure which was to be "the acme of comfort and luxury."[6] Land changed hands almost faster than the recorders could write. So much construction was going on that an El Paso Building and Loan Association was obviously needed and was therefore organized with a long list of prominent citizens as stockholders.[7] The meetings of this body had definite social overtones and might as well have been called parties.

The native adobes, which had served the community for two centuries, were now passé. Lumber, when it could be had, was the thing to build with, and brick was even better. There was plenty of good clay near the town and at least two firms — Parsons and Newell, Stout and Hills — promptly began to process building brick, as many as ten or eleven thousand per day.[8] Zach White soon installed a brick kiln on his property at what is now called White's Spur, a few miles above the Pass. The demand for materials kept well ahead of the supply.

Suddenly El Paso realized how much it had done without and found its insufficiencies embarrassing. Where were the utilities, the schools, the social organizations, the churches? Well, they were not there, but they soon would be. And before 1881 was over, a good start had been made toward the achievement of all these blessings.

The utilities, as we have seen, were thought of early because somebody would make money out of them. In September of 1882 Sylvester Watts of St. Louis unveiled his water mains and hydrants. Electricity arrived in 1883, and in 1884 Zach White, W. J. Fewel, and E. C. Roberts organized the gas company. Mrs. Fewel lit the first gas jet in the Little Plaza before a triumphant crowd of her fellow townsmen on a Saturday night in February, and S. H. Newman remarked in the *Lone Star* that, seen from the hills in Mr. Satterthwaite's addition, "the entire center of the city is a blaze of light."[9] By 1885 "forty magnificent arc lights" were at work making the streets "as clear as day."[10] Some merchants took the extreme step of installing both gas and electricity in their stores, thereby deeply impressing their customers. Gas was even installed in the Grand Central Hotel, its first victim being Jesús M. Duran of Chihuahua, who carefully blew out his jet before going to bed on the evening of December 30, 1884, and nearly died as a result.[11] The first telephones were installed when Maurice Ullman connected his two stores by wire in 1882. By 1884 ninety-six phones were operating in the city.[12] The Southwestern Ice Company began operations in 1882.[13] It took several years more to install a sewer system,[14] and paving had to wait till after 1900, but one by one these conveniences and comforts arrived. Refrigeration and air conditioning were far in the future but compared with the way people got along in 1880, life in 1885 was luxurious and refined.

Schools, of course, had to be arranged for, and a beginning was made in the fall of 1881 when Alderman J. D. Ochoa provided a building[15] and Miss Nunn began meeting classes. Unfortunately the arbiters of El Paso's destinies furnished only the building and the teacher. In November, when cold weather set in, the *Herald* noted: "If the school board does not provide Miss Nunn with a stove soon, we understand quite a number of children will stop school."[16] The chilly children did not realize how well off they were, for in December Mr. Ochoa took his building back. He may have been dissatisfied with the ten dollars a month he was receiving in rent, but one story says he had a better offer from a member of the sporting element who wanted to make the building into a palace of pleasure. At any rate he ran the teacher and her students off, so there was no school at all. The *Herald* protested the "indecent haste"[17] with which the deed was done, but apparently the children stayed out until February, 1882, when W. S. Hills, the real estate promoter, donated a lot and somebody else donated a large tent in which classes were to be conducted "until the heats of June, July, and August, arrive."[18]

By such catch-as-catch-can methods the education of the young of El Paso was carried on until the formation of an independent school district in December, 1882, and the opening of the first public school in March of 1883.[19] This famous old shrine, which faced south on Myrtle Street close to what is now the heart of downtown El Paso, was considered to be on the outermost edge of the community by people whose children had to walk from west of El Paso Street. These same people were further shocked when the Mesa School was erected on Montana Street (the YMCA occupies the site as this is written) in 1889. A petition for putting in a plank walk to keep sand out of the children's shoes and protect them from rattlesnakes was favorably considered by the city council.[20]

Minority groups did not come off triumphantly in those days, but they were provided for. A school for Negroes was organized in a church building in 1885[21] and the poor children of Mexican families were taught after 1887 by one of our most unusual and devoted characters — a Spanish gentleman who had been a Jesuit priest, had lived with the Mayas in Yucatan, had joined the Mormons and helped to translate their sacred book into Spanish, and had published a newspaper in Silver City, New Mexico.[22] He called himself O. V. (for Olivas Villanueva) Aoy. In an old building back of Dan Reckhart's assay office on San Francisco Street he set up his school, providing seats, blackboards, and books himself, besides paying Mundy brothers five dollars a month rent.

When he broke a leg in 1890 and came to the attention of Dr. Baird, he had spent everything he had, was sleeping on a bench with a coat for a pillow, had no clothes besides the ones he was wearing, and was out of food. To the credit of his Anglo brothers be it said that they got him an appointment as principal of the "Mexican Preparatory School" at thirty-five dollars a month, with something extra for supplies. Eventually he was paid $75 a month and was given two assistants. He taught music, calisthenics, politeness, patriotism, and reverence for God, besides the ordinary subjects. He helped his students get jobs and listened to their troubles. When he died of dropsy and asthma, on April 27, 1895, he was deeply mourned and many barefooted children followed the hearse all the way out to Evergreen Cemetery. Aoy School, which has continued his work all these years under some of our most devoted teachers, bears his name.

Our schools have steadily grown in numbers and quality since those far-off days. The first highschool classes met in the old Central School in 1885.[23] The first high school building, completed in 1902,[24] became Morehead School when El Paso High School replaced it in 1916; it was torn down to make way for a new nursing school for Hotel Dieu Hospital in 1964. The University of Texas at El Paso was born in the shape of a State School of Mines in 1913.[25] And we have gone on from there.

Miss Mary I. Stanton, a beloved teacher, gave us a start toward a public library in 1894 when she started a "reading club" for boys. Her library of 600 to 800 books was installed in a room of the Sheldon building. The key was left with the elevator operator and the twenty boys who were members helped themselves to what books they wanted and signed them out themselves. Within a year so many El Paso women had asked for membership that the library was opened to the public. By 1899 the need for bigger quarters and the remodeling necessary to change the Sheldon Block to the Sheldon Hotel moved the library to City Hall, where it remained until Mr. Carnegie provided us with a handsome new building in 1904.[26]

Society did better than the school system and the library at getting an early start. The fall of 1881 saw considerable activity, beginning with the "First Annual Thanksgiving Ball" of the Knights of Pythias. Marshal Stoudenmire was the floor director, but even his impressive presence could not make a complete success of the occasion and the *Herald* noted that "attendance of ladies was rather small."[27] A major effort by the town's social leaders brought the beginning of better days. Some time during that fall the El Paso Social Club was organized and gave its first ball.[28] This was the élite group for many years. It presented plays[29] and organized many a historic party which the pioneer citizens looked back on with fond recollection, especially after the first courthouse was built in 1885 and the district courtroom became available for balls and receptions. All through these years society was international. The fine ladies and gentlemen from both countries invited each other to their functions as a matter of course, and the graciousness of the Mexican *caballeros* and the beauty of their ladies added a special charm to every important occasion.

We should add that the cultural life of the city received a definite impulse upward when W. S. Hills opened a large hall in the fall of 1881 to traveling theatrical performers — real dramatic artists, not the entertainers of the variety theatres. The Nellie Boyd troupe arrived and gave a series of performances — plays with titles like *A Celebrated Case, Kathleen Mavourneen,* and *The Banker's Daughter.*[30]

The church people were as active as the bankers and saloonkeepers in getting organized. In November the Episcopalians were ready to start building the little wooden church — the first Church of St. Clement — on land donated by Parson Tays. It was to be 36 x 60 feet and was to cost about $4,000.[31] At the same time the Catholics were preparing to erect their first church in downtown El Paso. The Methodists (who had been holding services in a tent) laid the cornerstone of their church on Thanksgiving Day, 1881.[32] And the Presbyterians were not far behind.[33]

An illustration of how far El Paso had come in a few months appeared in the *Herald* for December 21, 1881. "A Christmas tree," said the editor, "is the subject of discussion among the little folks and older ones as well. El Paso ought to celebrate her first Christmas Eve in some praiseworthy way."

It is a sad thought that in three centuries the El Paso Valley had never seen a Christmas tree. It probably did not see one that Christmas either, but greener times were on the way.

While the builders of El Paso were trying to construct a civilized community, the sin merchants were active too, and new buildings to house their wares were going up in many strategic locations. One of these was the Coliseum, which we have mentioned already, a huge adobe barn erected behind the El Paso House on South El Paso Street. S. H. Newman of the *Lone Star* noted on November 26, 1881, that James McDaniels and James Manning were the builders. "McDaniels," he added, "is an old showman and was in the variety theatre business in Leadville during the palmy days of that camp. The new theatre will be one hundred and ten feet long by forty-nine feet wide. It will be two stories high and will be fitted up with twenty-five private boxes."[34]

Seven musicians and seven entertainers came in from Leadville just before opening night on Monday, December 15,[35] and the management was soon inviting the public to see the "beautiful Parlor Soiree, the Character Sketches, Songs and Dances, and all that contributes spice and flavor to a first-class variety performance."[36]

Billy Bridgers, who helped bring the railroad in, adds some significant details. "The upstairs boxes," he said, "would accommodate six people each, three men in chairs with a chorus girl on the knee of each. There were some 25 girls who worked in the theatre, and they averaged about $10 a night in percentages on beer at a dollar a bottle and champagne at $5 a bottle."[37]

The Coliseum was the biggest and liveliest place of its kind in the Southwest. The managers were lively operators too. We know little of McDaniels, who went off to Kansas City in January of 1882 and came back only to die. James Manning, however, was one of five locally famous brothers, very firm citizens, who made considerable El Paso history. William was removed early from the scene but James, John, Frank and Dr. G. F. (Felix) were here for some time. Their characters are not easy to evaluate. "They would not pick a fight," says Billy Bridgers, whose reminiscences throw a good deal of light on those sulphurous times, "but they never dodged one. They stepped aside for no man and were deadly, unflinching foes who gave no ground once guns were drawn. They killed several men on the streets of El Paso in 1880 and 1881."[38]

In fairness it should be added that although they are often referred to as "hard cases" or "toughs" by historians of this period, they have had staunch defenders. Dr. Manning, the oldest and smallest of the brothers but the stable one who served as anchor man for the rest, is described by W. W. Mills as "modest in deportment, devoted to his family and his profession."[39] William M. Coldwell, city attorney at the time of these events, calls him "a reputable physician, and perhaps the most accomplished gentleman of early El Paso. . . . Everything about him suggested what he really was, a retired, cultivated, unassuming gentleman, a little too formally courteous, if there was any defect in his manner."[40] W. W. Bridgers adds that he was "quiet, friendly, and inoffensive." The feeling comes through in these evaluations that the Mannings were peaceful and amicable until they felt put upon. Then somebody got hurt.

Their childhood home was a plantation near Huntsville, Alabama, and their descendants might still be Southern gentlemen had it not been for the Civil War. George Felix, a graduate of the University of Alabama, was studying medicine in Europe in the late 1850's. When war between the states began to seem inevitable, he came home and resumed his studies at Mobile Medical College, only to give them up again when hostilities broke out. With his brothers James and Frank he enlisted to fight for the South, all three of them doing good service as Confederate soldiers.

After Appomattox Felix (as he was usually called) joined the migration of die-hard secessionists to Mexico, where he may have enlisted in the forces of Emperor Maximilian. When that episode was over, he returned to Mobile Medical College to take his degree. For a time he lived in Belton, Texas, and there he met and married Sarah Alexander. About the time the railroad arrived, he appeared in El Paso.[41] With him came his brother Frank, who never married and always stayed close to Felix. Jim seems to have reached El Paso first and was there to welcome them. The doctor practiced casually in West Texas, but about 1887 he moved to Prescott, Arizona, where he became a full-time medical practitioner, and spent the rest of his life delivering babies and prescribing for the ailments of his neighbors. His slender figure, neat attire, and well trimmed goatee are still remembered by many Arizonans who as children followed him around, hoping for a taste of the rock candy which he always carried in his pockets for his small friends.[42]

Doc's brothers were not as polished and urbane as he, but they had the manners of gentlemen and apparently tried to stay out of trouble. In El Paso in 1881 this was hard to do, however, and they were soon involved in a particularly dangerous and bitter feud. The very considerable force of their united resentment was concentrated on two men — Marshal Stoudenmire and Doc Cummings. The buildup began in April, 1881, as we have seen, when Stoudenmire killed Johnny Hale and Cummings backed him up. Hale was a friend of the Mannings and managed their Canutillo ranch.

Before or after this affair William, the youngest of the Mannings, was assassinated. The story has never been told in print, but tradition in the Manning family says that he was "bushwhacked" by parties unknown and Frank and Jim disappeared for several months while they followed the trail of the assassins. Presumably they completed their mission, to the great displeasure of Cummings and Stoudenmire.

To make matters worse, these two believed that the Mannings had egged ex-Marshal Johnson into his futile and fatal attempt at assassination two days after the Hale killing. They believed that some of the bullets fired at them came from Frank Manning's saloon, once Ben Dowell's place, where the Paso del Norte now stands, and Doc talked until his death about the desirability of eliminating the brothers, especially Jim. Whenever he dropped such a remark, helpful friends always hurried over to the Mannings, and these same friends contributed further by persuading Cummings that Jim Manning had hired a man to assassinate him, even providing the shotgun which was to do the job.[43]

Cummings, by all accounts, was dangerous, especially with liquor in him, a famous fighter and a good man to let alone. Jim Manning apparently tried to let him alone as much as possible, and although the tensions of the feud were building up behind the scenes, not much got into the open. All references to the principals in the public prints are cheerful and facetious. A man named Joe King early in 1882 tried to assassinate Stoudenmire, failed, and left town precipitately to the amusement of the by-standers.[44] About the same time Cummings returned from a trip out of town. "Dr. S. M. Cummings," said the *Herald*, "the popular caterer of the Globe, returned from an extended eastern tour Monday, looking as handsome as a bridegroom."[45]

Three weeks later Stoudenmire departed. He was on his way to East Texas to get married.[46] Deputy Marshal Gillett (formerly of Baylor's Rangers) was left in charge and his presence was as effective as Stoudenmire's in keeping the bad boys in line. But on Tuesday afternoon, February 14, Gillett stayed home sick. Immediately there was trouble.

Doc Cummings had apparently been brooding over the smoldering feud and at the same time hitting the bottle. Late in the afternoon, after more drinks at Bill Coffin's Old Boss Saloon on the corner of Overland and El Paso streets, he met Jim outside and began to express his views of Jim's character and conduct. Together they went into the Coliseum and stood at the bar while Doc had another drink and continued the discussion. Manning did his best to quiet Doc and even walked out into the street with him, but they were soon back and the storm had not subsided. Doc demanded that Jim drink with him and Jim agreed but asked for seltzer water. Doc knocked the glass off the bar and got into a hot argument with J. C. Kling, the bartender, whom he advised to keep his hands in sight.[47] Witnesses disagreed about where Manning was when the shooting started, whether or not Doc was threatening with his gun and calling for a fight, and who fired the first shot, but Cummings fell with two bullets through him and a nasty gash on his scalp. Only one chamber of Manning's pistol was fired, so the second bullet came from somewhere else. Gillett says, "It was generally understood that a barkeeper of Manning's really did the shooting,"[48] but Kling was never called to account.

Captain Baylor of the Rangers picked Manning up and held him until his lawyers went through habeas corpus proceedings, but in a case of this kind, where hard feelings were known to exist, where both men were armed, and where the dead man seemed to be the aggressor,[49] the killer was naturally congratulated and turned loose.[50]

Both sides of the river were in a fever of anticipation after this bloody encounter. What would Stoudenmire do when he got back? Would his new status as a bridegroom influence his reaction to his brother-in-law's death? Would he be a match for three Mannings in a pitched battle? Everybody waited in great suspense for Stoudenmire's return.

Gillett met him and his bride at the train and told him what had happened. "Stoudenmire was mad and made no effort to conceal his feelings," Gillett writes. "Said if the Mannings wanted a fight, they could get it, and the relations became more strained than ever. It reached such a point that it seemed a pitched battle between Stoudenmire and the Mannings might break out any time, and endanger the lives of those on the one crowded street of the town. Finally the best citizens of El Paso could stand the strain no longer. They appointed a committee to wait on Stoudenmire and the Mannings, and implore them for the benefit of the town and their friends, to come together and patch up their differences and try to be friendly."[51]

Gillett reproduces the strange document which was the outcome of these negotiations:

El Paso, Texas, April 16, 1882
We the undersigned parties, having this day mutually settled all difficulties and unfriendly feelings existing between us, hereby agree that we will meet and pass each other on peaceable terms and that bygones shall be bygones, and that we will never allude in the future to any past animosities that have existed between us.

Dallas Stoudenmire
J. Manning
G. F. Manning
Frank Manning

Both sides behaved circumspectly after this, no matter what fires were burning beneath the surface, and it was five months before the big trouble came.

Meanwhile whatever worm was working inside Dallas Stoudenmire gnawed deeper. His marriage apparently did not increase his happiness or peace of mind. He drank more and more, and became more and more impossible to live with or to do business with. It became necessary for the city to get rid of him. The question was how to do it — safely.

In March of 1882 the council managed to lay him temporarily on the shelf when he was unable to perform his duties. James B. Gillett was made Marshal Pro Tem and functioned for a week or so until Stoudenmire was sober.[52] By the time he was back in harness, another way of eliminating him had opened up. A letter from W. W. Mills was read before the council stating that Stoudenmire had accepted an appointment as Deputy United States Marshal in New Mexico, thereby vacating his office in El Paso. Hopefully but cautiously, the council referred the letter to the city attorney for an opinion.

We might add that W. W. Mills had been for some time an aspirant to the marshal's office himself. He claims to have secured Stoudenmire's job as United States Marshal in New Mexico, and if he did so, it was undoubtedly because he wanted the place which Stoudenmire would vacate.

As if to reprove the councilmen for what they were getting ready to do, Stoudenmire presented a report on April 8 revealing that between December 1, 1881, and March 26, 1882, he had brought 171 offenders before the mayor's court, enriching the city coffers by $971.75. He did not mention the fact that his accounts had been almost continuously in arrears for some time.[53]

The undercover work which followed the receipt of Mills' letter resulted in a showdown at the council meeting held on the evening of April 13, 1882. Following the reading of a letter from John Sherman, Jr., United States Marshal for New Mexico, confirming Stoudenmire's appointment as his deputy, the four aldermen present unanimously declared the office of city marshal vacant. When the question of naming Stoudenmire's successor was introduced, however, a very strange thing took place. Alderman Hague nominated W. W. Mills for the vacant office. Ben Schuster immediately rose and nominated the man they had just fired. On the vote the council split down the middle two and two. Mayor Magoffin broke the tie by voting for Stoudenmire.[54] The council allowed nothing to be set down in the minutes to explain this remarkable reversal of attitudes, but it looks as if three councilmen regarded Stoudenmire as the lesser of two evils.

Now began the most painful two months of the Stoudenmire period in El Paso's history. The marshal went from bad to worse. Editor Carrico of the *Times* demanded his removal. Some people left town and others refused to enter it as word of the troubles spread abroad. The aldermen were afraid to move, but on May 27 they met to take action. Stoudenmire entered the chamber, according to his deputy Jim Gillett, made "a dramatic and firey speech" in which he said they had not treated him fairly, invited them collectively and individually outside, and declared that he "could straddle them all."[55] The mayor adjourned the meeting without transacting any business.

The council had one card still to play, and it proved to be the high one. On May 29 Stoudenmire offered his resignation and an apology and gave up the fight.

"Believing as I do," he wrote, "that under the present administration of the City government my usefulness as City Marshal will be materially impaired and learning that there will be an attempt to reduce the pay of the Marshal all ready too low I hereby tender . . . my resignation. Before parting company with the officers of the City, whilst I feel that I have suffered injustice from certain members of your honorable body, I think it my duty to, and do hereby, apologize for my conduct in the council chamber on last Saturday evening and beg to assure you that I meant no disrespect to your body or the people whom you represent."

Stoudenmire being present in the council chambers as usual, the council moved to accept his resignation, following which Alderman Blacker offered a resolution which the group gladly passed complimenting the ex-marshal on "the fearless and faithful manner in which he has ever discharged the duties of the dangerous and difficult position he has for the last year held in our midst," and acknowledging that "to his faithful efforts in behalf of law and order, is and has been most largely due the quietude our city heretofore enjoyed."[56]

In an atmosphere which was calm, if not exactly friendly, the council went on to name James B. Gillett as the new marshal. Stoudenmire approached him afterward and said, "Young man, I congratulate you on being elected city marshal and at the same time I wish to warn you that you have more than a man's size job on your hands." It was certainly the Voice of Experience speaking.

So Stoudenmire bowed out of office, but not out of El Paso. He continued to live — and to drink — in the border town and it seemed inevitable that if he stayed, he would have to fight. He undoubtedly thought so too. Actually the trouble might have been postponed indefinitely had it not been for trouble-making busybodies who were industrious in spreading rumors.

All through the summer and into the fall the talk went on and the rift between Stoudenmire and the Mannings grew wider. On the night of September 17, 1882, the final moves began. Stoudenmire had spent the day in Deming on law business and got off the train at El Paso about eleven o'clock that night. He came directly to the Acme Saloon, where Neal Newland, Cliff Brooks and Walt

Jones, all his old friends from Colorado County in East Texas, had their place of business. Brooks was keeping the place open. He noted that Stoudenmire looked bad and told him so. The marshal admitted that he had been drinking some.

"You had better go home to your wife," Brooks said.

"No," he replied. "You close up and we'll go down to some of the houses."

"Can't do it," Brooks told him.

Stoudenmire walked out and went to Jim Manning's Coliseum. He may have gone in. He said later he did not. His story was that he had a warrant for somebody and had looked in to see if the man was there. Apparently a person or persons unknown went and waked up the Mannings and told them Stoudenmire had been in "looking for them." This convinced the brothers that Stoudenmire had broken their truce.

Leaving the Coliseum, Stoudenmire came back to the Acme and about the same time, according to Brooks, a brother-in-law of Alderman J. D. Ochoa appeared on the scene and began to tell a story about somebody who had threatened Stoudenmire's life. It seemed to Brooks that this was no time for such conversation, so he ran the man off and closed the saloon.

Stoudenmire was still in a mood to go down on the "line" and Brooks humored him, going as far as the door of Abbie Bell's place where he asked for Carrie, apparently knowing Stoudenmire's preferences among the inmates. Carrie had gone uptown for some food; Stoudenmire walked inside and Brooks went home.[57]

Marshal Gillett met the big man stalking down the middle of El Paso Street the next morning and offered to take him to his house. Stoudenmire flared up and said he didn't need Gillett's company, or anybody else's company, but when Gillett walked away, he did go home and was not seen again until after noon. Meanwhile Jim Manning had come to the Acme looking for Stoudenmire since the busybodies had persuaded him that Stoudenmire was looking for him.[58] Presumably Stoudenmire's friends tried to explain things to Manning, but he and his brothers were aroused and angry.

In the afternoon Stoudenmire came back to the Acme and sat in the gambling room in the rear, occasionally returning to the bar for more whiskey. Frank Manning came in once and Stoudenmire told Walt Jones that they were watching him, that he expected trouble. Dr. Manning entered and joined Frank. Stoudenmire passed them a couple of times without speaking. The atmosphere was heavy with the hatred and suspicion of the last six months. The break could come at any moment.

"I am sorry it has to happen this way," Brooks said to Frank Manning.

"Brooks," Manning replied, "it is not my fault. I have tried every way to keep this thing down." A little later he added, "The sooner it comes off, the better for all parties."

When the Mannings left, Stoudenmire asked Jones to go to them and explain that he had not entered their place the night before — that he wanted no trouble, though he would fight them if they were bound to fight.

Brooks and Jones went back and forth between the two parties and finally they accompanied Stoudenmire over to the Manning saloon to have a drink and settle the matter. It was about six P.M. The three of them entered the place and found Jim Manning at the bar. Stoudenmire asked where Frank was and Jim volunteered to go and get him. Dr. Manning, who had been playing billiards, walked up.

"Some lying s. o. b. has been trying to make trouble," Stoudenmire said to open the conversation.

"Stoudenmire," Manning replied, "you have not lived up to our agreement."

"Whoever says I have not tells a damned lie."

Manning went for his gun as Jones tried to separate them, and there was shooting on both sides. According to Jim Gillett, who did not see the action but was only a few steps away, Manning was the quicker of the two, placing his first shot right over Stoudenmire's heart, where a bundle of papers absorbed the impact. His second bullet wounded Stoudenmire in the left arm and breast. By this time Stoudenmire had managed to get off a shot which caught Manning in the right hand, causing him to drop his gun and wounding him so badly that his career as a surgeon was finished then and there.[59]

No two reporters agree on this part of the action, or on what followed, but Editor S. H. Newman of the *Lone Star* wrote his version on the flyleaf of a copy of Owen White's *Out of the Desert* as a correction. Newman got his story from Jim Manning. It may be the correct one:

Dr. M. . . . took his hat from his head and rushed upon S., pelting him in the face therewith and thus preventing him from shooting a second time. S. backed and backed trying to get away from M., but the latter followed him up with the hat until S. backed out of the door onto the sidewalk. Just as he reached the sidewalk Jim Manning came up from lower down on the sidewalk, having heard the shot fired, and shot S. in the back of the head, scattering his brains around on the sidewalk.[60]

Ranger Joe Deaver, who had been ordered by Captain Baylor to keep an eye on Stoudenmire in the Acme Saloon, heard the shooting as he was killing time at the pool table. Cue in hand, he hurried out and caught the last scene of the drama. He saw Stoudenmire sprawled across the sidewalk in front of the saloon, Doc Manning on top of him "hammering him on the head with a gun."

Ed Scott, a Ranger that was well acquainted with everybody in El Paso, came running up the sidewalk, grabbed Doc by the wrist and grabbed Doc's gun with the other hand, at the same time lifting Manning to his knees. Doc refused to let go his gun and it seemed pretty hard to convince him that Stoudenmire was dead and he, Doc, was out of all danger and under our protection. Scott had just got Doc's gun when Gillett and Jim Manning came on the scene. Doc's family lived in a back room of the saloon building so I helped carry Doc back to said room. I was placed on guard to watch Jim and Doc. I was relieved about ten that night.[61]

It will be noted that Deaver has Gillett and Jim Manning appear after Stoudenmire was dead. Gillett, who gives Jim Manning credit for the killing, says Doc seized one of Stoudenmire's guns and straddled the big man's body.

S. H. Newman was present at the inquest and tells what happened in his own peculiar way: "Evidence was that witness saw M. point his pistol at S.'s head, saw smoke, heard a report and when the smoke cleared away, saw S. lying on the ground. Question by the J. P. Do you know M.'s pistol was loaded? Answer, No. Q. Did you see the ball leave the pistol and strike S. in the head? Answer, No. Verdict: Came to his death at the hands of parties unknown."

The inquest as reported in the newspapers (the records have been lost) was actually a lengthier and more orderly proceeding than Newman reported, several witnesses giving complete testimony. They were wary, however, of naming the man who fired the fatal shot. Behind their reticence was undoubtedly the feeling that it was a fair fight and nobody was really guilty. Besides, it was a relief to have Stoudenmire out of the way. The Mannings answered for the killing in court, but the hearing was really only a formality.

The Masons buried him. On September 19 the lodge room remained open until six P.M. so that all might see their brother for the last time. The lumber for his coffin cost the lodge $4.50 and $11.55 went for his burial suit.[62]

Stoudenmire's wife of six months, who remains faceless and speechless for us, was probably well on her way back to Columbus by the time the grave was filled. A year later Isabella Sherrington Stoudenmire changed her name to Kerl[63] and began a new and, we hope, better life. It would be safe to state that for the rest of her time on earth she did her best to put El Paso and its wicked ways entirely out of her mind.

The rest of us have forgotten too. Which of us is conscious now as he enters the front door of the Paso del Norte Hotel, that he has just stepped across the spot where Stoudenmire lay dead with Doc Manning astride him?

Marshal Gillett continued to deal efficiently with the girls and the gamblers and the hoodlums after Stoudenmire's demise, and the city had some fine peace officers afterward — Sheriff Jim White, Jeff Milton, even John Selman, gunman turned constable, who seems to have done a good job of enforcing the law. The situation, however, was a peculiar one, and a few words of explanation may be needed.

From the eighties on El Paso was actually two towns. One was the beginning of the place we know now, a city of legitimate business enterprises, law-abiding citizens, churches, schools, personal decency, respect for law, and dawning culture. The other was the city of sinners: the daughters of joy and the gamblers, the madams and moochers, the cutthroats and con men.

For something like twenty-five years the two El Pasos existed side by side, worlds apart morally but closely linked financially. All this time the good people strove without much success to make a civilized community out of their uncurried little border metropolis. Reform movements were organized, but they always sputtered out because some Christian businessmen were making too much money out of the vice merchants. "My own banker boss, Mr. H. L. Newman," says Owen White, "told me frequently that reform would come to El Paso not because of the reformers but only when business interests demanded it."[64] There can be no doubt that the rulers of the underworld carried great weight in the town's affairs through the eighties and nineties and on into the 1900's. When they did not dominate, they at least had to be reckoned with. As long as frontier conditions and concepts controlled our way of life, it was impossible to get rid of these "sporting" people and their influence on the community. When El Paso stopped being a frontier town, we ran the rascals out.

We should remember that the good people were always here, people sincerely concerned for the decency and progress of their little city who did what they could to make it a better place. These included a core of extraordinary women who lived here in perilous times, women of talent and refinement and considerable culture — some from older communities in Texas, some from the East or the North or the South, some from Europe. They made a social life in the wilderness, welcomed the stranger (if he behaved himself), promoted religion, and tried to bring their children up properly in an environment where it was easy to learn the wrong lessons. Their names should appear on a tablet somewhere with the thanks of a grateful citizenry:[65] Mary Mills, Flora Hague, Octavia Magoffin, Olga Kohlberg, Eugenia Schuster, Carrie Fewel, Lemire Morehead, Elizabeth Irvin, Margaret Beall, Eliza Berrien, Laura Loomis, Carrie Race, Maude Austin, Harriett Shelton, Frances McCutcheon, Rebecca Falvey, Mary Voss, Carrie Sutherland. These and a dozen more, including Mrs. James L. Marr, Mrs. E. M. Bray, Mrs. Alward White, the Payne sisters-in-law, Mrs. Allen Blacker, Mrs. John M. Dean, Mrs. Wyndham Kemp, Mrs. W. M. Coldwell — there is really no place to stop — were active and useful during our growing-up period.

Dr. William Berrien, son of our first furniture-and-undertaking specialist, says no history of El Paso will be worth anything unless it mentions Mrs. Justice, wife of Dr. Justice.[66] With two beautiful sisters Mrs. Justice came out from New Orleans and added a special note to our social concert. She was *petite*, charming, well mannered, elegantly dressed, and completely fascinating to most of the town's males, married or unmarried. One of our pioneer mayors never did get over her and caused much headshaking thereby. The story of Mrs. Justice and her sisters, one of whom married a Chinese doctor and migrated to Mexico, would be worth a chapter to themselves.

The women of the other El Paso — Alice Abbott, Gypsy Davenport, Etta Clark, Tillie Howard — were no less attractive and no less influential than the ladies on the other side of the tracks. Their establishments were as luxurious and refined as they knew how to make them, and many gentlemen from the right side of town came there to have a drink, discuss a business deal, or associate with "the girls." In their turn the madams sometimes visited the world of ostensible virtue and decency. They shopped, they went to the theatre, and they took their young women — dressed and hatted and gloved in the latest fashions — for buggy rides down the town's residential streets.

Thus the two worlds overlapped and, on the fringe at least, intermingled. Nevertheless Utah Street, the street of sin *par excellence*, was one world and Magoffin Avenue was another, so distinct that they will be considered separately in the next two chapters.

It is easy to find out about the upper or decent half of El Paso. Plenty of information is available about education, church activities, amateur theatricals, population expansion and the doings of the social leaders. Our upward struggles can be traced in the newspapers, in the city records, and in the minutes of many organizations. The chronicles of virtuous endeavor are somewhat lacking in drama, however, and most readers find them a bit dull.

On the other hand, the gunmen, the gamblers, and the girls have been given ten times the attention accorded to the good people although their manner of life is ten times as hard to learn about. The brothels and clip joints kept no records, and the few remaining pioneers who could tell about them are mostly close mouthed or forgetful — probably for very good personal reasons. Something can be learned, however. A hint from an eyewitness, a paragraph from a newspaper, an entry in the vital statistics, and we have enough to start with.

We begin with the early days of the town we know now, a place of progress and growing prosperity, of culture and clean sports, of music and good manners and more or less innocent amusements, in short, the Sun City.

CHAPTER XX

Sun City

IN 1880 EL PASO was not much more than a village. In 1885 it was beginning to be a big town and had to take the consequences.

A village can do with kerosene lamps and outdoor plumbing, cows in the back yard and an iron pot over an open fire for washing clothes. A city needs bathrooms and dairies and laundries, gas lights and places for parties, hotels and restaurants and banks. All these things require investment and know-how, and until people with money and know-how arrive, progress is apt to be slow.

It took a little time to accumulate the money and the know-how, but the people arrived fast enough. The population jumped from 700 to 10,000 in ten years,[1] and almost doubled in each decade after that for some time. A remarkable assortment of people flocked in with the locomotives. The girls and the gamblers came early and stayed late, but reputable citizens were there in large numbers too: railroad workers and soldiers, investors and builders, merchants and cattlemen. The mining boom in Arizona sent new business and new people to El Paso, where a smelter was in operation as early as 1885.[2] The drift of Texas cattlemen to New Mexico in the eighties did its part. More and more farm lands were opened to irrigation on the American side of the river, employing more people to raise food for still more people. In 1885 four Chinamen had started truck gardens between El Paso and Ysleta.[3]

The Chinamen, incidentally, are said to have been "dumped" here by the Southern Pacific when their usefulness as track workers was over.[4] A considerable number remained to start laundries, restaurants, and a few opium dives.[5] They were numerous enough and prosperous enough to stage New Year's celebrations complete with huge paper dragons,[6] administer their own brand of justice without interference from the police,[7] and populate a Chinatown on South Oregon Street.

The first thing needed was housing for the incoming thousands. Adobe — the natural building material of the country — was, as we have said, no longer good enough. All forward-looking citizens demanded frame or brick, and the *Times* called for the landmarks around the Little Plaza to be cleared out. "The old filthy adobe buildings at the head of El Paso Street ought to be torn down and removed from sight. They are a disgrace to El Paso."[8]

Well, these disgraces had two advantages. In the first place they were cool, and in the second place they were almost fireproof, virtues which could never be ascribed to the smart new houses and stores. The result of the new dispensation was a radical readjustment in the life of the town. Until the advent of air conditioning El Paso was too hot in the summer for anybody to stay in unless he had to, and the lack of refrigeration made it a perilous place for babies during the summer months.[9] As a result the wives and children of the well-to-do departed in a body for California in May or June, thus creating a need for one of our most distinctive early social groups — the Grass Widowers' Protective Association, which functioned for some fifteen years, often assisted and abetted by the Bachelors' Club, and made history with elaborate parties.[10]

The picture changed again with the opening of Cloudcroft in the Sacramento Mountains in 1900. Ladies and children went up for the summer and the men joined them on weekends. Cloudcroft was a lovely, carefree place in those days, pine scented and flower filled, and all those who were young in the early years of the century cherish its memory. The Baby Sanatorium, opened in 1911, saved the lives of some of them.[11]

One result of the decline of adobe as a building material was the birth of the El Paso Volunteer Fire Department. A ditch and a bucket brigade no longer served the purpose. Hotel owner W. H. Carter called the organization meeting on August 23, 1882, with twenty-six men present. That evening the El Paso Hook and Ladder Company was born with C. L. Pierce as Chief and Ben Levy as First Assistant.[12] The City Council agreed on September 1 to supply them with carts, hose reels, and 1,000 feet of "the best hose."[13] It should be added that the Council never did live up to its agreement.

A water supply had apparently been arranged for away back in April when a franchise was issued to the El Paso water company. Sylvester Watts of St. Louis sent his nephews William H. Watts and James J. Watts to El Paso to build the works. Billy Watts, in charge of construction, sank two wells in the bed of the Rio Grande, constructed a reservoir and settling tanks on top of the highest hill in Sunset Heights, installed pumps to force the water into the reservoir and prepared to supply the city's needs with the help of God and gravity. He installed water mains made of galvanized sheet metal and put in twenty-five hydrants which the city contracted to rent for one hundred dollars annually per hydrant.[14]

By the second week in September Mr. Watts' system was ready to be tested, and there was great and general satisfaction when the pressure proved great enough to throw water over the highest building in town (three stories). The galvanized pipes, however, developed leaks at various points. The editor of the *Lone Star* described them as "old stove pipes."[15]

In truth the system never gave much satisfaction to anybody. When the river went dry, so did Mr. Watts. The settling tanks never had time to operate, and sometimes the fluid which the town was supposed to drink was too thick to run through the pipes.[16] For many years people who could afford it drank water brought in from Deming in tank cars.

The first fire to put the Department to the test occurred on November 11, 1882. A frame building on El Paso Street housing the firm of Hogan and Dubell caught fire. The volunteers, summoned by six-shooter volleys, hooked up to the nearest hydrant and found that they had only 100 feet of hose – not enough to reach the front door of the burning building. When two adjoining structures were reduced to ashes, Chief Pierce announced cheerfully, "Well, boys, we could not prevent the buildings from burning but we saved the lot."[17]

Four days after this disgrace the Department was reorganized to provide for two hose companies and one hook-and-ladder company. The city council, under severe pressure, promised to provide better equipment,[18] but by now the men had learned the first lesson of volunteer groups – they were on their own financially. Their initial benefit ball was held on December 16, 1882, the first of many an entertainment which paid for equipment, uniforms, and quarters.[19]

The first vehicles, two two-wheeled hose carts and a hook-and-ladder truck, were acquired early in 1883.[20] They had to be propelled by the men themselves, and it was no small feat to drag them down El Paso's sandy streets, especially at night when no one could see where he was going. Lee Robinson was run over by a hose cart in 1886 and severely injured.[21] Electric lights had been installed in many places of business by 1885, but the moon provided the only street lighting and the firemen were bitter about it.[22] Add to these perils and difficulties the fact that when the firemen got to a fire, they were often too exhausted to go into effective action and one realizes that we were lucky to have any town at all in the eighties.

The second big fire, in April, 1883, was a worse disaster than the first. When the blaze started in the rear of Williamson's drug emporium and Pete Kern's jewelry store on El Paso Street, a roaring wind prevented many of the men from hearing the summoning shots and soon drove the fire so hard that it destroyed all the buildings on the west side of the street for an entire block. Property worth $37,000 was consumed, including eight sections of hose. Editor Newman of the *Lone Star*, always ready to place blame where he thought it was due, called for another dinner and ball to raise money for new equipment "since the city council seems more disposed to spend the public monies in paying superfluous salaries than in forwarding the real interests of the city."[23]

Step by step the department went forward, and 1883 saw the purchase of a fire bell (El Paso did not hear a siren until 1900).[24] The men practiced with their machines to develop speed and stamina[25] and engaged in "tournaments" to test their prowess, taking on teams from Texas and New Mexico and winning the state championship in 1885.[26] They joined the State Firemen's Association (organized in 1875) to keep their morale at top pitch and were hosts to the state convention in 1897.[27] Uniforms arrived in March, 1883, enabling the members to make a "splendid appearance" in the Washington's Birthday parade. For once Editor Newman could be generous. "No city anywhere can show a finer body of men," he remarked. "The company is composed of El Paso's best citizens and while they form a most useful adjunct of metropolitan life, the character of the members makes its membership honorable and pleasant."[28]

Actually the Fire Department came close to being the focus of the town's social life. The most prominent citizens belonged and it was no small distinction to be among them. Outsiders who donated money to the cause were made honorary members and given badges which they wore on special occasions as if they were decorations. Anson Mills, busy pursuing his army career but retaining his El Paso interests, was an honorary fireman and proud of it.[29]

As the city grew, the need for an adequate water supply began to be desperate. The citizens voted a $75,000 bond issue in 1890 but did not carry through, and Mr. Watts remained in business until 1902. Two spectacular fires pointed up the need for more water. The first was the burning of Pomeroy's Transfer Company in May of 1891, a $25,000 blaze. Low water pressure made it impossible to fight the fire effectively.[30] The second, a fire from which we once calculated time, broke out on the morning of February 12, 1892, in the Grand Central Hotel.

The Grand Central was the pride of El Paso. Built in 1883 by Josiah Crosby and Anson Mills,[31] it was considered the finest hostelry in the entire Southwest and was the focus of much of our social life in the eighties. To lose it was a sad blow to our civic pride, but lose it we did — because the firemen could not get water up to the fourth floor.

The entire town turned out to witness this disaster, which began at two in the morning and took the sleeping guests by surprise. Sad as the occasion was, there were moments of humor. Miss Ella B. Meekins, principal of the school and a lady of impressive dignity, appeared in slippers and a thin nightgown, mourning her lost clothing, jewelry and books. One fireman, exasperated beyond endurance by the jibes of his audience, revenged himself as best he could, moving the *Times* to comment next day: "A fireman has no right to get mad and turn his hose on a crowd of spectators when they laugh at something ridiculous. It is yet to be ascertained how many poor invalids will die from the effects of the drenching they received yesterday."[32]

After such a catastrophe the days of the volunteer fire fighters were numbered. The first steam fire engine arrived on November 1, 1892. Horses were purchased for locomotion and their daily practice runs were a popular part of El Paso's public entertainment.[33] In 1894 the old hook-and-ladder wagon was replaced by a sixty-five-foot aerial truck with wine-colored ladder, white wheels and gilt trimming. It weighed 7,000 pounds, required three horses to pull it, and made a tremendous impression in parades.[34]

In 1895 the Department made its first run across the river to fight a fire in our sister city. Since then it has been our custom to go when needed.

The late nineties saw the decline of the Department as a social institution. New clubs and activities came along, and there was a growing impression that the members joined in order to escape jury duty.[35]

The end came in 1905. On the evening of Saturday, November 4, the Myar Opera House on El Paso Street burst into flame. The citizenry turned out en masse to watch the volunteer firemen struggle with inadequate equipment and low water pressure to fight the biggest blaze since the loss of the Grand Central. The entire block went up in smoke.[36]

The Myar had been El Paso's stronghold of culture since its erection in 1887.[37] It gave ocular and audible proof that ours was not just another honky-tonk town. Tetrazzini came up from Mexico and gave her first American operatic performance there.[38] Edwin Booth and Sir Henry Irving, Sarah Bernhardt and Maxine Elliott, Adelina Patti and Lily Langtry — these names and many more had appeared on the marquee.[39] When you saw El Paso at its best, in tails and top hats, it was at the Myar.[40] To lose the Myar was to reduce El Paso to the level of an ordinary Western town. And the Myar was gone. Now, the citizens said, maybe somebody will get us a professional group of fire fighters.[41]

It took three years more. In 1909 Mayor Sweeney established a salaried department. From then on the fires were better handled but we lost some of the *esprit de corps* and the sense of civic responsibility which made the volunteer department a thing to be proud of.[42]

All during these years new residential districts were opening up as the Sun City grew and expanded. At first everybody who was anybody, including the owners of the better bawdy houses, lived west of El Paso Street and south of San Francisco Street — a district of mercantile establishments and small brick houses now.

Then the important people began to put up two- and three-story brick residences of considerable elegance on Myrtle and Magoffin Avenues, residences which in our time are mostly rooming houses and commercial property.[43] Several churches were erected in this section, adding to the respectability and decency of the neighborhood.

At the same time preparations were going on north of the tracks for the next migration, thanks to a remarkable individual named J. Fisher Satterthwaite, a New Yorker who had taken over most of the rocky, hilly terrain which seemed to other builders fit only for goats. In the opinion of these others, El Paso could expand only south and east and Satterthwaite was going to lose his shirt.[44]

Satterthwaite was not interested in their views. He was looking over their heads. Coming to El Paso in 1880 with the conviction that the town was to be the metropolis of the Southwest, he kept his New York offices at 71 Broadway and evidently intended to sell his dream to the people back East. While the property was still cheap, he bought up "all the higher lands in the present city" and began tearing down hills and grading streets. In 1882 he spent $35,000 on this apparently useless labor, provoking skeptics to make remarks about a fool and his money.[45] By 1884 water and gas mains were in below ground and telephone and electric light poles were visible above.[46] In 1885 he advertised that ninety new houses had been built and more were under way with plans for extending Upson and El Paso streets northward and opening up Oregon and Rio Grande streets. The Mesa Gardens, near the present corner of West Rio Grande and Yandell, originated in his fertile mind. The people who passed so many pleasant evenings there owed him more than they ever acknowledged. Most of the streets in his addition still bear the names he gave them.

There is evidence that J. Fisher Satterthwaite became a rather complete Westerner. In February of 1884 he was actually fined twenty-five dollars for gun toting. He defended himself by recounting the details of a disagreement he had had with one Fernandez who, he said, had beaten and kicked him, bruised him heavily, and threatened to do it again. Editor Newman remarked acidly that it would have been cheaper to kill Fernandez since undoubtedly Satterthwaite would have gone free.[47] Obviously the New Yorker's education had gone far, but possibly not far enough.

Satterthwaite was the first of a long line of developers who opened up new areas to settlement. One was Pete Kern the jeweler, who overextended himself in buying real estate, got caught in the panic of 1893, assigned everything he had to his creditors,[48] and left town, penniless, in 1897. He had foreseen the phenomenal growth that was to come, but he was twenty years too soon.

He had better luck in Alaska, where he joined the gold rush. He established a jewelry store and manufacturing business in Skagway and got rich. The symbol of his success was a palatial retreat called Castle Kern which he erected on the heights above the town.

In 1910, on his way home from a vacation in Mexico, he stopped to see his old friends in El Paso, found that the trustees who had managed his estate had husbanded his resources well, and learned that for a relatively small sum he could be back in business here. He decided to return to the border and start over.

Never one to dream small dreams, Pete Kern now let his imagination go. On the McKelligon tract, which we call Kern Place now in his honor, he planned to build our fanciest addition. In his mind's eye he saw a second Castle Kern high up on Crazy Cat Ridge, overlooking his development. Trolley cars from El Paso would come all the way to the top. There would be a lake in the *arroyo* just below where the citizens could "enjoy aquatic sports." "Hither," wrote Llew Davis with enthusiasm almost equal to Pete's own, "on hot summer nights will the heat-stricken people of the lower sections of the city go to recreate and cool their feverish brows and quaff the cool nectar of the gods. . . . In the winter time it will be a mecca for the thousands of northern tourists who will visit this sunland."[49]

Pete didn't bother to open an office and wrote his letters at Bob Mullin's book and stationery store,[50] but he spent his money freely. He had his tract surveyed and streets laid out — streets which curved and wound gracefully through the creosote brush and *lechuguilla*. He built a fantastic gateway, embodying many Indian symbols and carrying 444 electric-light bulbs, at the top of North Kansas Street where his development began. His sales campaign opened with a spread of sandwiches and beer laid out on the scenic point above El Paso High School but, ominously, a big dust storm came whirling in and sent everybody home before he could make his pitch.[51]

Only a few houses were erected in his private wilderness. His money ran out. Once again he was twenty years too soon, lost all he had, and gave up the battle. Aging and disappointed, he retired to the Masonic Home at Arlington, Texas, where he was living when he stepped in front of a train on February 8, 1937.[52] The boys who play touch football in Madeline Park (named for Pete's daughter) never realize that they are enjoying themselves in the midst of Pete Kern's broken dreams.

A whole volume could be written about the developers who followed in his footsteps. There would be a chapter on Stormville, a shanty town on the first big mesa north of the city, between Kern Place and the downtown area. In the twenties Mr. Storm's adobe hovels gave way to a glamorous procession of fine houses overlooking the river and the town with a view of the mountains far down in Chihuahua. There would be another chapter on Frank Tobin who, after making money from four additions in the Washington Park area, tried to organize a community ten miles or so beyond the city limits on the way to Alamogordo.[53] He too was ahead of his time and wasted his money, but El Paso has grown far beyond Tobin Town now.

Mesa Avenue, Sunset Heights, Montana Avenue, and Austin Terrace had their day, and the Country Club District took its turn. Now new names are in the news — Coronado Estates and Eastwood and Mountain Park and a dozen more. The center of population has shifted to a point near the airport in East El Paso, and the city limits extend to Ysleta on the south and past the Country Club on the north. It is hard to believe that Joseph Magoffin's house was once considered a rural residence.

A good deal of this expansion might never have happened at all if it had not been for the "lungers" — health seekers — who at one time flooded the town and added many a name to the roster of distinguished citizens. To the "Four C's" (Cattle, Copper, Cotton, and Climate) which are said to have built our community, a fifth "C" — Consumption — might well be added.[54]

Josiah Crosby left his home in Brenham in 1852 and brought his weak lungs to the Valley. Just before his death in 1902 he told a reporter that he "was feeling as well and enjoying life as much as any man in El Paso."[55]

When the railroad came and the boom began, the virtues of the climate were played up in superlatives. "This climate," the *Times* boasted, "is the paradise of the pulmonary invalid."[56] In 1885 a group of doctors, headed by the much-respected Dr. C. T. Race, issued a flowery report calling the town "the home of health";[57] and as late as 1905 the El Paso County Medical Society published a eulogy called "A Story of Sunshine" which ran for three months in every issue of the *Times* — a reprint of the paean of 1885. "The atmosphere is unsurpassed for its dryness and purity," the article declared; "full of electricity, it is wonderfully exhilarating. . . . The asthmatic invalid or the consumptive may sit out of doors, ride or walk in the sunshine 350 days in the year. . . ."[58]

For twenty-five or thirty years the consumptives crowded in. Some were doctors. At least one mayor (C. E. Kelly) and one collector of customs (Charles Davis) came because of lung trouble. In the 90's the *Herald* featured a columnist who called himself Wun Lung. Baldwin's Sanatorium, now St. Joseph's Hospital, was built for the health seekers. Hendricks-Laws, Long's and Price's sanatoria were famous in their day.[59]

Many of the invalids were short of money and actually camped out by the hundreds in the Highland Park section. Others built small houses with sun porches on the hills near Southwestern Hospital. Consumptives might still be seeking us out had the doctors not discovered that rest is more important than climate in treating the disease.

Culture came slowly to this raw and sometimes rowdy metropolis, though we were fiercely proud of what we had and were hospitable to talent which came our way. At the same time we had ambition and ability enough to produce a good deal of our own entertainment. Our people organized amateur theatricals, sang Gilbert and Sullivan, and could always provide duets, quartets, and solos when occasion demanded. In the earliest times, however, there was a minimum of cultural depth. Music, especially, took a long time to progress beyond the William Tell Overture and military marches.

At first about all we had to supplement the native string and brass groups was band music.[60] The musicians at Fort Bliss were available for dances on and off the post,[61] appearing about as often in Paso del Norte as in their own territory. At the same time the *tipica* orchestras, which we still love to listen to at festive times, were popular for dances and informal concerts. The *tipica* consisted of almost any number of instruments in almost any combination, but there had to be violins, guitars and a string bass plus trumpets, clarinets, and any odd strings available. The natural musicianship and fine ears of the Latins always made for good listening. Governor Ahumada of Chihuahua was partial to a band of this type from his own city, and sometimes brought his musicians to the border.

A brass band was organized by Professor Darrow in December of 1882[62] and the community was never without band music after that. The Fort Bliss musicians began a series of summer concerts before almost 6,000 people on May 13, 1890;[63] the El Paso Cornet Band made its debut on July 1, 1892; and Professor Rogers' Plaza Band and Orchestra concertized in 1893.[64] There were others, all occupying the bandstand in the Plaza as everybody turned out to listen to marches and polkas and classical arrangements on those magic summer nights so long ago.

A byproduct of the musical urge was the beautification of San Jacinto Plaza, heart of the downtown area. Once the town's dump heap and site of a manure pile produced by the livery stable on the St. Regis corner, the Plaza had been a disgrace. In 1881 Editor Newman campaigned successfully for the removal of John Woods' run-down blacksmith shop from the northwest angle of the square, but the first attempt at actual beautification came in 1883 when the council gave J. Fisher Satterthwaite $600 to do what he could.[65]

Mr. Satterthwaite's difficulties were great indeed. El Paso had never been a green town and was not likely to become one overnight. Mr. Newman complained early in 1883 that "burros, goats, and cows are allowed to run loose in the streets and all show a particular fondness for the tender bark and shoots of young trees and anything else green at this season of the year." Only two months later, however, improvements were visible. Iron posts and a chain fence surrounded the Plaza. Walks and flower beds had been installed. A handsome stone basin and a bandstand were taking shape; and in December seventy-five Chinese umbrella trees were planted.[66] Our central square, if not a temple of the muses, was at least no longer hostile to art.

Sadly we must admit that the umbrella trees did not live,[67] and neither did the plantings which followed,"[68] but gradually, a step at a time, El Paso grew greener. Major Fewel installed the first Bermuda-grass lawn at 907 East San Antonio, and progress continued until the great days of the nineteen twenties when Hugo Meyer set to work in earnest to make El Paso a city of trees and flowers. The alligators in the Plaza pool remained the same through the years, but everything changed around them.[69]

In time other musical centers besides the Plaza became available. Mr. Satterthwaite's Mesa Gardens was one. In the nineties the Golden Eagle and Castle Hall offered entertainment in an outdoor setting. Some years later Chopin Hall rose from the sand and cactus of a vacant lot on Myrtle Avenue (the United States Courthouse stands there now) and was given a gala opening on the evening of January 11, 1896. Its founder was Professor Ferdinand Dewey, a gray-haired health seeker from the East, a fine pianist and teacher who yearned to do his part in bringing civilization to the border. El Paso turned out in white gloves and evening dress to hear Miss Kate Moore, Miss Marie Shelton and other local performers assist Professor Dewey in presenting a program of Beethoven, Chopin and Schubert for the delighted audience.

In the years that followed the Professor brought many a world-renowned performer to the stage of Chopin Hall and sometimes participated in the programs himself. In January of 1896, for instance, Herr Anton Schott, a *heldentenor* of formidable bulk and volume, sang a program of Schubert and Wagner to ecstatic applause. Dewey collaborated with Herr Fickinscher, the accompanist, in a two-piano rendition arranged by himself of Schubert's *Marche Militaire*.[70]

What all this was leading up to was the birth of our most impressive cultural asset, the El Paso Symphony Orchestra, now a semi-professional group of seventy musicians which presents about eight concerts a season with a variety of visiting artists as soloists.

It was not always thus. The orchestra had to be born again, and yet again, the first birth occurring in the fall of 1893 when Frederick R. Koch assembled a group of amateur instrumentalists and began rehearsals.[71] Koch was a teacher of music with studios in the Franklin Club, a real professional. He presented his first concert in the district courtroom of the old courthouse on December 29. A crowded and attentive house listened to selections from

Balfé's *Bohemian Girl,* to Mascagni's *Intermezzo Sinfonico,* and to Von Flotow's overture to *Stradella.*[72] A second concert, scheduled in February of 1894, included music by Wagner, Mozart and Schubert.[73]

These volunteer musicians made strenuous efforts to present the best in music but disbanded in 1905.[74]

The next surge forward came in 1914 when Major H. E. Vansurdam, a man of many talents, reorganized the orchestra and presented a series of programs of classical and lighter music in the Crawford Theatre on Sunday afternoons.[75] The crowds were good but financial support was meagre.[76]

By this time James Graham McNary, a musical banker, had arrived in El Paso and had begun to organize the vocal talent of the town. He was a man of great energy and great zest for living as well as great musical ability. His wife was a fine pianist and organist and worked closely with him.[77] With the help of James A. Dick, a musical grocer, McNary organized the El Paso Choral Society in 1907. Within a year his 150 singers were good enough to present Haydn's *Creation* with the touring Chicago Symphony Orchestra, and El Paso was talking about an annual Music Festival.[78]

McNary was always looking for ways to upgrade El Paso music. In 1912 he was in search of a knowledgeable bank employee and found one in the person of J. Louis Coggeshall of Rhode Island, who just happened to be a fine bass singer. Mr. Coggeshall is still with us and still singing.[79]

Meanwhile the orchestra was being born again, this time as the child of a chamber-music society organized by C. T. Bates, a bassoonist who learned his instrument because no bassoon player was available.[80] Biagio Casciano, a native Italian, brought his French horn. L. R. Wosika, a cultivated second-generation Czech from Nebraska, was the nucleus of the cello section, and gentle, French-born Salvador Souflée, one of the few professional musicians, played the flute.[81] Peter Gustat, an Alsatian who arrived in 1915 to work for the El Paso and Southwestern Railroad,[82] made the chamber society into an orchestra.

A great occasion in our musical history was the first concert of this group, presented in Liberty Hall (still our concert hall) on November 7, 1919. Thirty musicians gave their best to the *Swedish Coronation March* and the *Unfinished Symphony* for about 1,000 listeners, and Miss Sarame Raynolds sang *Divinités du Styx* in a voice of "velvety richness."[83] The high point of the performance, however, was the rendition of Wagner's *Hail, Bright Abode* by the orchestra and Brahms Chorus, directed by James G. McNary. "With a sudden thrill," said the *Times* reporter, "the audience realized that something new had come into the civic life of El Paso."[84]

Gustat managed to get the city behind him financially. Between interested businessmen and the city council, $6,000 was raised to pay for six orchestra concerts that winter and twenty-four free band concerts the following summer.[85] Again, however, the group faced evil times. Gustat left El Paso in discouragement when the flooding Rio Grande damaged real estate in which he had invested. It was reborn once more in 1930 when H. Arthur Brown was sent to us from New York, part of his salary being paid by the Juilliard Foundation. Under his direction the organization made steady progress musically, and with the help of newspaper publisher Dorrance D. Roderick it achieved some financial stability — as much stability as symphony orchestras may hope to attain. Under Maestro Orlando Barera the competence of the musicians has steadily increased and audiences come close to filling the big hall.

It would not be good manners to leave out the most colorful and perhaps the most valuable group of musicians we have produced in seventy-five years of effort. This is the famous McGinty Club which at one time boasted a membership of some three hundred more-or-less-musical males and represents a high point in our independent and spontaneous production of joy, mirth, and music, all combined.

The Club was conceived one evening in 1889 in front of an assayer's office on San Francisco Street, on the spot where the Army YMCA is now. The business was operated by a remarkable El Paso personality named Dan W. Reckhart. Dan was a Columbia College graduate, an athlete, a friend of all mankind, a person of great enterprise and large appetite. He regularly ate a dozen eggs for breakfast and was the only man in town who could and sometimes did eat a whole turkey at one sitting.[86] He himself was heard to say that a turkey was a little too much for one and not quite enough for two.[87] His talents as a trencherman made him a broad-gauged human being, so broad indeed that he engaged three seats at the Myar Opera House — one for his wife and two (with the arms removed) for himself. In time he achieved the awe-inspiring weight of 310 pounds. As one would expect, he was charming and genial and the best company in the world. He was the first and only president the McGinties ever had.

On the evening we are speaking of, his partner, H. F. Heckelman, appeared at the office with an old, sweet-toned guitar and Reckhart decided that he would like to learn to play it. His musical education began then and there as Heckelmann initiated him into the mysteries of the key of G major. Eventually Reck rustled up a mandolin for Heck[88] and they played duets — always in G.

Ultimately they thought of organizing a club, and a number of young men began meeting for instrumental music, barbershop singing, gossip and beer at the assay offices. Sometimes on Sundays they gathered for an outing. "A crowd of fellows," Reckhart reminisced in 1909, "used to go out to the Mesa to hunt jack rabbits and quail and other game ahead of us toward Ysleta, and would come back to our camp wagon loaded with the fruits of the chase, which we would cook up in a big stew and invite our friends to help us eat it, with the amateur band furnishing the music after we had eaten our fill."[89]

A song which went well with beer and rabbit was in everybody's mouth at the time. It was called "Down Went McGinty" and told about a diver named McGinty, who dived not wisely but too well. The chorus went, in part:

> Down went McGinty to the bottom of the sea.
> He must be very wet, for he hasn't come back yet.

One Sunday in 1889 when the wagon was being loaded with beer for the regulation trip to the mesa, a waggish member named "Peg" Grandover (so called because he had a wooden leg) hung a sign on the vehicle: HUNTING FOR McGINTY.[90] That did it. The club had a name, and it was fun to belong to. "It grew," said Reckhart, "like a wart."[91]

The members amused themselves by setting up rules and objectives which nobody took seriously. The purpose of the club, officially, was to "put down liquor," but no saloonkeepers or bartenders were admitted. No political discussions were allowed, and a Committee on Murder was set up to throw out anybody who started one. It cost one dollar per month to belong, but there were special assessments for parties.[92]

Those parties were great occasions. Invitations went out on bright green cards which carried the notice that "Failure to attend forfeits all future recognition." Only death was accepted as a valid excuse for absence; but of course everybody wanted to come.[93] They gathered at Mesa Gardens and Castle Hall, and at such picnic spots as Orn's Grove, Rand's Grove, Hart's Mill, Woodlawn Park and Washington Park where the body was sustained by kettles of stew and barrels of beer (with soda water for "temperance" members) and the soul was elevated by music and song afterward. It is said that every member "watched himself" and nobody was ever drunk at a McGinty gathering.[94]

They liked to conclude a party with a display of fireworks and sometimes with the firing of the McGinty cannons — two venerable field pieces which were acquired early in the history of the club. In the nineties it was believed that Reckhart had wheedled them from Joseph and Samuel Schutz, who had picked them up when Camp Concordia was abandoned. Forty years later, however, Mrs. Mary S. Teel revealed that they had been captured from the Union forces at the Battle of Valverde in 1862 and buried in a vacant lot in Albuquerque by her husband, the late Major Trevanion T. Teel, until 1889. By this time Major Teel had moved his law practice to El Paso and wanted his favorite piece, called the Blue Whistler, to find a home here.[95]

When Al Lamour, "chief pyrotechnical artist" for the club, wanted a place to shoot off his cannon and his rockets, the management acquired the use of a big sandhill, the highest eminence in the downtown section, which rose near the future site of the Union Depot. Reckhart persuaded W. R. Brown and Billy Watts to go in with him and purchase it for speculation and incidentally for the use of the membership. It cost them $2,000, but when it was later sold to the El Paso and Southwestern Railway, it brought $19,000. Later still it was removed when steam shovels leveled the land around the railway station.[96]

When the Southwest Silver Convention met in El Paso in 1891, the club erected on top of the hill a canvas-and-lumber fort painted to look like stone. Entrenchments were dug around it. After a parade illuminated by red fire and Roman candles, the band played *Dixie* and *Down Went McGinty* and Peg Grandover's Light Guards stormed the hill while the cannon roared and the defenders blasted away with blank cartridges. A battery from Fort Bliss added to the pleasing uproar. At the climax of these heroics the fort was taken, set afire, and destroyed as an enormous supply of fireworks was touched off. It cost a lot of money, but it was so much fun and made such an impression on the spectators that it was repeated often thereafter.[97]

Members were apt to seize on anything unusual as an excuse for club activity. There was the time in 1891, for instance, when, during a bad drouth, the Department of Agriculture appropriated $19,000 for rain-making experiments, R. C. Dyrenforth had noticed during the Civil War that wet weather usually followed a violent bombardment and believed that explosives set off in the heavens would bring rain. He chose Mount Franklin as the site of one of his experiments. On its summit he set off dynamite and shot off mortars. He sent powerful charges up in balloons. The uproar went on for several days. One cloud formed, "about the size of a straw hat," but it disappeared in the direction of Albuquerque and the rainmakers gave up.[98]

At this point Reckhart stepped in and invited the scientists to a party at Mesa Gardens. They were seated outdoors close to the wall of the pavilion. At the high point of the entertainment Reckhart announced that the club had a squad of rainmakers of its own who would now show what they could do. A group on the roof overturned several barrels of water and drenched the guests sitting there in their pith helmets and canvas shoes. Everybody, including the visitors, thought it was funny.[99]

The main purpose of the club was music. "Professor" (everybody who played professionally was Professor) Offley came to Fort Bliss as a member of the Quartermaster Corps, led the choirs at St. Clement's Church and the First Methodist Church, and brought his talents to the McGinties. So did Professor Carl Pitzer, a fine band and orchestra man with a deep respect for good music well played. He was the one who made the club artistically respectable. These two men supervised the main musical groups but they could not be personally responsible for the ramifications which included no less than a dozen sub-groups — quartets, choir, fife-and-drum corps, tipica orchestra, string orchestra, banjo troubadours, and even a Chinese group which played "weirdly charming" airs on native instruments. As auxiliaries there were a couple of marching organizations and the military and pyrotechnical squads.

A "grand musical soiree" was held at the clubrooms in the spring of 1890,[100] but the first concert by the McGinty Band was heard on St. Patrick's Day, 1892, the musicians wearing long, dark coats and high hats. Later they acquired dark green uniforms with the word McGinty in white on the caps. They gave concerts in the Plaza, played for funerals and weddings, and welcomed every important visitor to town. Several concerts were presented in the Myar Opera House.[101] A special McGinty touch was achieved at one of these on February 20, 1895, when the ensemble played *The Forge in the Forest* with a real forge and three anvils on stage. Three strong-armed members, Brokenbrow, Pollard and Dold, hammered the sparks out of red-hot iron in time to the music to the great edification of a capacity audience.[102]

Great moments for the McGinty Club arrived with the visits of two presidents, Harrison and McKinley. The McGinty Band was the pivotal organization in the first one. The musicians convoyed Mr. Harrison and his party from his special train to the courthouse, where several thousand people were waiting. In a notably short speech he called El Paso a gateway of trade and also a gateway of friendship. He reminded his listeners, not too subtly, of their reputation as a sin city and advised them to do something about it. "You cannot attract foreign capital or increased citizenship," he said, "unless you have a reputation for social order."[103]

There were courtesies and felicitations in English and Spanish, and then the President was back in his carriage on his way to the station, to the musical accompaniment of the McGinty Band.

Ten years later William McKinley, his gentle, invalid wife, and a group of cabinet members and confidential agents stopped off on a similar swing around the country. Mexican and New Mexican dignitaries cooperated when the ceremonies began on May 6, 1901. "Following the carriages," the *Herald* reported, "was the most beautiful part of the parade, twelve hundred school children, kindergarten classes in the lead, carrying flags and marching to the music of the McGinty Band."

The *Herald* commented prophetically that McKinley's tendency to go his way without guards might have bad consequences: "Should an assassin desire to take his life, it would be a comparatively easy matter."[104]

By now the McGinty organization was nearing its end and the Band had to play second fiddle during the presidential visit, first place going to a group from Mexico. The *Herald* remarked rather frigidly that the McGinties presented "a good appearance." Obviously the good old days were over.

Perhaps the last full-dress appearance of the Band occurred earlier that same year. In January El Paso offered to the world its most elaborate celebration up to that time – a fiesta called the Midwinter Carnival. It originated in the teeming brain of the city editor of the *Times*, who suggested that a celebration capitalizing on El Paso's mild winter climate and almost perpetual sunshine was now in order. It would stimulate business, make fitting observance of the advent of the new century, and give the citizens a chance to release their pent-up energies. A group met at the Sheldon Hotel to get organized: A. S. Greig, Harry Alexander, T. M. Wingo, and Dr. H. H. Stark (chairman). W. W. Turney, Park Pitman and Julius Krakauer formed a selection committee to choose a queen. Two delightful young ladies, Claire Kelly and Leila Trumbull (later Mrs. Robert Holliday), were the leading contenders. Si Ryan, the portly and prosperous owner of the Astor House saloon and gambling hall, managed Miss Kelly's campaign and brought it to a victorious conclusion. One story says that he acted as grand marshal of the parade in which she appeared to her subjects.[105] Another places Tillie Howard, our most popular madam, on a white horse at the head of the procession. The prosaic fact, however, is that the rotund and bearded figure which headed the parade belonged to Joseph Magoffin.

On the second day a new set of floats included three prairie schooners which were attacked in front of the Orndorff Hotel by a band of Indians whose performance caused the female spectators to shriek as loud as the victims. Some of them are said to have fainted. At night fireworks seemed to make a volcano out of Mount Franklin and there was a ball to honor the queen. The McGinty Band was the heart of everything, marching and concertizing to the great satisfaction of twenty or twenty-five thousand spectators.

The next year wind and sand spoiled the show, and in 1903 a snowstorm ruined it. That ended the midwinter festivities until 1908, the first year of the Os-Aple celebrations. The war in Europe and the Mexican Revolution, plus bad weather, finished King Os-

Aple in 1912, and the Sunshine in January idea lay dormant again until 1935 when the Sun Carnival resurrected the Great Idea of 1899.[106]

The McGinties went out with the Midwinter Carnival. A few months before the third and final effort, the club disbanded. Men were dying, moving away, or finding themselves too busy for innocent amusement. Carl Pitzer's departure for Seattle in 1902 was the final blow. The band met for the last time in September. The club itself was already non-existent, and this was farewell. The musicians played the McGinty song and *Auld Lang Syne*. Then, as Dan Reckhart phrased it, they "tucked their instruments under their arms and took them home as relics of the greatest musical organization El Paso had ever known."[107]

With all the beer and horseplay, the club was the first organization in El Paso to be interested in serious music. Members filled the chairs of the first symphony orchestra and appeared at every reincarnation of that group. It is a sad thing that the only present-day reminder of the existence and influence of the club is the name attached to an oversize stemmed beer glass in Juárez bars. Produced in response to the demand of a member who could never get enough beer at McGinty meetings, the glass became familiar on both sides of the river and is still called a McGinty.

Captain Jack Crawford, Dan Reckhart's father-in-law, who was ambiguously known all over the country as "The Poet-Scout," was an honorary member of the club. He wrote an ode expressing his feelings toward the organization and its work. It concluded:

> And when in startling echoes, from heaven's high canopy
> You hear the final trumpet in great Reckhart's key of G,
> Walk right up to old St. Peter, though with fear you are depressed,
> Whisper in his ear, "McGinty," and the saint will do the rest.[108]

The McGinty Club was only one of a number of groups which counterbalanced the attractions of gambling halls, variety theatres, and parlor houses. Nobody thought of them as antidotes for the lure of the tenderloin, but they were, and were intended to be, gathering places for substantial citizens who were seriously interested in the progress of the town.

The Social Club was the ancestor of all later social organizations. Its birth coincided almost with the birth of the town, its first

ball being given on December 22, 1881, at Hills' Hall on San Antonio Street — a new meeting place erected by the town's pioneer
developer for just such occasions. The Chihuahua band was imported to provide the music. The supper tables were presided over
by Mrs. E. S. Newman, Mrs. Joseph Magoffin, and Mrs. Ben D.
Russell. This party began a tradition which lasted for some thirty
years. All functions were formal — white tie and long kid gloves.
The club met every other Friday at the courthouse, the Grand
Central, the Sheldon — later at the St. Regis, the Toltec Club, the
Del Norte. If it is good for all of us to dress in our best and put on
our finest manners, then the Social Club was a good thing for the
citizens of El Paso. After the Country Club was organized and the
social life of the town began to flow in many channels, the Social
Club declined and limited its activities to two dances a year — one
on New Year's Eve. But it was still going at the beginning of World
War I.[109]

An entirely different sort of thing was the Cactus Club, which
started out as a debating society. It was organized in the back
room of Llew Davis's drug store on San Antonio Street in the early
summer of 1882.[110] There must have been a few debaters present,
for one debate was actually held. The subject was the superior bliss
to be found in the married or in the single state. It developed, however, that debating was about the last thing the members wished
to do. What they really wanted was a gentleman's club with bar
and reading room where a man could go to meet his friends for a
drink, and where he could bring out-of-town guests whom he
wished to impress. And that is what they got — a very fancy layout on the second floor of Mr. Hills' new building. New officers
were elected and a new constitution and bylaws were drawn up.
It was pointed out, pridefully, that the rules were much the same
as those of the St. Louis Club, "one of the most aristocratic of the
West." In addition to the bar and reading room there was a pool
room with three tables. The atmosphere was cheerful and relaxed,[111] and sixty members spent considerable time enjoying it.

By 1890 one wing of the membership felt that it was time to
have a building of their own and a meeting was actually called and
attended by about a hundred members who discussed reorganization and the forming of a stock company to finance the new

program. Nothing came of this meeting – possibly because the McGinty Club was moving toward the center of community interest. But the organization was still in existence in 1918.[112]

Far outshining all other men's clubs in our history was the Toltec Club, founded in 1902. Nothing like it had been seen in these parts before, and nothing approaching it has been seen since. It was really the social high-water mark of an era when society, even down here on the border, was no shirt-sleeves affair. Quite typically, according to the men who were present at its birth, it was the product of emulation and irritation. For some time a very exclusive organization called The El Paso Club had flourished in the old two-story Mills Building which succeeded the Grand Central Hotel after the big fire of 1892 and preceded the present Mills Building. The El Paso Club was the last word in elegance and exclusiveness – so much so that a number of prominent citizens decided a new club was needed.[113]

Credit for the first suggestion is generally given to the Eddy brothers, J. Arthur and C. B., railroad builders and capitalists extraordinary, but most of the wealthy, prominent and successful men of the city were involved. The list of founding members includes such potent names as Britton Davis, A. P. Coles, W. W. Turney, Felix Martinez, T. M. Wingo, W. H. Burges, and 158 others who claimed El Paso as their residence. Sixty non-resident members were taken in. Members paid $100 for initiation and $50 a year dues.[114]

Quarters were rented at first, two floors upstairs in a building across from the Popular Dry Goods Company on Texas Street. The Club held forth there until 1909.[115] In those rooms practically every important visitor to our town was entertained, including President Díaz, President Madero, and Theodore Roosevelt.[116] The program of activities included a fabulous masquerade ball every New Year's Eve, but the really big affair was the annual stag dinner and election of officers. White tie and tails were mandatory. The menu was sumptuous and exotic, and the menu cards were embellished with the wit and learning of the erudite members, Will Burges usually taking the lead in the wit and wisdom department. Some memorable speeches were made on these occasions, for instance in 1914 when John J. Pershing was on the program.[117]

Without downgrading the McGinty Club, which certainly had top attractions of a different order, one can get an idea of what was happening at the Pass of the North by contrasting the rabbit stew and beer, enjoyed *al fresco* by the McGinty Club in 1890, with the viands and beverages served up by the members of the Toltec Club fifteen years later. The menu enjoyed at the annual reunion in 1907 appears on another page.

On October 14, 1910, the Club's new building was dedicated and opened to the membership. A fine, flatiron-shaped four-story brick building, it occupied the triangle where San Antonio and Magoffin Avenues come together and where the Baptist Church stood in the eighties. Its many rooms housed everything a clubman could desire or dream of in 1910. The ballroom was the best in town. The dining room was superb. The reading rooms, billiard rooms, card rooms, and lounging rooms were the last word. And there were ample quarters for members who wished to do all their living in the heart of such a male elysium.

The music, the flowers, the hospitality of the opening celebration remain in the minds of surviving guests as the most sumptuous social occasion of our early history.[118]

Prohibition dealt the club a body blow. The Depression finished it. After 1930 it ceased to exist as a live organization. It is worth noting that the Commonwealth Club, organized by El Paso residents who considered the Toltec Club too exclusive, was still going strong during World War II.[119]

As the Toltec Club declined, the El Paso Country Club blossomed. With Waters Davis — lawyer, athlete, crusader against vice — as the sparkplug, the first organization was set up in 1902.[120] A frame clubhouse and a nine-hole golf course close to the site now occupied by Dudley Field were in operation in 1906. Davis was president, W. T. Hixson was vice-president, directors were T. M. Wingo, J. F. Williams, W. E. Race, Owen P. White, E. Moye, and Carl Beers.[121] One hundred eighty-five names appeared on the membership rolls. Carl Beers donated a cup and arranged the first tournament in 1906. He is probably the only one active in that year who is still playing golf sixty years after.[122]

Two years later the club and golf course were moved to a site on Dyer Street near Fort Bliss where the new clubhouse opened brilliantly on January 16, 1909,[123] initiating ten years of activity which ended with the destruction of the building by fire on May 2, 1916.[124]

The present site of the El Paso Country Club, a *bosque* of trees and heavy brush in those days, was donated by Zack White in 1918 and the new clubhouse was unveiled with fanfare on January 7, 1922.[125] For many years it had the field to itself, but in recent years the Coronado Country Club, high up on the western slope of Mount Franklin, has provided healthy competition, and the *Club Campestre* across the river in Juárez challenges both of them in the quality of its golf course. The layout of the El Paso Club's course, product of the imagination of J. C. Wilmarth of the old *Herald,* is still regarded, however, as something of a work of art.[126]

Not everybody believes that gentlemen's clubs and golf courses are true measures of civilization, but in our case they have special significance. They measure our departure from frontier ways and standards. As they increase in importance, the tenderloin decreases.

Owen White, who was a moving spirit in the organization of the first Country Club, regrets, or pretends to regret, the change. Of his fellow club members he says, "These poor men now shaved daily, boasted of the cold shower every morning, whether they took it or not, changed their clothes twice a day, and began to play golf. That was the end. That settled it. El Paso had become entirely too 'nice' for me and so I decided to move."[127] Owen probably never suspected that somebody some day would look into the newspapers for 1906 and find his name leading all the rest as an organizer of golf clubs.

Speaking of organizations which helped to make El Paso a "nice" town, mention should be made of the YMCA, which was organized in 1886 and was operating in 1888 in rented rooms on San Francisco Street. A fine building, dedicated in 1908, went up on Oregon Street just north of the tracks and across from the Public Library. On that spot several generations of our young men swam and played handball and held meetings under the supervision of various capable secretaries until the much-beloved A. L. (Doc) Holm arrived in 1914 and began his twenty-two-year term in the office.[128] He and the old building went out of circulation at nearly the same time when the "Y" moved in 1955 to its new headquarters on Montana Avenue.

One last organization had more to do than all the rest, probably, in making El Paso a Sun City. This was the El Paso Woman's Club, something to be really proud of ever since the days of its beginning. It started when Mrs. W. W. Mills gathered a few of her friends at her home on San Francisco Street in 1894 and called the group the Current Topics Club.[129] The founding mothers were Mrs. Mills, Mrs. T. J. Beall, Mrs. Leigh Clark, Mrs. W. M. James, Mrs. Ernest Kohlberg, Mrs. E. R. Neff, Mrs. J. C. Townsend, Mrs. W. S. Tilton, Mrs. J. C. Voss, Miss Mary I. Stanton, and Mrs. Thirza I. Westcott. They met every Wednesday with Mrs. Mills, the president, until she moved to Chihuahua with her husband, the newly appointed U. S. Consul, in 1898.[130] In that year the club membership was increased from nine to twenty-five, but the Current Topics name was retained.

Since the Mills home was no longer available for meetings, the discussions were held in Miss Stanton's Reading Room for Boys (the first stage of our emerging public library) in the Sheldon Building. Later they were moved to the office of the county judge in the City Hall, then to Chopin Music Hall.[131]

All this moving indicated the need for permanent quarters for what was now the Woman's Club of El Paso with fifty members,[132] and the ladies began to think about raising money for a building. They opened their campaign with a Centennial Ball on January 1, 1900.[133] It was a really big show for such a time and such an organization, and its success gave them courage, but they had sixteen years to wait before the present handsome and spacious clubhouse on north Mesa Avenue rose in brick-and-concrete reality.[134]

Meanwhile the membership encountered opposition which a present-day woman could hardly take seriously. Many of the townspeople, including some conservative ladies, regarded the club activities as a waste of time at best and dangerous at worst. Why were those housewives out of their homes? What was happening to their children and their husbands? If they attended to their duties, they would be too busy to gad about and discuss politics and international affairs.[135]

Fortunately the club was too useful to be affected by these evidences of discontent. In 1899 it became a departmental organization with six specialties. These have multiplied until today a woman can find her place with almost any age group or with devotees of a dozen special interests.

The Woman's Club, of course, was not intended to keep the members out of saloons and gambling halls — perish the thought! But the role of women in bringing better things to the wilderness was clearly and completely exemplified. By building a richer life for themselves, they enriched the life of their community and thereby shortened the long reign of the gamblers, saloonkeepers and sports.

Since we are talking about the uplifting influences which prevented El Paso from relaxing completely with the sinners, something should be said of the outdoor and indoor activities which kept the young men out of the gambling halls and sporting houses, at least part of the time. Actually El Paso was a first-class sporting town in both the good and bad senses of the word. Leaving out boxing, bullfighting, and cockfighting as spectator sports with little to recommend them as character builders, we still have plenty to talk about.

During the eighties and nineties, for instance, El Paso was a baseball town, sometimes a fanatical baseball town. The times of great enthusiasm came, naturally, when we had a winning team, but even in the lean seasons, baseball was a passion with many a citizen.

The first green sprout of interest appeared on May 16, 1884, when an organization meeting was announced for the following Saturday in George Speck's saloon.[136] This shoot seems to have withered early, for nothing happened until October, when Mayor Magoffin responded to public demand and called for a conference in his office.[137] The result was the formation of two teams who were to play each other every Sunday afternoon. Should a contest be arranged with an out-of-town nine, the two groups would combine. After two weeks of practice, a game was scheduled with a Fort Bliss team. El Paso won 18-17.

The ball park, at the end of the San Antonio Street car line, immediately became a place of popular resort. There was a grandstand where it cost a quarter to sit down. The playing field was improved. And there the El Paso Browns did so well against all comers that in the spring of 1885 they had some difficulty in finding opponents.

The great test came in that year when they undertook a three-game series with Albuquerque on the Fourth of July. Albuquerque won all three, and there was gloom in El Paso.[138]

In 1888 the baseball fever rose to new heights. A game was scheduled every Sunday and the spectators were numbered in the hundreds, all passionately and loudly partisan. In January of that year L. B. Freudenthal called a meeting to form a stock company capitalized at $5,000 in shares of $25.00. A committee decided to build a diamond at Kansas and Seventh. Negotiations got under way to hire a good battery, Kittle and Gates, from Fort Worth. The great moment of the season came when El Paso played Las Vegas on the new grounds on July 21, 1888. Las Vegas had just shut out Albuquerque 4-0 and was regarded as the top team in the region if not in the world. The betting was three to one on Las Vegas, but El Paso won 8-3.

After that there was talk of organizing a league, but although the seasons of 1891 and 1893 were very successful, interest in the team declined from the heights of the late eighties, El Paso ceased to be a "city of baseball cranks,"[139] and the league idea never bore fruit. The citizens even stooped so low as to watch football matches of the grunt-and-shove variety on the sacred turf of the baseball field.

Other sports were added to the repertory as time went on. The Border Wheelmen organized in 1889 and were active in the nineties.[140] A Sporting and Athletic Club came into being in 1890. The fencers formed a brotherhood in 1892 and the tennis players did likewise in 1893. And so it went. Those who wished to enjoy themselves in the sweat of their brows always had ample opportunity to do so.[141]

At one time roller skating threatened to outdistance all other sports. A new rink was opened near the corner of Second Street and South El Paso on December 18, 1884, and the town went wild over the new activity. Whoever managed that skating rink was a master organizer with new ideas bubbling up in his brain every day. There was never a dull moment or a dull evening as special events followed each other in exciting sequence. New Year's parties, masquerades, ring tournaments, were advertised. There was a "Phantom Party" on February 26, 1885. A Dress Carnival was announced for March 11.[142] Business was so good that a rival rink was opened in Paso del Norte that spring.[143] For a few years the rink was the place to go.

Some years later came the Natatorium, a super-elegant indoor swimming pool with Turkish baths on the second floor and a skating rink on the third floor. From 1898 to 1906 there was no place like the Natatorium. Then the pool was covered over to make a floor for the Crawford Theatre, and the rest of the building merged with the Angelus Hotel,[144] which survived, battered but defiant, until 1965. As this is written, a parking lot now occupies the spot where the Crawford Theatre and the Natatorium once stood, near where Parson Tays called sinners to repentance in 1870.

With the help of these devices and activities, the young people of El Paso, along with some of their elders, were able to stay out of trouble and avoid the pitfalls of the Sin City. The chaperone had not disappeared from the scene in those days, and mothers were still solicitous about the conduct and companions of their daughters. El Paso was perhaps not an ideal place to rear girls, but such rearing could be, and was, done successfully. And our pioneer friends tell us now that the problems created by spoiled youth, permissive parents, early sophistication, and adolescent ownership of automobiles make the life of a young person more precarious today than it was in 1885.

CHAPTER XXI

Sin City

THE BAD ONES CAME IN ALL GRADES and sizes — little crooks and big crooks, high-grade and low-grade fancy women, tinhorns and big-time gamblers. Thanks to them El Paso was known, even before the railroad arrived, as a very sinful town, one of the nation's most important sporting centers. It was said that New York, New Orleans, El Paso, and the Barbary Coast were the four hottest spots in the United States. El Paso may have deserved this accolade, but the sinfulness was under pretty firm control.

The reason for our vigilance was the fact that sin was a business, like shoes and real estate. The city government for many years made ends meet by demanding payoffs from prostitutes and license fees from gamblers, money which paid the salaries of the policemen who kept the girls and the gamblers in line. Furthermore, the business of the sporting crowd was important to the town's merchants. "They knew," says Owen White, "that the thing that brought customers from afar into their stores was El Paso's invitation to step right up to the Sinners' bench, and they took advantage of it. They even encouraged it."[1]

Since sin was profitable, it had to be regulated and watched like any other financial asset. El Paso, says Owen in continuation, was "a town whose saloon keepers sold good whisky, whose gamblers ran square games, whose prostitutes paid their license fees, in the guise of 'fines,' with absolute regularity, and in whose dance halls visitors were not drugged, slugged, and rolled."

Considerable credit for this happy state of affairs is given by Mr. White and others to Mr. C. R. Morehead, the quiet little banker who came to El Paso in 1880 to grow up with the country. Before long, partly because of his financial influence and partly because of his instinct for management, he became the leading Democrat and political boss of the community — in the eyes of his adversaries the overlord of the town's vice. Mr. White speaks with admiration of his skill in riding his private whirlwind. "There wasn't a gambler, a saloon keeper, a dance-hall proprietor, not even a lady of ill-fame in the town who didn't know that any time he wanted to, C. R. Morehead could put them out of business. Therefore they had a great respect for him, and co-operated with him in keeping El Paso's vice industry on a level that was high indeed in comparison with other frontier towns."[2]

Mr. Morehead was to play a surprising and unexpected role in the cleanup of the Sin City, when it finally came. But for some twenty years he manipulated the affairs of the town from behind the scenes and put to use the forces he may have felt himself unable to resist. During most of this time members of the sporting fraternity were to be found in high places, even on the city council, and the underworld had some part, often an important one, in running the affairs of the municipality.[3]

It must be acknowledged that Mr. Morehead, or whoever was keeping matters in hand, did not reduce the tenderloin district to order all at once. At first the roughs of both sexes thought they could do as they pleased. Editor Newman of the *Lone Star,* who thought of himself as a guardian of the public morals, registered shock early in 1883 over a public display of vile language afforded by three or four men and as many prostitutes in a carriage in front of the post office.[4] During the following autumn a madam named Ann Myers lost her temper at Lou Howard, one of her girls: pinched her arms, tore her dress, pistol whipped her, and would have killed her if she had had a little more time before the police arrived.[5]

The managers of the vice industry were as dissatisfied with conditions as Newman was, but for a different reason. In 1885 several of the madams protested vigorously to the city council that the regular ten-dollar monthly assessments were too high and declared that the price must come down or they would have to go out of business. The council merely asked the Chief of Police to make sure collections were made, and the madams stayed on the job.[6]

Prostitutes and gamblers, the officials learned, were actually much easier to keep in line than the plague of tramps, thieves, burglars, confidence men, and miscellaneous small-time crooks who frequently drew exasperated comments from Mr. Newman.[7] Bunco steerers operated on both sides of the river, plying their trade when trains came in, at fiestas and celebrations, and even on ordinary weekdays on the main streets of either town in broad daylight.

Sometimes it was hard to tell the crook from the victims. In February, 1883, for instance, W. H. Price of Silver City came to town with $1,000 in gold which he was induced to exchange for what he thought was $4,000 in counterfeit money. When he found that his counterfeit bills were only strips of brown paper, he raised a vigorous outcry against the wicked swindlers who had deceived him.[8]

The *Times* described one particular swindle which was going on without interference on El Paso Street. "We refer to the man who sells envelopes. His scheme is to put money into envelopes in the presence of the crowd, and then puts cards into others with numbers to draw the money. He exhibits the prize-winning number, and pretends to use awkwardness in putting the number into the envelope, so that the silly purchaser thinks he knows just where the prize number is. Generally the persons who bite at this bunco bait are ignorant men or boys. . . . We hope for the credit of the town that prompt measures will be taken to rid the streets of El Paso of this pest."[9]

The bunco men reached their high-water mark in the winter of 1884-85. They heard the good news about El Paso and came swarming in from everywhere, defying the authorities and doing as they pleased. "They had a strong organization," says one survivor of those wild and wonderful years, "and plenty of money to hire lawyers and bribe jurors. The police would arrest them and the juries would turn them loose. They went to hotels for their victims and did not hesitate to drug and rob a man who refused to be buncoed."[10]

The citizens were on the point of organizing a vigilance committee, particularly after the council issued a badly timed announcement that the police force was being reduced for the sake of economy. This brought the businessmen out with "halters and lampposts" in their countenances. They met publicly in the quarters of the Board of Trade, and some of the confidence men actually had the gall to present themselves and attempt to speak. They were ejected, however, and after Uncle John Julian and Joe Schutz and E. V. Berrien had expressed their views, a committee was sent to the City Council, then in session, to present a set of resolutions. Diplomatically the committee offered "hearty cooperation in any way it may be necessary," but the councilmen heard the words that were not spoken, augmented the police force, and instructed the officers to jail any bunco men they found in operation. The result was an exodus of thugs and tricksters to Juárez, across the river.[11]

Some transients were not crooked — just hungry; and by 1896 so many of them were present that public-spirited citizens organized a soup kitchen. The city government was interested enough to start the project with an appropriation of fifty dollars, contributing forty dollars a month thereafter to keep it going. Sixteen prominent women formed a committee to organize the program and cook the soup.

The problem was to separate the bona fide cases from the free loaders. Cleofas Calleros, historian of those times, says that the intruders ceased to trouble when a wood pile was provided next to the soup kitchen and strangers were asked to work before they ate. For a large percentage of them work was a horror which could not be faced, and the next few freight trains reduced their numbers considerably.[12]

Several cuts above the tramps and confidence men were the professional gamblers who operated in the casinos behind and above the various saloons. The best of them attained a sort of magnificence beyond the reach of even the richest and sportiest of the town's permanent residents. W. W. Bridgers, who remembered and wrote about everything from 1881 on, says that "these were the days when gamblers wore heavy gold-linked watch chains and diamond shirt studs. Charlie Utter wore a watch chain that was a foot long and as thick as your little finger. He wore a low-cut vest and dazzling shirt front bedecked with glittering studs. He usually turned out on the street in a Prince Albert, a $50 broad-brimmed white Stetson and long hair . . . and boots the finest that could be made."[13]

The social scale among gamblers declined from this elegant figure down to the lowliest tinhorn who cheated and scrambled for small change. They were all transients, of course, unless, like George Speck or Si Ryan, they owned their places of business, and they left little mark on the community. Although in 1902 there were ninety-six saloons in which 600 gamblers made a living,[14] we know the identities of only the important ones, and then usually because some outbreak of violence or scandal brought their names to the fore. We should probably never have heard of Bob Cahill, a "lookout" for the faro game at the Gem, if two hard cases named Billy Raynor and R. B. Rennick had not fought over nothing.

Raynor was a well known member of the sporting set, a good talker who could be very entertaining when he chose, a neat and elegant dresser whose everyday attire included a Prince Albert coat, colorful tie, and white Stetson hat.[15] Unfortunately, he imagined himself to be a dangerous man, and he felt the obligation to test the mettle of strangers who might imagine themselves to be dangerous also. On April 15, 1885, Raynor and a friend of his, a former Texas Ranger named Buck Linn, were doing the town. When they got to the Gem, they were in such a state that Cahill undertook to separate them and send them home. While he was remonstrating with Linn, Raynor decided to look for a character named Harry Williams, with whom he wanted to pick a fight. Unable to locate this particular victim, Raynor belligerently approached a stranger in a white hat who was quietly watching the games.

He was dealing with R. B. Rennick, a much harder character than he knew, who, according to George Look, was investigating the Gem as a potential site for a holdup. Raynor demanded to know if this stranger was a fighter. Rennick told him mildly that he was not. In that case, said Raynor, he was something else which can't be mentioned on this page. After a little more talk, Raynor walked into another room. His departure gave Rennick a chance to get up and take a pistol from the drawer in the faro layout. Raynor saw him do it, came charging back with his gun out, intercepted Rennick as he was trying to leave by the back door, and started shooting. He missed, but Rennick didn't, and that was the end of Raynor.[16]

Meanwhile Buck Linn was after Cahill, probably because the latter had allowed Rennick to take the gun out of the drawer in the faro layout. He fired once at Cahill as the gambler scurried through the front door of the saloon and into the street, followed as fast as he could, and fired four more shots, none effective, as Cahill disappeared into the Ranch Saloon.[17]

Cahill thought this was the end of it. He waited fifteen minutes and came back to his faro layout. Linn was not ready to give up, however; in a saloon nearby he was declaring with alcoholic earnestness, "Bob Cahill has killed my friend and I am going over to kill him."

A couple of the "boys" sprinted across to the Gem and warned Cahill. He took his .45 out of the money drawer in the faro table and headed for the front of the saloon. George Look slowed him down for a minute, but when Linn steered himself unsteadily through the door, Cahill walked up and shot him twice in the heart, killing him instantly.[18]

One of the witnesses, incidentally, who testified at the hearing on April 15 was Wyatt Earp.[19]

The names of men like Bob Cahill are not often found in the records. The ones we hear are those of such important operators as J. J. Taylor, who owned the Gem at this time and did some dealing. George Look, who owned it in partnership later on, was not a gambler, but he ran a gambling saloon. Si Ryan of the Astor House was a gambler. George Speck of the Senate Saloon was a gambler. Rip Whitney was a gambler. Owen White mentions Fred Fenchler, a well-to-do merchant, as one who would sit in a game with the best of them, though he was not a professional.[20] The little ones were here today and some place else tomorrow.

These gamblers, no matter how well they dressed and behaved themselves and how regularly they paid their license fees, were a destructive element in the community. Their business was to take other people's money, and they were good at their business. "The games were open, defiant, and brazen," says Dr. Howard Thompson. "The tables any time from 1 p.m. to 4:30 a.m. would be surrounded three or four deep with men and boys looking on." The tenderfoot from back East with a little money which he hoped to double had no chance whatever among these wolves and inevitably lost all he had, sometimes capital belonging to somebody else. The easy way out was a bullet in the head. In 1898 the *Times* called El Paso "a Mecca for suicides." The unsuccessful gamblers were joined in boosting the death rate, we might add, by unhappy prostitutes who could face the world no longer. When Dr. George Brunner was answering calls on Utah Street, he always carried a stomach pump or two for use in case some desperate young woman had swallowed poison.[21]

The gay world only appeared to be gay, and the daughters of joy were joyful only for money, yet the most interesting part of the sin business for most people, then as now, was the part played by the girls in the dance halls, cribs, and parlor houses. Utah Street (South Mesa to us) was the heart of the tenderloin district and it brought us wide if not favorable notice. "There is not an old timer in the Southwest," says John Selman, Jr., who served on the police force during his father's incumbency as constable, "who does not remember this famous old street. During the nineties this street was a seething beehive of activity after nightfall. It was lined from East Overland street to the Rio Grande with dance halls, saloons and girls."[22]

There were two big dance halls — the Monte Carlo on South Oregon and Jim Burns' Red Light Dance Hall on Utah Street — where girls to suit every taste, no matter how eccentric, stood ready for action. Young Selman takes a charitable view of these entertainers. "For a dime," he says, "a man could dance with some of the finest dancers that ever came out of Old Mexico. . . . I knew a good many girls of good families, both in El Paso and Juárez, who made their living dancing at the Monte Carlo. A popular dancer could earn as much as three dollars in a night. . . . Many of these girls were accompanied by their duenas. . . ."[23]

It is a pleasing thought — the idea of the beautiful Mexican girl of good family, accompanied by her chaperone, dancing every night to keep her mother and father in groceries — but one which can hardly be taken seriously. The women who infested Oregon and Utah streets were anything but high class, though of course the fancy parlor houses provided a better type of merchandise for a better clientele. The Red Light, where the worst of them hung out, has been described by one good Baptist as "a deadfall, a plague spot, a dreadful disgrace to any community." Proprietor Jim Burns, he adds, was widely known as "the wickedest man in El Paso" although "no poor unfortunate woman in distress ever appealed to him in vain . . . he was a living example of the truth of the quaint Spanish proverb, 'en la tierra de los ciegos, el tuerto *es Rey'* " (in the country of the blind, the cross-eyed man is king).[24]

A graphic description of what actually went on in such places as the Red Light was printed in the *Times* for June 22, 1890, by a reporter who made the rounds of the dives and dance halls convoyed by a couple of policemen:

> Here amid the clinking of beer glasses and vulgarity, drunken men, reeling and yelling, danced with Mexican women to the strains of the devil's music, staggering between dances to the bar for liquid refreshments and enthusiasm. Women, long since sunk from respectability, joined the terrible brawl. Hair streaming in masses of disorder, dresses rent by the yanking and howling of the intoxicated men, and lending their shrill voices to complete the chaos of debauchery. Here and there were stretched-out men overcome with liquor, while the wooden benches surrounding the apartment were occupied by burly sons of toil holding upon their laps these women of prostitution. . . .

Dance halls such as the Red Light offered entertainment to the lower half of the sporting population, and the women who worked in them had their quarters nearby. Interspersed between the big houses on Utah Street were rows of cribs where a dollar was the going price. Colored prostitutes operated in a subdistrict on the south side of Overland Street in Selman's time. They were mostly controlled by an iron-muscled, thick-skulled gorilla named John Woods, a man so tough a pistol bullet fired point blank would flatten itself against his forehead.[25]

Of the operators and inmates of the cribs and cheap assignation houses we know very little. Mostly they are just names in the city directory. Occasionally one of them rated a paragraph in the news when something especially unfortunate or scandalous happened in her corner of the street. We wouldn't know about Winnie Messenger, madam of a place called The Electric Light, if she had not been terribly burned on December 1, 1884, when a hanging lamp fell and scattered coal oil all over her parlor. A patron named W. H. Mitchell, a gambler at the Diamond Palace, tore off her burning clothes (and singed himself in the process), but Dr. Justice found her beyond help and she died three days later. Her last moments and her funeral aroused some sentimental interest but a Baptist sociable and a meeting of the German residents interested in organizing a *Gesangverein* captured the interest of the town within a few hours and poor Winnie was forgotten.[26]

We know a little more about what went on in the big houses —

sumptuous places with expensive furnishings, fine rugs and draperies, and prices to match. Each had a cook and a staff of servants, often a small orchestra for dancing and entertainment, always a "buffet" (a fancy word for a small bar). There would be a carriage house alongside or in the rear with a shiny rig of some sort and a coachman ready to take Madam and a few of her girls on shopping expeditions, airings, or social calls at other houses. So resolute were the proprietors in maintaining an air of refinement and decency that these places were seldom called by their right names. Usually they were described as boarding houses, sometimes as residences; and on more than one occasion they were pictured in chamber-of-commerce propaganda as among the architectural glories of the city.[27]

You seldom saw the girls unless you went down on "the Line." In early days they never came uptown until after midnight, when they sometimes gathered in the wine rooms of the saloons for a brief convivial hour. After the turn of the century, they were allowed to shop in small groups on one day of the week, usually Wednesday at noon when the stores were comparatively clear of customers.[28] They spent their money bravely and copiously and their business was welcome. As a little girl, Rosalie Behr used to enjoy remaining in the White House against the wishes of the floor walkers to see them come in, all beautiful and all strikingly dressed.[29] Some were heavily made up and trailed clouds of perfume. Lily Smith Howard, the postmaster's daughter, remembers that they could always be recognized, when they came for the mail, by their wonderful smell and by the fact that they all smoked cigarettes – in public.[30] Louis Hubbard, who became a college president, listened as well as looked and noted that they used much profanity.[31]

If their dress and manners were a little conspicuous, and if their arrival in Madam's carriage, complete with colored driver, was a bit ostentatious, we must remember that they were in a highly competitive business and only a few of their patrons could appreciate the quiet charm of good taste.

In the early days, when there were not many places for a man to meet his business associates or friends in a relaxed atmosphere, the parlor houses served as gentlemen's clubs. They were certainly the most elegant places of entertainment the town could boast, and it was not necessary to avail oneself of all the hospitality of the establishment if one came there to meet friends or have a social drink.

A striking example of this sort of thing occurred in 1890 when Doc Bolton and Jeff Clayton, who may have been involved in smuggling arms into Mexico for plotters against the Díaz régime, killed a partner of theirs named Cavitt on a street corner in Juárez and were confined in the Juárez jail. These men had many great and good friends in El Paso who were anxious to do what could be done for them, and the first thing these friends tried to do was to get some action out of the mayor. He was not at home. He was not in his office. He was apparently not anywhere until somebody thought to look for him at one of the houses, and there he was — probably conducting city business. Nobody thought it was particularly odd that the first citizen of El Paso should be spending an afternoon in a sporting house.[32]

Considering the purpose of even the fanciest of the parlor houses and the kind of men who patronized them, it is a wonder they were kept as decent and orderly as they were. Madams and girls alike tried to act like ladies, sometimes succeeding too well to be convincing. If liquor or high spirits got the better of a patron, the madam had a police whistle which she would blow loudly from the front porch, and the nearest officer would come on the run. It was the least he could do in view of the fact that Big Alice or May or Gypsy was the means of providing him with a salary.

The ideal situation was for the place to become a haunt of well-heeled gentlemen whose discretion would be matched only by the discretion of Madam and her girls. Sometimes a mining tycoon or a rich cattleman from Mexico would "buy" the place — take over the whole house for the night. Then the front door would be locked; and if joy was unrefined, nobody knew it but the people behind the drawn curtains.[33]

The maidens and the madams were discreet, but discretion is only one of the reasons why so little can be told of the inhabitants of those houses. Another is the fact that the girls did not stay around long enough to make much history. It was bad business to keep them too long in one place. Girls who did not move were apt to concentrate on a few favorites and sometimes committed the supreme sin of getting married and leaving the industry. To keep them in circulation, the men in charge maintained a regular circuit which the women customarily followed.

The organizers were almost always Frenchmen. Their headquarters was in San Francisco, but they had local agents.[34] At one time there were three of these living in El Paso but they haunted the shadows and nobody now can tell you their names. They managed girls of every nationality, but the real pros were imported from Paris. The French girls attended to business, saved their money, returned after a few years to their homeland, used their dollars to attract husbands, and immersed themselves in respectability.[35] At least many people think they did.

Some of the American girls married too, in spite of all precautions. Several married El Paso men, and the folklore of the subject says that they made wonderful wives. At least three madams married locally likewise, to the scandal and dismay of all virtuous women.

There were five important madams between 1881 and 1915 — all of them shrewd and capable businesswomen of considerable personal force and (we must admit it) charm. The folklore says that every one of them was of good family and education, and of high social position in her native city, wherever that was, in the days beyond recall. Some of them may indeed have been from top-drawer families, but it would not be safe to generalize.

The five who have survived, at least as names, in the legendry of the border were Alice Abbott, Etta Clark, Gypsy Davenport, May Palmer, and Tillie Howard. Gypsy Davenport, May Palmer, and Tillie Howard were professional names and their owners kept quiet about who they really were. Whether the others went by their right titles or not we do not know, and there is nobody left to tell us.

First on the scene was "Big Alice" Abbott, who seems to have arrived in 1881 very shortly after the coming of the railroad.[36] Etta and Gypsy were not far behind, and by 1885 the three of them were established on Utah Street in large and expensively furnished houses. May and Tillie arrived in the early nineties[37] and outdid their predecessors in the elegance of their establishments.

Big Alice, most striking of the Big Five, was a massive Magdalene who weighed 195 pounds, most of it bone and muscle. A reporter in 1886 spoke of her "magnificent physique" without any overtone of satire.[38] Supposedly she was the wife of a prominent lawyer in Louisville, Kentucky. Why she exchanged the amenities of this metropolis for the crudities of the Mexican border the record does not say. She was twenty-seven years old when she arrived in the fall of 1881.

Etta Clark was an entirely different type. According to one El Paso pioneer who remembered her without being acquainted with her, she was a "voluptuous redhead" with a temper to match her hair, a lyric figure, and a way with some of El Paso's better-heeled business men.[39] Her family name was Mercier and she was said to belong to a "prominent French-Canadian family." She had a sister, Eva Mercier, who lived with her and helped her run her business in the eighties.

We know a little about Alice and Etta because of a dispute they got into in 1886 which ended in a shooting and a sensational trial. Alice had moved to Utah Street from a location in the west end of town not long before the trouble, and the fact that she was now occupying a big house almost directly opposite Etta's mansion may have created bad feeling. Another factor was a practice which certainly existed but about which we know very little — the custom of luring girls away from one house by the madam of another.

In this case a popular attraction named Bessie Colvin got behind in her "rent" at Alice's place, resented Alice's reminders, worked herself into a passion with the help of alcohol, and decided to leave. She stormed across the street to the rival sex emporium, had a conference with Etta, and came back to declare herself. When she marched over to Etta's place the second time, Alice, with a couple of her girls, was right behind her but not close enough to catch Bessie before she disappeared inside. The bell brought Etta, who opened the door a crack. Alice asked to see the girl.

"Bessie doesn't want to see you," was the answer.

Aroused and indignant, Big Alice put her weight against the door and flung it inward, bruising Etta's tender flesh in the process. When Etta reached for a gas lighter standing in the hall and tried to use it as a weapon, Alice hit her a resounding slap in the face. "I owe you that one, anyhow," she remarked.

"I have always treated you like a lady."

"Yes, you have. You tried to rope my woman away — you and your sister."

XXI – *Sin City*

Bessie now appeared at the scene of action. Alice laid hold of her and tried to jerk her through the door, thought better of it, and started for home. Meanwhile Etta had stepped into her bedroom and picked up a pistol. She appeared on the porch as Alice was getting out of the yard. The big woman turned just as Etta pulled the trigger and the bullet hit dead center.

The *Herald* the next morning described the affair and tried to say, at the climax, that Alice was shot in the pubic arch, but the phrase came out "public arch" — a more accurate statement of the case, perhaps, than the one which was intended.

There was a well publicized trial, one session being held in Alice's bedroom. It might have gone hard with Etta if Alice had died, but her powerful constitution turned the tide and she recovered quickly. The authorities apparently thought that the battle ought to be considered a draw, and the case was dropped.

Repercussions were heard, however, outside the courtroom. In 1936, when El Paso was celebrating the Texas centennial and was in a reminiscent mood, Frank Wells Brown added another episode to this story. He told Marshal Hail of the *Herald-Post* that the editor of the old *Herald* in 1886 was an Irishman named Brady who indulged in some "witty remarks" about Alice and Etta at the time of their trouble. The *Herald* file is incomplete for this period, but Mr. Brown (who was co-owner of the paper) indicated that the "public arch" error was involved. The morning after the story appeared, Etta descended upon the *Herald* office, armed with a big pistol and accompanied by a female friend bearing a bull whip. Brady happened to be out at the time, but he was scared when he heard about the visitation and asked Brown what he should do. "Get out of town for a while," said his friend. "I bought him a ticket to Albuquerque," Brown concluded, "and I have never seen him since."

Big Alice waited two years for her revenge, but she got it. She burned Etta's house down.

It would seem that she had a burning bee in mind all the time, for the reporters remembered in 1888 that "one or two attempts were made to burn the house about a year ago." It was not until July 12, 1888, however, that the fire bug was successful. He picked the middle of the afternoon for his attempt, that being the time when ladies of the evening are most likely to be asleep. He brought a can of kerosene to the premises (a one-story frame fire trap), poured generous portions in three outside doorways, and struck a match. The whole building exploded into flames. While the old cracked fire bell "called all within range of its still, small voice," the frightened inmates struggled to get out with their lives, leaving their clothes, their money, and their pets.

The suffering of the poodles and parrots grieved them most. A particularly strong character named Verdie Love got safely out and then remembered her menagerie. She rushed back in, but the smoke and flames were too much for her and she barely escaped with her life, "her feet and back being terribly burned" as the *Times* reported the next day.

Etta herself was alert enough to save her money, jewelry and birds. All the rest, valued at $7,000, went up in smoke.

A month later, on August 14, Big Alice and three Negro employees were arrested for the crime. John Duncan, probably the one who had set the fire, was arrested at Colorado City by somebody who was interested in the thousand-dollar reward posted by J. P. Dieter (part owner of the building) and the board of underwriters. Duncan probably implicated Ben Johnson and Will Ragland, and Johnson put the finger on Alice. They were brought into court on August 13 but apparently the evidence was not conclusive, for nothing seems to have been done to them.

Big Alice was in the news again some years later when she fell out with another member of the Big Five — this time Gypsy Davenport. Gypsy had been doing business on Utah Street almost as long as Alice had, that is, since the early eighties. Her real name was Maria Blakeley, but naturally she did not use it. Born in New York State, she apparently grew up in Davenport, Iowa, and called herself after her home town. Why she considered "Gypsy" a suitable first name we do not know, but perhaps she thought it descriptive of a pleasing wildness in her nature. She was probably the most ornamental of the El Paso madams. A "good" woman who disapproved of her completely once described her as "wholly and utterly beautiful."[41]

Big operator though she was, she was not in the same league ethically, if the word may be used in such a connection, with Etta Clark and Alice Abbott, who came as close to running legitimate businesses as circumstances would permit. Gypsy was shrewd and unscrupulous. She would get a rich cattleman drunk and put him to bed. Then she would change things around in his room while he was unconscious. She would bring in a few pieces of broken furniture, scatter empty champagne bottles around, and charge him for drinks and damages when he came to in the morning.[42]

In 1894 she apparently tried one of her tricks on Alice Abbott and didn't get away with it. They were in District Court on April 24 – Gypsy charged with getting illegal possession of $1,300 worth of diamonds rightfully belonging to Alice. Apparently Gypsy had returned part of the stones she had borrowed or purloined and insisted that everything had gone back to the owner. Mr. Susen of Hickox and Hixson, jewelers, testified that what Alice now had on hand was worth $790. Jewels worth $600 had been withheld, and Alice was going to have them back. She won her suit.[43]

It is interesting to note that a year later, Gypsy was having diamond trouble again, charging a character named Kid Richards with "hooking" her jewels. He was arrested but the police let him go for lack of evidence.[44]

Big Alice died on April 7, 1896. The circumstances must remain mysterious, for the newspapers took no notice of her demise. Owen White, however, records some facts about her death in his autobiography. He came home that afternoon to find his father shedding real tears, and when Owen questioned him he said, "Son, Alice Abbott is dead, and by God, even if she wasn't respectable, if she doesn't go to Heaven, I don't want to go there. And you don't either. It will be no place for us."

Dr. White knew Alice very well, partly because of his profession and partly because she was the one he went to when he needed money for the sick and the down and out. "He always got it, and there was never but one stipulation: 'Here, Doc, take it and spend it wherever you want to. The only thing is: don't ever tell where it came from.' "[45]

From the evidence we have, it looks as if she had given away almost everything she had by the time she died. Horace B. Stevens was named administrator of her estate when he applied for the job. He listed her assets as furniture worth $40, a diamond ring worth $50, and a pair of diamond earrings worth $125.[46] The wages of sin, in her case at least, were low indeed.

Since we have mentioned Gypsy Davenport, we may add that

she disappears from the directory after 1900[47] and she may have gone to Chihuahua to open a house.[48] After a few years there she returned to the border. At some time after she left the big house, she ran a second-story place on East San Antonio Street near the Toltec Club.[49] Eventually she gave up business entirely and may have spent some time in Davenport, Iowa, recapturing the joys of her innocent youth. She had invested in an apartment house at 2912 Madera Street, however, and occupied Apartment 3 most of the time. The late Maury Kemp was her lawyer and Kemp and Coldwell handled her real estate problems.

Maury used to tell about his first meeting with her. He was in his law office some months after the death in February, 1909, of his father and partner, Judge Wyndham Kemp. An elderly, rather striking woman in black came in and asked for Judge Kemp.

"Judge Kemp is no longer with us," Maury told her. "He died a few months ago. Could I be of any service?"

His visitor looked at him long and hard. Finally she said, "You look pretty young, but you might do." She introduced herself as Maria Blakeley, said she had been living with a niece in Fort Wayne, Indiana, and had come back to El Paso after many years' absence to straighten up the taxes on her property and see about selling it. She also wanted to make a will. In the course of discussions about the latter enterprise she said to Maury one day, "You don't know me, do you?"

"Well, no," Maury admitted.

"I used to be known around here as Gypsy Davenport."

The lawyer found this information interesting but kept it to himself and continued to advise his client. She lived in her apartment until morphinism and edema of the lungs caused her death on January 22, 1920.[50] Kemp and Coldwell, in charge of her property, arranged the funeral.

Maury Kemp was a man of considerable force and dignity, but he loved a joke, and when an old-timer named Manny Turner thought of a way to make humorous capital out of Gypsy's passing, Maury joined him with great good will. They telephoned five leading politicians, including the mayor and the county judge, and asked them to act as pallbearers at the funeral of Mrs. Blakeley, a pioneer lady known to all of them. They all accepted, naturally, and saw the coffin decently laid away. On the way back one of them remarked to Maury, "I am ashamed to confess it, but I am not sure I ever met the woman we just buried." Kemp and Turner savored the joke a while longer but finally confessed. The county judge said, "Well, somebody had to put the old girl away and it had just as well be me."[51]

To return to Etta Clark, the *pistolera* of 1886, the record shows that in 1889 one of our prominent wholesale liquor dealers developed such a deep personal interest in her that he built her a $75,000 house on the corner of Utah and Second streets. Decorations cost $50,000, it was said. There was a red room, a green room, carved woodwork, expensive murals, and all the plush and gilt that the eighties admired. There were thirty-two rooms in the place.[52] The wife of Etta's patron divorced him, but he went ahead with the building, and the monument to his infatuation with the red-haired madam stood for almost fifty years.

By now Eva Mercier, Etta's sister, had married a man from Georgia — "prominent," of course — and left town, but Etta continued in business in the big house till after the turn of the century. She may have given it up by 1905, for in that year she disappears from the directory. When the Myar Opera House burned on November 4, Etta was the "proprietress" of a rooming house located on the third floor of the building. She was carried out, unconscious, by Acting Fire Chief Mitchell. All her roomers escaped likewise, though without the personal attentions of the fire department.[53]

She was in charge of rooms at 219½ San Antonio in 1907. In 1909 she was helpless in Hotel Dieu and a trial to the nurses, according to Mrs. Hugh White, who saw her there.[54] Presumably she died in that year but the papers did not notice her passing and nobody remembers how it happened.

Her house was kept by a variety of madams and boardinghouse keepers until the red-light district moved to Ninth and Santa Fe in 1916. Very shortly after this event Eva Mercier Johnson, now a widow, came back from Georgia to see about the property. She lived in the big house with very little company, unregarded by the world, and probably would have died there had it not been necessary in 1947 to tear the place down to make way for a new thoroughfare — Paisano Drive. Then all the old skeletons, including Eva, came forth into the light of day, and senior El Pasoans were startled to find that these relics of thirty years before had been lurking at their elbows all the time.[55]

Eva barricaded herself in one of the rooms with a shotgun and two pistols and gave the officers a few bad moments. She was induced to give up without bloodshed, however, a guardian was appointed, and a lawyer took charge of the estate, which yielded something like $50,000 to the Georgia relatives. For several years she lived in an El Paso rest home but went back to Atlanta for her last days and died there in January, 1957. Her passing rated two paragraphs in the *Herald-Post* — two more than her notorious sister had rated when she died forty years before.[56]

We know less about May Palmer, fourth of the big madams, than we do about her colleagues, but she may have done more business than all the rest of them put together. Maury Kemp's memoirs say that her right name was Eisenmend. Legend adds that she came from a rich Chicago family and had a good education. Somewhere she developed a flair for organization and is rumored to have operated not just one but a whole chain of bawdy houses. The impression prevails among some pioneer citizens that she had a place in Salt Lake City.[57] Bud Rutherford, pioneer newsman, says she had one in the vice district in Chicago.[58] Others credit her with ownership of the Palmer House in Tucson.[59] Her El Paso headquarters was a sumptuous mansion on the west side of Utah Street — number 309. Her name appears first in the City Directory for 1902 and disappears after 1910, when she gave up business for matrimony.

Her husband was Harland (Pete) Adams, a tall, attractive young man who came out from Bryan, Texas, to help Captain Charles Davis, a fellow townsman, when he became Collector of Customs in 1893. At first he was much admired and much sought after by men and women of the first families, but apparently the Sin City was too much for him. He became a wholesale liquor dealer and later kept the Lobby Saloon at various locations. As a result he lost out with his upper-class friends and finally married May. It seems to have been a great irritation to the respectable people who knew them that May and Pete got along so well together. The ladies were scandalized when the two of them drove out of a Sunday in May's carriage, "her plumes billowing in the wind."[60]

When May died after some ten years of connubial felicity, Pete was grief stricken but not so much so that he was incapable of enjoying her money. He bought a stable of race horses with it.[61] His old friends hoped that his final separation from May might be the beginning of his reclamation, but they were disappointed. Pete established a reputation for consistency by marrying one of May's colleagues.

This was a madam familiarly known as Moonface[62] and described by an old acquaintance as "round-faced, big-bottomed Myrtle Phillips."[63] She managed Tillie's place for a time after Tillie gave it up and gave it up in her turn when "the line" was moved to Ninth Street. About that time she and Pete Adams made their lives a duet. After prohibition became a painful reality, Adams moved to Juárez, where he operated the Lobby Saloon for a few years and then died. Pete had owned a good-sized piece of valley land in the vicinity of Anthony, New Mexico, where he and May Palmer had lived and where he and Myrtle were living when he succumbed. In 1925 Myrtle moved back to town and bought a big house on North Mesa Avenue, still standing, where she kept a few girls to the great discomfort and scandal of her eminently respectable neighbors.[64] Eventually she too faded from the scene, leaving few traces of her passage.

Last and best remembered of the Big Five was Mathilde Weiler — Tillie Howard to several generations of border residents. Her solicitude for the welfare of her girls, her sympathy for men in difficulties, the good order she kept in her parlor house made her almost respectable and a legend all over the Southwest.

A well-proportioned, amply endowed woman with a full, round face, a low, husky voice, sharp eyes which could shine and twinkle, and an unusual vein of sentiment, she bought a house on Utah Street in 1892[65] for $2,200 and opened up for business.

Ordinarily Tillie was as reticent as most women in her line of work, but occasionally she would confide in someone she liked, and the tales got around. John Selman the younger was one who knew a little about her. "When I became better acquainted with her," he says in his unpublished memoirs, "she told me her story. She had come from a prominent family in the East. She had run off with a young fellow and had married him. He soon deserted her and she was ashamed to go home and had drifted west. Finally she landed in El Paso and opened a parlor house. I could readily believe her story because Tillie, which was not her right name, was well educated and had the queenly bearing of good breeding."[66]

This was the story Tillie told when she needed to say something about herself. None of it was true, but it had the authentic ring of a standard piece of folklore. To people who had done her valuable service she sometimes told the truth. One of these was young Will Burges, her lawyer, who valued her as a human being and won her confidence. In 1945 he wrote for historian Evetts Haley what is probably the true story as she told it to him.

Her people were not "a prominent family in the East." They were of German stock, probably country people, with very little in the way of worldly goods. Her mother died when Tillie was born; her father some three years later.[67] There was at least one uncle and two cousins, but apparently she went to a neighbor rather than to her relatives. The neighbor expected her to work her way, and whipped her when he thought she was shirking. She stood it until she was twelve and then, after a particularly vicious beating, ran away with the intention of committing suicide.

Drowning seemed the cheapest and easiest way, so she headed for the nearest stream and sat on the bank, sobbing and trying to get up nerve enough to jump. It happened that a railroad trestle crossed the river at this point and trains sometimes stopped there for water. A freight crew on the Wisconsin Central picked her up and made her at home in the caboose. For some time — perhaps several years — she rode with the trainmen, sharing their lunches and sleeping aboard. Before long she had accumulated a good deal of basic information about men.

She left the railroad for Sells' Circus when she met Willie Sells, a trick rider, after a performance in some county-seat town. She traveled with him for several years more and might have gone on in this fashion, but something happened; she found herself stranded in San Antonio;[68] and the next we know of her, she had gone into business in El Paso. The Sells connection must have been profitable, for she had money enough to buy her real estate. In 1892, when she set up her "house," she was twenty-three years old.[69] Young, beautiful, and extremely good at her business, she was soon famous all over our part of the West.

A young Texas Ranger named Alonzo Oden, who made a pilgrimage to her shrine in 1893, gives us our best closeup of Tillie in action. Alonzo joined the force in 1891 and wrote down in a diary his day-by-day experiences. For a while he was stationed at Alpine, but moved to Ysleta with Captain Hughes' company in 1893. His fourth entry (none of the entries is dated) says: "I'm going to El Paso tomorrow. It will be good to get a bath in a long tub. . . . Maybe, I shall meet a beautiful lady in El Paso, and that would be hard on me."[70]

On arriving, his first act was to order a pair of boots from Charley Rokahr. His second was to pay a call on Tillie Howard. "I've been anxious to visit Tillie," he writes. "She is the talk of the border. Jim said he'd introduce me, so we went down there. It is a regular saloon, and sort of hotel and dance hall combined; but Tillie makes the place different. She is tall, and I imagine she doesn't need those artificial bosoms the ladies are using now; hers look natural enough — I'll ask her when I know her better. She seems to take a shine to me. She has the blackest hair, and she is one of the most beautiful women I've ever seen. I'll be seeing more of Tillie — as an experience."

He did, too, and records his impressions as follows:

What a madam this Tillie is. Had a long talk with her — was curious to know what set her on the crimson highway of sin. She is glad to talk about everything interesting except Tillie. She took me all over her establishment and introduced me to all the girls. She is proud of the fact that all the girls are refined. She allows no loud talk, no vulgarity, and the girls are not allowed to get drunk. They are paid a straight salary. Tillie thinks this is more protection for the girls, and she thinks it also keeps them honest; on commission they are sometimes inclined to cheat.

I made a remark about betrayed womanhood in a pitying tone. Tillie looked at me with those unreadable blue-black eyes of hers and said, "Lon, my dear, a woman is never betrayed except by her own emotions." I asked her if she meant that a man is not responsible for a girl's downfall. She smiled: "A girl usually follows her own desires. She may be a victim of love; but when love is done, she should be brave enough to share the blame equally, if not more than the man."

I asked her if she didn't think she'd be punished for being in the sporting house business. She rose from her chair, walked to the window, pulled back the heavy red curtains and looked out. I walked over and stood by her. We stood this way a few minutes, and then she turned and looked deeply into my eyes and said in the queerest voice. "Punished! Alonzo Oden, I know Hell."

She held out her long, slim hand to me and said, "Thank you, my friend, for treating me as a human with brains — and now, good bye."

I left the house; I walked down the street, and I kept hearing that voice say, "I know Hell." I think I know the scarlet sister Christ forgave. I can hear his voice cry: "Let him without sin cast the first stone."[71]

This unusual closeup of our most famous madam was written, conjecturally, in 1893, long enough after Tillie's arrival for her fame to spread. We next hear of her in 1894 when one of her girls died in harness and was given a funeral so sumptuous that the *Times* noticed it in a story which was copied throughout the territory. Tillie saw to it that her girls traveled first class even on a trip to the cemetery.

The body of the unfortunate young woman "Vernice Valentine," who died at the house of Miss Tillie Howard yesterday morning at 3 o'clock, has been embalmed and is laid out in Powell's undertaking rooms on West Overland Street. The corpse is attired in a white satin-silk and occupies an elegant coffin, ornamented with beautiful wreaths of flowers placed there by sympathizing friends. The lid bears her true name, but it is cautiously kept away from public view. The hands of the deceased hold a bunch of white roses, from the center of which a white dove in natural position and opened wings is ready to fly heavenward. The face indicates that deceased, when living, was surprisingly handsome, and from its general appearance one would naturally conclude that she came from a good family. It is sad indeed to look down upon so beautiful a corpse that has neither friends nor relatives to shed a tear or cast a sigh for it. What a lesson her fate has been to fallen women!

Every effort has been made to hear from her friends in Eagle Lake, Wisconsin, and undertaker Powell has concluded to keep the body no longer, and it will be buried at 5 o'clock this evening in Evergreen cemetery, Rector Cabell Martin of the Episcopal Church, conducting the funeral services.[72]

The mixed emotions aroused in most people by affairs on Utah Street appear quite clearly in this story. Those affairs were mentioned among close friends with leers and earthy laughter; among strangers with a mincing mock-seriousness like that of the *Times* reporter. At the same time it seems to have been expected that any reference in print should be accompanied by a sigh for the fallen creature and a comment on the lesson to be drawn from her fate.

The next three years of Tillie's life are a blank, probably indicating that she was attending to business and keeping out of trouble, but she comes back into focus in 1897. The Kimberley diamond mines had been opened and news filtered in of the fortunes that were being made in South Africa. It sounded like a wonderful opportunity for a madam who knew her business. Tillie decided to go.

She may have been influenced by a fire which broke out in her house and damaged some of her possessions. Relics of this fire are to be seen to this day. Colonel Walter Stevenson has two big steel engravings which still show some smoke damage from that fire (Walter's father attended Tillie in her last illness), but it is hard to find out when it happened. If it occurred in 1896 or 1897, it started Tillie on her pilgrimage.[73]

Some time in 1897 she closed up and left, accompanied by a handsome half-Indian gambler named Rufus Nimmo. Will Burges says an army captain went along, and that the three of them bought a wine shop in Johannesburg, sold it at a profit, and invested in a better one. Eventually Tillie parted company with her friends and ran the shop alone with great advantage to herself.

The truth may have been a little less glamorous. Tillie was granted a license to open a "house" in Kimberley. The license still exists, dated December, 1897. Among her effects is a picture of an aristocratic-looking stone mansion which is probably where she operated. She came back rich. Estimates of her take run as high as $400,000.[74] Her lawyer, Will Burges, says she "sold out for $65,000, invested in gilt edge securities, and with her jewels and a tiger skin from Africa"[75] came back to her native heath.

Apparently Tillie's taste of life in foreign lands made her eager for more contact with the beautiful, wonderful world, and when she left the diamond fields, she took the long way home. Traveling by way of the Suez Canal to Egypt and the Holy Land, she saw Italy, Switzerland, Germany, England, and Scotland. These were the days before color film and post cards, but Tillie found plenty of large, colorful pictures of the sights she liked best to remember — royal palaces, the avenues of Europe's most venerable cities, gorgeous landscapes. After her return she had the whole collection put into a huge scrapbook which has been preserved in the family of her physician almost as she left it, though some of the great and good El Paso friends whose pictures she cherished have taken pains to remove their photographs since her death.

In this book we find what can be learned of Mathilde Weiler Howard's soul and mind — things about which her friends were almost totally unconcerned. She had a tender heart. Her sympathies were easily aroused and she had a passion for the sentimental verses which were featured in so many American newspapers a few generations ago. The scrapbook is loaded with them, all about unrequited love and the deaths of little children and the sorrows of the fractured heart. Tillie was not a hard woman by any means.

A vein of something else comes through in a large picture called *The Secrets of the Wedding Night* showing a surprised but knowing Cupid with his hand over his mouth just outside a drawn velvet curtain. Another shows a Hawaiian girl with her breasts exposed. The legend underneath in Miss Howard's irregular writing reads: "The Innocence of Youth." There are many pictures of cats, creatures of which she was very fond, and along with the cats are pictures of the interiors and exteriors of local bars and bistros owned by friends of hers.

Tillie didn't spell very well (for example, she always wrote Swissland for Switzerland) and her handwriting was not well formed, but she was interested in things outside the sphere in which, for better or for worse, she was fated to live. Her book, for instance, contains a genealogical chart of the English royal family.

Her first objective after her return was to build the biggest and best parlor house in El Paso. She didn't quite manage to outdo Etta Clark in the size of her place, but she certainly equaled her in the high tone of the appointments. From all accounts she was far ahead of Etta in matters of taste. Only the best was good enough. The roof was of solid copper. The finest hardwood was used throughout. The bathrooms were the last word. Oriental rugs and velvet drapes flattered the eye, expensive art objects were displayed here and there, and good pictures hung on the walls. Four large parlors occupied the ground floor, and in each Tillie had a special chair (a "throne," said the witty ones) where she sat in silks and diamonds when her girls were on display and where Aunt Sallie, the motherly colored maid, helped the butler to serve drinks. Nothing so vulgar as a bartender was allowed to function in sight of the guests.[76]

It was a place designed to attract gentlemen, gentlemen patronized it, and it is possible that a gentleman helped to build it. Captain W. H. Fenchler, one of three brothers with fingers in the El Paso financial pie, is said to have put up the money,[77] though if Tillie did as well as they say in her African venture, she didn't need any help.

The last touch of elegance was achieved, it is said, in the dissemination of 1,500 engraved invitations to a select list of citizens for the festivities marking her opening night.[78]

Chamber-of-commerce advertising of the period says the house was erected in 1899, and maybe it was, but Tillie's familiar address — 214 Utah — is first mentioned in the city directory in 1902. In 1901 she occupied an unnumbered dwelling "between Overland and Second."

Tillie "just loved a good home,"[79] and now that she could afford it, she decided that she was going to have a place of her own a good distance from her business. As a result she was soon in possession of a fine two-story red-brick house at 1201 San Antonio Street in an excellent residential district. On the other side of the street lived Waters Davis, eminent lawyer, athlete and leader in the reform movement which was eventually to outlaw Tillie's kind of life. Her establishment included a fountain in the yard featuring a boy with an umbrella, a coach house and coachman, and all the appurtenances needed for gracious living in the style of 1900. She had a buggy which was drawn by a horse named — appropriately — Rowdy, but the buggy did not occupy the coach house. That was reserved for Miss Tillie's cats. The little girls in the neighborhood referred to it as "Tillie Howard's Cat House."[80]

A picture in the scrapbook shows Tillie's apartment on the second floor of this house — a sitting room and bedroom. Curtains sweep from ceiling to floor around the bed. A life-size statue stands before a window. Furnishings are expensive and elegant. It looks as if Tillie meant to live as much like a member of the British Royal Family as possible.

She was famous for taking good care of her girls, whom she seems to have regarded as part of an extended family, and she wore herself out trying to keep things decent and orderly in an indecent and disorderly part of town. She proved this to the wife of one of our best early-day doctors, a pretty young woman who liked to accompany her husband on his rounds even when his calls took him to Utah Street. She would sit in the car (this must have been about 1910) while the doctor was inside, and she feared no evil. But Tillie feared it for her. She came out to the car one evening in her finery and diamond anklets and told the young wife she wished she would go elsewhere. "I have told my bouncer to make sure nothing happens to you, and it takes him away from his work every time you come by. You haven't any business coming here, and I wish you would stay away."[81]

Ordinarily she was gracious and friendly, at least to those who merited graciousness and friendliness, and she was the soul of generosity. Will Burges remembered that at one point in her career the inevitable happened: a man from her home town came to the place by chance and recognized her.

"You," he said, "are Tillie Weiler."

"My name is Tillie Howard," she replied, firmly.

"And I say you are Tillie Weiler and I knew you back in Wisconsin."

She gave in and began to think back, probably for the first time in years, to her miserable childhood. "Do you know if any of my people are living?" she asked him.

"Just your aunt and uncle," he replied, "and they are sick and old, and the mortgage is about to get them."

So Tillie got on the train and went back to the world she had left in 1882. She was not equipped to record her feelings in any sort of diary, but her ready emotional responses must have worked overtime. When she came back with the information she needed, she took $5,000 in securities to the First National Bank and tried to use them as collateral for a loan. The president turned her down. But when Will Burges took the same securities to the bank and asked for the loan, he got what he wanted, and the mortgage was lifted for Tillie's uncle.[82]

She tried to make life better for herself as well as for others. She did some traveling. In 1903 and 1904 the directories assign other names to 214 Utah,[83] and perhaps it was during these years that she voyaged to the Hawaiian Islands. Her scrapbook has a full section of views of San Francisco after the earthquake and fire of 1906. She must have been there too.

Of the scraps of available information which show her mind reaching out beyond the parlor house, the most touching is the one Rita Faudoa tells. Rita was working at Cannon's store on South El Paso Street in 1906 at a time when china painting was popular. A teacher was available at the store to show interested ladies how it was done. And who should ask for lessons but Tillie Howard? She applied under an assumed name, calling herself Mrs. Sanderson, and she came at noon when the store was almost empty, but she came, and she painted. Before she finished, she had about a barrel of decorated china. Rita has a piece of it, which Tillie gave her, to this day.[84]

Woman, of course, does not live by travel and china painting alone, and Tillie was a woman. She had her friends, men who perhaps did not touch her heart, and then she met George Ogden. It happened some time in the early 1900's, and after it happened George had the field to himself.

The man was a well-known saloonkeeper whom everybody knew and liked. He is remembered as a big man, verging on plump, with a handsome face and a genial disposition, a good piano player, a cheerful companion, a lover of fine horses and the things that go with them. Red haired and red mustached, he had a special kind of attractiveness which one El Paso girl found "electrifying,"[85] and which Tillie found irresistible. He appears in the 1903 directory as operator of the Parlor Saloon, which Tillie owned from 1903 to 1908; in 1904 as resident at 1201 San Antonio, Tillie's house. After that he changed residences frequently, giving addresses on Chihuahua Street and Leon Street, then the Ramona Hotel and the Angelus Hotel. For several years, beginning in 1906, he ran the Bank Saloon on San Antonio Street. All this time he had a wife and child,[86] though by 1909, when he took up residence at the Angelus Hotel, his domestic arrangements may have been crumbling. His association with Tillie was so close and so well known that many old timers will tell you in all seriousness that they were married.

There is actually no record of their association except in Tillie's scrapbook, the latter pages of which are full of snapshots of George in all sorts of interesting situations — on picnics surrounded by bottles, playing with Tillie's cats, just resting. There are no snapshots of her. Apparently George was not as anxious to preserve her image as she was to record his, and since she grew shapeless in her last years and lost much of her charm, she may have been unwilling to pose.

She was, one can see now, a sick woman. In 1906 Rita Faudoa noted that she was heavy and quite large around the waist. Rita could not know that Tillie's trouble was a uterine tumor which proved to be malignant. In 1910 she knew she had to give it up.

In that year George again took over the venerable Parlor Saloon on the corner of San Antonio and El Paso Streets. Tillie probably helped him to embark on this venture, which may have been a desperate attempt to save his failing fortunes. Her name appears in the directories for the last time in 1911. In early April she entered Providence Hospital and Dr. W. O. Wright prepared to operate.

Tillie's world was dying with her. The gamblers had been driven into holes and corners, and prostitution was in evil plight likewise. A new era was being born as the old days disappeared. The Mexican Revolution was well under way. Francisco I. Madero was in camp near Chihuahua at Bustillos hacienda issuing statements against President Díaz; fighting was in progress at Torreón and Culiacán. There was a circus in town that day. J. D. and Thomas Mayfield had just sold three lots on West Missouri Street to Thomas Kelly, who planned to erect an apartment house on them. As El Paso concentrated on such developments, Tillie's plight went almost completely unnoticed. When she slipped out of existence at 6:15 that evening, Eleanor Eubanks, the Calhoun sisters, Ruth Critchett, and a few more were coming home from the party which Marian Bowden had just given for Janet Grove.[87]

Tillie was buried the next day, Sunday, April 9, in Evergreen Cemetery. The *Times* failed to notice her passing. On Monday the *Herald* gave it very brief mention under "Deaths and Burials": "Tillie Weiler, aged 42 years, died at a local hospital Saturday evening. The funeral was held at 4 o'clock Sunday afternoon. The body was interred in Evergreen Cemetery. The woman was better known as Tillie Howard and owned quite a bit of El Paso property. She died from the effects of an operation."[88]

"The woman" was one of El Paso's authentic pioneers, once "the talk of the border," a human being of whom Will Burges wrote later, "I'll argue her case in the hereafter, if I can, though I do not expect to be called as counsel."[89]

She left an estate valued at $15,000 and named George Ogden as executor, a choice which set off a lawsuit. One of Tillie's two cousins was living in town, a Mrs. A. E. Bartlett who was as painfully righteous as Tillie was not. Her husband was a railroad man and she herself was a conscientious visitor of the sick and caller at the Old Folks' Home who was so helpful that she became something of a pest.[90] This lady, with the encouragement of the second cousin, Mrs. Annie Anglicka, hired Coldwell and Sweeney to try to break the will on the grounds that Tillie was incompetent when she made it and that George was no fit person to administer it. At the making of the will, said their plea, and for many years previously, George "had been more intimately acquainted with said deceased and possessed irresistible influence over her, which said influence he often used to his own advantage, and to the loss of said deceased.

"That at the time of the making of said will and continuously for many years previously thereto said deceased was in great fear of the said Ogden and apprehensive of suffering violence at his hands;

"That, notwithstanding said fear and apprehension, deceased was infatuated with said Ogden and pliant to his will; that said Ogden, well knowing said sickness and its effect upon the will of the deceased and her affection for and fear of him and of her inability to resist his wishes, and desiring to take advantage of the same prevailed upon said deceased to make said sections of said will in favor of him, the said Ogden, who was in no wise related to deceased, and to the disinheritance of the natural and statutory heirs of the deceased, to-wit, contestant, Mrs. A. E. Bartlett, and the said Mrs. Annie Anglicka. . . .

"That the said George Ogden is insolvent and has failed in his business, that of a saloon keeper, and is not a proper person to be executor without bond of the estate of the deceased. . . .

"That the said estate consists of personal property easily portable, and readily to be disposed of, and is of the value of some Fifteen Thousand Dollars; that the value of the property bequeathed by deceased to contestant Mrs. A. E. Bartlett, and Mrs. Annie Anglicka by said will is at least six thousand dollars which they will probably lose."[91]

Mrs. Bartlett lost her case. The suit was dismissed on July 31, 1911. George Ogden took over the executorship and within the year was gone from El Paso, probably taking Tillie's portable property with him.

For almost fifty years Tillie's mansion stood as a reminder of El Paso's palmy days. Ora Curtis, a lesser madam, managed it for a year as The Palace. The impulse to marry claimed her, however, and she became the wife of a Kentuckian named Walter Nahm, with whom she lived in apparent content for many years. She was succeeded by Bess Montell, who lasted only one year (1913), and then by Sam Dudley, who shot herself after a few months because of unrequited love for a pimp.[92] So it went through cycles of respectability and dilapidation until Karl Goodman bought the place for speculation. His father had an automobile business in the same block with offices in a building across the street which used to be a row of cribs. The house came down in 1958 to make room for a parking lot — the last of the great parlor houses to go.[93]

Almost everyone is gone now who could remember the Sin City of the eighties and only a few are left who remember it in the nineties. It is still a vivid memory, however, to people whose recollections go back to the early 1900's when Tillie Howard's magnificent house was the first place on "the Line" and the other big ones rose up in that block and in the block below. In between were dance halls, saloons, eating houses, dives of various kinds, and rows of cubicles where the second- and third-class prostitutes lived. The farther south one went on Utah Street, the cheaper and more degraded the places became, the older and uglier the occupants.

It was a pitiful business. The girls in the big houses, who were extremely handsome and mostly well-bred, may have done all right for a while, but as their years multiplied and their charms diminished, they were likely to wind up in the cribs, where they had to contend with brutality in many forms — often from the P. I.'s or "Macs" (for *macarons*) who brought business to them and shared the take.

"The poor things," says one old-time policeman turned reporter. "They comprised a society that had a class of its own, yet were absolutely classless and faceless in legal eyes. They had no more ground to stand upon than the vagrant. . . ."[94]

They constituted the number-one problem in El Paso for many years and eventually had to be got rid of, but then as now they were objects of curiosity and wonder. Younger citizens, boys and girls alike, were always inquisitive about what went on in the Tenderloin, and almost always frustrated in their attempts to find out. Every senior citizen whose memories go back before 1920 can tell a story of how he set foot, or tried to set foot, in the forbidden precincts. Walter Stevenson got as far down Utah as Overland Street with a band of fearful friends one evening and found a rope across the intersection to keep such as they from penetrating further.[95] A policeman was there to watch the rope. Some boys had better luck when they went on official business. Owen White tells how his father sent him to collect bills for medical services from the girls in the District.

"You mean you want *me* to go down there and collect bills?" said the son, hovering between horror and anticipation.

"Of course, Son," replied the father. "Those women won't hurt you. They're not nearly as bad as most people say they are; in fact many of them are very good."

"It cured me of curiosity," Owen adds, "because by calling on the Utah Street ladies between three and four in the afternoon, when they were just getting up, many of them nursing hangovers, and all with their warpaint off and their face grease on, and their hair in curlers and their rooms reeking with the odor of liquor and cigarette smoke, I unavoidably came to the conclusion that the beauty of sin, as they peddled it, was entirely mythical."[96]

Bob Mullin, who later became an alderman and after that an oil-company executive, had a similar experience at the age of nine. He was doing odd jobs for Blakesley, Freeman, and Fennell's Book Store on El Paso Street, the predecessor of today's Norton Brothers. The place carried, among other things, a fine supply of fashion magazines including *Elite Style* and various periodicals from Paris. Clothes — not ready made but creations of the dressmaker's art — were apparently close to the hearts of the Utah Street ladies, and every Wednesday a shiny brougham carried three or four of them, elegantly turned out, to the store to see those magazines. Among them was one with a soft, husky voice who impressed young Mr. Mullin deeply. She had, he says, "the laughingest eyes I had ever seen" and a way of attracting males of any age.

It was beneath the dignity of these parasoled phenomena to carry their own magazines. They always left orders that the magazines should be delivered, and that was how Bob Mullin came to ride his pony down Utah Street one morning and deliver a magazine to Tillie Howard in person. "My parents would have killed me if they had known," he says now. He found Tillie in bed looking "like an overdeveloped Juno" and not at all seductive at that hour of the day.[97]

Even the local girls sometimes came for a quick look, particularly if they were allowed to ride horseback. Eleanor Eubanks rode her pony down Utah Street one time when she was in her teens and the girls in the cribs called to her in friendly fashion and asked her to come in — an invitation which she did not accept.[98]

Another of our prominent and charming ladies tells how she did accept such an invitation. She actually rode down Utah Street to Tillie Howard's place one afternoon and went inside. The attraction was a poodle which belonged to one of the girls. The enthusiasm for dogs which brought them together led to a charming friendship and frequent calls at Tillie's house where wonderful cookies and the best lemonade were provided in quantities and the ladies, all lounging around in Japanese kimonos ornamented with butterflies and morning glories, were so hospitable and friendly that Mary found herself completely at home. No doubt the girls were glad enough to make contact with somebody who was not in their business.

This idyll came to an end when Mary and her father were walking together down Oregon Street past the present location of the American Furniture Company, and met the owner of the poodle. Mary ran to her, threw her arms around her in genuine affection, and introduced her to her father — a very rich and important man. When they separated, he asked his daughter with what seemed to her unnecessary seriousness, how she came to know the girl. Mary told him.

"You are not to see that girl any more," he warned her. "If you do, I will take away your horse."

"You are mean. You are the meanest man in the world. But if you are going to take away my horse, I suppose I will have to do what you say. But it isn't fair."

Not long after that Mary went East to school.[99]

The City of Sin probably had more effect on the virtuous half of town than most of us realize. Some people could see practical value in the presence of a flourishing red-light district. There was less wear and tear on adolescent girls from good families, for one thing. Fathers told their sons to let their sisters' friends alone and satisfy their curiosities down on the Line. And without any telling from anybody, many unmarried (and some married) men found themselves at home there. When you get to know the survivors of those days rather well, they will talk a little about the way they

"ran around" before they married and settled down and may add
what they know about respectable girls who ended up at May
Palmer's or Etta Clark's or about the protegés of Tillie who married and left the business. Most of these latter found husbands in
the sporting world but some of them — perhaps half a dozen —
invaded the fringes of society. One married a scion of a prosperous
pioneer family and tried, they say, to get herself accepted socially.
When this did not work, she took him off to California where life
is said to be freer and easier. So far as I know, only one ever established herself in good society and she did it by marrying a much-
liked politician and becoming a member of the Catholic Church
devoted to good works. Once they had accepted her, her fellow
townsmen defended and protected her, never mentioning the past
and keeping all knowledge of her history from outsiders.

Only a sociologist with much more information than comes
readily to hand could give a true picture of the impact of Sin City
on the life of the community, but it was undoubtedly strong and
will last a long time in non-measurable ways.

The outward symbols of these remarkable and regrettable times
are gone now. South Mesa is just another street in Little Chihuahua
lined with tenements, modest dwellings, and hole-in-the-wall grocery stores. There are no reminders of the teeming underworld
life which once flourished there except at the far end of the street,
at Mesa and Ninth, where one can still see some of the buildings
built by George Look for use in the restricted district and occupied
until the middle thirties by prostitutes. They are used now as
apartments by respectable Mexican families, and only a few of
the passersby can remember what once went on there.

These few, however, will always hear an echo as they drive down
that street of the voice of Gypsy or May or Tillie calling, "Company
in the parlor, girls," as their painted and perfumed charges, smiling
and gracious, troop down those vanished stairs to brighten the
lives of a generation gone long ago, one hopes, to mansions of a
better kind.

CHAPTER XXII

Six Shooter Capital

 NINE YEARS have gone by since the railroad opened El Paso to the world and brought the world to El Paso. It is 1890 now, and the population is over 10,000. The City of Virtue is flourishing with churches and schools, social clubs, and musical organizations. The City of Vice is doing just as well, and El Paso is known far and wide as "The Monte Carlo of the United States."[1]

The entire Southwest is booming. The ranges of New Mexico and Arizona have been stocked with Texas cattle; miners are swarming over the mountains; speculators move in and out of Mexico; and El Paso is their good-time town. Whenever anybody has a dollar in his pocket, says Owen White, "he heads hell-bent to El Paso to get rid of it."[2]

Thus there is a market for all the diversions El Paso can invent or import. These include, on the one hand, such comparatively harmless institutions as baseball, bicycle racing, boxing, cockfighting and horse racing, and on the other, gambling and gunfighting. They all are interesting to the sporting world, and the barrooms serve as centers for information, debate, and the placing of bets.

The presence of Juárez across the river is a determining factor in the situation. A sport who gets in trouble on our side takes a few quick steps and is safe on the other, and it works the same way in Mexico. The availability of this escape hatch is instrumental in attracting to the border an extraordinary group of gunfighters and fast-draw artists, some on one side of the law and some on the other, who add to our other distinctions the title of Six-Shooter Capital of the Southwest. Some people think it ought to be our pride and joy that for a few years we ranked as a murder metropolis with Fort Griffin and Dodge City, Tombstone and Tonopah.

The palmy days of the gunfighters were the middle nineties, but the breed was not disposed of finally for another ten years.

The world of the girls, gunmen, and gamblers, we should add, was on the whole self-contained. The roughs broke up no Sunday School picnics at Rand's Grove, and they mostly killed each other. As a result every survivor from those times insists that El Paso was a more secure and orderly place in the days of John Wesley Hardin than it is today. "Women could go anywhere then and be perfectly safe," says Page Kemp. "I wouldn't let my wife go down town alone at night now."[3]

Outside El Paso as well as inside, the nineties were years of violence. Frontier conditions died out slowly, and during this time they were kept alive by gangs of thieves and rustlers who flourished in the rough country above and below town. North of the Pass toward Canutillo a band of home-grown outlaws operated out of a river-bottom *bosque* or tangled thicket. Below town a larger *bosque,* nearly ten miles long and as much as five miles wide, sheltered several hundred suspicious characters who protected each other and defied the law.

This latter stronghold was known as "The Island." In 1854 the river moved several miles north and east. The old bed was dry, except during flood times, but occasionally both channels were full of water, giving the Island its name. The International Boundary ran through the brush and cottonwood groves on the western side but the whole area was a sort of no-man's land, inhabited by people who claimed citizenship in either country as occasion warranted and who flouted the authorities of both.

It was said that by keeping to the brush and avoiding the highways, a native of either *bosque* could arrive at the other without being seen.[4]

The men who lived in the north *bosque* had a fine little rustling business going. In a canyon high up on the west side of Mount Franklin they owned a rock corral far removed from prying eyes where they could hold a few head of stock. Their favorite trick was to drop across the crest of the mountain, steal a couple of cows from one of the ranches on the east side, and drive them back through a pass so stony that trailing was impossible. This gap is still called Smuggler's Pass, though few of us know why.[5]

In 1890 the killing of Charley Fusselman threw a spotlight on these activities. A group of thieves from the lower *bosque* on their way to the upper refuge passed the present site of Fort Bliss (then called "the Mesa"), headed for the Pass, and picked up several horses belonging to John Barnes at Mundy's Spring. Barnes got on their trail almost immediately and actually caught up with them — something he had apparently not counted on, for he was unarmed. When a "villainous-looking Mexican" confronted him in the canyon leading to the Pass, he backed off and went to El Paso for help.[6]

Within a very short time he was back on the trail with two companions, policeman George Herold and Deputy United States Marshal Charles H. Fusselman of Presidio. Fusselman was in town to attend court and had time on his hands.

For some reason, perhaps a sublime self-confidence, the rustlers had gone into camp in the canyon to which Barnes had trailed them. It was said that the Bosque gangs had never lost a fight and would take on anybody from either side of the river.[7] They did put out a sentry who nodded at the wrong moment and was taken by surprise as the three officers moved cautiously up the canyon. He looked up to see three pistols pointed at his belt buckle, threw up his hands, and went meekly along. They recognized him as a well-known thief named Ysidro Pasos.

The main body of the outlaws was only a short distance away. Topping a rise, the little posse came suddenly and unexpectedly upon them. Lead began to fly at once. At the first fire Fusselman was shot off his horse and Herold and Barnes left the canyon fast, some eight or ten outlaws after them.

A few hours later Deputy U. S. Marshal Bob Ross led a ten-man squad into the hills and found Fusselman lying where he fell, shot through the neck. Well aware that they would be pursued in force this time, the thieves had decamped, leaving eighteen horses, two cows, a calf, a whole beef, and a bucket of tortillas. The officers picked up their trail on the other side of the Pass and followed them to the heavy brush along the river where the rustlers were at home and the pursuers were not. The trail led eventually to the Mexican border, and it was obvious that the fugitives intended to circle Juárez and take refuge in the lower *bosque* on the Island.[8]

No doubt existed in anybody's mind as to who was responsible for Fusselman's death. Herold and Barnes had seen a notorious outlaw named Geronimo Parra fire his rifle twice at the dead man.

It took ten years to bring Parra to justice, and the man who did it was Captain John R. Hughes, a corporal when Fusselman was killed. He finally located the man in the New Mexico penitentiary but was unable to get him out until he ran down a fugitive in Texas who was wanted in Las Cruces by Sheriff Pat Garrett. According to the Captain's biographer, a deal was arranged and late in 1899 Hughes brought Parra back to El Paso, where he was tried and sentenced to hang.[9]

The story of that hanging, on January 6, 1900, is a gruesome chapter in our history. On their way to execution in the old El Paso jail, Parra and a companion named Flores whipped out improvised daggers and nearly cleaned out the El Paso Police force before the sentence was finally carried out.[10]

The canyon where Charlie Fusselman lost his life is still called Fusselman Canyon. The route of the new trans-mountain highway runs near the place where he fell.

This regrettable episode slowed the activities of the Bosque gangs for a while, but they were soon doing business as usual. The Island group was particularly troublesome. The nucleus was a family named Olguín, sons and grandsons of old Jesús-María Olguín[11] who in his youth had been a first-class border man himself but was now too old to keep up with his hard-riding sons.[12] During the spring of 1893 these outlaws became so troublesome that a determined effort was made to stop them. Sebastian Olguín got ten years for horse stealing; Prisciliano (sixteen years old) was sentenced to three years in the State Reformatory for stealing a cow.[13] This left Severo, Antonio, and old Jesús-María still at large. Severo, the most dangerous of the lot, was under indictment but still free and living in the midst of some three hundred friends and supporters. The situation was bad enough to call for drastic action, and in June, 1893, a detachment of Rangers prepared to take on the Island gang in a finish fight.

Captain Frank Jones knew what he was getting into and told the Adjutant General before he left Alpine that he would need manpower. "There must be fully 50 in the gang," he said, "and they are well organized too. They are part of the mob who murdered Howard some years ago." A small force, he thought, would "simply be murdered."[14]

Jones was a good man to take along. Thirty-six years old, better educated than most of his group, he was a brave officer and a good leader. He had been married for about a year to a daughter of the famous Ranger and peace officer Colonel George W. Baylor.¹⁵ His presence was a great reassurance to the harried lawmen of the Valley when he went into camp with his men at Ysleta.

About the time of his arrival, as if to let the Rangers know what they had to contend with, Severo Olguín and some of his men got drunk at the little Mexican town of Guadalupe, killed one citizen, wounded three more, and rode away, unscathed and unpursued, to their headquarters at a place called Tres Jacales (Three Shacks) on the Island.¹⁶ The news came by some branch of the grapevine to Deputy Sheriff Ed Bryant at El Paso that Severo had hunted his hole, and Bryant sent word to Captain Jones that he was ready to move. The next day, June 29, Bryant and Jones with four Rangers — Corporal Karl Kirchner, Privates Aten, Saunders and Tucker — moved out of Ysleta and stopped for the night at the old campground below Fabens. At daybreak on the thirtieth they struck out through the brush for the heart of the Island. A guide took them to the Olguín ranch, where they found nobody at home. Turning northward, they fell into a trail that followed, roughly, the International Boundary until their guide admitted that he was lost. Jones gave the order to turn back.¹⁷

They chose a path which seemed to run eastward toward Clint, Texas. Jones and Tucker were in the lead, Alden and Saunders, with the packmule, followed.

As they approached a tiny Mexican village, two men on horseback turned into the road and came to meet them. Realizing what they were running into, the men whirled their horses and dashed for the village with Jones and Tucker in hot pursuit. The road rounded a sharp corner at the entrance to the settlement, and when the two Rangers made the turn, they saw their quarry take shelter behind one of the houses. Immediately rifle fire burst from doors and windows.

What followed happened faster than it can be told. Tucker was off his horse first, kneeling in the road and blasting away at the hidden assailants. Before Jones could get both feet on the ground, he was hit in the thigh and a few seconds later received a bad wound in the neck.

"Are you hurt, Captain?" Tucker inquired.

"Yes, shot all to pieces."[18]

Now the other two Rangers, who had been held back by the pack mule, came charging around the curve so fast they could not stop at once. The fire from the houses grew more intense as they turned around and came back. Jones, at the point of death, told them to take cover, and when they saw he was gone, they did so, working their way through the brush and eventually making their way to Clint, where Kirchner wired El Paso for help.

Next day Sheriff Simmons and a posse demanded the body of the dead Captain, but got nowhere until the Mexican authorities were asked to help. Lieutenant Rafael García Martínez, the Juárez *jefe político*, rode with Simmons down the Mexican side of the border with a Mexican police escort. They had better luck than they expected, for not only did they bring home the body of Captain Jones — they met three members of the gang making their way out of the brush and rounded them up without a fight. These turned out to be Jesús-María Olguín and his sons Severo and Antonio, undoubtedly on their way to the upper *bosque*. Captain Jones had got Severo in the shoulder and Antonio in the hand. The brothers might not have been so easy to corral had they not been disabled. They wound up in the Juárez jail, but what happened to them after that we do not know.[19]

It is worth noting that a member of Simmons' posse was George Scarborough, a preacher's son turned cowboy and peace officer from the Fort Griffin country[20] who was destined to play a prominent role in El Paso's six-shooter history. Another familiar name was affixed to a telegram which came to the sheriff after his first trip to the Island: "Arriving this morning with a posse. United States Deputy Marshal Bass Outlaw, Alpine, Texas."[21]

Two results of this affair were the erection of a monument to the memory of Captain Jones in 1938 at the place of his death and the appointment of John R. Hughes, one of the great Rangers, as his successor.

The Bosque gangs were by no means the only outlaw organization in the area. The tide of violence and crime had been rising in New Mexico and West Texas since the eighties, partly, at least, as a result of a migration from farther east. Rain had fallen on the arid slopes and swales of the Tularosa and Three Rivers country for several years and the grass was thick and high — thick, at least, for that area — and thousands of cattle were moved in to take advantage of it. The owners of these herds brought their own codes with them. They quarrelled among themselves and with the people already on the ground, and things went from bad to worse. Little ranchers fought big ranchers. Cattlemen fell out with town men. And rustling became a way of life.

The Fountain murder case — the disappearance of Colonel A. J. Fountain and his little son Henry near the White Sands on February 2, 1896 — grew out of these conditions,[22] and many another life had to be lost before the wild men were tamed. The shootings which made El Paso notorious in the middle nineties, however, were not battles for law and order. They involved the elimination of each other by more-or-less professional killers.

This brings up the case of Uncle John Selman, a once-notorious pistol wielder whose various lives and exploits have only recently been fully unraveled.[23] His youth and early manhood were spent in Shackleford County near Fort Griffin. There he became involved with a plausible and popular character named John Larn who married into the county's most prominent family and was for a while sheriff. When his killing and rustling activities came to light and he was jailed, a party of vigilantes, some of them supposedly his relatives by marriage, walked in and executed him. Selman, his lieutenant, was on the wanted list but fled in time.[24]

A short time later he joined a band of itinerant desperadoes in New Mexico who were murdering and stealing under cover of the confusion caused by the Lincoln County War.[25] The Rangers finally caught up with him and brought him back to his home county to stand trial. His former neighbors asked only to be rid of him, however, and he was encouraged to "escape." He went to Mexico with his second wife and stayed several years. When he thought the heat was off, he came back to the United States and after some adventures in the Magdalena country of New Mexico he became a citizen of El Paso.[26]

By now he was somewhat mellowed, as became his graying hair, and he decided to get on the right side of the law. This meant honest toil, and to make ends meet he worked for the American Smelting and Refining Company until 1889. After that he gathered cattle in the Sacramento Mountains, worked for the Mexican Central Railroad, bounced undesirables out of the Wigwam Saloon, and chased horse thieves. His activities in running down rustlers resulted in an attack on the dark streets of El Paso which laid him up for months and almost cost him his life.[27]

He finally found a place on the regular police force in 1892 when he ran for the office of constable and, to everybody's surprise, beat Republican E. C. Jones.[28] By this time he was a well-known figure in the little border town, and most people thought of him kindly although his connections were mostly among the sporting element, his best friend being Jim Burns, proprietor of the Red Light Dance Hall and dealer in liquor, sex, and political influence. John's son tells how he and his father helped Jim round up and "influence" Mexican voters who were herded to the polls to vote for the Democrats.[29] Not that the Republicans were any better, for both parties bought as many illegal votes as they could. It was just that the Democrats were able to round up more of them.

So old John became a constable in 1892, was reelected in 1894, and was still in office in 1896 when he had his rendezvous with destiny.[30] In the meantime he was probably the hardest working officer El Paso ever had. The dockets show that he was constantly bringing offenders before the courts for offenses of all types.[31] His son tells of various occasions when would-be bad men challenged him unsuccessfully, and the natural conclusion is that he showed considerable talent and energy in carrying out his duties.

The Bass Outlaw affair clinched John's reputation as a handy man with a gun, but he paid a high price for his status.

Outlaw was one of those incredible characters produced by frontier conditions. Born supposedly in Georgia, he had a good family background and a good education. He was short (about five feet four) but wiry and well coordinated, a good athlete and a famous pistol shot. He had a rather refined-looking face with delicate features and a receding chin – a face that did not go with the rest of him – symbolic, perhaps, of the fact that he was a very much mixed-up young man.

The stories say that he left his home state because he had killed somebody. In 1885 he became a member of Company E of the Texas Rangers, later transferred to Company D, attained the rank of sergeant, and in the early nineties was stationed at Alpine under Captain Frank Jones.[32] Captain Jones was not happy with him because of his one fatal flaw. A likable, friendly, winning fellow most of the time, he became a wild man, dangerous to friends as well as foes, when he was drunk. And he got drunk with increasing frequency as time went on. After repeated warnings, Captain Jones dismissed him from the Ranger Service for being intoxicated while on duty.[33]

Bass's friends took care of that. He got an appointment as Deputy United States Marshal and was so popular that large numbers of Alpine citizens petitioned Marshal Dick Ware to keep him on duty there. Marshal Ware did so, with some misgivings.[34]

Bass was in and out of El Paso during these years, and his reputation as a fast man with a gun preceded him. Some of the most dangerous characters in town were afraid to bring him to a showdown. John Watts, for instance, the iron-headed colored man who ran a Negro house of prostitution on Overland Street, was understandably resentful when Bass ended an evening of revelry in June, 1892, in bed with Watts' white mistress. After thinking the matter over very carefully, Watts filed a complaint, but when Bass sobered up, he gave the woman back with great good will and all was as before.[35]

It is said that after a few such episodes as this the El Paso city authorities sometimes assigned a policeman just to watch over Bass when he honored the town with a visit.[36]

The climax came in April, 1894, when he was back as a witness in a court case. Having considerable leisure time, he employed it in getting drunker and angrier than usual. He was unhappy with Marshal Dick Ware who, he thought, had allowed another deputy United States marshal to enter his territory to serve papers and collect the fees. The more he drank, the more resentful he became. In this frame of mind he dropped in for a visit at Tillie Howard's place, where a girl named Ruby comforted him for a while and sent him out in a better frame of mind. On the street he met Selman and Frank Collinson, to whom he told his troubles, his anger reviving as he talked. When they suggested that he go to his room and sober up, he decided that he needed Ruby's therapeutic attentions once more, and back he went to Tillie's, Collinson and Selman keeping him company.[37]

As Frank and John sat chatting in the parlor, Bass wandered off toward the back of the house, and a few minutes later they heard a shot in the bathroom. Selman looked at his companion and re-marked, "Bass has dropped his gun."[38]

At that moment Tillie herself came charging out of one of the downstairs rooms, headed for the rear entrance, and began blowing her police whistle — the normal procedure for a madam in distress. By the time Selman and Collinson reached the back door, Outlaw had caught up with her and was attempting to take her whistle away.

The first notes had caught the ear of a Texas Ranger named Joe McKittrick, or McKidrict as he spelled it (it was not his right name),[39] and he came running around the corner into the back yard as Selman emerged onto the porch.

"It was an accident, Joe," Selman told him. "He's all right."

McKidrict was not satisfied. "Bass, why did you shoot?" he inquired.

"You want some too?" Bass spat at him, and shot him through the head. As McKidrict fell, Bass put another bullet into his body.

Selman was in action by now. Pulling his gun, he jumped off the porch and went for Outlaw, who turned and fired at him point blank. They were so close together that Selman was blinded by the powder blast, which caught him directly in the eyes. The ball, fortunately for him, whistled past his ear. Reflex action brought his gun into position and he placed a bullet directly over Outlaw's heart — then he stood there holding his eyes with his left hand, unable to see a thing.

The incredible little ex-Ranger now showed the vitality that was in him. Mortally wounded and unable to raise his pistol above his waist, he got off two more shots, one striking Selman in the thigh, the other above the right knee. He still had strength to stagger around the house into the street, surrender to Ranger Frank Mc-Mahon, and walk into the Barnum Show Saloon, where Dr. Turner came to see him. He did not die until four hours later on a bed in the back room of the saloon. His last desperate question was, "Where are my friends?"[40]

No friend was there to answer him, but Alonzo Oden mourned his passing. "Bass Outlaw is dead. Bass, my friend, is gone," he wrote in his diary. "Bass, who was so brave and kind; who could laugh louder, ride longer, and cuss harder than the rest of us; and who could be more sympathetic, more tender, more patient than all of us when necessary."[41] Outlaw was undoubtedly the only one of his kind on record about whom such things were ever said, or could have been said.

Selman was tried for murder but of course came clear.[42] As a result of this episode, however, his vision was permanently impaired — he could hardly see at all at night, says his son — and he walked with a cane for the remaining two years of his life.[43]

Selman was only one of an impressive concentration of pistol men who made El Paso and Juárez their headquarters in the middle 90's. Jeff Milton, who already had a massive reputation in Arizona as a peace officer, became City Marshal during a brief flurry of reform activity in 1894. Deputy United States Marshal George Scarborough, known as a dangerous man in a fight, was already on the ground. Several other efficient hand-gun artists were on the side of the law. On the other side were all sorts of local sports, drifting desperadoes, men in flight from other regions — a wide assortment of loose-living characters who came and went in pursuit of their own nefarious ends.

A particularly interesting bunch came to town in the spring of 1895, stopped briefly, and fled to Juárez just ahead of a posse from Eddy (Carlsbad), New Mexico. There were at least four of them, probably more, their leader being a remarkable personality named Martin Morose. The newspapers spelled him M'Rose, but Dee Harkey, who helped to break up his rustling activities and rush him out of New Mexico, spells his name Morose, gives an account of his origin in a Polish community in Karnes County, southeast of San Antonio, and tells how he learned to be a cowboy at the same time he was learning to speak English. He was big, blond, crude, unwashed and immoral, but he had a gift for getting hold of other people's property and was tough enough to kill if necessary to keep what he stole. Tom Finnessy, range manager for the VVN's (Eddy-Bissell Cattle Company) and a man after Martin's own heart, hired him as a cowboy and started him on his career.[44] His prosperity began when he drove a herd to Kansas and picked up enough stray stock along the way to start him in business for himself. He adopted the Ladder brand, which would cover almost anything, and made so much money that he spruced up, began to wear boots and possibly underwear, and assumed a position of leadership among the outlaws and thieves who dominated the county.

Dee Harkey, his boyhood acquaintance, came to Eddy about this time and noted the change. The two did not have a happy reunion, however, for the legitimate cattlemen of the region were fed up with Martin and his friends and they hired Harkey to go after them. They got Dee an appointment as United States Deputy Marshal and Inspector for the Livestock Association.

There was a meeting at which Harkey met Martin and his fellow thieves, who included Tom Finnessy, a desperado named Vic Queen, and the Sheriff of the county. In all there were twenty-five or thirty hard cases in the group. Martin proposed to match Dee's salary and brand a thousand calves a year for him if he would let them alone. Dee says he refused; and during the years that followed he sent the gang off, a few at a time, to prison.[45]

Early in 1895 he ran Morose, Queen, and Finnessy out of the country for stealing horses. Finnessy and Queen went directly to El Paso and on to Juárez. Morose went overland to Midland, where he met his "wife," a handsome blonde woman named Beulah whom he is said to have married in "the sheriff's whore house at Eddy."[46] She had a child as a result of some former connection, and seems to have been in all ways a lady of great energy and no inhibitions. Together they took the train to El Paso, carrying at least $3,500 in cash with which they planned to buy a ranch in Mexico.[47] The news that Morose and his men were wanted reached El Paso almost as soon as he did, but he had to be run down in the interior of Chihuahua before he could be arrested and brought back to the border. Beulah was with him. True to her explosive nature, she was ready to fight the arresting officers and had to be disarmed.[48] Officer Beauregard Lee, whom she tried to kill, noted that she was carrying $1,880 in money.

The stage was now set for the dramas and difficulties of 1895. Morose was locked up. Beulah was in El Paso trying to take the heat off him. Vic Queen and Tom Finnessy, though not in jail, were pinned down in Juárez and unable to cross the international bridge. They had been joined by Sam Kaufman and a Mr. Lightfoot of New Mexico.[49] Eventually a Texas cattleman, "General" Gene Mackenzie, with whom Morose had once been in partnership,[50] brought a bag of money to Juárez and bought his friend's release from jail,[51] though he couldn't bring him out of Mexico. To add extra interest, Dee Harkey advertised in El Paso and Juárez that the cattleman's association which he represented would pay $500 to anyone who would deliver Martin Morose to the American side of the river, dead or alive.

Matters were in this situation when the greatest gunman of them all got off the Southern Pacific train and appeared on the streets of El Paso to the horror and joy of the citizens. This was John Wesley Hardin, still a great name in Texas sporting circles though fifteen years in the State Penitentiary, from which he had only recently emerged, had subtracted some of the glamor from his public image. Still, a first-class pistol man could not be taken lightly and one who had killed somewhere near forty men was certainly first class. As he appeared in the saloons and eating houses, El Paso regarded him with respectful curiosity and devoted considerable attention to him and his doings throughout the four months of his residence. Young John Selman says that the general attitude approached hero worship.

Hardin was almost forty-three years old at the time of his arrival. He had put on some middle-aged flesh but was still a handsome man, well coordinated, forceful, full of life and ambition. Outwardly he was a gentleman of good manners and prepossessing appearance, at home in a Prince Albert coat and striped pants. Inwardly, he was a sick man. Dee Harkey calls him "the most tortured soul I have ever known."[52]

If he had been born in a different time and place, he might have turned out differently, but he was a boy during the Civil War in Texas and grew up during the terrible times that followed. He first saw the light in May, 1853, at Bonham, the county seat of Fannin County, a hotbed of trouble between Southerners and Union men. Later the family moved to Southeast Texas where things were no better. Although John Wesley was named for the founder of Methodism and his father was a circuit-riding preacher, he learned and lived by a frontier code which had little to do with the teachings of Christianity. He was a Southerner and Texan of the touchiest variety. In his personal creed the first principle was to back down for no man. The second was to revenge to the hilt any reflection on his personal honor.

The fact that everybody, including schoolboys, carried pistols in those days had a good deal to do with his initiation as a killer. At the age of fifteen he shot a colored boy who aroused his indignation, and he was almost constantly in trouble after that until in 1878 the law finally caught him and he went to prison — for shooting a deputy sheriff whom he describes as a glory hunter looking for a fight.[53] He had killed upward of thirty men when he began his fifteen-year stay at the Huntsville penitentiary.

In the hundred or more books which have followed John Wesley Hardin's lethal career, the picture usually presented is that of a ruthless and efficient destroyer, the "fastest gun in Texas," a specialist in homicide who lost his nerve and ended his career in degradation and despair.[54] It is true that disappointment and defeat altered him for the worse during his last months on earth, but the John Wesley Hardin known to his friends and relatives in the days of his youth and early manhood was not the character painted by the frontier historians.

The letters which he wrote to his family from prison are apparently the product of a well educated Christian gentleman, master of a rather florid but competent English style, and upholder of ethical standards high enough to satisfy Preacher Hardin himself. "My dear son," he begins one letter to John Wesley, Jr., "your father is again permitted to write his noble, his brave boy. Then with gratitude to God for this privilege together with the many blessings and benefits received by me during these many years, I offer with reverence that divine one my sincere thanks and bestow upon him my praises with the hopeful assurance that his blessings and his comfort will not be withdrawn from me and mine in the near or distant future."[55]

A man who could go on like that was bound to become the superintendent of the prison Sunday school, and who shall say that he was not sincere!

He admonishes his son to be brave and strong, to protect his mother and sisters, and to behave so that his parents will be proud of him. In the principles he recommends to his boy it is easy to distinguish the principles which John Wesley aimed to live by himself. There can be no doubt that in those days he thought himself a good and brave man in whom there was no weakness and no compromise with evil and wrong. His autobiography, which he brought to a conclusion just before his death in El Paso, shows that the famous gunman's picture of himself had been battered by time, but had not changed in its essential features.

The explanation for this almost incredible situation comes to this: John Wesley Hardin was two distinct persons — killer and Christian hero. He could kill without compunction, and he could preach and pray when circumstances called for preaching and praying. The bridge between these two personalities, the device which kept the halves from flying apart, was his sincere and constant conviction that every single one of those thirty to forty killings was right and necessary. His victims had forced the quarrel or needed killing or were stupid enough not to throw up their hands when he told them to. On occasion he could regard shooting a man as a public service. In 1871 he punctured two Mexicans over a monte game and closed his account of the affair in his autobiography with the observation: "The best people of the vicinity said I did a good thing."[56]

He undoubtedly expected, when he got out of jail, to lead a different and better life. He thought he would like to be a lawyer and actually absorbed a good deal of legal knowledge during those fifteen years behind bars. Less than a year before his time was up, however, his dream fell in ruins with the death of his wife Jane Bowen Hardin. He emerged in February, 1894, into a world which had passed him by and into a frustrating relationship with his almost-grown children, who loved him dearly but hardly knew him and could not fully understand him.

At first things went well enough. The Governor gave him a full pardon; he passed his bar examinations, rating first in a group of seventy candidates; and he hung out his shingle in the town of Gonzales, where he had been very much at home as a boy. He made the mistake, however, of getting involved in a political dogfight and when his side lost, he left his children with a close friend while he went off to look for a new home.[57]

The pilgrimage which was to end at El Paso began in the hill-country town of Junction, lost in the brush out west of Austin, where he stepped into a nest of Hardin relatives. There in December of 1894 Wes opened a law office. One month later he married a young girl named Callie Lewis, who left him a few hours after the wedding, refused to see him again for reasons still mysterious, and sent him off on the next lap of the journey.[58]

After a brief pause at Kerrville, he headed west once more in response to a call for help from one of his less creditable relatives. "Killin' Jim" Miller, a cousin by marriage, was in need of his legal services. A man whose gun was for hire, Miller had been involved in a number of bloody little episodes whose consequences he had escaped by fast footwork and the good offices of friends he had made in church. This time he was the plaintiff. At the climax of a private feud between himself and ex-Sheriff Bud Frazer of Pecos, Bud had shot first and put Miller in the hospital. Jim was now charging Bud with attempted murder. The case had been moved to El Paso,[59] and the family lawyer was needed there. Hardin's cousin Jenny, Mrs. Frank Powers, was an El Paso resident and may have added her persuasions to Miller's.

Thus destiny of some sort brought Hardin to El Paso on or about the first of April, 1895. The police were interested, of course, and the *Times* for April 2 commented sourly that the Miller and Frazer outfits "will no doubt be taught the lesson that El Paso has her own peace officers. The day for man killers in El Paso has passed." Jeff Milton says he made John Wesley take off his pistol, and no doubt Hardin obliged him when he made the request, but he was certainly wearing it a few days later.[60] At Miller's trial Wes made himself useful, though he had no official part in the proceedings.[61]

A hung jury delayed the case and the Pecos people went home, but Hardin liked El Paso and resolved to stay. On April 17 he was the inspiration for a sketch in the "Caught on the Fly" column of the *Times*. John Middagh, the historian of this newspaper, thinks he paid to have the notice inserted.[62]

"In his younger days," the column stated, "Mr. Hardin was as wild as the broad western plains upon which he was raised. But he was a generous, brave-hearted youth and got into no small amount of trouble for the sake of his friends. . . . Young Hardin, having a reputation for being a man who never took water, was picked out by every bad man who wanted to make a reputation, and there is where the 'bad men' made a mistake, for the young westerner still survives many warm and tragic encounters." In contrast to the wild youth of former days, the article went on, the Hardin of 1895 is "a quiet, dignified, peaceable man of business . . .

but underneath the modest dignity is a firmness that never yields except to reason and the law."

If the writer of this piece was not John Wesley Hardin, he certainly saw Wes as Wes saw himself.

The people who knew Hardin best at this time were convinced that he meant to go straight. Judge Wyndham Kemp used to say that during these days Wesley made a "heartbreaking" effort to establish himself as a lawyer.[63] He rented an office on the second floor of the old First National Bank Building (you can look up at his window as you stand on the front steps of the Hotel Paso del Norte). He solicited any sort of legal business and welcomed even calls to act as a notary. Gradually he came to see that a man with his record was not the sort of lawyer people went to with their troubles, but for a month or so he tried to practice his profession.

One piece of legal business which came to him he would have been better off without. Mrs. Martin Morose, blonde, beautiful, and belligerent, appeared at his office door one morning and asked him to see what he could do for her husband. Hardin took the job in good faith but almost immediately — within a few days — their relationship changed to a personal one. They both had rooms at Mrs. Herndon's lodging house on Overland Street, and the word soon got around that they were living together. Martin Morose heard all about it and nearly went out of his mind while his little knot of sympathizers in Juárez began to talk about ways and means of eliminating Hardin. They may have given the matter some extra attention because Mrs. Morose was taking care of a part of the Morose money. They sent word to Hardin that "he had better make himself scarce" in Mexico.[64]

Things happened rapidly in this affair. Morose and Beulah were arrested at Magdalena, Chihuahua, on April 11, 1895. Hardin's first encounter with the Morose party happened on April 21, only ten days later. He was taking a Sunday stroll in Juárez all by himself, apparently thinking no evil of anybody, when he met Tom Finnessy and several of Martin's friends. Seeing that they had him at a disadvantage, they proceeded to work him over verbally, probably intending to provoke him into a fight. They "tried to bulldoze him," the *Times* reported, "and grew quite saucy in their talk." Hardin swallowed his wrath and got away without trouble, but the next day he was back in Juárez again, this time with "a friend" whose identity was not mentioned in the papers. The two joined forces with Police Chief Milton and a friend of his, and the four of them sought the back room of Dieter and Sauer's saloon. They found five of Morose's friends already in the room having a consultation with Beulah herself. One senses all sorts of currents and undercurrents in this meeting. It is hard to believe that it was accidental.

"The conversation soon became general," the *Times* reported, "M'Rose's case was brought up and hot words passed between Hardin and Finnessy. Both men sprang to their feet. In an instant Mr. Hardin had slapped Finnessy's face and had his gun at his breast. In another instant Finnessy would have been a dead man, but quick as thought Chief Milton grasped the pistol and . . . it was quickly agreed the matter should be dropped."[65]

The Juárez police were at hand and apparently took everybody to the Mayor for a hearing, but Jeff Milton made a speech good enough to get them off.

It was one of Milton's last efforts as chief of police, for on the first of May he was replaced by Ed Fink. At the city elections on April 9 the reform element had been voted out and R. F. Campbell, the new mayor, wanted his own man.[66] A gambler of some note himself, Campbell was by no means hostile to gaming and the town knew it. On the evening of Ed Fink's appointment "quiet" games opened up here and there in the gambling rooms of the saloons.

John Wesley Hardin was in attendance at a poker session at the Acme. Perhaps he went out of curiosity. Perhaps he was already so discouraged over his law business that he was looking for a diversion or another way of life. At any rate he became discontented with the way the game was being conducted, scooped up the pot, and walked out with it.

From what we know about Wes Hardin, there must have been something odd about that poker game. His own explanation, made three days later, was: "I would not stand a holdout."[67] He did not display a gun and nobody objected to his action, indicating that other people thought there was something odd about the poker game also.

The next night he did it again, under different circumstances and with far different results. The attraction was a crap game at the Gem, across the street from Wes's law office. The man in charge was a gambler named Phil Baker. Hardin's luck was bad but he endured it until Baker made a sneering remark reflecting on his ability as a crap shooter. The next thing Phil knew, he was looking down the barrel of a .45 and listening closely as Wes remarked: "Since you are trying to be so cute, I'll just take over the money I lost here."

"Yes, Sir," the startled gambler said as he began counting out bills. Wes added, "You can't win my money and hurrah me too." He stopped the count when $95 was lying in front of him. "That's all I want. Just my money and no more," he said, and so saying he scooped up the cash and left.

In a minute he was back. Somebody had made a remark he objected to. He invited those who did not like what had happened to get in line and "show your manhood." As witness Charles F. Jones expressed it at the trial on May 16: "After getting the money, he went out, but soon returned and challenged the people in the room to trot out if they did not like his play, and as no one trotted out, I guess they liked his play."[68]

Apparently two such high-handed performances on two successive nights were more than even El Paso could adjust to, and there was a good deal of talk — so much, in fact, that Hardin felt he had to explain himself. In the columns of the *Times* on May 4 he did so. In a way he was explaining the code he had always lived by — the code which had made him what he was:

> I wish to announce right now that in the past my only ambition was to be a man and you bet I draw my own idea, and while I have not always come up to my standard, yet I have no kick to make against myself for default . . . my only aim is to acquit myself manly and bravely. . . . I admire pluck, push, and virtue wherever found.

Whatever other people thought, John Wesley Hardin was convinced, as he always was, that his conduct had been courageous and correct.

His fellow townsmen probably understood his point of view better than we can, for when he was brought to trial two weeks later, he was charged only with carrying a concealed weapon and was fined only $25 for doing so. His defense was that his life was in danger from the Morose crowd.[69]

Late in May he was tried for robbery — aftermath of the holdup of the crap game at the Gem Saloon. Hardin charged that the dice used in Baker's game were loaded, and he must have convinced some of his listeners, for the proceedings ended in a mistrial. The case was continued until October, an October which Hardin never saw.[70]

A surprising aspect of his activities, one which raises some interesting questions, was mentioned in the concluding lines of the May fourth notice in the *Times*. "I have bought an interest in the Wigwam Saloon," Wes announced, "and you who, whether in El Paso or elsewhere, that admire pluck, that desire fairplay, are cordially invited to call at the Wigwam where you will have everything done to make it pleasant for you. All are especially invited to our blowout on the 4th."

It took ready cash to buy into the Wigwam, one of El Paso's busiest and most profitable liquor-and-gambling emporiums. Where did the money come from? Specialists in border history suspect that he got it from Mrs. Morose.[71] In an interview three months later, Beulah said she had "advanced" Hardin a large amount of cash[72] – possibly as a retainer, possibly as an investment in the autobiography which he was writing. John Selman's biographer thinks that Wes liked Martin's money and wanted the rest of it.[73]

Morose had been out of the Juárez *juzgado* for some time, possibly because he had taken the oath of allegiance to Mexico,[74] but he was still a wanted man in the United States. Several El Paso police officers, including Jeff Milton, George Scarborough, and ex-Ranger Frank McMahon (Scarborough's brother-in-law) were eager to get their hands on him. This Morose knew, but he wanted desperately to come back. He wanted a crack at Hardin and was even more eager for an interview with Beulah. George Look, the man of many lives who left a manuscript telling what he knew, says Selman tried to arrange a meeting between Morose and Beulah in the back room of Look's Gem Saloon.[75] He does not say whether or not the meeting came off, but other sources make it clear that Morose was looking across the river with longing eyes.

Scarborough, the blue-eyed, buck-toothed little Deputy United States Marshal, was Morose's contact man. He says Morose "had been sending messages" to him for a month before the showdown,[76] and George took the initiative in leading the victim into the trap. There is reason to believe that Scarborough, Milton and

Selman made some sort of bargain with Hardin and that this bargain cost several people their lives.

By the middle of June Martin was ripe and ready to be plucked. On June 21 Scarborough went to meet him in the middle of the Mexican Central Railway bridge, talked Martin out of his suspicions, and led him back to the American side. His hope of meeting Beulah was shattered when Milton and McMahon rose up from the little jungle of sunflower stalks beyond the bridge end and challenged him. Morose was game. He jerked his gun and succeeded in getting off one ineffectual shot before he fell with eight bullets in his body,[77] All that was found on him was a letter addressed to Mrs. Helen Beulah Morose.

Nothing could have been more secret than this midnight assassination, but there were witnesses. Two Mexican smugglers who happened to be in the neighborhood told what they had seen to Vic Queen, Martin's partner. Queen fired off a letter to the El Paso *Times* accusing Scarborough of "a systematic course of deception" and of the cold-blooded murder of a man who had trusted him.[78] Public sentiment in El Paso took about the same view.

Milton, Scarborough, and McMahon were tried for the killing and came clear when Milton showed that he had a warrant for Morose's arrest.[79] It is quite possible that John Wesley Hardin and John Selman were as deeply involved as the three who stood trial. In the files of historian R. N. Mullin are the recorded statements of several men close to the principals who say that Hardin arranged the killing. There is also the fact that Morose had a considerable amount of cash which he is not known to have left with anybody and which was not found on his person.[80] George Look says Hardin got it, and paid dearly for it later on.

An ironic aspect of this sordid business came out at the time of Morose's burial. He was so little known that undertaker Powell had to pick up four young men on the street to serve as pallbearers, and the only mourners at Concordia Cemetery when the hearse arrived were Beulah Morose and John Wesley Hardin.[81]

With Martin out of the way, life should have been simpler for Wes and Beulah, but there were serpents in their desert Eden. On August 2, when Wes was out of town, Beulah got drunk and disorderly and was arrested by young John Selman for carrying a pistol. Although she paid her fine and apologized the next morning, it was abvious that things were not well with her.

They were not well with Hardin either. A temperate man in his youth, he too was drinking more than was good for him and seemed to be pursued by some personal devil. The Morose killing was haunting him and once when he was not himself he made some incautious remarks about George Scarborough — remarks for which he apologized the next morning.[82] The apology was not enough for George, and a few days later he forced Wes to print a retraction in the *Times*. "While under the influence of liquor," the statement read, "I made a talk against George Scarborough, stating that I had hired George Scarborough to kill Morose. I do not recollect making any such statement and if I did, the statement was absolutely false, and it was superinduced by drink and frenzy."[83]

When he released this statement, John Wesley Hardin, the incarnation of pluck and manliness, touched the lowest possible point of personal humiliation. He could no longer believe in himself and it was time for him to go.

These troubles brought on violent quarrels between Wes and Mrs. Morose. At one time Beulah and Annie Williams, keeper of the boarding house where they were now living together, had him arrested for threatening Beulah's life. The Court put him under a peace bond. They went back together again, but it was obvious that there was not much future in their association. Beulah felt this herself, and about the middle of August she left for Phoenix, where she seems to have had connections. She got as far as Deming, New Mexico, and changed her mind. A wire came through to El Paso: "I feel you are in trouble and I'm coming back."[84] And Beulah was not far behind her wire.

It was no use. A few days later she left again, and this time she went all the way. Hardin was deprived of even the doubtful benefit of Beulah's concern when he went forth to meet his destiny on the evening of August 19, 1895, at the Acme Saloon on San Antonio Street.

Undoubtedly pressures had been building up behind the scenes through July and August. The story most often heard (both Selmans told it) says that Hardin and Selman fell out over young Selman's arrest of Beulah. The two men had been meeting each other without incident, however, ever since the arrest and had been rolling dice together that evening.[85] It may be that Martin Morose's money was involved. George Look declared in 1909 that Hardin took $3,600 out of Martin's pockets a few seconds after the killing and bad blood resulted when he refused to split.[86]

After the Gem holdup Selman came to Look in a cold rage and said, "George, you people may stand for it, but I won't. He has to come across or I'll kill him. . . . I believe he has cut with Scarborough, but he has not cut with any of the rest of us. What do you say? Shall I get the son-of-a-bitch?"

Whether his motives were personal or financial, Selman was in an ugly mood that night. About eleven o'clock he had left the Acme when his friend E. L. Shackleford, afraid he had had a drink too many, urged him to go outside. As he stepped into the fresh air, Owen White, too young to be on the streets at that hour, caught his eye and he advised the boy to go home.[87]

Inside, Hardin was standing at the bar rolling dice for quarters with a young fellow named H. S. Brown. He apparently had his game won. Looking at what he had just thrown, he remarked, "You have four sixes to beat." At that moment E. L. Shackleford came through the swinging doors. Selman was right behind him, and as Shackleford stepped aside, Uncle John sent a bullet through Hardin's head and shot him twice more as he lay on the floor. He put up the pistol when young John Selman ran in and stopped him: "Don't shoot him any more. He's dead!"

In a matter of minutes the saloon was full of curious people who stared at the body until it was carried off to Nagley's undertaking parlors. Two days later Texas' most famous gunman was carried to Concordia Cemetery, where he rests today a few feet from Martin Morose in a grave which until 1965 was untended and unmarked.[88]

The end of John Wesley Hardin, however, was the beginning of an argument which threatens to go on for the foreseeable future. The testimony of the doctors and most of the witnesses indicated that Hardin was shot in the back of the head before he could turn around and face his slayer. For years Judge Howe retained possession of Hardin's hat and could show you the bullet hole in the back.[89] Nevertheless John Selman declared positively that he had shot Hardin in the eye — that Wes had whirled and reached for his

gun just before the bullet struck. We don't know yet who was right.
A story which may be pure legend says that A. B. Fall was
brought down from Las Cruces to help with the defense and that
he threw the proceedings into confusion by establishing the fact
that Hardin was a famous "mirror shot" – could draw and fire
over his shoulder with deadly speed and accuracy.[90] The credibility
of this story is destroyed, as R. N. Mullin has shown, by the fact
that a man entering the south door of the Acme could not have
been seen in the mirror.[91]

Fall actually did take a hand in the case. The truth as it involves
him seems to be that Selman was convinced he had shot Hardin
in a face-to-face encounter and nothing could make him change
his story though Davis, Beall and Kemp, his lawyers, tried their
best. Finally Selman asked them to call in Fall, in whom he had
confidence.[92] Although the young lawyer was not *persona grata*
to the members of the firm, they did as Selman asked. Fall could
not shake John Selman's conviction either, so he made the most of
the two or three witnesses who swore that Hardin had turned and
reached for his gun as Selman came into the saloon. Interestingly
enough, some present-day ballistics experts are inclined to believe
that the bullet holes in Hardin's head and chest, as they appear
in the photograph taken in the morgue, are very likely entrance
holes.[93]

After hearings in two local courts the preliminary examinations
came to an end. On October 12, Selman was indicted and trial
began in the district courtroom on February 8. Four days later
the jury declared itself unable to agree and the case was reset for
the next term. It was never called, for Selman was summoned, as
the *Times* expressed it, "to a higher court."[94]

For the sake of the record it is worth noting that the only good
man involved in these doings seems to have suffered the most.
This was young Henry Brown, usually described as a grocer. He
was really a dairyman and had come to the Acme to collect a bill.
It never occurred to him that he need not set up the drinks or roll
the dice a few times. Everybody else did, and probably he had
done it a hundred times himself. He was not required to finish
his competition against Hardin's four sixes, but he found himself
up against worse odds as soon as the news of the shooting got
around. He was engaged to Mattie Robertson, daughter of a Meth-

odist minister, who was shocked to hear that her beloved was involved in a sordid saloon killing. Her father was more horrified still and they told Henry he would be on probation for a year; one drink and it would be all over.

Before the year was up, Henry had been given his dismissal although he hadn't touched a drop, and, as people said in those times, he "went to the dogs."

Interestingly enough, his sweetheart's father suffered the same fate. He left town, left the ministry, became a school teacher in a community far away from El Paso, and was sent to prison for shooting an ex-sheriff who had made improper remarks to Mattie. Attorney Robert T. Neill went to Governor Lanham's house to plead for a pardon, and Robertson went free.[95]

John Selman apparently got little satisfaction from his triumph. Revenge turned out to be a hollow thing, and in addition there was the fact that people still refused to believe he had shot his enemy in a fair fight. "In the back of the head. . . ." That was the phrase that kept echoing in his mind. He drank more and more, and the more he drank, the more he brooded. He felt compelled to persuade an occasional stranger that he was really a great fighter. To add to his burdens, a rumor started that Mannen Clements, one of John Wesley's relatives, intended to take the matter up.[96] Selman's sons never let him go out alone, especially at night.[97]

Thus matters stood for several months. Then John Selman, Jr., made the move which brought on the finale. Young John was in love. His Juliet was a fifteen-year-old Mexican girl, the daughter of a storekeeper named José María Ruiz. Late in the afternoon of April 2, 1892, the lovers rode bicycles across the bridge to Juárez and disappeared from view. The girl's mother was not far behind, and she got the Juárez police force into the act. It took the officers until after midnight to locate the couple, but eventually they were flushed out of their retreat — the house of a Mexican friend of Selman's — and John was taken to the Juárez jail.

Young Selman says the elopement took place when the girl brought him the news that her father was moving his family to El Salvador. They meant to get married, tried repeatedly to see the mayor about it, could not locate him, and finally sought refuge with Selman's friend.[98] After the arrest the girl's mother took her home — lost to Selman for good. Young John was crushed. His father came to see him on April 4 and spent the afternoon. It was a gloomy meeting and the old man seemed to have a premonition of trouble to come. As they said goodbye he remarked, "Well, I will have to be going, but tomorrow I will come back with George and we will get you out of here."[99]

"George" was George Scarborough, whom Selman considered his best friend.

That evening George shot Selman to death in the alley alongside the Wigwam Saloon.

Selman's death is, in its way, as mysterious as Hardin's. It happened in the small hours of Easter morning, April 5 – perhaps four A.M. Scarborough had been spending his time in the gambling rooms of the Wigwam, which were on the second floor. He came down the outside stairway, where Selman met him. One or the other proposed that they have a talk, and they turned into the alley. A few seconds later four pistol shots fractured the early-morning silence. The crowd which gathered almost instantly found Selman stretched out on the ground and George Scarborough standing over him with his gun in his hand.

Bud Selman, the second son, was called by telephone from the Santa Fe station where he was night watchman. His father was still lying in the alley when he arrived, and was conscious. "Bud," he said, "it is too bad this had to happen. I don't know what became of my gun. If I had had my gun, things would of been different."[100]

Why he didn't have his pistol is still a mystery. It turned up in possession of a barroom character named Cole Belmont who said he had picked it up in the alley at the time of the shooting. Uncle Jimmy Watts used to say, "Scarborough saw Selman sitting in the Wigwam saloon asleep. He paid a Negro $20 to steal Selman's gun out of his holster. Then he sent someone in to tell Selman he wanted to see him outside." Maybe Uncle Jimmy knew.[101]

Scarborough's story was that Selman had asked him to talk, had spoken about the possibility of getting John, Jr., out of jail, and had taken offense when George refused a drink. When he threatened to kill Scarborough, the shooting followed.[102] The jury believed him when the case came to trial and turned him loose.[103] Belmont, who had picked up Selman's gun but had not killed anybody, got sixty days in jail.[104]

George Look says that Martin Morose's money caused his death as it may have caused Hardin's. Selman was still unhappy about not getting his cut after Hardin was dead, and he incautiously let fall some words about the split Hardin supposedly had made with Scarborough. So Scarborough called him out and shot him.[105]

Now it was Scarborough's turn to face the consequences of what he had done. He resigned his job as Deputy United States Marshal and moved to Deming, New Mexico, where the Grant County cattleman's association hired him as a detective. On April 5, 1900, in a battle with cattle thieves or bandits, he was shot in the leg and had to wait until the next day for medical help. A doctor at Deming took the leg off, but George did not survive the amputation. He died on April 6.[106]

If the size of a funeral is any indication of the standing and importance of a man in the community, John Selman's was a sort of triumph. The Confederate Veterans, assisted by the GAR, took charge. Pallbearers included Judge Wyndham Kemp, Dr. W. M. Yandell, and other prominent citizens. Children who had been fond of Uncle John followed his coffin. No such tribute was extended to Morose, Outlaw, or Hardin. Selman was no better than the others, but he had represented law and order in El Paso for three years and worked at his job, so El Paso, ignoring his shortcomings, paid tribute to his services.

With the death of George Scarborough the era of the gunman in our town was almost over, though violence could never be entirely eliminated in this border community. By 1900, says Morgan Broaddus, "each weekend in El Paso proved to be a brief episode of bloodshed," and between 1903 and 1906 fifty killings occurred without a single execution.[107] The cold-blooded professional murderers of the nineties, however, existed only in memory.

Actually there was one belated chapter in the story — a chapter held over until the end of 1908 when Manning or Mannen (as most people called him) Clements came to the end of his string. Mannen was the offshoot of a rough-and-ready cattle-raising family from Southeast Texas. The Clementses were allied with many other pioneer clans; Mannen's father, for instance, was a double cousin of John Wesley Hardin's father. A prominent trail driver who left some legends in the Kansas cowtowns, Mannen Senior operated in Brown County and died in a shoot-out at Ballinger in 1889.

Young Mannen was twenty years old when this happened. Shortly thereafter he migrated to Pecos. Jim Miller was his brother-in-law, and this may have prompted the move. He supported Killin' Jim in his feud with Bud Frazer and appeared in court several times as a result.[108]

Already he had some reputation as a bad man. The Rangers had taken him in at San Angelo[109] for what must have been good and sufficient reason, and he added to his dubious laurels at various times and places after that. No one has yet followed the crooks in his career during this period, but one story says that he spent some time at Alpine, known as Murphysville in those days, where he and a man named Webb took a contract to eliminate a very rugged citizen named Pink Taylor. It was agreed that they would both try for the kill and would split the proceeds no matter which one succeeded. The legend says that Mannen climbed up in a tree outside a Murphysville bar where he could shoot through a window when Pink came in. He got his chance, but managed to kill the wrong man. Webb was found dead some time later. Mannen left the community at high speed and went to El Paso.[110]

Newspaper stories at the time of his death say that he arrived in 1894, some months ahead of his cousin John Wesley Hardin. They were seen together at Big Spring, however, and may have reached the Pass at the same time.[111] When the reformers went out and Mayor Campbell came in, Mannen got a job as constable. He turned out to be a moderately efficient police officer, but ambition bit him and he decided that he wanted to be captain. When word got round that he was being considered for the place, a number of responsible citizens reacted negatively. A petition circulated recommending that the job be given to somebody else.

Mannen went to the Mayor. "Mr. Campbell," he said, "I am going to get every one of those names off the petition." According to the late Maury Kemp he did get them off — all but one. Judge Falvey was stubborn enough and brave enough to refuse to remove his, and Mannen did not get the appointment.

Nevertheless he became a fixture in the border city and spent the next fourteen years in one police job or another — deputy constable, constable, deputy sheriff. Everybody recognized his long, narrow-shouldered body, small round head, and stiff, irregular walk. He seemed to have a nose for trouble, loved excitement, and always turned up where things were happening. "Because he was always around when there was trouble," said one of his old acquaintances, "people concluded he was mixed up in it."[112]

Sometimes he was mixed up in it. One of his escapades became an open scandal in the spring of 1908. It started when a man named Samuel Van Rooyen, an employee of a Chicago manufacturer of rubber cement, came in from Mexico and registered at the Sheldon. Somewhere south of the border he had struck up a friendship with a shady character named William A. Naill whom he promised to call when he got to town. The two made contact, had dinner together, and went for a tour of the city in a rented buggy. As a climactic experience, Naill promised to show his guest the racetrack at Washington Park, and they drove out Missouri Street as far as the Southern Pacific roundhouse. At this point two men stepped into the road and held them up. Van Rooyen was wearing two diamond rings, a diamond horseshoe pin, and a diamond stud, the whole collection being worth about $1,500. The men steered him and his host into a clump of bushes, relieved them of diamonds and money, and turned them loose.

Van Rooyen, though he seems to have been a friendly soul, was not about to put up with this sort of treatment and went at once to Night Captain Ten Eyck of the El Paso police force. He was sure Naill had lured him into an ambush. The police were experienced and energetic in those days and they went to work on a woman named Catherine Williams, with whom Naill was living at 539 Magoffin Avenue. Convinced that Naill was in trouble, she put the finger on his accomplice, another young man whose only local address was May Palmer's parlor house on Utah Street. When she called him to report the situation, the police went over and picked him up. His name was J. W. Gill. He was currently and contentedly unemployed but had once worked for the Southern Pacific as a switchman. They found in his possession correspondence and equipment for sealing freight cars which linked him with the ring engaged in smuggling Chinese into the United States.[113]

The officers felt sure they had one of the hold-up artists but had no idea who the second one was until assistant district attorney Maury Kemp came into the picture. The day after the robbery

Judge Caleb Marshall called him on the phone and asked him to come to his office. "Don't send a deputy," he said. "Come yourself." As Kemp was preparing to leave, Mannen Clements arrived with a story to tell. Two friends of his were accused of holding up a Jewish traveling salesman and were being held in jail, but there was nothing to it. One of them had been with the salesman at the time of the robbery. The other was sitting on the Clements' front porch engaged in conversation. Would Maury do something about it?

"I'm just going over to tend to it now," Maury told him, and they set off together. The Judge's office was in front of his living quarters on San Antonio Street. Maury and Mannen entered, and shortly thereafter Mannen headed for the back of the house. Van Rooyen was present and watched him move away with his peculiar gait. "That's the man," he said, "who walked ahead of me when they held me up."[114]

It seemed best to the authorities not to make any charges against Clements at the moment, but he suspected that they were going to and Kemp felt that Van Rooyen's life was in danger as a result. He told the man to stay near the center of town, and whenever he felt that there was any special reason for caution, Maury stayed as close to him as possible. Van Rooyen survived to testify after the grand jury indicted Clements a month later. Mannen did his part by selling his house to help raise Gill's $3,000 bail and[115] by putting up a bold front after the indictment was brought in. "There is no truth," he said, "in the statement that I had mortgaged my home for the purpose of assisting Gill in making his bond. I sold the place outright to Volney M. Brown. I have been jobbed in this case by my enemies, as the trial will show, and I had no other purpose in making bond for him than a confidence in his innocence."[116]

The trial came on in November. Mrs. Clements testified that she had left her husband and Gill talking on her front porch the night of the robbery when she went to bed, but she couldn't be positive what Mannen was doing between 7:30 and 10:30 that night. The jury was inclined to go along with the alibi, however, and when Victor Moore attacked Van Rooyen, calling him an actor who had quit acting to become a diamond smuggler, their minds were made up. They turned Mannen loose.[117] The papers reported that the jurors took "only a few moments" to decide. It has been said, however, that "Clements' eye never left the jury box," and he let it be known that if he should be convicted, it would be a bad day for every juror who voted to send him up.[118]

Mannen's career as a peace officer was ended by the robbery. Guilty or not, he was a candidate for reelection to the office of constable, and the election was held just before his trial. It was no help to an aspirant to public office to be under indictment for armed robbery, and Clements lost by the margin of four votes to W. F. Mitchell. It was a terrible blow to his pride, and his personality seems to have undergone a radical change as a result. "He was not the Manny of old," one citizen commented. "He had grown reserved and at times even quarrelsome." Defeat "seemed to break his spirit."[119] Like Hardin and Selman, Mannen went through a sort of psychological shipwreck just before his end.

A particular kind of underground activity was going on in El Paso at this time, and Mannen undoubtedly knew something about it. Smuggling Chinamen into the United States was beginning to be big business. Behind it was the Exclusion Act which kept Orientals out of the country and arranged for their deportation if they were caught. Many Chinamen were smuggled in because they wished to live in the United States. Others were smuggled across the border from Mexico so that they could give themselves up and get a free ticket back to China. El Paso and Juárez were headquarters for the business.

As a result the border was flooded with Chinese, permanently settled or in transit. Most of them seemed to have the proper papers. In El Paso, said the *Times,* "there are a hundred 'Celestials' where there was one twenty years before." They have certificates which "bear the inspection of the immigration officials. Every train brings a dozen or two to Juárez, all intent on getting across the border, and in the course of a few years hundreds of them have been taken off trains on the American side."[120]

The trainmen, particularly the conductors, were supposed to be deeply involved. They would stop at Newman or some other place a few miles out of town where a group of contraband human beings would be waiting. The Immigration officials knew what was going on and made life difficult for the smugglers, but the ring was too big and powerful for them to wipe out the abuse entirely.[121]

Ancient gossip says that Manny, who "always liked to be where there was excitement," knew all about these activities and just before his end had threatened to tell what he knew. There is no real evidence to back the story up, but it is worth noting that a citizen testified under oath in May of the following year (1909) that on the evening of his death Mannen had offered, for money, to "go down to the stock yards where they were loading Chinamen and cut Charles F. McClanny in two" with a load of buckshot.[122]

The place where the trainmen hung out was a famous dive known as the Coney Island. It was a saloon, with a billiard parlor adjoining and gambling rooms upstairs, belonging to Tom Powers and G. E. Truesdale. It may be significant that Powers and Truesdale were Gill's bondsmen. One-eyed Tom was a hard but likable character about whom many stories still circulate. He was the particular friend whom Pat Garrett took along to San Antonio to meet President Roosevelt at a reunion of the Rough Riders — a gesture of friendship which is supposed to have cost Pat his job as collector of customs.[123] The Coney Island stood just across the alley from the Sheldon Hotel, where the First National Bank Building now raises its dignified façade. At one time or another every male in El Paso, with the possible exception of a few preachers, had passed through the Coney Island's swinging doors. It was a very popular resort, particularly with shady characters and the sporting crowd. One lawyer called it the rendezvous for "all the uncaged convicts in the west."[124] During World War I it was placed off bounds for soldiers because of some of the things that went on inside.[125]

A place of this kind was the appropriate site for the murder of Mannen Clements, which took place at 6:10 P.M. on the evening of December 29, 1908. Mannen entered about six o'clock a little tipsy but in control of himself. He asked Colonel Hunt and two racehorse men to have a drink with him, but they were occupied and refused. He turned to Elmer Webb, who had just come in, and offered him a drink. Webb said no, he wanted to talk with him. They went to the back of the saloon, near the wine booths and the telephone booth, and engaged in conversation. Some witnesses thought they were quarrelling. The place was full of people. At least twenty were standing at the bar drinking or waiting to be

served. Three bartenders, including Joe Brown, a regular employee, were mixing and pouring as fast as they could. It was a
typical old-time saloon scene, the place abuzz with talk and laughter, glasses clinking, doors swinging, people coming and going.
In the midst of it there was a muffled explosion — a witness later
said it sounded like somebody striking a match — and an instant
later Mannen Clements' head dropped, his knees buckled, and he
sank lifeless to the floor, a bullet hole oozing blood and brains in
the back of his head. W. H. Fryer, a young lawyer, stepped into
the place at this moment and asked Tom Powers what had happened. Powers replied, "Mannen Clements just committed suicide."

A scene of monumental confusion followed. People came running in to see what had happened. Those already inside tried to
leave *en masse* so as not to be involved in the investigation which
was sure to follow. Police officers were present and in the neighborhood, but it never seemed to occur to any of them to close an
exit or get the names of witnesses. Nobody, absolutely nobody, had
a word to say about what had happened or who had done it.[126]

Good citizens were outraged, of course, by this cynical dodging
of responsibility. While Mannen was being laid out in the undertaking parlors of McBean, Simmons and Carr and while the Eagles,
Woodmen and Maccabees were preparing to bury him, editors
throughout the Southwest were commenting on the incredible fact
that a man could be shot down in a crowded saloon before a hundred witnesses and the slayer could walk out unhindered and un-
detected.[127] Chief George C. Campbell, who was accused of spending his days at the Washington Park race track instead of running
the police force,[128] absorbed so much criticism that Mayor Kelly
had to find another job for him and appoint Ben F. Jenkins as
chief of police in his place.[129]

Stimulated by public disapprobation, the officers arrested a number of more-or-less innocent bystanders and let them go when it
became obvious that there was no case against them. Finally they
struck what seemed to be pay dirt, put their case together, and
arrested bartender Joe Brown.[130]

Joe qualified as the number-one suspect. He had quarreled with
Clements for attempting, as he said, to "rope him into" the diamond
robbery. Mannen may have threatened his life. As a matter of fact

the diamonds lifted from Mr. Van Rooyen are said by competent witnesses to have been reposing in the Coney Island safe at the time of Mannen's death,[131] but what, if anything, Joe Brown had to do with that is by no means clear.

The trial, which began on May 11, 1909, was sensational. It went on for three days before a crowd which jammed the courtroom and overflowed into the corridors and onto the grounds. District Attorney Walter Howe and his understudy Joe Nealon were in charge of the prosecution. Two young lawyers with their spurs to win, Victor Moore and Dan M. Jackson, defended.

It looked as if the prosecution had a sure thing when Howe produced three eyewitnesses who swore they saw the gun in Joe Brown's hand. One of them said he saw Joe put it in his right hip pocket after the shot. The defense proceeded to show that the witnesses were unworthy of credit and produced witnesses of their own who made it appear beyond question that Brown could not have fired the shot. A bartender on temporary duty stated that Joe was serving drinks at the other end of the bar when the killing took place and could not have done it. Another witness had seen a stranger come in from the pool room, fire the shot, and leave. Now it seemed that the defense was in charge; but the prosecution was able to show clearly that the defense witnesses were not worthy of credit either. Although Dan Jackson bore down hard in his final speech on Joe Brown's "beautiful trusting babe" and "loving wife," nobody could predict the outcome when the case went to the jury.[132]

The jury, quite naturally, was confused also. At first the men were eight to four for conviction, then eleven to one for acquittal, then unanimous in believing that there was a reasonable doubt about Joe's guilt.[133]

The case was discussed for years, and everybody had a theory about how such a killing could be managed in a busy saloon without any credible witness seeing it happen. Owen White spends considerable time in his autobiography analyzing the possibilities and comes up with the explanation that a bartender was the killer, that he concealed the gun in a bar towel, and that he dropped his weapon into the dishwater as soon as he fired the shot. Owen does not mention the name of the bartender, but he indicates that Tom

Powers, co-owner of the saloon, assured him many years later that this is the way it happened.[134]

It might be worth adding that Judge W. D. Howe remarked in an interview toward the end of his life that for many years he had given Joe Brown credit for the killing but had finally come to the conclusion that Tom Powers was really the man.[135]

More than one of Joe Brown's friends asked him if he did it and how he did it. He usually answered, "I was acquitted of that one." Once he replied, "I didn't do it, but I know who did, and he didn't get his money."[136]

In any case Mannen Clements was dead, and his passing marked the end of an era.

CHAPTER XXIII

The Cleanup

FOR THE FIRST FIFTEEN YEARS of its existence as a city, El Paso remained frankly and more or less unashamedly a wide-open town. There was no thought of a cleanup. For a while the sports and the non-sporting citizens who lived off them may have been actually in the majority. In any case the good people were so convinced that what their neighbors did was none of their business that any attempt at interference would have seemed to them highhanded if not actually immoral.

Besides, there was the Theory. This was a typical piece of Western philosophy, based on a disillusioned view of human nature and the economic situation, which has its exponents even today. It was divided into two parts. The first said that sin was here to stay, or, as a locally famous character called Give-a-Damn Jones expressed it during the reform fever of 1904, "As long as there is money there will be gambling, and as long as there is liquor distilled there will be drunkards."[1] The second part declared that the revenue produced by the saloons and gambling halls and parlor houses provided such a large part of the community income that it would be suicide to cut it off. "Grass will grow in your streets," they said, "if you close them up." And they could give you statistics on the number of liquor dealers who paid license fees, the number of gamblers who did likewise, and the proportion of the policemen's salaries paid by "fines" from the red-light district.

The good women and the preachers were against liquor and vice, of course, and so were many businessmen, but their voices were almost inaudible above the clink of glasses, the click of poker chips, and the seductive notes of the daughters of joy.

We were as cynical in our politics as in our public morals, and the party bosses of the region were past masters in the art of controlling the electorate. Mexican voters tended to follow a *patrón* who told them how to vote, so the *patrones* were lined up first. Then the leaders went to work on the uncommitted voters. Sometimes these were paid off at a standard rate (when the system got organized it was two dollars apiece),[2] but there were other expenses. Since the other side always found ways to seduce the weak of will, the bosses had various places where they kept their voters overnight, gave them food, drink, and entertainment, and held them until the polls opened for business the next morning.

Whenever there was a political contest, both sides rounded up all the men they could. Frank Faudoa used to take a buggy and a bag of silver dollars and collect Democratic voters in all the Valley towns. His boys were treated to barbecue, beer, music and dancing.[3]

The system was put to its first important test in 1882 when the matter of a new county seat came up. County affairs were still being conducted in traditional leisurely fashion at Ysleta — once, like San Elizario, a Valley metropolis; now, in comparison with the community at the Pass, a sleepy rural village. In 1882 the justice of the peace at Ysleta could not speak English. The courthouse was neglected and inadequate.[4] A change seemed to be indicated.

County-seat elections could be called only once in five years, and this fact made thoughtful citizens hesitate to bring the matter to an issue. A loss would mean five more years of Ysleta-type government.[5] The Ysleta politicians, on the other hand, were confident that they could win an election, and as a result of their efforts a vote was called for on December 4, 1883.

El Paso realized that it must make a supreme effort. "Every man who is legally qualified should vote," said Mr. Newman of the *Lone Star* on November 7. "There is no registration required nor any vexatious preliminaries . . . the large body of Mexicans . . . have but to go before the clerk of the district court and declare their intention to become citizens of the United States and then, if they have lived the legal period in the state and county, they are entitled to vote . . . every ballot counts in piling up a two-thirds majority."

On election day the town rose up as one man to get out the vote. Businesses were closed. People with buggies and wagons were busy bringing citizens to the polls. The Santa Fe offered free rides to voters coming from the north. When the score was in, El Paso had 2,252 votes; Ysleta had 476.[6] Since every Mexican who could be rounded up on either side of the river had been induced to vote at least once, the total number of ballots was far in excess of the number of qualified voters in the county. Ysleta protested vigorously but nobody listened. El Paso was the county seat, and she made her title secure in 1885 by building the largest and finest courthouse in Texas.

This structure, incidentally, was the cause of the biggest scandal since the Salt War and gave the town one of the most dramatic moments in its early history. A contractor cut corners on the construction and tried to bribe the city officials to look the other way. James P. Hague set a trap for the rascals, accepted the money offered him while concealed witnesses listened in, and made a public exposure of the whole scheme the next day.[7]

The brand of political ethics displayed in the county-seat contest was characteristic of our town for a good many years. No man ever objected when his side won by these tactics, but he was always indignant when the other side used them. During the city election of 1884, for example, there was great resentment in the south-side Second Ward when M. E. Flores and Ben Schuster marched about thirty Mexicans in column of twos to the polls.[8] "Instantly," said the *Times*, "the crowd set up a protest against voting such specimens." Two or three fights started, and when a known alien approached the ballot box, the bona fide voters ran him off.[9]

John Selman, Junior, tells how it was done in 1892. Jim Burns announced a big dance with free beer at the Red Light dance hall on Utah Street the night before the election and imported girls from Juárez for dancing partners. Jim gave young John his instructions: everybody got in but nobody got out. As Jim left, he handed the boy a big walking stick. When John asked what it was for, Burns replied, "If any of them try to leave, hit him over the head and make a damn good Democrat out of him."

"As soon as the polls opened the next morning," John adds, "the hacks started coming for them and they would be taken away in groups of four to the polls where they voted right."[10]

With such characters as Jim Burns in control, reform was obviously out of the question. Yet as early as 1883, a "reform" movement started. S. H. Newman started it. The Republicans on the city council were repulsive to him, especially James P. Hague. After the Salt War Hague succeeded Cardis as the friend of the people, and Newman thought rightly that Hague had the Council "in his vest pocket."[11]

In July forty or fifty citizens who agreed with Mr. Newman organized a Citizens' Reform League and published a Statement of Purpose.[12] Their first act was to petition Joseph Magoffin to run for mayor. Two hundred and thirty-seven men signed the paper, including preachers and saloon keepers, businessmen and plain citizens. In 1883 party affiliations were still unimportant; both Democrats and Republicans were involved.[13]

The strange feature of the whole business was the fact that Mr. Magoffin was mayor at the time and would probably have run without being asked. The reason for the demonstration was the situation in the council. For a least a year the aldermen, led by Mr. Hague, had thwarted and ignored the mayor, even meeting and doing business under a mayor pro tem when Magoffin was at home and within call.[14] It was the council, not the mayor, which the citizens wished to reform.

Nowhere in the protests and plans of the Reform League, nowhere in the files of The Rescue, a three-column, four-page daily edited by Major W. J. Fewel during the height of the campaign, was there any mention of gambling or prostitution or the proliferating saloons.[15] "Reform" in 1883 had none of the connotations it picked up during the next decade. When the reformers won 431 to 190[16] and Magoffin's supporters announced that "the city is safe," nobody even thought of disturbing the dispensers of vice and liquor.[17] Magoffin and his administration got along with the sinners as was customary while the citizens went back to business.[18]

Through the middle eighties the situation remained stable. In 1885 R. C. Lightbody, a Democratic haberdasher, was elected mayor without the help of party apparatus, and in 1887 he was returned to office. By this time, however, a change had begun. More and more Republicans had come in with the expansion of the population, and during the presidential campaign of 1888 the GOP in El Paso became active for the first time since carpetbagger days. For a few years the Republicans were the party of reform and the Democrats were the conservatives who held onto the old ways, tolerating if not encouraging the saloonkeepers and gamblers.

The most powerful man among the Democrats was Charles R. Morehead, and behind him was the money and prestige of the State National Bank plus the influence of what James P. Hague called the "Morehead Bank Gang."[19]

Hague's vehement language was the audible and outward sign of deep divisions which were beginning to split the community and stir up resentments undreamed of in the first years of the boom. As time went on, these partisan feelings focused more and more on the question of cleaning up the town. Should El Paso continue to be the Monte Carlo of the United States, or should it be something else?

The great rift began to widen in the fall of 1888 as the presidential election drew near. The El Paso Republicans, riding a nation-wide wave of popular feeling, met at Ysleta and put out a "People's Ticket" of candidates for county office. The Democrats took fire at once and the two groups began sniping at each other. The *Times,* aimed and triggered by Juan Hart, raked the Republicans fore and aft, and the *Herald* went after the Democrats. The *Times* did more damage, for Hart was a handy man with a lampoon and had practiced hacking at his "weak and brainless" rival since the time of the courthouse scandal in 1885. Now he rose to new heights of invective. The *Herald* became a "hired mud gun and filth mortar" and the voice of Republican chairman W. W. Mills was "a bloody bray."[20]

The election was a passionate and colorful affair with bands, carriages, banners, and crowds in the streets. When the Republicans were reasonably sure that Harrison would be the next President, they began arranging for a celebration, and on November 10 they organized a magnificent torchlight parade followed by a triumphal rally at the Myar Opera House. Editor Hart admitted sourly that the GOP had exhibited some "get up and go." "The number of torches," he said, "was not large, but the procession as a whole was a pretty spectacle worthy of a better cause."[21]

Locally the Republicans were unsucessful that fall of '88, but Harrison's election to the presidency was strong medicine, and they resolved to make the municipal elections in the spring of 1889 a supreme party effort. A new city charter had been approved by the Texas Legislature,[22] and the time seemed ripe for a new deal all round. Waters Davis, president of the Republican Club, called his forces together on March 4, 1889. The Democrats responded to a call from S. H. Newman on March 12, and both parties conducted primaries shortly thereafter for the first time in history with "rattling resolutions and stirring speeches."[23] The Republican candidate for mayor was Adolf Krakauer, a Jewish merchant small and frail of body but well on his way toward being the richest man in town. He was opposed by none other than Charles R. Morehead, who for years had been the real boss of the city.

Mr. Morehead did not want the job. Twice he refused to accept the nomination. Only when W. H. Austin (to whom he had not been speaking) took him by the hand and offered to "take off his coat and go to work" did Morehead accept.

Our first excursion into full-scale party politics was an untidy business. Krakauer, in the innocence of his heart, declared that the campaign would be clean and devoid of mudslinging, but within a few days he was so thoroughly spattered that he began hurling mud himself. Among other things he was accused of voting to enfranchise the street railway company some years before in exchange for a block of stock.[24]

His former Democratic friends made impolite fun of him. "Upon what meat has he [Morehead] fed," inquired the *Herald*, "that he should be considered so superior to the nominee of the Republican party?" "Pork, of course," replied the *Times*. "Give us something harder."[25]

The *Times* made great capital of Morehead's record during his incumbency as mayor of Leavenworth some twenty years before. Day after day the story of his success was repeated. The *Herald* made no reply but went quietly to work and rounded up a citizen of Leavenworth who testified that Morehead had used his office as mayor for personal profit. The story broke the day before the election. Too late the *Times*, screaming "fraud and filth," revealed that the *Herald's* informant was a "liar, thief, scoundrel and murderer."[26]

The cries of fraud and frameup did not discourage either side from buying votes. The Republicans had more money and corralled the greater number of "qualified" voters, many imported from Mexico. The Democrats bought as many as they could, but their resources were inadequate. When the votes were counted,

Krakauer had 892 and Morehead 855. The number cast exceeded the number of qualified voters by several hundred.

"Black Fraud," was the *Times* headline: "How Krakauer's Heelers Did Their Dirty Work." Mexicans were brought in from as far south in Chihuahua as Santa Rosalía and were "herded together in droves" the day before the election.[27] Every Democrat in town demanded an investigation, and a petition went to the city council. The Republican members, led by Alderman Hague, put the decision off as long as possible, but on April 17, after speeches from both sides in which such words as "coward," "liar," and "sneak" were pointedly used, the investigation was authorized.[28]

At this point Mayor Lightbody stepped into the limelight. Apparently convinced that an election was an election and the Republicans had won, he opened and canvassed the returns on April 18 and installed the entire slate of officers in spite of the anguished cries of the Democratic councilmen, who left the room in a body when the mayor revealed his intentions.[29]

Relieved of opposition by this walkout, the Republicans took over control of the city government. Then they made a fatal mistake. Although Mr. Krakauer had declared, "we must keep the peace at all hazards," twenty-five new police officers were sworn in, two cases of Winchester rifles were brought over from Ketelsen and Degetau's hardware store on El Paso Street, and City Hall was stocked with provisions, as if for a siege. J. A. Smith and J. F. Satterthwaite were the ringleaders — Uncle Jimmy Smith, one of our best-loved men, editor of the *Herald* and later El Paso's postmaster; Satterthwaite, the same New Yorker who had brought his tender feet to the border in 1881 and started developing the town. He had picked up a good many Western ways since then.

The records do not reveal why the Republicans took this extreme stand, but they undoubtedly felt that the Democrats would do it if they did not do it first. Frank Wells Brown, part owner of the *Herald,* said in later years that the Republicans "armed themselves and took the City Hall by force when the Democrats refused to give it up," and that the Democrats armed themselves likewise and threatened a battle.[30] Feelings were aroused on both sides, and a small spark might have touched off the powder keg.

Mayor-elect Krakauer was much disturbed by this show of force and foresaw disastrous consequences if the warlike spirit were allowed to develop in his belligerent community. He called on all good citizens to keep their heads and the peace,[31] but his words rang hollow in view of what was going on at City Hall.

The Democrats, contrary to Republican expectations, decided not to shoot it out. Instead, after appointing R. F. (Bob) Johnson as acting mayor, they got out an injunction forbidding the Republicans to occupy the council chambers until the votes were canvassed and their victory confirmed or denied.

The choice of a man to serve the papers gave the Democrats some concern. What if the Republicans shot first and listened afterward? The man selected was Sheriff James H. White, modest and unassuming but afraid of nothing. He marched up to City Hall and took charge without the least opposition. Smith and Satterthwaite and their little army marched out, leaving Winchesters and provisions behind, and the Democrats marched back in.[32]

Judge Falvey upheld the legality of the injunction and ordered the old council to canvass the votes to see who had actually won the election. Since the majority of the councilmen were Democrats, the Republicans were nervous about starting over. On the other hand, their man had won, and the count might show him still the winner. Besides, as long as the Democrats' rump council continued in power, there was no future for the Republicans. A showdown was their only hope, and they demanded one.[33]

Again Mayor Lightbody went his own way. He had served his two terms and would serve no longer. Aldermen Hague and Detweiler (Republicans) and Ben Schuster (Democrat) stood with him and refused to enter the council chamber. The Democratic aldermen regarded this as an opportunity rather than as a defeat. They met, chose three aldermen to replace the absentees, and appointed a large, calm, efficient Democrat named G. E. Hubbard as acting mayor.[34]

The final blow to the Republicans came with the disclosure that Krakauer was not eligible to hold the office of mayor, even if his election had been confirmed. He was not an American citizen. He had taken out his first papers, but that was all. Whatever face the Republicans had left was lost with this discovery,[35] even though their entire aldermanic slate was certified and installed.[36] At a special election held on June 29, Democrat Richard Caples was elected mayor with only feeble Republican opposition. Ironically, Caples was Irish born and, according to Owen White, in exactly the same position as Krakauer had been a month before. The discovery was made in time, however. Caples rushed down to the courthouse the day before election and emerged with his final citizenship papers.[37]

And now, with the Republicans in eclipse, the Democrats made the first real gesture toward reform. Prodded by the Law and Order League, the Council passed an Ordinance to Restrain Gambling. Their idea of "restraint," however, was simply to raise the price of license fees so high that only a few gamblers could stay in business. After January 1, 1890, it would cost $800 a year to operate a gambling establishment. The councilmen were pretty well agreed that gambling would "go on anyhow in spite of the law and order league," and that the city should get the revenue.[38]

The statutes, of course, said that gambling was illegal, and a good many businessmen were not satisfied with Mayor Caples' high-price-tag method of controlling sin. They thought gambling should be outlawed. The result was a split in the Democratic ranks. A group known as the Independents, disenchanted with the graft and cynicism of the party regulars, came out in 1893 with a ticket headed by Judge C. R. Loomis, a lawyer of great respectability and responsibility and a life-long Democrat. W. H. Austin, the conservative banker who had offered to take off his coat for Morehead in 1889, was the rival candidate for mayor.[39]

Even now, in 1893, the reformers hardly dared to name their objectives. They never mentioned gambling in their platform but merely called for an end to "corrupting influences."[40]

Again the reform party went down to resounding defeat. Austin won by a two-to-one majority, leaving the Democrats a house divided.[41]

The city government was divided too. Young Will Burges, called a "radical" because his enthusiasm for reform knew no bounds, was the new city attorney. He was backed by his younger brother Richard and by his uncle, the city health officer, Dr. William Yandell. Most of the members of the council were reform minded also. Prodded by the councilmen and by Juan Hart of the *Times*, the police officers began picking up prostitutes and bringing them into court. Jim Burns' Red Light Dance Hall on Utah Street seemed to be the focus of these official attentions. "The mills of justice cannot grind up the Red Light fast enough to suit the *Times* so that paper grinds Jim Burns a little every morning," remarked the editor of the *Tribune,* and the results appeared when Burns was handed a stiff fine which induced him on May 10, 1893, to close his place of business for a while.⁴²

The *Herald,* for the moment, was in tune with the *Times* and supported the Law and Order League with articles on "framed games" which slaughtered the innocent and with comments on the desirability of moving gambling "upstairs." All through this period people seem to have felt that if the gamblers could not be got rid of, the next best thing was to get them out of sight. Hence the attempts to move them to second-story locations.⁴³

The gamblers got more attention than the prostitutes, but these were not ignored. "It is time," said Editor J. A. Smith of the *Herald,* "they were asked to give other people a show. Prostitutes should be treated as if the authorities considered their calling a shameful one. They act now as if they have a few more rights than respectable people."⁴⁴

The campaign continued into the fall, at least in the newspapers. Rooming-house operators who rented quarters to prostitutes off the reservation were threatened with arrest and prosecution,⁴⁵ but apparently arrests were few. In the following spring the *Herald* noted the lack of progress in a piece called "Our Shame." Girls from the tenderloin, said the story, are scattered all over the city. "On West Overland respectable citizens are forced to give up their homes or live in a neighborhood with . . . lewd women. It does no good to make complaint to the authorities as there seems no proof sufficient to satisfy a jury that these women come under the penalties of the ordinance of the city . . . until our people go to the polls determined to elect officers who consider it their duty to see that every law upon the statute books is enforced, there will be a general disregard of law by prostitutes and gamblers."⁴⁶

One symptom of the prevailing disease was the frequency of suicides. Despondent lovers, discouraged health-seekers, and depressed neurotics might be expected to do away with themselves as they do in other communities, but here the rate was certainly boosted by the presence of so much vice and sin. In February, 1894, the son of a Mexican millionaire killed himself. In March G. C.

Ford, with ten cents left in his pocket after several days of "dissipation," ended his problems with morphine.[47] With disturbing frequency young men who had sat too long at the gambling tables took the easy way out.

Symptomatic also was the nonchalance with which young men flaunted their vices in the faces of respectable citizens. The *Times* in the fall of 1894 printed a significant paragraph borrowed from another paper and entitled "Young Men and Prostitutes":

Several young men have been in the habit lately of buying reserved seats in the opera house and presenting them to prostitutes. It is bad enough for them to buy the seats for these women at all, but it is a thousand times worse when they take advantage of the management to purchase seats in parts of the house where they know full well these women are not allowed to sit. Several prostitutes occupied such seats on the night of "Charley's Aunt," and the managers are anxious for the public to understand how it occurred, and to know exactly where the blame should rest. Fallen women are not allowed in any seats in the opera house except from the third dress circle row back, and in the gallery. And if they impose upon the management again as they have been doing, they will have to occupy the gallery or not enter the house. And further than this, the name of the person who buys tickets for them in the wrong part of the house will be published. . . .[48]

It is probable that these developments had something to do with the high turnover rate in the mayor's office during the next few months. Mr. Austin became ill and could not serve out his term. He was replaced by Adolf Solomon, a dignified Jewish gentleman who carried on until the election of 1894. In April of that year a wholesale druggist named A. K. Albers was elected, arousing high hopes among the reformers. But although Mr. Albers chose to run, he did not choose to serve and resigned almost as soon as he had taken his oath. So the council appointed a successor, as they were charged to do, this being Robert F. Johnson, a wholesale liquor dealer.[49]

This set up another explosive situation. Bob Johnson was certainly poles away from the Law and Order League in his thinking, but the pressure from the Puritans was more than any wholesale liquor dealer should be asked to bear. Juan Hart and Will Burges and the preachers and the indignant housewives pressed the mayor so hard that he determined to enforce the anti-gambling laws. Burges went down to Del Rio in July and asked the district court for an injunction closing the Gem, the most frequented of the gambling halls. Before the month was out, the mayor had taken a firm stand and issued orders for closing the rest.[50]

Johnson waited to issue his proclamation until he was sure he had a man at the head of the police force who could handle the situation. This was Jeff Milton, a young fellow with a reputation in Arizona and Texas as a bandit tamer, who was working at the moment for the Pullman Company. On August 10, 1894, Milton took the oath of office and the slaughter began.[51]

To make it impossible for the mayor to fire Milton, Burges had him confirmed by the city council. The next morning Jeff went to work. According to his own story, he forced John Selman to stop mulcting the prostitutes. Then he got a list of all the gamblers in town and ran them out or put them in jail. He gave a public beating to the only gambler who dared to defy him. And when he caught Juan Hart and Charley Davis (top citizens and leading reformers) raising sand in George Look's Gem saloon, he sent them across the river to sober up.[52]

For a time the mayor's popularity seemed to be enhanced by his action. The ministerial union congratulated him and he was praised for what he had done "for the salvation of boys and the comfort of many a hard working wife."[53] Then the tide turned. A few months of reform was all the town could stand. Bob Johnson, fed up, resigned before his term was finished,[54] and when it was time to elect a new city government in the spring of that year, the demand for a clean city had weakened considerably. E. A. Shelton, a non-professional making his first and last excursion into politics, was the Law and Order League's candidate for mayor but he and his supporters talked more about municipal ownership of the water works than they did about gambling and prostitution.[55] The chief argument in Shelton's favor seemed to be the decency of his constituents and the indecency of his opponents. "Theirs is a campaign of boodle and beer," said the *Herald*, "which would not be tolerated by the class of people supporting Mr. Shelton."[56]

Robert Campbell, Shelton's opponent, was nauseated by all this respectability. "Oh, they are so pious," he sneered, speaking at the Republican rally the night before election. The Independents had accused him of playing poker. "As I was brought up," he countered, "it was the understanding that a gentleman wasn't fit for society unless he could play an average game of poker."[57] His audience seemed to share his point of view.

The regular Democrats were unable to put out a full slate of candidates for this election. Some of them, including Morehead and Magoffin, joined the Shelton forces. Others took the once unthinkable step of voting Republican. S. H. Newman, whose *Lone Star* had long since succumbed to pressure of one kind or another[58] but whose political influence remained strong, urged his fellow Democrats to cross the party line. "In this election there is no politics," he assured them. Morehead and Magoffin "promise us nothing but reversion to moss back rule."[59]

In a spirited finale Will Burges and the witty Dr. William Yandell addressed a mass meeting in the Plaza and marched with the McGinty Band in a torchlight procession, but the poker players still outnumbered the pious citizens and the conservatives won.[60] Campbell took over the mayor's office to the great relief of the sporting population.[61] One of his first acts was to fire Jeff Milton and install Ed Fink, whom Milton had dismissed from the force, as Chief of Police. Immediately the gamblers reopened for business and all was as before. John Wesley Hardin held up two games on successive nights, as we have noted, and began the last chapter of his career.

This was the darkness before dawn, but as usual the obscurity was dense and deep — so dense and deep that the Law and Order League petitioned the Governor to send more Rangers to help the Ysleta detachment and the local officers in the almost hopeless task of curbing vice and lawlessness.[62] Not content to depend on outside help, the League found a way, three months after the election, to catch the opposition off balance. Their weapon was the injunction. Their lawyers swore out a complaint in the district court at Del Rio, Texas, against the owners of two buildings which housed El Paso's biggest gambling saloons and persuaded Judge Gillis to forbid them to continue in business.[63] Twenty gamblers were enjoined from operating in these casinos.

The injunction was upheld after a legal battle,[64] but it proved to be ineffectual. You could not stop gambling in El Paso by stopping twenty gamblers, or by closing two saloons.

On the other hand things had gone so far that a setback could not stop the reformers, either, and a situation came along in 1896 which enabled them to flex their muscles with considerable effect. In the spring of that year El Paso was chosen as the site of a world's championship prizefight, and the impending horror of this brutal and degrading spectacle brought the reformers out in full cry.

There was considerable buildup to this situation, beginning back in 1892 when Bob Fitzsimmons, the red-headed, Cornish-born Australian blacksmith, knocked out Peter Maher, the dour champion of Ireland. Fitz's victory persuaded him that he was ready to take on Gentleman Jim Corbett, the champion of the world. Corbett was willing, and promoter Dan Stuart began to make arrangements to hold the match in Texas, one of the few states without an anti-prizefight law. Governor Culberson, however, called a special session of the state legislature and made prizefighting illegal in his territory. When Hot Springs, Arkansas, was chosen as a site for the brawl, the governor of that state had the fighters arrested when they crossed the boundary.

Corbett, who was not much excited about fighting anyway, now lost interest in his title and offered to vacate it in favor of the winner of a proposed match between Peter Maher and a heavyweight named O'Donnell. This contest was actually held, and Maher won. So Stuart had his buildup for a world's championship match and Fitzsimmons had his chance at the title. The big question, as before, was Where? A tentative arrangement in Florida fell through and the promoters were at their wits' end.[65]

While Stuart was engaged in fruitless pondering over this question, he was surprised by the arrival of a telegram from a group of El Paso businessmen offering him a six-thousand-dollar bonus if he would stage the fight in the El Paso vicinity. He accepted the offer.

Actually El Paso had much to recommend it under the circumstances. It was far from the parts of Texas infected by virtue. Mexico was just across a shallow watercourse. New Mexico was only a handful of miles away. Arizona could be reached overnight. By keeping the location of the fight secret until the last minute, Stuart could protect himself in some degree from injunctions and policemen and indignant citizens. He decided that Valentine's Day, February 14, 1896, would be a propitious date.

What happened after that was without example in all border history. Two months before The Day the forerunners of the sporting crowd began to arrive and the innkeepers and restaurateurs and saloon operators and madams got ready for an overflow crowd.

Fitzsimmons arrived on Christmas Day and set up training quarters in Juárez, where he boxed and jumped rope, rode his bicycle and wrestled with his pet lion.[66] Fitz was a friendly fellow and enjoyed being seen at the bullfight, at Noakes' blacksmith shop, at evening entertainments. Maher, when he finally arrived on January 11 from New York, was described as "quiet," by which the reporter meant "surly." He stayed in El Paso only two days and then went off to train at Las Cruces.[67]

On February 9 Promoter Stuart, a portly, polysyllabic man, stepped off the train exuding confidence. Many people were saying that the fight would never be held. Stuart called such opinions "malicious rot."[68]

In his heart, however, he well knew that he was playing a dangerous game which could make or break him, and he would be lucky if he ever got his men in a ring together. Nevertheless he went about the business of getting chairs, selling tickets, and building confidence. "Nothing short of lightning or the destruction of the earth by fire or flood can stop the contests," he told the newspapers, and went on to announce that he had arranged a "Fistic Carnival" which would last a week and bring prosperity to the border. The heavyweight match would be fought on February 14, the date announced, for a purse of $10,000. On the four days following, four other fights would be held, three of them for world's championships.[69]

The sideshows were almost as beguiling as the main tent. Half a dozen prime attractions were known to be en route to El Paso or already on the ground. John L. Sullivan and Paddy Ryan, with their theatrical troupe, were on the way. So was Señor José de Moreno of Spain, who was bringing six talented bullfighters from Madrid. A big "cowboy tournament" (ancestor of the rodeo) was in operation on the outskirts of town. A boy evangelist named Mysonheimer, with nine thousand converts to his credit, was battling sin nightly at the First Methodist Church. Dixon, Walcott, Everhart, Leeds and other famous fighters scheduled to take part in the Fistic Carnival began arriving. Bat Masterson, self important and full of sporting information, came in and regaled the reporters with his opinions. Even Science was represented, for Thomas A. Edison's Kinetoscope (forty pictures a minute for two hundred minutes) was to record the big fight for posterity.[70]

As time went on, however, Stuart's difficulties increased. Captain Hughes of the Rangers, quartered at Ysleta, received instructions from Austin to be on the lookout for violations of the anti-prizefight law, and to make sure that there were no slip-ups. Adjutant General Mabry arrived in person with reinforcements. The Governor of Arizona alerted the state militia in case the fighters came to his state, and Governor Ahumada of Chihuahua brought 150 cavalrymen to Juárez to keep Stuart out of Mexico.

These threats Stuart might have weathered, for he was a resourceful man, but he had against him a far mightier force than governors and militia, namely the united ministry of El Paso led by L. R. Millican of the First Baptist Church. Early in Stuart's campaign members of the ministerial alliance had attacked boxing as primitive and brutal and unrefined. Stuart had not bothered to answer them in person, but had turned the job over to his secretary, W. K. Wheelock, who informed the world, including El Paso, that boxing might have been brutal once but was so no longer. "There is nothing," he declared, "that occurs in the present glove contests that would bring a flush to the cheek of the most refined lady in the land. . . . I do not make the comparison with either base ball, foot ball, or polo, as they are so brutal and dangerous that a comparison would not be fair. This opposition is simply a fad, born of ignorance or a desire for notoriety. . . . More physical culture and less six shooter is my idea."[71]

This tongue-in-cheek defense served only to irritate the ministers, who published a reply in the *Herald* for January 17. "Did not Fitzsimmons kill his trainer in New York City while simply training?" they asked. "We are convinced . . . that it is a brutal relic of barbarism, disgraceful to a civilized nation."[72]

The card was signed by only four men: A. Hoffman of the First Methodist Church, L. R. Millican of the First Baptist Church, E. R. Hallam of the Christian Church, and C. J. Oxley of Trinity Methodist, but the ministers' union and most of the church members were behind them. Sunday, January 26, was mostly devoted to boxing in the El Paso churches. Mr. Millican told his congregation at the Baptist Church that he had been in Baltimore lately and learned that El Paso "had such a bad name that Eastern people were under the delusion that it was not safe to pass through." The implication was that if the prize fights came off, the people in the East would be correct in their assumptions.

The ministers had some good practical ideas along with their emotional reactions. They were sure that Stuart meant to stage his fights somewhere in New Mexico and they made contact with Governor Thornton, who told them, "I will do all I can to keep this disgrace from being visited upon the territory."[73] Unfortunately there was no anti-prizefight law in New Mexico and he was powerless, or at least he said he was.

The ministers would not take his no for an answer. On February 4 they wired to Congressman Cockrell in Washington: "Undoubtedly prize fights in New Mexico, neither territorial law nor federal law prohibiting. Can't Congress prohibit immediately?"

Congress, under pressure from Delegate Tom Catron, could and did, and the President signed the measure into law.

Now it was the turn of the churches to feel pressure. Mr. Millican let it be known that his life had been threatened and that there was talk about "starving the preachers out." Members who saw no more than a business opportunity in the Fistic Carnival took their names off the church rolls and withdrew their financial support. "Let them starve [us]," said the Reverend Mr. Oxley from his pulpit. "I can live on cornbread and water, if it is necessary."

When the city council passed a resolution censuring Governor Culberson for passing the anti-prizefight law, the ministers union passed a resolution criticizing the council for criticizing the Governor and went on to point out that prizefighting was only a symptom. Business houses and saloons were violating the law by staying open all day Sunday. Games and races were charging admission on the Sabbath. Gambling houses were running day and night. The authorities were conniving at "shameless prostitution in the heart of the city."

Whether the ministers knew it or not, El Paso was coming around to their point of view. "The town is full of tin horns and busted sports, and more are coming," said the *Herald*. We were learning the hard way that being a big-time sports center has its drawbacks.[74]

On the morning of the fourteenth Stuart announced that the fight had been postponed. Peter Maher had got some Las Cruces dust in his eyes and couldn't see. That broke up the great Fistic Carnival. The pugs and their camp followers began to pack up and move out. Stuart said the fight would take place on the twenty-first, but not many people believed him, and probably even Stuart had no idea what to do next.

Three days before the deadline a way opened. Old Roy Bean, the Law West of the Pecos, kept Stuart's defeat from becoming a rout by inviting him to bring his boys to Langtry. Stuart agreed to come.

It is one of the well-known facts of boxing history that Maher and Fitzsimmons actually met in a ring set up on the Mexican side of the Rio Grande 400 miles southeast of El Paso, and that some 300 fans, plus the Ranger force watching from the top of the bluffs, saw Fitzsimmons knock Maher out in the first round after something less than two minutes of fighting. The peace which descended at that moment on West Texas was more than welcome, and although non-Methodists continued for some time to twit the Reverend Mr. Oxley about his cornbread diet, most of our citizens were glad to forget the whole sorry business and start putting the town back together.[75]

In those days the reformers seemed able to win only temporary victories. Two months after Peter Maher's defeat they lost out in the county elections,[76] and in the municipal election the following year they lost again. This time Republicans and Democrats were fighting it out on party lines with John O'Keefe and Joseph Magoffin as standard bearers. Magoffin became mayor in 1897.

The Independents, who had been so hot for reform in 1893 and 1895, were not heard from in this election. When the Republicans showed signs of life, the Democrats always closed ranks and tended to forget their differences. Magoffin's majority was only twenty-nine votes out of the 1351 cast, but he won. Only one Republican, O. E. Scott, became an alderman, and his success was probably due to the fact that George Look, the Democratic candidate, was so closely identified with the early-day liquor-and-gambling business. The rest were all Democrats and non-reformers, if not anti-reformers.[77]

The demand for a cleanup, however, was slowly growing. A

newcomer from Washington named H. D. Slater was now conducting the affairs of the *Herald* and demanding that the prostitutes be kept off the street. "Our miserable mayor," he fumed, "fails to stop this gross abuse. A few days ago the Herald was reliably informed that a petition had been presented to Mayor Magoffin by a large body of women requesting that prostitutes be kept off the public streets during the day. It was supposed that the petition would have its desired effect, but on Sunday there were hack loads of them gaudily dressed parading the main streets."[78] In the editor's view, Mayor Magoffin was worse than useless.

Mr. Slater's sentiments, however, were not shared by the majority of his fellow townsmen, for Magoffin was reelected in 1899 by a much larger and safer majority than in 1897.[79] The Republicans made no effort to beat him. In fact, they were through as an effective opposition party for many years.

This left the way clear for the reform-minded Democrats to go into action once more and in 1901 they did so, though not with the old dash and drive. The contest in that year was between safe, unspectacular Richard Caples and good, inoffensive B. F. Hammett. In a particularly quiet election[80] Mr. Hammett, bearded and benevolent, came out on top and went on to conduct a quiet administration. Supposedly reform oriented, Hammett aimed a few light blows at the sporting people but caused them no serious trouble. His object was to get them out of sight — not to close them up. In May of 1902 he told the gamblers that they would have to move upstairs, and at the same time he informed the saloon keepers that their front doors would have to be closed all day Sunday.[81] Even these mild measures were offensive to El Paso businessmen, who missed the "Sunday money" that was going to Juárez. No more was heard from the mayor,[82] and the reformers decided that the time had come to do or die. In that spirit they approached the campaign of 1903.

The reform candidate was no less a figure than the much-respected and beloved former sheriff James H. White, firm and fearless, high principled and persuasive. He was the man who had talked the embattled Republicans out of their last-ditch stand in the city hall in 1889. He had been on the side of the reformers ever since. If anybody could throw the mossbacks out, he was the man.

Such a challenge brought out the ultimate resistance of the traditionalists in the Democratic Party, and White's opponent in the elections turned out to be Charles R. Morehead himself. Morehead hated publicity and contention and liked to work behind the scenes. He had manipulated the city's affairs from his office in the State National Bank for at least twenty years. It was with great reluctance that he appeared at the head of his forces.

Vice was not the paramount issue and never had been, as far as he was concerned. What he stood for was municipal ownership of the water works. The reformers, however, would not limit themselves to Mr. Morehead's favorite subjects for debate. From the very first they discussed gambling, drinking, and disorderly women. And the language they used was like nothing ever heard before on the banks of the Rio Grande.

The rally in the Plaza the night before election was conducted by a wildly cheering crowd and a series of passionate orators. All the reformers were there — Slater, the editor; James A. Dick, merchant; R. C. Walsh, attorney; the Burges brothers; and several hundred more. Waters Davis, two hundred pounds of thunder and lightning, declared that El Paso was going to stop being a wide-open town. At the end he told the story of the traveling salesman who received a wire from home: "Your mother-in-law is dead. Shall we bury or cremate?" The salesman wired back, "Take no chances. Do both!"

"That," promised Davis, "is what we are going to do to gambling in this town."

Will Burges was the only man present who could dig deeper than that, and he did. Billy Bridgers reports what he said:

The question is whether or not the honest men who have administered the affairs of this county for the past two years are going to administer them for another two years, or whether we will revert to that state when the violation of every law was looked upon as a matter of right; whether we are going to have in power men who are willing to fight under the banner of Tom Powers [of the Coney Island Saloon] and a man who answers to the euphonious appellation of Barrel House Steve.

You might believe from reading the Afternoon Assassin that no promises have been made by the candidates on that ticket to Tom Powers and his people. J. F. Mitchim has turned his paper loose for the purpose of vilifying and reviling every man who stands for honest government. He holds up his hands reeking with the blood of young Harrell, shot down in cold blood at night, and he knows it. If there was ever a man who would want a county attorney or district attorney that would not prosecute, Mitchim is that man.

Burges paused for a moment while this sank in. Mitchim was the editor of the *News,* a non-reformer who had tried to steal the reformers' thunder by sending a photographer down to the red-light district to see what he could catch. He caught Harrell, a young employee on the *News* advertising staff, relaxing at a dance hall. Harrell told Mitchim he would kill him if he ran the picture. Mitchim shot him, and was acquitted some months later on a charge of murder. To this dangerous man Burges was now paying his respects.

"My real objection to Mitchim," he concluded, "is esthetic rather than moral — an official libeler and cowardly assassin who would look better if his neck were three inches longer."[83]

There was an instant of dead silence as the crowd digested the implications of this statement. Then the cheering broke out louder than ever.

Next day the reformers stormed the polls, full of hope and confidence. And again the fundamental political fact was demonstrated: enthusiasm is no match for organization. Morehead was in, and it looked like two more years of prosperity for the sporting crowd.

It would not be fair to imply that Morehead and his friends were on the side of lawlessness or that they were foes of good government. A great many good people believed in Morehead's dedication to the welfare of his city and in the validity of his ideas of what could and what could not be done for and in the town. These people thought of the reformers as wild-eyed idealists touched with exhibitionism, people who wanted change for the sake of change. They questioned the frankness of some of them. Maury Kemp, who was a Morehead man, used to growl when these matters were recalled: "Our side was no worse than the other. The Burgeses and the Coldwells were not so lily-white either."[84] And as a matter of fact, there were some tough, practical politicians on both sides. In this very election both parties brought "hordes" of voters in from the Mexican side of the river and voted them. Conscience yielded to cash, as usual.[85] Reform lost again.

It seemed this time, however, that a defeat was what the reformers needed, for they went to work as never before to get ready for the next round. Richard Burges and Waters Davis organized a

Citizens' Reform League and started a publicity campaign against the gamblers. They pointed out that there were in the city 600 men who made their living at the gambling tables—that there were forty licensed gambling halls—and that as much as $29,000,000 passed across the tables every year.[86] They bore down on the fringe evils that accompanied gambling, the cheats and tinhorns and con men who formed the lowest stratum of the sporting fraternity. They talked about the money these people took in, to the great detriment of legitimate enterprise. They demanded action and they raised money — $7,500 — to keep the battle going.

Those who argued on the other side made only a feeble showing. Chief of police Wooten's defense of bunco men sounded particularly hollow. "The bunco men get money from strangers that might not otherwise be left here," he declared, "and the money is put into circulation in this city, thus adding to the general prosperity."[87]

The constant pressure had its effect, sooner, perhaps, than the reformers expected. A year after his election, Morehead began showing signs of a change of heart. In September, 1904, the talk went round that he meant to close the gambling houses down.[88] Morehead issued a public denial, and gossip said the gamblers had told him he had better.[89]

Now began a game of political cat and mouse as the people and the newspapers tried to find out what was going on while Morehead stayed behind the scenes and said nothing for publication. The day after the mayor's denial of any intention to interfere with the status quo, Alderman Harry Charman, interviewed in his cigar store, told a reporter that the cribs and gambling houses on Utah Street had been told they must close, but that no cleanup would be attempted in the rest of the city. No new licenses for gambling, however, were to be issued.

Charman was quite sure the cleanup was undesirable, and furthermore, that it would not work. "We are not trying to make a Sunday school out of El Paso," he said.[90]

The mayor said nothing, but the places on Utah Street remained open.

Police Chief Wooten was the first to crack under the strain. On October 5 he resigned. On October 19 the Citizens' League assembled and presented a petition calling for the end of open gambling. One thousand men signed it.

One week later Florence J. Hall became the new chief of police, and when he was interviewed, he said he thought the mayor meant to limit gambling. The mayor, as usual, said nothing.

Another mass meeting was called to order on November 10 in the open-air theatre and pavilion across from City Hall. So many people attended that they could not all get in and many had to stand outside on the sidewalks. The consensus of the meeting was that gambling had to go.

Next morning a committee called on the mayor and put the question to him point blank: Was it or was it not true, as they had heard, that he was going to put the gamblers "upstairs"? Morehead said he had made no such statement. "There are more liars in El Paso than in any other place I ever saw," he snapped.[91]

The Citizens' Reform League rejected this sort of trifling. Over 1,300 of the members by now had signed the petition calling for enforcement of the anti-gambling laws and had presented it to Sheriff J. H. Boone. After some preliminary shuffling, Boone said that he would indeed enforce the law.[92]

This can only mean that the Morehead forces had yielded to pressure. Virtue was being forced upon them. Their real sentiments were betrayed during a council meeting when the aldermen discussed raising taxes to make up for the loss of revenue from the gamblers and the madams. Nevertheless in mid-November the order went out to close the houses down. And at three A. M., when the graveyard shift was supposed to go on in the all-night gambling saloons, they closed.

The mayor moved next against the dance halls in the red-light district and closed them too, to the surprise of almost everybody but Mr. Morehead, who seemed anxious to make up for all his years of inactivity by getting rid of all the vice at once.

The closing order brought El Paso to one of its most memorable nights, the evening of Saturday, November 19, 1904. Everybody thought it was the end of the tenderloin. A wave of nostalgic regret swept through the district, and on the last evening crowds of boozy sentimentalists went from house to house saying goodbye. The next day the exodus began. The gamblers mostly moved to Juárez. The girls scattered out to other towns less hagridden by virtue.

The sporting crowd did not give up without at least talking a fight. Will Burges used to tell how a leading gambler came to him at the height of the tension and told him that the end of gambling would be the end of Will Burges. Will sat in his office all day, his pistol in a drawer within easy reach, but the gambler made no attempt to carry out his threat.

"The reason," said Richard Burges to the writer of these pages, "was that he knew I would be after him in about twenty minutes with a 30-30 rifle."

As the years have separated us from the early stages of the reform period, there has been a tendency to give Mr. Morehead credit for beginning the cleanup. "He first issued an order closing the dance halls," says Owen White, "and next handed the gamblers their passports and told them to 'git.' They got."[93]

It is possible that Mr. Morehead, who never commented publicly on his motives during these historic times, was willing to join the reform movement when he saw that the town wanted it and that it had a chance to succeed. What happened in the days after the closing, however, makes one suspect that the mayor's plans were much more deeply laid than most people imagined. Sheriff Boone informed the city, through the columns of the *Times,* that if he was expected to enforce the laws, he was going to enforce all of them. And he printed the sections of the Texas "Blue Laws" which were still in force and as valid, legally, as the anti-gambling ordinances. All commerce would have to cease. Even bootblacks and cigar stores were forbidden to do business. There would be no performances on Sunday at the Myar Opera House. El Paso wanted law and order, and El Paso was going to get law and order.

The sheriff carried his campaign to ridiculous lengths, as Mr. Morehead no doubt intended that he should. He told the brewery and the smelter that Sunday closing applied to them too, and he actually arrested the smelter employees for working on the Sabbath. The climax came when the word went out that a group of citizens who had participated in the time-honored rite of a turkey shoot (on a Tuesday) were to be arrested for violating the anti-gambling laws.[94]

It did not take long for Mr. Morehead to make his point. The citizens squirmed when papers all over the West — San Francisco, Saint Louis, Denver — took note with sneering incredulity of El Paso's "moral spasm" and wondered how long it would last. More galling still was the painful truth that nobody stopped drinking just because the saloons were closed. The crowd simply moved to Juárez. On Sunday, November 20, the day after the houses on Utah Street turned off the lights, 4,429 people crossed the international bridge.

That did it. The *Times* on the following Wednesday morning printed a letter signed by six well-known businessmen concluding with these words: ". . . we believe that carrying out the prohibitory laws on the statute books of the state would ruin any business community, especially with Juárez across the river." They asked to have their names taken off the Citizens' League petition which had triggered the whole catastrophe.

For three weeks and no more the town endured its ordeal of righteousness. The turning point came on Sunday the third of December when a venturesome saloonkeeper named Max Miller kept his Legal Tender bar open and gave the sheriff and his deputies all the evidence they wanted. In justice court the next day, a jury said that Mr. Miller had not broken the law. Immediately the bars began to open again on Sundays, and shortly afterward the gamblers came back. This time, however, they voluntarily removed themselves from public view. The Wigwam and the Astor House built outside stairways to their second-story rooms, and gamblers and equipment moved upstairs.[95]

When Sheriff Boone, urged on by the Citizens' League, began a series of systematic arrests and prosecutions, he was defeated by the juries, often composed of hangers-on around the courthouse, who just as systematically turned the prisoners loose.[96]

The end was not reached until Will Burges and T. A. Falvey went to Austin and managed to get legislative support for a law which would make it possible to enjoin any property owner from using his building for the purpose of gambling. The law was passed and tested in other cities. When it stood up, the gamblers were through as an open, organized group in El Paso.[97]

The change, of course, was more ideal than real, and what actually happened was that for a short time vice went underground. Four months after election, as Jack Vowell points out, "slot machines were creeping back into the bars and back rooms of the saloons and sporting houses."[98] These gambling devices showed clearly enough that the reformers could not keep their foothold, and although the mayor got rid of the slot machines, he could not get rid of the indifference and laxity which encouraged the Old Guard to take a new grip on the town.

The Old Guard, we need to remember, included some very good people who believed that the Democratic Party was the party of progress and enlightenment and that the Republicans and reformers were lesser breeds without the law. They were convinced that Mr. Morehead was a bulwark of good sense and civic responsibility holding back the tide of new-fangled progressivism and irrational efforts at moral uplift. These people were temporarily—only temporarily—out of power in 1905, but they never lost heart or stopped trying and they had two emerging leaders ready to leap into the fight. These were C. E. Kelly and County Judge Joseph U. Sweeney, good friends who saw eye to eye in political matters and despised the reformers.

A small but dynamic man with sandy red hair, a sanguine complexion and a rugged Irish face, Kelly (known for some reason as "Henry" or "Uncle Henry") dominated El Paso civic history for the next ten years and deserves a page to himself. Grandson of an Irish immigrant and son of a Civil War private on the side of the South, Kelly grew up in Mississippi during the dark days of Reconstruction. His educational opportunities were limited but he was shrewd, intelligent, and had a remarkable memory which he put to good use in the study of pharmacy. He came west in 1883 when his health broke, lived on a ranch till he was able to go back to work, and started putting up prescriptions in the old Rio Grande pharmacy. In 1887 he went into business for himself, and in 1893 he joined J. H. Pollard in a retail drug business. He was married in 1897 to Willie Word, a Mississippi girl who was to become one of El Paso's great ladies and the mother of a remarkable group of sisters.[99]

The drug business kept C. E. Kelly going, but politics was his life. His active career began in 1902 when he became city treasurer, an office which he held until he became mayor in 1910. The treasurer's post was an ideal one for him. He controlled the financial life blood of the body politic and was able to build a political machine which was known for a dozen years or so as "The Ring," a machine which in its day was responsible, resourceful, ruthless, and unbeatable.

PRESIDENT TAFT *and* PRESIDENT DIAZ, *Juarez Customhouse, 1909*
[Aultman Collection]

Dedication of the Juarez Monument, 1909
[Aultman Collection]

Program and Menu, Annual Banquet of the Toltec Club, 1909
[Jane Burges Perrenot]

Peter Gustat and the Symphony Orchestra, 1919
[El Paso Musicians Union]

The dream of Pete Kern, archway at the entrance to Kern Place
[Aultman Collection]

The Border Wheelmen, Late 1880's
[Aultman Collection]

The El Paso Browns, 1887, Give-a-Damn Jones, Manager
Top Row: Hart, Kelly, Edwards, Davis, Beneke, Greenland, Hawley
Bottom Row: Cook, Jones, Spencer
[George Simpson]

Tournament Team, El Paso Fire Department, 1891
Top Row: Fred Edelsten, Dauterman, Weesey Lyons, W. C. McGown, C. C. Kiefer, Peyton Edwards, Red Herbert, George Flory (below) John Julian. Bottom Row: B. Tackaberry, M. B. Proctor, Dr. Herbert Stevenson, Tom Robinson, Jim Conklyn, John Whitaker. In Front: Felix, shine boy and mascot   [El Paso Fire Department]

First El Paso Football Team, featuring Bob Fitzsimmons
[Aultman Collection]

Tillie Howard's Residence on San Antonio Street

Tillie's Parlor House on Utah (South Mesa) street
[Colonel Walter Stevenson]

TILLIE HOWARD *and her horse Rowdy*
[Colonel Walter Stevenson]

The Parlor Saloon, George Ogden in Dark Coat
Insert: George and Canine Friends
[Colonel Walter Stevenson]

The Gem Bar, second location, July 11, 1914
Insert: George Look, Proprietor
[Aultman Collection; Mrs. Lee Gibson]

El Paso and San Antonio Streets, 1910
Clearing for West San Antonio under way
[Aultman Collection]

Mrs. Buckler's House Party, 1898

Standing: Mrs. E. V. Berrien, Mrs. A. G. Wilcox, Mrs. J. A. Eddy, Mrs. John Dean, Mrs. Moses Dillon, Mrs. Oscar Baum, Mrs. Max Weber, Mrs. Will Race, Mrs. U. S. Stewart, Mrs. S. T. Turner, Hattie Race Blumenthal. Seated: Miss Kate Hague, Mrs. J. Wk's, Mrs. Lyand Moreffer, Miss Lillian Hagne, Mrs. C. N. Buckler, Mrs. Jack Hanner, unidentified,

Mrs. Gist's Boarders, the El Paso Bachelor's Club

Top Row: Foley Woods, Lewis M. (Manny) Turner, J. H. (Pete) Adams, M. H. Webb. Bottom Row: James A. Murdock, Rupert Moore, Harry Flato, C. E. (Henry) Kelly, Frank S. Ainsa. [Aultman Collection]

The Coney Island Saloon and the Sheldon Hotel
[Aultman Collection]

JOHN WESLEY HARDIN
as he looked in 1895
[Mercaldo Archive]

BEULAH MOROSE *and child*
[E. D. Spellman]

JOHN SELMAN
Gunman and Peace Officer
[Leon Metz]

Rangers in El Paso in 1896
Front Row: Adjutant General W. H. Mabry; Captains John R. Hughes, J. A. Brooks,
Bill McDonald, and J. H. Rogers   [Aultman Collection]

The El Paso Police Department in 1897
Standing: George Cole, Pat Dwyer, Bob Roos, Joe Rogers, Frank Winkler, John
Denniston, Carl Schmidt. Sitting: George Herold, Captain Tom Bendy, Chief Con
Lockhart, Mannen Clements, Juan Franco.
[J. H. Daross and El Paso Police Department]

Revolutionary Leaders, Juarez, 1911
José de la Luz Soto, Francisco I. Madero, Jr., Abraham Gonzalez, and Eduardo Hay
[Aultman Collection]

The Battle of Juarez begins, May 7, 1911
Revolutionary troops start down the dry ditch
[Aultman Collection]

Insurrecto Camp opposite the Smelter, March, 1911
[Aultman Collection]

ᴀꜱᴄᴜᴀʟ Oʀᴏᴢᴄᴏ *and* Dʀ. I. J. Bᴜꜱʜ
in consultation
[Aultman Collection]

Negotiators at Peace Grove, May, 1911
Norman Walker (a reporter), Pino Suarez, Francisco Carbajal, Dr. Francisco Vázquez Gómez
[Aultman Collection]

The Mutiny against Madero, May 1911
(Villa and Orozco are inside)
[Aultman Collection]

Pancho Villa and Pascual Orozco (at table)
in the Elite Confectionery, 1911
[Aultman Collection]

Let us admit at once that Boss Kelly was scrupulous in his handling of public money. Reports were always available on expenditures and collections, and nobody could say truthfully that the people's resources were spent on buying votes. But machines do not run without cash, and Kelly managed to find it. Old-time city employees will tell you that they kicked back part of their salaries to finance operations (we would say now that they contributed to the campaign fund) and expected to do so when they accepted their jobs. Kelly himself was not interested in either wealth or the trappings of office. What he wanted was power, and he preferred to exercise it quietly and effectively from behind the scenes. When you ask an old timer if Kelly was ever to his knowledge unethical, he is apt to reply, "No, he wasn't crooked. He was practical — just practical."[100]

Undoubtedly Kelly was convinced that his tactics were the only way to get the results he wanted, and it must be admitted that many of the results he wanted were for the good of his town. As early as 1892 he began to work for municipal ownership of the water works, though the transfer of title was not consummated until 1910. He pressed for lowering of the Southern Pacific tracks, which bisected the city and blocked traffic often enough to qualify as a nuisance.

In smaller ways he ran the town in patriarchal fashion, especially when his Irish temper was up. Louis LeVeaux, his friend and supporter, remembers the time when Stone and Webster, who supplied the town with electricity after 1902, distributed current through a complex of wires which came together at the top of a pole near the Union Depot. Two men were electrocuted here. After the second death, Kelly called Superintendent Potter at the power plant and asked him how many more people he was going to kill. "I want that pole out of there," he said.

Mr. Potter replied that he was willing but he would have to consult Stone and Webster.

"Stone and Webster are not running this town," said Kelly. "I am. And if that pole is not out of there by six o'clock tonight, I am coming with an axe and chop it down."

Well knowing that Mayor Kelly meant what he said, Mr. Potter had the pole out long before the deadline.[101]

The list of advances made during C. E. Kelly's reign is a long one: paving, sewers, fire protection, the School of Mines (now The University of Texas at El Paso), the Scenic Drive, and a hundred other forward-looking projects were conceived during Kelly's days in power or in office. But he ran his show his own way and he believed in controlling rather than suppressing vice. Naturally the reformers thought he was non-progressive and unscrupulous. In some ways he probably was, but certainly not in all.

This was the man who took charge in 1905, and he was more than impatient with the traditional Democratic leadership—Joseph Magoffin and C. R. Morehead and the rest. In his view they had shown fatal weakness in allowing the reformers to take over, and it was time to send them out to pasture.

The result was a division in the High Command of the Democratic Party. Morehead was on one side, supported by many of the old timers and served by his own machine with the two Dwyer brothers, Jim and Sam, as his strong boys. Kelly and his streamlined political organization occupied the other. Bad blood developed, and after a while there was shooting. In a mob scene at the Coney Island saloon on the evening of November 8, 1905, the two parties fell upon each other. In the course of events Jim Dwyer shot and wounded a visiting outsider, a brother-in-law of Alderman Grant, and got well beaten for his pains.[102] Although the factions appeared to patch up their differences, especially when the Republicans, hopeful of a rebirth, staged their state convention in El Paso in 1905,[103] the feeling persisted.

The tension showed in various eruptions of emotion, for instance the outbreak in a city council meeting on January 7 when the matter of paving El Paso's streets was being debated. Major W. J. Fewel was a passionate advocate of street improvement and had acquired considerable information about paving by visiting other and better-paved cities. In the course of the discussion tempers flared and Mayor Davis and Alderman Fewel had a falling out "amounting almost to a personal encounter," according to the Times.[104]

Meanwhile the reformers had shot their last bolt in the form of a new city charter, drawn up by Richard Burges and approved by the Legislature in February, 1907.[105] Ward politics were abolished by this new instrument and councilmen were elected at large by the voters. This much accomplished, the reform party signed its own death warrant by dividing its already weakened ranks. A nonpartisan ticket announced for the next city election, splitting the Independent vote, and clearing the way for C. E. Kelly's friend Judge Joseph U. Sweeney to become mayor in the election of 1907.

Sweeney was a powerful leader, a dynamic personality, and a man of great public spirit. He had an Irish temper, however, which was eventually to take him out of politics, and his opponents accused him of relying on the traditional political methods which had determined the course of events in El Paso for so long. To make sure of his election, says Jack Vowell, Sweeney's supporters "merely took their poll taxes from the safes of their saloons and sporting houses and marched their . . . imported Juárez voters to the polls."[106]

Sweeney was in by a comfortable majority and the reformers were out once more, but Morehead's men were no longer in the center of the picture. Pat and Sam Dwyer were in trouble again as a result of a shooting in Pete Adam's Lobby saloon on May 2, 1907. Special Officer John L. Taylor was shot in the back of the head and died instantly. Joseph Magoffin, uncle of the Dwyer boys, hired the best legal talent to defend them and they were exonerated, but the affair was a serious blow to their party.[107]

Mayor Sweeney tried to satisfy the reformers without rocking the boat too much. He ordered gambling to cease, but took no positive steps to stop it. He closed the front doors of the saloons on Sunday but the back doors opened for business as usual.[108] It was a help, of course, to get the ungodly off the sidewalks when the righteous were on their way to church.

In this atmosphere of compromise and tolerance events rocked along until September of 1907, when District Judge James Goggin resigned and it became necessary to name a successor. Kelly and Sweeney wanted Maury Kemp appointed. Morehead wanted somebody else. Kelly and Sweeney won, and thereby removed the last vestiges of opposition within their own party.[109] They clinched their supremacy at the next county election[110] and reelected Sweeney as mayor in 1909.

During all this time Mayor Sweeney forged ahead on many fronts. He set up machinery for studying and settling the vexed question of municipal ownership of the water works, labored to extend and improve the street-railway system, paved miles and miles of streets, put the electric wires underground, and raised teachers' salaries. Meanwhile gambling and prostitution were tolerated, regulated, and made to pay part of the expenses of the city government.

The water problem finally proved to be too much for Sweeney to endure. He himself was opposed to putting the city in hock in order to buy out the water company, but some of the town's most influential citizens were against him, including the editors of both papers. When the company got in difficulties and wanted to raise rates, something had to be done. Sweeney appointed a committee to make recommendations and as a result elections were scheduled, first in October and then in November, to determine the will of the people on the question of municipal ownership. Both elections were called off because one side or the other wanted more time to present its case. The last straw was laid on the mayor's back when his committee turned against him and accused him of "nullifying" their work. Much exasperated, he began to think about leaving the frustrations of his office behind. At this time Mr. Sweeney was still a bridegroom, having married Miss Nell Humphreys a few months before. He had promised her that he would get out of politics with all convenient speed, and it seemed to him that the time might as well be now. On January 19, 1910, he announced his intention of resigning no later than the following April, and in April he stepped out.[111]

His successor, W. F. Robinson, was killed by a falling wall during a fire on August 14, 1910. The Council appointed C. E. Kelly to fill out the term.[112] He was no more in control than he had been before, but he was out in the open.

One thing you could say for Mayor Kelly — he kept things quiet. His reelection in 1911, in spite of vigorous opposition, was at least partly due to his handling of the explosive situations created by the revolution in Mexico. The exit of gamblers to Juárez when the race track opened in 1909 quieted the town to some extent, but this blessing was more than counterbalanced by the appearance on the scene of Francisco Madero and Pancho Villa. Two battles were fought only a few feet away from American soil. El Paso was jammed with plotting revolutionists, *porfiristas* in exile, refugee Mormons from the colonies in Chihuahua. Some American lives were lost and many more were in danger. During this troubled time Mayor Kelly kept a firm grip on the reins and allowed no trouble to start. When Villa appeared at the Sheldon hotel, bearing pistols, and announced that he was going to shoot Giuseppe Garibaldi, grandson of the Italian liberator and leader of a group of foreigners in the revolutionary army, the mayor did not send police. He appeared in person at the hotel and told Pancho to put up his guns and go home. Pancho did. Exploits like that convinced the voters that it would be unwise to change mayors in midstream.[113]

Gambling and prostitution still flourished, however, and even though the gamblers and the girls were kept well in hand, the reformers felt that their victory of a few years before had been nullified and their cause betrayed. "If we have to fight the fight all over again," said Slater of the *Herald* with understandable bitterness, "let's go to it. We can't start any sooner."[114]

To prepare for the campaign of 1913, the reformers began to gather evidence. The grand jury, headed by J. C. Wilmarth of the *Herald* with the full support of his editor, sent undercover workers to look into the conduct of the city's vice. Investigations began in the summer of 1912, but the big push came in March and April, 1913, just before election. Operatives, both male and female, moved into the district and found that beer was being sold in violation of the law in all the houses and cribs; that everybody in business there hoped for the triumph of the "Ring" in the election. The number of night-life women operating on Utah Street was given as 367, and the report was that the demand for girls exceeded the supply.[115]

In spite of all this undercover activity, no attempt was made in 1913 to challenge or expose the Ring. Probably the reformers did not feel ready to make a real battle of it. Their hunch was correct, for the Kelly administration was returned to office by a large majority. By 1915, however, the time for a massive effort seemed to have come, and the reformers made it.

Kelly was opposed at the primary election by a rising young attorney named Tom Lea, one of the great characters in our history. An exceptional trial lawyer, he combined a fine oratorical talent with deep emotional involvement in whatever cause he was working for. He would shed genuine tears before a jury in a murder trial. Young and persuasive, he was irresistible to the voters, Mexican and Anglo alike.

A combination of overconfidence and Tom Lea was too much for Mayor Kelly. He was heard to say during his last term in office that he could be mayor for the rest of his life if he wanted to. He didn't even bother to campaign during the election of 1915 until he saw himself in danger, and then it was too late.[116] He promised to push the project for a scenic drive above the city around the nose of Mount Franklin and to improve the streets in south El Paso. He pointed to his accomplishments: lower fire rates, municipal ownership of the water works, miles of paved streets, park improvement, and reduced rates for garbage collection.

It was not enough. Slater was belaboring him in the *Herald* every day for tolerating and even exploiting vice. And Tom Lea was promising the voters all the improvements Kelly stood for, plus equalization of taxes and a clean, businesslike administration.

Lea held his final rally in a skating rink because the Ring had taken pains to engage every other place of assembly. He spoke for an hour to a crowd which grew more enthusiastic by the minute.[117] The next day his supporters swamped the polls in the largest turnout of voters ever seen in the city and sent Lea to the mayor's chair by a vote of 4,218 to 3,149.[118]

The new mayor moved cautiously, but he moved. His first step, taken on May 5, 1915, was to put an end to the practice of collecting fines from prostitutes. He was resolved, he said, not to conduct his administration "with the blood money of these unfortunate women."[119] By the end of the year he was ready to close the red-light district, and the order was given. Frank Spence and Fred Fenchler, owners of tenderloin real estate, asked for legal redress, took their case to the supreme court on appeal, and lost when Justice Hawkins wrote an opinion that a city operating under a special charter could not legally designate a restricted area.[120]

Still cautious, Mayor Lea did not close the district. He just moved it. The council obliged him on January 15, 1916, by shifting it as far as possible from the heart of town — to a block close to the river between Eighth and Ninth streets. The madams and their girls were given until March 1 to move.[121]

Meanwhile the Law and Order people, now assembling as the Good Government Club, were thankful for this sign of progress but were unwilling to relax or slow down. They knew what could happen, and what would happen if they went to sleep. Ex-Mayor Kelly talked seriously once or twice of making a comeback.[122] Troops sent to the border to watch or chase Villa attracted vultures of both sexes. It seemed impossible to eliminate vice entirely, but the battle went on. Almost as soon as the new district opened, there was a movement to close it. Dr. Paul Gallagher presided over a large and enthusiastic meeting at the Chamber of Commerce. Reverend Miles Hanson of the First Congregational Church made the first speech. Again the good people of the town were on the move, determined once more to clean the place up. This time they presented a petition to the grand jury asking that the vice district be closed by injunction.[123] Their efforts came to nothing and the district stayed open, but they and their successors kept on trying to make El Paso a decent town.

They never succeeded entirely. Cleaning up a city is a chore that can never be completed, but there has been progress. We are a long way from the wide-open days of five decades ago. For many years after Mayor Lea's term was over, the police department kept busy raiding, arresting, fining and deporting prostitutes. The city-county health board was always making rounds and examining the girls. The fact that El Paso is a military center and has sometimes had many thousands of troops to look out for has created problems.

A great policewoman, Mrs. Callie Fairley, made a career of restraining girls when she had to and helping them when she could. People called her "the moocher," because she was always tapping somebody for money to help an unfortunate who was not beyond redemption.

"We had many, many girls that were runaways from home," she once said after her retirement, "not El Paso homes but sometimes far east, north, or west. They were not the type of girls that you would lock up — that you wanted to turn the key on — and there were no finances to help anybody, and that was why I obtained the name of the Moocher. I could always manage to get fare and enough for them to eat on till they got home."[124]

A sample of her work was reported in the *Herald* in 1940 after the district had been closed. In one day she brought in twenty-nine girls operating in South El Paso hotels. The raids touched off serious talk about reopening the district at Ninth and Mesa. At the same time Chief of Police Robey was planning a drive on "bar girls," who, he said, "were a greater menace to health than the regulars." [125]

This sort of thing, of course, is part of the daily life of any city, and in 1940 El Paso was no worse off in the vice department than Fort Worth or Kansas City or Atlanta. There were hotel-room poker games. Professional and non-professional prostitutes continued to operate. Confidence men fleeced an occasional lamb. They still do. But the old days of big-time gambling, fancy women displaying their silken charms in open carriages on Sundays, saloon fights every night and killings every few days — these times are gone, we hope forever. If El Paso is a less colorful town as a result, it at least gets a good deal less unfavorable advertising in the Eastern papers and no longer is thought of as the Sin City *par excellence* of the American West.

CHAPTER XXIV

Across the River

 THE CLEANUP of vice and ring politics ended the last survivals of frontier times for us. The Mexican Revolution did the same for Juárez. By 1918 and the outbreak of World War I, the curtain had descended on one world and was rising an another for both peoples.

In Mexico, however, the Revolution was not the only thing involved. The transformation of Mexican life and society from the traditional patterns to what we know now began a long way back and was shaped by many forces.

When Americans came to the left bank of the river, the old families and the old customs were still dominant on the right. The Rio Grande made them so. The country for ten miles below Paso del Norte was one great garden, rich with grain and fruits, vegetables and flowers. It was a paradise — but not a modern paradise. The tools of agriculture were primitive and most of the work was done laboriously by hand. The great families owned most of the property and the poor ones owned hardly anything, yet even the *peones* had a flair for living, for taking their time and making the most of the present, for extracting joy and reassurance from their communal life — or so it has seemed to those who looked back in later times.

Weddings, Sunday visits, dances and parties were naturally times of good feeling, but working together was pleasant also. The *fatigas* which every irrigator owed his community for work on the communal ditch brought him and his neighbors out in the spring for toil which seemed easier because everybody shared it. The *peonadas* or labor exchanges worked the same way. "They would present themselves," says Romulo Escobar, "with their tools in their hands or their yokes of oxen. . . . In exchange the owner would set out a tub of good wine." They got together on Sundays for *corridas de liebres* (rabbit hunts) which provided food as well as pleasure and were great occasions for everybody except the rabbits. These ancient customs "have disappeared along with the unity and brotherhood of the country people,"[1] Mr. Escobar wistfully remarks.

The well-to-do families were kindly, hospitable, polite and amiable. They were also industrious and shrewd. Don Ynocente Ochoa, the richest man in town, started as a helper in a mercantile establishment, married a Samaniego and worked his way up. His great house on *Calle Comercio* (now Sixteenth of September Street) was the showplace of the whole region, good enough to house the President of Mexico when Porfirio Díaz visited the border.

His neighbor across the street, where the city market now stands, was José María Flores, who got tired of working for a demanding stepfather in San Antonio and came out with Isaac Lightner, operator of a freighting business and a connection by marriage of all the great families through his wife Carmen Valdéz. José María followed the standard pattern. He worked for Lightner and Don Ynocente, married Hugh Stephenson's daughter Margarita, and soon had a business of his own. It was quite typical of him and his group that when his son José Jacinto was big enough, he sent him across to the American side to work in Sam Schutz's store and learn to be a merchant. J. J. swept the place out every morning and worked on the books.

The life that went on in the many-roomed adobe home of José María Flores was leisurely and sociable. Relatives and dependents lived close to the mansion and visitors came in a steady stream. The ladies breakfasted late and usually sat down to *malilla* (a complicated card game) about eleven. They smoked the tiniest possible *cigarros,* often made with corn husks, and sipped *aguardiente de uva,* colorless but potent, dulcified with a little rock candy. Meals were lengthy, ample, and full of calories. Conversation was lively but limited to local topics. The great world was still a long way off.

The men were really country gentlemen at heart. They all owned land and were interested in agriculture. Dr. Mariano Samaniego specialized in grapes and experimented with cuttings imported from France (he found that nothing succeeded like the mission grapes introduced by the Spanish fathers). J. M. Flores worked with apples, strawberries and peaches.[2]

These were civilized and agreeable people whose relations with their American neighbors were close and cordial. Through the seventies and on into the eighties parties were international — Mexican society attending dances on the American side and the Social Club going en masse to Mexico when Don Ynocente had a ball in his big *sala* with the huge black grand piano and the red drapes.[3]

The great event of the year was the *feria,* the *Fiesta de Guadalupe,* a winter celebration which antedated the Sun Carnival and its predecessors by perhaps two hundred years. Announcements appeared in November. People began to arrive in December — cockfighters, bullfighters, circus performers, merchants of all descriptions, along with confidence men and gamblers. The early days of January were given over to food, dancing, games, and joy.[4]

As stable as it seemed, the whole interwoven fabric of life was and had always been dependent on a capricious and headstrong stream — the Great River of the North. The whole social and business organization was precipitated out of those muddy waters, and when the water failed, the organization failed also.

A hundred years ago there was always water. The floods of spring were a menace and changes in the river channel during these times could be destructive and dangerous, but a farmer could be reasonably certain of making a crop. If there was hunger, it was likely to be the result of politics. For instance the troubles of 1858 dislocated the border community, as they did the rest of Mexico. People were hungry. Exports and imports stopped. Thieving was common. The United States Consul described the situation as "deplorable."[5]

This, however, was a short-term calamity. The big trouble began in the 1870's when the river began to fail. The reasons for this failure could be summed up in one phrase: more people and less water. More and more immigrants were coming to the Valley; the acreage under cultivation was increasing and with it the demand for irrigation. The real source of difficulty, we know now, was six hundred miles away in southern Colorado, where the Denver and Rio Grande Railroad had opened up new areas to settlement and placed new demands on the river. At the same time lumbermen and ranchers were denuding the hillsides in Colorado and New Mexico of the vegetation which in the past had slowed down run-off and tamed the floods of spring. So there was less and less water, and what came down the channel was likely to come all at once.

Nature did her part to make it a real catastrophe. All through the seventies, and again into the nineties, prolonged droughts ruined the crops and brought misery to the land. These were followed by floods, for instance the big one of 1874, which washed away a number of villages above El Paso,[6] and then would come rainless months when the wheat shoots withered and the apples dried up on the trees.

In 1880 the farmers at San Elizario petitioned the county judge to forgive their taxes because the drought of the preceding year had wiped them out. In 1884 they petitioned again — this time because a flood had wiped them out once more.[7]

Nevertheless homeseekers came in by the trainload in the eighties, and the Texas and Pacific provided the trains.[8] The immigrants bought and developed new land where there had been only tornillo and catclaw *bosque,* and they changed the Valley from a fruit-and-vegetable garden to a granary. The days when every Mexican had his little field and orchard, his cow and his chickens began to recede into the past.

The greatest burden the Mexican had to bear was the pressure of *yanqui* ways and *yanqui* wealth. An aggressive, acquisitive, technically minded culture was in contact, sometimes in conflict, with an ancient tradition of acceptance and respect and resistance to change. Neither group was prepared to understand or appreciate the other, and even today a very small episode will bring the old feelings to the surface.

"Americans," says Cecil Robinson, "in their Protestant individualism, in their ideas of thrift and hard work, in their faith in progress through technology, in their insistence upon personal hygiene, in puritanism and racial pride, found Mexico much to their distaste."[9]

The border Latins formed their impressions of the Americans from limited evidence—from contacts with adventurers and mountain men in the early days; from merchants and lawyers and land speculators, all on the make, in later times — and their opinion of all gringos was apt to be very low.

Each party loved and respected individuals on the other side but generalized unfavorably about the group as a whole.

It is strange but true that now, more than a century after our first contacts with Mexico, Americans tend to go to the other extreme and admire the Mexican for the very traits they disliked before. "The American writer, especially in recent years," critic Robinson continues, "has often turned to the Mexican out of a sense of his own deficiency or of the society in which he grew up." The result has been an oversimplification in the direction of "one of the various types of noble savage."[10]

After the railroads came, one circumstance was especially galling to the patriotic Mexican: quite obviously life was easier on the American side. El Paso and its people flourished. Business was good most of the time. Work and food were plentiful except in the very worst depressions, and necessities were cheaper. No crossing cards were required in those days, and very little risk or trouble was involved in fording a shallow stream, moving one's family into a vacant house on somebody's farm, and becoming an American like the rest of one's cousins. The result, especially in times of economic hardship, was a noticeable shrinkage in the population of Juárez and its tributary communities. In the nineties, when conditions were at their worst, the count may have been down by as much as fifty per cent.[11]

"Beyond the Rio Grande," one Mexican historian says, "was free commerce, lowest customs duties, and sale of European and American articles without import tax. On this side prohibitive tariffs, absurd duties and voracious treasuries were added to the already mentioned failure of natural resources." The result was "the depopulation of the Mexican side to the benefit of the American side. Misery appeared. The Mexicans who remained did so at the expense of severe sacrifice."[12]

No wonder Rubén Darío exclaimed, "Poor Mexico, so close to the United States!"[13]

To protect the Mexicans who stayed south of the Border from the pressures of the American economic system, a *zona libre,* or Free Zone, operated more or less effectively from 1849 until 1905, when it was discontinued by Limantour, Porfirio Díaz' financial genius. It allowed merchants in Juárez and other border towns to import products free of Mexican duties, shipped in bond from

Mexican seaports or through American ports of entry, thereby giving their countrymen an inducement to "buy Mexican." The *zona libre* was a political football which was forever causing resentment and protest, sometimes on one side of the border, sometimes on the other. It never gave the Mexicans a really fair shake against the Americans, but, as one of them said in 1890, it was "the backbone of Juárez."[14] Ten years later another one commented, "As long as we have no water, we don't want the free zone abolished. If it were we would all have to move into Texas to get anything at all to eat. We can't raise anything without water and so have to import everything in order to live. If we had to pay full duties, the prices would be so high that we would starve."[15]

"Poor Mexico, so close to the United States!" The water failed in the ditches. The roses on the banks disappeared. The orchards gave way to fields of grain, when any crop at all would grow. Following the lead of the gringos, who were having their water troubles too, the Mexican farmers took to raising alfalfa in the late eighties because alfalfa roots will go down many feet after water. Even the mission grapes, once the pride of the valley, had to give up the struggle. When the great flood of 1897 washed out many of the vineyards, grape culture was at an end, and it has never come back as an industry on either side of the river.

It is only fair to add that the drouth was responsible for bad times on the American side too. Shortly after 1900 water shortages and changing agricultural practices dislodged large numbers of Mexican workers who left to seek employment elsewhere. The situation became so bad that in 1903 strenuous efforts were made to attract Anglo farmers to the Valley.[16]

From the earliest times people were aware that the river was the problem and the answer. Something had to be done to stabilize the water supply. In September of 1888 Anson Mills, sent to Fort Bliss to take part in a survey of arid government lands, addressed the city council and proposed the building of a dam "near the Southern Pacific Bridge"— the neck of the gorge of the Rio Grande. Mills wanted it to be an international project, Mexico participating and sharing in the water.[17]

From this time on, irrigation was a subject of major interest in both El Paso and Juárez. Irrigation congresses met yearly to discuss the needs and prospects of various arid sections of the country. In 1904 the convention was held at El Paso with dairyman and journalist Uncle Jimmy Smith as chairman of the executive committee and various prominent El Pasoans helping with the arrangements.

By this time a good deal of progress had been made toward finding a suitable site for the dam which would make controlled irrigation a reality. El Paso and Juárez wanted it just above town, but the farmers in the Mesilla Valley, who would be drowned out, were naturally against that. The other favored site was at Elephant Butte, a hundred miles above the Pass. In 1893 a group of speculators, including several El Pasoans, had organized the Rio Grande Dam and Irrigation Company to consider dam building on that site.[18] Failing to make any headway, this group in 1896 conveyed its rights and privileges to an English corporation called the Rio Grande Irrigation and Land Company. El Paso and Juárez did everything in their power to defeat this project. Progress was delayed for a while by getting the American Secretary of War to intervene on the grounds that the Rio Grande was a navigable stream and that it was his right and duty to prevent obstructions from interfering with navigation.

At the 1904 meeting a committee of fifteen, appointed to study the question, adopted a resolution favoring the Elephant Butte site. The representatives from Texas were Felix Martínez, A. P. Coles, Zach White, Alfred Courchesne, and J. A. Smith.[19]

The dam was begun in 1912 and finished in 1916. An agreement was reached whereby Mexican farmers got a share of the water,[20] and in spite of drouths and difficulties, life has been much richer and happier in both countries since the dam went in.

The happiness and enrichment were delayed in Mexico, however, by the great event of modern Mexican history — the Revolution of 1910, a national convulsion which tore Mexico apart and changed the entire social and political structure in ways which are still working themselves out.

The city of Juárez, isolated at the northernmost point of Mexican territory, was not typical. The extremes of poverty and wealth were not so pronounced as in communities farther south. The sense of injustice and the burning desire for reform were possibly less intense. But "the wind that swept Mexico" first began to blow in the north-Mexican desert, and several times Juárez was the revolutionary capital — the center of everything.

The beginnings are a much-told tale: how the great Porfirio Díaz, eighty years old but hale and strong, set aside the month of September, 1910, to celebrate a century of Mexican independence and thirty-four years of personal rule by himself — how Francisco Madero, the rich little idealist, wrote a book called *The Presidential Succession in 1910* and became the leader of the anti-reelectionist party which called for the retirement of Díaz and for free elections. Land reforms, so badly needed, were not in the forefront of Madero's thinking at the moment, but they soon became a principal object of the Revolution.

These were desperately important issues to the Mexican people. Díaz had done much for Mexico since 1876. He had given his country the appearance of a great nation with massive public buildings, international financial respectability, a surplus in the treasury. He had kept the peace. He had enlisted foreign capital in the development of Mexican resources. Most of the well-to-do families were for him. The church was for him. In September, 1910, he seemed invulnerable and invincible by anything but time, and time had been kind to Don Porfirio.

But dry rot was spreading rapidly at the root of his tree of government. The wealth of the country was finding its way into the hands of fewer and fewer people, and in 1910 less than one per cent of the families of Mexico possessed eighty-five per cent of the land.[21] The Terrazas family of Chihuahua controlled the state and owned an enormous amount of it. Agrarian reform was badly needed, but under Díaz it could never be realized, for the aging president favored his little circle of friends and advisors, got rid of the few who disagreed with him, and saw to it that the right people owned and ran the country.

The industrialization of which he was so proud, carried on by foreigners with money to invest, was actually a continuous process of selling out to capitalists from other lands, or so the Mexican people believed, and was in reality another way of taking Mexico out of the hands of the Mexicans. Since no expression of opposition was tolerated, Porfirio Díaz did not know, probably could not have believed, the depth of the unrest in the hearts of his supposedly loyal fellow countrymen. He learned quickly, however. In less than eight months after his centennial celebration, he was in flight and his country was in the hands of *insurrectos*.

Quite understandably, Díaz never admitted that his methods and ideas were wrong, and when he left Vera Cruz to die in exile, he was still convinced that his way was the only way to run the affairs of Mexico. There are still good *porfiristas* with us who think he was right — that he was developing Mexico as fast as she was able to go; that he would have given the people the power they wanted as soon as they were ready; and that events have shown how unready the people were for the power they assumed when they drove him out. The vast majority of contemporary Mexicans, however, are children of the Revolution and can see only evil in the long reign of Porfirio Díaz.[22]

Díaz' prestige was never as high in Chihuahua as in other Mexican states. Here Benito Juárez had found his refuge in the desert, and the city of Juárez has always been loyal to his memory. Díaz, his betrayer, was cheered and viewed with patriotic interest when he came to the border for his historic meeting with President Taft on October 16, 1909 — an affair of great pomp and circumstance on both sides of the boundary. But only a year later the whole northern country was in the process of rising against him.

The people of Chihuahua had as much reason as any of the citizens of Mexico to be tired of dictatorship. They were a sturdy and hardy group who were more willing than some of their fellow countrymen to fight for what they considered just and right, and they found the *caciquismo local* (the local or regional autocracy of the great landowners) a hard thing to put up with. The "odious monopolies and humiliating privileges" which were characteristic of the Díaz régime aroused their special resentment, and the pretentious symbols of greatness that arose in their capital city of Chihuahua left them cold. The monuments and public buildings, characterized by "the ornate and the superfluous and by all that would contribute to consolidate the authority and respect of the régime," were a scandal to the masses, landless, miserably housed, uneducated, defenseless, and resentful,[23] and to some of their more prosperous countrymen.

All they needed was a leader, and they found one — an unlikely one, it must be admitted, in Madero. His book on the Presidential

Succession made him known throughout Mexico, where so many had wished to protest against the Díaz autocracy and so few had dared to do it. It did not seem possible that he could be a menace to the monolithic porfirian dictatorship; Don Porfirio himself did not take seriously this little man with the high-pitched voice and nervous hands, this country capitalist who had no military experience and very little political background, a sentimentalist who wept when he heard great music, a spiritualist who took advice from his contacts in the next world. But Madero founded a newspaper and in articles and speeches carried his message to the people everywhere. In April his upstart party nominated him for the presidency with the one-time Díaz family physician, Dr. Francisco Vázquez Gómez, as his vice-presidential running mate. Dr. Vázquez was a solid and practical little man who knew his way around in the Mexican government and was idealistic without being visionary. His participation added respectability to Madero's movement and people flocked to their standard. In May 30,000 of them demonstrated outside the Presidential palace in Mexico City and convinced Díaz that Madero had better be taken care of. Madero went to prison in San Luis Potosí, charged with inciting armed rebellion.[24] Díaz, of course, was reelected to the presidency — for the eighth time — and massive petitions to have the election declared invalid were ignored.

Madero was soon released from his confinement, subject to his remaining under surveillance in San Luis. He "escaped," however, and came to the United States. From his hotel in San Antonio, he announced that the Revolution was about to begin. His manifesto was called the Plan of San Luis Potosí. In it he declared the Mexican elections null and void, named himself Provisional President of Mexico, and summoned his countrymen to rise against their oppressors and exploiters on November 20.

They rose. The first to do so were easily suppressed, but the movement spread across the country like a prairie fire. Chihuahua was a focal area. The great Terrazas family, owner of everything, was a natural target for the dissatisfied and disgruntled. Pascual Orozco, a man of the people, a well regarded freighter and storekeeper from the western part of the state, lean, grim, and determined, raised a force of irregulars which the harrassed Federal troops were unable to catch up with most of the time, and unable to destroy when they did catch up. Allied with Orozco was an unlettered but dynamic young leader named Francisco (Pancho) Villa, who had made a local reputation as an extremely successful, though unwelcome, participant in Don Luis Terrazas' cattle business. Though he has become the Robin Hood of Mexico, he was at that time an outlaw. By the end of December, 1910, the *insurrectos* controlled most of the southern part of the state and had appeared (they stole a train) within twenty miles or so of Juárez.[25] Prophecies were heard that they would assault the city in a matter of days. The papers published stories of fighting at widely separated points in the northern states; Chihuahua was practically under siege; and Governor Terrazas issued futile calls for volunteers to prepare for defense.[26]

By this time El Paso was beginning to move into the center of the revolutionary picture. It could almost have been called the headquarters of revolutionary Mexico and the Sheldon hotel was practically the capitol building. South El Paso — *Chihuahuita* (Little Chihuahua) they called it then — sheltered dozens of organizers, agents, undercover workers, exiles. The local Mexican population was largely in sympathy with the *insurrectos*, gave them refuge, and encouraged them in all possible ways. Several ephemeral newspapers succeeded each other as time went on, produced on small presses in basements and back rooms.[27] One famous novel, *Los de abajo* (Those Below, The Underdogs) by a passionate revolutionary exile named Dr. Mariano Azuela, appeared in 1915 in one of the Spanish-language newspapers and was later published in El Paso in paper-back form without fanfare. It has become the classic of the Revolution.[28] Abraham González, the Provisional Governor of Chihuahua, rented offices in the Roberts-Banner Building and gave his fellow *maderistas* an official headquarters.[29]

All this was done without the encouragement of the American Government. Washington was not about to sponsor a revolution against a friendly power — at least not until the Revolution had made some progress. In that month of December, 1910, observant citizens noted the presence on our streets of a considerable number of out-of-town deputy sheriffs, all alert for agitators from south of the border. "Every Mexican who apparently has nothing to do is being followed to his domicile," declared the *Times*. "If the Mexican meets two or three others and talks with them, they are all watched, and if they have a common meeting place that also is being watched." It was an accepted article of local gossip in saloons and stores and even churches that men were being recruited in El Paso and arms were being gathered and stored.[30]

The day after Christmas brought a new kind of excitement to both sides of the Rio Grande, and scenes which were to become familiar during the succeeding years began to be enacted. First came the rumors — rumors which spread "like wildfire." The *revoltosos* were marching on Juárez. There would be a battle — probably a bloody one. It was something one must not miss. And so a mass movement began toward the border. The banks of the river were lined with curious citizens, including the entire population of Chihuahuita, all the way from the Stanton Street bridge to the smelter. The Mexicans followed suit, and the hills west of Juárez were crowded with spectators until the *rurales* made them go home. General Navarro and and Mayor Portillo were frantically busy getting organized — they hardly knew for what. The *Fiesta de Guadalupe,* the annual fair, was in progress and doing very well until the mayor issued orders for discontinuance. The gamblers brought $40,000 to El Paso banks and dismantled their equipment.[31]

New Year's came and went amid rumors of death and destruction in communities to the south in Chihuahua and prophecies of invasion for Juárez. The Revolutionaries on New Year's Day circulated a red-lettered broadside calling on all Mexicans to shed their blood for Liberty.

Through the month of January the tension continued, though the would-be spectators of the horrors of war left the river banks and went home. Government troops came and departed as battles were reported at Casas Grandes and points south. Colonel Rábago left for the mountains of Western Chihuahua with a detachment of government troops, and about the same time Orozco appeared on the Mexican Central railroad ninety-four miles below the city. On the first of February the news came that he was marching on Juárez and would be there almost at once. This time the rumors were correct.[32] Had it not been for the announcement that "seven world-famous bird men" were to put on an aviation show at Washington Park, the coming battle would have been the sole subject of conversation.

Orozco had indeed moved up to Samalayuca within twenty-three miles of Juárez and on February 2 the first of a long series of extras issued by the *Times* in the morning and the *Herald* in the evening announced: OROSCO NOW AT THE OUTSKIRTS OF JUAREZ. A picture of the famous leader appeared on the front page showing him in boots and breeches with two cartridge belts around his waist, a white shirt and wrinkled tie, an American hat on his head, a repeating rifle in his hand. His lean face with the smoldering eyes was looking grimly into the camera.

The rebels had destroyed bridges on the way up from Chihuahua to protect their rear, and the Federals had played the same game by placing dynamite on the track and blowing up a troop train filled with Orozco's men. A party of four American reporters made a dash by automobile to the scene of the wreck and came back with pictures and stories.

Provisional Governor González engaged Dr. I. J. Bush of El Paso to improvise a hospital at Second and Campbell streets. Dr. Bush had already done good service for Orozco in the skirmishing between his troops and the Federal forces in the desert country south of the city.[33]

The agitation in Juárez was tremendous. The banks moved their funds to the other side, and the Mexican post office followed suit. Horse races at the new track in the park named for Don Alberto Terrazas were called off. Prominent families crossed the bridge in an uninterrupted stream. And a large portion of the population of El Paso joined in the activities by taking positions on the river bank, or in the foothills where they could get a view of whatever was going to happen.

Mayor Kelly did his best for his people, ordering the police to move them back from the danger zone and warning them that in case of a battle, "bullets will rain" on the American side. The citizens did not seem to share Mr. Kelly's alarm. They did not even heed Consul Edwards' admonition to stay out of Juárez. Until street-car traffic was stopped at three p.m. on February 3, they flocked across for a look around. It was quite obvious that Americans of whatever origin had had no experience with the perils of conflict.

On February 6 the first of the rebel troops reached the river opposite the smelter. The Federals marched out to meet them and then marched back again. They seemed to feel that it was their first duty to herd their fellow countrymen away from the river where anything could happen. There was no fighting.

Now the Americans had the chance they had been wanting. Orozco's men came to the river in force and camped on the banks. Some fifteen thousand citizens (estimate by the *Times*), curious and cheerful, descended upon them. Most of these people stayed on their own side and satisfied themselves with looking, but the more intrepid, many of them "kodak fiends," crossed the suspension bridge at the brick plant and mingled with the *insurrectos*. It is possible that the crowd would have been smaller on account of the aviation show at Washington Park, but high winds had grounded the aviators.[34]

Orozco was low on ammunition and seems to have planned to capture Juárez to get it. He had no difficulty in smuggling adequate supplies from the American side, however, and was in a position to attack when Colonel Rábago returned from western Chihuahua, broke through the rebel defenses, and reinforced the garrison. Frustrated, Orozco moved his troops off to the south, leaving Juárez unmolested and hardly able to believe its own good luck.

During the fighting outside the city limits carloads of El Pasoans went over to watch, among them some women. "I never saw a crazier-acting bunch of folks," says Dr. Bush. "They seemed to think that battle was something pulled off for their especial amusement." One strong-minded female told the doctor to mind his own business when he spoke a word of warning, but she tore down a mesquite bush getting away when a bullet knocked some gravel in her face.[35]

About this time Madero, getting ready to join his forces in the field, came incognito to El Paso and remained for several days, issuing orders and trying to guide his troops by remote control. One of his official acts was the appointment of Dr. Bush to a colonelcy in the Medical Corps. As a matter of fact, Colonel Bush was the Medical Corps. On the morning of February 14, 1911, the President crossed the river near Ysleta, stopped for a short time in the village of Guadalupe, then faded into the desert in the direction of Chihuahua with General José de la Luz Blanco's volunteers and a group of some seventy-five American adventurers known as the Foreign Legion.[36]

This motley group of stragglers spent the next month and a half skirmishing with government troops in western Chihuahua. At Casas Grandes, in the mountains southwest of El Paso, they were defeated and scattered and Madero himself was wounded.[37]

Here the Revolution came close to foundering. Hardly anybody expected it to grow, or even to continue. Most of the talk was about peace; Madero himself was willing to negotiate. When Díaz appointed a new cabinet and sent a message to his Congress advocating reforms, almost everybody (not including Madero) hoped the worst was over. When the United States sent twenty thousand troops to the border and when American warships visited the coast of the Latin republic, both sides in Mexico grew indignant at the thought of Yankee intervention and wished for a peace which would prevent such disgrace.[38]

About the only actual intervention on the part of the United States at this time was an informal one involving the McGinty cannon. The old Blue Whistler, salvaged by Major Trevanion T. Teel twenty years before and used by the McGinty Club to add emphasis to its celebrations and mock battles, had been sitting for some time in the little triangular park in front of the city hall. Ownership had passed to the Pioneer Society upon the demise of the McGinty organization.

Dr. Bush tells how he and Abraham González passed the old gun one day after having lunched at the Elks Club.

"We could use that gun if we had it in Mexico," González remarked.

"Then let's put it in Mexico," Bush replied.

González hesitated, but Bush did not forget, and when the Governor joined Madero for the crossing into Mexico on February 14, the doctor began to make arrangements. With the encouragement and assistance of Mrs. Monroe Harper, former wife of Major Teel, and her son Albert Hatcher, they towed the old cannon away behind Mrs. Harper's car, and on April 17, 1911, they buried it in a back yard until they could smuggle it into Mexico. It was hauled all the way to Ojinaga, across the roughest kind of country, and blasted the garrison there, after which it was put to use pulverizing adobe walls many miles away at Camargo. On August 18, 1911, after the first stage of the Revolution was over, it was brought back to El Paso with appropriate ceremonies and reinstalled in the City Hall plaza.[39]

Since his defeat at Casas Grandes, Madero had planned to attack Juárez — first moving toward Chihuahua to force the Federals to concentrate there, then cutting the railway and moving to the strategic northern city. There he would have a port of entry, a source of supply across the international bridge, and a major Mexican center of population in his hands. But first he was willing to negotiate, particularly since his father and his brothers said he should. They came to El Paso on April 2, while Díaz was recommending reforms to his Congress. With them at the Sheldon Hotel was a lawyer named Rafael Hernández, supposedly an unofficial representative of the Díaz government. For several days they conferred, but no announcements of progress were forthcoming. The supposition was that they hadn't made any.[40] News stories said that their next move was to go into Chihuahua to confer with the Provisional President.

It turned out they didn't need to. On April 15 a *Times* extra announced that he was at Bauché, a siding on the Northwestern only a few miles outside Juárez, and a battle was going on. At once curiosity and panic started up again. Refugees began to trickle across the international bridge. Mayor Kelly announced that the police would form a line in the neighborhood of Seventh Street, two blocks from the river, and everybody would be kept back from the danger zone in case of a battle[41]

Madero took his time. He approached the city by way of the Flores ranch, where there was a little water, and his men did not filter down through the canyons to the river until April 19. Other bands camped east of town across from Washington Park in plain view of the fascinated citizens on our side.

Madero arrived with the vanguard and let it be known that he would attack Juárez unless the garrison surrendered by six P.M. of the twentieth. He had set up his headquarters in a small adobe house, little more than a hut, across from the smelter, and his followers were scattered about on the flat land and back in the hills from a point opposite Hart's Mill to the vicinity of the brick plant.

In those days the bottom land near Madero's adobe residence was covered with grass and shaded by a grove of native cottonwoods. The events of the next few days caused these trees to be known, as long as they remained, as the Peace Grove. They disappeared years ago.[42]

The President did not carry out his threat to attack at six P.M. He was short of supplies and ammunition, and besides he was under heavy pressure to negotiate a peace. His family wanted him to. The Central Government wanted him to. His representative in Washington, Dr. Vázquez Gómez, agreed to come to the border and join the negotiators. A five-day truce, later extended to ten, was agreed to.[43]

The truce freed Madero and his *insurrectos* for some of the most concentrated fraternizing that the Valley had seen since the arrival of Doniphan's Missourians in 1847. The suspension bridge at the brick plant "groaned" under the weight of a constant stream of visitors who invaded the camp ground. With curious eyes they watched the *soldaderas* cooking and doing their chores, they talked endlessly, they waited for a glimpse of Madero or Orozco or Pino Suárez, and they took pictures of everything. Those who did not care to cross threw oranges and silver dollars and other objects of interest or value across the stream for the troops.

One man complained that he was left with the chickens, the cow and the children while his wife spent her time throwing cookies across the river. Everybody, old and young, at least came and looked.[44]

Some sentimental scenes occurred when Reyes' band, a fine amateur organization from El Paso, crossed the river with a "vast crowd" of sympathizers and gave a concert for the President. After the playing of the Mexican national anthem, Madero came to the door of his little adobe headquarters and made an impromptu speech. His eyes flashing with emotion, his hands moving restlessly, he told them of the difficult and dangerous crisis Mexico was passing through and quoted with deep feeling the words of the song: If we must fight, "our country has a soldier in each son and a hero in each soldier."[45]

All the leaders were there: Orozco (whom Madero made a brigadier general the next day), Villa, Garibaldi, and the rest — still friendly, still working together.

The delay as they waited for the negotiators was helpful in more than one way, but its greatest value was in the time it gave the insurgents to build up their supplies. Although the Twenty-Third Infantry was on patrol duty and one of its objectives was to prevent sympathizers on the American side from giving aid and comfort to the invaders, the sentries had to meet, turn, and move away from each other as they walked back and forth, and when they turned their backs, food and ammunition went across to Mexico.[46]

Sometimes one or another of the important Revolutionaries would slip across to El Paso. Orozco did it on the night of April 20. He registered at the Sheldon and ate his dinner at a restaurant on San Antonio Street, where he was recognized by a friendly mob as he left. The Secret Service, noting his name on the Sheldon register, had rushed a man off to headquarters to ask if they should arrest him. Before an answer could be returned, the crowd had put Orozco into an automobile, driven him to a point across the river from his camp, and sent him splashing to safety.[47]

These were boom times for El Paso merchants. The armistice allowed the rebels to import food and clothing (no arms or ammunition) through the Juárez customs house, but many of them preferred more direct action and found their way to Cannon's department store, Mr. Lightbody's haberdashery, the Bazaar, the Popular, and every place else that had something to sell. Their leaders were joined at the Sheldon, the Coney Island, May Palmer's, and all the other male haunts by a small army of Secret Service men, soldiers of fortune, newspaper correspondents, freelance writers, photographers, and refugees from Mexico. For a while El Paso was in the national news almost every day, and the Chamber of Commerce was so grateful that it gave a banquet (a moist one), after the worst was over, for all the visitors who had "put El Paso on the map." This celebration was remembered for many years by those who could remember it at all as a high point in their lives.[48]

Our own contribution to the cause of photographic history was Otis Aultman, who came in 1907, just in time to get set for his great opportunity. He took pictures of everything and everybody along the border and down into Mexico, and although he never got around to putting names and places on his pictures, his negatives and plates, now in our public library, are the best pictorial record of the Revolution in northern Mexico and carry us back, as words fail to do, to those extraordinary times.

The peace commissioners finally assembled. Judge Francisco Carbajal arrived to negotiate for the Díaz government. Dr. Vázquez Gómez came in from Washington. Pino Suárez, Madero's special friend who became his vice-president later, and the elder Francisco Madero were already on the ground. Conferences began at once.

Sad to say, the negotiations came to nothing. They foundered on the question of Díaz' resignation. This, said the revolutionists, must come first. No, insisted Díaz; he would step down when he was sure the country was not on its way to anarchy.[49] The critical day was Sunday, May 7. Hopeless of success, Madero addressed his troops (he liked addressing his troops) and informed them that he was ordering a withdrawal from the border; that he was leaving a three-man peace commission in case the government had a change of heart. He admitted that several of his leaders were insisting that Juárez must be taken, but to avoid trouble with the United States he was overruling them.

Among those who were demanding a showdown were Orozco and Villa. The volunteers in the Foreign Legion were determined to fight also. Madero's address set them in motion. At 11 A.M. a small scouting party of *maderistas* edged in toward Juárez and came under fire from a detachment of Federals who were intrenched at the outskirts of town. Under cover of this engagement a larger force made its way into the very heart of the city by way of the *acequia madre*, the mother irrigation ditch, dry now and its banks raised by the spring cleaning. Entering where it left the river opposite Hart's Mill, they crouched along, unperceived, until they actually reached the central plaza. They drove the *Federales* out of a trench in front of the city jail, occupied it themselves, and refused to be dislodged. The Foreign Legion, led by Giuseppe Garibaldi (grandson of the Liberator) in his green velour hat, went in along the ditch bank without bothering to take cover.[50]

Word of the attack came back to Madero, who was perfectly frantic at this brazen disregard of his orders and wishes, and a man with a white flag rode desperately toward Juárez to order the troops back. General Navarro, in command in the city, was as anxious as Madero to prevent a battle, but neither of them could stop what had been so long in starting, and at four o'clock Orozco told his chief that the front-line fighters would be lost if not reinforced. Unhappy but helpless, Madero ordered him to attack. Villa marched his men around the town for an assault from the south by way of the railroad station. Madero found an observation post in the hills near the western outskirts.[51]

May 9 was a day of hard fighting on both sides, but the rebels' unusual methods of warfare were a trial to the few European-trained officers. Everybody fought his own war — left the front when he felt like it and went back for food and sleep, returning when he was ready. The best snipers mounted the house tops, knocked out the wooden gutters to make loopholes, sheltered themselves behind the adobe parapets, and harassed the Federals, whose trenches and barricades were ineffectual against this sort of warfare. Where the firing was heaviest, the *insurrectos* moved forward by knocking holes in the adobe walls between the houses, traveling in this fashion a block at a time without exposing themselves. By nightfall Madero's men had all the city but the bullring, the barracks, and the old church.

Their two pieces of artillery were not as effective as their rifle fire and their improvised hand grenades. Newsman Timothy Turner, who was close to the battle front, says the McGinty cannon was there and did some execution with charges of scrap metal. The hope of their small corps of artillerymen, however, was a home-made piece, long of barrel, small of bore, created in the machine shops at the lumber camp at Madera beyond Casas Grandes. Turner calls it "a sort of mammoth early American squirrel rifle mounted on a pair of small locomotive wheels." It was fired only three times. The first charge went off into the wild blue somewhere. The second by some miracle penetrated the Federal water tank in the patio of the *cuartel*. The third blew the breech block off and left the gunner in despair and tears.

The rebels, ragged and hungry for so long, had the time of their lives looting. They outfitted themselves with clothes and shoes, loaded their pockets with trinkets taken from the captured houses, ate wherever they found food, and cheered themselves with confiscated liquor.

Now at last the people of Juárez were up against the real thing, and they passed some dreadful hours. Bullets were flying everywhere and dead men were lying in the streets. Block by block the rebels took the city. J. J. Flores and his family were more or less typical. They lived a considerable distance from the heart of town and the center of conflict, but bullets kept hitting their house. Mr. Flores, his wife, his daughter María Luisa and several others took refuge in a closet and stayed there the best part of two days, but on May 9 the rebels had penetrated to the next block and something had to be done. Mr. Flores went to his back door and waved a white towel. Somebody started shooting at him and he ducked back inside.

A little later he waved his white flag from an upstairs window and Colonel T. D. Edwards, the American consul, saw it from his office across the street. He came out and motioned for them to come over and take refuge with him. They did. But some of the invaders, knowing well that soldiers had escaped before in women's clothes, began to fire at them just as they reached Edwards' door.

Soon after, they had a call from Colonel Juan Medina, a former friend of the family, who came to the consulate with ten or twelve soldiers, asked for Mr. Flores, and told him that he would have to come to the *jefatura* and open the safe (Mr. Flores was city treasurer). On promise of safe return, Mr. Flores went, amid the tears of his wife and children. Most of the city funds were in a bank in El Paso, and Pancho Villa was unhappy to find so little ready cash available. He took what there was, of course, and when Mr. Flores asked him for a receipt, he growled that he did not give receipts, motioning Mr. Flores to go away.[52]

That afternoon Juan Hart, editor of the *Times*, called the consulate to find out about the Flores family. His mother was an aunt of Mrs. Flores. His journalistic connection and his known sympathy with the rebel cause got him a pass through the lines and about five o'clock he came to the consulate in his big Reo automobile and took the Flores family to his place at Hart's Mill. They lived there until 1920, sometimes going back for short periods to their house in Juárez, but always returning in times of stress. J. J. Flores became *presidente municipal* (mayor) in 1913 and was a respected citizen until his death in 1929.[53]

This was the beginning of a great exodus from Mexico. Many of the best people of Juárez and Chihuahua took refuge in the

United States. The Flores family were joined by the Luhans, the Urruetas, the Cisniegas, the family of Dr. Márquez, and a hundred more. In December of that year (1911) the great Don Luis Terrazas arrived by way of Ojinaga and Presidio from Chihuahua, bringing as much of his great wealth as possible in twenty wagons. He first rented an entire floor of the Paso del Norte hotel and then moved into Senator Fall's mansion on Arizona Street, where he lived in patriarchal style and provided a haven for other top-ranking refugees, most of whom were related to him or obligated to him one way or another.[54]

He used to have a sort of levee or reception every morning at which time he gave away American quarters to the children of his relatives and dependents. Young William Berrien, son of the pioneer furniture dealer and undertaker, found out about it and used to travel from his home on Magoffin Avenue in time to arrive at nine o'clock and participate in the tribal ceremonies of the Terrazas clan. Don Luis had so many connections he could not possibly remember them all and it never occurred to him that William might be an impostor.[55]

All this came later. The evening of May 8, 1911, saw almost all of Juárez in the hands of the revolters. Sharp, positive little Colonel Tamborrel, who had accused the rebels of cowardice, was found hanging out of a window of his office, his hands tied behind him and the top of his head blown off. General Navarro had been forced to give up almost all his outlying positions and retreated to the barracks. His water and electricity had been cut off, and as the third day of battle dawned, his position appeared hopeless. His men were hungry and thirsty and exhausted after two days of fighting. Early in the afternoon, "to avoid useless sacrifice," he raised the white flag and surrendered to Captain Alejandro Aranzubia, the first *maderista* officer to arrive.[56] Colonel Garibaldi, who understood these formalities, accepted his sword.

The excitement on the American side was almost as intense as it was in Juárez, and the risk to the citizens was almost as great. Mayor Kelly did his best to keep his people in line, but they were too much even for him. They found points of vantage anywhere they could. Leslie Reed was back of a brick chimney at the Santa Fe depot, and bullets kept hitting the chimney. In the railroad yards people lined up on top of boxcars, just asking to be killed.

Jane Burges was on top of an apartment house (now the Medical Arts building), without her father's knowledge. Everybody else was trying to find a fairly safe spot where he could see what was going on. Five people were killed and fifteen were wounded—some near the Union Depot, some a mile down the river at the Madera lumber plant. Bullets left their marks at many places in El Paso. Mrs. J. C. Wilmarth, among others, could show bullet holes in her house in Sunset Heights until the freeway moved her and it out. A slug came through Miss Leona Black's window at Aoy School and hit the blackboard. Fortunately, the children had been sent home at the beginning of the battle.[57]

With Navarro's surrender an uneasy calm settled on both towns. The ambulatory wounded began to come across the bridge to Dr. Bush's improvised hospital, and many American doctors rushed to the other side to do what they might for the ones who could not be moved. In the midst of the shooting and looting little evidences of humanity appeared which were hardly to be expected at a time like this. Tough Orozco told his men to assist the wounded of both sides. Madero came to the enclosure where the Federal prisoners were confined and made them a speech full of sympathy and encouragement, telling them he knew they had only done their duty and praising them for the bravery of their resistance.[58]

Hatred and revenge were present, however. Orozco and Villa resented the fact that Navarro had not been shot in reprisal for his supposed cruelty to revolutionary troops in the past. On the morning of May 13, they came with 150 soldiers to the customhouse, where Madero was sitting in council. Orozco entered the room, pistol in hand, and demanded Navarro's execution. Villa waited outside. There are many versions of what happened in that room. Madero's biographer says that Orozco told the President he would have to submit to arrest.

"I will die first!" shouted Madero. "You are dismissed!" And dodging the hands that reached for him, he made his way outside and told the soldiers what was going on. Before it was over, Orozco and Madero had publicly proclaimed their undying loyalty to each other, but it was a most regrettable and revealing incident, prophetic of divisions to come.[59]

Timothy Turner, the *Herald's* on-the-spot reporter, was involved in what followed and tells about it in his sprightly autobiography,

Bullets, Bottles and Gardenias. Madero behaved toward stiff, un-bending General Navarro like the gentleman he was. He commandeered a house in the eastern part of town (probably Don Ynocente Ochoa's) and entertained his prisoner there. Turner, driving through Juárez in an automobile in search of news, heard the tipsy soldiers beginning to shout the slogan *muera Navarro* — death to Navarro. He drove to Madero's headquarters, told the President what he had heard, and persuaded him that Navarro must be smuggled into the United States to avoid a blot on the revolutionists' honor. They took the general, now in civilian clothes, to the house of Max Weber, the German consul. Mrs. Weber, who had great beauty and a great soul, had also a great horse which she gave to the fugitive and went along in the newsman's car to the river to point out a suitable place for crossing.

Navarro asked them to go back before he entered the river. When they were out of sight, he stripped off his clothes, tied them on his back with his suspenders, and put them on when he was safely across.

Turner was back at the *Herald* office writing his story when he was called to the telephone. Mr. A. Schwartz of the Popular Dry Goods Company was on the line. "General Navarro is here," he announced, "and asks you to please come to see him. He is in Chinaware in the basement."

Shortly thereafter the sister in charge at Hotel Dieu was asked to admit a sick man who was really Navarro using another name. He remained quietly at the hospital until it was safe to leave.[60]

The fall of Juárez was the beginning of triumph and tragedy for Madero. After a great formal ball in the customhouse, attended by many Americans, he assembled his troops on May 20 for a fare-well speech and departed for Mexico City to gain the presidency and lose his life. That was the end of the first phase of the Revolution.

Nothing as bad as that three-day battle happened again to the border cities, but the excitement and danger were by no means over. In fact, for several years it was one scare after another as no less than ten revolutionary parties in Mexico split off, realigned, and jockeyed for position. A counter revolution started in January, 1912, when Madero's former friend and supporter Emilio Vázquez Gómez assumed the provisional presidency, but Orozco managed the matter so that there was no bloodshed.[61] General José Ines Salazar occupied Juárez with 400 *vazquistas* on February 23, again with no fighting.[62] A month later Orozco himself turned against Madero, supporting Vázquez Gómez and declaring Juárez the capital of the Republic.[63]

By this time the mass exodus of foreigners was in full swing: cattlemen, lumbermen, mining men, and a great many Mormons from the colonies in Chihuahua. These latter swarmed across the border in all manner of conveyances, each one with a hair-raising story to tell. For a time some 500 of them were quartered in a lumber shed on Cotton Avenue near the Texas and Pacific tracks.[64]

In August it was all over with Orozco, and again El Paso was full of refugees, intrigue, and suspicion. When Huerta made himself president, over Madero's dead body, Villa broke with him and for several months lived in exile in El Paso.[65] Returned to good standing by Carranza, he was soon in the field again and threatening to take Juárez by storm as he had in 1911. As a consequence, in July of 1913 El Paso was again looking for a place to watch the expected battle.[66] Nothing happened this time, but in November Villa did take the city for the second time. There was no real fighting, though a great many bullets flew, some of them landing on our side of the river.[67] Mayor Kelly met Pancho on the bridge on November 15 and arranged matters between Mexican and American authorities. In repayment for this courtesy Pancho managed to fight the battle of Tierra Blanca some distance south of town so as not to endanger international relations. He had tactical reasons for this arrangement, of course, but these he did not mention. His firing squads were active during this occupation of Juárez. Dr. Cathcart took his daughter Florence across with him when he went to do what he could for the wounded, and the sights she saw taught her to hate war. Those were the hours when Mexicans showed that they knew how to die.

Nineteen hundred and fourteen was a bad year for Americans in Mexico. The wanton murder of fifty-one of them by fire and suffocation in the Cumbres tunnel on February 14,[68] the killing of W. S. Benton, a British cattle rancher, about the same time,[69] the death or disappearance of others (for instance San Francisco writer and newsman Ambrose Bierce)[70] brought more *yanquis* scurrying out of Mexico. Villa's men were responsible for the heartless cruelty and wanton destruction which brought grief and ruin to so many people, but Villa's prestige and power were at their height at this time and he was the most potent man in the north, if not in all Mexico.

General Hugh Scott, watching the border and trying to keep the two countries from flying at each other's throats, met Villa twice — once on January 9, 1915, and again on August 10 of the same year. Pancho became quite a familiar figure in El Paso, where he liked to come to buy clothes and supplies and to eat ice cream at the Elite confectionery. As Mexico fell into complete confusion, however, with as many as four presidents (including Villa) at once,[71] Pancho had less and less time for such diversions.

Orozco and Huerta, now in exile, came to the Pass in June, 1915, and were detained by the authorities.[72] They were not alone. As many as 5,000 "prisoners" were here at one time, along with hundreds of assorted refugees.[73] Orozco escaped and was killed by a party of ranchers near Van Horn on September 1.[74] Three thousand Mexicans attended his funeral, and in their bitterness against all Americans came close to rioting.[75] Huerta moved into a house at 415 West Yandell and died there on January 13, 1916.

By now Villa had lost some of his influence in Mexico and was not in the good graces of the United States. We were backing Carranza, now Villa's enemy, and Pancho was resentful. The savage Santa Ysabel massacre by *villistas* on January 10, 1916, widened the breach and provoked great indignation in El Paso. When the bodies of the murdered Americans were brought out, there was danger of mob violence to innocent Mexicans in Chihuahuita, and Mayor Tom Lea had to call out the entire police force to stop it.[76]

Then came the Columbus Raid on March 9, 1916, and after that the "Punitive Expedition" into Mexico, so futile and so much resented by the Mexicans. El Paso was the center of military activity. Sixty thousand soldiers camped on the mesa near Fort Bliss and moved across the border under General Pershing. They were back in January, 1917, and within a few months were preparing for a bigger conflict on the other side of the Atlantic Ocean.

World War I took our minds off the troubles in Mexico, but for eight years those troubles had been the number-one fact of our existence and the number-one topic of conversation. Along with the expectancy and the excitement and the dread came suspicion and resentment and distrust. Americans remembered the bandits and the expropriations and the executions. Mexicans remembered the interference, the threats of intervention, the invasion of 1916, and the entry of our troops into Juárez in June of 1919 when Villa took the town and Americans were being killed and wounded.[77] The old friendly feelings were impaired. Thoughtful people were distressed by the change and mourned for the old days.

"Five years ago," said H. D. Slater in an editorial on the front page of the *Herald*, "no two nations, no two peoples, were on better terms of friendship, respect, appreciation, cooperation than were the Mexicans and the Americans. Today no two nations are farther from the point of agreement on mutual interests." The United States and its citizens have had much to endure, he continued. "Scores, perhaps hundreds, of American citizens have been killed, assaulted, outraged, robbed by Mexicans in Mexico; American border cities have been fired upon repeatedly. On its part the government of the United States under two national administrations has done everything that could possibly be conceived — to goad the Mexicans into war; to harm Mexico, to ruin Mexico, to destroy Mexico . . . to set back for 50 years the restoration of good feeling . . . to invite reckless reprisal. . . . Between us only the river's thread. It seems such a little way. And we all used to be such good friends."[78]

In the fifty years since Slater wrote these words we have come a long way towards being friends again. The Pan American Round Table promotes understanding among women of both backgrounds. Our military leaders entertain each other. Our chambers of commerce discuss common problems. Our police assist each other. We have made a beginning in establishing cooperative programs in our colleges. As time goes on we shall have more to give each other, and our ties may grow close once more.

CHAPTER XXV

Afterword

THIS IS REALLY only the beginning. Besides all the stories that didn't fit into the chapters already written, the miraculous half century since 1917 is waiting for a historian, and the story gets better with the years.

Whoever tells it ought to be reminded of some things he must not leave out. He will have to start with the tremendous community effort that went into the First World War, beginning, perhaps, with the company of volunteers that peppery lawyer Richard Burges led to the battle-fields of France and telling how he was known forever after as Major Burges, as if he had just been through the Civil War.

There will have to be a big chapter on the wild days that followed in the wake of Prohibition, when smugglers and bootleggers and rum runners fought the Border Patrol and the sheriff's deputies almost every night and ended the careers of some first-class men. That will naturally bring on a discussion of the dope traffic, which still has to be battled on the border, and will introduce La Nacha (supposed to be the Queen of the Dope Ring) and her operatives, who can always think of a new way to get the stuff across — like attaching it to a mother dog who will not let anybody stop her as she rushes back across the bridge to her pups.

All this will have to be tied in with the fight against the Ku Klux Klan in the early twenties when the El Paso school board was in the hands of the organization and City Hall was in some danger of being taken over. After that will come the depression years when banks and businesses folded and the tops of freight cars were lined with sad-faced men making hopeless journeys to and from California; the Second World War and the action in Korea when the young men left again; the German rocket experts, some of whom slipped in through Mexico to work with captured V-2's and help us get our own program organized; the expansion of the missile ranges until they have taken over most of the Tularosa Valley for two hundred miles north of El Paso.

Our writer will have to reach for potent adjectives as he describes the population explosion of the 1950's which spread new housing developments and shopping centers across a thousand hills where purple verbenas and prickly pear and mesquite had flourished only a few months before. He must not leave out the "parachutists" — squatters — whose shacks and hovels, crowding the slopes west of Juárez all the way to the foot of the mountains, are being replaced by good adobe in *colonias* which already show signs of becoming decent subdivisions.

He will have to tell about the transformation of the border itself, the moving of the river to the new international boundary and the fine buildings and boulevards in the area opened for development by the Chamizal settlement; the Border Improvement Program in Mexico which has begun the transformation of Juárez into a city of parks and museums and spacious avenues; the housing projects which have made life better for small-income and retired people on our side and will do the same for those across the boundary line.

Whoever writes the story must tell something about the other and darker side of the picture — about the indigent people and the blighted areas and what is being done about them — about the vice and crime which are so hard to suppress in border towns, the closing down of the great gambling casinos in Juárez and the campaign which moved *calle diablo* (the Street of the devil) away from the downtown section to the outskirts of the city — the car thieves, the stick-up men, the swindlers, the fake real-estate promoters, the gang wars in South El Paso and the efforts of such men as Father Harold Rahm to get the delinquents into boys clubs and make useful citizens out of them.

There has never been a place like El Paso for characters with the bark on, and the best part of the book could very well be a sampling of the life stories of the people who have come here to make their homes since the First World War and to swell a population which is well over half a million now in the sister cities and will be a million before we know it.

There should be a corner somewhere in the book for the soldiers of fortune — Sam Dreben, Tracy Richardson, and the rest — who made the Sheldon Hotel their headquarters while they rounded up supplies for Villa or prepared to man his machine guns, and who went on to bigger and bloodier battlefields in Europe in 1918. There might well be a chapter devoted to H. D. Slater, tough-minded editor of the *Herald,* who chaired the first City Planning Commission and was responsible more than any other one man for the construction of the Scenic Drive around the point of Mount Franklin. He too went off to war in 1917, leaving his paper in charge of Zach White, and was always Captain Slater after that — a strange and rather lonely figure devoted to fine music and the nude in sculpture, as crochety as a New England spinster and never understood or appreciated by the townspeople who owed him so much.

For contrast there would be Roy Martin, known today among the capitalists of New York and California as Royce G. Martin, who was once the gambling czar of El Paso and Juárez, husband of saloon man Theo Eggers' beautiful blond daughter, and un-official partner of Pancho Villa. He left us to become president of the Electric Autolite Corporation, a director of the Chrysler Company, a close friend and confidant of Walter P. Chrysler himself. Alongside Roy's name should appear that of Elbridge A. Stuart, whose first business enterprise was a grocery store in a tent across from the St. Charles Hotel on South El Paso Street. He moved to Mundy's meat market, where the Capri theatre is now, and eventually left to found the Carnation Milk Company.

Bill Greet must be got in somehow, W. D. Greet, a gentleman of the Old South who came West for adventure, married a preacher's daughter, and became one of history's most unusual policemen — gentlemanly, helpful, completely fearless, and beloved by all. The worst people trusted him and behaved like lambs when he told them to. He kept $20,000 of Pancho Villa's money in the county clerk's safe until Pancho was ready to use it, and he went through the most unbelievable scrapes and perils in the day-to-day exercise of his functions.

As deserving of our grateful remembrance as Cap Greet is Dr. Hugh White, who fathered the County Hospital and almost single handed wiped out smallpox, a perennial scourge until, with the help of Father Cordova, he managed to vaccinate just about the entire population.

Examples come crowding in — like the distinguished Chinese diplomat who stopped in El Paso after the Boxer Rebellion and left his son there and finally went home. He bought a printing press which had been used to make passports for his countrymen on their way back to China. It would seem that nothing could be more useless than a Chinese printing press in the United States when the need for passports was over, but Mr. Yee was a man of ideas. He put his press to work printing Chinese lottery tickets. His descendants, who include teachers and lawyers, still run a successful job-printing business.

Then there was the young Syrian whose business career had its roots back in his native country at the time of his marriage. A large group of friends and relatives assembled to celebrate the occasion. After the ceremony, following the custom of the country, the bride and groom retired to the nuptial chamber, from which a short time later, again according to custom, the groom emerged to announce to the assembled guests that the bride was really a virgin. This was the signal for the firing of guns and an outburst of general rejoicing. It happened that on this particular evening a group of insurgents was planning to rise against the French, the call to action being the discharge of firearms. When the groom made his announcement, the wedding party responded in the time-honored way. The rebels went into premature action and suffered severe losses. It occurred to one of the survivors that there was something a little too coincidental about the timing of the gunfire at the wedding feast, and as a result one of our leading rug merchants made his appearance on our creosote-and-cactus-covered stage.

While he is at it — this historian of the period since 1917 — he should remember to say something about the survivals of an earlier time which add a special flavor to the typical twentieth-century way of life we share with Peoria and Poughkeepsie and Portland: the *luminarias* — lighted candles in paper sacks — which outline houses and sidewalks during the Christmas holidays; the Mexican dancers and *tipica* orchestras; the *chile con queso* (chile with cheese) which is standard equipment at all our parties; the words of *Allá en el rancho grande* which everybody knows and bellows gladly at all festive gatherings which last long enough.

We would not trade it for any other city, including New York and Los Angeles. Newcomers call it the Gravel Pit, the Dust Bin, the Rock Pile until they develop a companionable feeling for Mount Franklin and begin to find themselves at home with the enormous sky and the vast, gray-green desert. Before long they will be going out once or twice a week for Mexican food, and it is a short step from there to picking up a little Spanish and trying it out on the waiters in the cafés across the river — to sending out Christmas cards with Spanish mottoes and collecting Mexican pottery or glass. They may even develop an interest in what happened a century or two ago in this very Valley. After that, they belong here.

Day by day and year by year both communities become more internationally minded, and there is great hope for a future of cooperation and mutual understanding and respect. We are learning each others' languages (American grade-school children are taught Spanish by native speakers) and exchange programs are being organized in our colleges. What the end will be no man can know, but on this spot where there has been conflict and cruelty and misunderstanding for so many years, the door is open to friendship and good will. We have only to walk through the door.

ACKNOWLEDGMENTS

SOURCES

REFERENCES

INDEX

ACKNOWLEDGMENTS

THIS BOOK has been growing for over thirty years and owes so much to so many that the indebtedness can only begin to be acknowledged.

Librarians and their staffs naturally come first: Librarian Baxter Polk of the University of Texas at El Paso and his always-helpful people; Elizabeth Kelly, Donald Foos and John Wayne Smith (Librarians) with Marcelle Hamer, Virginia Hoke, and other staff members of the El Paso Public Library; Dr. Myra Jenkins of the New Mexico Records Center; Gertrude Hill, Ruth Rambo, and the staff of the New Mexico State Library; Nettie Lee Benson and Mrs. Evan S. Reese of the Latin American Collection of the University of Texas at Austin; Frederick Hall of the Newberry Library; Daniel J. Reed of the Manuscript Division, Library of Congress; Librarian David O. Kelly of the University of New Mexico; Charles Van Ravenswaay of the Missouri Historical Society; former Texas State Archivist James Day; Chester Kielman, The University of Texas Archivist; Llerena Friend of the Texas Collection, The University of Texas at Austin.

Special mention should be made of the indispensable file of theses and seminar papers on El Paso subjects accumulated in the U.T. El Paso Library over the past thirty-five years as a result of the efforts of Dr. John L. Waller, Dr. Rex Strickland, Dr. John H. McNeely and other members of the Department of History. Likewise indispensable are the articles in Dr. Eugene Porter's *Password*, organ of the El Paso County Historical Society, and the files of El Paso newspapers available through the early-day efforts of Major Richard F. Burges.

For friendly counsel through letters or by word of mouth much gratitude is due to many dedicated historians: Dr. Eleanor B. Adams, Dr. Odie B. Faulk, Dr. George P. Hammond, Fray Angelico Chávez, Dr. Jack D. Forbes, Dr. Donald Worcester, Dr. Ralph Smith, Dr. Robert C. Stevens and (from El Paso) Dr. John L. Waller, Dr. Rex Strickland, John Middagh, Morgan Broaddus, John W. Denny, Father Gerard Decorme, Esther Darbyshire MacCallum, Richard K. McMaster, Leon Metz, Marshall Hail, Bob Chapman, Bill McGaw, plus all the generous people whose names appear in the list of interviews.

Those who shared important material include Kathy White, Gordon Frost, Anton Gutiérrez, Eleanor Goodman, Jane Burges Perrenot, Mrs. J. C. Wilmarth, Wyndham White and Simeon H. Newman — all of El Paso; Sonja Fojtik of Fayetteville, Texas, Gene Bowden of Dallas, Frank Manning of Phoenix, Arizona, E. D. Spellman of Burnet, Texas, Frances Newman Thiel of Pacific Palisades, California, Fletcher Newman, now Brother M. Robert, O.C.S.O., Nona Barrick and Mary Taylor of Mesilla, New Mexico.

Most of the pictures are from the Aultman Collection and are used by permission of the El Paso Public Library. Those from the archive of the Pioneer Society of El Paso are used by permission of the officers of the

Society. Special thanks go to Roland Dickey, former Director of the University of New Mexico Press, for permission to use the portrait of de Vargas from J. Manuel Espinosa's *First Expedition of Vargas into New Mexico* (Albuquerque: University of New Mexico Press, 1940); to Leon Metz for the photograph of John Selman; to E. D. Spellman for the photograph of Mrs. Morose; to Chief Marion Coleman for the 1891 photograph of the El Paso Volunteer Fire Department; to George Simpson for permission to reproduce the 1887 photograph of the El Paso Browns; to Biagio Casciano for permission to copy the 1919 picture of the El Paso Symphony Orchestra; to Colonel Walter Stevenson for making available Tillie Howard's famous scrapbook; to Walter Stout of Stout-Feldman Studio for care and skill in reproducing portraits credited to him; to Commander Millard G. McKinney, U.S.N., Ret., historian of Fort Bliss and Biggs Field, whose skill with words and pictures has contributed much to this book. Thanks for help in completing the picture section are due also to Charles Teed, Mrs. Lee Gibson, Ed. Bartholomew, Vincent Mercaldo, the Museum of New Mexico, Mrs. E. F. Flores, and Miss María Luisa Flores.

Friends who have had the patience to read parts of the manuscript include Mrs. Frank Coles, Miss Elizabeth Kelly, Mrs. Mary K. Quinn, R. N. Mullin, Frank Manning, Leon Metz, Major General F. S. Ross (USA, Ret.), Laurence Stevens, and Mrs. Anne Kemp White. Dr. S. D. Myres, Editor of Texas Western Press, supervised the work at every stage and gave invaluable help.

For hours spent in typing the manuscript special thanks go to Claudia Arnold, Jean Carran, Sheryll Van Pelt, Jean McNeil and Ruby Telles. Mary Susan Gary earned my gratitude for work on the index.

The most deeply felt acknowledgment of all goes to my wife Carol, who was patient, cheerful and helpful as her husband toiled to bring the book into being.

SOURCES

INTERVIEWS

Mrs. Manuel Aguirre and Al Jennings, July 4, 1948
Dr. William Berrien, November 26, 1958
Karl Blumenthal, March 31, 1965
Mrs. Jess Boykin, March 20, 24, 1965
Frances Rosser Brown, Muskogee, Oklahoma, October 30, 1964
Mrs. George Brunner, January 7, 1963, July 14, 1965
Dr. George Brunner, January 17, 1963
Emma Adair Fall Chase, Alamogordo, New Mexico, January 15, 1964
William J. Chesak, Sr., July 1, 1966
Mr. and Mrs. Joe Clements, April 26, 1963
J. L. Coggeshall, July 7, Nov. 20, 1965
Colbert Coldwell, October 8, 1964, June 11, 1965
Mrs. Eleanor Coldwell, May 4, 1965
Mrs. Frank Coles, March 25, July 9, September 16, 1965
Lillian Hague Corcoran, February 8, 1950, Nov. 4, 1959, March 7, April 20, 1960
Francisco Faudoa, June 26, 1948
Rita Faudoa, July 14, 1965
María Luisa Flores and Mrs. E. F. Flores, June 1, 17, 27, 1960
W. H. Fryer, July 8, 1961
Mrs. Lee Gibson, March 25, 1966
Mrs. W. D. Greet, August 14, 1965
S. G. Gonzalez, June 7, 1965
Karl Goodman, May 26, June 5, 1965
Marshal Hail, November 23, 1964
Lily Smith Howard, June 8, 1965
Mrs. W. D. Howe, September 30, 1965
Elizabeth Kelly and Mary Kelly Quinn, January 24, 1965

Maury Kemp, Oct. 4, 1953, Aug. 13, 1954
Page Kemp, June 11, 1965
Noel Longuemare, November 26, 1965 (with Leon Metz)
A. A. Lane, September 12, 1965
Louis Le Veau, June 4, 22, 1965
Jim McKinney, Big Spring, Texas, June 2, 1944
Frank Manning, November 25, 1965
Flournoy Manzo, May 27, June 7, 1965
John Middagh, April 23, 1965
R. N. Mullin, August 12, 1966
John Neff, March 26, 1965
Robert T. Neill, Austin, Tex., Apr. 25, 1959
Jane Burges Perrenot, Apr. 5, Aug. 7, 1965
Ed Redding, July 30, 1965
Arthur Schuster, July 15, 1965
Irene Reckhart Shontz, July 15, 1965
George Simpson, June 10, 1965
Mattie Hardin Smith, Fort Worth, Texas, June 12, 1964
Fred Souflee, November 16, 1965
Laurence Stevens, March 26, April 2, 23, June 30, 1965
Rex Strickland, January 26, 1966
Mrs. J. U. Sweeney, January 24, 1965
Rachel Teel Vordermark, November 20, 1965
E. C. Wade, December 25, 1965
Rosalie Behr Waters, August 24, 1965
Pearson Wosika, November 16, 1965
Mrs. Hugh S. White, January 1, 15, 1966
Interviews not precisely dated in 1944 with Cleofas Calleros, Josefina Escajeda, Francisco Gonzalez, Jesús Montes, and G. N. Phillips

LETTERS

Will C. Burgie to C. L. S., June 19, 1965
J. J. Deaver, Calallen, Texas, to J. M. Deaver, El Paso, Tex., Oct. 4, 1937 (in possession of Wyndham Kemp White)
Sonja Fojtik to C. L. S., January 12, 1965
M. G. McKinney to C. L. S., Oct. 21, 1965
R. N. Mullin to C. L. S., June 26, July 21, December 30, 1965

L. M. Rutherford to C. L. S., June 7, 1965
M. H. Thomas, Curator of Columbiana, Columbia University, to C. L. S., January 8, 1954
Anson Mills to Richard F. Burges and T. A. Falvey, Washington, D. C., May 28, 1906 (describing his surveys of the townsite of El Paso), El Paso Public Library

NEWSPAPERS

Austin *Daily Statesman*
Austin *Weekly Statesman*
Weekly Austin Republican
Daily State Journal (Austin)
Texas State Gazette (Austin)
Dallas *Daily Herald*
Dallas *Weekly Herald*
Denison *News*
El Paso *Evening Post*
El Paso *Herald-Post*
El Paso *Lone Star*
El Paso *Times*

Galveston *News*
Flake's Daily Bulletin (Houston)
Flake's Semi-Weekly Bulletin (Houston)
Houston *Telegraph and Texas Register*
Newman's Semi-Weekly (Las Cruces, New Mexico)
Mesilla *Independent*
Mesilla *Times*
San Antonio *Express*
San Antonio *Ledger*
San Antonio *Light*
Santa Fe *New Mexican*
El Fronterizo (Juárez, Chihuahua)

BOOKS, ARTICLES, DOCUMENTS, ARCHIVAL MATERIAL

Abel, Annie Louise (ed.), *The Official Correspondence of James S. Calhoun while Indian Agent at Santa Fe and Superintendent of Indian Affairs in New Mexico.* Washington: Government Printing Office, 1915

Adams, Eleanor B. (ed. and trans.), *Bishop Tamaron's Visitation of New Mexico, 1760.* Albuquerque: University of New Mexico Press, Historical Society of New Mexico Publications in History, Vol. XV, 1954

Adams, Eleanor B., and Fray Angelico Chávez, *The Missions of New Mexico, 7176: A Description by Fray Francisco Atanasio Domínguez with other Contemporary Documents.* Albuquerque: University of New Mexico Press, 1956

Adams, Eleanor B., and France V. Scholes, "Books in New Mexico, 1598-1680." *New Mexico Historical Review,* XVII (July, 1942), 226-255

Almada, Francisco R., *Geographía del Estado de Chihuahua.* [Chihuahua, Impresora Ruiz Sandoval, 1945]
Resumen de Historia del Estado de Chihuahua. Mexico: Libros Mexicanos, 1955

Ayeta, Father Francisco, Letter to the Viceroy, February 11, 1682, Biblioteca Nacional de Mexico, Provincias Internas, Legajo 35, University of New Mexico Library transcript
Letter to the Viceroy, April 30, 1682, *Ibid.,* Legajo 2, No. 5, University of New Mexico transcript

Arlegúi, Joseph, *Crónica de la provincia de N. S. P. Francisco de Zacatecas.* Mexico. J. B. de Hogal, 1737

Bailey, Jessie Bromilow, *Diego de Vargas and the Reconquest of New Mexico.* Albuquerque: University of New Mexico Press, 1940

Bancroft, Hubert Howe, *History of Arizona and New Mexico.* Works, Vol. XVII. San Francisco: The History Company, 1899
North Mexican States and Texas. Works, Vols. XV, XVI. San Francisco: The History Company, 1890

Bandelier, Adolph, "Documentary History of the Rio Grande Pueblos, New Mexico" (Part I, 1536 to 1542, Concluded), *New Mexico Historical Review,* V (April, 1930), 130-138

Bandelier, Adolph, and Fanny R. Bandelier, *Historical Documents Relating to New Mexico, Nueva Vizcaya, and Approaches Thereto, to 1773* (ed. Charles Wilson Hackett). 3 Vols., Washington: The Carnegie Institution, 1923, 1926, 1937

Bandelier, Adolph, and Edgar L. Hewett, *Indians of the Rio Grande Valley.* Albuquerque: University of New Mexico Press, 1937

Barreiro, Antonio, *Ojeada sobre Nuevo Mexico* (ed. Lansing B. Bloom). Historical Society of New Mexico, Publications in History, Vol. VI, October, 1932

Bartlett, I. S., "Personal Account of Benito Juárez, 1865-66." *El Paso Herald,* June 5, 1909

Bartlett, John Russell, *Personal Narrative of Explorations and Incidents in Texas, Mexico, California, Sonora and Chihuahua, Connected with the United States and Mexican Boundary Commission during the Years 1850-1853.* 2 Vols., New York: D. Appleton Co., 1854

Barton, John Vinson, *El Paso in 1890.* Unpublished M. A. Thesis, Texas Western College, August, 1963

Baylor, Colonel George W., "Historical Sketches of the Southwest." *El Paso Herald,* January 20, 1900

Benavides, Fray Alonso, *Revised Memorial of 1634* (ed. F. W. Hodge, G. P. Hammond, and Agapito Rey). Albuquerque: University of New Mexico Press, 1945

Bender, A. B., "Opening Routes Across West Texas, 1848-1850." *Southwestern Historical Quarterly,* XXXVII (October, 1933), 116-135
The March of Empire. Lawrence: University of Kansas Press, 1952

Benton, Thomas H., *Thirty Years View.* 2 Vols. New York: D. Appleton and Co., 1856

Beristain de Souza, Dr. Don José Mariano, *Biblioteca Hispano-Americana Septentrional. . . .* Mexico, 1916.

Bieber, Ralph P., *Southern Trails to California in 1849.* Glendale: Arthur H. Clark Co., 1937

Bieber, Ralph P., and A. B. Bender, *Exploring Southwestern Trails, 1846-1854.* Glendale: Arthur H. Clark Co., 1938

Billard, J. B., "Stained Records Show Hart Bought His Land for 50 Cents an Acre." *El Paso Herald-Post,* May 10, 1938

Billington, Ray Allen, *Westward Expansion: A History of the American Frontier.* New York: The Macmillan Company, 1949

Binkley, William Campbell, *The Expansionist Movement in Texas.* Berkeley: University of California Press, 1925

Bishop, Morris, *The Odyssey of Cabeza de Vaca.* New York: The Century Company, 1933

Blake, Robert N., A History of the Catholic Church in El Paso, Texas. Unpublished M. A. Thesis, Texas Western College, 1948

Bloom, John P., "Johnny Gringo at the Pass of the North." Password, IV (October, 1959), 134-140

Bloom, Lansing B., "Early Bridges in New Mexico." New Mexico Highway Journal, III (January, 1925), 5-7, 18-19

"The Diego de Vargas Notes." New Mexico Historical Review, X (April, 1935), 170-171

"The Governors of New Mexico," New Mexico Historical Review, X (April, 1935), 152-157

"The Vargas Encomienda." New Mexico Historical Review, XIV (October, 1939), 366-417

Brinckerhoff, Sidney, and Odie B. Faulk, Lancers for the King. Phoenix: Arizona Historical Foundation, 1965

Bolton, Herbert Eugene (ed.), Spanish Exploration in the Southwest, 1542-1706 (Original Narratives of Early American History). New York: Charles Scribner's Sons, 1930

Texas in the Middle Eighteenth Century. Berkeley: University of California Press, 1951

Borah, Woodrow, New Spain's Century of Depression. Berkeley: University of California Press, 1951

Bowden, J. J., The Ascarate Grant. Unpublished M. A. Thesis, Texas Western College, 1952

El Rancho de Ponce, History Seminar Paper, TWC, 1951

"The Magoffin Salt War." Password, VII (Summer, 1962), 95-121

"The Texas-New Mexico Boundary Dispute Along the Rio Grande." Southwest Historical Quarterly, LXIII (October, 1959), 220-237

Brady, Donald V., The Theatre in Early El Paso (Southwestern Studies, IV. No. I, Monograph 13). El Paso: Texas Western Press, 1966

Bridgers, W. W., "El Paso was 'Wide Open' Border Town back in the Eighties." El Paso Herald, October 24, 1929

Just Chatting (typescript). 4 Vols., El Paso Public Library

Broaddus, J. Morgan, Jr., The Legal Heritage of El Paso. El Paso: Texas Western Press, 1963

Bronson, Edgar Beecher, The Red-Blooded Heroes of the Frontier. New York: Grosset and Dunlap, 1910

Buchanan, A. Russell (ed.), "George Washington Traherne: Texan Cowboy Soldier from Mier to Buena Vista." Southwestern Historical Quarterly, LVIII (July, 1954), 60-90

Budke, Maralyn, Albert B. Fall in New Mexico, 1888-1912. Unpublished M. A. Thesis, University of New Mexico, 1962

Burges, Richard F., Burges Collection (newspaper clippings, interviews, miscellaneous material in scrapbooks), in possession of Mrs. Jane Burges Perrenot, El Paso, Texas

Bush, Dr. I. J., Gringo Doctor. Caldwell, Ida.: Caxton Printers, 1939

Bustamante, Don Carlos María de, El nuevo Bernal Diaz o sea historia de la invasion de los Anglo-Americanos en Mexico compuesta en 1847 por D. Carlos Ma de Bustamante. Introduccion de Salvador Noriega. Vol. II. Mexico: Secretaria de Educación Publico, 1949

Calleros, Cleofas, "Chopin Music Hall Was Cultural." El Paso Times, September 7, 1952

El Paso Then and Now. El Paso: American Printing Company, 1954

La Antorcha de El Paso del Norte. El Paso: American Printing Company, 1951

"20th Annual Sun Carnival Recalls Festivals of Yesteryear." El Paso Times, January 9, 1955

Calleros, Cleofas, and Marjorie Graham, Queen of the Missions: Our Lady of Guadalupe. El Paso: American Printing Company, 1952

Campbell, John Logan, Autobiography of John Logan Campbell. Oakland, California: Privately Printed, 1940

Cardona, Ing. Manuel I., El Chamizal: Estudio Presentado a la VIII Reunion del Congreso Mexicano de Historia. Mexico, 1940

Carroll, H. Bailey, and J. Villasana Haggard, Three New Mexico Chronicles: The Exposición of Don Pedro Bautista Pino, 1812; The Ojeada of Lic. Antonio Barreiro, 1832; and the Additions by Don José Agustín de Escudero, 1849. Albuquerque: The Quivira Society, 1942

Castañeda, Carlos, Our Catholic Heritage in Texas, 1519-1936. 6 Vols., Vol. I., The Mission Era: The Founding of Texas, 1519-1693. Austin: Von Boeckmann-Jones Company, 1936

Cervantes M., Federico, Francisco Villa y la Revolución. Mexico: Ediciones Alonso, 1960

Chamberlain, Samuel E., My Confession. New York: Harper and Brothers, 1956

Chapman, Bob, "Hotel Angelus History" El Paso Times, February 24, 1952

Chávez, Fray Angelico, Origins of New Mexico Families in the Spanish Colonial Period. In Two Parts: The Seventeenth (1598-1693) and the Eighteenth (1693-1821) Centuries. Santa Fe: The Historical Society of New Mexico, 1954

418   BIBLIOGRAPHY

Chávez M., Armando B., *Historia de Ciudad Juárez Chih. Segunda Edición, Corregida y Aumentada.* [Juárez, Chihuahua: Privately Printed], 1951
Sesenta Años de Gobierno Municipal. Jefes Políticos del Distrito Bravos y Presidentes del Municipio de Juárez, 1897-1960. Mexico: Gráfica Cervantina, 1959
Clendenin, Clarence C., "General James Henry Carleton," *New Mexico Historical Review,* XXX (January, 1955), 23-43
Cline, Howard Francis, *The United States and Mexico.* Cambridge: Harvard University Press, 1953
Coldwell, W. M., "Gillett Book Revives Pioneer's Memories." Undated clipping from an El Paso newspaper, probably 1921, in El Paso Public Library copy of *Six Years with the Texas Rangers*
"Recollections of Early El Paso." R. F. Burges Collection, Book L, 33-43 (33-43)
Colton, Ray C., *The Civil War in the Southwest.* Norman: University of Oklahoma Press, 1959
Colyer, Vincent, *Peace with the Apaches of New Mexico and Arizona. Report of Vincent Colyer Member of Board of Indian Commissioners, 1871.* Washington: Government Printing Office, 1872
Commissioner of Indian Affairs, *Annual Report.* William P. Dole, Commissioner, to Hon. Caleb B. Smith, Secretary of the Interior, 1861
Conkling, Roscoe P., and Margaret B. Conkling, *The Butterfield Overland Mail 1857-1859.* 2 Vols. Glendale: Arthur H. Clark Co., 1947
Connelly, William Elsey, *Doniphan's Expedition and the Conquest of New Mexico and California.* Kansas City Mo.: Bryant Book and Stationery Co., 1907
Conway, G. R. G., "Antonio Espejo as a Familiar of the Mexican Inquisition 1572-1578." *New Mexico Historical Review,* VI (January, 1931), 1-20.
Corcoran, Lillian Hague, "He Brought the Railroad to El Paso — the story of Judge James P. Hague." *Password,* I (May, 1956), 45-54
Consular Despatches (U. S.) from Ciudad Juárez, April 10, 1850, to December 23, 1859; January 16, 1889-July 1, 1891. Microfilm, U.T. El Paso Library
Cornish, Beatrice Quijada, "The Ancestry and Family of Juan de Oñate," in *The Pacific Ocean in History.* H. Morse Stephens and Herbert E. Bolton, eds., New York: The Macmillan Company, 1917
Coues, Elliott (ed.), *The Expeditions of Zebulon Montgomery Pike.* 3 Vols. New York: Francis P. Harper, 1895

Cox, C. C., "From Texas to California in 1849" (Diary of C. C. Cox). Ed. Mabelle Eppard Martin. *Southwestern Historical Quarterly,* XXIX (July, 1925), 36-50
Cox, Sanford, *The State National Bank.* History Seminar Paper. n.d. U.T. El Paso Library
Creel, Enrique C., *El Estado de Chihuahua Su Historia, Geographía, y Riquiezas Naturales. Disertación Leida en dos Sesiones de la Sociedad Mexicana de Geographía y Estadistica.* Mexico: Tip. El Progreso, 1928
Cremony, John C., *Life Among the Apaches.* San Francisco: A. Roman, 1868
"The Apache Race." *Overland Monthly,* I (September, 1868), 201-209
Crimmins, Col. Martin L., "Colonel Buell's Expedition into Mexico in 1880." *New Mexico Historical Review,* X (April, 1935), 133-149
Cross, Jack L., "The El Paso-Fort Yuma Wagon Road: 1857-1860." *Password,* IV (Jaury, 1959) 4-18, (April, 1959) 58-70.
Cumberland, Charles Curtis, *The Mexican Revolution, Genesis under Madero.* Austin: University of Texas Press, 1952
Cunningham, Eugene, *Triggernometry: A Galley of Gunfighters.* Caldwell, Idaho: Caxton Printers, 1947
Cunningham, Mary S., *A History of the Woman's Club 1894-1945.* El Paso: Privately Printed, March, 1945
Current Topics Club Year Book, 1898, MS. El Paso Woman's Club
Cutts, James Madison, *The Conquest of California and New Mexico by the Forces of the United States in the Years 1846 and 1847.* Albuquerque, New Mexico: Horn and Wallace, 1965 (Facsimile reproduction of the original edition of 1847)
Daniel, James M. (trans. and ed.), "Diary of Pedro José de la Fuente, Captain of the Presidio of El Paso del Norte." *Southwestern Historical Quarterly,* LX (October, 1956), 260-281
Davenport, Harbert, and Joseph K. Wells, "The First Europeans in Texas." *Southwestern Historical Quarterly,* XXII (October, 1918), 111-142, (January, 1919), 205-259
Davis, L. H., "P. E. Kern, the Pioneer, Is El Paso's Monte Cristo." *El Paso Times,* January 28, 1912
Davis, W. W. H., *El Gringo; or, New Mexico and Her People.* New York: Harper and Brothers, 1857
Decorme, Father Gerard, *Las Misiones del Valle del Paso,* MS
Demarest, David D., *Diary.* Bancroft Library (MS)

Denny, John W., *A Century of Freemasonry at El Paso*. El Paso: Privately Printed, 1956

De Wetter, Charles Safford, "The Smelting Works as Remembered by Noel Longuemare." *Password*, VIII (Winter, 1963), 133-134

De Wetter, Mardee, *Revolutionary El Paso, 1910-1917*. Unpublished M. A. Thesis, Texas Western College, January, 1946

Diffenderfer, Mary M., *By Wagon Train from St. Louis to El Paso in 1865* (Diary of F. R. Diffenderfer). Clippings bound in the files of the Missouri Historical Society, St. Louis, Missouri

Dunn, William Edward, "Apache Relations in Texas, 1718-1750. *The Quarterly of the Texas State Historical Association*, XIV (January, 1911), 198-269

Dwyer, James Magoffin, Jr., "Hugh Stephenson," *New Mexico Historical Review*, XXIX (January, 1954), 1-7

Eastland, Thomas, and Joseph Eastland, "To California through Texas and Mexico. The Diary and Letters of Thomas B. Eastland and Joseph G. Eastland, His Son (Foreword by Douglas S. Watson, notes by Dorothy H. Huggins. *California Historical Society Quarterly*), XVIII (June, 1939), 99-135; (September, 1939), 229-248

Edwards, Marcellus Ball, "Journal of Marcellus Ball Edwards," in Ralph P. Bieber's *Marching with the Army of the West, 1846-1848, by Abraham Robinson Johnston, Marcellus Ball Edwards, Philip Gooch Ferguson*. California: Arthur H. Clark Co., 1936

El Paso Chamber of Commerce, *Missions of the El Paso Valley and Juárez, Chihuahua, Mexico*. n.d. (mimeographed)

El Paso, City of, El Paso City Council Minutes, Books B, C and H (typescript), El Paso Public Library
Vital Statistics (Death Records), El Paso County Courthouse

El Paso, County of, County Commissioners Court Minutes, El Paso County Court House
Deed Records, Book C, El Paso County Courthouse
Probate Records, El Paso County Courthouse

El Paso County Historical Society, *El Paso and the Mexican Revolution*, typescript made from tape recording of Old Timers Night program, April 26, 1962 (reminiscences of María Luisa Flores, Laurence Stevens, Mrs. J. C. Wilmarth, and others)

El Paso Pioneers Association, *Biographical and Historical Sketchbook*, M.S. U.T. El Paso Library

El Paso *Times*, Midsummer Trade Edition, August, 1887

El Paso Troubles in Texas. House Executive Document No. 93, 45th Congress, Second Session, 1878

Emory, William H., *Notes of a Military Reconnoissance, with Introduction and Notes by Ross Calvin*. Albuquerque: University of New Mexico Press, 1951

Erskine, M. H., "A Cattle Drive from Texas to California." *Southwestern Historical Quarterly*, LXVII (January, 1964), 404-405

Escobar, Romulo, "Memorias del Paso del Norte." *Boletin de la Sociedad Chihuahuense de Estudios Historicos*, VI (20 de Octubre y Noviembre de 1946), 61-62

Espinosa, Aurora M. de, "Platica de la Señora Aurora M. de Espinosa en el Ateneo Fronterizo." *El Fronterizo* (Juárez, Chihuahua), October 14, 1943

Espinosa, J. Manuel (trans. and ed.), *First Expedition of Vargas into New Mexico, 1692*. Albuquerque: University of New Mexico Press (Coronado Cuarto Centennial Publications, 1540-1940, Vol. X), 1940
"The Legend of Sierra Azul." *New Mexico Historical Review*, IX (April, 1934), 113-158
"Notes on the Lineage of Don Diego de Vargas, Reconqueror of New Mexico." *New Mexico Historical Review*, X (April, 1935), 112-120

Ex Parte James Manning. Habeas Corpus Proceedings before Judge T. A. Falvey, February 15, 1882 (A 63-page document devoted to testimony of eyewitnesses and character witnesses in the Cummings - Manning shooting — original document in the possession of H. Gordon Frost of El Paso)

Farris, Frances Bramlette, *South of the Alamo*. Unpublished MS in possession of C. L. S.

Fatout, Paul, *Ambrose Bierce, The Devil's Lexicographer*. Norman: University of Oklahoma Press, 1951

Faulk, Odie B., "The Controversial Boundary Survey and the Gadsden Treaty." *Arizona and the West*, IV (Autumn, 1962), 201-227

Ferguson, Philip Gooch, "Diary of Philip Gooch Ferguson" in *Marching with the Army of the West*, ed. Ralph P. Bieber. Glendale, California: The Arthur H. Clark Co., 1936, 343-344

Fernandez Duro, Cesareo, *Don Diego de Peñalosa y Su Descubrimento del Reino de Quivira. . . .* Madrid: Imprenta y Fundación de Manuel Tello, 1882

Fierman, Floyd S., "Ernest Angerstein — Soldier, Merchant, Accused Secessionist, and Post Trader." *Password*, VII (Spring, 1962), 43-62

Figueroa, Father Francisco Antonio de la Rosa, *Bezerro General Menologico y Cronologico de todos los Religiosos que* de las tres Parcialidades conviene a saber Padres de España, Hijos de Provincia, y Criollos ha avido in esta Sta Prova del Sto Evango desde su fundación hasta el preste año de 1764. . . . MS, Newberry Library 1990, Ayer Collection

First Regiment of California Infantry, Company E, Muster Rolls, 1861-1864 (record of A. J. Fountain). General Services Administration, National Archives

Flores, J. J., Diario (MS), in possession of María Luisa Flores

Libro Memorial (MS), in possession of María Luisa Flores

Foley, Edna Snowden, The William Elveus Robinson Water Treatment Plant. History Seminar Paper, Texas Western College, August, 1950

Forbes, Jack D., Apache, Navaho and Spaniard. Norman, Oklahoma: University of Oklahoma Press, 1960

"The Janos, Jocomes, Mansos and Sumas Indians." New Mexico Historical Review, XXXII (October, 1957), 319-334

"Unknown Athapascans: The Identification of the Jano, Jocome, Suma, Manso. . . ." Ethnohistory, VI (Spring, 1959), 97-159

Force, Fred P., The Life Story of L. R. Millican. Unpublished M. A. Thesis, Texas Western College, July, 1956

Fort Bliss: One Hundredth Anniversary (Commemorative brochure designed and produced by Carl Hertzog and Tom Lea). El Paso: Guynes Printing Company, 1948

Fountain, A. J., Answers to Interrogatories in Case Pending in McLennan County, George B. Zimpelman Plaintiff, Frank Howard et al defendants, answered before L. W. Lenoir, Notary Public, Las Cruces, New Mexico, April 6, 1887. MS. Copy in the Library of The University of Texas at El Paso.

Freeman, Leola, James Wiley Magoffin. Course Thesis, Texas Western College, 1942 (MS in files of C. L. S.)

Fugate, Francis, Frontier College. El Paso: Texas Western Press, 1963

Gallaher, F. M. (trans.), "Official Report of the Battle at Temescalitos (Brazito)." New Mexico Historical Review, III (October, 1928), 381-389

Gallegos, Hernán, "Relación." New Mexico Historical Review, II (July, 1927), 239-268, (October, 1927), 334-362

Galvez, Bernardo de, Instructions for Governing the Interior Provinces of New Spain, 1786 (trans. and ed. Donald L. Worcester). Berkeley: The Quivira Society (Publications, Vol. XII), 1951

Garber, Paul Neff, The Gadsden Treaty. Gloucester, Mass.: Peter Smith, 1959

Gerald, Rex E., "Portrait of a Community." The American West, III (Summer, 1966), 38-41

Gibson, A. M., The Life and Death of Colonel Albert Jennings Fountain. Norman: University of Oklahoma Press, 1965

Gibson, George Rutledge, Journal of a Soldier under Kearny and Doniphan, 1846-1847. (Ed. Ralph P. Bieber). Glendale: The Arthur H. Clark Co., 1935

Giddings, Emily Chase. and Emmie Wheatley Mahon, "The Jackass Trail." Password, II (August, 1957), 91-96

Gill, Mario, Nuestros Buenos Vecinos (Cuarta Edición Ampliada). Mexico: Editorial Azteca S. A., 1959

Gillett, James B., Six Years with the Texas Rangers, 1875 to 1881. Austin, Texas: Von Boeckman-Jones Company, 1921

"The Killing of Dallas Stoudenmire." Frontier Times, I (July, 1924), 24-25

Godbold, Mollie M., "Comanche and the Hardin Gang." Southwestern Historical Quarterly, LXVIII (July, 1963), 55-57

Goetzman, William H., Army Exploration in the American West. New Haven: Yale University Press, 1950

Golley, Frank B., "James Baird, Early Santa Fe Trader." Missouri Historical Society Bulletin, XV (April, 1959), 171-193

Gonzalez Flores, Lic. Enrique, Chihuahua de la Independencia a la Revolución. Mexico: Ediciones Botas, 1949

Greenwood, C. L., "Opening Routes to El Paso, 1849." Southwestern Historical Quarterly, XLVIII (October, 1944), 262-274

Gregg, Josiah, The Commerce of the Prairies (ed. Max L. Moorhead). Norman: University of Oklahoma Press, 1954 (originally published in 1844)

Gregg, Kate L., The Road to Santa Fe. Albuquerque: University of New Mexico Press, 1952

Gregory, Gladys, The Chamizal Settlement: A View from El Paso. El Paso: Texas Western Press (Southwestern Studies, I, No. 2), 1963

Guzmán, Martín Luis, Memoirs of Pancho Villa (trans. Virginia H. Taylor). Austin: University of Texas Press 1965

Gustat, Jennie B., His Band Marches On: The Story of Peter Gustat. New York: Vantage Press, 1954

Hackett, Charles Wilson, Revolt of the Pueblo Indians of New Mexico and Otermin's Attempted Reconquest, 1680-1692 (ed. C. W. Hackett, trans. Charmian Claire Shelby). Coronado Cuarto Centennial Publications, 1540-1940, ed. G. P. Hammond, Vols. 8 and 9. Albuquerque: University of New Mexico Press, 1942

Hail, Marshall, "What's Happened to the City's Health Seeking Visitors?" El Paso Herald-Post, April 26, 1961

Hakluyt, Richard, The Voyages, Traffiques & Discoveries of Foreign Voyagers. . . in the "Navigations" by Richard Hakluyt (ed. Ernest Rhys). (Vol. 2 of the Foreign Voyages; Vol. 10 of the Principal Voyages). London: J. M. Dent and Sons, Ltd.; New York: E. P. Dutton & Co., 1928. (Vol. 10 contains Juan González de Mendoza's Brief Relation of Espejo's entrada.)

Haley, J. Evetts, Fort Concho and the Texas Frontier. San Angelo, Texas: San Angelo Standard-Times, 1952

Jeff Milton: A Good Man with a Gun. Norman: University of Oklahoma Press, 1948

"A Log of the Texas-California Cattle Trail, 1854." Southwestern Historical Quarterly, XXXV (January, 1932), 208-237

Hall, Martin Hardwick, Sibley's New Mexico Campaign. Austin: University of Texas Press, 1960

Hallenbeck, Cleve, Alvar Núñez Cabeza de Vaca. Glendale: The Arthur H. Clark Company, 1940

Hammond, George P., "Oñate a Marauder?" New Mexico Historical Review, X (October, 1935), 249-270

Hammond, George P., and Edward H. Howes (ed.), Overland to California on the Southwestern Trail, 1849. Berkeley and Los Angeles: University of California Press, 1950

Hammond, George P., and Agapito Rey, "The Crown's Participation in the Founding of New Mexico." New Mexico Historical Quarterly, XXXII (October, 1957), 293-309

Expedition into New Mexico Made by Antonio de Espejo, 1582-1583 as Revealed in the Journal of Diego Pérez de Luxan, a Member of the Party. Los Angeles: The Quivira Society (Publications No. I), 1929

Obregon's History of 16th Century Explorations in Western America Entitled Chronicle, Commentary or Relation of the Ancient and Modern Discoveries in New Spain and New Mexico, 1584. Los Angeles: Wetzel Publishing Company, 1928

Don Juan de Oñate Colonizer of New Mexico, 1595-1628. (Coronado Cuarto Centennial Publications, 1540 - 1940, ed. George P. Hammond, Vol. V). Albuquerque: University of New Mexico Press, 1953

The Rediscovery of New Mexico, 1580-1594 (Coronado Cuarto Centennial Publications, 1540-1940, ed. George P. Hammond, Vol. III), Albuquerque: University of New Mexico Press, 1966

"The Rodriguez Expedition to New Mexico, 1581-1582." New Mexico Historical Review, II (July, 1927), 239-268; (October, 1927), 334-362

Hammons, Nancy Lee, A History of El Paso County, Texas, to 1900. Unpublished M. A. Thesis, Texas Western College, September, 1942

Haney, P. L., The International Controversy over the Waters of the Upper Rio Grande. Unpublished M.A. Thesis, Texas Western College, August, 1948

Hanke, Lewis, The Spanish Struggle for Justice in the Conquest of America. Philadelphia: University of Pennsylvania Press, 1949

Hardin, John Wesley, The Life of John Wesley Hardin as Written by Himself. Norman: University of Oklahoma Press, 1961 (original publication in 1896)

Harkey, Dee, Mean as Hell. Albuquerque: University of New Mexico Press, 1948

Harper, Mary S. Teel, "True Story of the Cannon, the Old Blue Whistler." El Paso Times, March 13, 1937

Harris, Benjamin Butler, The Gila Trail: The Texas Argonauts and the California Gold Rush (ed. Richard H. Dillon). Norman: University of Oklahoma Press, 1960

Hastings, D. H., "With Doniphan in Mexico," in Diaries, Recollections and Memoirs of the War with Mexico. Documents and notes collected by Justin H. Smith, Part II. Latin-American Collection, University of Texas, MS

Hening, H. B. (ed.), George Curry, 1861-1947: An Autobiography. Albuquerque: University of New Mexico Press, 1958

El Paso Herald, The Great Southwest, Souvenir Edition of the El Paso Daily Herald, 1880-1900. The Herald Company, 1900

Hodge, Frederick W. (ed.), "The Narrative of Alvar Núñez Cabeza de Vaca," in Spanish Explorers in the Southern United States (Original Narratives of Early American History). New York: Barnes and Noble, 1907

Horgan, Paul, Great River: The Rio Grande in North American History. Vol. I, "Indians and Spain." New York: Rinehart and Company, 1954

The Habit of Empire. Santa Fe: Rydal Press, 1938

House Executive Document, 36th Congress, 2nd Session, No. 537, 129, 1848 (Colonel John Ralls' commendation of Simeon Hart)

Hubbard, Louis H., Recollections of a Texas Educator. Salado, Texas: Anson Jones Press, 1964

Hughes, Anne E., The Beginnings of Spanish Settlement in the El Paso District. Berkeley: University of California Press, 1914 (Reprint, El Paso Public Schools, 1935)

Hughes, George W., *Report of the Secretary of War, Communicating a Map.* . . . March, 1849. Senate Executive Document No. 32, 31st Congress, 1st Session

Hughes, W. J., *Rebellious Ranger: Rip Ford and the Old Southwest.* Norman: University of Oklahoma Press, 1964

Hunt, Aurora, *The Army of the Pacific.* Glendale: The Arthur H. Clark Company, 1951

Illustrated History of New Mexico. Chicago: The Lewis Publishing Company, 1895, 656-658 (A. J. Fountain)

Irigoyen, Ulises, "El Problema Economico de las Ciudades Fronterizos." *Boletin de la Sociedad Chihuahuense de Estudios Historicos,* IV (Julio 20 de 1942), 64-68

Jackson, W. Turrentine, *Wagon Roads West.* Berkeley: University of California Press, 1952

Jones, Daniel, *Forty Years among the Indians.* Los Angeles: Westernlore Press, 1961

Jordan, Mildred L., *Railroads in the El Paso Area.* Unpublished M. A. Thesis, Texas Western College, 1957

Karnes, Harry J., and Associates (trans.), *Unknown Arizona and Sonora 1693-1721* (From the Francisco Fernandez del Castillo version of *Luz de la Tierra Incognita* by Captain Juan Mateo Manje). Tucson, 1954

Keleher, W. A., *The Fabulous Frontier.* Albuquerque: University of New Mexico Press, 1963 (original publication, 1945)

Turmoil in New Mexico, 1846-1848. Santa Fe: The Rydal Press, 1951

Kelly, Henry W., "Franciscan Missions of New Mexico, 1740-1760." *New Mexico Historical Review,* XV (October, 1940), 345-368; XVI (January, 1941), 41-69, (April, 1941), 148-183

Kelly, J. Charles, "Juan Sabeata and Diffusion in Aboriginal Tribes." *American Anthropologist,* LVII (October, 1955), 981-995

Kemp, Maury, *From the Memoirs of Maury Kemp.* Typescript, El Paso Public Library

Kendall, George Wilkins, *Narrative of an Expedition across the Great Southwestern Prairies from Texas to Santa Fe.* . . . 2 Vols. New York: Harper and Brothers, 1844

Kinnaird, Lawrence, *The Frontiers of New Spain: Nicolas de Lafora's Description, 1776-1778.* Berkeley: The Quivira Society (Quivira Society Publications XIII), 1958

Kohlberg, Walter, *A Translation of the Letters Written by Ernest Kohlberg, 1875, 1876, 1877.* MS in possession of Mrs. Leonard Goodman

Lafora, Nicolás de, *Relación de un viaje que hizo a los Presidios internos situados en la frontera de la America Septentrional* (Vito Alessio Robles, ed.) Mexico: Editorial Pedro Robledo, 1939

Lane, Lydia Spencer, *I Married a Soldier.* Albuquerque: Horn and Wallace, 1964 (first published in 1893)

Leach, Joseph, "Stagecoach Through the Pass — the Butterfield Overland Mail Comes to El Paso." *Password,* III (October, 1958), 130-137

Leonard, Irving A. (ed.), *The Mercurio Volante of Don Carlos de Sigüenza y Gongora.* . . . Los Angeles: The Quivira Society (Quivira Society Publications III), 1932

Leonard, O. B., *The Manning Family,* MS (copy in possession of C. L. S.)

Lesley, Lewis Burt, *Uncle Sam's Camels.* Cambridge: Harvard University Press, 1929

Levy, Estelle Goodman, "The Cloudcroft Baby Sanatorium." *Password,* VII (Fall, 1962), 136-148

"El Paso Defends Her Culture—Opera at the Pass of the North." *Password,* IV (July, 1959), 90-95

"The Myar Opera House and other Theaters in Old El Paso." *Password,* V (April, 1960), 65-73

Lofton, Monk, "John Wesley Hardin: Cunning Cruel Fighter." El Paso *Times Sundial,* April 28, 1963

Long, Grace, *The Anglo-American Occupation of the El Paso District.* Unpublished M. A. Thesis, The University of Texas, 1931

Look, George, *Reminiscences.* M. S. Copy in possession of Wyndham K. White

Loomis, Noel M., *The Texan-Santa Fe Pioneers.* Norman: University of Oklahoma Press, 1958

Lord, Walter (ed.), *The Fremantle Diary: Being the Journal of Lieutenant Colonel Arthur James Lyon Fremantle, Coldstream Guards, on his Three Months in the Southern States.* Boston: Little, Brown, 1959

Lummis, Charles F. (trans.), "Pioneers of the Far West." *Land of Sunshine,* XI (November, 1899), "Relating all the things that have been seen and known in New Mexico as well by sea as by land from the year of 1538 till that of 1626 by the Father Geronimo de Zárate Salmeron, etc."

MacCallum, Esther Darbyshire, *The History of St. Clement's Church, El Paso, Texas, 1870-1925.* El Paso: The McMath Company, 1925

McConville, James Edward, "El Paso–Ciudad Juárez: a Focus of Inter-American Culture." *New Mexico Historical Review,* XL (July, 1965), 233-247

McGaw, Bill, "James Baird, First Anglo Settler in El Paso, Died of Pneumonia after Trappers Doused Him in the Gila." *The Southwesterner,* IV (May-June, 1965), 2, 11

McMaster, Richard K., "Canby's Captains of the Southwest: 1860-1862." *Password*, VI (Summer, 1961), 79-95; (Fall, 1961), 123-140
"The Evolution of El Paso County." *Password*, III (July, 1958), 120-122
"The Mansfield Report." *Password*, IV (July, 1959), 96-112
Musket, Saber, and Missile: A History of Fort Bliss. El Paso: Complete Printing and Letter Service, 1962
McNary, James Graham, *This Is My Life.* Albuquerque: University of New Mexico Press, 1956
Magoffin, Susan Shelby, *Down the Santa Fe Trail and into Mexico: The Diary of Susan Shelby Magoffin, 1846-1847* (ed. Stella M. Drumm). New Haven: Yale University Press, 1962 (original copyright, 1926)
Mahon, Emmie Giddings W., and Chester V. Kielman, "George H. Giddings and the San Antonio-San Diego Mail Line." *Southwestern Historical Quarterly*, LXI (October, 1957), 220-239
Mahon, Emmie Wheatley, *George H. Giddings and the San Antonio-San Diego Stage Coach Line.* History Seminar Paper, Texas Western College, n.d.
The History and Development of the Southwestern Sun Carnival. Unpublished M. A. Thesis, Texas Western College, August, 1956
Malooly, Gilbert, *The First National Building.* History Seminar Paper, Texas Western College, May 21, 1953
Mangan, Frank, *Bordertown.* El Paso: Carl Hertzog, 1964
Marshall, Thomas Maitland, "St. Vrain's Expedition to the Gila in 1846." *Southwestern Historical Quarterly*, XIX (January, 1916), 251-260
Martin, Jack, *Border Boss: Captain John R. Hughes.* San Antonio: The Naylor Company, 1942
Martin, Mabelle Eppard, "California Emigrant Roads through Texas." *Southwestern Historical Quarterly*, XXVIII (April, 1925), 287-301
"From Texas to California in 1849: Diary of C. C. Cox." *Southwestern Historical Quarterly*, XXIX (July, 1925). 36-50; (October, 1925), 128-146; (January, 1926), 201-223
Martin, Mary Jean, *C. E. Kelly: Mayor of El Paso, 1910-1915.* History Seminar Paper, Texas Western College, August, 1956
Mecham, J. Lloyd, "Antonio de Espejo and His Journey to New Mexico." *Southwestern Historical Quarterly*, XXX (October, 1926), 114-138
"The Second Spanish Expedition to New Mexico." *New Mexico Historical Review*, I (July, 1926), 265-291
"Supplementary Documents Relating to the Chamuscado-Rodriguez Expedition." *Southwestern Historical Quarterly*, XXIX (January, 1926), 224-231
Meriwether, David, *My Life in the Mountains and on the Plains* (ed. Robert A. Griffen). Norman: University of Oklahoma Press, 1965
Metz, Leon, *John Selman, Texas Gunfighter.* New York: Hastings House, 1966
"Why Old John Selman Died." *Frontier Times*, XXXIX (October-November, 1965), 30-31, 64-65
Dallas Stoudenmire: El Paso Marshal, MS
Middagh, John, *El Paso after Dark.* Lecture, YWCA, El Paso, April 23, 1965
Frontier Newspaper: The El Paso Times. El Paso: Texas Western Press, 1958
Mills, Anson, *My Story.* Washington: Byron S. Adams, 1921 (second ed.)
W. W. Mills, *El Paso. A Glance at Its Men and Contests for the Last Few Years: The Election Fraud, the Marshes, Williams, Pearson, Verney, Stine and Fountain the Infamous.* Austin: Republican Office, 1871
Forty Years at El Paso, 1858-1898 (ed. Rex W. Strickland), El Paso: Carl Hertzog, 1962 (original copyright, 1901)
Mitchell, Guy Elliott (compiler and ed.), *The Official Proceedings of the Twelfth National Irrigation Congress Held at El Paso, Texas, November 15-16-17-18, 1904.* Galveston: Clarke and Courts, 1904
Moorhead, Max L., *New Mexico's Royal Road.* Norman: University of Oklahoma Press, 1958
"Spanish Transportation in The Southwest, 1540-1846." *New Mexico Historical Review*, XXXII (April, 1957), 107-122
Morehead, Charles R., "Personal Recollections of Charles R. Morehead," in William Elsey Connelley's *Doniphan's Expedition.* Kansas City, Mo.: Bryant and Douglas Book & Stationery Company, 1907 (Appendix C, 600-622)
Morrell, Elaine Lewis, *The Rise and Growth of Public Education in El Paso, Texas.* El Paso: Privately Printed, 1936
Mosier, Leanora, *History of the El Paso Fire Department 1882-1910.* History Seminar Paper, Texas Western College, August, 1956
Mullin, Robert N., "David Meriwether, Territorial Governor of New Mexico: a Sidelight on the Mexican Boundary Controversy of 1853." *Password*, VIII (Fall, 1963), 83-98
"In El Paso, John Wesley Hardin Tried to Live Down Gunman Reputation." *The Southwesterner*, II (December, 1962), 2

Neighbors, Kenneth, "The Expedition of Major Robert S. Neighbors to El Paso in 1849." *Southwestern Historical Quarterly*, LVIII (July, 1954), 36-59.

Newman, S. H., Notation on flyleaf of his copy of Owen White's *Out of the Desert* describing the killing of Stoudenmire. Used by permission of Frances Newman Thiel *Reminiscences* (MS)

Nicoll, Marian C., *A History of the El Paso Sewage Treatment and Pumping Plant*. History Seminar Paper, Texas Western College, January, 1951

Nordyke, Lewis, *John Wesley Hardin: Texas Gunman*. New York: William Morrow and Company, 1957

Ocaranza, Fernando, *Establicimientos Franciscanos en el Misterioso Reino de Nuevo Mexico*. Mexico: Privately printed.

Oden, Alonzo Van, *Ranger's Diary and Scrapbook*. Dallas: The Kaleidograph Press, 1936

Ogle, Ralph Hedrick, *Federal Control of the Western Apaches, 1848-1886*. New Mexico Historical Society Publications in History, Vol. IX, July, 1940

Orndorff, Helen, *History of the Development of Agriculture in the El Paso Valley*. Unpublished M. A. Thesis, Texas Western College, May, 1957

"The Development of Agriculture in the El Paso Valley—the Spanish Period." *Password*, V (October, 1960), 139-145

Otermin, Don Antonio, Letter to the Viceroy, March 24, 1682, Archivo de las Indias, Provincias Internas 35, Legajo 53, No. 14. University of New Mexico transcripts

Owens, Sister M. Liliana, *et al*, *Reverend Carlos M. Pinto, S. J., Apostle of El Paso, 1892-1919*. El Paso: Revista Catolica Press, 1951

Parkes, Henry Bamford, *A History of Mexico*. Third Edition. Boston: Houghton Mifflin Company, 1960

Parrish, Joe K., *Coffins, Cactus and Cowboys. The Exciting Story of El Paso, 1536 to the Present*. El Paso: Superior Publishing Company, 1964

"Hanged by the Neck till Dead." *Password*, III (April, 1958), 68-75

"Mrs. Mary M. Phillips Lives El Paso History." El Paso *Times*, January 7, 1951

"Ranger Killed in Gun Battle." El Paso *Times Sun Dial*, September 26, 1965

Parrish, Joe, and Cleofas Calleros, "Has Daughter of El Paso's first Settler Been Found?" El Paso *Times*, January 17, 1965

Pattie, James O., *The Personal Narrative of James O. Pattie of Kentucky* (ed. Timothy Flint), Chicago: Lakeside Press, 1930 (first publication, 1831)

Pérez de Luxan, Diego, *Expedition into New Mexico Made by Antonio de Espejo, 1582-1583* (trans. and ed. George P. Hammond and Agapito Rey). Los Angeles: The Quivira Society, 1929

Pérez de Villagrá, Gaspar, *History of New Mexico, Alcala, 1610* (trans. Gilberto Espinosa, ed. F. W. Hodge). Los Angeles: The Quivira Society, 1933

Pérez, Santos, *Baseball in El Paso*. History Seminar Paper, Texas Western College, n.d.

Phelan, John L., *The Milennial Kingdom of the Franciscans in the New World*. Berkeley: University of California Press, 1956

Pichardo, José Antonio, *Pichardo's Treatise on the Limits of Louisiana and Texas. . . .* (ed. Charles Wilson Hackett). 2 Vols. Austin: University of Texas Press, 1931

Phillips, Mrs. Mary, "Statement of Mary M. Phillips of Early Days in El Paso, Texas, May 26, 1934." R. F. Burges Collection, Book L, 14-30

Pike, Zebulon M., *The Southwestern Expedition of Zebulon M. Pike* (ed. Milo M. Quaife). Chicago: R. R. Donnelley and Sons, 1925

Exploratory Travels through the Western Territories of North America. . . . (London, 1811). Denver: H. Lawrence & Co., 1889.

Ponce de Leon, José M., *Reseñas Historicas del Estado de Chihuahua*. Segunda Edición, Tomo I. Chihuahua: Imprenta del Gobierno, 1910

Pope, Captain John, *Report of Exploration of a Route for the Pacific Railroad near the Thirty-Second Parallel of Latitude, from the Red River to the Rio Grande*. House Executive Document 129 (1855), 33rd Congress, Second Session

Porter, Clyde and Mae Reed, and LeRoy R. Hafen, *Ruxton of the Rockies*. Norman: University of Oklahoma Press, 1950

Porter, Eugene O., "No Dark and Cold and Dreary Day—El Paso, Texas, as a Health Resort." *Password*, IV (April, 1959), 71-74

"The Founding of San Elizario." *Password*, IX (Fall, 1964), 87-98

"Map No. Two of Satterthwaite's Addition to El Paso, 1884." *Password*, I (May, 1956), 68

"San Elizario, a Century of History." *Password*, IX (Winter, 1964), 137-146

Powell, Philip Wayne, *Soldiers, Indians and Silver: The Northward Advance of New Spain, 1550-1600*. Berkeley: University of California Press, 1952

Prestwood, Nadine H., *Social Life and Customs of the People of El Paso*. Unpublished M. A. Thesis, Texas Western College, 1949

Prince, L. B., *Concise History of New Mexico*. Cedar Rapids: The Torch Press, 1912

Puckett, Fidelia M., "Ramon Ortiz, Priest and Patriot." *New Mexico Historical Review*, XXV (October, 1950), 265-295

Ramsdell, Charles William, *Reconstruction in Texas*. New York: Longmans, Green, 1910

Reed, S. G., *A History of the Texas Railroads*. Houston: St. Clair Publishing Co., 1941

Report of the Adjutant General of the State of Texas for the Fiscal Year Ending August 31, 1878. Galveston: Book and Job Office of the Galveston *News*, 1878

Richardson, Albert D., *Beyond the Mississippi . . . 1857-1867*. Hartford: American Publishing Company, 1867

Richardson, William H., *Journal of William H. Richardson. . . .* Third Edition. New York: Privately Printed, 1850. Reproduced in the *Missouri Historical Review*, XXII (October, 1927 - July, 1928), 193-236, 331-360, 511-542

Rives, George Lockhart, *The United States and Mexico, 1821-1848*. 2 Vols. New York: Charles Scribner's Sons, 1913

Robinson, Cecil, *With the Ears of Strangers*. Tucson: University of Arizona Press, 1964

Robinson, Jacob S., *A Journal of the Santa Fe Expedition under Col. Doniphan*. Princeton: Princeton University Press, 1932 (first printed in 1848)

Robles, Vito Alessio (ed.), *Diario y derrotero de lo caminado, vista y observado, en la visita que hizo a los presidios de la Nueva España Septentrional el Brigadier Pedro de Rivera con una introducción y notas por Vito Alessio Robles*. Mexico: Taller Autographia, 1946

Rogers, Betty, *Reminiscences of Old El Paso* (Based on conversations with Judge W. D. Howe). Course thesis, Texas Western College, May, 1946

Rosen, Evelyn R., *Henry Cuniffe: The Man and His Times*. Unpublished M. A. Thesis, Texas Western College, August, 1961

Ross, Robert Stanley, *Francisco I. Madero, Apostle of Mexican Democracy*. New York: Columbia University Press, 1955

Ruhlen, George, "Brazito—the Only Battle in the Southwest between American and Foreign Troops." *Password*, II (February, 1957), 4-13

"The Battle of Brazito—Where It Was Fought." *Password*, II (May, 1957), 53-60

Rush, Thomas Herman, *El Paso YMCA, 1886-1918*. History Seminar Paper, Texas Western College, Summer, 1950

Rutherford, Bud, "Tillie Howard's House End of Line on Broadway, Near Cleo Starr's and Beebe's." *The Southwesterner*, IV (May-June, 1965), 7-8

Ruxton, George F., *Adventures in Mexico and the Rocky Mountains*. New York: Harper & Brothers, 1848

Sanderlin, Walter S. (ed.), "A Cattle Drive from Texas to California: The Diary of M. H. Erskine, 1954." *Southwestern Historical Quarterly*, LXIII (October, 1959), 397-412

Sanger, Donald Bridgman, *The Story of Fort Bliss*. El Paso: Privately Printed, 1933

Sauer, Carl, *The Distribution of Aboriginal Tribes and Languages in Northwestern Mexico*. Berkeley: University of California Press, 1934

Schaer, Bertha Archer, *An Historical Sketch of Aoy School*. History Seminar Paper, Texas Western College, n.d.

Scholes, France V., "Church and State in New Mexico." *New Mexico Historical Review*, XI (January, 1936), 1-71; (April, 1936), 145-178; (July, 1936), 283-294; (October, 1936), 297-349; XII (January, 1937), 78-106

"Documents for the History of New Mexico Missions in the Seventeenth Century." *New Mexico Historical Review*, IV (January, 1920), 45-58

"Civil Government and Society in New Mexico in the 17th Century." *New Mexico Historical Review*, X (April, 1935), 71-111

"The First Decade of the Inquisition in New Mexico." *New Mexico Historical Review*, X (July, 1935), 195-241

"The Supply Service of the New Mexican Missions in the Seventeenth Century." *New Mexico Historical Review*, V (January, 1930), 93-115; (April, 1930), 186-210; (October, 1930), 386-404

"Troublous Times in New Mexico." *New Mexico Historical Review*, XII (April, 1937), 134-174; (October, 1937), 380-452; XIII (January, 1938), 63-84; XV (July, 1940), 249-268; (October, 1940), 369-417; XVI (January, 1941), 5-40; (April, 1941), 184-205; (July, 1941), 313-327

Selman, John, Jr., *John Selman of El Paso*, MS

Sherman, Edward F., *A Decade of Exploration in the Southwest*. Unpublished M. A. Thesis, Texas Western College, 1962

Simpson, Lesley Byrd, *The Encomienda in New Spain: The Beginning of Spanish Mexico*. Berkeley and Los Angeles: University of California Press, 1950

Smart, Charles Allen, *Viva Juárez*. Philadelphia: Lippincott, 1963

Smith, Justin H., *The War with Mexico*. 2 Vols. New York: Macmillan, 1919

Smith, Ralph, "Apache Plunder Trails Southward, 1831-1840." *New Mexico Historical Review*, XXXVII (January, 1962), 20-42

"Apache 'Ranching' below the Gila, 1841-1845." *Arizoniana*, III (Winter, 1962), 1-17

"Mexican and Anglo-Saxon Traffic in Scalps, Slaves and Livestock, 1835-1841." *West Texas Historical Association Yearbook*, XXXVI (October, 1960), 98-115

"The Scalp Hunt in Chihuahua — 1849." *New Mexico Historical Review*, XL (April, 1965), 117-140

"The Scalp Hunter in the Borderlands, 1835-1850." *Arizona and the West*, VI (Spring, 1964), 4-22

Sonnichsen, C. L., *Billy King's Tombstone*. Caldwell: Caxton Printers, 1941

I'll Die before I'll Run. New York: The Devin-Adair Co., 1962

"Major McMullen's Invasion of Mexico." *Password*, II (May, 1957), 38-43

Tularosa: Last of the Frontier West. New York: Devin-Adair, 1960

Spanish Archives of New Mexico, New Mexico Records Center, Santa Fe

Stevens, Robert C., "The Apache Menace in Sonora, 1831-1849." *Arizona and the West*, VI (Autumn, 1964), 211-222

Stoes, K. D., "Smuggler's Gap Offered Protection to Many Lawless Men along Border." El Paso *Times*, August 21, 1955

Streit, Robert, O. M. I., *Bibliotheca Missionum, Zweiter Band*. Amerikanische Missionliteratur, 1493-1699. Aachen: Franziskanus Xaverius Missionverein, Zentrale, 1924

Strickland, Rex W., "James Baird," in *The Fur Trade and the Mountain Men* (ed. Leroy R. Hafen), III, 27-37. Glendale: Arthur H. Clark, 1966

"P. T. Herbert: Ante-Bellum Resident of El Paso." *Password*, V (April, 1960), 43-52

"W. W. Mills, El Paso Politician." *Password*, VII (Summer, 1962), 83-94

Six Who Came to El Paso. El Paso: Texas Western Press (Southwestern Studies I-3), Fall, 1963

Tamayo, Jorge L., *Epistolario de Benito Juárez; selección, prologo y notas de Jorge L. Tamayo*. Mexico: Fondo de Cultura Economica, [1957]

Taylor, Mary, and Nona W. Barrick, *El Tratado de Mesilla*. MS

Testimonio a la letra de la causa criminal, que ha seguido contra el Maestro de Campo Juan Domínguez de Mendoza y los demás que con el hicieron fuga incurriendo en pena de la vida y traidores al Rey por quebrantadores del bando promulgado que contenía la

dicha pena (Testimony in the trial of Juan Domínguez de Mendoza in absentia, September 28 to October 6, 1685, New Mexico Archives No. 35)

Thomas, Alfred Barnaby, "Antonio de Bonilla and Spanish Plans for the Defense of New Mexico, 1772 - 1778." *New Spain and the Anglo-American West*, Historical Contributions Presented to Herbert Eugene Bolton, Vol. I (New Spain). Lancaster, Pennsylvania: Lancaster Press, 1932, 183-209

Teodoro de Croix and the Northern Frontier of New Spain, 1776 - 1783. Norman: University of Oklahoma Press, 1941

Forgotten Frontiers: A Study of the Spanish Indian Policy of Don Juan Bautista de Anza, Governor of New Mexico, 1777-1787. Norman: University of Oklahoma Press, 1932

The Plains Indians and New Mexico, 1751 - 1778. Albuquerque: University of New Mexico Press, 1940 (Coronado Cuarto Centennial Publications, 1540-1940, Vol. XI, ed. George P. Hammond)

Thomlinson, M. H., *The Garrison of Fort Bliss, 1849-1916*. El Paso: Hertzog and Resler, 1945

"The Dragoons and El Paso, 1848." *New Mexico Historical Review*, XXIII (July, 1948), 217-224

Thompson, Dr. Howard, *Builders of El Paso* (ed. C. L. Sonnichsen). Typescript, 1945

Timm, Charles A., *The International Boundary Commission, United States and Mexico*. Austin: University of Texas Press (University of Texas Publication No. 4134), September 8, 1941

Tittman, Edward D., "The Exploitation of Treason." *New Mexico Historical Review*, IV (April, 1929), 128-145

Tully, Jim, *Ladies in the Parlor*. New York: Greenberg, 1935

Turner, Timothy, *Bullets, Bottles and Gardenias*. Dallas: Southwest Press, 1935

Twitchell, Ralph Emerson, *The Leading Facts of New Mexican History*. 5 Vols. Cedar Rapids, Iowa: The Torch Press, 1911-1917

Spanish Archives of New Mexico. 2 Vols. Cedar Rapids, Iowa: The Torch Press, 1914

The Story of the Conquest of Santa Fe, New Mexico, and the Building of Old Fort Marcy, A. D. 1846. Albuquerque: Historical Society of New Mexico (Publications No. 24), 1920

Utley, Robert M., *The International Boundary, United States and Mexico: A History of Frontier Dispute and Cooperation, 1848-1963*. Santa Fe: U. S. Department of the Interior, National Park Service (Mimeograph), 1964

Vetancurt, Fr. Agustín de, *Teatro Mexicano*, III. *Cronica de la provincia del Santo Evangelio*, IV *(Menologio Franciscano de los Varones mas Senalados, que con sus vidas ejemplares, perfección religiosa, ciencia, predicación evangelica, en su vida y muerte ilustraron la Provincia del Santo Evangelio de Mexico)*. Mexico: Imprenta de I. Escalante y Ca, 1871

Vowell, Jack, *Politics in El Paso, 1850-1920*. Unpublished M. A. Thesis, Texas Western College, 1950

Walker, Rosalie, *A History of the Woman's Club of El Paso*. History Seminar Paper, Texas Western College, January, 1954

Waller, J. L., "The Civil War in the El Paso Area." *West Texas Historical Association Year Book*, XXII (October, 1946), 3-14

Walz, Vina, *History of the El Paso Area, 1680-1692*. Unpublished Ph.D. Dissertation, University of New Mexico, 1951

Want, Marguerite T., "The Crumbling Adobes of Chamberino." *New Mexico Historical Review*, XXXIX (July, 1964), 169-180

The War of the Rebellion Records: A Compilation of the Official Records of the Union and Confederate Armies. Series I, IV, IX, XV, XXVI, XLVII (Vol. II), L (Parts I, II). Washington: Government Printing Office, 1882, 1883, 1897

Ward, Charles Francis, *The Salt War of San Elizario* (1877). Unpublished M. A. Thesis, The University of Texas, 1932

Webb, James Josiah, *Adventures in the Santa Fe Trade* (ed. Ralph P. Bieber). Glendale: The Arthur H. Clark Company, 1931

Webb, Walter Prescott, *The Texas Rangers: A Century of Frontier Defense.* Boston: Houghton Mifflin, 1935

Webster, Martha, *History of San Jacinto Square and Pioneer Plaza*. History Seminar Paper, Texas Western College, August, 1957

White, Alice M., *History of the Development of Irrigation in the El Paso Valley*. Unpublished M. A. Thesis, Texas Western College, May, 1950

White, Mrs. Hugh, *My Little History Story*. MS [1965]

White, Katherine H., *The Recognized Spanish and Mexican Land Grants of the El Paso Area*. History Seminar Paper, Texas Western College, Spring, 1950

White, Owen P., *The Autobiography of a Durable Sinner*. New York: G. P. Putnam's Sons, 1942

My Texas, 'Tis of Thee. New York: G. P. Putnam's Sons, 1936

Out of the Desert: The Historical Romance of El Paso. El Paso: The McMath Company, 1924

White, Zach T., "Zach White Tells Story of Famous City Marshal. . . ." *El Paso Evening Post*, May 30, 1928

Williams, Gladys, *Orchestras and Bands, El Paso Music, 1880 - 1960*. Unpublished M. A. Thesis, Texas Western College, 1960

Williams, O. W., *In Old New Mexico, 1879-1880*. Privately Printed, n.p., n.d.

Wise, Clyde, "The Effects of the Railroads upon El Paso." *Password*, V (July, 1960), 91-100

Wilson, Neill C., and Frank J. Taylor, *Southern Pacific*. New York: McGraw-Hill, 1952

Wislizenus, A., *Memoir of a Tour through Northern Mexico; Connected with Colonel Doniphan's Expedition, 1846-1847*. Senate Miscellaneous Document No. 26, 30th Congress, 1st Session. Washington: Tippin and Streepen, Printers, 1848

Woodward, Arthur, "Great Western Was Earliest Inn-Keeper in Old El Paso." *The Southwesterner*, III (August, 1963), 1, 22

The Great Western: Amazon of the Army. San Francisco: Johnck and Seeger, 1961

Wright, Lyle H., and Josephine Bynum (eds.), *The Butterfield Overland Mail*. San Marino: Henry E. Huntington Library, 1954

Zingg, Robert M., "The Importance of the El Paso Area in the Conquest and Reconquest of New Mexico." *Password*, I (August, 1956), 82-89, (November, 1956), 134-139

REFERENCES

Chapter I

Men With Beards and Armor

1 The story is told by Philip Wayne Powell in *Soldiers, Indians and Silver* (Berkeley, 1952)
2 Castañeda, *Our Catholic Heritage* (Austin, 1950), 1
3 Hakluyt, *Voyages* (London, 1928), II, 185
4 Espinosa, "The Legend of Sierra Azul" MMHR, IX (April, 1934), 113-158
5 Bishop, *Odyssey of Cabeza de Vaca* (New York, 1933), 137, thinks they crossed "probably at San Elizario" twenty miles below El Paso. Cf. Hallenbeck, *Alvar Núñez Cabeza de Vaca* (Glendale, 1940), 183-215
6 White, *Out of the Desert* (El Paso, 1924), 14
7 Hodge (ed.), "The Narrative of Alvar Núñez Cabeza de Vaca" in *Spanish Explorers* (New York, 1907), 111
8 Bolton, *Spanish Exploration* (New York, 1930), 137 (Introduction)
9 Hughes, *Beginnings of Spanish Settlement* (Berkeley, 1914), 297
10 Mecham, "Second Spanish Expedition," NMHR, I (July, 1926); 266; Hammond and Rey, "Rodríguez Expedition." NMHR, II (July, 1927), 253, n.15
11 Hammond and Rey, *Rediscovery of New Mexico* (Albuquerque, 1966), 127-129; Bolton, *Spanish Exploration*, 144, n.1. Calleros, following Arlegúi (*Cronica*, 214-215), thinks Rodríguez may have made a preliminary trip to the Pass (*La Antorcha*, El Paso, 1951, 20-21).
12 Bandelier, "Documentary History of the Rio Grande Pueblos," NMHR, V (April, 1930), 259
13 Bolton, *Spanish Exploration*, 158 (Report of the Viceroy to the King)
14 Mecham, "Second Spanish Expedition," 242
15 Hammond and Rey, *Rediscovery*, 143
16 *Ibid.*, 68
17 *Ibid.*, 80
18 Baltasar de Obregón and Hernando Barrado gave testimony in Mexico City (*Ibid.*, 133, 139)
19 Mecham, "Second Spanish Expedition," 280; Zárate-Salmeron, *Relación*, translated as "Pioneers of the West" by C. F. Lummis in *The Land of Sunshine*, XI (November, 1899), 340-341
20 Mecham, "Supplementary Documents," 244; Forbes, *Apache, Navaho and Spaniard* (Norman, 1960), 53; Hammond and Rey, *Rediscovery*, 121-122
21 Hammond and Rey, *Rediscovery*, 96

22 Calleros, *La Antorcha*, 24
23 Mecham, "Second Spanish Expedition," 285
24 Mecham, "Supplementary Documents." SWHQ, XXIX (Jan., 1926), 227-228
25 Hammond and Rey, "The Rodríguez Expedition," 356-357
26 *Ibid.*, 359
27 Mecham, "Second Spanish Expedition," 289
28 Conway, "Antonio de Espejo." NMHR, VI (January, 1931), 1-20
29 Mecham, "Antonio Espejo." SWHQ, XXX (October, 1926), 114-122, shows that there is considerable confusion about how and when Espejo became leader.

Chapter II

The Tread of a Conqueror

1 Bolton, *Spanish Exploration* (New York, 1930), 202
2 Villagrá, *History of New Mexico* (Los Angeles, 1933), 7, 83
3 *Ibid.*, 9; Hammond and Rey, *Don Juan de Oñate* (Albuquerque, 1953), 974
4 Villagrá, *History*, 15
5 *Ibid.*, 107
6 Paul Horgan's *The Habit of Empire* (Santa Fe, 1938) is an account of the enterprise with emphasis on the exploits of the Zaldívar brothers.
7 For Oñate's background see Cornish, "The Ancestry and Family of Juan de Oñate" in *The Pacific Ocean in History* (New York, 1917), 452-464
8 There were two wildcat *entradas*: the first (1590) led by Gaspar Castaño de Sosa; the second (1593) under joint command of Francisco de Leyva Bonilla and Antonio Gutiérrez de Humaña. See Hammond and Rey, *Oñate*, 5
9 Hammond and Rey, *Oñate*, 11-14
10 *Ibid.*, 15. For Crown expenditures see Hammond and Rey, "The Crown's Participation in the Founding of New Mexico." NMHR, XXXII (October, 1957), 293-309
11 During the period of waiting Oñate may have evened the score with his enemy Don Juan Bautista de Lomas de Colmenares. See "Oñate a Marauder?" NMHR, X (October, 1935), 249-270, by George P. Hammond
12 Villagrá, *History*, 108; Hammond and Rey, *Oñate*, 15
13 Villagrá, 114
14 *Ibid.*
15 *Ibid.*, 115-116
16 *Ibid.*, 126-128
17 *Ibid.*, 127

18 *Ibid.*, 129
19 *Ibid.*, 130-135
20 *Ibid.*, 144
21 *Ibid.*, 144n; Hammond and Rey, *Oñate*, 95
22 Chávez, *Historia de Ciudad Juárez* (Juárez, 1951), 62
23 For an excellent account of this conflict see Scholes, "Church and State in New Mexico" (NMHR XI, January-October, 1936; XII, January, 1937) and "Troublous Times in New Mexico" (NMHR XII, April, October, 1937); XIII (January, 1938); XV (July, October, 1949); XVI (January, April, July, 1941)

CHAPTER III

Laying the Foundation

1 The problem of who the Jumanos were and what became of them has been much debated. Sauer, *Distribution of Aboriginal Tribes* (Berkeley, 1934), 68, thinks there was "no clear difference between Jumano and Suma."
2 Forbes, "Unknown Athapaskans" (*Ethnohistory* VI, Spring, 1959), 110; "Janos, Jocomes, Mansos, and Suma Indians," NMHR, XXXII (October, 1957), 319-334
3 Vetancurt, *Teatro Mexicano* (Mexico, 1871), IV, 24, says they were a "barbarous nation which by their ferocity discredited the title."
4 Hammond and Rey, *Oñate* (Albuquerque, 1953), 315
5 Benavides, *Revised Memorial* (Albuquerque, 1945), 52-53
6 Adams, *Bishop Tamaron's Visitation* (Albuquerque, 1954), 40
7 Bandelier, "Documentary History of the Rio Grande Pueblos" (NMHR V April, 1930), 383
8 Scholes, "The Supply Service of the New Mexico Missions" (NMHR V, January, 1930), 93-97; (April, 1930), 186-210
9 Benavides, *Revised Memorial*, 53
10 Hughes, *Spanish Settlement* (Berkeley, 1914), 304, says Fray Antonio de Arteaga baptized the Mansos some time after 1629
11 Walz, *History of the El Paso Area, 1680-1692* (MS), 12. Dr. Walz bases her conclusions on an unpublished paper, "Documents on the Beginnings of the Manso and Suma Missions," by France V. Scholes.
12 Vetancurt, *Teatro Mexicano*, III, 300-310
13 *Ibid.*, IV, 24
14 *Ibid.*, III, 309
15 *Ibid.*, IV, 25
16 *Ibid.*, IV, 24
17 Hughes, *Spanish Settlement*, 304-305

18 Vetancurt, *Teatro*, IV, 25
19 Mrs. Walz in her *History of the El Paso Area* follows Dr. Scholes in believing that the date should be 1657 or 1658 (pp. 15-16).
20 Cleofas Calleros in *La Antorcha* (El Paso, 1951) reproduces the *Auto de Fundación* from a copy of the lost document made by Bandelier in 1888 (pp. 41-42). See also Hughes, *Spanish Settlement*, 306-307.
21 Vetancurt, *Teatro*, IV, 25
22 *Missions of the El Paso Valley* (El Paso, n.d.). Cf. Calleros, *Queen of the Missions* (El Paso, 1952), 8. Rex Gerald in his discussion of the Urrutia map of Paso del Norte ("Portrait of a Community," *The American West*, III, Summer, 1966, 38-41) thinks the present church is smaller than the original though it may incorporate parts of the original structure.
23 Vetancurt, *Teatro*, III, 308
24 Ocaranza, *Establicimientos Franciscanos* (Mexico, 1934), 65
25 Vetancurt, *Teatro*, III, 308
26 Hughes, *Spanish Settlement*, 309
27 Walz, *History*, 22-23. Hughes lists from burial records the names of thirty-one Spaniards living in El Paso before 1680.
28 Scholes, "Documents for the History of the New Mexican Missions in the Seventeenth Century," NMHR IV (January, 1929), 56
29 Walz, *History*, 19; Vetancurt, *Teatro*, III, 309. Forbes, *Apache, Navaho and Spaniard* (Norman, 1960), 201, says it was "at present-day Janos."
30 Walz, *History*, 22
31 Chávez, *Historia*, 49, thinks García brought roses and apples to the Valley.
32 Forbes, *Apache, Navaho and Spaniard*, 71
33 Scholes, "Troublous Times," NMHR XIII (January, 1938), 66

CHAPTER IV

The Loss of Everything

1 Hackett, *Revolt of the Pueblo Indians* (Albuquerque, 1942), 28
2 The whole miserable story is told by Scholes in "Church and State in New Mexico" and "Troublous Times in New Mexico." Cf. Forbes, *Apache, Navaho and Spaniard* (Norman, 1960), 129, 136
3 Hackett, *Revolt*, I, 126. Walz, *History*, 31, says they had been leaving for ten years.
4 Scholes, "Civil Government and Society in New Mexico," NMHR, X (April, 1935), 71-111; Adams and Scholes, "Books in New Mexico, 1598-1680," NMHR, XVII (July, 1942), 226-255

5　Scholes, "The First Decade of the Inquisition in New Mexico," NMHR, X (July, 1935), 225

6　Scholes, "Church and State," 104

7　Scholes, "Civil Government and Society," 89

8　For the encomienda system see Barber, *Indian Labor* (Albuquerque, 1932); Simpson, *The Encomienda* (Berkeley, 1950); Bloom, "The Vargas Encomienda," NMHR, XIV (October, 1939), 366-417

9　Hackett, *Revolt*, I, xxii

10　Bandelier and Hackett, *Documents* (Washington, 1937) III, 177 (Declaration of Thomé Domínguez de Mendoza)

11　Hackett, *Revolt*, I, 62, Declaration of Pedro García

12　Espinosa, *First Expedition* (Albuquerque, 1940), 14: "Between 1645 and 1675 there were several attempts at armed rebellion all of which were easily suppressed." Forbes, *Apache, Navaho and Spaniard*, 163, mentions revolts which were planned for 1650 and 1667. He notes that by 1677 the Apaches had invaded the El Paso region, "a fact previously unknown" (172).

13　Forbes, *Apache, Navaho and Spaniard*, 171-172

14　Hackett, *Revolt*, I, xxii, ff.

15　*Ibid.*, I, 251

16　*Ibid.*, I, lxxix, lxxxiv; Bandelier and Hackett, *Documents*, III, 286-288

17　Scholes, "The Supply Service of the New Mexico Missions, NMHR, V (October, 1930), 401: "So long as the missions could make a strong appeal to the Indians by furnishing food in time of disaster, the Indians maintained a certain loyalty to the church. But now, with food scarce, the missions could no longer make the same appeal."

18　Hackett, *Revolt*, I, lxxxii; Bandelier and Hackett, *Documents*, III, 296-308, 343

19　These facts come from Father Francisco Antonio de la Rosa Figueroa's manuscript volume, *Bezerro General.* . . . Father Figueroa worked over the archives in the convent of San Francisco de Mexico. His book is now in the Newberry Library.

20　Bandelier and Hackett, *Documents*, III, 297, Royal Cedula of June, 1678. The King thanks Ayeta for his "zeal and diligence."

21　Hackett, *Revolt*, I, 216. On his way to Mexico City he resolved "to gallop forty leagues in four days" to visit Don Bartolomé de Escamiela

22　*Ibid.*, I, 92. Ayeta to Otermín, September 8, 1680

23　He did this during Otermín's attempted reconquest (*Ibid.*, II, 305)

24　*Ibid.*, I, 31

25　*Ibid.*, I, 34. He asked for and got certification in writing of his promptness and willingness in caring for the refugees (42-43).

26　*Ibid.*, I, 51

27　*Ibid.*

28　*Ibid.*, I, 52

29　Bandelier and Hackett, *Documents*, III, 293, 304

30　Hackett, *Revolt*, I, 94

31　*Ibid.*, I, 130, 212-213; Bandelier and Hackett, *Documents*, III, 341

32　Hackett, *Revolt*, I, 126, 153; II, 154; Forbes, *Apache, Navaho and Spaniard*, 183; Walz, *History*, 31

33　Hackett, *Revolt*, I, 214

34　*Ibid.*, cvii-cxvi. The muster showed 1956 persons, 155 of them men able to bear arms. Not counted in the muster were 317 Piro Indians.

35　*Ibid.*, I, 215

36　Hughes, *Spanish Settlement* (Berkeley, 1914), 310

37　Hackett, *Revolt*, I, 215; Hughes, 316, quoting Ayeta

38　Hackett, *Revolt*, I, 249-250

39　*Ibid.*, 254-262; Bandelier and Hackett, *Documents*, III, 347-348

40　Hackett, *Revolt*, II, 17

41　Scholes, "Church and State," NMHR, XI (October, 1936), 344

42　Hackett, *Revolt*, II, 21-22

43　*Ibid.*, II, 29-31

44　*Ibid.*, II, 64

45　*Ibid.*, II, 90, 92

46　*Ibid.*, II, 143-146

47　*Ibid.*, II, 147-149

48　*Ibid.*, II, 146-147

49　*Ibid.*, II, 311-312

50　*Ibid.*, II, 153

51　*Ibid.*, II, 160-181

52　Walz, *History*, 63

53　Forbes, *Apache, Navaho and Spaniard*, 187

54　Walz, *History*, 68

CHAPTER V

The First Reentry

1　Hackett, *Revolt* (Albuquerque, 1942), II, 203-204

2　*Ibid.*, II, 215-217

3　Walz, *History* (MS), 217

4　Chávez, *Origins of New Mexico Families* (Santa Fe, 1954), 24-26

5　Hackett, *Revolt*, II, 94

6　*Ibid.*, II, 266

7　Bandelier and Hackett, *Documents* (Washington, 1937), III, 354 (Memorial of Juan Domínguez de Mendoza)

8　*Ibid.*, III, 364. Father López says: ". . . he is fully experienced in matters of war, and moreover is known to be a man of singular good fortune in it." Scholes, "Civil Government in New

Mexico," 99, calls him "the most distinguished soldier in New Mexico in the seventeenth century."

9 Included in *Servicios Personales*, copy in possession of C. L. S. A somewhat different version, including mention of the "letter of favor and privilege," was brought to Mexico City by Father López and is printed by Hackett in *Revolt*, II, 357-358.

10 Forbes, *Apache, Navaho and Spaniard* (Norman, 1960), 140, 143

11 *Ibid.*, 140, quoting an unpublished letter supposedly signed by Governor Fernando Argüello, who did not take office until after the date given.

12 Bandelier and Hackett, *Documents*, III, 363. López says Domínguez has served his Majesty "from the age of fourteen years up to fifty-four."

13 Forbes, 146, cites testimony of Juan Samaniego y Jaca, given January 12, 1653, to show the Domínguez' story was a "false account."

14 *Ibid.*, 147

15 *Ibid.*, 148. Juan's brother Tomé was involved in something like this in 1657.

16 *Ibid.*, 154. Walz, *History*, 203-204; Scholes, "Troublous Times," XIII (January, 1938), 69; *Testimonio* (MS), 1685, Statement of Felipe Serna

17 One charge against López was that he had "sold the office of lieutenant-captain general of the Sandía area to Juan Domínguez de Mendoza for three hundred pesos" (Scholes, "Troublous Times," XIII, 73).

18 Bandelier and Hackett, *Documents*, III, 138-139

19 "The Vargas Encomienda," NMHR, XIV (October, 1939); Scholes, "Troublous Times," NMHR, XV (July, 1940), 251

20 Scholes, "Troublous Times," XV, 253, gives an example.

21 *Ibid.*, XVI, 315-317

22 Forbes, *Apache, Navaho and Spaniard*, 165

23 Walz, *History*, 205

24 *Servicios Personales*, certificate supplied by the Cabildo

25 Hackett, *Revolt*. II, 69

26 *Ibid.*, II, 228-231; 233-252

27 *Ibid.*, II, 372

28 Bandelier and Hackett, *Documents*, III, 355

29 Hackett, *Revolt*, II 255-272, 398-400; Forbes, *Apache, Navaho and Spaniard*, 188

30 Hackett, *Revolt*, II, 400

31 *Ibid.*, II, 316

32 *Ibid.*, II, 350

33 *Ibid.*, II, 396, 398

34 Walz, *History*, 74-76

35 Barber, *Indian Labor in the Spanish Colonies* (Albuquerque, 1932), 125

36 Ayeta to the Viceroy, February 11, 1682. Biblioteca Nacional de Mexico,
University of New Mexico Transcripts; Walz, 68, 75; Hughes, 37

37 Walz, *History*, 77-78

38 *Ibid.*, 98. The messengers included Captain Joseph Padilla, Lazaro de Mizquia, Don Fernando Duran y Chávez, and Estevan López. Padilla was a nephew of Don Pedro. The complaints obviously came from the Chávez-Domínguez faction. The papers accused Otermín of every sort of peculation and mismanagement, recommended that his salary be cut 2,000 pesos, and his rank be reduced to that of *alcalde mayor* (*Ibid.*, 82, 92).

39 *Ibid.*, 87

40 Otermín to the Viceroy, March 24, 1682, Biblioteca Nacional de Mexico, University of New Mexico transcripts

41 Ayeta to the Viceroy, Parral, April 30, 1682. Biblioteca Nacional de Mexico, University of New Mexico transcripts

42 Especially *Defensa de la Verdad. . . .* Madrid, 1683; *Crisol de la Verdad. . . .* Madrid, 1693; *Verdad Defendida. . . .* Madrid, 1694 (See Streit and Figueroa)

43 Robert Streit, *Biblioteca Missionum* (Aachen, 1924), Zweiter Band, 579

44 Beristain de Souza, *Biblioteca Hispano-Americana Septentrional* (Mexico, 1816), 132

45 Figueroa, *Bezerro General* (MS)

46 Walz, *History*, 93-94

47 *Ibid.*, 94

48 *Ibid.*, 95

49 *Ibid.*, 96

50 *Ibid.*, 97-98

51 *Ibid.*, 101

52 *Ibid.*, 100-101

CHAPTER VI

Ambitions and
Disappointments

1 Walz, *History* (MS), 104-109; Karnes, *Unknown Arizona* (Tucson, 1954), 2-3

2 Walz, 115-118

3 Hughes, *Beginnings of Spanish Settlement* (Berkeley, 1914), 327, 364-368; Walz, 120

4 Walz, 118

5 *Ibid.*, 89

6 El Paso *Times*, January 15, 1956 (dedication of plaque at San Elizario), May 20, 1956. In 1964 Dr. E. O. Porter, "The Founding of San Elizario," *Password*, IX (Fall, 1964), 87-88, and "San Elizario, a Century of History," *Password*, IX (Winter, 1964), 137-146, argued that the San Elizario presidio was not established until 1780. Mrs. Walz, p. 76, quotes Father Ayeta as he lists the settlements in order from north to south in 1680: Paso, Real de San

Lorenco, San Pedro de Alcántara, Corpus Christi [Ysleta], Tzenecu, Presidio, Santa Gertrudis, Soledad, Thoma. This places the presidio below Ysleta in the neighborhood, at least, of San Elizario.

7 Walz, 124

8 *Ibid.*, 143

9 Kelley, "Juan Sabeata," *American Anthropologist*, LVII (October, 1955), calls his subject "an inveterate gossip and a master of frontier intrigue."

10 Father Leclerc (Pichardo, II, 350) writing to the Count of Paredes in 1685, says, "many of those nations had begged repeatedly at the mining camp of Parral for the water of baptism." They complained of serving in the mines and fields of Parral without ever having religious instruction.

11 Kelly, 181, expresses this view.

12 Pichardo II, 350

13 Bolton, *Spanish Exploration* (New York, 1930), 314, 316; Walz, 128

14 Jironza's letter is reproduced in Pichardo I, 137-139

15 Walz, 129

16 *Ibid.*

17 Bolton, *Spanish Exploration*, 316

18 Bandelier and Hackett, *Documents* (Washington, 1926), II, 361

19 Bolton, 331

20 *Ibid.*

21 *Ibid.*, 336

22 *Ibid.*, 338, n1

23 Bandelier and Hackett, III, 362 (López to the Viceroy in 1686)

24 Bolton, 340

25 Kelly, "Juan Sabeata," 985-987, puts together the Indian's record.

26 Forbes, *Apache, Navaho and Spaniard* (Norman, 1960), 198

27 *Testimonio* in the trial *in absentia* of Juan Domínguez de Mendoza, September 28-October 6, 1685, testimony of Diego de Luna and others.

28 *Ibid.*, testimony of Hernando Martín Serrano and others

29 *Ibid.*, testimony of Diego de Luna and others

30 *Ibid.*, testimony of Juan Ruiz and others.

31 *Ibid.*

32 Hughes, *Beginnings of Spanish Settlement*, 336

33 Walz, *History*, 141

34 Forbes, "Unknown Athapaskans," *Ethnohistory*, VI (Spring, 1959), 106

35 Walz, 145

36 *Ibid.*, 146-148; Hughes, 358

37 Walz, 154

38 *Ibid.*, 133; Hughes, 361

39 Walz, 158; Hughes, 371

40 Walz, 162-163; Hughes, 372, summarizes the Governor's reply.

41 Walz, 193

42 *Ibid.*, 196

43 Hughes, 374-380

44 The trial *in absentia* lasted from September 28 to October 6. A copy of the transcript of testimony is in the New Mexico Archives.

45 *Testimonio*, declaration of Sargento Mayor Diego López and others

46 *Ibid.*, declaration of Adjutant Antonio Lucero and others

47 *Ibid.*, declarations of Sargento Mayor Diego López and Salvador Holguin

48 Walz, 212

49 *Ibid.*, 206

50 Bandelier and Hackett, *Documents*, III, 356

51 Hughes, 319, note 12a

52 Walz, 219, 221-222

53 Bandelier and Hackett, III, 363

54 *Ibid.*, 364

55 *Ibid.*

56 Walz, 219

57 *Ibid.*, 238, note 8

58 *Ibid.*, 227

59 *Ibid.*, 222. Mrs. Walz gives details of his execution of Juan de Montoya, ten days after his arrival. See pp. 225, 241-243 for his "embezzlement" of the presidio payroll.

60 Karnes, *Unknown Arizona* (Tucson, 1954),4

61 *Ibid.*

62 Walz, 261-263

63 *Ibid.*, 236-238, 245

64 Pichardo, II, 345-346, quoting Barcia's *Ensayo Cronologico para la Historia General de la Florida* (1686). This entire letter, which was included with the *Servicios Personales* drawn up by Domínguez for presentation to the King, is quoted in Fernández Duro, *Don Diego de Peñalosa* (Madrid, 1882), 74-77

65 Walz, 245

CHAPTER VII

The End of Rebellion

1 Espinosa, *First Expedition of Vargas, 1692* (Albuquerque, 1940), 19-23, summarizes the achievements of the house of Vargas. Dr. Espinosa's volume is the indispensable essay on the reconquest.

2 The original was lost during the Spanish Civil War. See Espinosa, 25, for his analysis of Vargas' dress and personality as indicated in the portrait.

3 Espinosa, 24, notes that we have only his baptismal date, November 8, 1643. See Bailey, *Diego de Vargas* (Albuquerque, 1940) for sources of information.

4 Bloom, "De Vargas Notes," NMHQ, X (April, 1935), 170

5 Espinosa, 26

6 *Ibid.*, 45
7 *Ibid.*, 27-29. Mrs. Walz (*History*, MS) discusses the campaign (275-280, 290, 292 n.45), recording Vargas' protests against using his troops for anything but the reconquest and his eventual yielding to viceregal pressure. She thinks less of Vargas than Espinosa does in his "rapturous" book, and considers him "glory thirsty" and "status conscious" (226).
8 Espinosa, 44
9 *Ibid.*, 49, 52, 53
10 Bancroft, *Arizona and New Mexico* (Albuquerque, 1962), 198
11 Espinosa, 155
12 *Ibid.*, 125, 181. Bailey, 37-48, tells what happened at Santa Fe.
13 Espinosa, 70
14 *Ibid.*, 134. This was his way of describing his actions when he did not burn the Indians' crops.
15 *Ibid.*, 219, 276
16 *Ibid.*, 165
17 *Ibid.*, 262
18 *Ibid.*, 262-263
19 *Ibid.*, 299
20 *Ibid.*, 306 n
21 Bancroft, *Arizona and New Mexico*, 202-203, notes 13, 14
22 Espinosa, 280
23 *Ibid.*, 298
24 *Ibid.*, 34; Bancroft, 202 - 203. Mrs. Walz, 301-309, gives an account of the serious trouble between Vargas and the local clergy at this time.
25 Bancroft, 203-205; Espinosa, 35-37
26 Espinosa, 40
27 Zingg, "The Importance of the El Paso Area in the Conquest and Reconquest of New Mexico," Part Two, *Password*, I (November, 1956), 139, n.11

CHAPTER VIII

A Century of Trouble

1 Dunn, "Apache Relations in Texas," TSHA *Quarterly*, XIV (January, 1911), 266, quoting Father Santa Ana (1745); Bolton, *Texas in the Middle Eighteenth Century* (Berkeley, 1915), 3
2 Bandelier and Hackett, *Documents* (Washington, 1937), III, 377
3 Bancroft, *Arizona and New Mexico* (Albuquerque, 1962), 227-230
4 Forbes, *Apache, Navaho and Spaniard* (Norman, 1960), 283-284
5 The first was Bishop Benito Crespo, who got as far as Paso del Norte in 1725 and went all the way to Santa Fe in 1730. The next was Martín de Elizacoecha, who made a visitation of New Mexico in 1737 (Adams, *Bishop Tamaron's Visitation*, Albuquerque,

1954, 14-17; Kelly, "Franciscan Missions," NMHR XVI, January, 1941, 161).
6 Adams, *Bishop Tamaron*, 1-19, and Kelly, "Franciscan Missions," 148-183, discuss this controversy in detail. Some of the original documents are reproduced in Bandelier and Hackett, especially III, 425-431, and 468-501.
7 Kelly, "Franciscan Missions," 162
8 *Ibid.*, 165
9 Bandelier and Hackett, *Documents*, III, 428-429
10 Chávez, *Historia de Ciudad Juárez* (Juárez, 1951), 72. The material is from the Juárez Archives.
11 Bancroft, *Arizona and New Mexico*, 253 n.51
12 Thomas, *The Plains Indians and New Mexico* (Albuquerque, 1940), 16
13 *Ibid.*, 20, 36
14 Bandelier and Hackett, III, 406-407
15 Adams, *Bishop Tamaron*, Appendix II, 107-109
16 Bandelier and Hackett, III, 460
17 *Ibid.*, Father Fray Juan Sáenz de Lezaún, writing in 1760, says that there were two Indian uprisings in Paso del Norte during the preceding decade (*Ibid.*, III, 496).
18 Adams, *Bishop Tamaron*, "Introduction," 21
19 *Ibid.*, 35, 36
20 Daniel, "Diary of Pedro José de la Fuente," SWHQ LX (October, 1956), 262
21 *Ibid.*, 263-264
22 *Ibid.*, 265
23 Bolton, *Texas in the Middle Eighteenth Century*, 102-105
24 Kinnaird, *The Frontiers of New Spain* (Berkeley, 1958), 83
25 Thomas, *The Plains Indians and New Mexico*, 41
26 Thomas, *Forgotten Frontiers* (Norman, 1932), 5
27 Thomas, *Teodoro de Croix* (Norman, 1941), 29
28 Thomas, *Forgotten Frontiers*, 10
29 This spot, as pointed out by Eugene O. Porter in "The Founding of San Elizario," *Password*, IX (Fall, 1964), was far to the southeast of present-day San Elizario. In 1780 the presidio and its name were transferred back to the site called Los Tiburcios on or near the place where San Elizario stands now, and about where the presidio had been when it was moved during the Indian troubles of 1684.
30 Thomas, *Forgotten Frontiers*, 13
31 *Ibid.*
32 Adams and Chávez, *The Missions of New Mexico* (Albuquerque, 1956), xviii
33 Thomas, *Teodoro de Croix*, 28-37

34 Thomas, "Antonio de Bonilla and Spanish Plans for the Defense of New Mexico, 1772-1778," (Lancaster, Pa., 1932), 195
35 *Ibid.*, 199
36 For a translation of the proceedings see Thomas, *The Plains Indians*, 193-211
37 *Ibid.*, 211
38 Thomas, *Forgotten Frontiers*, 66-71
39 Thomas, *Teodoro de Croix*, 46
40 *Ibid.*, 96
41 *Ibid.*, 38-39
42 *Ibid.*, 42
43 *Ibid.*, 125-126
44 *Ibid.*, 129
45 *Ibid.*, 62
46 *Ibid.*, 43-44
47 *Ibid.*, 42
48 *Ibid.*, 42-56; Bancroft, *Arizona and New Mexico*, 378-379
49 Gálvez, *Instructions* (Berkeley, 1951), 43
50 *Ibid.*, 46-47
51 *Ibid.*, 47
52 Bancroft, *North Mexican States and Texas*, 683-684
53 Spanish Archives of New Mexico, No. 1715: "Extracto de las Novedades Ocurridas en la Provincia . . . desde 20 Noviembre Pasado hasta 30 de Marzo de 1804"
54 *Ibid.*, 291, Pedro de Nava to the Governor, July 16, 1799
55 *Ibid.*, 2009, Isidro Rey to Joaquín del Real Alencaster, August 31, 1806
56 *Ibid.*, 1463, September 14, 1798
57 Pike, *The Southwestern Expedition* (Chicago, 1925), 166-167

CHAPTER IX

Prosperity and Peril

1 Spanish Archives of New Mexico, no. 1204, Governor Fernando de la Concha to Lieutenant Governor Uranga, July 23, 1792
2 *Ibid.*, 1833, Report of Surgeon Larranaga on children vaccinated, his work having been handicapped by an epidemic, Santa Fe, May 25, 1805
3 *Ibid.*, 1900, Joaquín del Real Alencaster, Santa Fe, October 12, 1806
4 Moorhead, *New Mexico's Royal Road* (Norman, 1958), 44-48; Carroll *et al*, *Three New Mexico Chronicles* (Albuquerque, 1942), 106
5 Gregg, *Commerce of the Prairies* (Norman, 1954), 267, n.5, quoting J. A. Escudero, *Noticias Estadísticas*, 186
6 Levels listed are as follows: *Niños Inscritos, Leyen Cartas, En Libro, En Carton, En Cartilla, Restando.*
7 Spanish Archives of New Mexico, 2061

8 Barreiro, *Ojeada* (Santa Fe, 1928), 29
9 Reports on the building and maintenance of the bridge are preserved in the Spanish Archives of New Mexico, Bernal's letter being numbered 1383, June 20, 1797. See also Lansing B. Bloom, "Early Bridges in New Mexico," *New Mexico Highway Journal,* III (January, 1925).
10 Spanish Archives nos. 1494, 1495a, Fernando Chacón to Pedro de Nava, August 30, 1800
11 W. M. Coldwell, "Recollections," Burges Collection, Book L, 41. Coldwell says his father (Doniphan's interpreter at the battle of Brazito) once showed his wife (W. M. Coldwell's mother) the place.
12 Spanish Archives, 1512, unsigned, to Pedro de Nava, October 17, 1800
13 *Ibid.*, 1584 (Santiago Abreu to Pedro de Nava, January 7, 1802); 611 (to Pedro de Nava, June 15, 1802); 1613 (to Pedro de Nava, July 21, 1802) 1613 (Joseph Joaquín Ugarte to Pedro de Nava, July 14, 1802)
14 *Ibid.*, 1893, no. 3, Isidro Rey to Joaquín del Real Alencaster, September 26, 1805
15 Pike, *Exploratory Travels* (London, 1811), 334-336
16 It was rebuilt in 1816 (Spanish Archives 2658, Rafael Montes to Pedro María de Allande, April 4, 1816)
17 *Ibid.*, 2814, Father Sebastian Alvarez to Governor Melgares, May 8, 1810
18 Almada, *Resumen* (Mexico, 1955), 194
19 Stevens, "The Apache Menace," *Arizona and the West,* VI (Autumn, 1964), 213
20 Chávez, *Historia de Ciudad Juárez* (Juárez, 1951), 101; Long, *Anglo-American Occupation* (MS, 1931), 16
21 Chávez, 103
22 *Ibid.*, 106
23 Stevens, "Apache Menace," 214; Almada, *Resumen*, 197
24 Almada, 201
25 Moorhead, "Spanish Transportation," *NMHR*, XXXII (April, 1957), 117
26 Ogle, *Federal Control of the Western Apaches* (Santa Fe, 1940), 29
27 Smith, "Apache Plunder Trails," *NM HR*, XXXVII (January, 1962), 29-32
28 Smith, "The Scalp Hunter," *Arizona and the West*, VI (Spring, 1964), 8
29 Smith, "Apache Plunder Trails," 32
30 *Ibid.*
31 Much new material on Kirker has been assembled by Bill McGaw in *The Southwesterner*, Vols. II and III, in seventeen issues beginning in November, 1962. Ralph Smith concentrates on Kirker's activities in Mexico, his best articles being "Apache Plunder Trails" and "The Scalp Hunter."

32 Almada, *Resumen*, 225-236; U. S. Consular Reports as cited by Max Moorhead in *New Mexico's Royal Road*, 148; Smith, "The Scalp Hunter," 9

33 Smith, "Apache Plunder Trails," 37-42

34 Smith, "The Scalp Hunter," 15

35 Ruxton, *Adventures in Mexico and the Rocky Mountains* (New York, 1848), 156

36 Bill McGaw, a Kirker specialist, says (El Paso, March 22, 1965) that Kirker turned in only one non-Indian scalp. It belonged to a half-Indian Mexican who was accidentally killed and Kirker included his scalp as a sort of joke.

37 Smith, "The Scalp Hunter," 18-19, names most of them.

38 *Ibid.*, 20

39 Pope, *Report* (Washington, 1885), 69. Cf. Bartlett, *Personal Narrative* (New York, 1854) I, 174. This must have been a famous victory.

40 Gregg, *Commerce*, 206-207

41 Smith, "The Scalp Hunter," 20

42 Joe Parrish and Cleofas Calleros, "Has Daughter of El Paso's First Settler Been Found?" *El Paso Times*, January 17, 1965

43 Anastacia died on April 23, 1965, at the age of 103 (*Times*, April 25, 1965)

44 Gregg, *Commerce*, 273, 313

45 For instance Gibson, *Journal of a Soldier* (Glendale, 1935), 312; M. B. Edwards, "Journal" (Glendale, 1936), 245; Connelley, *Doniphan's Expedition* (Kansas City, 1907), 393. An exception was J. R. Bartlett. He says (*Personal Narrative*, I, 186) that little of the wine is "above mediocrity" and that it produces headaches.

46 Orndorff, *Development of Agriculture* (MS, 1957), 141-142

47 Decorme, *Las Misiones del Valle del Paso*, MS. The chapter used here is called "Folklore del Valle en la Epoca Mexicana, 1793-1848."

48 Moorhead, *New Mexico's Royal Road*, 45, referring to Spanish Archives of New Mexico 2218, Manrique to Salcedo, April 1, 1809

49 Barreiro, *Ojeada*, 30

50 Magoffin, *Down the Santa Fe Trail* (New Haven, 1926), 211-213

51 Parkes, *History of Mexico* (Boston, 1960), 153 ff.

52 Americans underestimated the culture of the Mexicans. Col. J. K. F. Mansfield in 1848 remarked: "They as a body are ignorant. . . . There are not more than two schools in the whole Territory of a population of 50,000 Mexicans. One of these is organized by the Catholic Bishop for the children of the most influential persons and the other is kept by the Rev. Henry Smith, a Baptist missionary, who has 12 or 14 scholars, the children of American fathers and Mexican mothers, and both located in Santa Fe (McMaster, "The Mansfield Report," *Password* IV, July, 1959, 100).

53 Chávez, *Historia*, 80

54 *Ibid.*, 92

CHAPTER X

The Americans Arrive

1 Rex Strickland (January 26, 1966) thinks the men were members of a "flying company" of Indian fighters from Santa Fe who wished to settle in the country and were on their way to Chihuahua to make arrangements. Pike (*Exploratory Travels*, 314-316) may have seen Purcell later in Santa Fe; see Long, *Anglo-American Occupation*, 36, for commentary.

2 Spanish Archives of New Mexico, no. 2009, Rey to Alencaster, August 31, 1806. He was described as "the Anglo-American, Dimas Proscel."

3 Pike, *Exploratory Travels* (London, 1811), 285-286

4 Carroll, *Three New Mexico Chronicles* (Albuquerque, 1942), 105

5 Gregg, *The Road to Santa Fe* (Albuquerque, 1952), 267

6 For Baird see Gregg, *Commerce of the Prairies* (Norman, 1954), 12, n.9; Golley, "James Baird," *Missouri Historical Society Bulletin*, XV (April, 1959), 171-193; McGaw, "James Baird," *The Southwesterner*, IV (May-June, 1965), 2, 11; Strickland, "James Baird," in LeRoy Hafen's *The Fur Trade and the Mountain Men*, III, 27-37

7 Marshall, "St. Vrain's Expedition to the Gila in 1826," SWHQ, XIX (January, 1916), 244-250. Baird's complaint was passed on to the governor of Chihuahua, who forwarded it to Mexico City. The United States Minister was requested to have his government restrain the interlopers, but there is no record that anything was done.

8 Pattie, *Personal Narrative* (Chicago, 1930), 155-156

9 Gregg, *Commerce*, 273

10 *Ibid.*, 313-314

11 Webb, *Adventures in the Santa Fe Trade* (Glendale, 1931), 191-192

12 Broaddus, *Legal Heritage of El Paso* (El Paso, 1963), 22, takes a different view: ". . . those who settled in the area appear to have abandoned American democratic ideas to become avaricious Anglo-American *gachupines*."

13 Miss Maria-Luisa Flores and Mrs. E. F. Flores, El Paso, June 27, 1960

14 Dwyer, "Hugh Stephenson," NMHR, XXIX (January, 1954), 3

15 Bowden, *The Ascarate Grant* (MS, 1952), 52-54
16 Dwyer, *op. cit.*
17 Strickland, *Six Who Came to El Paso* (El Paso, 1963), 36
18 Magoffin, *Down the Santa Fe Trail* (New Haven, 1962), xxv-xxvii
19 Thomlinson, *The Garrison of Fort Bliss* (El Paso, 1945), 7
20 Strickland, *Six Who Came*, 27
21 Bowden, *El Rancho de Ponce* (MS, 1951), 11
22 *Ibid.*, 13
23 *Ibid.*
24 El Paso *Herald*, Souvenir Edition, March 22, 1897
25 For the legends about Ponce's "hacienda" see Strickland, *Six Who Came*, 9: Bowden, *El Rancho de Ponce*, 16-17; Conkling, *Butterfield Overland Mail* (Glendale, 1947), I, 70
26 Bowden, *El Rancho*, 15; Strickland, *Six Who Came*, 9-10
27 Bexar County was extended to include El Paso in 1837
28 For details see Loomis, *The Texan-Santa Fe Pioneers* (Norman, 1958)
29 Kendall, *Narrative* (New York, 1844), II, 34-41
30 See Puckett, "Ramon Ortiz," NMHR, XXV (October, 1950), 265-295
31 Smith, *The War with Mexico* (New York, 1919), I, 298-299
32 Moorhead, *New Mexico's Royal Road* (Norman, 1958), 164-168, recounts the trials of the traders.
33 Porter and Hafen, *Ruxton of the Rockies* (Norman, 1950), 168
34 Ponce de León, *Reseñas* (Chihuahua, 1910), Tomo I, 345
35 Chávez, *Historia* (Juárez, 1951), 123
36 Gibson, *Journal of a Soldier* (Glendale, 1935), 93 (quoting *Diario Oficial*, September 10, 18, 1846)
37 Cutts, *Conquest of California and New Mexico* (Albuquerque, 1965), 91
38 Wislizenus, *Memoir* (Washington, 1848), 26
39 Smith, *War with Mexico*, I, 300
40 Chávez, *Historia*, 127
41 *Ibid.*, 124-125 (from the Juárez Archives)
42 *Ibid.*, 125
43 Smith, *War with Mexico*, I, 293
44 Almada, *Resumen* (Chihuahua, 1945), 223-224; Gibson, *Journal*, 93 (quoting Ramon Alcaraz, *The Other Side*, New York, 1850, 168)
45 Ponce de León, *Reseñas*, 323
46 Chávez, *Historia*, Appendix, seventh document: "Arenga a los Ciudadanos del distrito de Paso del Norte, con motivo de la invasion Norteamericana — 1846."
47 Ruhlen, "The Battle of Brazito—where It Was Fought" (*Password*, II, 53 ff. Colonel Ruhlen has made a convincing attempt to locate the battle field.

Temescales are "oven-shaped Indian sweat-bath houses," which the sand hills probably resembled. He places the engagement "600 yards to the northeast of a point on U. S. Highway 80 two miles northwest of the intersection of that highway with the road leading to Berino." See also Conkling, *Butterfield Overland Mail*, II, 94-95.
48 Colonel Ruhlen ("The Battle of Brazito," 8) estimates that Ponce's force consisted of 500 men. Other estimates run as high as 1200.
49 Gallaher, "Official Report," NMHR, III (October, 1928), 385. Colonel Ruhlen thinks the plan "might well have succeeded."
50 Smith, *War with Mexico*, I, 301
51 Connelley, *Doniphan's Expedition* 370, note
52 M. B. Edwards, "Journal" (in Bieber, *Marching with the Army of the West*, Glendale, 1936), 229
53 Hughes calls him Thomas Coldwell, but his descendants say his name was Colbert, nicknamed Tobe. He accompanied Kit Carson on the latter's first trip to Mexico, learning Spanish on the way. M. B. Edwards (244) says Coldwell "became offended" shortly after his arrival in El Paso and went back to Missouri. His son settled in El Paso in the seventies and the family has been important here ever since (Colbert Coldwell, El Paso, October 18, 1964).
54 Cutts, *Conquest*, 77-79 (letter of C. H. Kribben); Connelley, *Doniphan's Expedition*, 377 (Doniphan's report of the battle)
55 Connelley, 376-377
56 Almada, *Resumen*, 224, says part of the Mexican trouble was "a trumpet call wrongly interpreted." A story repeated in El Paso and attributed to Tobe Coldwell says that a piece of white cloth, displayed somewhere in the American lines, misled the Mexicans into expecting a surrender.
57 M. B. Edwards, "Journal," 235, says the cannon was abandoned, not taken.
58 Smith, *War with Mexico*, I, 302. Accounts of the battle are found in Connelley, 370-378; Gibson, *Journal*, 95-96; F. S. Edwards, *A Campaign in New Mexico* (Philadelphia, 1847), 82-88; Cutts, *Conquest*, 77-79.
59 Gallaher, "Official Report," 387-389
60 The fleeing regulars brought word to Chihuahua that the El Paso volunteers were the ones who ran: "The seven hundred men of El Paso fled; but our line held firm" (Carlos Nava de Bustamente, *El Nuevo Bernal Díaz*, Mexico, 1949, II, 224).
61 Connelley, 383-384
62 F. S. Edwards, 240
63 Gibson, 313, n.428
64 Connelley, 391, 397

65 F. S. Edwards, 243-244
66 M. B. Edwards, 244
67 Connelley, 92, 387
68 *Ibid.*, 92
69 *Ibid.*, 94-95. Hastings, "With Doniphan in Mexico," MS, describes some of the senseless destruction of property which went on.
70 Gibson, 323
71 M. B. Edwards, 242
72 John P. Bloom, "Johnny Gringo at the Pass of the North," *Password*, IV (October, 1959), 140. John Hughes in his notes expresses much the same opinion, but when he worked his jottings up for publication, he changed his tune, declaring that "the universal kind treatment which the El Pasenos received from the Americans, not only induced them to think well of the conduct of the army, but disposed them favorably toward the American government. . . ." (Connelley, 389).
73 Gibson, 314
74 Robinson, *Sketches of the Great West* (Plymouth, 1848), 69
75 *Ibid.*
76 Connelley, 392-394
77 Ferguson, "Diary" (in Bieber, *Marching with the Army of the West*, Glendale, 1936), 348
78 Gibson, 316
79 Connelley, 396, n.102: "The question was put to a vote of the troops." Cf. Robinson, ix
80 Gibson, 323; Connelley, 386
81 Hastings, "With Doniphan in Mexico," 30-40, describes vividly the hardships endured by the men who brought the guns.
82 Strickland, *Six Who Came*, 37
83 House Executive Document, 30 Cong., 2nd Sess., No. 537, 129, 1848
84 Miss María-Luisa Flores and Mrs. E. F. Flores, June 17, 1960
85 Billard, "Stained Records," El Paso *Herald-Post*, May 10, 1938; Hunt, *The Army of the Pacific* (Glendale, 1951) 125
86 Mullin, "David Meriwether," *Password*, VIII (Fall, 1963), 91-92; Davis *El Gringo* (New York, 1857), 375-376

CHAPTER XI

The Pivotal Fifties

1 Binkley, *The Expansionist Movement in Texas* (Berkeley, 1925), 153-156
2 McMaster, "The Evolution of El Paso County," *Password*, III (July, 1958), 120-122
3 Reproduced in *Fort Bliss: One Hundredth Anniversary* (El Paso, 1948). See Bender, "Opening Routes," SWHQ, XXXVII (October(1933), for the government's program of exploration following the Mexican War.
4 Martin, "California Emigrant Roads," SWHQ, XXVIII (April, 1925), 290
5 Sherman, *A Decade of Exploration* (MS, 1962), quoting David D. Demarest's Diary for May 10, 1849 (Bancroft Library MS)
6 The "Ignorance" of an Indian guide led the Hays expedition astray (Bender, "Opening Routes," 118).
7 Mabelle E. Martin says that "acute" jealousy between the towns led to the sending out of exploring parties ("California Emigrant Roads," 292).
8 Hughes, *Report of the Secretary of War. . . March 1, 1849.* 31st Cong., 1st Sess., Senate Exec. Doc., 32, 1850; Goetzmann, *Army Exploration* (New Haven, 1959), 149-151
9 Bender, "Opening Routes," 118
10 Neighbors, "The Expedition of Major Robert S. Neighbors," SWHQ, LVIII (July, 1954), 36
11 Chamberlain, *My Confession* (New York 1956), 241-242, 256, tells of her career in Mexico, picturing her as a loose woman.
12 Buchanan, "G. W. Traherne," SWHQ, LVIII (July, 1954), 84
13 Hughes, *Rebellious Ranger* (Norman, 1964), 68, quoting Ford's Memoirs (MS) III, 521. Hughes adds (note 13) that in the 1860's "she was operating a brothel in Arizona and was noted there for her pistol dexterity."
14 Martin, "From Texas to California in 1849," SWHQ, XXIX (January, 1926), 219 (letter from Lewis B. Harris to his brother published in the Houston *Telegraph*, August 23, 1849)
15 Rex Strickland has located her in Socorro, New Mexico, in 1850 and found her name to be Sarah Bourgett. Arthur Woodward (*The Great Western*, San Francisco, 1961) traces her later movements. She died at Fort Yuma in 1866.
16 Jackson, *Wagon Roads West* (Berkeley, 1952), 41
17 According to Thomas Eastland, *To California through Texas and Mexico*, CHSQ, XVIII (June, 1939), 121-122, the troops camped six miles below the town for several days after the date given for their arrival. He says Coons leased the buildings and six acres of ground to the government for $4,200 per annum.
18 It hangs in the Texas Memorial Museum in Austin.
19 Thomlinson, *The Garrison of Fort Bliss* (El Paso, 1945), 7
20 McMaster, *Musket, Saber and Missile* (El Paso, 1962), and Thomlinson give details.

21 Martin, "California Emigrant Roads," 294. This was the first large party. Led by Captain Mays, it started from Fredericksburg on March 17. Its route across the Sacramentos has not been located.

22 *Ibid.*, 294

23 Martin, "From Texas to California," 128

24 Greenwood, "Opening Routes to El Paso," SWHQ, XLVIII (October, 1944), 270

25 Martin, "California Emigrant Roads," 301

26 Martin, "From Texas to California," 130

27 *Ibid.*, 131

28 *To California through Texas and Mexico*, 127

29 Smith, "The Scalp Hunter," *Arizona and the West*, VI (Spring, 1964), 19

30 *Ibid.*, 21. Cf. Greenwood, "Opening Routes," quoting the Houston *Telegraph* for January 3, 1950: "Their great hostility is ascribed to attacks on them by parties of Americans . . . principally those under command of Chevallie and Glanton. . . ."

31 Martin, "From Texas to California," 131

32 Chávez, *Historia de Ciudad Juárez* (Juárez, 1951), 130; Almada, *Resumen Chihuahua*, 1945), gives a somewhat different figure.

33 Smith, "The Scalp Hunt," NMHR, XL (April, 1965), 132

34 Greenwood, "Opening Routes," 272. The story was brought to Houston by Major B. W. Gillock and published in the *Telegraph* for January 3, 1850.

35 Bartlett, *Personal Narrative* (New York, 1854), I, 152-153

36 Quoted in Sherman, *A Decade of Exploration* (MS, 1962), 45

37 Chávez, *Historia*, 130

38 Mills, *My Story* (Washington, 1921), 50

39 Conkling, *Butterfield Overland Mail* (Glendale, 1947), II, 46-47, traces the old channel.

40 The fixing of the boundary is a complicated story and has been told by many historians. Recent accounts include Robert M. Utley, *The International Boundary* (Santa Fe, 1964), and Odie B. Faulk, "The Controversial Boundary Survey," *Arizona and the West*, IV (Autumn, 1962), 201-227.

41 The basic work on the Gadsden Purchase is Paul Neff Garber, *The Gadsden Treaty* (Gloucester, 1959). See also Utley, *The International Boundary*, 18-25.

42 Mullin, "David Meriwether," *Password*, VIII (Fall, 1963), 88, 90-91; Meriwether, *My Life* (Norman, 1965), 226

43 Almada, *Resumen*, 292; Galveston *News*, July 9, 1867; Dallas *Weekly Herald*, August 10, 1867 ("El Paso Washes Away")

44 Bowden, "The Texas-New Mexico Boundary Dispute," SWHQ, LXIII (October, 1959), 220-237, discusses recent litigation.

45 Many volumes have been published in both Spanish and English about the Chamizal. For a summary see Gladys Gregory, *The Chamizal Settlement* (El Paso, 1963). Charles A. Timm, *The International Boundary Commission* (Austin, 1941), treats fully events up to 1941.

46 See El Paso papers for this date. The hose incident was not played up.

47 For instance, see Mario Gill, *Nuestros Buenos Vecinos* (Mexico, 1959).

48 Bartlett, *Personal Narrative*, I, 156-157

49 Binkley, *Expansionist Movement*, describes attempts to attach eastern New Mexico to Texas. Long, *Anglo-American Occupation* (MS, 1931), has done important research on early county officers as has Morgan Broaddus (*Legal Heritage*, El Paso, 1963), 29-44.

50 Broaddus, *Legal Heritage*, 43

51 Bartlett, *Personal Narrative*, I, 160-161

52 *Ibid.*, 163

53 As a result of this episode word came back to San Antonio that "lynch law was prevailing at El Paso. . . . Within two weeks, fifteen persons, Americans and Mexicans, had suffered by hanging or shooting, at the hands of self constituted jurists" (San Antonio *Ledger*, May 22, 1851).

54 See Haley, "A Log of the Texas-California Trail," SWHQ, XXXV (January, 1932), 208-237; Erskine, "A Cattle Drive from Texas to California," SWHQ, LXVII (January, 1964), 404-405.

55 *Texas State Gazette*, August 27, 1853, quoting the San Antonio *Ledger*

56 Broaddus, *Legal Heritage*, 50-51, quoting reports of U. S. Consuls in Juárez

57 *Ibid.*, 56

58 *Ibid.*,

59 *Ibid.*, 62-63. The Prefect and Judge Josiah Crosby held a conference to "find some solution to the clashes between people on both sides of the river."

60 Conkling, *Butterfield Overland Mail*, I, 90

61 Broaddus, *Legal Heritage*, 31, quoting the San Antonio *Ledger*, August 9, 1852

62 Bartlett, *Personal Narrative*, II, 397. Bartlett describes one of Bigfoot's fights which delayed but did not stop him.

63 See Mills, *Forty Years* (El Paso, 1962), 19, n. 25, for a discussion.

64 Farris, *South of the Alamo* (MS in possession of C. L. S.)
65 Strickland, *Six Who Came* (El Paso, 1963), 7-8
66 Conkling, *Butterfield Overland Mail*, I, 91
67 Mahon, *George H. Giddings* (MS, n. d.), 17-20; Mahon and Kielman, "George W. Giddings," SWHQ, VI (October, 1957), 220-239
68 Giddings and Mahon, "The Jackass Trail," *Pass-Word*, II (August, 1957), 93
69 Conkling, I, 94
70 *Ibid.*, I, 95
71 The El Paso-Fort Yuma wagon road was being constructed in 1857-58, but Giddings' operations began before the building started (Cross, "The El Paso-Yuma Wagon Road," *Password*, IV (January, 1959), 58-70.
72 Conkling, I, 95
73 *Ibid.*, 96
74 Leach, "Stagecoach through the Pass," *Password*, III (October, 1958), 130-137, quoting Waterman L. Ormsby of the New York *Herald*, who took the trip and wrote it up for his paper. See Lyle H. Wright and Josephine M. Bynum, *The Butterfield Overland Mail* (San Marino, 1954), for Ormsby's full account.
75 In August, 1859, the route was changed to reach El Paso by way of Fort Stockton and Fort Davis and the stations near Guadalupe Peak were abandoned (Conkling, I, 393).
76 Conkling, II, 60
77 Mesilla *Times*, November 1, 1860 (Huntington Library)
78 Conkling, II, 52
79 *Ibid.*, II, 52-53, quoting Report of Lieutenant E. F. Beale in House Executive Document No. 124, 35th Cong. Ist Sess., 28
80 Lesley, *Uncle Sam's Camels* (Journal of Major Humphreys Stacey), Cambridge, 1929, 170-171
81 Diffenderfer, *By Wagon Train from St. Louis to El Paso* (Clippings, files of Missouri Historical Society), Sunday, September 17, 1865
82 Richardson, *Beyond the Mississippi* (Hartford, 1867), 238
83 Mills, *My Story*, 50
84 Prestwood, *Social Life and Customs* (MS, 1949), 13
85 Mills, *My Sory*, 48
86 Anson Mills to Richard F. Burges and T. A. Falvey, Washington, May 28, 1906 (El Paso Public Library). Mills wrote describing the events of 1858-1859 because a Mrs. Porter had sued to retain title to some downtown property, basing her claim on one of Mills' preliminary sketches of the area. See also

The Great Southtwest, Souvenir Edition of the El Paso *Daily Herald*, 1900, quoting Judge Falvey.
87 Mills, *My Story*, 51-52
88 Lillian Hague Corcoran, "He Brought the Railroads," *Password*, I (May, 1956), 45-54

CHAPTER XII

Life on the Border

1 *Forty Years at El Paso*. The original edition of 1901 (now extremely rare) was reprinted in 1962 with drawings by Tom Lea and annotations by Rex Strickland.
2 *Ibid.*, 5. The river ran then near the future site of the Santa Fe Station, half a mile north of its present course.
3 *Ibid.*, 69-70
4 Mary M. Phillips' "Statement," Burges Collection, Book L, 14 ff.; El Paso *Herald-Post*, May 28, 1936 (interview with Mrs. Phillips)
5 Joe Parrish, "Mrs. Mary M. Phillips Lives El Paso History," El Paso *Times*, January 7, 1951
6 Mills, *Forty Years* (biographical sketch), 178
7 San Antonio *Herald*, August 28, 30, 1856
8 Mills, *Fory Years*, 70; City Council Minutes, Book B, December 1, 1880 (testimonial resolutions on Dowell's death)
9 Mills, *Forty Years*, 5, n. 11. The figures are Rex Strickland's
10 *Ibid.*, 9
11 *Ibid.*, 21
12 *Ibid.*, 18
13 *Ibid.*, 22
14 Diffenderfer, *By Wagon Train from St. Louis to El Paso*, Sunday, September 17, 1865 (newspaper clippings)
15 Mills, *Forty Years*, 5-6. S. H. Newman in his unpublished *Reminiscences* says that in 1876 "two ash trees, one on either side, stood at the bridge crossing the ditch at El Paso Street and Little [Pioneer] Plaza and these served as bulletin boards. . . ."
16 Mills, *My Story* (Washington, 1921), 57-59
17 Strickland, "P. T. Herbert," *Password*, V (April, 1960), 44-49
18 Mills, *My Story*, 60
19 Dr. J. L. Waller found Mills' letter in the Amnesty Papers in Washington (see Strickland, *Six Who Came*, El Paso, 1963, 39).
20 This extraordinary document, dated April 25, 1862, was advertised for sale by W. M. Morrison of Waco, Texas, in 1960 (List 171), reproducing the text in his advertisement.

21 Mills, *Forty Years*, 23
22 Richardson, *Beyond the Mississippi* (Hartford, 1867), 242-243
23 Mills, *Forty Years*, 195, Appendix III. Editor Rex Strickland synthesizes what is known about the Cooke's Spring fight. O. W. Williams, *In Old New Mexico* (n. p., n. d.), adds details

CHAPTER XIII

War in the Desert

1 Waller, "The Civil War in the El Paso Area," *West Texas Historical Association Yearbook*, XXIII (October, 1946), 3-4
2 Mills, *My Story*, 60
3 *Ibid.*, 60-61
4 Mills, *Forty Years*, 38-39. Some did get out. Ernest Angerstein, for instance, moved to Mexico. See Fierman, "Ernest Angerstein," *Password*, VII (Spring, 1962), 43-62.
5 ORR (War of the Rebellion Records, Washington, various dates), Series I, IV, 50, Lt. A. L. Anderson to Major I. Lynde, June 30, 1861: ". . . this robbery was not the unauthorized act of a band of robbers but was planned at Hart's Mill. . . . The horses were stolen for. . . Texas troops now on their way to Fort Bliss."
6 Mills, *Forty Years*, 50
7 Hall, *Sibley's New Mexico Campaign* (Austin, 1960), 30-31; ORR, Series I, IV, 55 (Sibley at Hart"s Mill)
8 Hall, *Sibley's New Mexico Campaign*, 32 (quoting Major T. T. Teel)
9 ORR, Series I, IV, 133
10 *Ibid.*, Series I, IV, 134
11 Hall, *Sibley's New Mexico Campaign*, 54, n. 30
12 ORR, Series I, IV, 89
13 *Ibid.*, Series I, L, Part I, 1013
14 *Ibid.*, Series I, IX, 722
15 *Ibid.*, Series I, L, Part I, 1013; XV, 916 (Baylor's account)
16 *Ibid.*, Series I, IV, 89, 133
17 H. C. Wright, *Reminiscenses*, MS, University of Texas Archives, quoted by Grace Long, *Anglo-American Occupation* (MS, 1931), 172
18 ORR, Series I, XV, 916 (Magruder to Cooper, December 9, 1862)
19 *Ibid.*, Series I, L, Part I, (Carleton to Drum, July 22, 1862), 89-90
20 Hunt, *The Army of the Pacific* (Glendale, 1951), 125-126
21 Quoted by Owen White in *Out of the Desert* (El Paso, 1924), 79
22 ORR, Series I, IX, 567
23 *Ibid.*, Series I, IX, 580, 583
24 *Ibid.*, Series I, L, vol. I, 598: Lt. Col. Edwin A. Riff, writitng to Col. J. R.

West on November 11, 1862, says, ". . . their party has increased to 80."
25 *Ibid.*, Series I, XV, 598, Rigg to West, November 11, 1862
26 Uranga to McMullen, December 24, 1862, Ritch Collection, No. 1173
27 McMullen to Uranga, December 25, 1862, *Ibid.*, no. 1174
28 Uranga to McMullen, December 29, 1862, *Ibid.*, no. 1175
29 McMullen to West, January 16, 1863, *Ibid.*, no. 1187
30 West to McMullen, January 18, 1863, *Ibid.*, no. 1168
31 ORR, Series I, XXVI, Vol. I, 917
32 Santa Fe *New Mexican*, February 27, 1864
33 Report of the Commissioner of Indian Affairs, 1861, Commissioner William P. Dole to Caleb B. Smith, Secretary of the Interior, 123
34 Santa Fe *New Mexican*, December 22, 1865
35 ORR, Series I, XLVIII, Vol. II, 390. Confederate forces arrived at Fort Davis in the spring of 1863. Baylor was busy in 1864 urging the Confederate Congress to reoccupy West Texas and Arizona (Long, 182).
36 González Flores, *Chihuahua de la independencia a la revolución* (Mexico, 1949), 124
37 Bartlett, "Personal Account of Benito Juarez, 1865-66," El Paso *Herald*, June 5, 1909
38 *Ibid.*; W. W. Mills, *Forty Years*, 89-90
39 ORR, Series I, XXVI, 27-28, Carleton reporting
40 Juárez collected several forced loans in Paso del Norte, of which American businessmen had to pay one sixth. They asked Henry Cuniffe, the consul, to protest (Rosen, Henry J. Cuniffe, MS, 1961, 59)
41 Mary Phillips remembered in 1934 that a great party was actually held on the American side for Juárez' cabinet (Burges collection, Book L, 26)
42 Tamayo, *Epistolario* (Mexico, 1957), 320-321
43 Juárez. Correspondencia, Letter 90, Biblioteca Nacional, quoted by Rosen, *Henry Cuniffe*, 53
44 Tamayo, *Epistolario*, 322
45 Mills, *Forty Years*, 91-93
46 Tamayo, *Epistolario*, 335
47 *Ibid.*, 191; Smart, *Viva Juárez* (Philadelphia, 1963), 330-331, 361-362
48 Tamayo, 323
49 Smart, 334
50 Parkes, *A History of Mexico* (Boston, 1960), 273
51 Smart, 354-355

CHAPTER XIV

Peace at Last

1 Broaddus, *Legal Heritage* (El Paso, 1963), 79, 82, 85
2 Mills, *Forty Years* (El Paso, 1962), 179
3 El Paso *Herald-Post*, March 28, 1936
4 Mills, *Forty Years*, 68-69
5 Rosen, *Henry Cuniffe* (MS, 1961), 48
6 Santa Fe *Weekly New Mexican*, January 16, 1872; Mills, *Forty Years*, 70
7 El Paso *Times*, February 8, 1948, recollections of Mrs. Mary Phillips
8 Santa Fe *Daily New Mexican*, July 16, 1875; Mills, *Forty Years*, 70
9 Tittman, "The Exploitation of Treason," NMHR, IV (April, 1929), 129
10 *Ibid.*, 139
11 Long, *Anglo-American Occupation* (MS, 1931), 189
12 Deed Record C, El Paso County Courthouse, 1-256
13 Mills, *Forty Years*, 135
14 Tittman, "Exploitation of Treason," 142-145
15 El Paso *Times*, Midsummer Trade Edition, August, 1887
16 Strickland, *Six Who Came* (El Paso, 1963), 40
17 *Ibid.*, 33 (material from the Amnesty Papers, Box C, National Archives, and Santa Fe *Gazette*, May 19, 1866)
18 Long, *Anglo-American Occupation*, 191; Tittman, 141-143
19 Long, 191; Broaddus, *Legal Heritage*, 81-82
20 Mills, *Forty Years*, 134-135
21 *Ibid.*, 135
22 Strickland, "W. W. Mills," *Password*, VII (Summer, 1962), 90
23 Mrs. L. H. Corcoran, November 4, 1959

CHAPTER XV

Buildup to Trouble

1 The El Paso *Sentinel* was published, probably irregularly, between 1871 and 1873 (See *Times* Midsummer Trade Edition, August, 1887). The *Times* and the *Herald* appeared almost simultaneously in 1881 (Middagh, *Frontier Newspaper*, El Paso, 1958, 3-4).
2 Census returns show 464 people in 1870; 736 in 1880
3 S. H. Newman, *Reminiscenses*, MS
4 Galveston *News*, July 26, 1866: The stage to El Paso "is now in operation." On July 7 this coach was attacked by Indians at Barela Springs. The Mesilla *Weekly Times* for July 15, 1867, an-

nounces schedules from the States and from California. The San Antonio *Herald* for December 5, 1872, prints this notice: "The El Paso coach will leave on Tuesdays, Thursdays, and Saturdays at 8 a. m. and arrive on Sundays, Wednesdays, and Fridays at 6 p. m. (barring Indians)."
5 Mills, *Forty Years* (El Paso, 1963), 137-141; Galveston *News*, June 2, 1868
6 Jones, *Forty Years among the Indians* (Los Angeles, 1961), 242
7 Kohlberg, Walter, *A Translation of the Letters Written by Ernest Kohlberg, 1875, 1876, 1877* (MS)
8 Jones, *Forty Years among the Indians*, 251-252
9 Mrs. Berthold Spitz (Sam Schutz' daughter) in El Paso Pioneer Society Scrapbook, TWC Library; Mills, *Forty Years*, 181
10 Mills, *Forty Years*, 137-141, 192
11 Long, *Anglo-American Occupation* (MS. 1931), 192, Appendix, Table I
12 *Illustrated History of New Mexico* (Chicago, 1895), 656
13 W. Halsey Thomas, Curator of Columbiana, to C. L. S., January 8, 1954
14 Al Jennings and Mrs. Manuel Aguirre, El Paso, July 4, 1948. A. M. Gibson, *The Life and Death of Colonel Albert Jennings Fountain* (Norman, 1965), has assembled much new material but still calls Fountain a "man of mystery."
15 *Illustrated History of New Mexico*, 656-658
16 Muster Rolls, First Regiment California Infantry, Company E, 1861-1864
17 *Illustrated History of New Mexico*, 657; Mesilla *Independent*, August 11, 1877
18 Twitchell, *Leading Facts of New Mexican History* (Cedar Rapids, 1911-1917), II, 494
19 *Illustrated History of New Mexico*, 656-658; Mesilla *Independent*, August 11, 1877
20 *Weekly Austin Republican*, December 1, 1869; Mills, *Forty Years*, 120-121
21 Long, *Anglo-American Occupation*, 192
22 *Illustrated History of New Mexico*, 657
23 Broaddus, *Legal Heritage* (El Paso, 1963), 93
24 *Austin Weekly Statesman*, July 20, 1876 (Legislative Directory--Representatives); Galveston *News*, October 16, 1877
25 Fountain, *Answers to Interrogatories* (MS, UTEP Library)
26 Mills, *Forty Years*, 149
27 Galveston *News*, January 31, 1869, announces the opening of the line from Fort Smith, Arkansas.
28 *Ibid.*, October 16, 1877 (personal description)

29 Jesus Montes (son of Telesforo), San Elizario, July 21, 1934; *El Paso Troubles in Texas* (House Ex. Doc. no. 93, 45th Cong., 2nd Sess.), 66 (E. Stine), 70 (Blanchard), 77 (Kerber)

30 G. N. Phillips (Ben Dowell's grandson), historian Cleofas Calleros, Jesus Montes and Josefina Escajeda told me about Borajo at various times and places in 1934.

31 Jones, *Forty Years among the Indians*, 242-244

32 Broaddus, *Legal Heritage*, 109, sketches the career of Aranda and refers to several of the others.

33 Broaddus, 85-86

34 *El Paso Troubles*, 127-129 (Fountain), 69-70 (Blanchard), 100 (Aranda); Mesilla *Independent*, October 6, 1877; Bowden, "The Magoffin Salt War," *Password*, VII (Summer, 1962), 120, n.72

35 Bowden, "Magoffin Salt War," 95-121

36 *Ibid.*, 120, n.75

37 Colonel Fountain in 1877 said that the surveyors mistakenly located Maverick's land "a considerable distance from the lakes, 12 miles I have been informed" (*Answers to Interrogatories*, MS)

38 Fountain in his *Answers* names them.

39 *Ibid.*

40 Mills, *Forty Years*, 41

41 Broaddus, *Legal Heritage*, 90, quoting William M. Pierson, U. S. Consul

42 *Weekly Austin Republican*, September 29, 1869

43 *Ibid.*, December 1, 1869

44 *Ibid.*, June 16, 1869: "Mr. Mills has been removed for political reasons."

45 San Antonio *Herald*, September 15, 1870. The *Republican* for June 16, 1869, defends the "gallant Mills" and traces Marsh's career.

46 Mills, *Forty Years*, 120-121

47 *Ibid.*, 145

48 MacCallum, *History of St. Clement's Church*, 30-31

49 Mrs. MacCallum reproduces several of his poems.

50 *Ibid.*, 29

51 Mary M. Phillips, "Statement," Burges Collection, Book L, 22 ff. Mrs. Phillips went to school in El Paso del Norte to a Frenchman named Peter Lafayette, who taught English and Spanish. When she came to the American side after the Civil War, a teacher named Wright carried on where the Caples Building stands. Lawyer M. A. Jones succeeded him, conducting classes where, until recently, the Angelus Hotel stood — later in the Overland Building. Mrs. Reed came in 1867 and Mrs. Clarke was next.

52 Mills, *Forty Years*, 146

53 *El Paso Troubles*, 127-129; Fountain, *Answers to Interrogatories*

54 Fountain, *Answers*

55 *Weekly Austin Republican*, December 21, 1870; San Antonio *Herald*, January 23, March 18, 1873

56 Fountain's descendants still have the watch. See Gibson, *Life and Death*, 57-88, for his legislative career.

57 *El Paso Troubles*, 129

58 Mills, *Forty Years*, 147

59 Broaddus, *Legal Heritage*, 99. Mr. Broaddus found the petition in the El Paso folder, County Petitions and Protests, State Archives, Austin.

60 *Weekly Austin Republican*, December 21, 1870

61 San Antonio *Herald*, December 17, 1870; *Weekly Austin Republican*, December 21, 1870. Gibson, *Life and Death*, gives a full account drawn mostly from the Austin *State Journal* for December 22, 1870.

62 Austin *Daily Statesman*, December 14, 1871, quoted by *Flake's Semi-Weekly Bulletin*, December 20, 1871

63 *Flake's Daily Bulletin*, March 13, 1873

64 There was dissatisfaction with the verdict. See *Ibid.*, March 30, 1872, and the San Antonio *Express* for May 30, 1872.

65 Fountain, *Answers to Interrogatories*. Joseph Magoffin swore before Judge Newcomb on October 12, 1871, that during the preceding April Cardis had offered Antoine Leroux a loaded shotgun and a hundred dollars to kill him (Magoffin). The original deposition is owned by Anton Gutiérrez of El Paso.

66 For more on Fountain see Keleher, *The Fabulous Frontier* (Albuquerque, 1963); Sonnichsen, *Tularosa* (New York, 1960); Gibson, *Life and Death*.

67 *Flake's Semi-Weekly Bulletin*, October 11, 1871

68 Mills, *Forty Years*, 123, gives his view of Newcomb.

69 Broaddus, *Legal Heritage*, 102-107 (Newcomb's career); Dallas *Weekly Herald*, August 18, 1874 (his removal)

70 Corcoran, "He Brought the Railroad," *Password*, I (May, 1965), 45-54

71 Galveston *News*, October 16, 1877

72 Ward, *The El Paso Salt War* (MS, 1932), comments on his marksmanship; Galveston *News*, October 16 1877, adds details.

73 Mills, *Forty Years*, 149

74 MacCallum, *History of St. Clement's*, 32-51

75 Austin *Daily Journal*, November 4, 1870 (Webb Papers, University of Texas Archives)

CHAPTER XVI

The Storm Breaks

1 See Ramsdell, *Reconstruction in Texas* (New York, 1910), 295-318
2 Fountain, *Answers to Interrogatories* (MS)
3 San Antonio *Herald,* November 19, 1872
4 *Ibid.,* December 17, 1872
5 Denison *News,* October 14, 1877
6 Austin *Daily Statesman,* December 9, 1874
7 Mesilla *News,* June 13, 1874
8 The San Antonio *Herald* for July 24, 1875, describes some of these attacks.
9 Montes to Steele, May 31, September 27, October 20, November 29, 1874; September 18, November 20, 1875 (Adjutant General's Files, Texas State Library)
10 Austin *Daily Statesman,* March 28, 1874
11 Ward, *The Salt War* (MS, 1931), 34-35
12 Austin *Weekly Statesman,* June 28, 1877. Howard was genuinely fond of her. Judge Wyndham Kemp had a copy of a very tender poem which Howard wrote to his wife (Maury Kemp, October 4, 1953)
13 *El Paso Troubles in Texas* (House Ex. Doc., no. 93, 45th Cong., 2nd Sess.), 65 (Stine); Fountain, *Answers to Interrogatories;* Joseph Magoffin to Governor Hubbard, October 5, 1877, W. P. Webb transcripts, University of Texas Archives
14 Mesilla *Independent,* October 6, 1877
15 *El Paso Troubles,* 122-123 (Blacker); Fountain, *Answers to Interrogatories*
16 *El Paso Troubles,* 120-121 (B. S. Dowell and Miguel García); 96 (J. N. García says he was offered money to kill Howard.)
17 San Antonio *Herald,* July 17, August 12, 17, 21, September 8, November 4, 1875
18 Austin *Weekly Statesman,* April 6, 1876
19 *El Paso Troubles,* 65 (Stine); Ward, *Salt War,* 36
20 *El Paso Troubles,* 120-121 (Dowell), 69-70 (Blanchard), 71 (Clark)
21 Fountain, *Answers to Interrogatories,* says Zimpelman furnished the capital; Howard acted in his interest. Cardis told Fountain that Howard promised to make the locations in his own name and divide with Cardis and Borajo, but he broke his word.
22 Mesilla *Independent,* August 25, 1877. An Ysleta correspondent says they located 3840 acres. For the arrest see *El Paso Troubles,* 106 (G. N. García), 118 (Kerber and Blanchard); Mesilla

Independent, October 6, 1877 (Howard's statement).
23 Mesilla *Independent,* October 6, 1877
24 *El Paso Troubles,* 99 (Wesley Owens)
25 Mesilla *Independent,* October 6, 1877
26 *El Paso Troubles,* 151
27 *Ibid.,* 89-99 (Bourgade), 66 (Stine); Mesilla *Independent,* February 2, 1877
28 *El Paso Troubles,* 107 (G. N. García)
29 Fountain, *Answers to Interrogatories*
30 *El Paso Troubles,* 141-142 (Blacker to Hubbard)
31 AGF, Cardis to Hubbard, October 9, 1877
32 Mesilla *Independent,* October 6, 1877
33 *El Paso Troubles,* 59 (Owens)
34 *Ibid.,* 113 (Wahl), 59-64 (depositions describing the killing); Mesilla *Independent,* October 13, 1877
35 *El Paso Troubles,* 64
36 *Ibid.,* 100, 102, 154
37 Atkinson's letter, quoted by Ward, *Salt War,* 65-66, is in the AGF
38 Jones' visit to San Elizario is covered in EPT (Jones to Hubbard), 90-100 (Bourgade), 26 (Jones' Minority Report)
39 *El Paso Troubles,* 139-140 (testimony of several citizens); Galveston *News,* December 20, 1877
40 Tays to Jones, AGF. Frank Faudoa (Interview, June 26, 1948) says that Howard had an Airedale which ran under his buggy. It had trouble with another dog at Canutillo and Wesley shot the local animal.
41 Mesilla *Independent,* September 29, 1877
42 Cardis to Steele, October 12, 1877, AGF
43 Cardis to Steele, October 11, 1877, AGF
44 Kohlberg, *Letters* (MS), June 28, 1876
45 *Ibid.,* November 26, 1876
46 *Ibid.,* June 5, 1877
47 Austin *Daily Statesman,* November 4, 1877
48 *El Paso Troubles,* 67-68 (Father Ortiz' letter to General Hatch)
49 Galveston *News,* November 7, 1877
50 Kohlberg, *Letters,* August 8, 1877
51 Austin *Daily Statesman,* November 4, 1877; Mesilla *Independent,* November 3, 1877
52 *El Paso Troubles,* 73 (V. García), 130-131 (Magoffin), 126 (Blacker)
53 Fountain, *Answers to Interrogatories*
54 Jesús Montes, notes taken by Josefina Escajeda in 1944; Luján to Jones, November 15, 1877, AGF: ". . . the people employed Mr. Hague to perfect title to their lands."

55 The late Lillian Hague Corcoran had the letter.

56 Ward, *Salt War*, 85, quoting Bourgade to Jones, AGF

57 Mesilla *Independent*, January 5, 1878

58 Francisco González, Chico's son-in-law, told me about Pancha in 1934

59 Mesilla *Independent*, January 5, 1877

60 *Ibid.; El Paso Troubles*, 88 (Atkinson's actions), 102-103 (Ball), 73 (V. García)

61 Mesilla *Independent*, January 5, 1878

62 *El Paso Troubles*, 98 (J. N. García)

63 Mesilla *Independent*, January 12, 1878;; *El Paso Troubles*, 74 (Mary Antonia Cooper), 97-98

64 *El Paso Troubles*, 82, 113, 158; Tays to Jones, quoted by Ward, 118

65 *El Paso Troubles*, 148 (telegrams), 28 (Major Jones' report), 146-150 (official communications), 78-79, 102-103, 113-117, 145, 149; Mesilla *Independent*, December 22, 1877, January 5, 1878; *Report of the Secretary of War for the Year 1878*, 51

66 *El Paso Troubles*, 1-33

67 Thomlinson, *The Garrison of Fort Bliss* (El Paso, 1945), 23

68 Ward, *Salt War*, 145

CHAPTER XVII

The Boom Begins

1 Mesilla *Independent*, July 28, 1877

2 The census of 1880 gave the number as 736

3 S. H. Newman, *Reminiscenses* (MS)

4 Wilson and Taylor, *Southern Pacific* (New York, 1952), 73-77

5 Adjutant General's Files, State Library

6 Wahl to Jones, October 15, 1878, AGF

7 Tays to Jones, November 25, 1878 (telegram), AGF; Tays to Jones, November 26, 1878 (letter), AGF; Tays to Jones, December 16, 1878 (letter), AGF

8 Webb, *The Texas Rangers* (Boston, 1935), 396

9 Gillett, *Six Years with the Texas Rangers* (Austin, 1921), 227-230

10 Webb, *Texas Rangers*, 402

11 *Ibid.*, 403-406

12 White, *My Texas, 'Tis of Thee* (New York, 1936), 152

13 Wilson and Taylor, *Southern Pacific*, 76-77

14 Jordan, *Railroads in the El Paso Area* (MS, 1957), 149-151

15 Wise, "Effects of the Railroads upon El Paso," *Password*, V (July, 1960), 91, quoting the *Lone Star* for July 30, 1884

16 El Paso Pioneer Society Sketchbook, MS, U. T. El Paso Library

17 *Ibid.*, quoting the *National Cyclopedia of American Biography*; White, *Out of the Desert* (El Paso, 1924), quoting Morehead's diary.

18 Middagh, *Frontier Newspaper* (El Paso, 1958), endpaper reproduces the front page of the first issue of the *Times*, April 2, 1881. O. T. Bassett advertises "Lumber, Shingles, Lath, Sash, Doors," etc.

19 White, *Out of the Desert*, 146-147; Personal Recollections of Charles R. Morehead," in Connelley's *Doniphan's Expedition* (Kansas City, Mo., 1907), Appendix C, 600-622; Sanford Cox, *The State National Bank*, History Seminar Paper, n. d., Texas Western College

20 El Paso Pioneer Society Sketchbook, MS

21 *Ibid.*

22 Tays to Jones, December 16, 1878, Adjutant General's Files, Texas State Archives

23 El Paso City Council Minutes, Book B, July 31, 1880

24 Betty Rogers, *Reminiscences of Old El Paso*, MS

25 Bridgers, *Just Chatting* (typescript), I, 203; Brady, *The Theatre in Early El Paso* (El Paso, 1966), 9-11

26 Bridgers, I, 203

27 El Paso *Lone Star*, June 2, 1883

28 Gillett, *Six Years with the Texas Rangers* (Austin, 1821), 323

29 Coldwell, "Gillett Book Revives Pioneer's Memories" (newspaper clipping). Leon Metz, *Dallas Stoudenmire* (MS) has assembled the available information about early El Paso peace officers.

30 Coldwell, *op. cit.*

31 El Paso City Council Minutes, Book B, December 23, 1880

32 Metz, *Dallas Stoudenmire*, MS

33 Coldwell, *op. cit.*

34 Gillett, *Six Years*, 312: "In the latter part of the summer of 1881 Captain Baylor moved his company of rangers from Ysleta to a site three miles below El Paso."

35 Details are from a sketch of Stoudenmire apparently provided by himself and printed in the El Paso *Herald*, April 19, 1882

36 El Paso City Council Minutes, Book B, April 11, 1881

37 W. M. Coldwell, *op. cit.*

38 As El Paso expanded and former fields became building lots, the ditches fell into disrepair. The *Herald*, February 8, 1882, remarked, "In case of fire the absence of water from our ditches would be serious." The Southern Pacific Railroad at this time offered to

clean the main ditch from Hart's Mill to the Railroad Station.

39 El Paso City Council Minutes, Book B, August 11, 1881

40 Gillett, *Six Years*, 325

41 George Look, untitled Reminiscences, dated Sunday, June 13, 1909, MS; *Newman's Semi-Weekly*, April 20, 1881. The Mexicans were killed on April 13.

42 Gillett says Deputy Sheriff Melitón Gonzáles led the party which went after the bodies and that Krempkau merely served as interpreter at the inquest. Johnny Hale objected to his translation and the trouble started ("The Killing of Stoudenmire," *Frontier Times*, I, July, 1924, 24-25)

43 Look, *Reminiscences*, MS. Look's version of this affair differs from the half dozen others which exist. He was remembering after twenty-five years, but at least he was an eyewitness and he must have got some of it right.

44 El Paso *Herald*, December 28, 1881

45 "Zach White Tells Story of Famous City Marshal," El Paso *Evening Post*, May 30, 1928

46 *Newman's Semi-Weekly*, April 20, 1881; George Look, *Reminiscences*

47 Bronson, *The Red Blooded Heroes* (New York, 1910), 94-95

48 Chapman, "Old Hotel Pierson," El Paso *Times*, January 27, 1952

49 Middagh, *Frontier Newspaper*, 1

50 El Paso City Council Minutes, Book B

51 Clyde Wise, "The Effects of the Railroad on El Paso," *Password* V (July, 1960), 95

52 El Paso City Council Minutes, Book B, April 14, 1881

CHAPTER XVIII

The Great Day

1 El Paso *Herald*, June 1, 1881 (from the collection of Mrs. L. H. Corcoran)

2 Corcoran, "He brought the Railroads to El Paso," *Password*, I (May, 1956), 51

CHAPTER XIX

The Boom Continues

1 El Paso *Herald*, June 1, 1881. The Santa Fe arrived on June 11, 1881.

2 Jordan, *Railroads in the El Paso Area* (MS, 1957), 151

3 *Ibid.*, 166-174

4 El Paso *Herald*, January 4, 1882: "Merchants say they will not ship by the Santa Fe Railroad, even if they come down from their outrageous tariff to the same rate as the Texas and Pacific."

5 Jordan, *Railroads*, 102

6 El Paso *Times*, January 1, 1885

7 *Herald*, December 14, 21, 1881

8 *Ibid.*, January 25, 1882

9 Mrs. Adele Fewel Coles, September 16, 1965; El Paso *Lone Star*, February 27, 1884; El Paso City Council Minutes, Book C, November 3, 1883 (Will J. Fewel's bid to supply gas accepted)

10 *Times*, January 1, 1885

11 *Ibid.*

12 Prestwood, *Social Life and Customs of the People of El Paso* (MS. 1949), 42

13 *Herald*, January 25, March 8, 1882

14 *Times*, December 14, 1884; Nicoll, *History of El Paso Sewage Treatment and Pumping Plant* (MS, 1951),

15 Bridgers, *Just Chatting*, I, 55, June 29, 1934, says the first school building was on Myrtle Avenue where the old Federal Bank later stood. This may have been Miss Nunn's school.

16 *Herald*, November 9, 1881

17 *Ibid.*, December 7, 1881

18 *Ibid.*, February 8, 1882

19 White, *Out of the Desert* (El Paso, 1924), 185-186

20 *Times*, November 1, 1891; E. A. Shelton, "Reminiscences," *Times*, December 8, 1963

21 Morrell, *Rise and Growth of Public Education in El Paso* (El Paso, 1936), 46

22 Schaer, *An Historical Sketch of Aoy School* (MS, n. d.), 1-5, quoting mostly G. W. Hare, "Life and Character of Olivas Villanueva Aoy," in *Quien Sabe* (El Paso High School Year Book), 1900; *Herald-Post*, April 29, 1933

23 Morrell, *Rise and Growth*, 47

24 *Ibid.*, 58

25 Fugate, *Frontier College* (El Paso, 1963)

26 *Herald-Post*, May 28, 1936, August 26, 1946; *Times*, July 4, 11, 1954, July 25, 1963

27 *Herald*, November 23, 25, 1881

28 *Ibid.*, December 21, 1881

29 *Lone Star*, December 20, 1882. The Play was *Lady Audley's Secret*

30 *Herald*, November 23, 24, 1881

31 *Ibid.*, November 2, 1881

32 *Ibid.*, November 23, 1881

33 *Ibid.*, November 30, 1881; 'We will soon have four churches, a Methodist, Catholic, Presbyterian, and Episcopal one. . . .'

34 *Lone Star*, November 26, 1881; Brady, *Theatre in Early El Paso* (El Paso, 1966), 8-10

35 *Lone Star,* December 14, 1881
36 *Ibid.,* December 21, 1881
37 *Times,* May 30, 1942; Gillett, *Six Years with the Texas Rangers* (Austin, 1921), 323. The Coliseum was doing well in December, 1882 *(Lone Star,* December 27). By the following spring it had been reorganized and was trying to present legitimate theatre *(Lone Star,* February 17, 1883). In 1887 the Myar Opera House was erected on the site.
38 Bridgers, *Just Chatting,* I, 28; *Lone Star,* January 3, 1883: John Manning, the new Deputy U. S. Marshal, is "sober, gentlemanly, reliable."
39 Mills, *Forty Years* (El Paso, 1963), 165
40 Coldwell, "Gillett Book Revives Pioneer's Memories" (newspaper clipping, early 1921, pasted in El Paso Public Library's copy of *Six Years with the Texas Rangers)*
41 Leonard, *The Manning Family,* MS; *Herald,* June 1, 1881
42 Frank M. Manning, El Paso, November 5, 1965. Jim's name appears in the census records of 1880. Doc's arrival is noted in the *Herald* for June 1, 1881. The issue of December 7 notes his purchase of a house.
43 Ex Parte James Manning (Habeas Corpus Proceedings), February 15, 1882, testimony of John Evans, J. C. Kling, and John Webb (document in possesion of Leon Metz, El Paso). Compare Gillett, "The Killing of Dallas Stoudenmire," *Frontier Times,* (July, 1924), 24
44 *Herald,* January 11, 1882
45 *Ibid.*
46 Colorado County records at Columbus, Texas, show that a marriage license was issued on February 20, 1882, to Dallas Stoudenmire and Isabella Sherrington (Volume C-2, 246).
47 Ex Parte James Manning, testimony of J. C. Kling. Family tradition among the Mannings says that Jim had stopped drinking and would take nothing alcoholic.
48 Gillett, "Killing of Dallas Stoudenmire," 25
49 James H. White and other respected citizens of the community testified at the *habeas corpus* proceedings that Cummings was a "desperate and dangerous man."
50 *Herald,* February 15, 1882; *Lone Star,* February 15, 1882
51 Gillett, "The Killing of Dallas Stoudenmire," 25-26. The *Lone Star* gave special note to the feud on March 25, 1882.
52 El Paso City Council Minutes, Book C, Part I, 46
53 *Ibid.,* Book C, April 8, 1882, 61; Mills, *Forty Years,* 159-164; *Lone Star,* April 5, 1882

54 El Paso City Council Minutes, Book C., Part I, 62
55 *Lone Star,* April 8, 1882; Middagh, *Frontier Newspaper* (El Paso, 1958), 8-9; Gillett, *Six Years,* 329
56 El Paso City Council Minutes, Book C, May 29, 1882, 72-73
57 *Herald,* September 20, 1882, testimony of L. C. Brooks
58 Gillett, "The Killing of Dallas Stoudenmire," 26
59 *Ibid.,* Frank H. Manning, November 5, 1965. Leon Metz has found an account of the fight in the *Colorado County Citizen* (Columbus, Texas) quoting from a lost issue of the El Paso *Times.* Jones stepped between the two men, giving Doc a chance to draw first and wound Stoudenmire in the arm and chest. His second shot hit the papers in Stoudenmire's pocket. Stoudenmire did not fire until they were outside.
60 Quoted by courtesy of Frances Newman Thiel
61 J. J. Deaver, Calallen, Texas, to J. M. Deaver, El Paso, Texas, October 4, 1937
62 Denny, *A Century of Freemasonry* (El Paso, 1956), 48
63 Colorado County Court Records, Book C-2, 341, shows that Belle Stoudenmire and Charles S. Kerl applied for a marriage license on December 4, 1883.
64 White, *Autobiography* (New York, 1942), 43
65 Dr. Howard Thompson lists most of these ladies in *Builders of El Paso,* MS
66 Dr. William Berrien, November 26, 1958

CHAPTER XX

Sun City

1 The population in 1880 was 736; in 1890, 10, 338
2 Hammons, *History of El Paso County* (MS, 1942), 118; de Wetter, "The Smelting Works," 133
3 *Times,* January 1, 1885
4 Bridgers, El Paso *Herald,* October 24, 1929
5 *Times,* July 28, 1884
6 *Ibid.,* March 1, 1885
7 Bridgers, *Just Chatting,* I, 64-65; *Times,* August 20, 1884
8 *Times,* July 21, 1884
9 Mrs. J. C. Wilmarth, July 5, 1965
10 *Herald,* July 8, 10, 1890
11 Levy, "The Cloudcroft Baby Sanitarium," *Password,* VII (Fall, 1962), 136-148
12 *Lone Star,* August 23, 1882; *Herald,* May 13, 1897 (Firemen's Special Edition)

13 El Paso City Council Minutes, Book C, 126

14 Mosier, *History of the El Paso Fire Department* (MS, 1956), 5

15 *Lone Star*, December 16, 1882; E. A. Shelton, "Reminiscences," *Times*, December 8, 1963

16 Mosier, 29-30

17 *Herald*, May 13, 1897

18 Mosier, 7-8

19 *Lone Star*, December 16, 1882

20 *Ibid.*, January 27, February 7, 10, 1883

21 Mosier, 32

22 *Ibid.*

23 *Lone Star*, April 14, 21, 1883

24 Mosier, 84-86, 91

25 *Times*, August 19, 1884: "P. E. Kern Hook and Ladde Co. made a record run with a hose cart--44 seconds to get to the plug and get water through 250 feet of hose."

26 Mosier, 33

27 *Herald*, May 12-15, 1897

28 *Lone Star*, March 7, 1883

29 Mosier, 28

30 *Times*, May 6, 1891

31 *Lone Star*, January 16, 1883 (bids called for)

32 Mosier, 42-45; *Times*, February 12, 13, 1892

33 *Herald*, February 27, 1894

34 Mosier, 48-57; *Times*, December 23, 1893, January 27-29, 1895; *Herald*, May 13, 1897

35 Mosier, 66, 67, 78; Cleofas Calleros, *Times*, August 16, 1953, describes the officials and activities of the Department in 1896.

36 *Times*, November 5, 1905

37 Brady, *The Theatre in Early El Paso* El Paso, 1966), 24-32

38 Mrs. W. D. Howe, September 30, 1965

39 Levy, "The Myar Opera House," *Password*, V (April, 1960), 66-67; "El Paso Defends her Culture," *Ibid.*, IV (July, 1959), 91-92

40 Brady, 35

41 Levy, "Myar Opera House," 70; *Times*, November 5, 1905; Mosier, 78

42 The organization is still in existence as this is written (1968) and meets once a year (*Times*, June 6, 13, 1967).

43 *Lone Star*, December 30, 1882: "A number of handsome and costly residences will shortly be commenced in Magoffin's addition."

44 Bridgers, *Just Chatting*, I, 138

45 *Times*, January 1, 1885

46 Porter, "Map No. 2 of Satterthwaite's Addition," *Password*, I (May, 1956), 68

47 *Lone Star*, February 27, 1884

48 *Times*, November 27, 1894

49 L. H. Davis, "P. E. Kern, the Pioneer, Is El Paso's Monte Cristo," *Times*, January 28, 1912

50 R. N. Mullin to C. L. S., June 26, 1965

51 Louis Le Veaux, June 22, 1965

52 *Times*, February 9, 1967

53 The El Paso papers in the spring of 1908 carried full-page advertisements for Tobin Town.

54 Francis Rosser Brown, Muskogee, Oklahoma, October 30, 1964

55 "Judge Crosby's Interesting Story," *Times*, January 14, 1902

56 *Times*, November 9, 1881

57 *Ibid.*, December 21, 1952

58 Calleros, "Climate Here Unexcelled," *Times*, August 2, 1953. There were full-page spreads in 1895 (*Times*, May 2, 4).

59 Hail, "What's Happened to City's Healthseeking Visitors?" *Herald-Post*, April 26, 1961

60 *Lone Star*, July 28, 1883, describes a visit of the Nellie Boyd Theatrical Troupe complete with marching band.

61 *Times*, April 18, 1885: "The Tenth Cavalry Band presented a concert on the Plaza last night."

62 *Lone Star*, December 15, 1882

63 *Herald*, May 13, 14, 1890

64 *Ibid.* May 4, 1893

65 *Ibid.*, October 24, 1929 (W. W. Bridgers); *Lone Star*, October 12, 29, 1881; City Council Minutes, Book C-1, 178, February 6, 1883

66 *Lone Star*, March 17, 1883

67 *Ibid.*, May 24, August 2, 1884; *Times*, March 19, 1885; Webster, *History of San Jacinto Square* (MS, 1957), 1-8

68 Williams, *Orchestras and Bands, El Paso Music 1880-1960* (MS, 1960), 9

69 Mrs. J. F. Coles, July 9, 1965; Mrs. J. C. Wilmarth, July 5, 1965. Major George Zimpelman gave Major Fewel the idea of planting Bermuda grass and showed him how to do it. The date of the arrival of the alligators is much debated. One story (*Herald-Post*, February 6, 1962) says that Satterthwaite brought them in 1883. Mrs. K. F. MacCallum credits her father, B. F. Darbyshire (Texas and Pacific Agent from 1880 to 1906) with importing them. Cf. W. W. Bridgers, *Herald*, October 4, 1929, and *Herald-Post*, April 28, 1956; *Times*, August 28, 1946.

70 Calleros, "Chopin Music Hall was Cultural," *Times*, September 7, 1952; Mrs. W. D. Howe, September 30, 1965; *Herald*, January 3, 4, 1896. See *Herald*, April 15, 1895, for more on Professor Dewey.

71 *Times*, December 24, 28, 1893; *Herald*, April 27, 1916

72 *Times*, December 29, 1893

73 *Ibid.*, February 23, 1894
74 Williams, *Orchestras and Bands*, 32
75 *Herald*, November 8, 1913, December 18, 19-20, 1914
76 *Ibid.*, December 19-20, 1914
77 McNary, *This Is My Life* (Albuquerque, 1956), 52-53
78 *Times*, June 20, 1965; Louis LeVeaux, June 22, 1965
79 J. L. Coggeshall, July 7, 1965
80 Williams, *Orchestras and Bands*, 41
81 Pearson Wosika, November 14, 1965; Fred Souflee, November 16, 1965
82 Williams, 41; Jennie B. Gustat, *His Band Marches On* (New York, 1954). Gustat died in 1952. He was a famous leader of young people's bands in Florida (W. J. Chesak, July 1, 1966).
83 *Times*, November 10, 1919
84 *Ibid.*
85 *Ibid.*, November 8, 1919
86 Irene Reckhart Shontz, July 15, 1965
87 Mayo Seamon, June 3, 1965
88 *Herald*, August 7, 1909
89 *Ibid.*, July 17, 1909
90 *Ibid.*
91 *Ibid.*
92 *Ibid.*, August 14, 1909
93 *Ibid.*
94 Calleros, *El Paso Then and Now* (El Paso, 1954), quoting J. J. Watts, 129
95 *Times*, July 4, 1895, March 13, 1937; Mrs. Rachel Teel Vordermark (the Major's daughter), November 20, 1965. S. H. Newman (*Times*, August 19, 1911) denied that the gun was ever called the Blue Whistler or had been used in the Civil War.
96 *Herald*, July 31, 1909
97 *Ibid.*
98 *Ibid.*
99 *Ibid.*, July 24, August 7, 1909
100 *Ibid.*, May 15, 1890
101 *Ibid.*, July 8, 11, 1892
102 *Ibid.*, February 21, 1895, September 18, 1909
103 *Ibid.*, April 21, 1891
104 *Ibid.*, May 6, 1891
105 *Ibid.*, January 17, 19, 20, 1901; Prestwood, *Social Life* (MS, 1949), 127; Calleros, "Twentieth Annual Sun Carnival," *Times*, January 9, 1955
106 Mahon, *History and Development of the Southwestern Sun Carnival* (MS, 1956), 2-6; *Herald*, January 11-20, 1903
107 *Herald*, August 7, 1909
108 *Ibid.*, October 5, 1904, October 2, 1909
109 Prestwood, *Social Life*, 40, 50-52; *Herald*, December 21, 1881 (first ball), August 26, 1916
110 *Lone Star*, March 24, 1883; *Herald*, July 26, 1882
111 *Lone Star*, June 17, 1885
112 *Herald*, February 20, 1918. The *Times* for January 22, 1893, mentions the Franklin Club and the Winter Evening Club. There were doubtless others.
113 R. N. Mullin to C. L. S., June 26, 1965
114 Prestwood, *Social Life*, 143-144
115 *Herald*, February 23, 1909
116 *Ibid.*, May 30, 1938
117 Prestwood, 150
118 *Herald*, July 23, 1909, October 15, 1910
119 Laurence Stevens, June 30, 1965
120 *Herald*, July 19, 1902. The first El Paso golf club in 1898-99 had a six to nine-hole layout in the area of Arizona and Brown Streets (M. G. McKinney to C. L. S. October 21, 1965).
121 *Herald*, April 23, 1906; *Herald-Post*, January 14, 1939
122 *Herald*, June 5, 7, 1906, December 31, 1908
123 *Ibid.*, February 15, 1906, December 31, 1908
124 *Times*, May 3, 1916; *Herald*, August 16, 1916
125 *Herald-Post*, January 14, 1939; *Herald*, March 8, 1920, January 7, 1922
126 Mrs. J. C. Wilmarth, July 5, 1965
127 *Autobiography* (New York, 1942), 91
128 Shelton, "Reminiscences," *Times*, December 8, 1963; Calleros, *El Paso Then and Now*, 67, 196; Rush, *El Paso YMCA* (MS, 1950), 20-22, 48-55, 62
129 *Current Topics Year Book*, 1898 (MS); *Times*, February 22, 1931; *Herald-Post*, September 21, 1928
130 Mills, *Forty Years* (El Paso, 1963), xxi. Mills was appointed on October 1, 1897.
131 Prestwood, *Social Life*, 113
132 *Ibid.*
133 *Herald*, January 2, 1901
134 Cunningham, *History of the Woman's Club* (El Paso, 1945), 9
135 *Herald*, October 9, 1909
136 *Times*, May 16, 1884
137 *Ibid.*, October 14, 1884
138 Pérez, *Baseball in El Paso* (MS, n. d.), 4
139 *Ibid.*, 12
140 *Times*, December 28, 1889, announced the first annual supper and ball of the wheelmen.
141 Hammons, *A History of El Paso County* (MS, 1942), 146-148, gathers these facts.
142 *Times*, December 17, 1884 (opening), December 10, 24, 1884; January 3, 1885 (New Year's Party); February 4, (ring tournament), 6, 7 (Grand Carnival), 1885
143 *Ibid.*, March 18, 1885
144 Chapman, "Hotel Angelus History," *Times*, February 24, 1952

CHAPTER XXI

Sin City

1 *Autobiography* (New York, 1942), 43
2 *Ibid.*, 71
3 White, *Out of the Desert* (El Paso, 1924), 229
4 *Lone Star*, January 27, February 14, 1883
5 *Ibid.*, September 1, 1883
6 El Paso City Council Minutes, Book D, Part 3, 111
7 *Lone Star*, December 27, 1882, January 6, 1883
8 *Ibid.*, February 7, 1883
9 *Times*, September 17, 1884
10 *Ibid.*, August 8, 1909
11 *Ibid.*, January 17, 18, 1885
12 Calleros, *El Paso Then and Now* (El Paso, 1954), 60-62
13 Bridgers, *Just Chatting*, I, 202 (September 17, 1934)
14 Broaddus, *Legal Heritage* (El Paso, 1963), 164
15 W. W. Bridgers, El Paso *Times*, August 22, 1909
16 George Look, *Reminiscenses* (MS); testimony of A. P. Criswell and M. W. Criswell in Justice Court, El Paso, Texas, June 26, 1885 (documents in possession of Gordon Frost, El Paso); *Times*, April 15 16, 17, 19, 1885, August 15, 1909.
17 *Times*, April 16, 1885, Frank Grafenberg's testimony at Cahill's preliminary trial
18 George Look, *op. cit.*; Broaddus, *Legal Heritage*, 145; *Times*, August 22, 1909
19 *Times*, April 16, 1885
20 *Autobiography*, 44-45. See Thompson, *Builders of El Paso* (MS, 1945) for Si Ryan
21 Thompson, *Builders*, 66; *Times*, March 24, 1898; Mrs. George Brunner, July 14, 1965
22 Selman, *John Selman of El Paso*, MS
23 *Ibid.*
24 Thompson, *Builders*, 72
25 Selman, *John Selman*, MS
26 *Times*, December 2, 4, 5, 7, 1884
27 A fine example from 1908 pictured bedrooms, bathrooms and parlors in the "residences" of Miss Etta Clark and Miss Tillie Howard.
28 R. N. Mullin to C. L. S., June 26, 1965; Page Kemp and Colbert Coldwell, June 11, 1965. Girls in Juárez could appear in that city only between 11 a.m. and 1 p.m. (*Times*, August 7, 1909).
29 Rosalie Behr Waters, August 24, 1965
30 Mrs. Lily Smith Howard, June 8, 1965
31 *Recollections of a Texas Educator* (Salado, Texas, 1964), 19

32 The *Times* for April 3, 6, 10, 11, December 19, 20, 1890, surveys the Bolton-Cavitt business. The official explanation was that Cavitt had settled a claim, contrary to agreement, with a man named Doak. Bolton escaped from the Juárez jail in December. The late Maury Kemp thought there were deeper reasons for the trouble. The story about the missing mayor comes from him.
33 Selman, *John Selman* (MS)
34 Sonnichsen, *Billy King's Tombstone* (Caldwell, Idaho, 1941), 93-116
35 S. G. González, June 7, 1965. A study of names on Utah Street can be revealing. In 1912 the City Directory lists such tenants above and below Tillie's place as Misses Marie Fontaine, Marthe Montesquieu,, Belle Marceuse, E. Gonsoulin, and Merci du Bignon.
36 *Times*, April 20, 1886
37 Tillie appears in the City Directory for 1892-93; May Palmer in 1895-96
38 *Times*, April 20, 1886
39 Mrs. L. H. Corcoran, February 8, 1950
40 *Times*, April 20-25, 1886. Marshal Hail, November 23, 1964. The *Herald* for April 20 has not been found. Hail got his information from Frank Wells Brown, former owner of the *Herald*, and printed the story in the *Herald-Post*, May 28, 1936.
41 Anne Kemp White, *My Little History Story* (MS). Her death certificate says she was born in New York.
42 *Times*, August 2, 1947
43 *Ibid.*, April 23, 24, 1894
44 *Herald*, January 9, 1895
45 *Autobiography*, 48
46 County Court Probate Minutes, Book 3, pp. 533, 610; Book 4, 374-375
47 Page Kemp and Colbert Coldwell, June 10, 1965
48 Louis Le Veau, June 5, 1965
49 Grace Davenport appears at a Utah Street address in 1903, probably a lesser madam trying to cash in on Gypsy Davenport's reputation.
50 Death Records, El Paso County Courthouse, 1920, Certificate 1312. She is listed as a widow, age 65.
51 Kemp, *From the Memoirs of Maury Kemp* (typescript)
52 *Times*, August 2, 1947
53 *Ibid.*, November 6, 1905
54 *Ibid.*, August 2, 1907; Anne Kemp White, January 18, 1966
55 *Times*, August 2, 1947; *Herald-Post*, July 29, 1947
56 A. A. Lane, September 12, 1965 (Mr. Lane was co-executor); *Herald-Post*, January 9. 1957
57 Laurence Stevens, June 20, 1965

58 Rutherford, *The Southwesterner*, IV (May-June, 1965), 8
59 Arthur Schuster, July 15, 1965
60 Flournoy Manzo, May 27, 1965, quoting Ora Davis Neal
61 Rutherford, *op. cit.* Laurence Stevens, El Paso, April 23, 1965, says May left her money to Florence Forrest, one of her girls.
62 Karl Goodman, El Paso, June 5, 1965
63 L. M. Rutherford to C. L. S., June 7, 1965
64 Karl Goodman, June 5, 1965
65 Laurence Stevens (August 1, 1965) found this and other records of Tillie's ownership of real estate.
66 Selman, *John Selman* (MS)
67 Her father, Henry Weiler, was from Pennsylvania; her mother, Eva Lucke, was born in Germany (Vital Statistics, Death Records, El Paso County Courthouse, Death Certificate 573, 1911).
68 Haley, *Jeff Milton* (Norman, 1948), 216-217
69 Tillie's death certificate says she was forty-one years old in 1911
70 Oden, *Texas Ranger's Diary and Scrapbook* (Dallas, 1936), 17
71 *Ibid.*, 22
72 Eddy *Daily Current*, September 20, 1894, quoting the El Paso *Times*, n. d.
73 The companion engravings show lifeboats leaving the harbor in a storm to pick up survivors of a wreck, and the same boats returning with the unfortunates.
74 John Middagh, April 23, 1965
75 Haley, *Jeff Milton*, 216-217
76 Arthur Schuster, July 15, 1965
77 *Ibid.*
78 Jane Burges Perrenot, August 5, 1965
79 Rita Faudoa, July 14, 1965
80 John Middagh, Lecture, El Paso YWCA, April 23, 1965
81 Mrs. George Brunner, July 14, 1965
82 Haley, *Jeff Milton*, 215 216
83 J. Ostrander in 1903; Leona Reed in 1904
84 Rita Faudoa, July 14, 1965
85 *Ibid.*
86 Irene Reckhart Shontz, July 15, 1965
87 *Herald*, April 8, 1911
88 *Ibid.*, April 10, 1911; *Times*, April 25, 1911 (Tillie's will probated. She left only her clothes, cut glass and china to her cousins).
89 Haley, *Jeff Milton*, 216
90 Irene Reckhart Shontz, July 15, 1965
91 Probate Records, El Paso County Courthouse, No. 1576, Estate of Tillie Weiler, Contest of A. E. Bartlett and Mrs. A. E. Bartlett
92 Bud Rutherford to C. L. S., June 17, 1965
93 *Herald-Post*, June 25, 1958; Karl Goodman, June 5, 1965
94 Rutherford, *Southwesterner*, IV (May-June, 1965), 8
95 Interview, April 5, 1965
96 *Autobiography*, 49-50. A pioneer woman, who knew the White family well, says, "He didn't do it. His mother would have skinned him alive if he had gone down there."
97 R. N. Mullin to C. L. S., June 26, 1965
98 Mrs. Eleanor Coldwell, May 4, 1965
99 Mrs. Jess Boykin, March 20, 24, 1965

CHAPTER XXII

Six-Shooter Capital

1 El Paso *Times*, November 12, 1903
2 *Autobiography* (New York, 1942), 43
3 Interview, June 11, 1965
4 *Times*, July 2, 1893
5 Laurence Stevens, April 2, 1965
6 *Times*, April 18, 1893
7 *Ibid.*, April 19, 1890
8 *Ibid.*; Parrish, "Ranger Killed in Gun Battle," El Paso *Times Sun Dial*, September 26, 1965
9 Martin, *Border Boss* (San Antonio, 1942), 147-148
10 Parrish, "Hanged by the Neck," *Password*, III (April, 1958), 72, 75; *Times*, January 7, 1935
11 Baylor to Mabry, July 9, 1893, Hughes to Mabry, September 6, 1893, Adjutant General's Files, State Library, Austin
12 Webb, *The Texas Rangers* (Boston, 1935), 442
13 *Times*, April 4, July 2, 1893; *Herald*, June 30, 1893
14 Jones to Mabry, April 16, 1893, AGF. *Herald*, April 5, 1893: "Body after body has been brought to town . . . not a party has been arrested."
15 *Times*, June 30, 1893
16 Webb, *Texas Rangers*, 441-444
17 *Times*, July 2, 1893
18 Webb, 443
19 *Times*, July 2, 1893
20 Haley, *Jeff Milton*, 234
21 *Times*, July 1, 1893
22 Sonnichsen, *Tularosa*, (New York, 1960), 107-201; Hening, *George Curry* (Albuquerque, 1959), 100-119; Gibson, *The Life and Death of Col. A. J. Fountain* (Norman, 1965), 256-288
23 Leon Metz, *John Selman: Texas Gunfighter* (New York, 1966), has followed Selman's trail to the end.
24 Sonnichsen, *I'll Die Before I'll Run*, 150-166 ("Justice after Dark"), covers this part of Selman's career.
25 Metz, *John Selman*, 96-111
26 Selman, *John Selman of El Paso* (MS)
27 Metz, *John Selman*, 133-135
28 *Times*, November 9, 1892
29 Selman, *John Selman of El Paso* (MS)
30 Metz, 138
31 *Ibid.*, 152-153
32 Cunningham, *Triggernometry* (Caldwell, Ida., 1947), 236-244

33 Metz, 146-147
34 *Times*, April 7, 1894
35 Metz, 137
36 *Times*, April 6, 1894
37 *Ibid.*
38 Oden, *Ranger's Diary* (Dallas, 1936), 40
39 *Times*, April 17, 1894
40 *Ibid.*, April 6, 7, 12, 1894; Oden, 41
41 Oden, *Ranger's Diary*, 40-41
42 *Herald*, June 30, 1894; District Court Minutes, 34th District Court, El Paso, Texas, Case 1753
43 Selman, *John Selman of El Paso* (MS)
44 Haley, *Jeff Milton*, 229
45 Harkey, *Mean as Hell* (Albuquerque, 1948), 114
46 Haley, 232
47 *Ibid.*, 233
48 *Times*, April 12, 1895
49 *Ibid.*, April 24, 1894
50 Haley, 233
51 Harkey, 131
52 Dr. George Brunner (El Paso, January 17, 1963) remembers the Prince Albert. Harkey gave his impressions to Monk Lofton (*Times*, April 28, 1963).
53 Hardin, *The Life of John Wesley Hardin* (Norman, 1961), 88-106; Godbold, "Comanche and the Hardin Gang," SWHQ, LXVIII (July, 1963), 55-57; Galveston *News*, October 7, 1877 (Hardin's trial). Mrs. Godbold and some testimony at Hardin's trial place the blame on JWH.
54 Haley, *Jeff Milton*, 226-251, paints him in the blackest colors.
55 JWH to his son, JWH, Jr., Huntsville, July 3, 1887 (letter in possession of C. L. S., used by courtesy of E. D. Spellman, J. W. H.'s grandson-in-law).
56 Hardin, *Life*, 34
57 Nordyke, *John Wesley Hardin* (New York, 1957), 235-255. Mrs. Mattie Hardin Smith (JWH's sister) says he was first in the group of examinees (Fort Worth, June 12, 1944).
58 Nordyke, 258-261; Mr. and Mrs. Joe Clements, April 26, 1963
59 Sonnichsen, *Ten Texas Feuds* (Albuquerque, 1957), 200-210
60 Haley, 228
61 *Times*, May 4, 1895; *Herald*, April 10, 11, 1895
62 Middagh, *Frontier Newspaper* (El Paso, 1958), 66
63 R. N. Mullin to C. L. S., July 21, 1965, quoting statements made by Judge Kemp to Mr. Mullin's father
64 *Times*, April 24, 1895
65 *Ibid.*
66 Middagh, *Frontier Newspaper*, 70
67 *Times*, May 4, 1965
68 *Ibid.*, May 16, 1895
69 *Ibid.*

70 Minutes, 34th District Court, El Paso, Texas, Case 1815; *Times*, October 2, 1895. Judge Buckler dismissed Hardin's case and the cattle-stealing charges against Morose because of the death of the principals.
71 Metz, *John Selman*, 179
72 *Times*, August 27, 1895. The issue of November 14 mentions a contract.
73 Metz, 178-179
74 The *Times* for June 30, 1895, says Morose had applied for citizenship. In the issue of July 2 Consul Zayas denies the story.
75 George Look, *Reminiscences*, (MS)
76 *Times*, June 30, 1895
77 *Ibid.*, July 2, 1895
78 *Ibid.*, June 30, 1895
79 Haley, *Jeff Milton*, 242
80 Metz, *John Selman*, 178
81 *Times*, July 2, 1895
82 *Ibid.*, August 7, 1895
83 *Ibid.*, August 11, 1895
84 *Ibid.*, August 15, 22, 1895; George Look, *Reminiscences* (MS)
85 Testimony of Frank McMurray before Justice W. D. Howe, August 20, 1895, copy in possession of C. L. S.
86 Look, *Reminiscences* (MS). R. N. Mullin's files on this case contain statements by Ed Bryant, a policeman, and Roy Barnum, a saloon keeper, giving Hardin credit for arranging the killing.
87 White, *Autobiography* (New York, 1942), 57
88 *Herald*, August 20, 1895 (statements of H. S. Brown, E. L. Shackleford, and John Selman before Justice Howe), August 22, 1895; *Times*, August 21, 22, 1895. Hardin's descendants marked the grave in 1965.
89 Betty Rogers, *Reminiscences of Old El Paso* (MS)
90 Budke, *Albert B. Fall in New Mexico* (MS, 1961), 23-24
91 *The Southwesterner*, II (December, 1962), 3
92 Emma Adair Fall Chase, Alamogordo, January 15, 1964; *Times*, February 6, 1896; *Herald*, February 12, 1896
93 Metz, *John Selman*, 190-192
94 The *Times* for October 15, 1895, lists Zack White, Charles R. Morehead, O. T. Bassett, and W. J. Fewel as Selman's sureties on a $5,000 bond. The issue of February 12, 1896, describes the trial.
95 Robert T. Neill, Austin, April 25, 1959. Mrs. Anne Kemp White (January 15, 1966) says her father, Judge Wyndham Kemp, conducted the defense.
96 Metz, 195
87 *Ibid.*
98 Selman, *John Selman of El Paso* (MS); *Times*, April 3, 4, 1896; Metz, "Why Old John Selman Died," *Frontier Times*, XXXIX (October-November, 1965), 30-31

99 Selman, *John Selman* (MS). Young John missed his father's funeral but later made a sensational jail break and left the country (*Ibid.; Times,* May 9, 10, 18, 19, 1896).
100 Selman. *op. cit.; Times,* April 5, 7, 1896
101 *Times,* April 29, 1951
102 *Ibid.,* June 20, 1896
103 *Ibid.*
104 Metz, *John Selman,* 201
105 Look, *Reminiscences* (MS)
106 *Times,* April 11, 1896; April 5, 6, 1900
107 Broaddus, *Legal Heritage,* 164
108 Helen and Joe Clements, April 26, 1963; *Times,* December 30, 1908
109 Haley, *Jeff Milton,* 39
110 Maury Kemp, October 4, 1953
111 Jim McKinney, Big Spring, Texas, June 2, 1944, told me that Hardin and Clements rode through Big Spring together on their way to El Paso.
112 *Times,* December 30, 1908
113 *Ibid.,* July 28, 1908
114 Maury Kemp, October 4, 1953. The *Herald* for December 30, 1908, says Van Rooyen accused Clements in the Coney Island Saloon a month after the robbery.
115 *Times,* December 31, 1908
116 *Ibid.,* October 8, 1908
117 *Ibid.,* November 12, 1908
118 Middagh, *Frontier Newspaper,* 126-127
119 *Times,* December 30, 1908
120 *Ibid.,* January 2, 1909
121 Louis Leveaux, June 22, 1965. A conductor and a negro porter were arrested at San Marcial on January 16 for "aiding and abetting" illegal entry. This was the second arrest (*Times,* January 17, 1900). Newspapers in 1908 are full of stories about smuggled Chinamen.
122 *Times,* May 13, 1909
123 Maury Kemp, August 13, 1954
124 *Times,* May 14, 1909
125 Will C. Burgie to C. L. S., June 19, 1965
126 *Times,* December 30, 31, 1908, January 1-4, 1909; W. H. Fryer, July 8, 1961
127 *Times,* January 4, 1909
128 *Ibid.*
129 *Ibid.,* January 8, 9, 1909
130 *Ibid.,* May 12, 13, 1909
131 Louis Le Veaux, June 22, 1965
132 *Times,* May 15, 1909
133 *Ibid.*
134 White, *Autobiography,* 103-104
135 Rogers, *Reminiscences of Old El Paso* (MS)
136 Louis Le Veaux, June 22, 1965; Maury Kemp, October 4, 1953

CHAPTER XXIII

The Cleanup

1 El Paso *Times,* November 20, 1904
2 Broaddus, *Legal Heritage* (El Paso, 1963), 138. Ysleta had replaced San Elizario as the County seat in 1878.
3 El Paso *Lone Star,* November 7, 21, 24, December 1, 1883
4 *Ibid.,* December 5, 1883; Broaddus, *Legal Heritage,* 141
5 El Paso County Commissioners Court Minutes, II, 187-191, 324; *Times,* May 16, 1885, January 21, 1886; *Lone Star,* May 23, 27, June 27, July 15, 18, 25, 1885
6 *Lone Star,* November 21, 1883
7 Bridgers, *Just Chatting,* I, 108 (July 30, 1934)
8 Frank Faudoa, El Paso, June 26, 1948
9 *Times,* November 4, 5, 1884
10 Selman, *John Selman of El Paso* (MS)
11 El Paso *Lone Star,* April 11, May 19, 1883
12 *Ibid.,* August 1, 1883
13 Vowell, *Politics at El Paso 1850-1920* (MS, 1950), 84
14 *Lone Star,* August 1, 1883
15 *Ibid.;* El Paso *Herald,* March 1, 1882, August 1, 1883
16 *Times,* January 7, 1949, quoting *The Rescue* for August 15, 1883
17 *Lone Star,* August 15, 1883
18 Vowell, *Politics,* 86
19 *Lone Star,* August 11, 1883
20 *Times,* November 3, 6, 1888
21 *Ibid.,* November 11, 1888
22 *Ibid.,* March 3, 1889
23 *Ibid.,* March 17, 1889
24 *Ibid.,* April 9, 1889
25 *Ibid.,* March 16, 1889
26 *Ibid.,* March 20, 22, April 9, 1889
27 *Ibid.,* April 10, 11, 1889; White, *Out of the Desert* (El Paso, 1924), 217-218
28 *Times,* April 18 1889
29 *Ibid.,* April 19, 1889
30 Interview reported by Marshal Hail in the El Paso *Herald-Post,* May 28, 1936 Cf. *Herald,* April 19, 1889
31 *Times,* April 18, 19, 20, 1889
32 *Ibid.,* Hubbard was elected mayor on April 23 (*Times,* April 24, 1889)
33 *Ibid.,* April 24, 25, May 7, 9, 1889
34 *Ibid.,* May 7, 8, 9, 1889
35 *Ibid.,* May 3, 12, June 7, 1889. The canvass showed Krakauer winning by three votes.
36 *Ibid.,* June 13, 1889
37 White, *Out of the Desert,* 220; *Times,* June 28, 29, 1889
38 *Herald,* December 28, 1889; *Times,* December 29, 1889, January 1, 1890
39 *Herald,* March 22, 23, 26, 1893
40 Vowell, *Politics,* 109; *Herald,* April 11, 1893
41 *Times,* April 11, 12, 1893; Vowell, 107-109

42 El Paso *Evening Tribune,* April 1, 12, May 5, 10, 11, 1893; *Times,* May 4, 6, 12 (Red Light closed), 1893; June 24, 1894 (Burns opens again)
43 *Herald,* January 25, 30, 1893
44 *Ibid.,* October 18, 1893
45 *Ibid.,* October 31, 1893
46 *Ibid.,* May 25, 1894
47 *Times,* March 24, 1894
48 *Ibid.,* November 27, 1894
49 Haley, *Jeff Milton* (Norman, 1948), 211-212, bases his analysis of the political situation in 1893 on his correspondence with W. H. Burges.
50 *Herald,* July 18, 30, August 4, 1894
51 *Times,* August 11, 1894
52 Haley, 218-225
53 *Times,* August 5, 1895
54 Haley, 234; *Times,* March 31, 1895. Compare El Paso City Council Minutes, Book H, Part II (March 1, 1895), p. 542.
55 Richard F. Burges Collection, Book E, 75-79
56 *Ibid.,* Book E, 76
57 *Herald,* April 9, 1895
58 Maury Kemp's explanation for the demises of the *Lone Star* was that the gamblers, tired of Newman's sniping, told him to stop or they would refuse to do business with his advertisers. When he continued his attacks, his paper died for lack of support. Newman himself said, when he printed his last issue on January 6, 1886, that there were too many newspapers and he could not compete any longer.
59 Burges Collection, Book E, 80
60 *Herald,* April 10, 1895
61 *Ibid.*
62 Broaddus, *Legal Heritage,* 164
63 *Herald,* July 18, 1895
64 *Ibid.,* October 12, 21 1895; Vowell, *Politics,* 114
65 *Ibid.,* December 6, 1895
66 *Ibid.,* January 3, 6, 7, 1896
67 *Ibid.,* January 11, 13, 1896
68 *Ibid.,* January 1, 1896
69 *Ibid.,* January 4, 9, 13, 16, 31, February 8, 13, 1896
70 *Ibid.,* February 10, 1896
71 *Ibid.,* January 14, 15, 1896; Force, *The Life Story of L. R. Millican* (MS, 1956), 47-49, 105. Mr. Force gives most of the credit for the energy of the ministerial campaign to Millican. He persuaded the Governor to pass the anti-prizefight law.
72 *Herald,* January 17, 1896
73 *Ibid.,* January 30, 1896
74 *Ibid.,* February 6-10, 11, 15, 18, 1896
75 *Ibid.,* February 15, 17-25, 1896
76 *Times,* April 15, 1896
77 *Ibid.,* April 14, 1897
78 *Herald,* April 5, 1899. Editor Slater "exposed" Magoffin's gambling record.
79 Vowell, *Politics,* 117
80 *Herald,* April 1, 2, 3, 10, 1901

81 *Herald,* May 1, 1902; Middagh, *Frontier Newspaper,* 101-102
82 *Herald,* January 8, 1903; *Times,* June 18, 19, 1902; Middagh, *Frontier Newspaper,* 99-100
83 *Times,* May 12, 1946; *Herald,* March 3-9, 13-28, April 2, 13-15, 1903
84 Maury Kemp, October 4, 1953
85 Prestwood, *Social Life* (MS, 1949), 131
86 *Times,* September 1, 1904; *Herald,* January 26, July 9, 1904, January 10, 1912
87 *Herald,* January 25, 26, 1904
88 *Times,* September 1, 1904; *Herald,* January 11, 1912
89 *Herald,* September 16, 1904
90 *Ibid.,* September 17, 1904
91 *Ibid.,* November 10, 11, 1904
92 *Times,* November 12, 1904
93 White, *Autobiography* (New York, 1942), 90
94 *Times,* November 20-25, 1904; White, *Out of the Desert,* 240
95 *Times,* November 26, 1904, January 3, 1905; Middagh, *Frontier Newspaper,* 110-111
96 Noel Longuemare, interview with Leon Metz, November 26, 1965
97 *Times,* April 14, 1905; Middagh, 114
98 Vowell, *Politics,* 125; *Herald,* August 2, 4, 1905
99 Martin, *C. E. Kelly* (MS, 1956), 3-6
100 R. N. Mullin to C. L. S., December 30, 1965
101 Louis Le Veaux, June 5, 1965
102 *Herald,* November 9-13, 1905; Vowell, *Politics,* 106
103 *Herald,* May 8, August 13-16, 1906
104 *Times,* January 8, 1907. Trouble began when Fewel was about to begin paving Mesa Avenue and Davis moved the machinery to Stanton (R. N. Mullin, August 12, 1966).
105 *Herald,* February 19, 1907
106 *Ibid.,* March 8, 1907; Vowell, 128; E. C. Wade, December 25, 1965
107 *Herald,* May 3, 4, October 1, 1907
108 Vowell, 131
109 *Herald,* September 18, 1907; Vowell, 132
110 *Ibid.,* July 27, 1908
111 *Ibid.,* September 8, 28, December 10, 11, 1909, January 19, 1910; Mrs. J. U. Sweeney, January 24, 1966. Middagh, *Frontier Newspaper,* 115-141, gives an excellent account of the last stages of the water controversy. See also Parrish, *Coffins,, Cactus and Cowboys* (El Paso, 1964), 65-67
112 *Herald,* August 15, 17, 18, 1910
113 *Ibid.,* December 20, 22, 1911. Mary Kelly Quinn and Elizabeth Kelly (January 24, 1966) tell about Villa. Many versions exist of the Villa-Garibaldi quarrel. See Guzmán, *Memoirs* 42-43, and White, *Autobiography,* 115
114 *Herald,* January 10, 1912

115 Grand Jury Report, "Restricted District," March 28, 1913. Copy in possession of C. L. S.

116 Louis Le Veaux, June 5, 1965

117 Vowell, *Politics,* 140

118 *Herald,* January 22, February 17, 1915

119 *Ibid.,* May 5, 1915

120 *Ibid.,* December 8, 1915

121 *Times,* January 15, 1916

122 *Herald,* January 4, 1917

123 *Ibid.,* June 23, 1916

124 Mrs. Callie Fairley, "Law Enforcement in Early El Paso," Tape Recording, El Paso County Historical Society, October 24, 1963

125 *Herald,* November 26, 27, 1940

CHAPTER XXIV

Across the River

1 Rómulo Escobar, "Memorias del Paso del Norte," Boletín de la Sociedad Chihuahuense de Estudios Históricos, VI (20 de Octubre y Noviembre, 1964), 61-62

2 María Luisa Flores and Mrs. Henry Flores, June 1, 1960; J. J. Flores, *Diario* (MS), March 19, 1872, *Libro Memorial* (MS), January 1, April 7, July 19, 1869

3 María Luisa Flores, Mrs. Henry Flores, June 1, June 17, June 27, 1960

4 Escobar, "Memorias," 61-62

5 Consular Despatches from Ciudad Juárez, April 10, 1850, to December 23, 1859, Report No. 1, April 10, 1858

6 Mesilla *News,* June 13, 1874

7 White, *History of the Development of Irrigation* (MS, 1950), 36-37, 48

8 Orndorff, *History of the Development of Agriculture* (MS, 1957), 80

9 Robinson, *With the Ears of Strangers* (Tucson, 1964), "Introduction," vii

10 *Ibid.,* 68

11 The El Paso *Times* for February 5, 1896, says that the population of the Juárez Valley has been reduced by more than half in the preceding years. The United States Consul in Juárez, however, reported in 1889 that the population of that city had increased from 7,000 in 1886 to 9,000 in 1889 (Despatches from United States Consuls in Ciudad Juárez, January 16, 1889, July 1, 1891, No. 35, March 20, 1889).

12 Irigoyen, "El problema Económico de las Ciudades Fronterizas," *Boletín de la Sociedad Chihuahuense de Estudios Históricos,* IV (Julio 2 de 1942), 64

13 Quoted facing the first page of Mario Gill's *Nuestros Buenos Vecinos* (México, 1959).

14 Irigoyen, "El Problema Económico," 64; Almada, *Resumen* (México, 1955), 294; *Lone Star,* May 24, 1884; *Times,* January 14, 21, 28, 29, February 25, 1890 (El Pasoans were petitioning Congress to pressure Mexico into abolishing the Free Zone), May 3, 4, 1895 (Díaz reestablishes the Free Zone)

15 *Herald,* April 5, 1900

16 Orndorff, *History of Agriculture,* 94-95; *Herald,* Industrial and Investment Edition, 1903

17 White, *History of Irrigation,* 51-68; *Times,* November 15, 1888, January 5, 1890. Mills actually proposed two sites, one near Hart's Mill (Haney, *International Controversy,* MS, 1948(35).

18 Haney tells the whole story. John Logan Campbell in his *Autobiography* outlines his part in the two private organizations which were chartered to build the dam. He was Chief Engineer, and installations of the Reclamation Service are about where he said they should be.

19 Mitchell, *Official Proceedings of the Twelfth National Irrigation Congress* (Galveston, 1904). 107-108

20 White, *History of the Development of Irrigation,* 100 ff.

21 Cumberland, *Mexican Revolution* (Austin, 1952), 22

22 María Luisa Flores and Mrs. Henry Flores, June 27, 1960

23 González Flores, *Chihuahua de la Independencia a la Revolución* (México, 1949), 209, 215

24 Parkes, *A History of México* (Boston, 1960), 317; Ross, *Madero* (New York, 1955), 91-121

25 *Times,* December 23, 25, 1910

26 *Ibid.,* December 26, 1910

27 de Wetter, *Revolutionary El Paso* (MS, 1946), 34 (interview with Tom Lea)

28 *Times,* February 22, 1911

29 *Ibid.,* February 4, 1911 (González has been in El Paso for two months.)

30 *Ibid.,* December 31, 1910

31 *Ibid.,* December 27, 1910

32 *Ibid.,* February 2, 1911

33 *Ibid.,* Bush, *Gringo Doctor* (Caldwell, Ida., 1939), 167-170. Bush says the *insurrecto* train was loaded with dynamite and a Federal bullet set it off. His story differs from contemporary accounts.

34 *Times,* February 7, 8, 9, 10, 1911

35 Bush, *Gringo Doctor,* 175

36 Turner in *Bullets, Bottles, and Gardenias* (Dallas, 1935), 25-26, gives a first-hand account.

37 Ross, *Madero,* 146-149; Bush, *Gringo Doctor,* 178; *Times,* February 12, April 12, 1911. Mexican affairs were front-page news every day.

38 *Times,* April 2-9, 1911; Ross, *Madero,* 139-141

39 Mrs. Mary Teel Harper, "True Story of the Cannon, the old Blue Whistler," *Times*, March 13, 1937; *Times*, August 13, 19, 1911; Bush, *Gringo Doctor*, 182-188

40 *Times*, April 3-5, 1911

41 *Ibid.*, April 20, 1911

42 Joe Goodell, *El Paso and the Mexican Revolution*, El Paso County Historical Society, April 26, 1962, typescript; *Times*, April 30, 1911

43 *Times*, April 23, 1911

44 *Ibid.*, February 10, 1911

45 *Ibid.*, April 27, 1911

46 Laurence Stevens, *El Paso and the Mexican Revolution* (typescript)

47 *Times*, April 21, 1911

48 Bush, *Gringo Doctor*, 194-195; Turner, *Bullets, Bottles and Gardenias*, 70-71; White, *Autobiography* (New York, 1942), 113-114

49 *Times*, May 3, 4, 5, 6, 7, 1911; Ross, *Madero*, 163

50 Guzmán, *Memoirs of Pancho Villa* (Austin, 1965), 45. White, *Autobiography*, 117, says the "American roughnecks" in the Legion resolved to deliver the town to Madero whether he wanted it or not and started the attack.

51 *Times*, May 8, 9, 1911; Guzmán, *Memoirs*, 45-46; Bush, *Gringo Doctor*, 200-201

52 María Luisa Flores and Mrs. Henry Flores, June 27, 1960

53 María Luisa Flores, *El Paso and the Mexican Revolution* (typescript); Chávez, *Sesenta Años de Gobierno Municipal* (México, 1959), 85-86

54 *Herald*, December 10, 1913; de Wetter, *Revolutionary El Paso*, 106

55 Dr. William Berrien, November 26, 1958; *Times*, December 13, 1915

56 Almada, *Resumen*, 386; Chávez, *Historia de Ciudad Juárez* (Juárez, 1951), 199

57 Leslie Reed, Jane Burges Perrenot, Laurence Stevens, Louise Wilmarth, *El Paso and the Mexican Revolution*, typescript; Frank Mangan, *Border Town* (El Paso, 1964)

58 *Times*, May 10, 11, 1911

59 Ross, *Madero*, 167-169. Villa's story (Guzmán, *Memoirs*, 49-51) was that Orozco wanted to maneuver him into having to kill Madero, but that Orozco could not go through with it. Federico Cervantes (*Francisco Villa y la Revolución*, México, 1960) is one who tells an entirely different story. Compare *Times*, May 13 1911.

60 Turner, *Bullets, Bottles and Gardenias*, 68-70; Bush *Gringo Doctor*, 212-213; *Times*, May 14, 1911. All sources but Turner say that Navarro was taken to the river by Madero in his own automobile, (cf. Chávez, *Historia.*) On page 202 he has a picture of Navarro in Madero's car.

61 *Times*, February 1, 3-5, 1912

62 *Ibid.*, February 28, March 1, 1912

63 *Ibid.*, May 4, 1912

64 *Ibid.*, July 29-August 7, 1912

65 *Herald*, January 21, 23, February 1, 1913; de Wetter, *Revolutionary El Paso*, 93

66 *Herald*, July 11, 12, 1913

67 *Ibid.*, November 15, 1913

68 *Ibid.*, February 16, 1914

69 *Ibid.*, February 19-21, 1914

70 Fatout, *Ambrose Bierce* (Norman, 1951), 325

71 *Herald*, January 25, February 1, 1915

72 *Ibid.*, June 28, July 1, 1915; de Wetter, 126

73 de Wetter, *Revolutionary El Paso*, 115

74 *Times*, September 1, 2, 3, 1915

75 de Wetter, *Revolutionary El Paso*, 133-134

76 *Herald*, January 11, 13, 14, 1916

77 Almada, *Resumen*, 422; Chávez, *Historia*, 246; *Times*, June 15-17, 1919. Middagh, *Frontier Newspaper*, 179-183, has an excellent account of this episode.

78 *Herald*, March 13, 1915

INDEX

9835

Sonnichsen, Charles Leland, 1901-
    Pass of the North; four centuries on the
Rio Grande, by C.L. Sonnichsen.   [El Paso]
Texas Western Press, 1968.
    xii, 467p. illus., map, ports. 25cm. index.

    Bibliography: p.416-456.

294805

1.Rio Grande Valley-History.   I.Title.